THE POLISH-LITHUANIAN COMMONWEALTH, 1733–1795

THE POLISH-LITHUANIAN COMMONWEALTH, 1733–1795

LIGHT AND FLAME

RICHARD BUTTERWICK

YALE UNIVERSITY PRESS
NEW HAVEN AND LONDON

Published with assistance from the Annie Burr Lewis Fund.

For information about this and other Yale University Press publications, please contact:
U.S. Office: sales.press@yale.edu yalebooks.com
Europe Office: sales@yaleup.co.uk yalebooks.co.uk

Set in Adobe Garamond Pro by IDSUK (DataConnection) Ltd
Printed and bound by CPI Group (UK) Ltd, Croydon, CR0 4YY

Library of Congress Control Number: 2020942540

ISBN 978-0-300-25220-0

A catalogue record for this book is available from the British Library.

10 9 8 7 6 5 4 3 2 1

MIX
Paper | Supporting responsible forestry
FSC www.fsc.org FSC® C013604

Góralce znad Warty

CONTENTS

ILLUSTRATIONS

PLATES

MAPS

ACKNOWLEDGEMENTS

During three decades studying the Polish-Lithuanian Commonwealth, I have incurred many debts of gratitude. Almost all of the thanks I have expressed in previous books also apply on this occasion. Particular debts are acknowledged in the endnotes and in the list of illustrations. I appreciate the generosity of the scholars, institutions and photographers concerned.

It has been a pleasure to work with Yale University Press's superb team in London. I thank Martin Brown, Lucy Buchan, Percie Edgeler, Lucy Isenberg, Marika Lysandrou, Richard Mason, Clarissa Sutherland and James Williams, and especially Heather McCallum who took on this book, long after we first the discussed the idea. The comments made by the anonymous reviewers were pertinent and constructive: I have gratefully adopted nearly all of their suggestions. The responsibility for the remaining faults is of course my own.

While long in gestation, most of this book was written while working full-time for the College of Europe Natolin in Warsaw and part-time for the UCL School of Slavonic and East European Studies. From the College I acknowledge the funding for a research trip to Gdańsk and several relevant conferences. My students and colleagues at Natolin (several of whose owners feature in this work) have widened my horizons. At SSEES I am particularly grateful to Simon Dixon and Thomas Lorman, with whom I have had the privilege of co-teaching two courses which have helped develop my understanding of the Commonwealth and its predicaments. I have also benefited from the responses and insights of our students.

As ever, I am grateful for the support of my friends, Lynda and Ian, and the unstinting love and encouragement of my parents. Many authors thank their spouses for tolerating their reading and writing during evenings, weekends and vacations. I am no exception in this regard, but can say more: Wioletta has not only understood my urge to study history, but has shared in and inspired it. Thank you, my beloved *Góralka znad Warty*.

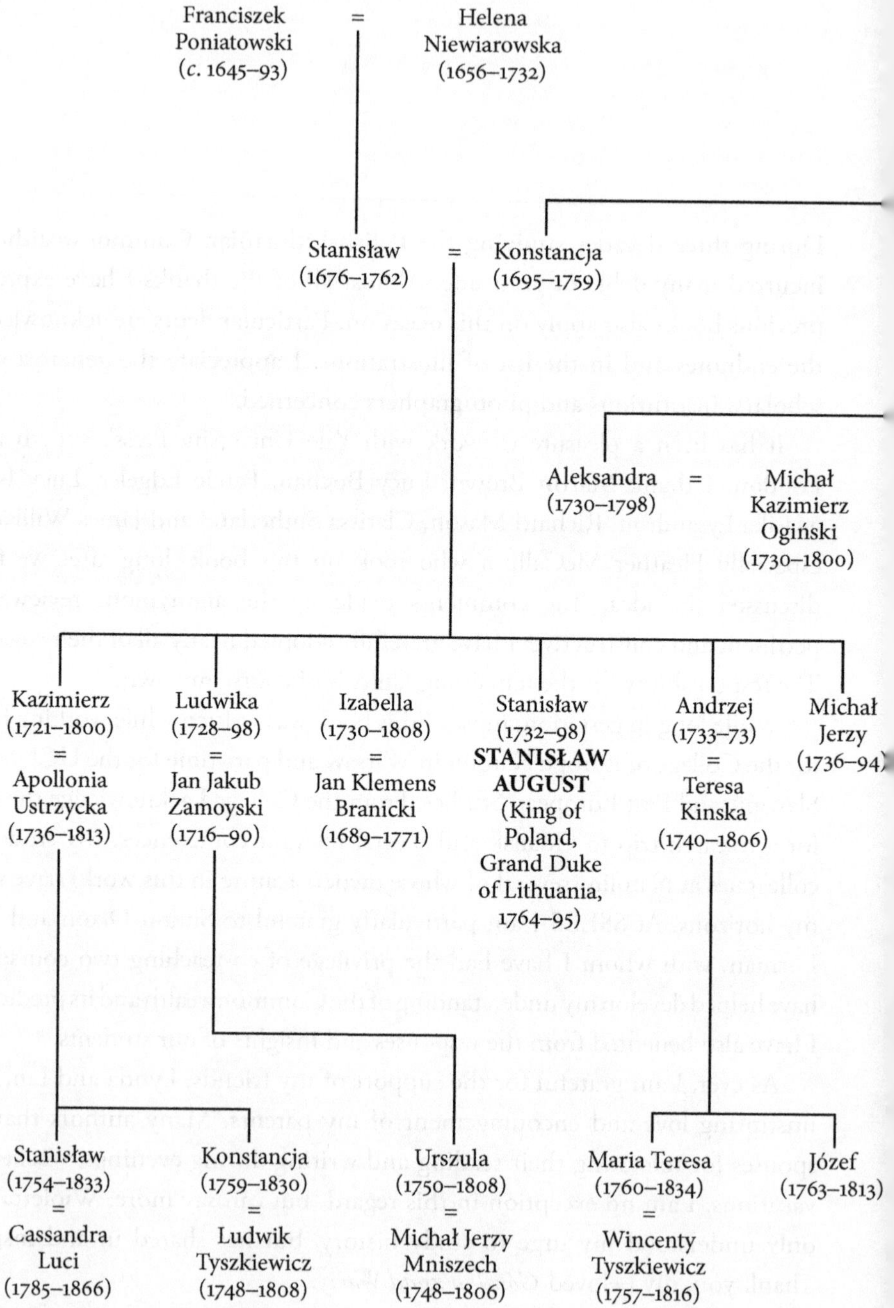
Franciszek Poniatowski (c. 1645–93)
=
Helena Niewiarowska (1656–1732)
Stanisław (1676–1762)
=
Konstancja (1695–1759)
Aleksandra (1730–1798)
=
Michał Kazimierz Ogiński (1730–1800)
Kazimierz (1721–1800)
=
Apollonia Ustrzycka (1736–1813)
Ludwika (1728–98)
=
Jan Jakub Zamoyski (1716–90)
Izabella (1730–1808)
=
Jan Klemens Branicki (1689–1771)
Stanisław (1732–98)
STANISŁAW AUGUST
(King of Poland, Grand Duke of Lithuania, 1764–95)
Andrzej (1733–73)
=
Teresa Kinska (1740–1806)
Michał Jerzy (1736–94)
Stanisław (1754–1833)
=
Cassandra Luci (1785–1866)
Konstancja (1759–1830)
=
Ludwik Tyszkiewicz (1748–1808)
Urszula (1750–1808)
=
Michał Jerzy Mniszech (1748–1806)
Maria Teresa (1760–1834)
=
Wincenty Tyszkiewicz (1757–1816)
Józef (1763–1813)

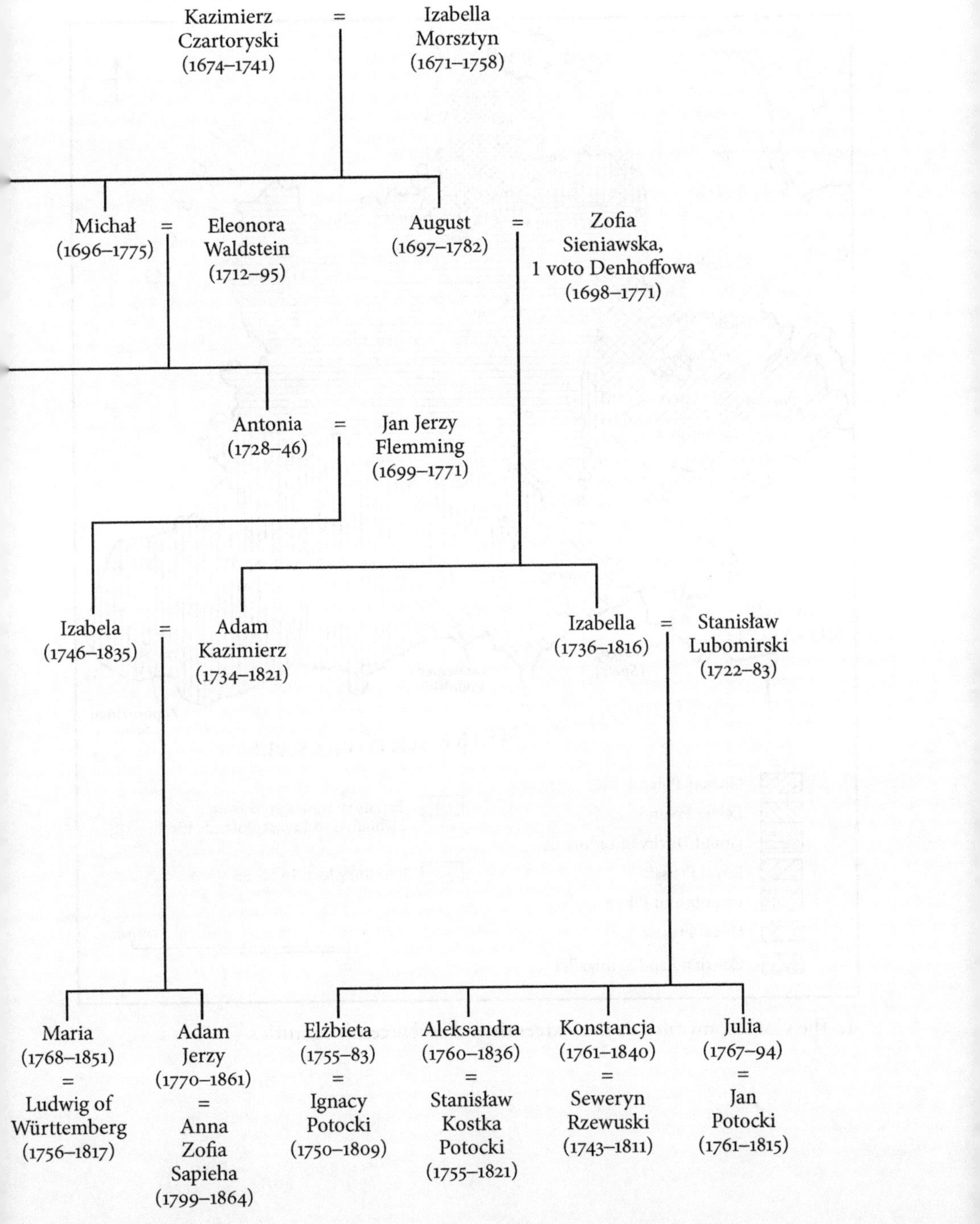

Kazimierz Czartoryski (1674–1741) = Izabella Morsztyn (1671–1758)
Michał (1696–1775) = Eleonora Waldstein (1712–95)
August (1697–1782) = Zofia Sieniawska, 1 voto Denhoffowa (1698–1771)
Antonia (1728–46) = Jan Jerzy Flemming (1699–1771)
Izabela (1746–1835) = Adam Kazimierz (1734–1821)
Izabella (1736–1816) = Stanisław Lubomirski (1722–83)
Maria (1768–1851) = Ludwig of Württemberg (1756–1817)
Adam Jerzy (1770–1861) = Anna Zofia Sapieha (1799–1864)
Elżbieta (1755–83) = Ignacy Potocki (1750–1809)
Aleksandra (1760–1836) = Stanisław Kostka Potocki (1755–1821)
Konstancja (1761–1840) = Seweryn Rzewuski (1743–1811)
Julia (1767–94) = Jan Potocki (1761–1815)

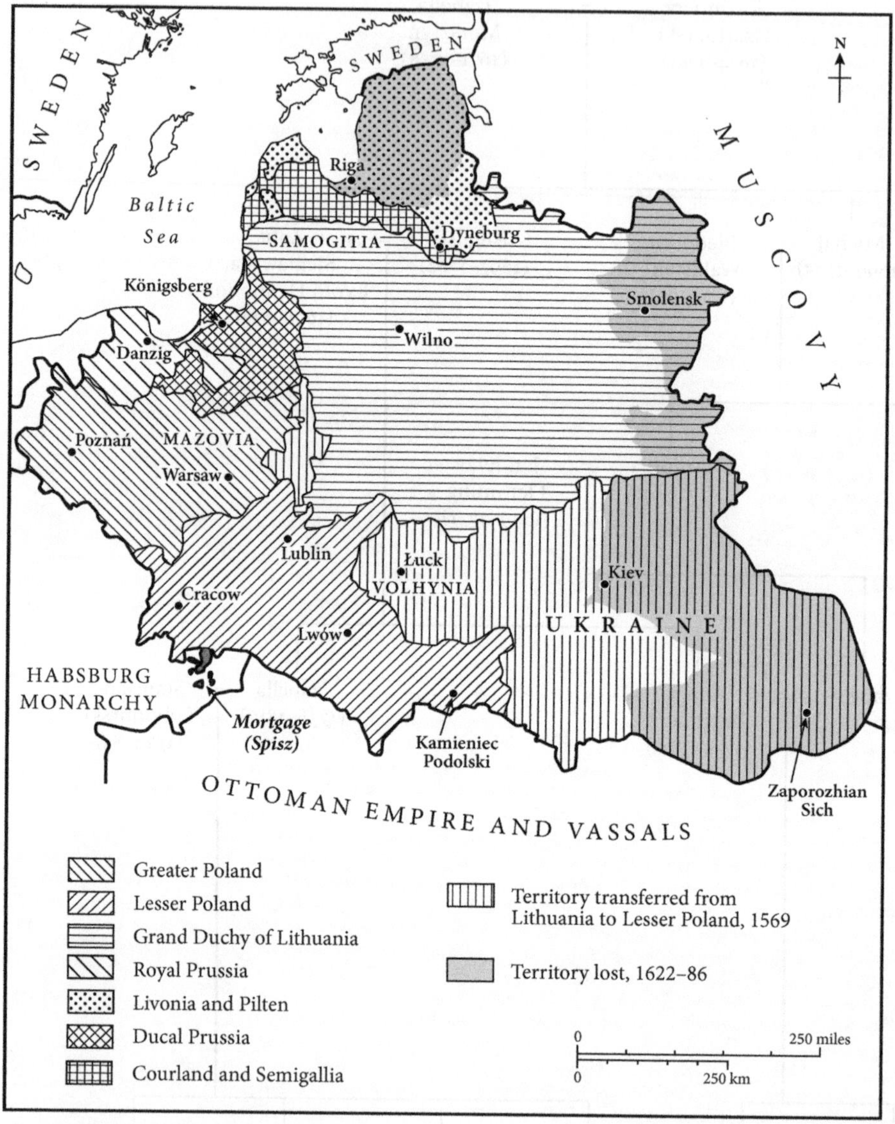

1. The Commonwealth in the sixteenth and seventeenth centuries

2. Christian confessions in the mid-eighteenth-century Commonwealth

3. The first partition, 1772

4. The 'referendum' of February 1792

5. The campaign in the Polish Crown, 1792

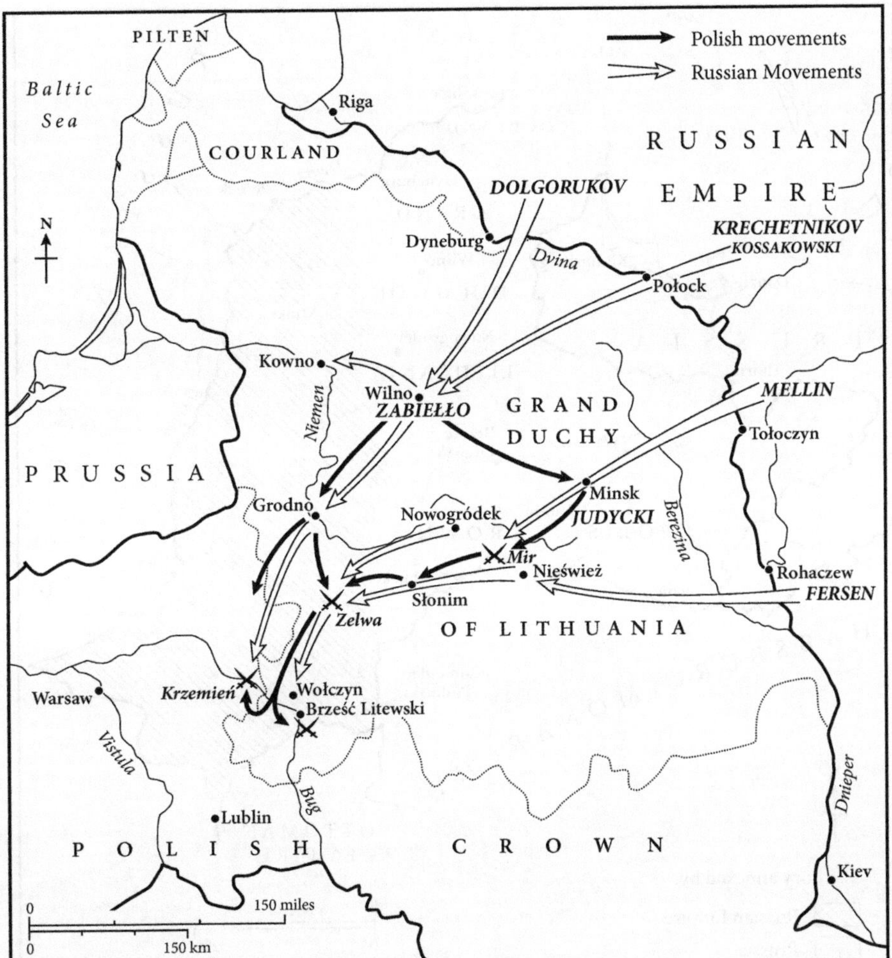

6. The campaign in the Grand Duchy of Lithuania, 1792

7. The second partition, 1793

8. The third partition, 1795

PRONUNCIATION GUIDE

Polish pronunciation looks worse than it is. Vowels are all of medium length, and the penultimate syllable is nearly always stressed. What follows is not for philologists.

a	as in 'jazz'
aj	as in 'lie' or 'bye'
au	as in 'how'
ą	nasal sound, approximating to 'om' or 'on'
c	'ts', as in 'lets'
ch	as in the Scottish pronunciation of 'loch'
cz	hard 'ch', as in 'chat'
ć, ci	soft 'ch', as in 'cheers'
e	as in 'best'
ej	as in 'say'
ę	nasal sound, approximating to 'em' or 'en'
i	like the 'ee' in 'cheese'. Softens a preceding consonant
j	'y' as in 'yet'
ł	'w' as in 'want'
ń, ni	soft 'n' as in 'new'
o	as in 'lot'
ó	as in 'nook'
r	rolled
rz	hard 'zh' as in 'treasure'
sz	hard 'sh' as in 'shop'
szcz	try 'wash-chops'
ś, si	soft 's' as in 'sheer'
ść, ści	like 'szcz' but softer

u	identical to 'ó'
w	'v' as in 'victor'
y	like the 'i' in 'win'
ź, zi	soft 'zh' as in the French 'gilet' (compare the hard 'zh' in 'jaune')
ż	identical to 'rz'

Other consonants are pronounced much as in English.
Example: *Kościuszko* approximates to Kosh´-CH´OOSH-ko

PROLOGUE
LIGHT AND FLAME

The morning of Sunday 6 May 1787 was bright and fresh. The strong spring sunshine was riven by sharp showers. The waters of the great River Dnieper, swollen by melted snow and ice from the north after a long winter, bore a flotilla of seven palatial galleys and about eighty lesser vessels southwards. This was the talk of Europe, the great progress of the Empress Catherine II of Russia. The empress was inspecting the southern lands being energetically settled by the colossus who was her effective co-ruler and probably her secret husband – Grigorii Potemkin. The imperial progress would later give rise to the term 'Potemkin villages' – based on maliciously exaggerated accounts of the hurriedly built or spruced-up settlements on the river banks. Catherine, long since called the Great by her admirers and flatterers, was *en route* to the newly annexed Crimea. War with the Ottoman Empire was in the offing. As the flotilla weighed anchor that morning at about ten o'clock, a battery above the small town of Kaniów on the Polish bank honoured its arrival with a 101- gun salute. The flotilla answered with nine salvos of its own.

Ashore, a well-groomed, rather plump man, aged fifty-five, with large dark eyes and an aquiline nose, waited nervously. He was Stanisław August Poniatowski, styled King of Poland, Grand Duke of Lithuania and twelve other lands, some of which had been lost. The length of his title was in inverse proportion to his powers as monarch. For at least two centuries, much of continental Europe had seen monarchs greatly increase their prestige, powers, revenues and armies, but the elective kings of Poland had been constrained by a numerous nobility – the szlachta – united by attachment to its liberties. These were given coherence by a shared ideology of republican freedom, which resonated in the name used for both the Polish-Lithuanian union and its community of noble citizens: the Commonwealth (*Rzeczpospolita*, a translation of *res publica*).

After twenty-nine years, Stanisław August was again to see the woman he had once loved. Having raised him to his throne, she had not only frustrated his ambitions to reform his country, but presided over its subjection and amputation. To see Catherine, he had traversed two-thirds of his kingdom in late winter. He had even suffered the indignity of a ducking when the ice cracked while his party (about 350 persons) attempted to cross the River Vistula. After arriving at Kaniów, he had waited six weeks in a specially designed and swiftly erected wooden residence. As the ice and snow slowly melted into mud, many of his leading subjects paid their court to the puissant empress upriver in Kiev. She paraded her piety in the city's venerable monasteries, especially during the Lenten religious rituals, while complaining privately at the tedium. The ancient capital of Rus′ had been seized from the Polish-Lithuanian Commonwealth by Muscovy in 1654 and formally annexed in 1686. It was now a backwater whose principal residents (if we are to believe the official account of the king's voyage) still kept their Polish speech, costume and hairstyles.[1]

Nearby were the sites of some of the Commonwealth's worst humiliations in the great Cossack revolt of 1648: a hammer-blow from which it had never fully recovered. As recently as 1768, the local Cossacks and peasants had again risen up against Polish lords, Catholic clergy and Jews, in an orgy of violence, fuelled by social, economic and religious grievances, before being equally brutally pacified. The far south-east of the Commonwealth was known as the Polish, or right-bank Ukraine, to distinguish it from the left-bank Ukraine which belonged to Russia. Even taken together, they covered a much smaller area than today's independent Ukraine. Here Catholic churches of the Latin rite were few and far between. The region remained afflicted by confessional tensions between Catholics of the Ruthenian rite (the Uniates) and the Orthodox. Close by was Potemkin's latifundium at Smila, which was fast becoming a state within a state. Its rapidly growing, overwhelmingly Orthodox population farmed the black earth and traded with the Russian Empire on the other bank of the Dnieper. Stanisław August had come to realize the political danger in the subordination of the Commonwealth's Orthodox clergy to St Petersburg. One item on his agenda was an oath of loyalty from the *de facto* bishop of the Orthodox Church in Poland-Lithuania. Among the king's other desiderata were trade agreements and the withdrawal of a Russian regiment which for some years had pillaged the south-east.

Above all, Stanisław August had long wanted to conclude a treaty of alliance and now saw his best opportunity. A Russo-Polish alliance, he reasoned, would secure the Commonwealth's remaining territory from its other neighbours – Prussia and Austria – and reactivate the Polish state on the international stage. Poles would fight alongside Russians in the impending war against the Ottoman Empire. He hoped this step would assuage national pride, dented by a passive decade and a half under Russian hegemony. He needed to convince Catherine that an alliance with a moderately strong Poland – albeit a very unequal alliance – was in Russian as well as in Polish interests. The problem he faced was that hitherto she had preferred to keep the Commonwealth weak. Only twice had she permitted relatively minor reforms to its system of government. Four times she had rejected an alliance.

If the empress agreed, such an alliance would require the holding of the next sejm (the Polish-Lithuanian parliament) under the aegis of a confederacy – a kind of legalized state of emergency. The szlachta sometimes formed confederacies from the 'bottom up' in the provinces against its monarchs, but confederacies could also be formed around the king. A confederated sejm was not subject to the usual requirement of unanimity and so could legislate by majority vote if necessary. The king needed the agreement of the sejm both to increase the size of the army and to raise the necessary additional revenues. He also signalled his intention to 'correct' parliamentary procedure and the administration of justice.

The king was also prepared to make the best of a rejection of his proposals. Even a polite reception from the empress might at least help to prevent his domestic opponents from completely wrecking the next sejm. This would allow him to continue his policy, adopted through necessity after the 1772 partition, of incremental improvements in apparently minor matters. Stanisław August's mood rose and fell according to the signals reaching Kaniów from Kiev. On the one hand, the leader of the magnate opposition, Franciszek Ksawery Branicki, was intriguing against the king. He held the office of Crown Grand Hetman, still the Commonwealth's highest military rank, but whose powers had been reduced during Stanisław August's reign. Branicki made much and more of this grievance. Given that the hetman was married to Potemkin's favourite niece Aleksandra, who was beloved of Catherine, his intrigues boded ill for the king. On the other hand, the empress had treated other opposition magnates with disdain, and warmly welcomed members of the king's own family.

The morning of 6 May passed. The imperial court slowly came to life, while the Poles waited. Two cosmopolitan princes travelling with the empress's suite, Charles-Joseph de Ligne and Charles-Henri de Nassau-Siegen, came ashore and were received by Stanisław August. At about one o'clock, Aleksandr Bezborodko (the empress's secretary and *de facto* foreign minister)[2] reached the Polish bank in a launch powered by nine oarsmen. Accompanied by the marshal of the imperial court, Fedor Bariantynskii, Bezborodko landed and invited the king to the empress's luxurious galley, the *Dnepr*. The journey took about an hour because of the sandbars and strong current. Doubtless wet and a little dishevelled from the squalls and choppy water, the king came aboard, accompanied by a small suite (Plate 1).[3]

Stanisław August had announced his intention to do so as 'Count Poniatowski' both for legal reasons (the king could not leave the territory of the Commonwealth without the permission of the sejm), and in an effort to save time spent on ceremony. Doubtless he also recalled that it had been as 'Count Poniatowski' that he had last seen Catherine in 1758. Nevertheless, Catherine greeted him with royal honours: rather than present her hand for the king to kiss, the empress offered her well-rouged and powdered cheek. Potemkin took the king as far as the door of the empress's private rooms. Stanisław August was allowed only a few minutes alone with Catherine. Their conversation was not recorded for posterity. After a few minutes, the doors were opened. The king brought in his niece Urszula, who received a hug from the tsaritsa. Then they came out, seemingly ill at ease.[4]

The monarchs' brief private reunion and the presentations were followed by conversation for about half an hour, before the company embarked on the imperial launch for dinner on another galley, with ostensible gaiety. The empress returned to the *Dnepr* and Potemkin invited the king aboard his own galley. Potemkin read the proposed treaty and approved its being submitted to Catherine. Then he tried to reconcile Stanisław August with Branicki. The king declared his willingness to forgive and forget past wrongs, but the hetman started to declaim, as the king put it, as if he were addressing the sejm. After further visits to court personages on other galleys, Stanisław August and Potemkin returned to Catherine. The king handed her the proposed treaty. According to the king's account, she promised to read it and reply. A christening followed, of the baby son of Count and Countess Tarnowski. The king's favourite clergyman, the poet and historian Adam Naruszewicz, performed the rite, and the empress and king stood as godparents. Then the company conversed and played cards.

The British minister to 'the king and Republick of Poland', Charles Whitworth, who had accompanied Stanisław August on board, noted that during the whole day the king had not the smallest opportunity to talk business with the empress.[5] This was but a slight exaggeration. Catherine found maintaining small talk with the anxious Stanisław August difficult. The following day she moaned to her secretary: 'Prince Potemkin uttered not a word; I had to talk incessantly, so my mouth dried up. The king bargained for three, then two days, in the end for dinner the next day.'[6] About eight o'clock she indicated that she was tired, and expressed regret that she could not accept Stanisław August's invitation to supper. There was no chance of her joining the celebrations of the king's nameday, the feast of St Stanisław, on 8 May. She would not even stay for dinner on the following day, because, she said, she could not keep the Holy Roman Emperor waiting. Indeed, Emperor Joseph II, the restless ruler of the Habsburg Monarchy, was already hurrying to meet her for their joint tour of the Crimea. Stanisław August looked strained, but after the empress had assured him of her 'most amicable intentions' he took his leave. Catherine seemed embarrassed – perhaps she sensed that she had badly used the second of her lovers, who had once stimulated her intellectual and emotional development.[7] The only comment she made to her correspondent of choice, Baron Melchior Grimm, was revealing: 'The King of Poland spent nine hours on board yesterday; we dined together; it is almost thirty years since I have seen him: you can judge how we found each other changed.'[8]

The empress usually retired at nine, but perhaps, as she had promised, she watched the illuminations and fireworks prepared and lit in her honour. Catherine's galley had the best viewpoint, which may indicate that the king had anticipated her refusal to come ashore. The spectacle of light and flame culminated in a simulated eruption of Vesuvius (Plate 2). This feat involved thousands of simultaneously fired rockets, and the representation of lava flows by the lighting of many smaller fires in specially dug ditches reaching down to the shore. The role of the volcano was played by the largest of the hills which sloped down to the river; it was aptly known as the *Moskiewka* (Little Moscow). This hill was topped by a huge obelisk featuring an imperial cipher. Volcanic fireworks were no novelty: later eighteenth-century European elites were fascinated with volcanoes. Nevertheless, these pyrotechnics undoubtedly impressed those who saw them. The audience included a local peasant, Omelek Derevianka, whose childhood recollections ('the moon and stars, flaming sheaves, columns or crosses shone above the town') were written down (and may have gained and lost much in the translation and editing) and published in 1854.[9] The following morning, the flotilla departed. Stanisław August began his return journey to Warsaw.

And then nothing happened. No answer came from the empress until September 1787. Her pared-down acceptance of an alliance only arrived a year after that. The Prince de Ligne, who had been sailing in the flotilla as a kind of public-relations specialist, had already quipped that Stanisław August had spent three million (ducats) and waited three months in order to see the empress for three hours.[10] Besides its factual inaccuracy, this *bon mot* failed to comprehend the significance of the event. In the first place, from the king's point of view the expedition to Kaniów was no fiasco – it avoided a political disaster. Second, both the expectations aroused by the journey and Catherine's delayed and partial acceptance of Stanisław August's proposals meant the king was unable to control the budding political transformation in the Commonwealth. He characterized the phenomenon thus: 'the ferment of minds continues apace, especially among youth'.[11] Perhaps he recalled his own youth, when an English friend had thought him 'capable of catching light and flame'.[12]

When the sejm commenced in October 1788, the Commonwealth began its frenetic, Valkyrian ride to immolation. That journey would bring moments of hope as well as despair, of glory as well as shame, of far-sighted statesmanship as well as selfish myopia. The perception of the Commonwealth, both by its own inhabitants and by foreigners, would be altered forever – and for the better. Without these metamorphoses of the Polish nation, the partitioning powers would have had a much easier task in their shared endeavour, solemnized in their secret 1797 coda to the third partition, 'to abolish everything which could recall the existence of the Kingdom of Poland', the which designation would 'remain suppressed, now and forever'.[13]

These transformations of the Commonwealth derived in part from a swell of reformist ideas and activity dating back to the 1730s. Not only King Stanisław August, but several thousand citizens involved in politics, the Churches, the law, public administration, education, science and trade, concluded that Poles had fallen behind other, 'more enlightened' nations and that fundamental changes were needed. These reformers provoked deeply felt reactions among a rather greater number of noble citizens in defence of a traditional 'Sarmatian' world that found itself under critical interrogation. This label, originally deriving from the widespread belief among Polish nobles in their descent from the ancient Sarmatians who had fought the Roman legions, came to be used both as an insult and as a badge of pride. The fraught encounter between reformers and traditionalists, which was often entangled with the threads of factional politics, is often caricatured as a struggle between 'whiskers' and 'periwig', between the cosmopolitan Enlightenment and home-grown 'Sarmatism', between 'Warsaw' and the provincial countryside, or even between 'republicans' and 'monarchists'. In fact it proved far more complex, and far more productive than any of these dichotomies. Otherwise divided citizens could – and sometimes did – meet on the common ground of a profound patriotism. Most reformers found many things to admire in the Polish-Lithuanian past; most traditionalists admitted that much in the Commonwealth was in need of repair. By 1791 something approaching a synthesis of republican and monarchist visions for repair and reform had flowered in the Constitution of 3 May, whose preamble contains some of the most magnificent patriotic rhetoric ever written in the Polish language.

Before the Russian invasion of May 1792, the 'patriot' coalition had the critical mass, including sufficient support in some of the Commonwealth's deepest provinces, to continue the work of evolutionary transformation begun by revolutionary means on 3 May 1791. The Commonwealth's peoples would have had a very different – and probably much better – future, had that work not been curtailed. But the combination of Russian military might and a small group of unreconciled domestic 'malcontents' launched a final spiralling descent into the flames: war, counter-revolution, partition, insurrection and annihilation.

This fatal mechanism, although it worked in the 1790s with unprecedented speed and force, was not only the result of the process set in train in 1787–88 or even the pressure for repair and reform that was building up by mid-century. It also derived from the creation by Peter the Great at the start of the eighteenth century of a Russian Empire which looked to project its growing power westwards out of the Muscovite core of its Eurasian 'heartland'. Control of the Polish-Lithuanian polity, Muscovy's long-term rival for hegemony in the lands between the Baltic and Black Seas, would enable the newly proclaimed *Rossiiskaia Imperiia* to pursue its goals as one of the great powers of Europe. Expansion provoked containment, and a Commonwealth restored to its original vitality and courted by other powers could well shut the Russian Empire out of European affairs. Such was Russian *raison d'état* throughout the eighteenth century. Those geopolitics remain relevant today.

The three partitions of the Commonwealth – in 1772, 1793 and 1795 – can also be understood as an outcome of the eighteenth-century inter-state system, albeit an unusual and in some respects unprecedented one. For those who shaped the policies of the great powers, the principal assumptions of the system involved the prevention of rival powers' hegemony and the pursuit of a favourable balance of power via alliances. Indemnification involved acquisitions of territory in return for efforts undertaken on behalf of allies, while territorial compensation was claimed when neighbouring powers made gains. Given that all these factors were notoriously difficult to calculate, and that most statesmen tended to overestimate their own strength and underestimate their rivals', wars, once they broke out, were hard to end. Few eighteenth-century wars were 'surgical strikes'.

In these transactions of alliance and peace, minor principalities served as currency. In a Europe full of 'composite monarchies', rather than 'sovereign, territorial, nation states',[14] it was natural to countenance such bargains. Self-determination was unthinkable. The inhabitants of neither Lorraine nor Tuscany were consulted in 1737 when the father-in-law of the King of France became Duke of Lorraine, while the displaced duke, the son-in-law of the Holy Roman Emperor, became Grand Duke of Tuscany. On the other hand, although relatively few Europeans had a say in *who* ruled them, many more had a say in *how* they were ruled. Monarchs could not ignore their subjects' privileges and customs, although some had to learn this lesson the hard way. Given the predominance of dynastic over national thinking, the division of princely inheritances, although often resisted, was easily contemplated and sometimes practised. This could be a destabilizing factor: the eighteenth century saw several wars of succession. The most destructive of these followed the failed attempts to negotiate a peaceful partition of the Spanish Empire at the death of the last Spanish Habsburg in 1700.

The partitions of Poland were rather different. To begin with, the Commonwealth was neither a minor principality nor a city-republic, but one of Europe's largest states. Second, for all the various routes by which its diverse territories had come together, the Commonwealth was no longer a composite polity. By eighteenth-century standards it was internally coherent. Among its noble citizens, strong local identities complemented a shared civic, republican culture. Not only was a large and consolidated territory sliced up, but a mature and numerous political nation was also divided.[15] Third, schemes to partition the territories of larger polities among neighbouring powers were relatively rare, although not unknown. Most of the Commonwealth's neighbours (and one of its magnates) had planned its carve-up in 1656. The Austrian monarchy was slated for dismemberment in the early 1740s, and the Prussian state was set to be cut down to a rump in the later 1750s. However, these and other schemes did not succeed. The predators fell out among themselves, allies rallied round, and the victims recovered sufficiently to fight off their remaining foes.

It was possible in the eighteenth century for weaker polities to survive because neighbouring powers sought to prevent other powers from gaining a relative advantage. Statesmen recognized that defenceless buffer-states could help to keep their neighbours' conflicts manageable. However, a weak state which threatened to become stronger could not only directly threaten the interests of one or more of its neighbours, but could also create an imbalance between them. That imbalance could be 'righted' by the eighteenth-century system of indemnification and compensation. This mechanism goes some way to explaining the destruction of the Commonwealth in the 1790s. At this point it is worth recalling the broadly analogous case of the Holy Roman Empire of the German Nation. For all the differences between the Commonwealth and the old Reich – including the significant degree of sovereignty enjoyed by many German princes, the tiny number of electors, and the 'amphibious', half-in, half-out position of the Habsburgs and Hohenzollerns – their essential similarity in the eighteenth century was geopolitical. As vacuums of power, the Reich and the Commonwealth were kept in existence for decades, because no combination of internal and external powers could prevail against those with an interest in the status quo. But this equilibrium did not last forever. Between 1772 and 1795 the Commonwealth was partitioned by the decisions of an inconvenienced Russian imperial hegemon, with compensation paid to Prussia and Austria. The thousand-year Reich did not last much longer. Between 1797 and 1806 it was trimmed back in the west, partitioned from within by its compensation-hungry princes, including Austria and Prussia, and finally abolished by the decisions of a French imperial hegemon. Reform might precipitate annihilation. But partition was a latent hazard in eighteenth-century politics.[16]

The meteoric trajectory of the last years of the Polish-Lithuanian Commonwealth was driven by the interaction of external and internal factors. The long-standing crisis of Poland's institutions facilitated Russian, Prussian and occasionally Austrian interference which usually weakened the Commonwealth further. It also provoked both moralizing handwringing and thoughts of serious reform among its citizens. Both reformers and traditionalists, for all their disagreements, keenly felt the abasement of their country by the neighbouring powers. Their efforts to reassert the Commonwealth's sovereignty provoked invasion and partition. In these exceptionally unfavourable circumstances, a wide-ranging renewal took place. It encompassed education, the arts and sciences, the economy, social relations, government institutions and finally, the conduct of politics.

Few periods in the Commonwealth's history were so energized by discussion, or so packed with incidents and initiatives, as the reign of Stanisław August. The fact that it was punctuated with trauma, and ended with the annihilation of the state, should not obscure the enormous potential for human development woven deep into the fabric of the Commonwealth. Beginning in the middle decades of the eighteenth century, this potential was illuminated before being enflamed.

— ONE —
COMMONWEALTH

Stanisław August, like his predecessors, was styled King of Poland, Grand Duke of Lithuania, Ruthenia, Prussia, Mazovia, Samogitia, Kiev, Volhynia, Podolia, Podlasie, Livonia, Smolensk, Severia and Czernihów. It was a shorter list than that of his Habsburg contemporaries, but it still evokes the composite monarchies assembled by competing dynasts who inherited, married, purchased, swapped or conquered realms, duchies, counties, lordships, overlordships, jurisdictions and reversions. Monarchs would typically govern each of their territories according to its own laws and customs. While they would try to ratchet up the revenues and recruits over time, they usually had to negotiate compromises with local elites. Few of these 'mildly centripetal agglutinations' became nation states.[1] Most have many successor states and nations. At first sight the Polish-Lithuanian Commonwealth looks the part of a composite monarchy: its territories were divided into overlapping hierarchies of nations, provinces, palatinates, districts and lands. They are now in Belarus, Estonia, Latvia, Lithuania, Poland, Russia and Ukraine. Their peoples and customs were diverse, but these territories were united by more than a shared ruler. The Commonwealth was a union of political communities, whose enduring value was liberty.

Things might have turned out very differently. At the turn of the thirteenth century two kings of Bohemia won the Polish throne. A king of Hungary inherited it in the late fourteenth century. In the mid-fifteenth century a king of Poland was chosen as king of Hungary. In the late sixteenth century one elected king of Poland inherited the kingdom of France and another inherited that of Sweden. In the eighteenth century two successive electors of Saxony were also kings of Poland. Most spectacularly of all, at the turn of the fifteenth century three brothers Jagiellon reigned over a third of Europe: the kingdoms of Hungary, Bohemia and Poland, and the Grand Duchy of Lithuania. But all these personal unions proved short-lived, while many other projects were stillborn.

The Polish-Lithuanian and Polish-Prussian unions put down deeper roots. Their auspices were unpromising, for the medieval Kingdom of Poland was a fragile construction. It was held together as much by the metropolitan see of Gniezno as anything else, and was usually overshadowed by Bohemia and Hungary. Poland's sudden emergence and rapid expansion at the turn of the first Christian millennium were followed by several generations of division and shrinkage. The kingdom's reassembly between the 1290s and the 1320s was incomplete. The western crescent of Silesia, Lusatia and Pomerania was lost. The north-eastern Duchy of Mazovia remained a feudal vassal and was not finally reincorporated into the realm until 1529. So the 'reunited' Kingdom of Poland essentially comprised Greater Poland (*Wielkopolska, Polonia maior*) centred on the cities of Poznań and Gniezno in the north-west, and Lesser Poland (*Małopolska*, *Polonia minor*), with the royal residence of Cracow, in the south-east.

Casimir III, the last of the native Piast dynasty to rule the Kingdom of Poland, did much with his inheritance. During his long reign (1333–1370), when he was not hunting or wenching, he fought wars, built churches and castles, founded a university, and issued laws and charters. The realm flourished. Uniquely among Polish kings, Casimir won the sobriquet of 'the Great'. Acknowledging territorial losses in the west, he recompensed them in the south-east. Kievan Rus′ had initially followed a similar historical trajectory to Poland: a strong monarchy split into multiple principalities. The difference was that Kiev was incomparably wealthier – until the Mongols or Tatars brought devastation and subjection from 1237 onwards. The least affected principality of Rus′ was Halych and Volhynia in the south-west. This was the inheritance claimed by Casimir. He made good his claim to the southern part of it, where he set the city of lions – Lwów – on its path to prosperity. Six hundred years later, with a neat symmetry, Polish Lwów became L′viv in the Ukrainian SSR, while the Silesian provincial capital of Breslau became Polish Wrocław. Expelled Leopolitans became 'repatriated' Vratislavians.

Casimir pushed his rule further east into Podolia, but Polish expansion into Rus′ was dwarfed by the rise of the Grand Duchy of Lithuania. During the thirteenth and fourteenth centuries, pagan Lithuanian warriors swept southwards and eastwards from their glades and groves. The conquerors were often welcomed by Rus′ian elites who saw them as protectors from the Tatar Golden Horde. Scions of the ruling Lithuanian dynasty – kinsmen of their overlord, Grand Duke Gediminas – married local princesses, adopted Orthodox Christianity, and ruled their new subjects according to existing laws and customs. Rivals in south-western Rus′, Lithuania and Poland shared a long and turbulent frontier. They also shared a common enemy.

In the thirteenth century, the crusading order of warrior-monks known as the Teutonic Knights established itself on the east bank of the Vistula estuary – in the land of the Prussians. Their mission, endorsed by popes and emperors, was to convert the Baltic pagan tribes to Christianity, by fire and sword if necessary. The Prussians and their gods were all but extirpated. The conquerors founded a strictly governed *Ordernsstaat*, and enlarged it with rich lands taken from the divided Polish realm. Towns grew. Woods and marshes became farmland. A sister order established itself further north in Livonia (now Latvia and Estonia). The Lithuanian heartland was caught in a vice, for all the spectacular expansion into Rus′. So Lithuania and Poland began the process of union.

The opportunity arose through a dynastic accident. Casimir the Great had no legitimate son, and was succeeded by his nephew, King Louis of Hungary (r.1370–1382). He too was sonless. To ensure his younger daughter's succession in Poland he made concessions, especially on taxes, to the lords, knights and clergy. Although crowned queen regnant, the barely nubile Jadwiga (r.1384–1399) needed a husband. The lords of the realm persuaded her to accept a hairy pagan three times her age – Jogaila, Grand Duke of Lithuania. At Kreva in 1385, in return for the Polish throne he promised to accept baptism, convert his pagan Lithuanian subjects, marry Jadwiga and '*Terras suas Litvaniae et Rusie Corone Regni Polone perpetuo applicare*'.[2] He delivered on the first three promises, but the meaning of the last one has been endlessly contested. The most persuasive explanation – advanced by Robert Frost – is that Jogaila undertook to incorporate (*applicare*) his Lithuanian and Rus′ian lands, not into the Polish realm (*regnum*), but into something less tangible – the Crown of the Kingdom of Poland. This was grounded in the medieval concept of the community of the realm, binding monarch and leading subjects with the pursuit of the common good. This idea evolved somewhat differently in Hungary, where the Holy Crown of St Stephen also took on a specific territorial meaning. In Poland the essence of the Crown was the political community. It took two fractious centuries for the different interpretations of this bargain to be hammered out. From the start, this was no ordinary dynastic or personal union.

In the meantime, enemies had to be dealt with. The Teutonic Order was soundly beaten by the combined forces of Poland and Lithuania at the battle of Grunwald (Tannenberg) in 1410, but it survived and kept most of its lands. Poland – unaided by Lithuania – was unable to finish off the Order during the Thirteen Years' War of 1454–66. This conflict was nonetheless decisive. A league of Prussian cities and nobles rose up against the burdensome rule of the Order and offered the conditional incorporation of the Prussian lands into the Kingdom of Poland. In the end, only the western, richer half of Prussia freed itself from the Order's rule. 'Royal Prussia' became Poland's commercial powerhouse. Its urban and landed elites guarded their privileges and liberties through more than three centuries of union. The Lutheran Reformation put paid to the eastern rump of the *Ordernsstaat*. On Cracow's spacious market square in 1525, the former grand master, Albrecht von Hohenzollern, swore a vassal's homage to King Sigismund I of Poland and was invested with the Duchy of Prussia.

By this time, the Grand Duchy of Lithuania was seriously threatened from the east. Jogaila's father, Grand Duke Algirdas (1345–1377), had twice reached the gates of Moscow. For the next century or so, Muscovy remained in the shadow of its huge western neighbour. However, perhaps sensing relaxation as the Jagiellonian dynasty moved into Bohemia and Hungary, the grand princes of Moscow chipped away at the fringes of Lithuanian overlordship. During a series of wars in the late fifteenth and early sixteenth centuries, they seized a third of the Grand Duchy of Lithuania. Polish aid helped to stem the tide, but in the late 1550s Tsar Ivan 'the Terrible' renewed the attack. This time the main prize was the power vacuum left by the collapse of the Teutonic Knights' sister order in Livonia. The principal contenders were Muscovy, Sweden and Poland-Lithuania, and the long-term stake was hegemony in the Baltic.

In the short term, Muscovite aggression persuaded the principal Lithuanian lords to accept closer union with Poland. Lesser Lithuanian nobles were keen to share the personal and political liberties enjoyed by the Polish szlachta, but did not accept Polish demands for the incorporation of the Grand Duchy of Lithuania into Poland as a mere province, equal not to the Crown as a whole but to Greater or Lesser Poland. The last Jagiellonian monarch, Sigismund II Augustus (r.1548–1572), squared the circle. At Lublin on 1 July 1569 a joint sejm (parliament) agreed a new act of union. Henceforth Poland and

Lithuania would share a jointly elected monarch and a common sejm. They would retain separate armies, treasuries, legal systems and hierarchies of ministers, officials and dignitaries. The crucial clause of the Lublin act (written in Polish rather than Latin) says 'that the Kingdom of Poland and the Grand Duchy of Lithuania is already one indivisible and uniform body, and also one uniform and common *Rzeczpospolita*, which has joined and united two *państwa* and *narody* into one *lud*'.[3]

Four crucial terms need to be translated here. *Państwo* is the modern Polish word for state, and at first sight this appears to make sense. However, as late as the end of the eighteenth century the plural form *państwa* was often used to mean territories, while at root it means lordship or dominion. *Naród* means 'nation', but that is a slippery term. We should not necessarily assume that it meant a political community as opposed to a linguistic one.[4] Just to complicate things, other clauses of the act feature a 'dual nation'. *Lud* has plebeian connotations and is usually rendered as 'people' or 'populace'. However, the Latin *populus*, used in a previous act of union, meant the wider political community. So did *Rzeczpospolita*. This was an early translation of the Latin *res publica*, just like its English contemporary – Commonwealth. The forms '*republika*' and 'republic' came later. So we can unlock the quotation as an assertion of 'one uniform and common Commonwealth, which has joined and united two dominions and nations into one political community'. In one way this formula was utterly simple: two political communities agreed that they were one. In other ways its studied ambiguity left much unsaid and unresolved.

It is a misperception that the Union of Lublin founded a state called the Polish-Lithuanian Commonwealth, whose formal name was 'the Commonwealth of the Two Nations, Polish and Lithuanian'. No such name was ever inscribed into an official document. Eighteenth-century diplomats were accredited to '*le Roi et la République de Pologne*'. Older historical atlases and textbooks feature the 'Republic of Poland'. However, this usage has been largely displaced in English by 'the Polish-Lithuanian Commonwealth' or 'Poland-Lithuania'. The habit has spread to Poland, and the reader may wonder why. To start with, it is a neat expression of the dual composition of the polity; it may suggest comparisons with Austria-Hungary. It also contradicts modern nationalist Polish narratives that posit a First and a Second Republic of Poland, in which other nations were of little importance. Still more recently, during the 'Third Republic of Poland', it has become fashionable to enthuse about a multilingual, multiconfessional and multicultural 'Commonwealth of many nations', but that term is even further removed from historical sources. For our purposes, 'the Polish-Lithuanian Commonwealth' is a useful and not inaccurate label, although it can suggest both too many and too few components of the political community.

The Commonwealth had an array of ethnic and confessional minorities, but essentially there were eight unequal parties to this marriage. Besides the monarch, the Polish Crown and the Grand Duchy of Lithuania, these were Courland and Livonia, Ducal and Royal Prussia, and the lands of southern Rus′. The south-western strip of the Livonian lands contested with Muscovy and Sweden became the vassal duchy of Courland in 1561 – a Lithuanian equivalent to Ducal Prussia. The Kettler dukes had to contend with powerful Estates dominated by a Germanophone, Lutheran nobility. The Estates' position was defined by a privilege issued by Sigismund Augustus in 1561, enabling them to appeal to the Polish-Lithuanian monarch. Most of the duchy's population were Latvian-speaking peasants, but Ugro-Finnic (Liv-speaking) fishing communities survived along its bleak north-western coast. The remainder of Livonia became a Lithuano-Polish condominium in 1569. Part now forms Latgola – this south-eastern corner of Latvia retains a distinct identity. Royal Prussian delegates participated in the Lublin sejm, and Prussian liberties were stoutly defended thereafter.

Greater changes affected the southern half of the Grand Duchy of Lithuania: Volhynia and the fertile Ukrainian lands that rolled away past Kiev, far to the south-east. Beyond the no man's land known as the 'wild plains' lay the shores of the Black Sea, ruled by the predatory Crimean Tatars. In these exposed territories grand ducal rule had always been looser than north of the Polesian marshes. Local princes and nobles had few reasons to trust the northern Lithuanian lords more than their monarch. Only in 1566 did Orthodox nobles finally gain equal rights with Catholics within the Grand Duchy. 'Polish liberties' were correspondingly attractive. In 1569 the nobles of the Volhynian and Kievan lands joined their brethren in the Polish Crown 'as equals', while retaining their own laws and customs. All of southern Rus′ now fell within the Polish Crown. The marshy and woody borderland of Podlasie, which had long attracted settlers from Mazovia, became part of the Crown at the same time. From the Lithuanian lords' perspective, echoed in the modern national historiographies of Lithuania, Belarus and Ukraine, this massive transfer of territory was a vengeful act by the monarch to gratify Polish appetites. But the balance of the evidence suggests it was welcomed by local elites (Map 1).

This may be a good moment to explain the terms which derive from Rus′. This was originally the name of a people – whose leaders hailed from Scandinavia – which came to be applied to their lands in the Dnieper basin. By the end of the fourteenth century most of post-Kievan Rus′ was ruled by the Grand Dukes of Lithuania and Kings of Poland, while Muscovy remained a weak principality at its north-eastern edge. A hundred years later, however, things had changed dramatically, as the grand princes of Moscow proclaimed themselves lords 'of all Rus′' (*vseia Rusi*) and assumed the imperial title of tsar. Polish-Lithuanian rulers fought a long rearguard action against the usage which served a Muscovite ideology of expansion into their territories. The standard Latin translation of Rus′ is *Russia*. In Byzantine Greek it was *Rhossia*, which in turn encouraged the Muscovite use of *Rossiia* alongside Rus′. In 1721 Peter I would proclaim the *Rossiiskaia Imperiia* – the Russian Empire. In medieval western Christendom, however, an alternative Latin translation of Rus′ appeared: *Ruthenia*. This was occasionally used as a translation for Rus′ in documents created in the Commonwealth, although *Russia* remained more common.

The potential for confusion is immense. From this point in the book onwards, 'Muscovy' denotes the pre-1721 tsardom, 'Russia' the post-1721 empire, and 'Ruthenia' the lands of Rus′ which remained in Poland-Lithuania through most of the eighteenth century. Similarly, 'Russian' refers to the Great Russian language while 'Ruthenian' means the *ruskii* spoken in the Commonwealth. Variants of the latter evolved into the modern Belarusian and Ukrainian languages. Chancery Ruthenian was used for legal documents in the Lithuanian and Ruthenian lands until 1697. It contained admixtures of Old Church Slavonic, Latin and Polish. This was the language of the three Lithuanian statutes or law codes of 1529, 1566 and 1588, the last of which remained in force until 1840. The Third Statute had to be translated into Great Russian. Exceptions to the above rule will be made for quotations. For example, many Polish-Lithuanian politicians and writers continued to refer pejoratively to Muscovy (*Moskwa*) and Muscovites (*Moskale*), even after the Commonwealth had ceased to exist.

Like the Livonians and Prussians, the Ruthenian elites were willing partners in the shared political community forged in 1569. The terms of Lublin rankled with the Lithuanian lords, but closer union with Poland soon paid dividends for the

Grand Duchy. The second elective monarch, Stephen Báthory (r.1576–1586), turned the tables on Ivan the Terrible. Cut off from the Baltic, Muscovy plunged into its Time of Troubles. Although the Muscovite state reconsolidated itself under the Romanov dynasty, it had to return Smolensk to the Grand Duchy of Lithuania, and that verdict was crushingly confirmed in 1634. Elsewhere the Commonwealth's record was mixed. Polish misadventures in Moldavia provoked an Ottoman invasion in 1620–21, but a strong defence secured an honourable peace. Wars against Sweden began when the Commonwealth reluctantly backed the efforts of King Sigismund III Vasa (r.1587–1632) to recover his inherited Swedish throne. The Polish-Lithuanian armies beat the Swedes in the field more often than not, but the Commonwealth failed to sustain the fiscal commitments needed to take and hold territory. Most of Livonia was lost. Nevertheless, by 1635, while the Holy Roman Empire was ravaged by the Thirty Years' War, peace was assured on all fronts, and the Commonwealth's territory approached a million square kilometres. Overall, a combination of talented commanders, highly manoeuvrable medium-weight cavalry (the *Husaria*), battle-hardened Cossack infantry and advances in artillery brought the Commonwealth a formidable military reputation in its first eight decades.

Blessed (or cursed) with hindsight, many historians have lamented the victorious Commonwealth's repeated failure to finish off its foes. But the purpose of this political community was not territorial expansion – certainly not for its kings' glory. It was liberty. This meant more than the accumulation of 'liberties' and privileges. Across later medieval and early modern Europe, incoming monarchs would generally grant lands, issue charters, and confirm existing privileges to gain support. Once established on their thrones, they would sometimes convene assemblies of the bishops, abbots, lords, knights and burgesses of their realms or provinces. These assemblies might be called Estates, diets or parliaments. In return for the funds needed to wage war or agreement to the succession of their progeny, monarchs would promise to redress grievances. Some managed to consolidate their revenues and extend their authority, but dynastic accidents could weaken their hand.

All this occurred in the Kingdom of Poland. Without a son to succeed him, King Louis felt obliged to concede that no taxes (beyond a minimal two groats per morg) would be imposed on the Polish nobles or clergy without their consent. Jogaila (Władysław Jagiełło in Polish) begat sons very late in life, so he promised that nobles would be protected from arbitrary arrest and imprisonment without trial. This was the privilege of *neminem captivabimus nisi iure victum*, which took its final form in 1433. His younger son, Casimir IV Jagiellon, in order to fight the Teutonic Knights, agreed in 1454 that assemblies of the nobility would first have to consent to taxes and the calling out of the general levy.

By the beginning of the sixteenth century, the Kingdom of Poland had a functioning bicameral parliament. According to the act of *Nihil novi*, agreed in 1505, the monarch would enact

> nothing new . . . to the prejudice and inconvenience of the *Res publica*, or to the detriment and injury of whatsoever private interest, or that alters the common law and public liberties, without the common agreement of our councillors and envoys of the lands.[5]

This law left the monarch considerable powers regarding royal towns, Jews, royal estates, fiefs and so forth. Moreover, its corollary was that the three Estates of the sejm – king, senate and envoys – could agree to new laws and new taxes. And they did.

The sixteenth century was exceptionally fertile in parliamentary legislation and taxation. The 'community of the realm' took on mature institutional forms. Many thousands of nobles participated in local assemblies. These sejmiks instructed and elected envoys to the sejm, received reports from them and often responded directly to royal appeals. They took on responsibility for much local business as well. As the landed nobles who frequented sejmiks grew more prosperous, educated and self-confident, they became disinclined to defer to the great lords. Some of their spokesmen accused the magnates of illegally holding royal lands. If these properties were returned to the Crown, the monarch would be able to defend the kingdom's frontiers without such frequent resort to taxation. This was the social foundation of the 'movement for the execution of the laws'.

Noble tribunes and grandees alike could draw on printed editions of works created or rediscovered during the Renaissance. Particularly influential were histories and rhetorical works from late republican and early imperial Rome. What ancient Romans had called *libertas* was essentially a system for civic participation in public affairs, rather than the sum of individual or collective privileges. Classical authors such as Cicero, Quintilian, Sallust, Livy and Tacitus provided sixteenth-century Polish statesmen with a vision of their polity as a free and balanced *res publica*. Besides the civic community, territories and institutions of the Polish-Lithuanian union, the capacious term *Rzeczpospolita* also represented the harmonious and virtuous exercise of liberty for which all citizens were expected to strive. However, the cult of virtue was not taken to sacrificial extremes. Citizens' right to participate in their own governance secured their tranquil enjoyment of individual liberties and properties. In other words, their personal or 'negative' liberty depended on their collective or 'positive' liberty.

This concept of the Commonwealth lasted more than two centuries and belongs within the early modern European republican tradition. During the last few decades, this 'neo-Roman' tradition has been in vogue as an alternative to classical liberalism (often stigmatized as 'neo-liberalism'). It distinguishes the factual 'non-coercion' of the individual by the ruler, which is at the heart of the liberal idea of freedom, from 'non-domination', whereby rulers are denied the possibility of exercising arbitrary power. In Poland-Lithuania, republicanism was the predominant persuasion of the established and aspirant political community, rather than a radical fringe, as it became, for example, in seventeenth- and eighteenth-century England.[6]

From the early sixteenth century, the Polish form of government – often conflated with the political community – was usually called a *monarchia mixta*. The forces of monarchy, aristocracy and democracy were thought to hold each other in check, preventing their descent respectively into tyranny, oligarchy and ochlocracy (mob rule). The concept dates back to Aristotle and Polybius and was popularized in Renaissance Europe. It corresponded nicely with the emergent three Estates of the sejm. The popular or democratic contribution was made by the chamber of envoys, comprising delegates of the 'knighthood'. The monarchical element was the king, while the senate (which had grown out of the group of senior royal councillors and representatives) provided the aristocratic component.

According to the more aristocratic interpretation of the theory of *monarchia mixta*, the senators mediated between 'majesty' and 'liberty'. They strove to prevent the former from sliding into tyranny and the latter from slipping into licence. This view was fully articulated in 1568 by a future bishop, Wawrzyniec Goślicki (Latinized as Goslicius). His work *De optimo senatore* was four times translated or adapted into English (in 1598, 1607, 1733 and 1992) and almost certainly inspired the character Polonius in Shakespeare's *Hamlet*.[7] Tribunes of the non-senatorial nobility expounded a competing interpretation of *monarchia mixta*. They denounced the pretensions of senators who sought to elevate themselves above the equality of all noble citizens. Either way, this was an argument how best to balance the body politic, but the latter, increasingly common interpretation tended towards a binary struggle between *maiestas* and *libertas*.

Roughly until the middle of the seventeenth century the theory of *monarchia mixta* could still plausibly be presented as an approximation of the working structure of the Commonwealth. One of the weaknesses of the senatorial position was that senators were not a hereditary aristocracy – to attain and maintain their status, they had had to please either the monarch or a significant number of nobles. Thereafter, as malcontent magnates took the role of demagogues rather than aristocratic arbiters, the theory lost touch with reality, although it continued to be referenced until the 1770s.

At the heart of the system was the sejm. During the 1560s a tidier version of the Polish parliamentary system was rolled out in the Grand Duchy of Lithuania. The Lithuanian sejm also comprised the monarch, a senate including the lords of the council, and a lower chamber of noble envoys elected by district sejmiks. The 1569 Union of Lublin fused the two parliaments. Lithuanian senators and envoys took places amidst their Polish colleagues, rather than after them. Although neither the Crown nor the Grand Duchy was permitted to hold a separate parliament, monarchs continued to convoke meetings of the Estates of the Grand Duchy of Lithuania when they needed to raise additional revenue and soldiers in an emergency.

The joint sejm of the Commonwealth reached its decisions by consensus among its three Estates. Compromises were thrashed out in public deliberations and private negotiations, taking account of the relative importance of speakers as well as the strength of their arguments. Proceeding by consensus was quite typical for deliberative institutions in sixteenth-century Europe. There were – and are – strong arguments for preferring forms of decision-making that involve listening to and weighing up opinions, over those which merely count votes. Given the diversity of interests at stake, the political community might otherwise have been ruptured. However, the failure to nip serious procedural problems in the bud would have baleful consequences. The sejm was ordinarily expected to meet every two years and complete its tasks within six weeks. However, the increase in business often necessitated extensions. As the decades passed, a growing number of sejms dispersed without reaching a successful conclusion. After the initial joint session in which the royal propositions from the throne were read out, the two chambers deliberated separately, communicating by messages. When they joined together at the end of the sejm, the laws (called constitutions) that had been agreed were read out to the assembled senators and envoys. Each could only be inscribed into the law books after a threefold and uncontested cry of agreement: '*zgoda!*'. This meant that if a sejm dispersed because there was no agreement to further prolongation, no new laws or taxes could take effect. Extraordinary sejms, supposed to conclude in two weeks, could usually resolve this problem on a case-by-case basis. Nevertheless, harmony was in short supply by the 1640s.

Much of the problem revolved around trust: a crucial component of the system of values and institutions. The division between king and citizen-subjects was often criss-crossed by rifts between senators and envoys, the Crown and the Grand Duchy, provinces, and rival personalities. During the interregnum that followed the death of Sigismund Augustus in 1572, many matters unprovided for in the Lublin act had to be pragmatically resolved *ad hoc*. A false step could have led to civil war and foreign invasion. The decisions included the mode of electing the king – in the end it was agreed that all nobles who wished to participate in person could do so. The location was the same as that envisaged for sejms by the Union of Lublin: the secondary royal residence-town of Warsaw, conveniently located between the two capital cities of Cracow and Wilno. The surrounding Mazovian lands were inhabited by numerous, poor and Catholic nobles. The choice of king carried geopolitical implications. Many senators, especially bishops, traditionally oriented themselves towards the Austrian Habsburgs, but an alliance with Vienna increased the risk of war with the Ottoman Empire. Each time a Habsburg came close to winning, he was frustrated, sometimes violently.

The first elective monarch, Henri Valois (r.1573–1574), absconded from Cracow after succeeding his brother as King of France. He was given an ultimatum to return within a year. When he did not, the throne was declared vacant. The next king, Stephen Báthory, swore to keep the 'Henrician articles' drawn up to bind his predecessor. These were henceforth entered into the *pacta conventa* – effectively the contract of employment agreed with each newly elected monarch. Besides his military victories, Báthory established supreme Tribunals – courts of appeal – for the Crown and Lithuania, crowning a judicial system based mainly on elected judges. However, his autocratic temper aroused fears for freedom.

Jagiellonian sentiments remained strong. To win the throne, Báthory had espoused Sigismund Augustus's unmarried sister Anna. The female Jagiellonian line continued through Sigismund III Vasa, son and heir of Anna's sister Catherine and the King of Sweden. However, the inexperienced young monarch was soon negotiating secretly with the Habsburgs. By 1606 his lack of understanding of the Commonwealth's political values provoked a major revolt among much of the nobility. It ended in stalemate, and Sigismund learned from his mistakes. His elder son Władysław IV (r.1632–1648) was elected unopposed with a substantial credit of popularity, much of which he squandered. Władysław's two younger brothers contested the next election. For all their faults, no Vasa would suffer the bloody fate of Charles Stuart.

The monarch was crucial to the functioning of the system. Besides his political and military leadership (albeit advised and monitored by senators), the king symbolized the majesty of the Commonwealth. Monarchs had occasionally to endure plain-speaking, but generally they were treated with great honour. They also had a great store of patronage at their disposal. The most important offices in royal gift were those of the marshals, chancellors, vice-chancellors, treasurers, and grand and field hetmans of the Crown and Lithuania, as well as chairs in the senate. Still more potently, kings could award thousands of Crown estates linked to the office of starosta – originally a royal representative in a locality. Some of these *starostwa* came with judicial responsibilities in the castle courts, while a few conferred immense wealth on the recipient. The targeted distribution of patronage allowed kings to reward faithful and meritorious servants and to construct a royalist party. The attempt could easily backfire, however. The grant of most offices and lands was for life or until promotion to a higher rank, so the promise of future reward was more efficacious than gratitude for past bounty. Moreover, the most prominent families considered the plumpest rewards their due; to withhold favour invited opposition. In the Grand Duchy of Lithuania, the highest offices had long since been almost hereditary within a small circle of families. This problem would worsen in the course of the seventeenth century.

A further strand in the Commonwealth's political culture was religious liberty. Unequal but peaceable co-existence between Catholics, Orthodox, Armenians, Muslims, Jews and Karaites had long been the norm across Poland and Lithuania well before the onset of the Protestant Reformation in the 1520s. King Sigismund I usually turned a blind eye to the novelties and 'heresies' he was supposed to eradicate, for it was by no means clear that Catholic Christendom was splitting into irreconcilable confessions. He found it politic to invest his kinsman Albrecht von Hohenzollern with the Duchy of Prussia: effectively Europe's first Evangelical state. As the dust settled, it became clear that the Lutheran Reformation had put down deeper roots in towns and cities, especially in Royal Prussia, dominated by German-speaking patricians. Calvinism, in contrast, offered noble patrons of churches clear and challenging doctrines, far-reaching autonomy from both royal and ecclesiastical authority, and low costs. Even nobles who kept the old ways in religion joined their Reformed brethren in pulling the teeth from the Catholic clergy. From the 1540s secular courts refused to execute the verdicts of ecclesiastical courts – for example on those nobles who had installed a Calvinist minister in their parish, or who simply refused to pay tithes. A smaller number of nobles embraced radical ideas – denying the Trinity and striving to live a simple and pacific life according to the Gospel. For all the fulminations against 'Arian heretics' and resentment of those who refused to wield the sword, noble solidarity won out – for now.

Despite his sympathy for many aspects of the Reformation, Sigismund II Augustus declined to break with Rome. By the time of his death in 1572, Catholicism had begun its post-Tridentine resurgence while Protestantism was on the defensive. It remained strong, however, especially among the wealthiest and most politically active nobles. Moreover, most of the magnates of the Grand Duchy of Lithuania were Calvinists. There were also a few Orthodox senators, so in the joint senate created by the Union of Lublin, Catholics were in the minority. Perhaps the greatest challenge faced by the Commonwealth after the extinction of the male line of the Jagiellonian dynasty was the avoidance of civil war along religious lines. The senators, nobles and representatives of the principal cities who gathered in Warsaw to make arrangements for the election took this threat seriously. By forming themselves into a confederacy, they could bypass many normal procedures and take the decisions necessary to preserve the Commonwealth and its liberty. Noting the disturbances in other kingdoms, they resolved that their unity should not be broken by any dissidence between them concerning religion. They swore neither to shed blood nor to deprive each other of property, honour or liberty on account of differences in faith. Henceforth every elected king had to swear to maintain peace '*in causa religionis*'.[8]

The 1573 Confederacy of Warsaw is often misrepresented as an act of religious toleration (or even tolerance). It was both less and more than that. On the one hand, its guarantees did not extend to the peasant subjects of lords. On the contrary, it endorsed their punishment for disobedience in spiritual as well as temporal matters. Nor did it endorse religious indifference. On the other hand, the act was not a concession made by those who professed the dominant religion to the adherents of merely tolerated faiths, but a pragmatic agreement between equal citizens to refrain from mutual persecution. This equality angered some – not yet all – of the Catholic bishops. They denounced it as a privilege obtained by the 'heretics' and 'schismatics' by blackmail when the Commonwealth was vulnerable. Supported by a growing number of hardline Catholic laymen, they were able to prevent the sejm passing any effective measures to protect Protestant communities from the tumults that affected many of the Commonwealth's towns during the following decades. Increasingly, the phrase '*dissidentes in religione*' came to apply to the minority of non-Catholic nobles, rather than to all Christians divided by faith. Encouraged by the Catholic clergy, most Catholic nobles came to believe that they did indeed tolerate – suffer – the errors of their brethren.

A number of factors combined in the Catholic recovery. One was the excellence of the schools established by the Society of Jesus, starting in 1564. Another was the effectiveness of confessional polemics, and here again the Jesuits excelled. However, the role played by other orders, notably the Dominicans, should not be underestimated. Compared to the austerity of Reformed Protestantism, Catholicism impressed the senses. Moreover, some post-Tridentine Catholic bishops were determined to raise standards among the secular clergy, and to win back lost parishes by fair means or foul. Last but not least, both Stephen Báthory and Sigismund Vasa favoured Catholics in their nominations of senators and starostas. It remained possible for Protestant and Orthodox nobles to rise to the very top, but it became more difficult to do so, especially in the Polish Crown. Despite the foundation by Báthory of a Jesuit university in Wilno, the Protestant cause was more resilient in the Grand Duchy of Lithuania. Much, although not all of its continuing strength can be attributed to the commitment, wealth and international network of the Calvinist branch of the Radziwiłł family, until it died out in 1669.

The worst effects of confessional hardening were felt in the south-east of the Commonwealth. Here religious tensions intertwined with social ones in ways that few could have predicted in 1569. Immediately after the union of Lublin, the southern Ruthenian elites could consider themselves strategically, politically and confessionally satisfied. Orthodox Christianity long remained the religion of most nobles, but radical currents of the Protestant Reformation attracted significant numbers of the wealthy and educated. The recovering Roman Catholic Church also began to make converts. The Orthodox Church in the Commonwealth was caught between the haemorrhaging of its lay elites and the threat of the Patriarchate of Moscow, established in 1589, as an alternative centre of spiritual authority. To shore up their eroding prestige, Orthodox hierarchs sought an accommodation with Rome.

The ecclesiastical union agreed in 1595–96 at Brest maintained much of the Eastern Christian tradition, including the Slavonic liturgy and a married secular priesthood, in return for the acknowledgement of papal supremacy and minor doctrinal adjustments. However, leading Orthodox laymen were not consulted. Two bishops, many monasteries and lay brotherhoods rejected the union, but their Church was deprived of legal recognition. In theory there was now one Catholic Church with two equal rites – Latin and Ruthenian. However, the eastern bishops who accepted the union were denied entry into the Commonwealth's senate alongside the Catholic bishops of the Latin rite. Many of the latter were far less enthusiastic about the compromise than the pope and the monarch. Starved of prestige, the 'Uniate Church' endured severe birth-pains and a continuing loss of elites to the Latin rite. The 'disuniates', as the non-conformists were pejoratively called, formed a discontented religious minority, just a generation after Orthodox nobles had finally secured equal rights with Catholics. In 1632, faced with a Muscovite invasion, the Commonwealth again recognized the structures of the reviving Orthodox Church, but the schism in Eastern Christendom would have bitter consequences.

The Orthodox cause was espoused by the Zaporozhian Cossacks. These freebooters of the steppes attracted tens of thousands of masterless soldiers, petty nobles in trouble with the law, and runaway peasants. They made their citadel, the *Sich*, in shifting locations on the lower Dnieper, below the thunderous cataracts – *porohy* – which vanished beneath a vast lake in the 1930s. The Cossacks had a chequered relationship with the Commonwealth. On the one hand, the nobles of the Ruthenian lands regarded them as a disruptive element. *Ukraina*, the name for the fertile lands straddling the Dnieper, experienced rapid population growth, attracting migrants of all ranks. Within a generation, the richest lords amassed immense fortunes from their latifundia. The Cossacks were supposed to defend the region from the Crimean Tatars, who had long sold many of its people into slavery, but just as often the Cossacks plundered the returning Tatars. They also raided the Crimea and occasionally even crossed the Black Sea, risking Ottoman retaliation against the Commonwealth.

The lure of the roving and reaving Cossack lifestyle made it harder for lords to exact labour dues from peasant settlers, drawn east by easy terms of settlement. Magnates and wealthy nobles kept detachments of Cossacks for security, but feared their disloyalty. On the other hand, the Cossack elite – the *starshyna* – admired and coveted the freedoms of the szlachta. Some had noble status themselves, but wider Cossack aspirations to civic participation were frustrated. The Commonwealth licensed many Cossacks as soldiers, who contributed mightily to its victories. But the 'register' was increased in military emergencies, only to be reduced afterwards. Nobles wished to reduce unregistered Cossacks to peasant serfs, tilling the land or herding livestock, which provoked rebellions. After their suppression, the register was trimmed further. And so it went on, until the great revolt of 1648 changed almost everything.

Several factors combined to create a perfect storm. First, King Władysław IV raised Cossack hopes of a war against the Ottoman Empire, before being forced to back down by the sejm. Then a senior Cossack officer, Bohdan Khmelnytskyi, was wronged by a magnate and denied justice. He made an astonishing alliance with the Crimean Tatars and raised the standard of revolt. The Commonwealth had put down Cossack uprisings before, but its finest commander, Hetman Stanisław Koniecpolski, had died suddenly two years earlier (reportedly after taking aphrodisiacs in order to satisfy his sixteen-year-old bride). His replacements made a string of errors, leading to the destruction of the Crown army in the Ukraine and the eruption of a massive peasant revolt. At this juncture the king died. The Commonwealth's politicians were divided on how best to respond to the emergency while they organized the royal election. A hastily raised army led by a committee melted away as the Cossacks and Tatars approached. The myth of Polish invincibility ended.

Under the new king, John Casimir Vasa (r.1648–1668), the revolt was contained, but could not be crushed. In 1654 Khmelnytskyi made his fateful submission to Tsar Aleksei of Muscovy, who invaded and occupied most of the Grand Duchy of Lithuania. Four years later, an abortive agreement (known as the Union of Hadiach) to create a Commonwealth of Three Nations, Polish, Lithuanian and Ruthenian, involving Cossack autonomy and an Orthodox monopoly in the south-east, could not undo the damage. The fortunes of war swung one way, then another. The Commonwealth was inundated from all sides, but rallied strongly. The Swedes, who had 'deluged' most of the Crown and part of Lithuania in 1655, were expelled and in 1660 peace was made at Oliva. The Commonwealth then concentrated its forces against Muscovy, to great effect. However, its civil war in the mid-1660s handed Muscovy what proved – in the end – to be a lasting advantage. The price paid by the Commonwealth for the truce of 1667, which became a treaty of 'eternal peace' in 1686, was the loss of Smolensk, Kiev and vast lands beyond the Dnieper.

The unprecedented challenges of continual warfare on the Commonwealth's own soil prompted the sejm to agree to raise large armies, paid for by heavy taxation. John III Sobieski (r.1674–1696) won several victories against the Tatars and Turks, culminating in the relief of Vienna in 1683, which have since warmed Polish hearts. But the political community proved unable to reach consensus on the institutional reforms needed to place this fiscal and military effort on a stable footing. The breakdown of trust had corrosive consequences.

The fact that most of the Commonwealth's foreign enemies were non-Catholic powers heightened suspicions of non-Catholics at home. Plenty of Catholic nobles had sworn allegiance to the King of Sweden or the Tsar of Muscovy in the mid-1650s, while many Lutheran and Orthodox burghers had not, but 'dissidents', 'disuniates' and sometimes Jews were scapegoated. Arians were the first to feel the consequences: in 1658 they were ordered to convert to recognized Trinitarian Christian confessions or leave, on pain of death. Eleven years later, 'apostasy' – conversion from Catholicism to another faith – became a capital offence. By this time it was becoming much harder for non-Catholic nobles to get a fair hearing in courts and tribunals dominated by Catholic judges, and much easier for Catholic bishops to harass them. In time they would look abroad for protection.

More damaging in constitutional terms was the emergence of the *liberum veto*. It was not uncommon for sejms to disperse without reaching agreement, but a disturbing precedent was set in 1652. A single envoy objected to the necessary prolongation and then left Warsaw before he could be persuaded to change his mind. Deep respect for the law and tradition ensured that the sejm would not resume its deliberations. The shock spurred proposals to reform procedure so that an individual could not wreck everything. However, a different view came to prevail: the *veto* was a recourse of virtuous citizens when liberty was imperilled. A much worse precedent occurred in 1669, when the sejm was curtailed by a single protest before its six-week term had elapsed. The next stage came in 1688, when an envoy ruptured the sejm before it could elect its marshal (speaker), that is, before it had been legally constituted. Roughly half of the sejms in the second half of the seventeenth century were broken up by the *liberum veto*, and the problem had become chronic by the end of Sobieski's reign. Although a *veto* cast by a single envoy was recognized as binding, in practice powerful domestic and foreign protectors stood behind the protests.

The Commonwealth's over-mighty citizens increasingly sought foreign aid for their political ends. This was particularly damaging when the belligerent Commonwealth needed allies. The mid-1660s brought a disastrous civil war between adherents and opponents of John Casimir and his Franco-Italian queen, Louise-Marie Gonzaga. The court had argued that the best way to prevent a recurrence of the 'Deluge' was to arrange the election of the next monarch *vivente rege*, that is, while the present king was still alive. But should the next king come with the backing of Versailles or Vienna? The court overplayed its hand, while the opposition exploited a current of xenophobia and misogyny among the szlachta in order to frustrate the royal plans. After his wife's death, the embittered John Casimir abdicated, offending the nation which had elected him. The ensuing royal election saw a furious reaction among ordinary nobles against the senate, and the tumultuous choice of a native-born non-entity, Michael Wiśniowiecki (r.1669–1673). Most of his mercifully brief reign was dominated by rival armed confederacies and military disasters. John Sobieski, who had exacerbated the former and mitigated the latter, was elected to a crown of thorns. The latter part of his reign saw the Grand Duchy of Lithuania descend into civil war. Sobieski was the first king of Poland not to be succeeded by any of his surviving legitimate sons – testimony to his political failure.

The interregnum of 1696–97 was long and violent, but the inauguration of a personal union between the Commonwealth and the prosperous and orderly electorate of Saxony seemed to herald a recovery in Polish-Lithuanian fortunes. Such appearances were deceptive. Soon after his election as King of Poland, Augustus II Wettin (r.1697–1733) sought the aid of Tsar Peter I. However, their joint attack on the young King of Sweden misfired (not least because the cannonballs did not fit the cannons brought by the Saxons to the siege of Dünamünde). In the opening acts of what became the Great Northern War (1700–21) King Charles XII defeated both his foes. He then concentrated on Augustus, dragging the unwilling Commonwealth into the conflict. Charles's implacable insistence on deposing the Wettin managed to consolidate a hitherto critical szlachta around its elected monarch. It also made both Augustus and the Commonwealth more dependent on Peter, who had a good grasp of Polish-Lithuanian politics. Charles cornered Augustus in Saxony in 1706 and forced him to abdicate his Polish throne in favour of a puppet king, Stanisław Leszczyński – a magnate from Greater Poland. Much of the szlachta refused to recognize the illegal abdication. Leszczyński failed to stabilize the Commonwealth – his support drained away because he could not restrain the rapacious Swedish forces. At the local level, the szlachta, gathered at sejmiks, responded as best it could to the rapidly shifting situation. In the meantime Peter learned from his defeat, reformed his army and institutions, marshalled his resources and reversed the fortunes of war at Poltava in 1709.

That epochal battle buried Leszczyński's chances of keeping the Polish-Lithuanian throne and enabled Augustus to return. It did not, however, lead directly to the establishment of a Russian protectorate. Indeed, the over-confident tsar was lucky to escape annihilation by the Ottoman Empire in 1711. Many historians have detected a window of opportunity for the Commonwealth at this point, and lamented Augustus's failure to find a lasting *modus vivendi* with the confederates who had refused to accept Leszczyński. Had agreement been reached, runs the argument, the Commonwealth might yet have restored its sovereignty. Augustus sought by every possible means to regain the initiative, but encountered armed resistance to his plans. Not without reason, the confederates in both the Crown and Lithuania feared the monarch conspired against their liberty; they had their own ideas of how to repair the battered Commonwealth. The Grand Duchy of Lithuania seems to have held up relatively well in the circumstances, raising substantial taxes and defying its reputation for being dominated by magnates subservient to Russia. The chances of an alternative scenario can be questioned, but without doubt, the complex conflicts between king, nobles and magnates were skilfully exploited by the tsar. Russia mediated a solution of sorts in 1716–17.

This half-baked loaf of fiscal, military and local government reforms, notoriously passed by a silent, one-day sejm on 1 February 1717, did not inaugurate a Russian protectorate – yet. The settlement was followed by Augustus II's most serious attempt to escape his tutelage, and bring the Commonwealth into an alliance with Austria, Great Britain and Hanover. However, by 1720 Peter had put him back in his cage. The key factor was the success of the tsar's diplomats in persuading the hetmans, whose powers had been trimmed by the reforms, to oppose the king's plans. It was only at this stage that the stalemate was petrified (if the reader will excuse the pun).

Although its outcome was no foregone conclusion, the Great Northern War did indeed change everything. By 1721, the freshly proclaimed Russian Empire had emerged as the hegemon in the Baltic region. Sweden was severely weakened and vulnerable to manipulation. The Commonwealth crossed its tipping point as a sovereign power. The collapse of its military potential had been exposed and defeat begat demoralization. Economically and demographically devastated, especially by the epidemics spread by marching armies, the Commonwealth badly needed the years of relative peace and stability that followed. However, the respite was not – and could not be – used for reform.

As the great Polish historian Władysław Konopczyński put it with characteristic relish, 'the new Emperor of All the Russias ensnared the Commonwealth in the web of his influence, as a spider enwraps a fly that it has caught'.[9] Peter I managed to frustrate all efforts to strengthen the Commonwealth institutionally, fiscally and militarily, or to activate it in the international arena. The five years after his death in 1725, when Russia's formal rulers were first his illiterate widow Catherine I and then his teenage grandson Peter II, just might have offered the Commonwealth a fleeting opportunity to slip the Russian leash. For France now challenged Russian influence, with a view to winning the next Polish royal election. Again and again, Augustus tried to free himself, changing alliances with the desperation, as Konopczyński would have put it, of a fly caught in a web (perhaps a sturdy Lithuanian 'noble' fly, of the type immortalized by the national Bard, Adam Mickiewicz, would have done better).[10] Even at this juncture, Russian interests were protected by the Commonwealth's own domestic rivalries. Following the accession in 1730 of a new empress, Anna, Russian hegemony was firmly reasserted. The window – if it had opened a chink – was closed.

Peter I laid the foundations of Russia's Polish policy for decades to come. The Commonwealth would be kept weak and passive, so it could serve simultaneously as Russia's gateway and buffer in European politics. The means of implementing this policy varied. Most of the time, St Petersburg sought to maintain hegemonic influence over the entire Commonwealth. When necessary, however, Polish-Lithuanian territory was used to pay diplomatic bills – as long as Russia took still more land. At no point was St Petersburg prepared to sanction the kind of major reforms that might once more permit the Commonwealth to block the projection of Russian power westwards. Geopolitical generalizations tend to fragment under the scalpel of the diplomatic historian, but this one has been verified by the research undertaken in long inaccessible Russian archives by the 'New Warsaw School' of eighteenth-century diplomatic history.

The chief means by which Russia and other neighbouring powers were able to prevent significant reforms in the Commonwealth was the *liberum veto.* During the later seventeenth century, foreign courts had begun to exploit this convenient means of preventing measures inimical to their interests. They deployed bribery, threats and propaganda. From the end of the Great Northern War, the practice became the rule, rather than the exception. However, in some cases, their efforts did not succeed, while in others, internal factors sufficed to break up the sejm. Of the ten sejms held between 1718 and 1733, six were broken up by the *liberum veto*. Russia played a major part in rupturing four of these. Russian and Prussian diplomats usually worked hand in hand. Frederick William I, King in Prussia, set out his '*negative Polenpolitik*' in his 'Political Testament' of 1722. He instructed his successor to ensure he always had supporters in Poland who were prepared to break up the sejm, so that royal power could not be strengthened. The principle of maintaining the Polish form of government unchanged was written into a number of international agreements concluded by Russia in these years, although the practical significance of these clauses varied with the circumstances. In the early 1730s, the rival French and Russian embassies were actually paying some of the same persons to wreck successive sejms. They failed, however, to break up the sejm of 1733, before it was cut short by the death of King Augustus II on 1 February.[11] An interregnum began.

The dramatic events of 1733–34 would reveal just how far the Commonwealth had fallen in less than a century. Poland had become the laughing stock of Europe. Its military reputation had collapsed, its disorderly politics were manipulated by its neighbours, its nobility was a byword for myopia and bigotry, and it had been economically and demographically devastated by decades of warfare on its own soil. Much would get worse before it got better. Yet in many walks of life, a remarkable recovery would soon begin, gathering confidence in the following decades. Polish-Lithuanian reformers could build on the half-buried foundations of their Commonwealth. Elsewhere, some of Europe's composite monarchies, assembled by happenstance, marriage and conquest, were being consolidated by fiscal, bureaucratic, military, confessional and propagandistic means into something approaching 'absolutist' states. Throughout much of continental Europe, representative institutions were in retreat, while nobles had become monarchs' partners in quests for glory. The Kingdom of Poland and the Grand Duchy of Lithuania, together with Royal Prussia and Livonia, had not taken that path. Their political communities had come together to enjoy liberty. The republican values of the Commonwealth, built by voluntary unions, retained their power to inspire.

— TWO —
IMPASSE

An interregnum served to cleanse the Commonwealth of the abuses of the previous reign. The wrongs done by the last king could be righted, and a new contract – the *pacta conventa* – negotiated with his elected successor. The primate, advised by the senate council, acted as *interrex* but did not exercise all of the royal prerogative, so some precautions against royal corruption and tyranny were no longer necessary. On the other hand, the 'orphaned' Commonwealth was more than usually vulnerable to disorder. The interim courts used abbreviated procedures, while the szlachta formed local confederacies. These subsequently joined into a general confederacy of the Two Nations at the convocation sejm, which met to make arrangements for the forthcoming royal election. Because the convocation was confederated, the requirement of unanimity did not apply and the sejm could decide by majority vote. For this reason the competition between parties was intensified. Whichever party could gain a majority of envoys and senators at the convocation would in effect rule the Commonwealth until the confederacy was wound up at the coronation sejm.

So much for the theory. Interregna, as everyone knew, tended to provoke civil war and foreign intervention. In the entire history of the Commonwealth, only the election of Władysław IV in 1632 was reasonably trouble-free. Even then, Muscovy had invaded the Grand Duchy of Lithuania. On that distant occasion, the political community and its newly elected monarch proved themselves equal to the challenge. Since then Polish-Lithuanian power had collapsed, while the Russian Empire had become the arbiter of east-central Europe. The Commonwealth's 'crisis of sovereignty' manifested itself during its penultimate royal election.[1] The thirty-year reign of Augustus III (1733–1763) saw this geopolitical situation worsen further. The germination of ideas for reform could not break the impasse of the Commonwealth's politics. The reasons were both external and internal.

In 1733–34, Russia took on France in a contest to choose the king of Poland, and won. The French court aimed to rebuild the *barrière de l'est* – its long-standing policy of checking the Habsburgs by arrangements with Sweden, Poland and the Ottoman Empire. From 1725 onwards, Versailles spent large sums preparing the re-election of Stanisław Leszczyński. The former puppet-king was living in straitened circumstances in France when his twenty-two-year-old daughter Maria was selected as a bride for the fifteen-year-old Louis XV. Louis's existing fiancée was a small child and France needed an heir. Although theoretically a king's daughter, Maria Leszczyńska threatened almost no one. This advantage would not have sufficed to choose this Polish Cinderella from among ninety-nine maidens, had it not been for the fact that her father was a ready-made candidate for the Polish throne. However, the prospect of the king of France's father-in-law reigning in Warsaw was unacceptable to Vienna, St Petersburg and Berlin.

In Berlin in December 1732 ministers of these three powers reached an agreement to exclude Leszczyński in the forthcoming election. This short-lived accord is often named after the Russian minister, Karl Gustav Löwenwolde. It is sometimes mythologized as the doom-laden 'Treaty of the Three Black Eagles'. The final text did not specifically rule out the Wettin dynasty, despite the fact that Augustus had for some years been moving closer to France, infuriating the Holy Roman Emperor Charles VI. Instead, a secret protocol confirmed that the three courts' preferred candidate was the brother of King John V of Portugal. Don Manuel de Bragança was an increasingly unwelcome guest of his cousin the emperor, and his candidacy had been suggested by Vienna in 1729. His intellectual and political weaknesses suited the allied courts, but he had little appeal to Polish-Lithuanian nobles. Within a few weeks of the death of King Augustus II (1 February 1733), all three courts concluded that Don Manuel had no chance of success, and that it would be better to agree terms with the new Elector of Saxony, Frederick Augustus. They did not ratify the 'treaty'.

The Wettin had two good cards to play. The first was the recognition of the 'Pragmatic Sanction'. This was a solution which the sonless Charles VI hawked round the courts of Europe. It guaranteed the integrity of the Habsburg Monarchy, so that his daughter Maria Theresa could inherit it all. This involved overriding the claims of the daughters of his older brother Joseph I: Maria Josepha, who was the wife of the new Elector of Saxony, and the younger Maria Amalia, who was married to the Elector of Bavaria. The second card was that the Duchy of Courland was expected soon to revert to its feudal overlord – the Commonwealth – as the last of the Kettler dukes had no heir. Frederick Augustus was prepared to offer the succession to Courland to Ernst Biron, favourite of the Russian Empress Anna, in return for her support. It seems surprising that Frederick William I, King in Prussia, was prepared to countenance the prolongation of the Saxon-Polish-Lithuanian union. One factor may have been his own hopes of Courland. Another could be that as an imperial German patriot, he was reluctant to break with the emperor. He probably fell into line in the hope that Charles VI would support his dynastic claims elsewhere in the Reich. If so, the Hohenzollern was soon disappointed. The emperor was the first to support the Saxon elector, but he was not willing to intervene militarily. This was partly because he did not wish to provoke France, but also because he needed to cover his exposed frontiers if war were to break out. Russian and Saxon forces should suffice to quell the Commonwealth. Empress Anna agreed, so on 11 August a Russian corps crossed the frontier and began a slow march towards Warsaw.

In the meantime, Leszczyński's Polish supporters seized the initiative. Not all this support was purchased by the energetic French ambassador, Antoine-Félix Monti. It helped, of course, that Monti bought up all the printing houses in Warsaw, which meant that most counter-propaganda had to be printed abroad. But it also helped that the envoys of the two imperial courts, Löwenwolde and Heinrich Wilhelm von Wilczek, had no clear message of their own. Leszczyński's principal supporter was Teodor Potocki: Archbishop of Gniezno, primate and *interrex*. Several other Polish-Lithuanian lords were eyeing up the crown for themselves. However, facing a crescendo of support for Leszczyński, first Austria and then Russia decided to back the Elector of Saxony. Well might the imperial courts feel threatened. The slogan of 'independence' was in the air, because for the first time in decades the political community felt itself sovereign. Poles would now decide on Polish matters. The general lack of trust in the late monarch fed the demands to elect a 'Piast' (this term for a native-born candidate referred to Poland's first royal dynasty). Polemics were plentiful and pungent, both in print and in manuscript.

The convocation sejm met in Warsaw between 27 April and 23 May 1733. Primate Potocki skilfully rode the wave of emotion, and the national cause overlapped with the confessional one. The sejm began by excluding eighteen Protestant envoys from Royal Prussia, confirming the precedent set in 1718 when the sole Evangelical envoy had been expelled. Previous legislation limiting the rights of the heterodox was reiterated. The convocation effectively became an election sejm itself by deciding that the next king must be Polish-born. The oath to the confederacy formed at the end of the sejm to oversee the election declared anyone who aided a foreign candidate an enemy of the Fatherland. This step overrode opponents' protests and ignored the declaration made to the primate on 14 May by the Austrian, Russian and Prussian envoys: their rulers would not permit Leszczyński to ascend the Polish throne. Most pre-election sejmiks in the Polish Crown were dominated by Leszczyński's supporters. Saxon supporters, although not negligible in number, were usually drowned out by the clamour for a 'Piast'. At Płock, some nobles threatened to 'throttle' the local bishop for favouring the Wettin.[2] However, opinion in the Grand Duchy of Lithuania was divided more evenly: in several districts nobles protested against the oath.

The news of the support of the imperial courts for the Saxon elector arrived too late to dampen the jubilant mood in Warsaw, where the election sejm opened on 25 August 1733. The Lithuanian chancellor, Michał Serwacy Wiśniowiecki, who had coveted the throne himself, recalled the disbelief in his earlier warnings about 'Muscovy', now there was nothing to oppose the forces that had just entered the Commonwealth. At this an envoy from Leszczyński's stronghold of Greater Poland had riposted that the chancellor had the Lithuanian army under his command. The latter answered 'that those three thousand soldiers would not suffice for breakfast, and what would be left for dinner?'. The reply came that if he lacked the heart to fight, he could resign his command to someone else. At that a fight had broken out.[3] The following day Wiśniowiecki and many Lithuanian nobles crossed to Praga, on the other bank of the River Vistula. Despite the hopes of the imperial diplomats, they did not form a new confederacy in opposition to the election sejm.

The bravura was bolstered by Ambassador Monti's announcement on 4 September 1733 that Louis XV would not only use all his own strength to defend his father-in-law, if elected, but would even pay for the expansion of the Polish army. On 11 September Leszczyński was cheered to the rafters after he publicly attended Mass in Warsaw's Church of the Holy Cross, wearing national dress. The same day Primate Potocki counted the votes of most of the palatinates. A delegation crossed the river to talk to the Saxon supporters. Before it could return, however, on 12 September, on the election field of Wola the primate nominated Leszczyński as king, and about 13,500 nobles responded with a threefold roar of '*zgoda!*'. At that, 'the nobility in the election field started to fire its handguns, amidst the universal acclamation "long live His Majesty King Stanisław". During the shooting several men and horses were killed, and others wounded, through carelessness.'[4] The *Te Deum* was sung twice – first on the field and later in the collegiate church of St John the Baptist, after which King Stanisław was led to his apartments in the Royal Castle in triumph.

The mood changed as the Russian corps approached Warsaw. Most nobles prudently headed home. Others joined the Saxon supporters on the right bank of the Vistula. King Stanisław declined to disperse them by force. Instead, he and Monti left during the night of 21–22 September 1733. They headed for the safety of Danzig, in expectation of French and Swedish reinforcements. So did many of his principal supporters. Nevertheless, Leszczyński's opponents felt insecure until the Russian vanguard arrived. On 5 October three to four thousand men acclaimed Elector Frederick Augustus as King of Poland and Grand Duke of Lithuania. Among the names, some appear to be Poles serving in Saxon regiments, while others had figured among Leszczyński's electors. Many were from Lithuania. Others were long-standing adherents of the late monarch. Be all that as it may, this second election was illegal. Although it took place just before the expiry of the term allowed for the election sejm, the sejm had already concluded. More importantly, however, the Russian army had arrived. On 9 October Józef Potocki, the primate's distant cousin, led soldiers loyal to King Stanisław out of Warsaw. Saxon supporters, protected by Russian soldiers, took charge of the city the following day.

Augustus III left Dresden with his wife, their suite and a substantial military escort. They entered Poland on 4 January 1734. On 15 January Augustus II and John III were buried in the crypts of Wawel Cathedral, before 17 January saw the last coronation of a King and Queen of Poland in Cracow. It was a modest affair. The few bishops and senators present barely sufficed for the roles envisaged by the ancient ceremony. The coronation sejm was so poorly attended that it was promptly abandoned. The best thing about the event – at least for posterity – was the music, which included a cantata composed by Johann Sebastian Bach.[5]

The siege of Danzig began towards the end of February 1734 (Plate 3). The Russians had up to 30,000 men, later joined by almost 10,000 Saxons. The city, defended by around 8,000 soldiers and almost as many armed citizens and apprentices, was well prepared. The Danzigers hoped for at least diplomatic support from all the trading powers of the north. Encouraged by Monti, King

Stanisław rested his hopes in his son-in-law, who had proclaimed that France would defend Poland's freedom of election and consider its breach a *casus belli*. An imposing squadron had left Brest on 31 August 1733, bearing Leszczyński's *Doppelgänger*, while he himself crossed Germany in disguise. However, on receiving the news of his election, the squadron remained at anchor off Copenhagen, before most of the ships turned back for France. About two hundred Swedish volunteers and some weapons did arrive in Danzig between January and March 1734. By the time ships bearing 2,400 French soldiers finally appeared on 11 May 1734, the Russians had cut the city off from the sea and were shelling it with heavy artillery. The officers of the outnumbered French regiments refused to fight their way through the Russian positions. They sailed back to Copenhagen before being persuaded to return and try again. They failed to break through on 27 May and surrendered four weeks later. The city's situation was now hopeless. Danzig capitulated after Leszczyński escaped in the night of 28 June. Disguised as a peasant, he was guided through the Vistula delta to safety on neutral Prussian territory. By this time Frederick William I was so jealous of his Saxon rival's success and so angry at being denied Courland that despite his parsimony, he maintained Leszczyński and his followers in Königsberg until the end of the war.

The fall of Danzig decided the war in the Commonwealth, but the dust took longer to settle. Although some of Leszczyński's adherents soon submitted to the Wettin, many joined the separate confederacies in the Grand Duchy of Lithuania and the Polish Crown, which were formed in 1734 and not dissolved until 1736. New reigns tended to begin with a 'pacification sejm' at which the discords of the interregnum were calmed by royal largesse. Because of the extended conflict that followed his election, Augustus III did not try to hold a pacification sejm until the autumn of 1735. It was broken up by the *liberum veto*, necessitating a second attempt, held in the 'extraordinary' two-week mode, in the summer of 1736. The king, who took an active part in the deliberations, agreed to withdraw Saxon troops from the Commonwealth. The bargain struck with some of Leszczyński's leading supporters, notably the Potockis, lubricated agreement to several laws and resolutions. These included a reconfirmation of existing prohibitions on non-Catholics holding office or sitting in the sejm.[6]

This delayed resolution was linked to the general European conflict, whose usual name – the War of the Polish Succession – is rather misleading. Neither the French nor the Austrians sent significant military forces to Poland. They focused on the Rhineland and Italian *theatri belli* where the serious fighting began in

October 1733. France's first minister, Cardinal André-Hercule de Fleury, was a realist – as well as averse to spending money. Sweden and the Ottoman Empire would be welcome to fight for Leszczyński, but France would concentrate on matters closer to home. Fleury's first objective was Lorraine, whose duke, Francis Stephen, raised in Vienna, was desired as husband by the emperor's daughter and heiress, Maria Theresa. Although Sweden and the Ottoman Empire did not attack Russia, Spain and Savoy actively supported France against Austria, while Great Britain and the Dutch Republic remained neutral. Things went badly for the Habsburgs in Italy, but the emperor, drawing on the resources of the Reich, was able to halt the French advance into Germany. The bones of a peace were negotiated by 1735, just as a Russian corps was approaching the Rhine. However, it was only finally sealed in 1738, after the Grand Duchy of Tuscany had been vacated by the death of the last Medici the previous year. This was assigned to Francis Stephen, by now husband to Maria Theresa. His hereditary duchy of Lorraine and Bar went to Leszczyński. Louis XV would inherit it in 1766.

Leszczyński's unexpectedly long reign in Lorraine has burnished his reputation. He shone as a '*philosophe bienfaisant*', a generous patron of the arts and education, and a prolific, moralizing writer. As a Polish politician he was far less impressive, remaining passive at crucial junctures. His first reign in the Commonwealth was little more than a facade for Swedish pillage. The second time round he did at least function as a symbol of national sovereignty. For some Polish historians, Leszczyński epitomized the modern idea of Polish independence, based on resistance to Russia. However edifying this tradition for later generations, at least some of Leszczyński's opponents believed such a geopolitical choice to be madness. They supported the Saxon precisely because he would not bring down the wrath of imperial Russia on the near-defenceless Commonwealth.[7]

Once Augustus III was settled on his Polish throne, he could pay an important debt. In 1737, following the extinction of the Kettler dynasty, the king invested the Empress Anna's favourite, Ernst Biron, as duke of Courland and Semigallia. However, having briefly become regent to the infant Ivan VI in 1740–41, Biron was arrested and condemned to death by his rivals during the palace coup which raised Peter I's younger daughter Elizabeth to the Russian throne. She commuted his sentence to internal exile. The duke's long absence allowed the duchy's Estates considerable autonomy, as long as Russian interests were upheld. The new empress, who had earlier feared that Anna and Biron would confine her in a nunnery, led the reaction against their decade of 'German rule' in Russia. However, despite the cultural Gallicization of her court, she maintained Russia's geopolitical hostility to France – especially in Poland.[8]

Elizabeth had good reason to do so. The *barrière de l'est* began to be turned less against Austria than against Russia – to considerable effect at first. France nullified Russia's military successes against the Ottoman Empire between 1735 and 1739 by 'mediating' the peace. At the same time, Poland's role within the *barrière* became less important than those of the Ottoman Empire and Sweden (which fought an unsuccessful war against Russia in 1741–43). If Prussia, strengthened by its annexation of Silesia from the Habsburg Monarchy in 1740–41, had become part of the *barrière*, the consequences for Russia's ability to project its power westwards would have been severe. Between the mid-1730s and the mid-1750s Vienna was usually allied to St Petersburg, and Potsdam was usually aligned with Versailles. However, the intensity of these relations varied. Frederick II was never content simply to carry out French instructions, and during the 1740s he twice ditched Louis XV. The Russian Empire twice sent corps to aid Austria against France, but in both 1735 and 1748 preliminary peace terms ended the fighting before the Russian reinforcements arrived.

Within this external framework, it was easy for outsiders (such as British diplomats) to misread the Commonwealth's politics as a binary contest between two magnate factions and their foreign protectors. On the one side, so it seemed, was the *Familia*, led by the Czartoryskis and Poniatowskis, which was oriented towards Russia, Austria and Great Britain. On the other side was a faction centred on the Potockis, oriented towards Prussia and France. In practice things were messier, in part because the Grand Duchy of Lithuania had its own political dynamics, affected by its proximity to Russia. The view from Dresden was different again. The Elector of Saxony had still had some freedom of manoeuvre in European politics (not least as vicar of the Holy Roman Empire during an imperial vacancy). Augustus III initially allowed the Potockis much leeway in the Commonwealth and sought to mend his fences with France. However, when the Potockis were suspected of planning confederacies supported by the Ottoman Empire, France, Sweden and Prussia, the monarch lost patience. Following Saxony's ill-starred involvement in the attempt to carve up the Habsburg inheritance in 1741–42, the royal court shifted to an alliance with the

Familia, and drew closer to Russia. This did not prevent Augustus III from pulling off the diplomatic coup of marrying his daughter Maria Josepha to Louis, the Dauphin of France, in 1747. A further shift came in the early 1750s. The royal court broke with the *Familia* and sought a rapprochement with the Potockis and other families hitherto in opposition. The *Familia* responded by pursuing still closer links with Russia. However, Dresden avoided a confrontation with St Petersburg. Despite Russia and France both being allied to Austria against Prussia after 1757, Russo-French relations remained frosty. Against the advice of his ministers, Louis XV continued his secret and chaos-inducing efforts to influence the next Polish election.

Twice it seemed possible that Saxony and the Commonwealth could make a useful military contribution to an allied cause. The first apparent opportunity was during the war waged by Russia and Austria against the Ottoman Empire from 1735 to 1739, and the second during the War of the Austrian Succession (1740–48). These alignments gave rise, at the time and subsequently, to the conviction that at certain favourable moments Russia was prepared to support the 'repair' of the paralyzed Commonwealth. This would have involved the expansion of its tax base and army and the revitalization of its judicial and administrative institutions. There were even hopes of Russian acquiescence in the limitation or bypassing of the *liberum veto*.

However, in 1738, 1740 and 1744 genuine hopes that the sejm might agree to expand the army were crushed. These sejms ran out of time, without agreement to prolong the deliberations. Neither the Potockis nor the *Familia* could trust the other with control of an expanded army. But in addition to this – sufficient – cause of failure, neither Russia nor Prussia would support such an expansion, even when carried out by its own supporters. For St Petersburg, having a dependent party in the Commonwealth facilitated the projection of its power into European politics. However, given that the Russian-oriented and Prussophobic *Familia* was committed to reform, Russian ambassadors were secretly instructed not to disabuse its hopes. It was better for St Petersburg if the odium for the failure of sejms fell on Prussia and/or the Potockis, but if Prussian bribes did not suffice, Russia would step in. Berlin was more than welcome to block reforms, but could not be permitted to contest Russian hegemony in Poland.[9]

The failure of these sejms showed that the chances of passing major fiscal and military reforms at an ordinary sejm were infinitesimal. However, the forbidding ramparts of the *liberum veto* could in theory be bypassed by holding the sejm under the aegis of a confederacy. Normal procedures, such as unanimity, could be set aside in order to save the Commonwealth from peril. During the next few years the leaders of the *Familia* repeatedly urged the Saxon court to confederate the sejm 'from above'. This method was in contrast to the Potockis' traditionalist preference for confederacies formed 'from below' – first in the palatinates and later united. Either way, St Petersburg let Dresden know that such steps were unacceptable.[10]

The laws passed by the pacification sejm of 1736 proved to be the modest sum of legislation passed during Augustus III's reign. The sejms held between 1738 and 1748 ran their course without reaching agreement. They dispersed when consent for their continuation was refused. During the 1750s and early 1760s the rupture of the sejm became routine; the *liberum veto* was often invoked even before a marshal could be elected. By the early 1750s, the premature end of a sejm often came as a relief to the king and his first minister, Count Heinrich Brühl, who were eager to return to Dresden. The sejm had become a biennial rite of pious phrases about the public good that barely masked cynical manoeuvring between the court, camarillas and cliques.

But life went on. The Commonwealth could subsist – for a time – without a functioning legislature. To some extent this situation reflected the conservative values of the szlachta. As the *pacta conventa* of 1669 put it, no novelty could be introduced '*sine periculo et revolutione magna*' – 'without danger and great revolution'.[11] The essential purpose of the sejm, like most other institutions, was to defend the status quo, not alter it. The repeated rupture of the sejm was often denounced as an abuse of liberty and a grave sin, but only rarely as a constitutional flaw that required reform. For this ultimate bastion of liberty could not be abandoned. The slogan which later became notorious – '*Polska nierządem stoi*', usually translated as 'Poland subsists by anarchy' – did not mean the endorsement of chaos or licence. It implied no disrespect for the laws. It did, however, convey the conviction that some disorder was unavoidable in a free republican form of government. It accorded with the popular motto, taken from the ancient Roman historian Sallust, *potiorque visa est periculosa libertas quieto servitio* – 'it is better to live in perilous liberty than in tranquil servitude'.[12]

One of the reasons why the Commonwealth continued to operate was that other institutions than the sejm could take on functions necessary for subsistence.

Decentralized structures of governance had enabled the szlachta to cope as best it could with the misfortunes of war, aggravated by famine and plague, during the first decade and a half of the eighteenth century. Its ability to do so was weakened when the sejmiks lost many of their self-governing entitlements, including their ability to levy local taxes, through the settlement of 1716–17. Nevertheless, some of them, such as that for the combined palatinates of Greater Poland, could still effect minor improvements, for example in communications, and even maintain a small militia. The sejmiks of the Grand Duchy of Lithuania also remained the natural fora for the discussion and resolution of local problems. However, like the sejm, sejmiks were liable to be broken up by the *liberum veto*. This right was liberally used at those weightier assemblies where more was at stake. Worst affected was the Royal Prussian general sejmik or *Landtag*, but after the political situation stabilized in 1736, almost three-quarters of the conjoined sejmiks of Greater Poland were ruptured. There are some signs of the local szlachta losing patience: these included more frequent reports of sabres being drawn against those wielding the *veto* towards the end of Augustus III's reign.

Many disputes between nobles were still resolved, however tardily and venally, in the courts. However, it is a measure of the crisis of the Commonwealth's judicial institutions that the death of a judge could curtail the operation of the district land court for years, as no successor could be chosen by an election sejmik that was repeatedly ruptured. Boundary suits were particularly affected. Patience and tenacity were the virtues of litigants. The losing party could appeal indefinitely, so lawsuits occasionally lasted for generations. Sometimes a verdict was 'executed' by an armed incursion of neighbouring nobles – this was the 'foray' gently satirized by Adam Mickiewicz in his epic poem *Pan Tadeusz* (1834). As the *liberum veto* itself suggests, the law was venerated in noble political culture; law and liberty were inextricably linked. The inability of the Crown Tribunal to constitute itself in quorum in 1749, because too few judges (known as deputies) had incontestably been elected legally, provoked more concern than the routine paralysis of the sejm.

The senate council, established at the time of the Commonwealth's foundation as a check against the abuse of monarchical power, also served to transact pressing business when the sejm could not meet. Participation was not confined to the senators appointed to reside by the king between sejms, but to all those willing and able to attend. However, Augustus III held fewer senate councils than his father (fourteen as opposed to 106). Not all of these meetings were held in

Warsaw or (God forbid) Grodno; four were held in the nearest Polish town to Dresden: Wschowa, called Fraustadt by its mainly Germanophone inhabitants. Having distributed *starostwa* and dignities, the monarch hurried back home.

Instead of relying on the senate council, Augustus III preferred ministerial channels. The ruler sought to supervise Polish-Lithuanian affairs by having at least one of his ministers (the marshals, chancellors and treasurers) always in Dresden. The courier post covered the distance to or from Warsaw in about forty-eight hours. The chancelleries maintained by several Crown and Lithuanian ministers became important nodes for transacting business – a phenomenon begun in the previous reign. Ministerial prerogatives and responsibilities remained considerable, especially in the judicial sphere. So did the perks. Although they did not yet sit in the senate *ex officio*, the grand and field hetmans were even more powerful than the other ministers. These ranks were always held by senior lay senators. The king's reliance on ministers had mixed effects. Some gave sterling service, while others fought turf wars. The malversations of two successive Crown treasurers went unpunished because of the paralysis of the sejm.

With a mostly absent monarch, few noble citizens ever saw their king. At least until the court's involuntary move to Warsaw in 1757, communication between 'court' and 'country' rested in the hands of a few, mostly aristocratic intermediaries and their agents. Nevertheless, partly out of habit, and partly because of his increasingly obvious lack of ambition to change things in the Commonwealth, Augustus III did in time become quite popular among the szlachta. If familiarity breeds contempt, then Augustus, geographically and linguistically distanced from his citizen-subjects, and further shielded from them by elaborate etiquette, had regal dignity in abundance. On balance it probably helped that he was a foreign prince, who stood above the rivalries of the magnate families, rather than a 'Piast' who would have provoked jealousy among those he had leapfrogged. Most of the unpopularity of 'the court', which was to be expected in a republican political culture, could be borne by the talented but avaricious Brühl.[13]

The Commonwealth as a whole never had a stable aristocratic elite; it certainly had no oligarchy in the sense of a closed group which shared the fruits of power. For all the inflated pretensions of families who sported imperial or papal titles of prince or count, the Commonwealth had no upper, hereditary peerage, legally divided from the generality of the nobility. This was in contrast to the situation in the Reich and the Kingdom of Hungary. The Polish-Lithuanian szlachta did however contain (at any one time) a few dozen families who enjoyed great, and in some cases enormous wealth, running to dozens of towns, thousands of villages, hundreds of thousands of unfree subjects, yielding hundreds of thousands or even a few million złotys in annual income, placing them among the richest aristocrats in Europe.

With wealth came influence. Magnates could employ hundreds, occasionally even thousands of poorer nobles at their courts, on their estates and in their private militias. They could lease out lands and act as bankers. Moderately wealthy nobles, although neither employed nor directly tied economically to the magnates, were often their clients. Such 'unequal friendship' involved the support – at sejmiks, the sejm or the tribunals – of the client for the patron, while the patron could help the client win potentially ruinous lawsuits, make an advantageous marriage or receive some modest royal largesse (given the distance to Dresden, virtually all royal patronage was brokered). In most parts of the Commonwealth very few noblemen of middling fortune (owning perhaps a few or a dozen villages and a few hundred serfs) had the means, education or security to cut independent figures in politics comparable to the pillars of the 'movement for the execution of the laws' who had contested aristocratic predominance in the sixteenth century.

Fortunes could be made and lost with dizzying speed. Within three or four generations noble families could vault from obscurity to prominence before subsiding back into relative poverty. Partible inheritance and the biological lotteries of fertility, mortality and insanity meant that no family could take its continued material pre-eminence for granted. Families' matrimonial and procreational strategies responded to these dangers. Competition for heiresses was intense. August Czartoryski had every reason to spend years wooing the widow Zofia Denhoffowa, née Sieniawska, who had inherited one immense fortune from her parents and another from her husband. Having fought at least one duel, Czartoryski finally won her hand in 1731. By this marriage, an old and respectable but essentially second-rank family, which had only begun to rise again in the previous generation, instantly became a rival to the Radziwiłłs and Potockis.

Competition for royal largesse remained at least as important. Thousands of Crown estates paid a now grossly undervalued contribution to fund the small standing armies of the Polish Crown and the Grand Duchy of Lithuania. The offices and dignities in the king's gift ranged from seats in the senate and the central and court offices, to many of the offices in local hierarchies – the chamberlains, stewards, ensigns, cup-bearers and such like. Only a minority of these were subject to election at sejmiks – unlike most judicial offices. More offices were elective in Lithuania.

Not the least weapon in the royal armoury was ecclesiastical patronage. Many noble parents destined younger sons for the Catholic Church, expecting their clerical offspring to aid their families materially and politically. The king had long nominated bishops to their sees and senatorial chairs, the majority of prelates and canons to their cushioned stalls in cathedral and collegiate churches, and many provosts to their parishes. The wealthiest clergymen rarely resided in their accumulated benefices. As fewer than half of the bishoprics were sufficiently well endowed to enable their holders to lead an aristocratic lifestyle, poorer bishops sought to retain their previous benefices while angling for more lucrative sees. Those who served the king well in one of the offices of state reserved for clergymen might be rewarded with an abbey held *in commendam*. By the Concordat of 1737 the Holy See conceded the king the right to choose thirteen commendatory abbots. Each of this fortunate baker's dozen enjoyed two-thirds of the income of his abbey, while a claustral abbot, chosen by the monks, actually governed it.[14] In material terms, at the summit was the Bishop of Cracow, who enjoyed a vast annual income of about a million złotys, roughly twice that enjoyed by the primate and archbishop of Gniezno. Cracow was one of the richest bishoprics in Europe.[15] It is hardly surprising that following the death of Archbishop Teodor Potocki in 1738, Cardinal Jan Lipski turned down the primacy in order to remain Bishop of Cracow. In such circumstances, precedence was often at issue – between primates, papal nuncios and cardinal-bishops. That was why it mattered that in 1750 Pope Benedict XIV granted the archbishops of Gniezno the right to wear the purple-red attire of cardinals.

Rumours of the ill-health of an ageing bishop or prelate inevitably prompted intense lobbying not only for the imminent vacancy, but also for other benefices that could be vacated in a general promotion. The game of ecclesiastical thrones always left many disappointed supplicants, but some families specialized in picking up the choicest morsels. The Szembeks, for example, counted two primates and four other bishop-senators in the eighteenth century. Most bishops tended to be political royalists as a default position, but family politics could push them into opposition.

Besides these traditional benefits of royal favour, a small but growing number of nobly born Poles – laymen and clergymen alike – pursued careers at the court in Dresden. The rewards of such service were potentially immense, but falls from grace could be spectacular, as the royal favourite Aleksander Sułkowski discovered when he was suddenly stripped of his offices and perquisites in 1738. The king also conferred honorific baubles. Perhaps the most sought after was the Order of the White Eagle, instituted by Augustus II. Of course, royal largesse never sufficed. As the writer and pedagogue Stanisław Konarski put it:

> To give to some means, as we so often see, that others from emulation and revenge will rupture the sejm. Moreover, that which kings must give to the ambitious, they deny to the meritorious and worthy. And thus they do not oblige those who grasp unjustly, while they disoblige those who are thereby injured.[16]

A magnate clan that lost royal favour soon became tangibly poorer – it had fewer material means with which to reward or employ its followers. It was no longer able to procure the fruits of royal favour for its supporters, and it was well understood that a disappointed client could shift his support to a patron and protector who delivered on promises. If a declining family was outnumbered by its opponents at the tribunals, both among the judges and the crowds, then its socio-political position could become critically weak. For this reason, the sejmiks that elected deputies to the tribunals were more bitterly contested than those that elected envoys to the moribund sejm. The latter were by no means neglected, but they increasingly became warm-up matches. Although there is a tendency to associate the senate with the magnates and the chamber of envoys with the Knightly Estate as a whole, some senators – especially among back-bench castellans – came from middling noble backgrounds, while many scions of magnate families cut their parliamentary teeth as envoys.

Political tacticians calculated the relative strength of the magnate factions in the localities and plotted their shifting relationships with each other and the royal court. Given this intense rivalry, magnate families that aspired to play leading roles across the Crown, Lithuania or even the entire Commonwealth (rather than merely maintaining a steady regional position), organized themselves into 'parties'. These were ritually denounced as factions noxious to the public good. The ordering and reordering of the political landscape were carried out by forging marriage alliances, deepening cliental links and accepting – even seeking – the protection of foreign powers. We should not imagine the formal structures of modern political parties, even if the underlying mechanisms and mentalities of patronage and clientele seem eternal (not least in academic life). Attachments and alignments were fluid, and much depended on the attractiveness of the slogans with which noble opinion was courted.

That said, one grouping stood out for the united front which it presented to the world, its effective decision-making, and the determination with which it expanded its support in good times and maintained it in bad. This was the *Familia*. It had emerged in the 1720s, led by Stanisław Poniatowski the elder, a talented soldier and diplomat who had served Charles XII and Augustus II in turn. He was aided and later supplanted by his younger brothers-in-law. Michał Czartoryski, who became vice-chancellor of Lithuania in 1724 and grand chancellor in 1752, headed the *Familia* in the Grand Duchy. The material foundations, as well as a clientele, came from the marriage of August Czartoryski to Zofia Denhoffowa. Other notable magnates who joined the *Familia* included the three sons-in-law of Michał and August, as well as Andrzej Zamoyski, of whom more anon.

Less cohesive was the many-branched Potocki clan, especially after Primate Teodor Potocki died and Crown Grand Hetman Józef Potocki entered his dotage. The cleverest member of the family, Antoni Potocki, Palatine of Bełz, not having a large personal fortune, was on the Prussian payroll. He orchestrated the failure of several sejms. His less cerebral cousin Franciszek Salezy Potocki, Palatine of Kiev, was the Croesus of the south-east. It was here that the Potockis' client networks were strongest. After recognizing Augustus III in 1735, the Potockis were sated with offices and Crown estates at the expense of the *Familia*. For the next few years the Potockis held the political initiative, and their 'republican' slogans of an expanded army (on their terms) resonated among much of the szlachta. However, as we have seen, the geopolitical obstacles to their alliance with the royal court became insuperable by the early 1740s. Towards the end of the reign, relations between the court and the Potockis improved again, but there was no question of the clan recovering its position of the late 1730s.

In the Grand Duchy of Lithuania, the principal counterweight to the *Familia* were the Radziwiłłs, led by Grand Hetman Michał and later by his son Karol, Palatine of Wilno. Both were fêted for their extravagance, not their intelligence. The number of significant political players in the Grand Duchy was far smaller than in the Crown, but no grouping had ever managed completely to dominate its politics for more than a decade or two. The last such hegemony, exercised by the Sapiehas in the 1680s and 1690s, had provoked a civil war and the destruction of their power on the battlefield in 1700. It was only four decades later that another generation of Sapiehas began the partial rebuilding of the family's position.

The grim fate of the Sapiehas was cautionary. In general, magnate preponderance grew heavier as one went eastwards. However, in the Grand Duchy of Lithuania there were districts where local political life continued at a distance from the contest of the magnate factions and the royal court. For example, the sejmik of Kowno was never once broken by the *liberum veto*. Here the rising Zabiełło family managed to play off the bigger fish against each other. At the other end of the Grand Duchy, the Jeleńskis patiently built up their base in the district of Mozyrz. Their attention to detail is apparent from a request made in 1750 for game and wild fowl to be provided for the forthcoming sejmik, and 'that better mead be made than that at the last sejmik, which the szlachta did not want to drink' – necessitating the purchase of nobler mead from a local monastery.[17]

In much of the Commonwealth, even the greatest lords could not ignore nobles of middling and substantial fortune. In the palatinates of Poznań and Kalisz, the economic and cultural gap between several dozen notable families and those who counted as magnates was not unbridgeable. In Royal Prussia, the principal families had to deal not only with prosperous, well-educated nobles, including a substantial minority of Protestants, but also with self-confident urban patricians. Mazovia, by contrast, had no latifundia except for some Crown estates and the properties of the bishopric of Płock. The numerous, mostly impoverished Mazovian szlachta had the reputation of zealous Catholics and instinctive royalists, although they were by no means deferential to the clergy or always obedient to the monarch. The Commonwealth's best example of a meritocrat, Stanisław Poniatowski the elder, enjoyed particular authority in Mazovia, whose palatine he was between 1731 and 1752. He ended his career as the Commonwealth's first lay senator, the Castellan of Cracow: not bad for the son of a 'butler of Wyszogród' (as we can translate the district-level dignity of *cześnik wyszogrodzki*).

At one level, the gap between the rhetoric and the reality of political life was never wider than during the middle decades of the eighteenth century.[18] Declamations of republican virtue, ardent patriotism and imperilled liberty dominated political discourse (this term, so often needlessly complicated, boils down to a characteristic way of speaking or writing about something). Given the political culture of the szlachta, any proposals for change had to be couched in terms of restoration rather than reform. Rather startlingly, Antoni Potocki called for burghers to enter the sejm as a fourth estate. His sincerity has been questioned. Because he wished the sejm of 1744 to fail, this remarkable proposal may have been a distraction. Perhaps in the long term he helped to make the idea thinkable. Less controversially, rival slogans for 'the repair of the Commonwealth' included ideas for revitalizing trade and manufacturing, the unblocking of the law courts and, above all, the expansion of the army. One of the most intractable obstacles to the latter cause was the unequal distribution of the tax burden. Because of the exemptions agreed in recognition of the damage suffered in the Great Northern War, the south-eastern palatinates of the Polish Crown paid proportionately much less than other parts of the Commonwealth, especially Greater Poland and Mazovia. Unsurprisingly, equalization was demanded by the latter and resisted by the former.

Posterity has generally credited the *Familia* for embracing reform. During its period of close co-operation with the court (roughly 1743–52) it did try to implement a part of its programme. However, after the Czartoryskis parted company with the court, they showed no scruples in employing demagogic rhetoric and wrecking sejms for private ends. They clashed bitterly with the court, the Potockis, the Radziwiłłs and the Crown grand hetman, Jan Klemens Branicki, who aspired to the role of political arbiter and posed as the defender of republican liberty. In 1748, at the age of fifty-nine, he had married the elder Poniatowski's eighteen-year-old daughter Izabella, but refused to follow the *Familia*'s lead. It did not help that he felt patronized by the waspish Michał Czartoryski. Branicki's 'Podlasian Versailles' – an elegant palace, gracious park and exemplary private town at Białystok – expressed his lofty ambitions while also providing employment to poorer nobles. He had plenty of military patronage at his disposal, so serving and retired officers made up much of his clientele. He made blatantly political use of his command of the Crown forces. The impact of such leadership on an already demoralized and disorganized army may be imagined.

During the last decade of Augustus III's reign, Polish-Lithuanian politics plumbed the murkiest depths. The court, exiled in Warsaw during the Seven Years' War of 1756–63, no longer affected an interest in repairing the Commonwealth, but gathered supporters who openly sought preferment by making themselves useful. A 'camarilla' formed around Brühl's son-in-law, Crown Court Marshal Jerzy Mniszech. Although Mniszech did not appeal directly to middling nobles' sense of responsibility for the Commonwealth, he did pay close attention to the question of who became officials and judges at local level. Titular posts at court were multiplied as an incentive for wealthier nobles. Some of the Potockis put out feelers to the court, but Mniszech preferred to poach their clients. The *Familia* behaved just as cynically as its rivals. Having pushed the naturalization of Brühl's noble status through the Crown Tribunal in 1748, it denounced that verdict as illegal in 1762. The envoy who questioned the *ius indigenatus* of Brühl's son Aloysius and provoked the rupture of that year's sejm was Stanisław Poniatowski the younger.

Nevertheless, the fact that – Mniszech's camarilla apart – rival parties claimed and contested labels such as 'patriot' and 'republican' indicates that some appearances had to be maintained. Even the repetition of tired slogans attests to the underlying soundness and attractiveness of the Commonwealth's values at a time when republics were an endangered species in Europe. However cynically deployed in the political struggle, the inherited discourse of republican patriotism contained much – although not quite all – of the vocabulary with which genuine reformers could argue for an overhaul of the ship of state.

Historians who have waded into the political discourse of the Saxon period at the level of factional struggle have re-emerged from the mire with a sharply critical view of the Commonwealth's political culture. However, the study of ideas and concepts at the more abstract level that qualifies as 'political thought' has yielded interesting results.[19] One of the strongest criticisms made by scholars of Polish political thought and discourse during much of the seventeenth and eighteenth centuries is of its almost unrelenting call to return to ancestral virtue, rather than to reform institutions. But the one did not necessarily preclude the other. While most political writers merely lamented slippage from the ancestral virtue of the noble nation, a significant minority understood that calls for moral renewal were pointless without *also* addressing those aspects of the form of government which generated political corruption.

The prevalent strand in eighteenth-century reformist thought was republican. It located the source of the Commonwealth's troubles in the endemic struggle *inter maiestatem ac libertatem*, which made politics a zero-sum game between the king and the nobility (or between the court and magnate factions), rather than a co-operative enterprise for the common good. So a number of republican writers proposed to resolve the struggle decisively in favour of *libertas*. Once the monarchs had been deprived of their means of corrupting the political community, it would be possible to risk reforming – perhaps even abolishing – the institutions which prevented kings from overthrowing liberty. These were the *liberum veto* and, still more radically, free royal elections.

By far the greatest of the republican reformers was the polymath Piarist, Stanisław Konarski. During the interregnum and civil war, he articulated more clearly than anyone the dependence of all individual and corporate liberties on the collective freedom – or independence – of the Commonwealth. At the end of Augustus III's reign, between 1760 and 1763, he published a four-volume treatise: *On the Means of Effective Councils.* This magnum opus stripped away the justifications of the *liberum veto* and argued that all alternatives to simple majority voting in the sejm were worse. Konarski showed that it was ludicrous to imagine that a virtuous individual could resist a corrupted majority. On the contrary, a corrupt minority could use the *veto* to frustrate a virtuous majority. The resultant anarchy meant the strong could oppress the weak – the opposite of liberty. Moreover, the freedom supposedly defended by the *veto* would be lost should the Commonwealth fall as a result of the *veto*. In volumes three and four, Konarski sought to allay fears, compared the Commonwealth to other 'free states', notably England, and showed how a reformed government could work. The monarch would lose most of his prerogatives to a 'council of residents' with four departments. This rather unwieldy executive would emanate from and be responsible to the expanded sejm, which, startlingly, would be 'our monarch and absolute ruler'.[20] Konarski's vision rested on a realistic view of human nature, prompting Jerzy Lukowski to compare Konarski to Machiavelli. However, Machiavelli – in the *Discorsi* as well as in *Il Principe* – understood politics in secular terms, while Konarski's realism was ultimately grounded in the Christian doctrine of original sin. While most of Konarski's life's work sought to inculcate virtue, he recognized that men were not angels; their institutions should reflect their imperfections. A sejm capable of legislating and governing would help them improve.

As Polish-Lithuanian politics sank to their anarchic nadir, here was the kind of rigorous stocktaking and bold plan the Commonwealth needed. Even before the final volume had been published, another author had noted the revolutionary implications: 'the laws which we keep are not only those of our predecessors, but are written by ourselves, because we are all an absolute Commonwealth, able to change, correct, abolish everything, whatever we desire to do.'[21] The impact of *On the Means of Effective Councils* was aided by its lively but familiar political language. It became more difficult to defend the *liberum veto* – not many tried, and even some of Konarski's critics complimented him. However, this new beginning was also a peak. It is tempting to adopt a linear, teleological approach to the history of political thought, but ideas are as prone to fragmentation, irruptions and blind alleys as any other walk of life. Konarski had not resolved all the dilemmas of liberty. They continued to pose difficulties for the thinkers, writers and statesmen of the next two generations, who were faced by worsening geopolitics.

The Prussian invasion of Saxony in 1756 pushed Augustus III into the arms of Austria and Russia. He hoped that the two empresses – Elizabeth and Maria Theresa – would support the election of one of his sons as king of Poland in due course. Unfortunately for the Wettins, Elizabeth died first – on Christmas Day 1761 (5 January 1762 by the Gregorian calendar). Russia abandoned the Seven Years' War. The Commonwealth remained neutral throughout the conflict, but supposedly friendly Russian units did not always pay for their forage. Frederick II regarded Poland as an unlocked storehouse. Having captured the Saxon mint at the start of the war, he struck vast quantities of counterfeit Polish coins which soon drove good money from circulation and caused rampant inflation. Prussian military purchasers could thus easily afford to raise their prices for forage and other supplies to initially grateful Polish landowners. The profits of this mass fraud contributed mightily to the survival of the Prussian state.

As the Seven Years' War drew to an end, Frederick again displayed his ruthlessness. After seven weeks of negotiations, on 15 February 1763 Austrian, Prussian and Saxon diplomats signed the Treaty of Hubertusburg. Here, in this hunting palace, deep in the Wermsdorf forest, Augustus III had enjoyed his most carefree moments before the war. Now the diplomats were accommodated in a servants' pavilion, and furniture had to be brought from local inns, because in 1760 Frederick had ordered the pillage of the palace. It would be repaired and refurbished, but the glory days had passed forever. So it was with the electorate. As part of the peace settlement, concluded on the basis of the *status quo ante bellum*, Prussia returned Saxony to its legitimate ruler. Frederick refused, however, to pay any compensation for the occupation, which had pitilessly drained the country's wealth and blood. Tens of thousands of Saxon soldiers had been killed or maimed, having been forcibly conscripted into the Prussian army. In the final weeks of the war, the negotiations were spun out at Hubertusburg to enable still more money, foodstuffs and people to be threshed out of Saxony. Among them were many adolescent girls, forced to breed the next generation of Prussian subjects.[22] On 25 April 1763 Augustus left Warsaw, where he had resided since the autumn of 1756. He found the splendours of Dresden ruined. On 5 October 1763 he died, just short of his sixty-seventh birthday. It was thirty years to the day since he had been elected to the Polish-Lithuanian throne.

The direct impact of the Seven Years' War on the Commonwealth was less than the calamity that befell Saxony. However, the geopolitical balance sheet of the reign of Augustus III was equally disastrous for his elective realm and his hereditary electorate. The Wettin dukes of Saxony, who for centuries had played first fiddle in northern Germany, were definitively eclipsed by their old rivals, the Hohenzollern margraves of Brandenburg (kings in Prussia since 1701). Frederick II's conquest of Silesia from the Habsburg Monarchy ensured that Saxony and the Commonwealth were kept firmly separated. Vienna's determination to avenge the loss meant that it became less interested in maintaining the status quo in Poland than hitherto. In general Frederick, like his predecessors, was keenly aware of the vulnerability of his *arriviste* kingdom-in-the-making. He was also mindful of the former dependency of East (formerly Ducal) Prussia on the Polish Crown and of the liberties once enjoyed by its potentially rebellious nobility. A significant revival of the Commonwealth would have fatal consequences for his fragile, still congealing state. Given the chance, as he recorded in the confidential political testaments he addressed to his heir, Frederick would have consolidated his territories by annexing Royal (Polish) Prussia and parts of Greater Poland, which now formed an exposed salient. But he was still more mindful of the power of the Russian Empire, and careful not to challenge Russian hegemony in Poland-Lithuania.

Although Russian policy towards the Wettin dynasty reversed course in 1762, Catherine II would tighten, rather than loosen, the cords of an essentially coherent policy towards the Commonwealth which dated back to the Great Northern War. Besides the prevention of significant reform, it contained two further, linked elements – confessional and demographic.

Religious factors should never be underestimated in politics, but one myth best binned is that before the 1760s, Russia's rulers were interested in protecting the Commonwealth's Protestants. Peter I expressed outrage at the executions of Lutheran city councillors in Thorn after the 1724 tumult (discussed in the next chapter), but he had no intention of intervening militarily. Prussian hopes that a partition might come from the brouhaha came to nothing. The Commonwealth's Lutheran and Calvinist communities tended to look to Berlin for aid. While the number of Protestant noble families fell to five or six hundred, the number of Evangelical inhabitants of towns and villages was rising.

On the other hand, support for the Orthodox Church was a fairly consistent, albeit secondary component of Russia's Polish policy. The 1686 peace treaty between the Commonwealth and Muscovy contained a clause guaranteeing the rights of Catholics in the former and Orthodox in the latter. This wording would serve the eighteenth-century Russian Empire as a pretext to intervene on behalf of Orthodox co-believers in Poland-Lithuania. However, the position of the Orthodox Church in the Commonwealth was parlous. Only a few impoverished and mostly illiterate nobles still adhered to the Orthodox faith by the mid-eighteenth century. Orthodoxy had become an overwhelmingly plebeian confession, and thus counted for little in domestic political terms. The reasons were complex.

In 1667 the Commonwealth ceded to Muscovy lands in which Orthodoxy was predominant. These losses were confirmed in 1686. Reluctant to submit to the Patriarch of Moscow after being cut off from the Patriarch of Constantinople in 1676, most of the Commonwealth's remaining Orthodox bishops accepted the Union over the next three decades. Peter I was intermittently and violently interested in reversing the tide: in Połock in 1705 he personally killed a Uniate prior who had offended him, and ordered the drowning of four monks. The tsar did insist on the vacant bishopric of Mohylew being filled by an Orthodox nominee, but neither he nor his successors prioritized the cause of the Orthodox in the Commonwealth. Although the Orthodox clergy sent litanies of partly justified complaints of intimidation and coercion by their Uniate and Latin-rite Catholic counterparts, both to the Holy Synod in St Petersburg and to the Russian Embassy in Warsaw, diplomatic interventions on their behalf remained sporadic until the 1760s.

Deprived, at least beyond the vicinity of Mohylew, of effective leadership, the Orthodox clergy sank into demoralization and poverty, while the Uniates continued their advance. By the 1730s and 1740s, most Orthodox parishes in the Polish Ukraine had gone over to the Union, whose bishops and superiors were supported by local magnates and wealthy nobles of the Latin rite. The much lower costs to noble patrons of founding and maintaining parishes in the Ruthenian rite, compared to the Latin rite, encouraged their multiplication as the south-eastern reaches of the Commonwealth recovered from wartime devastation. The downside was that parishes' material bases were precarious. More generously endowed by patrons was the sole monastic order in the Uniate

Church – the Basilians. Besides training priests, its schools provided an education similar to that offered by the Jesuits to noble youth of the Latin rite. A number of szlachta families regularly had a son ordained in the Ruthenian rite so that he could rise through the Basilian ranks and become a bishop. The Basilians claimed a monopoly on promotions to the episcopate because of the requirements of celibacy, virtue and learning – which the mostly married, undertrained, plebeian and impoverished parish clergy were incapable of meeting. So the monks claimed anyway. While some Uniate bishops were poor, others had substantial incomes. The metropolitan archbishops had the wherewithal to live like magnates, and some behaved as such, engaging in complex property disputes.

The Union was not distinguished from Orthodoxy only by allegiance to Rome. Despite the poverty of the parish clergy and the low social status of most believers, significant changes in religious praxis (pejoratively labelled 'Latinization') took root. However, their impact was shallowest in the vicinity of the Russian frontier. Here most of the Uniate clergy and faithful belonged to the Catholic Church in name only. The long Orthodox slide was halted in the mid-1750s, not least through the efforts of three hierarchs: the Bishop of Mohylew, the superior of the monastery of Motrenin in the far south-east, and the Bishop of Pereiaslav in the left-bank, Russian Ukraine. The latter succeeded in exercising episcopal jurisdiction in the right-bank, Polish Ukraine. By the early 1760s, Orthodox emissaries were visiting villages close to the frontier, encouraging the abandonment of the Union. Uniate hierarchs sought to counter these moves, especially when they were backed by magnates' private militias or by detachments of the Crown and Lithuanian armies.

Whatever their nominal confessional allegiance, the peasants of the eastern reaches of the Commonwealth interested the Russian Empire as a human and economic resource. A constant thorn in neighbourly relations was peasant flight. Such movement occurred in both directions. There is no compelling evidence that Polish-Lithuanian lords treated their serfs more humanely than did their Russian counterparts. A deficit of labour compared to land and the light hand of the law meant that many peasants needed little encouragement to seek better conditions on another estate. The same factors ensured that most lords (or their estate managers) welcomed newcomers without asking too many questions. There is no doubt, however, that Russian landholders were vexed by peasant flight and petitioned their government to stop it. Relevant to the net flow of migrants was the heavier taxation imposed on Russian peasants and their greater chances of being drafted into the army. In any case, Polish-Lithuanian lords were incapable of revindicating their serfs, whereas Russian forces returning through the Commonwealth's territory would sometimes round up those deemed to be runaway Russian subjects and frogmarch them across the frontier. Brandenburg-Prussian forces would conduct similar abductions in the north and west. In order to hamper peasant flight, Russia occasionally demanded the delineation of the border (to Russian advantage, of course) and for an uncultivated belt to be left adjoining the frontier (on the Polish-Lithuanian side, of course). Pretexts were found by stretching the terms of the 1686 treaty.

The combined result of deepening Russian hegemony, the rising importance of Prussia, the waning influence of Austria and France and the link with Saxony was to maintain the Commonwealth in a precarious external equilibrium. It was cemented by an internal impasse. The rhythms of Polish-Lithuanian political life could be curiously disconnected from their wider European contexts. This could continue only as long as the Russian court remained content to prevent change in the Commonwealth, rather than impose it. Despite these unfavourable geopolitical shifts, territorial stability added plausibility to the widespread although not universal conviction among the szlachta that Poland's very weakness gave its neighbours an interest in its preservation. This belief was fortified by faith in Divine Providence and the protection of the Virgin Mary as Queen of Poland.

— THREE —
SACRUM AND *PROFANUM*

Reverend Stanisław Konarski excelled as a political and religious thinker, a pedagogue, and as a reformer of the art of rhetoric. Born into a middling noble family – his father briefly attained a back-bench castellany – he was orphaned in infancy. Schooled by the Piarists, he joined the order. During his studies at the Collegium Nazarenum in Rome in 1725–29 he was exposed to some carefully filtered ideas of the early Enlightenment, including those of Isaac Newton and John Locke. He then engaged in a project to collate and print the statute laws of the Kingdom of Poland and the Commonwealth – the *Volumina Legum*, still an essential resource for historians. This task prepared him for his intellectual dismantling of the *liberum veto*.

Frustrated in the political arena after the events of 1733–36, Konarski shifted his attention to pedagogy. He founded the Collegium Nobilium in Warsaw in 1740–41 as an elitist venture. Most of the traditional schools run by the religious orders catered for the sons of the ordinary szlachta, and often for plebeians as well. Boarding facilities were limited. This relative egalitarianism put off the wealthiest families, most of which engaged tutors to educate their sons at home. Konarski wanted to remove privileged youths from the corrupting influences of their parents and family retainers. Instead the Piarist order would educate a vanguard of leaders – equipped intellectually and morally to repair the broken Commonwealth. The reformed curriculum included modern languages and experimental science. Some modern philosophy *(philosophia recentiorum)* was checked against revealed Christian doctrine before being taught. This meant, for example, that the evidence for the heliocentric theories of Copernicus and Galileo could be openly discussed. Pupils presented supervised debates and plays to parents and guests on scientific, philosophical, literary, moral and even political subjects. It was not the first such venture – the Italian Theatine order had opened a small school in Warsaw in 1737 – but the Piarists' Collegium

Nobilium was larger and soon attracted an aristocratic roll call. The Jesuits, who ran three times as many schools as the Piarists, followed suit. During the next two decades over a dozen elite colleges were established across the Commonwealth.

Having gained the support of the scholarly and relatively enlightened Pope Benedict XIV, Konarski was able to reform the curriculum of other Piarist schools – including day schools – in the Polish Crown in 1753–54. His Lithuanian confrères resisted the new trend for several years. In contrast, the Jesuits of the Grand Duchy of Lithuania embraced curricular reform with more alacrity than most of their brethren in the Crown. The stimulus from the Jesuit University of Wilno had slowed the decline in Jesuit schooling in the seventeenth century, before accelerating its recovery in the eighteenth. The school reforms carried out by these three orders – Jesuits, Piarists and Theatines – together with the updated studies at the seminaries run by the Priests of the Mission (Lazarists), have been linked to the European or even global phenomenon of what is usually called the Catholic Enlightenment.

Few serious scholars would now see Catholic Enlightenment as an oxymoron. However, most of the phenomena usually claimed for it would be more accurately described as 'enlightened Catholicism'. In semantic terms, the essence is conveyed by the noun, the style by the adjective. Much of the essence of Enlightenment ultimately concerns the application of critical reason to improve this world, without reference to any transcendental dimension, although not necessarily in opposition to it. Catholic Christianity concerns – in large measure – access via sacraments, prayer and saintly intercessions to Divine Grace, thereby partaking in Divine Incarnation and Redemption, known through Revelation, to enable fallen humanity to ascend to the next world. However, the focus on transcendental spirituality does not preclude human efforts to live a better – and more useful – life on Earth. A significant role is usually assigned to human will and deeds, in contrast to Protestant convictions of justification by faith alone, and in the case of Calvinism – of predestination. So some overlap between eighteenth-century Catholicism and Enlightenment was philosophically and theologically possible.[1]

One thrust of enlightened Catholicism was philosophical and pedagogical. The pejorative connotations of the term 'eclecticism' do not do justice to the mind-broadening potential of this approach, in which Polish-Lithuanian Piarists and Jesuits were in the Catholic European vanguard. One of the motivations was to catch up with Protestant universities and seminaries. This applied particularly in the Holy Roman Empire, divided constitutionally between Catholics and

Protestants. Perhaps for this reason, German Catholic theologians, historians and philosophers tended to be bolder in challenging traditional teaching than their counterparts in the Commonwealth. In the Reich, much criticism was directed at the Jesuits, who controlled most Catholic universities.

The other main thrust of enlightened Catholicism was pastoral and episcopal. Individual bishops had long sought to implement the reforms of the Council of Trent, especially in raising standards of discipline and learning among the diocesan clergy and teaching the basics of sacramental Catholicism to the populace. The mid-eighteenth century brought a redoubled determination, now voiced in a more 'enlightened' discourse, to eradicate popular 'superstitions' and to contribute to the temporal improvement of society. Again, Catholic Germany led the way. Here many bishops were also territorial princes, which encouraged arguments in favour of episcopal, as opposed to papal, authority. The most famous case was made by Johann von Hontheim, suffragan Bishop of Trier. His treatise *De statu ecclesiæ*, published under the pseudonym 'Febronius' in 1763, was predictably condemned by Pope Clement XIII.

The heyday of the enlightened reforming bishop in the Commonwealth would not come until the 1770s, but some bishops of the Saxon period distinguished themselves in their love of science and learning, and their efforts to raise the standards of pastoral service and leadership. Political duties often kept them away from their dioceses, but through well-chosen subordinates they kept an eye on their flocks.

Most of the clergy, like most of the faithful, could not remotely be called 'enlightened'. For better or worse, few Catholics in the Commonwealth interiorized their religion intellectually; they experienced it through the senses, emotions and the rhythms of the calendar. Rites of passage – christenings, marriages and funerals – stood out. The *pompa funebris* that accompanied the exequies of lords and ladies was one of the most spectacular aspects of baroque Polish-Lithuanian culture. The lineage and real or imagined qualities of the deceased were proclaimed in florid panegyrics, endless libations, gargantuan feasting, and towering temporary architecture. The latter centred on the *castrum doloris* – castle of sorrow – over the catafalque. Scaled-down but still elaborate rites were expected of the Church not only by poorer noble, but also by burgher and even some peasant families. Some of the latter incurred onerous expenses to ensure their dead were decently consigned to God.

For the rich, who had lived well (perhaps too well) in this world, generous bequests to the Church assuaged their anxieties about their reception in the next one. Many legacies were for masses for their souls, but some were also directed to hospitals for the sick and dying. A similar function was expected of domestic chaplains, usually recruited from the mendicant orders – especially the Conventual, Reformed and Observant Franciscans (the latter, founded by St Bernardino of Siena, were known in Poland-Lithuania as Bernardines). Cultured Jesuits often fulfilled this role at magnate courts.

For the far more numerous poor, prayers to the appropriate saints, votive offerings, the keeping of fasts and holy days, and pilgrimages to shrines containing wonder-working pictures and figures, were a recourse against the vicissitudes of health and harvest. Few among the clergy – especially the poorer parish priests (drawn mostly from the petty szlachta) and the (mostly plebeian-born) vicars and friars, who actually did most of the pastoral work – were overly concerned about the far-reaching syncretism between Christian worship and older beliefs that affected not only the peasantry, but many burghers and nobles as well. Those conducting missions had to contend with a challenging nexus of beliefs and practices, and not only in confessionally mixed regions.

Even among wealthier and better-read nobles, 'superstitions' were rife. Stanisław and Konstancja Poniatowski seem to have taken seriously the prediction by a fortune teller of an extraordinary future for their fifth son, Stanisław the younger, born in 1732.[2] Astrological prognostics jostled for space with medical and agricultural advice, as well as tales for the credulous and standard hagiographic fare in the almanacs published by religious orders. Deep into the eighteenth century many educated Poles imagined a Ptolemaic universe, in which four elements and four humours were woven by the Fates into the rhythm of the Zodiac and the movements of the planets. However, we should not imagine that most readers' daily lives were paralyzed by the fear of poorly aligned stars, or that the authors of strange tales necessarily believed them.

The absence from the 1660s onwards of a major intellectual challenge to Catholic orthodoxy within the Commonwealth – outside Royal Prussia – and the manifestations of piety among the Catholic population might suggest harmonious relations between the lay and clerical estates. On the contrary. The very tightness of the weave between the *sacrum* and the *profanum* provoked countless disputes over the boundaries and duties of the temporal and spiritual powers. One anxiety felt by lay noblemen concerned the participation of clerical judges in the Crown and Lithuanian tribunals. These canons and prelates, chosen by cathedral chapters, adjudicated cases regarding anti-Trinitarian heresy, sacrilege, blasphemy, atheism, Judaizing and apostasy. Clergymen sat on mixed benches in cases between lay and clerical persons or institutions, while in the Crown Tribunal a clerical president sat alongside the lay marshal. This gave rise to fears that the clerical deputies, trained in both canon and civil law, would run rings around their lay colleagues.

Priests still enraged nobles by summoning them before ecclesiastical courts for non-payment of tithes or the interest due on capital sums located on noble estates, usually as a result of legacies or loans. Although the verdicts of these courts had not been enforced by the secular authorities since the mid-sixteenth century, a noble who ignored a summons, or else sued a clergyman in a secular court, might find himself threatened with excommunication, which was not to be taken lightly. The restrictions enacted in 1635 and 1669 on mortmain (once bequeathed to the Church, land and capital could never return to free circulation among the laity) did not stop donations, most of them to the religious orders. Many nobles were convinced that following the abolition in 1717 of the *hiberna* hitherto levied for the quartering of troops, ecclesiastical property was under-taxed. This was despite the fact that nobles paid less – mostly in hearth taxes – than clergymen making the so-called voluntary donation, or *subsidium charitativum*.

Sejmik instructions often voiced these complaints, particularly when funds were sought for the expansion of the army. In 1744 the sejmik of the Greater Polish palatinates urged an appeal:

> . . . to the hearts of the reverend bishops, abbots and the whole clergy in possession of ecclesiastical estates, that *ex zelo suo et amore erga religionem et regionem*, they either consecrate four thousand infantry, or 600,000 Polish złotys, or a *quartam partem* of their revenues *in usum* of the army *quotannis*, besides that which their reverences' serfs contribute.[3]

Two years later the sejmik repeated its demand at greater length, sententiously quoting St Augustine: '*Proventus spirituales ex natura sui* are the *patrimonium pauperum*'; after all, none could be poorer than the Fatherland. The instruction demanded a similar 'quarter' from the Uniate clergy.[4] Senior clergymen confronted such pressure directly. Preaching the sermon at the inauguration of the 1738 sejm, a canon of Gniezno warned that 'to ruin churches, taking their revenues, to burden the *Patrimonium Christi*, to weaken ecclesiastics' *authoritatem* . . . is to destroy one's own Religion, and *per consequens* to impoverish and destroy one's own Fatherland'.[5] On the other hand, instructions also contain recommendations of particular ecclesiastical institutions and requests to confirm foundations.

Long-standing expectations that the Catholic Church, which owned about a tenth of the land in the Commonwealth, should apply its resources to the commonweal were also expressed in an idiosyncratic book, *Anatomy of the Commonwealth*. Its author, Stefan Garczyński, crowned a long political career in Greater Poland as Palatine of Poznań. His treatise was mostly written in the mid-1730s, but first published in 1751. Monastic publishers twice removed passages censuring neglect by the clergy, prompting the author to have the full version, along with some further critical comments, republished across the border in Breslau in 1753. For Garczyński, who diligently looked after his own properties, cleanliness and sobriety came next to godliness. Levels of infant mortality were the key test for any healthy community. So was prosperity; he addressed similarly astringent admonitions to nobles who mismanaged their estates.

If the message of this zealous Catholic sounds rather Protestant, this is no coincidence. Garczyński had first-hand knowledge of the hard-working settlers from Protestant parts of Germany who peopled many of the growing towns along Poland's western borders with Silesia, Lusatia and Pomerania. He also appreciated the personally free farmers, called 'Ollenders' after the Dutch origins of the earliest such settlers, who set an example of industriousness to their Catholic neighbours. In the first half of the eighteenth century they were joined by several hundred Catholic farmers from the region of Bamberg in Franconia. Settled by the city of Poznań in its outlying villages, on similar terms to the Ollenders, the 'Bambers' soon prospered. In the long term, they assimilated into the neighbouring Polish-speaking peasantry (to the extent that the term is now used locally to signify a wealthy, albeit uneducated farmer). This process was fostered by a shared Roman Catholic religion; for the moment, however, they remained privileged exceptions. Greater Poland was a relatively prosperous region. Some substantial peasant families in the vicinity of Poznań accumulated valuable personal possessions including beds and bed linen, tables, chairs, cutlery, ceramics, and even silks and damasks. However, in most parts of the Commonwealth, the ballast of servitude and habitude slowed growth in the rural economy. No initiative could be expected from an unfree peasantry, overburdened by rising labour services.

Worst of all, not least for Garczyński, was despair-induced alcoholism, with its grim consequences for infant and adult mortality (never mind cleanliness and industriousness). In Greater Poland, the noble monopoly on the distilling, brewing and sale of alcohol, known as the *propinacja*, was less important than in the province of Lesser Poland. There, it could contribute more than half the income on some far-flung latifundia with sparse markets. In some cases peasants had to pay for quotas whether they drank the liquor or not. Many of them, perhaps most, drowned their sorrows. Because the *propinacja* was often leased to Jewish middlemen, along with other manorial monopolies such as the mill, and because these tavern-keepers and managers often also acted as moneylenders, Jews often bore the brunt of peasant hatred. This phenomenon was also commoner in the east. Jewish tavern-keepers were very rare in the westernmost palatinates of the Crown.

On private estates the lord or his nominee was judge, jury and executioner. On Crown estates, peasants had, in theory, the right of appeal to royal assessory courts; on clerical estates they could try their luck before ecclesiastical courts. On the other hand, a starosta, who had an interest in exploiting the property rather than investing for the long term, was less likely to feel a paternalistic sense of responsibility for the rural populace. One example must suffice. Between 1755 and 1758 the peasants of the *starostwo* of Libusza in the Carpathian foothills rebelled against increased obligations. Initially they had some success, and even beat off detachments of soldiers. The peasants seem to have had a touching faith in royal justice. Their case went to the assessory court, but the long legal process ended in failure. The royal commissars handed down five death sentences and many severe whippings. They also allowed the noble leaseholder to recoup as much of his losses as he could in the course of a year. Outside Crown estates, peasants' relationship to the king was much weaker. The idea of a common Fatherland was well-nigh non-existent.

Sabotage, obstruction and bloody-mindedness were the peasants' chief responses to exploitation beyond 'customary' practices. Violent rebellion was rare outside mountainous and remote regions. However, in parts of Lithuania, lesser nobles sporadically incited peasants to rebel against magnate lords. This was perhaps a reflection of these nobles' difficulty in asserting themselves through parliamentary politics. In the Polish Ukraine, rebellion was a more frequent threat to noble lives and livelihoods. Here religious and linguistic differences, as well as folk memories of the previous century, aggravated socio-economic grievances. The activities of the *haidamaky* – bandits who claimed some popular sympathy – prompted the nobles of the south-eastern palatinates to fund and organize their own militias in the 1750s. Nevertheless, repression was only a short-term fix. Hereditary landowners had a vested interest in the welfare of their own subjects, on whose labour they usually depended. Peasant flight helped restrain seigneurial tyranny. Custom also acted as a brake on lords who tried to raise dues. Such efforts could provoke representations from the village council (*gromada*). However, it was not unknown for the elected officials of the council to exploit their positions and defraud the community. In such cases the villagers' best hope of redress lay with the manor.

We may be sceptical about priests' pleas for peasants. But occasionally the parsonage tried to mediate between the manor and the cottage – at least where the peasants belonged to the Latin rite of the Catholic Church. The szlachta of Greater Poland was sufficiently concerned about the clergy educating peasants and encouraging vocations to demand 'that our serfs should not be admitted to schools without the express will and attestation of their lord, and that the reverend bishops should not admit these serfs *ad ordinem cleri* or ordain them as priests'.[6]

Inconveniently for post-war Poland's communist ideologues, not every eighteenth-century peasant could be characterized as a miserable, exploited serf, ever ready to rise up against oppression. To start with, peasants' state tax burdens were low compared to neighbouring monarchies, and very few were pressed into military service. Ground-breaking research on rural society undertaken before and after the Second World War yielded impressive empirical results, even if these were sometimes shoehorned into prefabricated paradigms of class conflict. This data in turn provided a platform for the most gifted historians to construct advanced models of 'peripheral feudalism' which ensured that Polish Marxist economic historiography was far from peripheral.

Rural society could be highly complex. We have already noted some pronounced regional differences. One of the most notable cases was the Vistula delta. Since the mid-sixteenth century this terrain, most of it below sea level, had been meliorated by industrious, peaceable and personally free Mennonite farmers whose ancestors had originally been religious refugees from the Netherlands. In the north, from Samogitia along the Dvina valley, a variety of factors, including the cultivation and export of hemp and flax, requiring specialist skills, combined to make cash rents common. The local peasantry became steeply stratified, with some becoming more prosperous than petty nobles. Still further east, the lands between the upper Dvina and upper Dnieper supported a relatively dense network of local market towns where peasants could sell what 'surplus' they had.

Among peasants, hierarchies were far from straightforward. An internal market in labour and land functioned. If, as on some Crown estates in Podlasie, sixteen days' labour in summer and twelve in winter were expected per *włóka* (just under eighteen hectares), this could only be performed by a team of hired hands with more than one plough pulled by horses or oxen. These were extreme cases, but demands for six days per *włóka* were common. Large plots were sublet and richer peasants hired the labour of poorer ones. In practice those with smaller holdings were liable for disproportionately heavy labour services. Another variation, particularly on latifundia, was in the tasks which peasants might be set – these included carting, punting, tree-felling, building, mining, manufacturing and even ballet-dancing. Many peasants were hired directly by lords and their agents, especially on larger estates. Some highly skilled craftsmen might earn a few hundred złotys a year – more than the income of many clergymen and nobles – whereas a herdsman or shepherd might get a handful of złotys. In other cases, however, additional tasks were compensated by a reduction in labour services. There was no strict divide between peasants obliged to provide labour services and those who were not. Some unfortunates were obliged to perform labour services *and* pay cash rents *and* hand over part of their produce and livestock to their lord's representatives.

Noble–peasant relations also varied according to the structure of the nobility. On latifundia and Crown estates in Volhynia, Podolia, the Ukraine and the eastern reaches of the Grand Duchy of Lithuania, the lord was usually a distant figure – increasing the role of leaseholders and reeves. At the other extreme, peasants in regions densely populated by petty szlachta – such as Mazovia and Samogitia – might even find their labour services shared among several noblemen or clergymen. They would moreover be the neighbours of serfless nobles who could be equally poor and illiterate, but nevertheless considered themselves to be almost a different species of human being.

The diversity and fluidity of peasant family structures at the end of the eighteenth century have been illuminated by the painstaking research of Mikołaj Szołtysek. He has applied computerized microsimulations to data on no fewer than 155,818 individuals in 26,654 households, regarding the ages of leaving home, marriage, fertility, mortality and so on. It transpires that on average, peasant family households were somewhat more complex in the eastern parts of the Commonwealth than in the west. On the other hand, eastern households had fewer servants, especially females. However, there was no sharp divide between a 'West' characterized by small, nuclear families formed at a relatively late stage (when economic independence had been achieved), and an 'East' of larger, complex families with much lower ages of marriage (where economic independence was rarely achievable). If anywhere, the latter pattern appeared in the Polesian marshlands.[7] One generalization that can safely be made is that within peasant families, wives were subjected to their husbands, and children to their fathers, sometimes brutally so.[8]

Despite the structural constraints on the rural economy, the reign of Augustus III saw significant economic and demographic growth. Most textbook statistics are 'guestimates', but scholars concur that by the first partition in 1772 the population of the Commonwealth had reached and perhaps surpassed the level of the mid-seventeenth century. Most historical demographers still favour a figure of 12–12.5 million, although a serious case has been made for 14 million. The seven decades or so after 1648 had brought a catastrophic sequence of wars, epidemics and famines, aggravated by a sharp drop in global temperatures and shorter growing seasons. A decade of post-war stagnation seems to have followed. Both the scale of the demographic losses and the rates and trajectories of recovery have provoked much debate. Allowances must be made for periodic, localized setbacks. That said, after the calamitous 'Deluge', it seems that most regions experienced a late seventeenth-century recovery before suffering comparable losses during the Great Northern War.[9] Figures calculated for the Grand Duchy of Lithuania suggest its population plummeted from 4.55 million in 1650 (on a larger territorial base), to just 1.85 million in 1717, before rebounding to 3.76 million in 1772. The Grand Duchy was exposed to harsher and longer winters, so if these astounding figures are remotely accurate, then both the fall and the rise in much of the Polish Crown would have been less dramatic.[10] Whatever the actual numbers, the overall tendencies are not in doubt.

More food was being produced. Grain yields, which had fallen as low as 2:1 during the 'Little Ice Age', began to rise again, reaching 5:1 or 6:1 in favoured places in the warmer second half of the eighteenth century. Partly this was due to closer supervision. Peace also underpinned the recovery, not least because more manure was available from more livestock. Cattle had been at least as vulnerable as humans to the epidemic diseases spread by armies during the Great Northern War.[11] Although foreign armies still marched through the Commonwealth's territory during later conflicts, sometimes spreading pestilence, more often than not they maintained their discipline and paid for their food and forage – if not the people they abducted. Especially dynamic was the growth in the fertile south-east. Here the recovery of the right-bank Ukraine in the 1710s opened up renewed opportunities for settlement. Social tensions worsened as mostly absentee landlords sought to raise labour dues from an unwilling rural populace.

Growth occurred in towns as well. The Commonwealth had more than two thousand of them. Although several hundred of these are often considered glorified villages, most of whose inhabitants lived from agriculture and rural trades and crafts, many of these towns benefited from the growing rural economy, meeting the rising need for local markets. Towns had a threefold status – royal, ecclesiastical and private. The latter two kinds were subordinated strictly to their owners – to bishoprics, chapters and abbeys, and to wealthy nobles respectively. Some owners collected their rents and allowed their towns to stagnate, while others founded markets, built urban infrastructure and sought new settlers with promises of self-government and low taxes.

The largest cities in the Commonwealth were royal towns, but only Danzig could be called a metropolis before the court moved to Warsaw in 1757. Mid-century Warsaw had about 25,000 inhabitants, a modest total which nevertheless significantly exceeded the populations of Wilno, Cracow, Lwów, Poznań, Lublin or Thorn.[12] Authority in most royal towns was contested between the starosta who represented the king (however theoretically) and the municipal corporation. The latter usually operated according to Magdeburg law, enshrined in royal charters. However, the municipal writ and taxes did not apply to *jurydyki* – properties belonging to nobles or the Catholic Church. These were sometimes the locations for business activities that undercut the registered tradesmen and artisans of the town. Where the town possessed the privilege *de non tolerandi Iudæis* and the competing trade in the *jurydyki* was in Jewish hands, the situation could become combustible. The tinder could ignite violently at times of crisis.

The number of Jews in the Commonwealth reached about three-quarters of a million during the 1760s. The rate of increase outstripped that of the szlachta.

Polin still attracted migrants, given relatively low taxes and extensive communal autonomy, at whose summit stood the Council of Lithuania and in the Crown, the Council of the Four Lands – until their abolition in 1764. Jewish communities were particularly numerous in the lands between the Rivers Vistula and Dniester. In the private towns of the east, the restrictions imposed by the Catholic clergy were more lightly felt, and the position of rival Christian burghers was much weaker than in the royal towns of the west. A magnate's Jews were legally at their master's mercy, and his economic interest generally outweighed prejudices against their settlement. Even owners of ecclesiastical towns were often persuaded that only Jews could kick-start trade. However, most of the Jews' demographic growth was internally generated. It can be attributed, among other things, to lower ages of marriage, better standards of midwifery and communal support for mothers and infants, and lower rates of alcoholism.

With this growing population came worsening socio-economic inequality. While some Jews prospered mightily, many more struggled to make a living as petty traders, craftsmen, labourers or tinkers. *Kahals* often struggled to meet their tax obligations and fell into debt. To many poor Jews, particularly those with grievances against communal authorities, scholarly arguments over finer points of the law (the Talmud) seemed irrelevant. This was fertile ground for emotional and even messianic religious revivals, although not for revolt against established elites. The most important of these movements came to be known as Hasidism, and it would have a huge long-term impact on central and eastern European Jewry. Israel ben Eliezer, known as Baal Shem Tov (the Master of the Good Name), was a poor Jew from Podolia, who acquired a reputation for both scholarship and saintliness, as well as miracles. His optimistic message of Divine love and immanence advocated the pursuit of blissful union with God through heartfelt prayer. Traditional rabbinical scholars criticized Hasidists for valuing the emotions more than learning. The greatest of these rabbis was Elijah ben Shlomo Zalman, known as the Gaon of Vilna (the genius of Wilno). His prestige and firm stance, extending to excommunications, helped to ensure that Hasidism was less successful in Lithuania than in the south-east of the Crown.

Baal Shem Tov and his followers drew the line at another movement which rejected Talmudism. Jakub Frank also hailed from Podolia – characterized by Paweł Maciejko as 'a seditious province where dissenters gathered and heterodoxy was practiced openly and publicly'.[13] Frank's father was a follower of the seventeenth-century 'messiah', Sabbatai Zevi. In 1755 Frank began to preach the heavenly revelations that he claimed to have experienced. He and other Sabbatians were excommunicated by the rabbinical authorities in Brody and Lwów the following year. He also proclaimed himself to be Sabbatai Zevi and the prophet Jacob reincarnated, as well as part of a divine trinity. Both sides appealed to an ecclesiastical court, despite it being an internal Jewish matter. Following a public disputation, the court declared the Frankists victorious, and ordered the public burning of the Talmud. Frank and thousands of his followers were effectively pushed by their rabbinical opponents into the arms of the Catholic Church. Mass baptisms took place in Lwów in 1759–60, despite the reservations of some clergymen about the Frankists' doctrine. Sure enough, in January 1760 Frank was arrested, charged with heresy by an ecclesiastical court, and imprisoned in the Pauline monastery at Częstochowa. Incarcerated there until his release by the Russians in 1772, he became a martyr to his numerous followers, who continued to send him money after he moved to the Habsburg Monarchy and later to Offenbach in central Germany.

The Frankist controversies referred to trials of Jews for the alleged ritual murder of Christian children – the infamous blood libel. In 1758 the Frankists, alongside a series of propositions regarding the Messiah, publicly contended that the Talmud taught that Jews needed to use Christian blood. This interested Kajetan Sołtyk, who was then lobbying for a translation from the impoverished see of Kiev to Cracow. For the most notorious trial of all had taken place in Żytomierz in 1753. Sołtyk, then the suffragan Bishop of Kiev, had brought charges of ritual murder against thirty-three Jews, who were tortured during interrogation. Eleven were executed in all, and the six who refused to abjure their faith were tormented further before being put to death. Jewish communities in the Ukraine later accused Sołtyk of extorting money by threatening further cases. In his memoirs, Stanisław August Poniatowski records the appalling impression this persecution produced among Dutch Jews. With a sullied reputation, Sołtyk had an interest in 'proving' the accusations during the Frankist disputes. The official position of the Holy See was then being drafted by Cardinal Lorenzo Ganganelli – the libel was declared false. But this was not yet published and the Commonwealth's ecclesiastical authorities hedged.[14]

The mass baptisms of the Frankists marked the problematic apogee of Catholic efforts to convert Jews in Poland-Lithuania. This process had recently been gaining momentum. The Mariavite congregation of nuns was established in 1737 in the Grand Duchy of Lithuania to provide help for converted Jewesses, many of whom became Mariavites themselves. No female order expanded faster. From the 1760s, the difficulty in assimilating into Christian society so many Frankist neophytes – many of whom still considered themselves essentially Jews – lessened enthusiasm among the clergy for conversion. The bitterest conflicts occurred when converts/apostates sought to baptize their children or grandchildren against the will of the rest of their families. Many nobles, moreover, regretted the ennoblement of large numbers of converts in the Grand Duchy of Lithuania, in accordance with the Third Lithuanian Statute of 1588.

Among Christian confessions, the Commonwealth's religious pluralism had shrunk markedly by the middle of the eighteenth century, at least in rural areas. In the Crown, villages with more than one place of worship of different confessions were nine times less numerous than those with only one (admittedly, most settlements had none at all). In general, the western half of the Commonwealth was overwhelmingly Latin; the east – Uniate (Map 2). The zone where the two Catholic rites were in approximate balance was not more than fifty kilometres wide at the western edge of Crown Ruthenia, but much broader in Podlasie and the Grand Duchy of Lithuania. The density of Latin-rite churches tapered off in an easterly direction, whereas with few exceptions the relatively denser Uniate structures ended abruptly. This 'cliff-edge' effect was probably due to the low social status of most Catholics of the Ruthenian rite – higher-status Ruthenians were often drawn to the Latin rite. Basilian monks were a partial exception. This pattern differed at the fringes of the Commonwealth. Most of the Orthodox lived close to the border with the Russian Empire, whereas most of the Lutherans, Bohemian Brethren and Mennonites lived along the western and north-western frontiers, as well as in Courland. The Protestant population of the towns close to the border with Silesia was rising fast. Here the Catholic hierarchy fought a losing battle to dissuade noble proprietors from settling 'heretics'.

The overall hegemony of the Catholic Church was not in doubt, but many towns remained confessionally and ethnically mixed. Jews and Ruthenians (Uniate and Orthodox) peopled the towns of the east, with Ruthenians predominant in the Polish Ukraine. In the southern parts of Crown Ruthenia much trade, not only with the Ottoman Empire, was in the hands of Armenians (who mostly belonged to the Armenian rite of the Catholic Church with an archbishopric in Lwów). In the western and north-western borderlands of the Polish Crown, German-speaking burghers, mostly Lutherans or Bohemian Brethren, mixed with Polish-speakers, mostly Catholics of the Latin rite. The proportion of Jews tended to be lowest when the percentage of Protestants was highest, but the Catholic prince-bishops of Warmia had prohibited their settlement altogether. Descendants of sixteenth- and seventeenth-century Scottish settlers – Calvinists and Catholics alike – could be found in the towns of Samogitia, Royal Prussia and elsewhere.

Co-existence was not always peaceful. For example, Kowno's Lutherans clung on to their representation in the town council, guaranteed by seventeenth-century royal privileges. However, their church had been rebuilt in the late seventeenth century – beyond the walls. Funeral processions had to make their way quietly through the backstreets to the Evangelical cemetery, in order not to offend Catholics. This discretion did not prevent a vicious attack on 20 April 1765. A crowd of carpenters assaulted the Lutheran pastor leading the funeral procession, while the Catholic parish priest personally beat him on the head with a stick, before presiding over his physical and ritual humiliation. It seems that a dispute over the rent for the Lutheran school building, which stood on land belonging to the Catholic Church, was a factor in triggering the violence. Later that year the leaders of the town's rival confessions agreed to maintain the local political status quo, but the Lutheran school had to close.[15]

Wilno, stronghold of the Jesuits, remained a polyglot city. Polish, Yiddish, Ruthenian and German were the most commonly spoken languages. Admittedly, the parity between 'Greeks' and 'Romans' in the city magistrature established back in 1536 had since 1666 been interpreted as Ruthenian- and Latin-rite Catholics; the hitherto strong Orthodox presence in the city faded as the decades passed. Lutheran and Calvinist Christians also maintained footholds, including in some of the guilds. They also maintained a well-organized system of charity – partly to prevent conversions to Catholicism of the destitute and dying. Tatars still lived and worshipped in their suburb beyond the walls, trading in the city itself. The large Jewish population of the 'Jerusalem of the North' not only multiplied in number, but from 1748 onwards could gain in wisdom by listening to the Gaon. Confessional tensions did not disappear. For example, the Latin Catholic Bishop of Wilno blocked the rebuilding of the Lutheran church after a fire in 1737. The Lutherans appealed to Primate Teodor Potocki, noting that the 'happy Jews' could worship under a roof.[16] The rebuilt church was reopened in 1744. However, no large-scale confessional violence had occurred since the 1680s. Those tumults – against the Calvinists and the Jews – had provoked firm reactions from John III Sobieski. The eighteenth century was probably calmer because Catholics of both rites felt far more self-confident than hitherto, having pushed their respective Christian rivals towards the margins of the city. But perhaps the persistently flexible markers of confessional allegiance, reflected in marriages across some of the religious divides, also played a part.

In this relatively easy-going environment, which retained enough of its former splendour to impress Stanisław Poniatowski the younger in 1755, cultural transfer was visible, not least because fires provided frequent opportunities for rebuilding.[17] The supremely elegant Vilnan late baroque and rococo style was adopted eagerly not only by Catholics of both rites, but also by the city's Lutheran, Orthodox and Jewish communities. The gifted architect Johann Christoph Glaubitz carried out much work for his own Lutheran community, including the rebuilding of the church. He also reconstructed several Latin-rite Catholic churches, built the lovely gateway of the Uniate Monastery of the Holy Trinity, designed the huge iconostasis of the Orthodox Church of the Holy Spirit, and even reshaped the deceptively large interior of the Great Synagogue. The characteristic Vilnan style of slender, tapering towers and rippling facades reached maturity in the 1750s, thanks to cross-fertilization between architects of various backgrounds. It spread across the Grand Duchy and into Livonia. Perhaps the finest example was the Basilian monastery and church at Berezwecz, constructed between 1756 and 1767. The Soviets turned the monastery into a prison in 1939, and around 1970 they blew up the church. As this book goes to press, a penal facility is still housed in the former monastic buildings (Plates 5, 6, 7).

The confessional mix caused complications in Royal Prussia. In the cities, unlike the surrounding countryside, Catholics (Polish, Kashubian and German-speakers) formed a reluctantly tolerated but growing minority, especially among the poorer plebeians. Mennonites and Jews, however, were excluded from urban citizenship and faced restrictions on their residence and business activities (doors were opened to Jews representing Polish lords). Predominantly Germanophone Lutherans dominated the urban patriciates, and in Danzig Lutherans constituted at least three-quarters of the entire population. Their preachers often engaged in learned but heated polemics with those of the small but influential Calvinist minority. Danzig and its suburbs also hosted five Catholic monastic houses. The Dominicans, Jesuits and Bernardines maintained an active presence in Thorn. These orders pursued converts from Protestant confessions across Royal Prussia, employing a mixture of polemical preaching and liturgical spectacle. The Prussian cities had to manage disputes arising from mixed marriages, changes of confession and affronted religious feelings.

Nobody forgot the events of 1724 in Thorn. Lutheran bystanders failed to show respect to a Catholic procession with the Host; insults and scuffles escalated into the demolition of the Jesuit college and the desecration and burning of religious artefacts by an enraged crowd. The city authorities did not intervene. Nobody was killed in the tumult, but in a draconian verdict the sejm court sentenced fourteen persons to death. Ten of them – including one of Thorn's burgomasters – lost their heads. In future half the city councillors would have to be Catholics – an analogous arrangement to that in some cities of the Reich. However, the Catholic burghers were never able to fill their quota. This reveals the strength of the Lutherans in the city. The Lutherans lost the city's principal church to the Catholics, but they were eventually able to build a new one on the market square, consecrated by royal permission in 1756. The papal nuncio vetted the design to ensure that the building did not look too much like a church – yet. Ironically, after the Second World War, as the city was repopulated with deportees from Wilno, the Jesuits received this church.

Uniquely, the cities of Royal Prussia had an entrenched institutional and political presence in their region. The Prussian *Landtag* had two houses. The upper house contained the representatives of the great cities of Danzig, Thorn and Elbing alongside the senators – palatines, castellans and bishops. The lower house comprised the non-senatorial szlachta of the three Prussian palatinates. Representatives of twenty-seven lesser towns had sat alongside these nobles until 1662; these towns continued to lobby for the restoration of their rights. The Prussian *Landtag* was entitled to send an unlimited number of envoys to the sejm. However, these higher stakes encouraged the use of the *liberum veto*: between 1713 and 1730, and again between 1735 and 1764, no *Landtag* reached a successful conclusion. The royal court had little interest in supporting a forum which could effectively defend the Prussian rights and privileges that it was gradually undermining, not least by granting offices and Crown estates to persons of doubtful Prussian status.

The paralysis of the *Landtag* did not really diminish the position of the great cities. Danzig, especially, could afford lobbyists – not least to foreign powers (many of which had their own residents in the city, mainly to keep an eye on trade). The carefully drafted and registered correspondence of Danzig City Council with other cities (in German), and with monarchs and senators (in Latin), bears witness to its status and influence.[18] However, from 1748 to 1752 the royal court took advantage of conflicts between the city council, dominated by the refined *Gelehrte* elite, and the increasingly vocal opposition led by active merchants and toiling guildsmen. Two royal commissars sided with the opposition and consolidated royal prerogatives in the city's affairs. There were limits, however: in 1760–61 the court tried and failed to take half of the port duties.

Danzig, with 40,000–50,000 inhabitants in mid-century, remained the Commonwealth's largest and wealthiest city, and its busiest port by far. Thorn, with about 11,000 people, was well behind.[19] Trade along the Vistula grew, even if the extraordinary prosperity of the early seventeenth century was never regained. The sheer variety of economic activity in Danzig emerges from the advertisements, notices and reports in its vibrant periodical press. The patricians continued to patronize the arts and sciences on a grand scale. Just as their ancestors had resisted Swedish besiegers in the mid-seventeenth century, so the mid-eighteenth-century Danzigers were determined to avoid subjection to the Hohenzollerns. The fate of Elbing served as a stark warning: that city was surrounded by land taken by Brandenburg-Prussia when Augustus II had failed to redeem its mortgage.

As Karin Friedrich has shown, 'liberty' had a particular resonance for the burghers of Royal Prussia – who believed themselves a Prussian branch of the 'Sarmatian nation'.[20] Prussian spokesmen had long claimed that theirs was a better version of the Sarmatian heritage, because liberty was not restricted to the szlachta. Such Prussian 'patriots', mostly Lutheran and mainly Germanophone, had an ambivalent relationship with the mostly Catholic and mainly Polonophone szlachta of the region. Not only did the cities themselves own considerable landed properties, but a diminishing number of patricians personally owned estates. When they did join forces, the nobles and patricians had some success in resisting royal encroachments on their liberties. The threat posed by Frederick II was of a different order. The Prussian burghers were more aware than most of their nobly born compatriots that their liberty would not survive Hohenzollern rule.

The erudition of Royal Prussian writers overlapped with the first impulses of the Enlightenment felt in the Commonwealth. The patricians had long employed graduates of north German universities as preachers and professors. As a result, the Lutheran *Gymnasien* of Royal Prussia adopted advances in mathematics, science and philosophy about a generation before any Catholic religious orders did likewise. We may question how far intellectual developments in the

Protestant, Germanophone world affected the rest of the Commonwealth, but there were points of contact. One was the syndic Gottfried Lengnich, who tutored the elder sons of Stanisław Poniatowski for two years, during their residence in Danzig in the 1730s, and dedicated his history of Poland to them when it was published in 1740.[21] Lengnich was steeped in the German natural law school of Christian Thomasius at Halle, but ultimately fell back on a historical justification of the Prussians' rights and liberties.[22]

Another link was through the migration to the Commonwealth of many Germanophone scholars – Catholics and Protestants alike – who found patrons among Poland's ecclesiastical and lay magnates. Particularly important was the erudite circle around the episcopal brothers Załuski. This group is perhaps better seen as an epigone of an early modern republic of scholars, rather than as a precursor of the Enlightenment, but it helped to keep open intellectual channels between Poland-Lithuania and the rest of Europe. Andrzej Stanisław Załuski even sought – albeit without success – to bring the rationalist philosopher Christian Wolff from Halle to the University of Cracow, of which the bishop was chancellor. This was at a time when many nobles – unlike many of their forefathers – were convinced that Poles had nothing to learn from abroad.

That was not a view taken in most magnate families. A voyage abroad continued to be part of the upbringing of aristocratic young men. From Italy, France, the Low Countries and Germany (other destinations were rare) they brought back cultural novelties. They employed foreign artists and architects to turn their palaces and ecclesiastical foundations into statements of wealth, status, power, piety and taste. Symbols of death, omniscient in the dark, heavy baroque forms of the seventeenth century, gave way after the Great Northern War to rococo frivolities in white, pastels and gilded stucco. Skulls were out, shells were in. Such frothy meringue proclaimed that these buildings' owners and founders were *au courant* with the well-sugared cream of the European elite. They were fit, in other words, to reign. This claim was at odds with the Commonwealth's republican political culture. Mixed messages resulted: the imperial princely mitre sat uneasily alongside the Sarmatian mace in the imagery of the Nieśwież Radziwiłłs. Similar tensions can be discerned in the patronage of Hetman Jan Klemens Branicki, recently characterized as a 'modern Sarmatian'.

Numerous magnates still shaved their heads, grew their whiskers and bedecked themselves in long robes (of which the inner one was called a *żupan*, the outer one a *kontusz*), silken sashes and soft boots, but others followed the latest European fashions, as many of their forebears had done. The mode for periwigs, frock coats, waistcoats, tight breeches, silk stockings and buckled shoes was advancing. Branicki abandoned foreign for national attire when he became field hetman in 1735, but half a century would pass before the tide turned decisively back in favour of 'Sarmatian' fashion among the Polish-Lithuanian noble elite.

Eighteenth-century moralists tended to be sceptical about the impact of foreign travel on the aristocracy. For every magnate who either applied himself diligently to the study of laws, customs and technology, or else prayed earnestly at shrines from Jerusalem to Compostela, there were more who took advantage of the opportunities for revelry. Travel was blamed for the export of wealth from the country and for diverse physical and moral maladies, whose underlying theme was effeminacy and degeneracy. In sharp contrast, in a 1744 pamphlet Stanisław Poniatowski the elder cast voyages by 'lordlings' as a patriotic duty: 'so that in acquiring experience of the world, they would inform themselves as well about the means of government, the economy, situation, power, forces and interests of various states and from this then choose that which could be proper and useful in the Commonwealth'. The result of such voyages, he believed, would be essential reforms, including the restriction or abolition of the *liberum veto*. Other free states from which Poles could learn were the Dutch Republic, Venice, Switzerland, and unusually for the time – England. Poniatowski looked towards a luminous future: 'Let us have forces, let us have order, we shall have it all, everything will go well, more than one [power] will seek our friendship and alliance, and we shall gain well-founded fame among neighbouring nations.'[23] He sent his own sons on voyages to western Europe.

Poniatowski's bright vision was the outcome of both the positive and negative sides of the ledger. The mostly peaceful reign of Augustus III brought significant economic and demographic growth. Replacing gloomier forms and shades, the lighter, sunnier art and architecture commissioned in these decades manifested prosperity. The self-confidence of the Catholic Church translated into a building boom. Many of the finest churches and monasteries were constructed in the east of the Commonwealth, where both principal Catholic rites were fast expanding.

Intellectually, a great advance had begun, although it proceeded on largely separate tracks in Protestant urban circles and among some of the Catholic clergy. Modern languages began to be taught systematically in boarding schools, rather than on an *ad hoc* basis by personal tutors. Partly as a result of a campaign by Konarski, the Polish language was purged. Texts from the 1760s are far less incrusted with Latin phrases and Latinate calques than those of the 1730s – including those by Konarski himself. Openness to new ideas enlivened much political writing. By 1763 Konarski and the *Familia* had drawn up coherent and plausible plans for the reform of the political system. Konarski published his project in the later volumes of *On the Means of Effective Councils*, while the Czartoryskis kept theirs under wraps. Understandably, the *Familia* assigned a greater role to senators than did Konarski, but both plans sought radically to reduce royal patronage powers, introduce a collegial executive, and prevent the rupture of the sejm.

However, while the elder Poniatowski had expressed much optimism and openness, he had also lamented the stasis of the system. The better the Commonwealth's finest minds argued for its repair, the more mired its politics became in corruption and anarchy, and the more vulnerable its international position. Politically, the balance sheet was decidedly negative. The profound crisis afflicting Polish-Lithuanian politics in the last decade of Augustus II's reign worsened under his son. The Commonwealth's neighbours had every interest in keeping it that way. Facilitated by Austro-Prussian rivalry, Russian hegemony seeped into the Commonwealth's politics, before being asserted in the 1760s.

Salutary the Czartoryskis' planned reforms may have been, but their implementation would have depended on a coup d'état and a Russian 'guarantee'. In 1762–63 the *Familia* counted on Russian power – although it also sounded out Versailles. Yet Catherine II had no more intention of permitting far-reaching reforms than had her predecessors. She decided that armed intervention in the Commonwealth was a premature risk before the death of Augustus III. She left her allies exposed. Outnumbered, outmuscled and outgunned by the Radziwiłłs, the *Familia* was worsted at the Lithuanian Tribunal in the spring and summer of 1763. It faced disaster at the Crown Tribunal in Piotrków. Just two days before this was due to recommence, the news arrived from Dresden that King Augustus had died on 5 October. The normal organs of justice ceased to function, as another interregnum had begun.

— FOUR —

'A NEW CREATION OF THE POLISH WORLD'

'We now seem to have a new, or rather a second creation of the Polish world before us. This is the critical moment . . . when it is necessary to move almost everything at once.'[1] Two years into his reign, King Stanisław August Poniatowski did not believe in doing things by halves. The 1763–64 interregnum had shattered the external equilibrium and internal impasse which had framed the Commonwealth's politics under Augustus III. On the one hand, long-germinating seeds bore fruit in tangible legislative, institutional and fiscal changes. Some citizens felt the benefits, but more were disturbed by the pace and scope of change. The tranquillity of the previous reign appeared greater in retrospect. The impasse could not have been broken without the decision of the new Empress of Russia, Catherine II, to intervene more deeply in the Commonwealth's affairs. Insisting on equalizing the rights of non-Catholic and Catholic nobles, she stirred emotions and released forces beyond her ken. Stanisław August's appeal to the sejm of 1766 proved a watershed. From this point onwards, things fell apart, and by the spring of 1768, the Commonwealth was in chaos.

Well before the death of Augustus III on 5 October 1763, the question of his successor had occupied the principal courts of Europe. The outcome of the contest was decided by the Seven Years' War. The natural supporters of a third Saxon reign in Poland were Austria and France, whose ruling dynasties were closely related by marriage to the now staunchly Catholic Wettins. The Habsburgs and Bourbons had put aside their long-standing enmity in the 'Diplomatic Revolution' of 1755–57, and they remained allies (if not exactly friends) after the war ended. However, France suffered a catastrophic maritime defeat to Great Britain and by 1760 had effectively abandoned the continental struggle. Britannia ruled the waves, but while British finances were in better shape than the French, the price of victory was eye-wateringly high. After the war ended, the two western great powers prepared for the next round in their global struggle. Europe's geopolitical centre of gravity shifted eastwards for a generation. The Commonwealth's fate would be decided by its immediate neighbours. Of these, as Paul Schroeder puts it, 'Russia had the widest choices, and would choose whichever combination would provide it the clearest hegemony and greatest profit at a given time'.[2]

The outcome of the Seven Years' War in central Europe had been decided at least as much by changes of policy in St Petersburg as by battles and sieges in the valleys of the Oder and the Elbe. In the mid-1750s the Austrian chancellor Prince Wenzel Anton von Kaunitz-Rietberg had assembled a grand coalition in order to retake Silesia from Prussia. The combined resources of the Habsburgs, Romanovs and Bourbons were furnished by about eighty million subjects, whereas the upstart Hohenzollern ruled just five million. The disparity should have been decisive. Notwithstanding Frederick II's early victories, by 1759 his cause seemed hopeless. The eastern parts of his kingdom were under Russian occupation when Empress Elizabeth died on 5 January 1762. Her successor, Peter III, who idolized Frederick, ended military operations. Russia was even preparing to re-enter the conflict on the Prussian side, when Peter was overthrown by his wife Catherine and killed after a reign of just six months. The Russian Empire stayed out of the war. Left without a major ally, Austria proved incapable of holding on to any of the fortresses it had regained. Prussia emerged from the war territorially intact.

Both at the time and subsequently, Elizabeth's death was considered 'the miracle of the House of Brandenburg'. It is easy to indulge in wishful thinking – of what the Commonwealth might have gained, had the tsaritsa lived just a little longer. However, the Russian Empire badly needed peace. Moreover, the sensual empress's health had long been weak, and the consequences of her demise had been calculated for years. For all her animosity towards the misogynistic Frederick, it was not in Russian interests to destroy Prussia. While a Prussia engorged by Silesia and allied to France was a serious threat to Russia and needed to be cut down to size, a victorious Austria allied to France might also obstruct the projection of Russian power westwards. Russian statesmen had long since chafed at the restrictions imposed by the Austrian alliance. Projects for Austria to recover Silesia and for Russia to gain East Prussia (the latter – possibly – to be exchanged for Courland and territories on the Dvina and Dnieper) remained speculative. Moreover, the Russians faced immense logistical difficulties in fighting so far from their bases. Thus the caution shown by Elizabeth's generals following allied victories derived from more than the peculiarities of her nephew Peter. That said, the course of the war demonstrated the power and potential of the Russian Empire. Given the systemic as well as the personal hostility between Maria Theresa and Frederick, the new Russian empress could, if she played her hand well, become the arbiter of central and eastern Europe. Only the Ottoman Empire would try to oppose Russia deciding the Polish election.

Augustus III's survival of Elizabeth was, however, a disaster for the House of Saxony. She had permitted the investiture of his favourite son Prince Charles as Duke of Courland in place of the exiled Ernst Biron in 1758. Augustus III's success in Courland – or its subsequent exchange for East Prussia – would have increased the chances of a Wettin succession. More importantly, while Elizabeth and Maria Theresa continued to wage war on Frederick, the courts of Vienna, St Petersburg and Versailles would probably have ensured that one of Augustus III's sons was elected to the Polish throne. However, following Elizabeth's death Charles left Courland before he could be ejected. In 1763, despite local and Polish protests, Biron was restored, on condition of his subservience to St Petersburg. Catherine II would not countenance a third Saxon king of Poland.

As in 1733, the court most interested in the Polish election was St Petersburg. This time, however, the opposition from other powers would be weaker. It became weaker still when Frederick Christian, the new Elector of Saxony, died a few weeks after his father. With his son still a minor, the courts of Versailles and Vienna lost their remaining appetite to support the Saxon cause. Augustus III's eldest surviving son, Prince Xavier, prudently decided not to put himself forward. The Saxon supporters in the Commonwealth plumped for Crown Grand Hetman Jan Klemens Branicki. The seventy-four-year-old Branicki was expected to keep the throne warm until the thirteen-year-old Elector Frederick Augustus III came of age.

Branicki squared up to his much younger brother-in-law, Stanisław Poniatowski the younger. Since the early 1750s, when the *Familia* had refused to support the *vivente rege* election of another Wettin without a commensurate commitment to reform, it had been clear that the *Familia* would seek to put one of its own on the throne with Russian support.[3] The obvious candidate was the son of August Czartoryski: Adam Kazimierz. At his wedding to his well-dowried younger cousin, Izabela Flemming, on 18 November 1761, Jagiellonian symbols – present in visual and versed panegyrics – proclaimed that this branch of the tree of Gediminas was ready to occupy the throne. The architectural centrepiece, inspired by the Temple of Sibyl in Tivoli, underlined the prophetic tone. However, the erudite and elegant Prince Adam rejected his destiny. According to the British envoy, the prince even threatened to flee the country rather than seek election as king.[4] His father, August, was thought to want the throne for himself, but he was, with good reason, not trusted on the banks of the Neva.

Stanisław Antoni Poniatowski was the fifth of the seven sons of the late Castellan of Cracow (two of his older brothers had died in early manhood, one in infancy). He held one of the Commonwealth's fairly prestigious central dignities – the stewardship of Lithuania. He was intelligent, well travelled, eloquent, handsome, generous, but sometimes naive. He had played a prominent role at recent sejms, but lacked wealth and seniority. His political significance derived from his relationship with the Grand Duchess Catherine. In 1755 he had travelled to St Petersburg as secretary to the British ambassador to Russia, Sir Charles Hanbury Williams, who introduced him to the grand duchess. Poniatowski subsequently returned to the banks of the Neva as a Saxon envoy in his own right, prolonging their love affair. The embers stayed warmer on his side.

After Catherine's coup d'état, Poniatowski became the *Familia*'s key channel of communication both with the Russian court and its experienced ambassador in Warsaw, Hermann von Keyserlingk (who had tutored him in logic during a previous posting). That was not all. Once Catherine had disposed of her husband, rumours crossed Europe that she planned to marry Stanisław. He hoped so. In his memoirs he explains that he was convinced 'that I would have done more good for my Fatherland as an individual at her side, than as king here'.[5] He may even have been right, but it was not to be. Catherine's tenure of the throne was expected to be brief and bloody. The last thing she needed was a Catholic and foreign husband, so she told him to stay where he was. She was, however, inclined to make him – or if necessary, Adam Czartoryski – king of Poland. He tried to persuade her that if he became king, he would need not only annual subsidies, but also direct command over part of the army and an undiminished royal prerogative.

Poniatowski probably did not send Catherine his more ambitious plans for reform, which he expressed in a literary 'Anecdote historique'. At their heart was the harmonious partnership of a revitalized legislature with a strengthened executive headed by the king. He would cherish this vision throughout his reign, and strive to realize it as circumstances permitted.[6] Stanisław was strongly influenced by the ideas of Charles-Louis, Baron de Secondat et de Montesquieu, whom he had briefly met during his stay in France in 1753–54. Poniatowski had next visited England, whose constitution had served Montesquieu as the idealized model for the famous sixth chapter of Book XI of his *Spirit of the Laws* (1748). Here Montesquieu reclassified the functions of government as powers – legislative, executive and judicial. If two out of the three were in the same hands, the liberty of each and every individual was endangered, while 'all would be lost if the same man or the same body of principal men, either of nobles, or of the people, exercised these three powers'.[7] Writing in the context of France, he saw the main threat to liberty in the aggrandizing monarchy of the Bourbons. For Montesquieu the principal hope lay in the mediating and tempering of royal power by the judiciary, which should provide impartial, proportionate and humane justice. However, his arguments just as explicitly applied to aristocratic and democratic republics as they did to monarchies. They still resonate today. Before his coronation Stanisław wrote to their mutual English friend, Charles Yorke, 'I have the noble and ardent desire to do what he [Montesquieu] wrote.'[8]

Despite Poniatowski's attempt to bargain over the details, he seemed to suit Catherine's purposes. Without a substantial fortune and following of his own, he would depend on Russia and wield the royal prerogative accordingly. However, Catherine and Stanisław misjudged each other. She, believing him to be infinitely pliable, underestimated his determination to reform the Commonwealth. His potential had been noticed not only by Williams, but also by Yorke:

> I can assure you, both of what I see, both of his judgement and his virtue, there is matter in him capable of catching light and flame. One is sorry at the same time to see a man of his quality and parts, without a theatre to act upon. For Poland is a country, where the unity of the Commonwealth is distracted, or its power annihilated, by the privileges of private men.[9]

As it turned out, the Polish scene was more flammable than anyone expected, and this was one of the main reasons why Catherine's misperception would sometimes inconvenience her. Poniatowski's delusion was tragic in its consequences: Stanisław sincerely believed that he could persuade the empress to treat an enlightened Commonwealth as a junior partner for an enlightened Russian Empire. Convinced that a Russo-Polish alliance – however asymmetrical – would benefit both states, he sought to win her over to his ideas even before his election. Poniatowski's arguments had both logic and merit but – alas – were never treated seriously by Catherine. She wanted Poland to remain in a state of tranquil subjection. Stanisław August would learn that lesson the hard way.[10]

The tsaritsa needed an early success abroad to shore up her rule. The Polish election was the ideal opportunity to show who ruled the roost in east-central Europe. Success in the Commonwealth would enable Russia to pursue an untrammelled foreign policy further west. It would help Catherine's chief adviser in foreign policy, Nikita Panin, to knit together his 'northern system', a web of alliances directed against the Catholic Bourbons and Habsburgs of the 'south'. Russia would take the lead, while Prussia, chastened by its near-death experience in the Seven Years' War, would be more of a client than an ally. Denmark would play a subsidiary part, while looser co-operation was envisaged with Great Britain. The two countries weakened by 'liberty' – Sweden and Poland – would be managed by St Petersburg. Russia would not share its hegemony in the Commonwealth, which would be permitted no independent foreign relations of its own. As Panin put it, 'the fewer international links Poland has, the easier for Russia to pursue its interests there, both by the way of friendship, and by the use of its forces'.[11] In geopolitical terms, this made the Commonwealth into the forward perimeter of the Russian Empire.

The proximity of this perimeter worried Frederick II. For all his appetite for Polish territory, his priority was to prevent Russia from reverting to the Austrian alliance that had brought his kingdom to the brink of collapse. When negotiating with St Petersburg he played a weak hand skilfully, even staging a flirtation with Ottoman envoys, but he had no illusions: Catherine would control the Commonwealth. In the unequal alliance treaty, signed on 11 April 1764, he not only agreed to support the empress's candidate for the Polish throne, but also to help restore Russian hegemony in Sweden and to aid Russia in the case of war with the Turks. The immediate consequence of the Russo-Prussian rapprochement was to deter Austria, France and the Ottoman Empire from significant opposition to Russia's military intervention in Poland.[12]

This weakness of international opposition to Russia proved crucial. Although the *Familia* and its allies had the better of most of the sejmiks held in February 1764, these assemblies revealed deep divisions among the szlachta. In a hypothetically 'free' election (that is, one decided by a civil war without foreign involvement) the militias of the pro-Saxon magnates, combined with most of the Crown army under Hetman Branicki, would have outnumbered the forces raised by the *Familia*. So

'John IV' would most likely have been elected. The *Familia*'s first success was to persuade the elderly primate Władysław Łubieński to delay the convocation and election for several months. Had a Potocki been archbishop of Gniezno, as in 1733, an early election might have allowed the 'republicans' to steal a march. On 23 December 1763 Ambassador Keyserlingk met the leaders of the *Familia*. All the arguments, not least the prospect of civil war, pointed to requesting Russian aid. Stanisław Poniatowski was the last to agree. It is difficult to judge whether he raised doubts merely for appearances' sake, but he carefully recorded them in his memoirs. A Russian corps duly entered the Grand Duchy of Lithuania.[13]

When the convocation sejm opened on 7 May 1764, the legality of its confederation was challenged. The pro-Saxon party also denounced the presence of foreign troops in the Commonwealth. The *Familia* argued that Russian forces were merely protecting the sejm from the opposition's violence and that the convocation was confederated by its very nature. After failing to rupture the sejm, the opposition leaders walked out. A Russian corps despatched the Radziwiłł troops and after further skirmishes Branicki realized the game was up. He and his leading supporters began to prepare for the expected 'pacification' – the targeted distribution of patronage to both sides – after the election of his opponent. At Russian insistence, Branicki and Karol Radziwiłł went abroad. This left the declared clients and supporters of the *Familia*, as well as a number of undecided envoys and senators. While the Czartoryskis could usually count on a majority, they could not offend the convictions of their supporters about Polish liberty. They were also constrained by the empress's refusal to countenance fundamental constitutional reforms. Andrzej Zamoyski had to cut some of the most radical passages from the eloquent speech he made on 7 May. He retained the reassuring rhetorical question: 'Of what does the republic consist, if not of us ourselves?' Nevertheless, the *Familia* was still able to achieve the most significant changes in living memory.[14]

For more than a generation the *liberum veto* had enabled the treasurers to avoid being held to account. The malpractice of the current Crown treasurer, Teodor Wessel, had been so scandalous that many envoys pressed for his exemplary punishment. The *Familia* cut a deal with the Russian ambassador. The treasurers' abuses would be curtailed by establishing elected, collegiate bodies – the Crown and Lithuanian Treasury Commissions. Although the treasurers could preside over these commissions, they could be outvoted. This new system promised to improve the transaction of routine business, but the greatest benefits would be nullified if the commissions' proposals were subject to the *liberum veto*.

In return for the sparing of Wessel, who would keep his ill-gotten gains, Keyserlingk affected not to notice that proposals from the Treasury Commissions would henceforth be transacted '*forma iudicaria*' – in the judicial manner. As the courts could (if necessary) reach their verdicts by a vote among the judges, this meant that the *veto* could be bypassed. For the moment its scope remained deliberately undefined.

A similar Military Commission was created to hamstring the Crown grand hetman. The confederacy had in any case appointed August Czartoryski to temporary command of the Crown army. He lost no time in assuming the hetman's authority and instructing the commanders of all regiments and squadrons to send him an officer with a tabular report. One unit after another accepted his orders.[15] For the moment, the need to keep Lithuanian Grand Hetman Massalski onside postponed the establishment of a military commission for the Grand Duchy. Tensions emerged over the question of raising the bishopric of Wilno – held by the hetman's son Ignacy – to an archbishopric. This project was put off indefinitely as the *Familia* withheld its support. Among other important reforms were long-planned (and long-blocked) improvements to the procedures and structures of the tribunals, land courts and castle courts, the ending (at least in theory) of the mandatory character of sejmik instructions, a law envisaging the establishment of a commission of 'good order' (*boni ordinis*) to supervise and improve the governance of Warsaw, the first survey of the Crown estates in a century, and a general customs duty in place of the myriad private customs that impeded trade. The fiscal measures promised substantially to increase the income of the state.

Catherine II's first concern was to document the 'legality' of her intervention by pressing the Czartoryskis and their allies to request her assistance and then to thank her for protecting Polish freedoms. The Russian Embassy distributed tens of thousands of ducats to the leading members of the *Familia*, including Stanisław Poniatowski, partly so that they could buy support for his election among the szlachta, but also to make them personally beholden to the Russian court.[16] August Czartoryski's ambitions to become king himself yielded to Catherine's preference for Poniatowski, officially conveyed by Keyserlingk to the primate on 7 August. Keyserlingk's audience before the election sejm was arranged for 4 September (the day after the papal nuncio and the day before the Prussian envoy). The ambassador was terminally ill, so his speech was delivered by the embassy's secretary. In florid Latin it evoked the 'dreadful domestic discords, the pestilence of civil wars, the ruin of the Fatherland', which had been the consequence of the 'ambitions of foreign lords excessively desirous of the Polish crown', and recommended the election of Stanisław Poniatowski, 'born of a heroic Polish father and a Jagiellonian mother'.[17]

On 6 and 7 September 1764, 5,584 electors and still more onlookers of both sexes gathered on the field of Wola (Plate 4). The number of electors who had come from the Commonwealth's palatinates, lands and districts varied, roughly correlating to their respective noble populations divided by the distance to Warsaw. So, for example, the act of election was signed by nineteen citizens of the faraway Mozyrz district, whereas 367 electors came from the nearby palatinate of Płock. However, the Mazovians were less preponderant than might have been expected, reflecting the low turnout.[18] When the primate asked the delegates of each palatinate in turn whom they desired as their king, they declared their wish for Stanisław Poniatowski. Then he led the *Te Deum laudamus*, that sonorous hymn of praise composed by St Ambrose in the fourth century. Amidst ceremonies proclaiming the unity between throne, altar and noble nation, Poniatowski was proclaimed King of Poland and Grand Duke of Lithuania, Ruthenia, Prussia, Mazovia, Samogitia, Kiev, Volhynia, Podolia, Podlasie, Livonia, Smolensk, Severia and Czernihów. On the election field all was peaceful, but on the very same day Prussian cavalry units crossed the border into Greater Poland and abducted over a thousand people. Berlin later claimed that they were seizing deserters.[19]

The new king took the regnal names Stanisław August. The choice was symbolic in more than one respect. He signalled his wish for reconciliation by joining of the names of his rival predecessors, Augustus II and III Wettin and Stanisław I Leszczyński. (The latter, still sprightly at the age of eighty-five, had considered a third attempt to win the throne, but in the end was pleased to receive a respectful letter from his namesake.)[20] The names also evoked the glorious past under Sigismund Augustus – from whose Jagiellonian dynasty Poniatowski tenuously claimed descent via his mother. Above all, the new king looked back to Augustus, who had brought peace and prosperity to the Roman world. But to do so, he had turned the stormy republic into a tranquil empire – a monarchy in all but name.

On 13 September 1764, in the capacious Church of the Holy Cross in Warsaw, the new king swore to uphold his *pacta conventa*. As usual, these contained not only the Henrician articles of 1573, which enshrined the Commonwealth's fundamental limitations on royal power, but also a series of personal obligations and permissions. These included the traditional promise to recover the lands torn away from the 'dominions of the Commonwealth', albeit 'according to time and circumstances'. Having abandoned his hopes of marrying Catherine II, Stanisław August was content to promise to marry only a Catholic, with a non-binding preference for 'the distinction of Polish blood'.[21] In a passionate speech he invoked Divine sanction for his desire to renew Poland:

> Great God! You who willed me in the post in which I now find myself, You do nothing in vain. You gave me this crown with the ardent desire of restoring the Fatherland. Accomplish Your design, and pour into the hearts of the whole nation that love of the public good with which mine overflows![22]

This would be a recurrent theme, not only of his public oratory, but also of his personal correspondence throughout his reign.

Stanisław August's personal means were modest. The annual revenues from his inherited landed estates have been estimated at 63,000 złotys.[23] He could theoretically have exchanged this sum for 1,750 pounds – less than the income of Jane Austen's Mr Bennet. In its own context, this was equivalent to the means of a fairly wealthy noble, a plurally beneficed prelate, or one of the poorer bishops, but definitely not a magnate. Yet he felt the need to show monarchical generosity to the Polish servants and retainers of the previous king. Anticipating future revenues, and thus contracting debts that would accumulate for the rest of his reign, he set about forming his court and acquiring more property of his own. Because Augustus III had resided in the Saxon Palace, which was the property of the Wettins, the Royal Castle was bare. Stanisław August began to refurbish the interiors and make ambitious plans for rebuilding.

In still worse condition was the Royal Castle on Wawel Hill in Cracow, so it was decided to hold the coronation in Warsaw. There was an inauspicious precedent: Stanisław Leszczyński had been crowned in the collegiate Church of St John the Baptist in 1705 – as Charles XII of Sweden's puppet-king. In tribute to the new monarch's imperial patroness, the date was set for 25 November 1764 – the feast of St Catherine of Alexandria. If that gesture was prudent, Stanisław August's decision, citing the pliant advice of his doctors, not to cut his tresses for his coronation, and to wear a stylized 'Spanish' costume with a ruff, gave needless offence to traditionalists (Plate 9). Worse was his continued rejection of Polish national dress in favour of his usual French-style attire in the following days. Even Augustus III had partly shaved his head, and donned a *kontusz* and *żupan* for three days during the icy January of 1734, before regrowing his shorn hair under a periwig. He later commissioned Louis de Silvestre to paint several coronation portraits displaying the Wettin dynast in full Sarmatian finery (Plate 8). These inspired the Meissen porcelain figures of King Augustus, which soon became collectors' items.

Despite the grumbling, the new monarch's youth, goodwill and mellifluence pleased those nobles not overcome by jealousy. Some hoped for an era of prosperity. Before Stanisław August became the object of vicious slanders, he could reasonably expect to win substantial support. He maintained an exemplary standard of public piety. On the vigil of his coronation he made his confession and said the traditional expiatory prayers to his patron, St Stanisław, in the Church of the Holy Cross – in place of the customary pilgrimage to the site of the saint's martyrdom just outside Cracow. The new king also sought reconciliation with the current Bishop of Cracow, Kajetan Sołtyk, who played a leading part in his coronation, as well as with other enemies of the *Familia*. He acceded to the Potockis' request to restore Aloysius Brühl, son of the late Saxon first minister, to his dignities. The younger Brühl regained his status as a naturalized Polish nobleman (his *ius indigenatus*) and was nominated general of the Crown artillery. He would serve the Commonwealth with distinction in the post – although panegyrics should not be taken at face value. Brühl was only the most visible of the Saxons who remained in the Commonwealth and entered the service of the new monarch.

Such actions were in themselves reasonable steps for the new king to take, but the Princes Czartoryski had other intentions. They claimed the spoils of victory for themselves and their clients. Having endured lean times during the last decade of Saxon rule, they did not want their nephew to give away the fruits of royal patronage to their rivals. Their hard-nosed determination ran counter not only to Stanisław August's inclination to munificence, but also to the tradition of a pacification sejm at which royal largesse reconciled the divided parties – for a while. The coronation ended the state of emergency which justified the general confederacy, but the Czartoryskis decided to maintain it indefinitely. Through its organs they could bypass many usual procedures and govern the country – sometimes for the common good, but often for their own. Whatever Stanisław August's conciliatory intentions, his uncles' uncompromising stance pushed the disappointed magnates back into opposition. The differences between the king and his uncles were effaced. The 'malcontent' families were joined by the Massalskis after the coronation sejm had completed the work of the convocation by establishing the Military Commission of the Grand Duchy of Lithuania.

Stanisław August carefully recorded in his memoirs the advice he received on the eve of his election from August Czartoryski – not to trust magnates, but to recruit supporters among the ordinary szlachta.[24] Nevertheless, the brothers Czartoryski looked askance at the monarch's efforts, encouraged by his brothers, to win over middling and wealthier nobles. According to the papal nuncio:

> The princes Czartoryski, who have long played a great part in the country's affairs, wish to maintain their credit, to act despotically, and keep the king and the Poniatowski family in need of recourse to their assistance. The king, under the pretext that his uncles are now much advanced in age, joins with the prince his brother, saying he needs to form a party entirely his own, not being sure that after his uncles' death, their friends will still be his supporters.[25]

This was the case, for example in Royal Prussia, where many 'Prussian patriots' nursed grudges against the *Familia*. Thanks to the king's conciliatory approach, in November 1764 the Prussian *Landtag* accepted his election and much of the convocation sejm's legislation. It also elected thirty-seven envoys to the coronation sejm and provided them with an instruction of thirty-six clauses. Many grievances had accumulated, for the *Landtag* had last reached a successful conclusion in 1735.[26]

The Czartoryskis also resented the king's inclusion of his brothers (adorned with a princely title by the coronation sejm) in the 'conference of the king and his ministers'. This informal body, effectively a privy council, complemented the senate council which functioned as a genuine advisory body. Another member of the 'conference' was the first head of the king's own Cabinet (or chancellery). This was Jacek Ogrodzki, an old family friend, who had represented the *Familia*'s interests in Dresden and thus provided continuity with the previous reign. A further member was Andrzej Zamoyski, the new grand chancellor of the Crown, with whom the king drafted legislation. Nonetheless, the weightiest opinions were those of Michał and August Czartoryski. They were supported by August's son-in-law Stanisław Lubomirski, who had been passed over in favour of Kazimierz Poniatowski for the rich *starostwo* of Spisz (nine small towns on the other side of the Carpathians, mortgaged to the kings of Poland by the kings of Hungary since

1412). Lubomirski was jealous of his wife's crowned cousin and confidant. In his memoirs he cast Stanisław August as lacking in respect for tradition, the laws and regal dignity, with a disturbing combination of democratic and despotic leanings. Nevertheless, the king raised Lubomirski to the grand marshalcy of the Crown when the office fell vacant in 1766.

Psychologically, there were bound to be tensions between the ageing uncles, who had achieved power after decades of political struggle, and their impatient nephew. The king, instead of meekly accepting their sage lessons in statecraft, had the temerity to pursue ideas of his own. Nevertheless, given the Czartoryskis' experience, wealth and above all, clients, he usually heeded their views. For example, he bowed to their pressure for the new Mint Commission, established to repair the damage done to the currency by Frederick II, to set a higher rate of exchange for the Polish złoty. The king had planned to set the silver content at the same level as that in the Hohenzollern lands. The resolution of the matter was further obstructed by Frederick's delaying tactics and complicated by the minting rights of the Royal Prussian cities. Stanisław August was proved right, but the error was only partly rectified after two decades, during which high-silver Polish coins continued to drain away.

More positively, Stanisław August and his uncles shared a broad vision of a Commonwealth repaired, reformed and renewed. Not the least benefit of their rule via the general confederacy was the easing of the logjam in the castle and land courts. The reforms of the convocation and coronation sejms regulated the number, election, qualifications, competencies, duties and remuneration of judges, as well as the appointment, competencies and duties of clerks, limiting the monarch's rights to nominate court officials. The duration of sessions was also fixed, while chanceries would be open all year round. Improvements were also ordained in the keeping of records, which grew steadily in volume. Towns which profited from the trade brought by court sessions were expected to provide and maintain suitable premises for archives. The tribunals ceased to be trials of strength between competing magnate factions. Ordinary nobles gained a chance of winning suits against magnates (as long as the latter did not belong to the *Familia*). Land courts were no longer suspended for years because of the election sejmiks' inability to elect key officials. While reaching a quorum continued to be problematic, and questions of procedure still caused doubts and disputes, on the whole justice became swifter, cheaper and probably fairer.

Other early initiatives included the implementation of the new survey of the Crown estates agreed at the convocation. This led to significant increases in the *kwarta* paid by starostas. There was also a demarcation and shake-up of the management of royal domain estates. A survey and reform of the Jewish poll tax also yielded more revenue (as well as demographic statistics). The results of the General Customs were especially impressive, despite the opposition of the Royal Prussian cities. In sum, the combined budget of the Commonwealth increased from about 8.4 million złotys annually to about 13 million.[27]

In order to lay the foundations of a military revival, the king prioritized the re-equipping and training of the regiments of the royal guard, established a cannon foundry and founded the Knights' School. Many monarchs had promised such a cadet corps; Stanisław August delivered it. The school was located in a palatial building purchased by the king, who continued to provide subsidies. Adam Czartoryski took his role as commandant seriously – his *Moral Catechism for the Students of the Cadet Corps* (1774) became a classic. Under the Englishman John Lind, director between 1767 and 1771, the school became a model of enlightened pedagogy, inspired by the child-centred thought of Locke and Rousseau. The curriculum featured natural sciences, modern languages, Polish law and history.

Within a few months of the coronation, the new essay-periodical *Monitor*, loosely based on the English *Spectator*, had begun to campaign for 'enlightenment', 'tolerance' and 'polish', employing a withering discourse against 'ignorance', 'superstition', 'fanaticism' and 'coarseness'. One aim was to convince the szlachta of the economic benefits of urban and rural immigration, and persuade them to welcome non-Catholic newcomers. The principal contributors were the king's chaplain Ignacy Krasicki (given the amply endowed prince-bishopric of Warmia in 1766), the Jesuit Franciszek Bohomolec and writers from the erudite circles of Saxon Warsaw. Stanisław August himself penned several essays. These almost certainly included the reflections of 'Theatralski', which cast mild doubt on the need to follow the unities of time and place, while recognizing the power of untamed genius – such as Shakespeare's. This essay was part of a lively discussion over the National Theatre, also founded in 1765. For the first time the nascent theatrical 'public', coming from diverse social backgrounds, enjoyed a venue. Hitherto theatre had been *either* an aristocratic *or* a plebeian entertainment, or else it comprehended school performances. Jesuit didacticism now had a wider audience. Some of Father Bohomolec's comedies of manners ponderously lampooned 'Sarmatian' prejudices, but more of them lacerated fashionable foreign follies. The monarch's call for 'a new creation of the Polish world' did not exclude the mining of nuggets from the seams of the Polish past.

'The king has talent, knowledge and above all a most ardent desire to reform in one day, if he could, all of the country, and all of the nation, and to raise it to the level of other, more cultured nations.'[28] These words of the papal nuncio, Antonio Eugenio Visconti, have often been quoted to demonstrate the king's boundless ambitions. It is not clear, however, whether the conviction that other nations were more cultured than the Polish nation better characterized the Polish monarch or the erudite Italian aristocrat. Despite the Holy See's understandable preference for another Wettin, once the enlightened and Anglophile Poniatowski had become king, the nuncio sought his friendship. They discussed cultural and intellectual novelties, to the point of comparing the peril to revealed religion posed by Rousseau and Voltaire (according to Stanisław August, Voltaire was the less dangerous, because he testified to Divine Providence and spirituality despite himself).[29]

The king wished to enlist the more 'enlightened' religious orders for his projects. Jesuit astronomers began the work of triangulation necessary for a detailed and accurate atlas of the Commonwealth. The king's confessor remained Father Piotr Śliwicki, a Priest of the Mission, while the monarch showed his appreciation of Stanisław Konarski by having a commemorative medal struck in his honour. The words *sapere auso* (to him who dared to be wise) applied the ancient Roman poet Horace's injunction *sapere aude* (dare to be wise!) almost two decades before Immanuel Kant famously employed it in his *Answer to the Question 'What is Enlightenment?'*. Jesuit and Piarist schools flourished, and the Priests of the Mission continued to train the Commonwealth's clerical elite, as the wave of enlightened Catholicism swelled to its crest.

Visconti and his superiors were nonetheless concerned to prevent the spirit of reform from assaulting the privileges of the Church in Poland. This was a time when one Catholic power after another was chipping away at papal jurisdiction and the battle to suppress the Society of Jesus was being fought in earnest. Winning over the king could help to avoid the disadvantageous resolution of long-standing disputes between the laity and the clergy over jurisdiction, tithes, interest payments on capital sums bequeathed to the Church, mortmain, inheritances, taxes, and fees due to the Holy See. These pressures had been evident during the interregnum. Numerous sejmiks had called for the restriction of the jurisdiction of ecclesiastical courts in disputes between laymen and ecclesiastical institutions and for the elimination of appeals to Rome in such cases. There were demands for a comprehensive regulation of relations between laity and clergy, and one postulate to ban male monastic vows below the age of twenty-four.

The nuncio blamed the *Familia* for encouraging the articulation of these sentiments. Andrzej Zamoyski's speech at the convocation contained a request to the clergy to devise a means by which cases begun in the country would be settled in the country: 'after all, this is the practice in all Christian states'.[30] But the leaders of the *Familia* would not have expended political capital had the cause been unpopular. The debates included an acrimonious discussion on secular and ecclesiastical courts. The sejm agreed the reiteration of seventeenth-century laws against legacies to the Church without the sejm's permission. During the coronation sejm, the primate conceded a mixed commission of laymen and clergymen to discuss contested issues and suggest solutions. It met at the end of September 1765, only to disperse within a month.

The jeremiad discourse of successive nuncios and secretaries of state cast such criticisms as an expression of the 'modern philosophy' and 'spirit of novelty' that were afflicting the Church,[31] but nobles' arguments against the privileges, accumulated wealth and jurisdiction of the Catholic clergy can be traced back two centuries and more. They expressed the conviction that the corporate interests of the clergy were often at odds with the common good. However, the Catholic szlachta's anti-clericalism was perfectly compatible with hostility towards 'heretics' and 'schismatics'. This republican anvil of confessional zeal was repeatedly struck by an imperial hammer. The reverberations of the so-called dissident question shook eastern and central Europe.

In 1766 the royal dreamboat hit the rocks of reality. In handing victory to the *Familia*, Catherine II had departed from a principle laid down by Peter I – to keep the Commonwealth internally divided among factions. She had done this expecting that the king and his uncles would gratefully do all she desired. Much indeed was done at the three sejms of 1764. The Russian imperial title proclaimed in 1721 was recognized, the Russo-Polish peace treaty of 1686 confirmed, and a 'delimitation' commission established. The latter in effect authorized the cession to Russia of a strip of territory along the frontier without the need to trouble the sejm further. For the empress, however, these were only the first items on the bill, which she expected to be paid in full.

After deciding the royal election in Poland, the tsaritsa turned her attention to the problem of restoring Russian hegemony in Sweden. There in 1765 the Russian-oriented 'caps' turned the Francophile 'hats' out of office. Stanisław August's aspirations to an autonomous role in European diplomacy, however minor, were an irritating distraction to Catherine. He sought recognition from the southern powers – France, the Habsburg Monarchy and the Ottoman Empire – with mixed results. Worse, from the Russian point of view, was his attempt (within the letter but not the spirit of his *pacta conventa*) to explore the possibility of marriage to a Habsburg archduchess. Nothing came of the soundings taken by his brother Andrzej, a general in Austrian service.

Catherine was further angered when Stanisław August appealed to her to uphold the Commonwealth's rights in its dispute with Prussia over the general customs duty established in 1764. Frederick II, determined to prevent the fiscal strengthening of his neighbour, had a fortified customs post built at Marienwerder where his territory touched the banks of the Vistula. Ships had to pay ruinous duties, swelling the Prussian treasury. After tortuous negotiations lasting until the spring of 1766, Russian 'mediation' led to a solution: the abolition of the general customs duty and the curtailing of the Prussian attempt to control trade on the Vistula. Back to square one. Catherine lectured Stanisław August that in his weak position, legalism must bow to *force majeure*, and that she had higher priorities than standing up for Poland. This much has long been known to scholars, but Zofia Zielińska has revealed that – contrary to the impression created by imperial Russian historians and editors – the Russian stance towards the Polish fiscal reform was in its way just as hostile as the Prussian one. Only the discovery that Frederick was again flirting with the Ottoman Porte led St Petersburg to insist on the dismantling of the customs post at Marienwerder.[32]

Russia could exert pressure: a corps of 8,000 troops was stationed in Royal Prussia until the end of 1765. Its arbitrary requisitions caused even Protestant nobles to protest, both to the Russian Embassy in Warsaw and directly to St Petersburg. It finally marched to Minsk, where the Lithuanian Tribunal was in session, leaving a trail of angry nobles in its wake. The original deployment and redeployment were intended to provide military support for possible confederacies of the dissident nobility.

If the problem of the General Customs irritated the empress, the dissident question enraged her. The sejms of 1764 had defied her wishes. The existing prohibitions on non-Catholic nobles holding office were extended to *starostwa* without judicial responsibilities. The advantages to the Catholic szlachta of excluding influential Protestant competitors were obvious. Stanisław August had managed to insert into his *pacta conventa* a clause protecting existing dissident starostas from this prohibition, but the dissident leaders continued to supplicate Berlin and St Petersburg for support. Following the coronation, on 28 November 1764 Ambassador Repnin, together with the lower-ranked diplomatic representatives of Prussia, Great Britain and Denmark, presented a memorandum to the king, formally demanding the restoration of all of the dissidents' former civil and political rights. As the papal nuncio realized, this demand was for equal rights with Catholic nobles, not merely for a greater degree of toleration.[33] While the empress's prestige and authority were certainly at stake, the main purpose of this policy appears to have been to procure for Russia a dependent party in the Commonwealth. This could veto any unwelcome reform initiatives and perhaps hold the balance between magnate factions if required.

From this point onwards, although his illusions were not yet completely shattered, Stanisław August was conscious of the hostility to his far-reaching plans for the regeneration of the Fatherland on the part of 'jealous and powerful neighbours' – as he confided to an English friend.[34] Following a second set of memoranda, seconded by Russian threats, the king agreed to a number of concessions which strengthened the position of the Orthodox clergy vis-à-vis the Uniates. To these measures were added analogous provisions for Protestants. When, with the acquiescence of the primate, this package was brought before the sejm on 20 December 1764, a roar of disapproval prevented it from being read out.

This rebuff was judged by enlightened European opinion as yet another case of Catholic 'fanaticism' in Poland. This question is still emotive, so it is important to distinguish between problems of practical toleration, such as the repair of existing churches and the building of new ones, or the conditions for worship, and the problem of participation in the legislature. On the former much progress would have been possible; on the latter it was not. Neither Stanisław August nor his uncles considered it either possible or desirable. The experienced princes knew how far they might press their clients. Even Repnin came to accept that the restoration of political rights would have to be limited or postponed. However, the empress took the refusal both of the king and of the Czartoryskis to recommend the acceptance of her demands in full as proof of their ingratitude. Her intransigent refusal to compromise eludes a purely rational explanation in the context of Russian political goals. Perhaps, as Isabel de Madariaga suggested, she simply did not understand

Catholicism.[35] The tsaritsa's stance is at least partly comprehensible in terms of her image within Russia. Strange as it may sound, the insistence with which she demanded equality for Polish-Lithuanian Protestants can be partly attributed to her need to burnish her domestic credentials as a champion of Orthodoxy.

By the early 1760s the long decline of the Orthodox Church in the Commonwealth had been halted. Georgii Konisskii, the energetic Bishop of Mohylew, pressed for stronger Russian intervention on behalf of his co-believers. Given an elevated role in Catherine's coronation ceremony in Moscow in 1762, he had delivered a speech comparing the persecution of the Orthodox in Poland to the Hebrews' Babylonian captivity. He would not have done so without encouragement, but the note he struck reflected Catherine's need to contrast her own *persona*, demonstratively Russophone and Orthodox, with the Germanophone and Lutheran sympathies of her late husband. The need was all the greater, because in the end she decided to implement Peter III's policy of sequestering Church lands and closing monasteries.

After the setbacks of 1764, Konisskii tried to regain momentum. At the end of July 1765 he arrived in Warsaw and shortly afterwards delivered a memorial to the king. It demanded an end to the harassment of the Orthodox clergy and population by the Catholic Church of both rites, the exemption of Orthodox clergy from taxation, and their subjection only to the jurisdiction of their own hierarchy. The Uniate episcopate demanded proofs of the alleged maltreatment. This produced some backtracking from Konisskii, whom Repnin regarded as a nuisance. The Uniate bishops were denied the opportunity to work out a coherent response to the Orthodox challenge by the nuncio's refusal to accept the king's demand to have representatives at the planned Uniate synod. This synod was postponed indefinitely. Stanisław August was probably concerned to prevent further escalation of the dispute, for on 3 March 1766 he confirmed all the existing privileges of the Orthodox Church.

The king was being pressed hard by Repnin, who in turn was under pressure from the empress over the restoration of political rights to dissident nobles. Stanisław August pleaded that Russia should not demand changes which the 'Polish nation' was not prepared to countenance. At the same time he argued that fiscal and military reforms would make Poland a useful ally to Russia. To obtain the security that an alliance would bring the Commonwealth, he was prepared to make far-reaching concessions on religion, albeit ones that fell short of political equality. But St Petersburg was no longer interested in an alliance.

Matters came to a head at the sejm of 1766. The leading dissidents hoped for a favourable resolution of their case, but if not, they were prepared to form confederacies under Russian military protection. The empress's demands, dated 4 September, for almost complete political equality, as well as the decision of long-standing disputes in favour of the Orthodox and Protestants, reached Warsaw on 15 September. It was communicated officially to the king a week later. Repnin received orders to threaten the Poles with the consequences of the empress's anger. Troops could be quartered in the estates of recalcitrant hierarchs. The ambassador mustered the leading dissidents behind the Russian demands, which Prussia, Denmark and Great Britain again agreed to support.

On the other side of the confessional divide, Bishop Sołtyk wrote to Europe's Catholic princes about the threat to the Faith in Poland. He despatched doom-laden letters to the sejmiks and ordained prayers in his diocese – that the dissidents might be righteously confounded. Many secular and religious clergy joined in the agitation. According to the Prussian envoy, Gédéon Benoît:

> The priests are extremely animated. They say that there is no more religion in Warsaw, that the king would be more dissident than Catholic, and that he would only serve in the name of the neighbouring powers as a mantle to cover his own ambition to relieve the dissidents under the pretext that he would be doing some good for the country. They assure all the old ladies that their husbands would certainly be damned, which is already to be feared in the case of the grand chancellor, Prince Czartoryski.[36]

Other diplomats and observers also noted the mobilization of *grandes dames*.

Only a few sejmiks, influenced by the king's closest associates, agreed to mildly pro-dissident instructions. Several expressly forbade any further concessions, even regarding worship. Most remained silent. Stanisław August's efforts to persuade the bishops to moderate their stance yielded minimal results. At some sejmiks the Czartoryskis, besides working for the election of their clients without reference to the king, encouraged an anti-dissident tone in the hope that this demonstration of the nation's sentiments would dissuade Russia from forcing the question at the sejm. Most of the envoys were linked more or less closely with the *Familia*, and a smaller number with the king directly. However, several opposition candidates were elected by some of the most prestigious sejmiks in the Crown, including those of Cracow, the conjoined Greater Polish sejmik, and the Royal Prussian *Landtag*. Provincial rights and privileges, fiscal questions and divisions among the Czartoryskis' supporters all weighed heavily at the latter assembly.

Leading patricians of Danzig and Thorn drew up a project to extend Royal Prussian autonomy. They opposed any diminution of their privileges and insisted that only the *Landtag* could agree to new taxes. In vain did Stanisław August appeal to the two cities' delegates to feel their 'Polish heart' and put aside their particular interests. At issue were the conditions of union between Royal Prussia and the Kingdom of Poland. So were two visions of the state – on the one hand, tenaciously defended provincial and urban liberties (albeit recast in a contemporary republican idiom); on the other, the enlightened reform of a unitary and sovereign Commonwealth.[37] In this context the king made a revealing comparison with the demands of the North American colonists:

> The worst of all would be if the will of the parliament of England would need the sanction of the American parliament to be implemented in America. By degrees the latter would become the sovereign of the [parliament] in Europe. This would be the same abuse which one sees in Poland where the sejmik of Prussia wants to arrogate the right to confirm or reject that which the sejm of the Kingdom of Poland has determined.[38]

Last but not least, the Royal Prussian urban elites defended their participation in the upper house of the *Landtag* – which might be threatened by the laws excluding non-Catholics from the legislature.

Most important of all was the dissident question. Repnin, like his superior Panin, was acutely aware of the insuperable obstacles to gaining the sejm's assent, but he concealed the Russian fall-back position. This would – for the time being – have reopened all *starostwa*, but not the legislature to the dissidents. Repnin kept this secret in order to increase the pressure on the king and the Czartoryskis, but thereby convinced the monarch that Russia would not be satisfied by any package with the slightest chance of being accepted by the sejm. On 5 October 1766, under pressure from his uncles to stiffen his stance, Stanisław August made a last attempt to convince Catherine to be satisfied with extended religious toleration and to refrain from using military force. The argument he employed was essentially a republican variant on the biblical theme that a house divided against itself could not stand:

> The nature of a free state such as ours is incompatible with even the most limited admission to the legislature of those who do not profess the dominant religion. The more national liberties there are in the constitution of a government, the more necessary are conformity of action and strict and respectful submission to the laws on the part of the citizens admitted to the movement of the machine. Otherwise, an avowed diversity of opinions on a matter as politically essential as religion can only produce frequent fragmentations, which are the most dangerous wherever a sufficiently prompt corrective to transgressions is not provided by a supreme absolute authority entirely concentrated in the person of the sovereign.

To buttress his case, Stanisław August cited foreign examples. No one suspected the Dutch Republic or England of being ruled by prejudice, but neither state permitted non-conformists to participate in lawmaking. Only the Thirty Years' War had led to both non-Catholic and Catholic judges sitting in the Imperial Aulic Council, and besides, he argued, the German Reich was a collection of warring and independent sovereigns, not a republic.[39]

Within a quarter-century, Stanisław August and most of his Catholic noble fellow citizens would willingly accept non-Catholic co-legislators in a sovereign Commonwealth. For the moment, his unexceptional reasoning (by the standards of the time) stood no hope of success. The slim chance of negotiating a compromise solution, based on re-admitting dissidents to judicial office, but not (yet) to the sejm, was lost. Catherine was infuriated with Stanisław August for what she took to be a '*negative absolue*'. She answered in an uncompromising and intimidating tone – although she could not resist the challenge of refuting his appeal to foreign examples.[40] Preparations began in St Petersburg to set up pro-Russian confederacies, backed up by military force. The die was cast – calamitously – even before the sejm opened on 6 October.

Stanisław August, still trying to defuse the situation, sought to postpone discussion of the dissident question until he had received an answer from the empress. However, on 11 October Kajetan Sołtyk overcame procedural obstacles and made an impassioned speech. The Bishop of Cracow condemned those who supported further concessions which would threaten the Catholic faith. Five days later his successor as Bishop of Kiev, Józef Andrzej Załuski, denounced 'the bat out of hell, the spirit of darkness' behind the Russian demands.[41] Thus fortified, the sejm received the notes presented both by the dissidents themselves and by the diplomatic representatives of Russia, Prussia, Great Britain and Denmark. The northern powers' demands on behalf of the 'Greeks and dissidents' were justified by references to the peace treaties concluded by the Commonwealth with Muscovy and Sweden, in 1686 and 1660 respectively. These contained vague formulations about the rights of Orthodox and Protestant believers, lending themselves to expansive interpretations. Accompanying the demands was a litany of complaints about the harassment and bad faith shown to non-Catholics and their foreign protectors. The march of a Russian corps towards Warsaw amplified the declarations.[42]

On 12 November Archbishop Visconti enjoyed an audience of the king and Estates. The nuncio – travelling in the royal carriage – was escorted to the Royal Castle by two episcopal senators, six envoys and a battalion of the royal guards in a carefully choreographed parade. On entering the senate chamber, he saluted the king three times as he approached the throne, to which the monarch thrice responded. The nuncio delivered his speech in Latin from an opulent chair at the king's right hand, placed closer than that of the primate. On each occasion that he named the pope, the king or the Commonwealth, he stood up, as did the senators and envoys. They did likewise during the brief but courteous reply, delivered by Chancellor Zamoyski. The assembled parliamentarians enthusiastically received Visconti's strongly worded speech, which amplified the trenchant *breve*, dated 6 September, that Clement XIII had sent to the primate. The Holy See not only opposed any concessions to the dissidents, but even demanded a prohibition on non-Catholic worship.[43]

By the time it transpired that there was in fact a little room for negotiation, the mood in Warsaw militated against compromise. The Holy See bore much of the responsibility. The Polish bishops, even Sołtyk, were prepared to make concessions, such as the exclusion of Protestant and Orthodox clergy from the jurisdiction of Catholic ecclesiastical courts, which Rome strongly opposed. Repnin declined to follow up the emergent possibilities. Bishop Massalski presented the bishops' project for the Estates' official reply to the diplomatic *démarche*. This, according to Visconti, 'was received with raptures of applause and tenderness', and was signed 'with such an excess of joy, and with a consent so unanimous, that the hand of God was visibly apparent'. On 29 November, the last day of deliberations, this reply was formally given to the four northern powers. It reaffirmed all the anti-dissident legislation of 1717, 1733, 1736 and 1764. Catholic Poland had thrown down the gauntlet.[44]

In the meantime Stanisław August had fought and lost a battle for majority voting. The king's clarion call on 11 October for 'a new creation of the Polish world' was the agreed prompt for Zamoyski to introduce a bill that supposedly clarified the procedure for transacting treasury business '*sub iudicaria*' – under judicial matters. In reality it would have extended majority voting to such crucial matters as new taxes and the size of the army. Malcontents revealed what was afoot to Repnin and Benoît. The manoeuvre used in 1764 would not succeed again. The opposition was backed by a broad constituency of noble opinion. Moreover, Repnin threatened that Russia and Prussia would invade and devastate the Commonwealth if the project was not withdrawn. Stanisław August resisted this ultimatum for six weeks, forlornly seeking help from Vienna and even London, until his uncles capitulated. Michał and August Czartoryski knew that their own supporters – the majority of envoys – were almost as suspicious of constitutional reform as they were hostile to the claims of the dissidents. On 22 November the sejm restored the *liberum veto* in full, thereby negating some of the key reforms passed in 1764. Indeed, the legal status of the *veto* had never before been spelt out so explicitly. The *Familia*'s defeat was sealed when the general confederacy, through which it had governed the Commonwealth since the convocation sejm, was wound up together with the sejm.

Hell hath no fury like an empress scorned. Catherine II was enraged by the further refusal of her demands on behalf of the dissidents. At her imperial command, Repnin organized dissident confederacies for the Crown and Grand Duchy of Lithuania. A few impoverished Orthodox nobles were rounded up for the Lithuanian confederacy, but like its Crown counterpart, it was led by Protestants. The dissident nobles demanded the full restoration of their rights, although some did so with foreboding. More assertive were the Lutheran elites of the Royal Prussian cities. Gottfried Lengnich, their legal and historical expert, produced a maximalist draft of a treaty between Russia and the Commonwealth, which would have secured all their desiderata. These arguably went beyond political equality for the non-Catholic nobility, by including minimum quotas for Protestant (or – theoretically – Orthodox) envoys, senators and ministers.

The latter demands went further than even Repnin was prepared to countenance. For the ambassador also sponsored confederacies for Catholic malcontents among the nobility. The Crown Confederacy of Radom and the Lithuanian Confederacy of Wilno later united themselves into a General Confederacy with a seat in Warsaw. They attracted the support of many magnates – the most important being Karol Radziwiłł who had negotiated his return from exile – as well as tens of thousands of ordinary nobles. These diverse confederates were united both by their detestation of the new monarch and his uncles and their fear of novelty. Poems circulated in manuscript and orally which depicted the king as both depraved and despotic, and played on the diabolical connotations of his uncles' name – *Czart* being a name for the Devil. Together they would, it was feared, incite peasants to slaughter the Catholic szlachta. In its place they would install docile and heretical burghers. Repnin encouraged the widespread belief among the confederates that the king would be deposed and his reforms nullified – mainly to exert further pressure on Stanisław August and the Czartoryskis to co-operate with him. The latter could still count on most of their clients. Some of the bishops bolstered the resistance of the sejmiks to any concessions to the dissidents, and added anti-dissident riders to their own accessions to the confederacy. It was only shortly before the extraordinary sejm met in Warsaw on 5 October 1767 that the ambassador shattered the confederates' illusions. The empress expected them to concede to her demands concerning the dissidents, but would not allow them to dethrone Poniatowski. An interregnum in Poland could have unpredictable and unwelcome consequences for Russia.

The Catholic confederates might have done well to draw conclusions from Repnin's choice of the next primate, following the death of Władysław Łubieński. Gabriel Podoski, the cathedral provost of Cracow, lived openly with his Lutheran mistress; he was so disdainful of his vocation and duties that he was rumoured to be an atheist. Stanisław August protested, but was warned by the ambassador that the consequences of opposition would be '*très-sérieux, je le repète*'. The king yielded. Having accepted the lesser evil, he sought to maximize his resulting credit with the empress. Podoski's diocesan bishop, Sołtyk, supplied a glowing character reference to overcome the pope's reluctance to confirm the elevation. Sołtyk also consecrated Podoski. Clement XIII's misgivings proved justified when Podoski drew up plans for what would effectively have been a national Church. Its governing synod, presided over by himself, would have been able to reorder benefices, dioceses, chapters, convents and monasteries without reference to Rome. Papal authority would have been reduced to the confirmation of candidates for sainthood. These decades saw the prerogatives of the Holy See assailed by Catholic monarchs and national episcopates alike, but Podoski's project was one of the most far-reaching. On this occasion it would serve to coerce the papacy into dropping its threat to excommunicate those who bowed to Russian demands, but the nightmare of a national synod would recur for successive nuncios in Warsaw.[45]

The sejm opened under the auspices of the united confederacy, with Karol Radziwiłł as its marshal. For all his alcohol-fuelled bravura, he had become a wretched, lachrymose puppet of the ambassador. With Russian soldiers quartered in and around Warsaw, Repnin demanded that a delegation formed of the most reliable envoys and senators should transact the sejm's entire business. The full sejm would reassemble to approve – not to amend, let alone reject – everything that the delegation had decided. The ambassador soon lost patience with those who stubbornly held out against the claims of the dissidents. He had the bishops of Cracow and Kiev, together with Crown Field Hetman Wacław Rzewuski and his son Seweryn, arrested during the night of 13–14 October 1767. Soon afterwards they were despatched under armed escort into the Russian Empire. They would remain captives at Kaluga for over five years. The violence worked – in the short term. On 19 October the cowed sejm agreed to form a delegation of seventy envoys and senators, chaired by Podoski. The sejm reconvened in plenary session on 27 February 1768, when Radziwiłł announced that no discussion would be permitted of the legislation agreed by the delegation. One of the envoys from Royal Prussia, the twenty-one-year-old Józef Wybicki, managed nonetheless to denounce the proceedings as a violation of Poland's liberty and sovereignty. In the uproar he slipped away and reached the mountain refuge of Spisz, where he deposited a formal protest with a local priest. The sejm concluded its business on 5 March.

The legislation of 'Repnin's sejm' was, in its essentials, dictated according to the tsaritsa's wishes by her ambassador. Whenever stirrings of resistance appeared among the delegation, threats quelled them. Under duress, something close to political and civil equality was restored between Catholics and non-Catholics (dependent, of course, on their social estate). The provisions relating to the cities and towns of Royal Prussia were particularly detailed, but still fell short of the burghers' hopes. The Lutherans of Thorn were unhappy with the equal political rights that so pleased the Commonwealth's Protestant nobles. They had sought to restore the effective exclusion of Catholics from municipal office, as well as the annulment of the sejm court's decree that had followed the 1724 tumult. Elsewhere, it was no small matter that Protestants and Orthodox could henceforth build new churches and schools and hold synods freely, especially where – as in

Warsaw – they had not been tolerated formally. Legal disputes between persons of different confessions would be handled by a mixed court, chaired by Konisskii. He, however, was disappointed that no bishoprics were transferred from the Uniate to the Orthodox Church. Moreover, 'apostasy' from Catholicism remained a crime, albeit now punishable by banishment rather than death. This solution suited the rulers of Russia and Prussia, for they had no advantage from conversions in Poland-Lithuania. On the contrary, they wanted new settlers in their own lands. Panin feared that a growing Orthodox population might induce more serfs to flee from the Russian Empire to the Commonwealth, while an increased number of Protestants might 'enlighten' the Poles and make them more formidable.

The repair of the Commonwealth begun in 1764 had certainly been halted, but had it been put into reverse?[46] For starters, a signal retreat from the high-water mark had already occurred at the sejm of 1766. While Russian diplomats usually sounded more open to the idea of a more orderly neighbour than their Prussian counterparts, in essence, Catherine was just as hostile as Frederick to the prospect of a revitalized Poland. Her idea of 'a fixed constitution, invariable and advantageous to all orders' entailed the equal and utter dependence of the king and his 'republican' opponents on Russian favour.[47]

Nonetheless, Russia permitted the Military and Treasury Commissions established in 1764 to remain in place. Sejmiks would be able to decide by majority vote when necessary. A threefold classification of legislation was introduced. First, cardinal laws defined such immutable republican foundations as free royal election, the *liberum veto*, *neminem captivabimus nisi iure victum*, and the nation's right to refuse obedience (all of which had recently been trampled on by Russia). Second came *materiæ status* – matters of state, including taxation, the army establishment, trade and money – the decision of which by the sejm required unanimity. Third were remaining 'economic matters' which were to be transacted before *materiæ status* and could be decided by a majority vote. The use of the *liberum veto* concerning *materiæ status* would not negate laws that had already been agreed, so its worst consequences would be avoided. Commissions 'of good order' similar to that already established for Warsaw were now authorized for other royal towns. These commissions would extend noble supervision of urban affairs, but chinks even appeared in the carapace of szlachta privileges. No longer would nobles be able to sentence their own serfs to death, while the murder of a peasant by a nobleman became a capital offence – in theory. Russia – but not Prussia – formally guaranteed both the treaties concerning the dissidents and the cardinal laws.

'A NEW CREATION OF THE POLISH WORLD'

The idea of 'a new creation of the Polish world' now looked like the grimmest of jokes. The reformist optimism of the first two years of Stanisław August's reign had evaporated. Russian interference in Polish affairs had culminated in the abduction of senators and the forcible imposition of a formal 'guarantee'. The Commonwealth was *de iure*, as well as *de facto*, no longer a sovereign state. It looked as though things could get no worse, but they did. By the time 'Repnin's sejm' had dispersed, the south-eastern reaches were ablaze.

— FIVE —
MARTYRDOMS

On 30 January 1774 a haggard monk crossed the Russo-Polish frontier south-west of Kiev. For almost six years he had been kept under guard in a cramped, dark cell, in the same filthy habit, permitted no communication with anybody. He had not even been interrogated. His name was Marek Jandołowicz, formerly prior of the Carmelite house in Bar in Podolia. Many revered Father Marek as a miracle worker and prophet; his religious and literary cult continued well after his death in 1799.

On 29 February 1768 a confederacy had been proclaimed at Bar in defence of the faith and liberty of the Polish noble nation. It constituted itself more formally on 4 March. The charismatic Jandołowicz fired the signatories with the belief that God would help them reverse hateful novelties, teach the 'heretics' and 'schismatics' a lesson, and end Russian domination of the Commonwealth. For the last two years he had been predicting the downfall of the godless Poniatowski. The prior set the tone for the confederates' intense and emotional Catholicism, which had strong Marian and millenarian streaks. Indeed, a shared religious culture best explains the sympathy for the confederates among many Catholic burghers. Jandołowicz's hopes for a Saxon restoration were shared by the initial leaders of the confederacy. The most intelligent was Adam Krasiński, the Bishop of Kamieniec, who realized that success depended on the Ottoman Empire and the powers of the Catholic 'South'. The confederates were cheered on by the new papal nuncio, Angelo Durini. However, his experienced predecessor, Visconti, counselled a more nuanced approach from his new posting in Vienna. The Holy See, beset by the culminating phase of the attack on the Jesuits following the election of Lorenzo Ganganelli as Clement XIV, hardly knew which way to turn.[1]

The confederacy was at first thought in Warsaw to be a protest against the proposed reform of the notoriously undisciplined National Cavalry units of the Crown and Lithuanian armies. The measure was hastily abandoned. Stanisław

August summoned the senate council which did not rule out joint Polish and Russian military action, but first despatched an emissary to negotiate with the confederates. The exultant confederate leaders, in no mood for compromise, rebuffed the approach. As the rising spread, fighting erupted between the confederates and Russian forces. The latter were joined by those units of the Crown army which had not gone over to the confederates. Commanded by the Crown master of the hunt, Franciszek Ksawery Branicki (no relation of Jan Klemens), they joined in the capture of Bar. Jandołowicz was among the prisoners, and received special treatment.

The Catholic fervour of the confederates collided with the zeal of the Orthodox clergy. The consequences were horrific. Encouraged by events in Warsaw and confident of Russian support, Orthodox hierarchs stepped up pressure on Uniate parishioners and their priests to convert or revert to Orthodoxy. This provoked counter-efforts from the Uniate bishops, who turned to local confederates for help. The epicentre of the Orthodox campaign was Motrenin. The monastery was crowded with sundry rebels and runaways, many of them formerly employed by nobles in their private militias as Cossacks. The approach of a detachment of confederates lit the torch of revolt. A glittering document was swiftly produced, possibly forged by one of the monks, which purported to be an injunction from the tsaritsa to drive out the Poles in the name of the true Orthodox faith. The mutineers and *haidamaky* were rapidly joined by tens of thousands of enserfed peasants. The bloodbath that followed later inspired major works of Romantic poetry in Ukrainian and Polish.

The engorged rebel forces burnt, raped and slaughtered their way across the south-eastern reaches of the Commonwealth. Nobles, Catholic priests and Jews who did not flee in time were butchered with gratuitous cruelty. Their corpses were sometimes strung up along with dogs, according to the maxim 'a Pole, a Jew and a dog are all of one faith'.[2] The bloodiest massacre took place at Humań, whose magnificent monastery and school, endowed by Franciszek Salezy Potocki a few years earlier, constituted the Uniate Basilians' chief stronghold in the region. The school's teachers and pupils were among the thousands of inhabitants and refugees killed in the slaughter. Most Uniate clergymen sought re-ordination in the Orthodox Church, but a significant minority either fled or chose martyrdom. The rebels ritually destroyed Uniate religious artefacts adopted from Latin-rite Catholicism – such as the tabernacle used to store consecrated hosts. While this testified to the intensity of confessional emotions, the revolt, somewhat mysteriously known as the *koliivshchyna* or *koliszczyzna*, was also fed by socio-economic grievances among the peasantry. Following several decades in which lands emptied by the long cycle of wars with the Cossacks, Muscovites, Tatars and Turks had been resettled by migrant peasants on relatively easy terms, the burdens of labour services, *propinacja* and other obligations were increasing. This had also occurred before the great revolt of 1648.

In the end Russian soldiers joined the detachments of the Crown army to extinguish the conflagration. Catherine II feared that the rebellion could spread uncontrollably into her empire. Józef Stempkowski, camp commandant of the Crown, who had already shown his mettle in organizing part of the Crown army against the Barists, put down the rebellion in the south-east in the first months of 1769. The ensuing repressions were as bloody as the slaughter perpetrated by the rebels. Stempkowski acquired a fearsome reputation by passing several hundred death sentences on those convicted of rebellion. Many suspects, however, were acquitted, and others, while not found innocent, were released after swearing allegiance. If the judicial procedure was quick, death came all too slowly to those condemned. Impalement, flaying, disembowelment and quartering were all employed liberally. Others had limbs amputated. Thousands of terrified peasants fled to Moldavia, the Crimea or Russia, where they were allowed to settle. Polish noble landowners began to fear for their labour force, but most were grateful to the jovial Stempkowski for restoring order. Indeed, the *koliivshchyna* proved the last revolt in the Polish Ukraine. Stempkowski would be well rewarded for his sanguinary services with a *starostwo* and a chair in the senate.

The Barist movement spread rapidly across the Commonwealth. Suppressed in one area, it would erupt again in another. The Carpathian Mountains, backing onto the frontier with the Habsburg Monarchy, afforded the confederates conditions for partisan warfare. They scored some notable local successes, which later generations of Polish patriots have proudly commemorated. But the confederates' requisitioning bore heavily on the highlanders. The Uniate Ruthenians of the Carpathian Mountains were treated with suspicion and hostility – they were mistaken for 'Russians' by the confederates. Many perished on hilltop gallows for real or imagined insubordination, leaving a lasting grievance which would be woven into later injustices in the Lemko people's collective memory.[3] Some Protestant communities also suffered violence and pillage from confederates. Some sought refuge abroad, while others, notably the city of Thorn in 1769, resisted forced requisitions and contributions.

It proved impossible to hold many sejmiks in September 1768, and the ordinary sejm planned for November could not take place. By this time the Ottoman Empire had had enough of the Russian armed presence in the Commonwealth. After Russia refused to admit responsibility for a detachment of Cossacks which pursued some confederates into Turkish territory and plundered the fort at Balta, the Porte lost patience and demanded a complete Russian withdrawal from Poland. No such assurance was forthcoming, so on 6 October 1768 the Ottoman Empire declared war on the Russian Empire. As tradition required, the Russian ambassador was imprisoned in Istanbul's Fortress of the Seven Towers. Neither side could launch an immediate offensive, so it was well into 1769 before the fighting began in earnest. By then, much of the Grand Duchy of Lithuania was in revolt.

In June 1769 Mikhail Volkonskii replaced Repnin. The new ambassador had instructions to prevent the dethroning of Stanisław August in favour of a candidate sponsored by France. He was expected to reach an understanding with the Czartoryskis in order to overcome the confederacy politically. However, the king recalled Branicki and tried to set conditions. Stanisław August had already sought to explain to Catherine that no pacification was possible until significant concessions were made to 'the nation': these should include the scaling back of the rights granted to the dissidents and the withdrawal of the Russian 'guarantee'. She would have none of it.[4] And so it continued. The senate council called by the king in October 1769 authorized diplomatic feelers to Britain, the Dutch Republic and France, causing consternation on the banks of the Neva. There, the Czartoryskis were often blamed for hardening their nephew's stance. They kept up their resistance despite the sequestration of valuable estates. The elderly princes could at least withdraw from public life temporarily; the king could not. Stanisław August was caught between unrelenting Russian demands and the implacable hatred of the confederates. The chaos also deprived him of most of his revenues. Volkonskii tried to increase the pressure on the king by seeking to organize a pro-Russian confederacy among the leaders of the pro-Saxon opposition. They refused the bait. Panin took the view that attempting to replace Stanisław August with a more pliable man might destabilize his entire 'northern system'. In 1770 there was a Russian military surge against the confederates, but victory proved elusive. The king, after a period of appearing to be more co-operative, again moved closer to his obdurate uncles. Finally, in February 1771 Volkonskii was dismissed.

His successor, the volcanic Caspar von Saldern, arrived two months later. Saldern's mission was not a last chance for the Polish court to avoid a partition of the Commonwealth through an understanding with St Petersburg. It was for other reasons that Saldern heaped pressure on the king and his uncles to agree to the renewed use of the Crown and Lithuanian armies to pacify the Commonwealth. Finally, in May 1771 the king gave way. Branicki was placed at the head of a joint Polish-Russian corps and sent into action against the confederates, alongside the crack troops commanded by Aleksandr Suvorov. However, many of the Commonwealth's soldiers had long since been fighting on the confederate side. Szymon Kossakowski led up to four thousand confederates on a raid deep into Russian territory, providing a welcome boost to morale and embarrassing the enemy.

The General Council (Generalcy) of the confederacy, based in the Kingdom of Hungary, hoped that France would turn the tide in their favour. French military advisers arrived, but Louis XV's chronically indebted kingdom could not afford war with Russia. The confederates also sought intellectual succour abroad, in the hope that victory would enable them to secure Polish liberty in perpetuity. The Generalcy's delegate to France, Michał Wielhorski (who had moved the motion to restore the *liberum veto* at the sejm of 1766), approached two *philosophes*. He asked the Ábbé Gabriel Bonnot de Mably and the more famous Jean-Jacques Rousseau to compose constitutional projects for Poland. Mably responded to the confederates' invitation with a broadly republican plan to tidy things up. The emasculation of the monarchy would make it safe to replace the *liberum veto* with qualified majority voting.

Rousseau's advice was radically different from anything that had gone before, but reassuringly appreciative of republican liberty and national traditions. His prescriptions have been somewhat mythologized. Jerzy Michalski, the author of the best work on the *Considerations on the Government of Poland*, has persuasively argued that Rousseau's famous aside that Poland's neighbours might do her the service of reducing her territory was probably not a prediction that partition was imminent. On the contrary, writing at the turn of 1770 and 1771, Rousseau hoped for an Ottoman and confederate victory that would give the Poles a twenty-year breathing space, during which his counsel could be implemented. In the long term, however, he did believe that Poles might come under Russian rule, for one of the aims of his advice was to ensure that they could never become Russians in their hearts. Nor is there any evidence that Rousseau's conviction that education was 'the important subject' had any direct influence on the establishment or the programme of the Commission of National Education, even if in retrospect he seems to have predicted its long-term achievements.[5]

Neither of these caveats diminishes the real interest of the *Considerations*, written in scintillating prose. Poles, argued Rousseau, should not aspire to emulate the commercial and military strength of other European nations, partly because this was a contest they could only lose, but chiefly because in doing so they would cease to be Poles. It has been argued that he was not recommending a return to a primitive agrarian economy, but rather searching for a kind of balanced economic growth which would not leave the countryside behind while the towns moved ahead. He recognized that it would be impractical for the economy to do without money altogether.[6] Nevertheless, even allowing for the rhetorical exaggeration to which Rousseau was prone, his hostility to modern, moneyed, cosmopolitan, enlightened and effeminate Europeans was palpable. They were, he fulminated, corrupted by luxury, fit only for slavery. He assumed that Poles would prefer to cultivate their own identity, by preserving and, if necessary, inventing their own national traditions. That applied to politics as well. Rather than centralizing and expediting decision-making, they should decentralize power, leaving as much as possible to the sejmiks, which Rousseau lauded as the 'palladium of liberty'.[7]

Inspired by the example of the ancient Roman Republic, Rousseau proposed an elaborate ladder of public service, from teachers and judges through envoys and senators to the kingship itself. It was the antithesis of professionalism, but profoundly meritocratic. The monarch would be chosen by lot from among the senior senators, and after his death, with his sons and grandsons excluded from consideration for the throne, would be subjected to the verdict of history: either honour or oblivion. An even more dramatic decision would be taken by the nation following any use of the *liberum veto* – a grateful reward for the saviour of the Fatherland or a traitor's death. Neither the *veto* nor confederacies should be abolished – they had saved the country before and might be needed again. In general, it would be better to change too little, too slowly, than too much, too fast, for fear of losing what had made the Poles themselves.[8]

Therefore the emancipation of the serfs should come gradually – very gradually. They must first be accustomed to the challenges of liberty, a food that most stomachs found hard to digest. For Rousseau, liberty was above all a matter of quality rather than quantity. He was not excessively disturbed by the condition of the helots in the Sparta he so admired. Although he envisaged not merely personal but political liberty for the Commonwealth's peasant farmers, this truly revolutionary idea was a misty prospect indeed. So the *Considérations* would provide apologists for serfdom with excuses to delay emancipation well into the nineteenth century.

For Stanisław August (who soon acquired a manuscript copy of the work) and for many subsequent interpreters, Rousseau's vision was wondrously beautiful in its romantic impracticality. However, following the publication of the work in Rousseau's posthumous *Oeuvres* in 1782 and then in Polish translation in 1789, the *Considérations* gave a shot in the arm to the 'Sarmatian' revival. They also accelerated a crucial shift in Polish republicanism. This concerned the sovereign power of the nation to effect major changes. The national will should be active rather than passive. Rousseau's eloquence also contributed to a kind of Utopian optimism about the perfectibility of humanity, given good laws and education, which eclipsed Konarski's sober realism about human nature.[9]

By the time Rousseau's prescriptions had been delivered, the confederacy had boxed itself in diplomatically. On 13 October 1770 the Generalcy issued a proclamation from its seat in Eperjes (now Prešov in Slovakia). It stated that the interregnum begun by the death of Augustus III seven years earlier had not ended. All laws passed since then were null and void, and the man apparently elected to the throne in 1764 was a tyrant and a usurper. Hyperbole evoked the nightmare of the last seven years:

> In a word, tears, misery, poverty, desolation, killings, rape, slavery, shackles, chains, registers, knives, stakes, hooks and various kinds of instruments of cruelty, these are the proper and essential attributes of Stanisław Poniatowski, intruder and usurper of the Polish throne![10]

Stanisław August made a cogent response, albeit in an anonymously and hurriedly published pamphlet, *Suum cuique* (To Each His Due). It also circulated in manuscript. If the monarch did not write the entire text himself, he certainly provided the concepts and arguments. The Latin version was more radical than the Polish. The pamphlet explained and defended the king's efforts for reform and exposed the intrigues and hypocrisies of his opponents. It argued that the roots of the present discontents reached down to the foundations of the Commonwealth, especially free royal election.[11]

This response made no impact on the Generalcy. Having declared Stanisław August's reign void, it decided to abduct him, probably in order to put him on trial. However, the attempt backfired badly, not least because only the king's version of events is known. In short, it is as follows.[12]

On the evening of 3 November 1771 Stanisław August was returning to the Royal Castle from a visit to the nearby residence of Michał Czartoryski, when confederate riders surrounded his lightly guarded carriage. After a brief struggle, they headed out of the city with the wounded monarch. One by one, they lost either their nerve or their bearings, until the king was able to talk round the last of his captors and find refuge in the house of a miller. Help soon arrived from Warsaw. Whatever else actually happened that night, afterwards Stanisław August was able to depict the confederates to all Europe as regicides, and himself as a man of mercy. Despite the pressure from Catherine II for the severest penalties to be applied to the 'regicides', he kept his promise to spare his last captor's life. He even paid him a pension in exile for the remainder of his reign. Royal propaganda surrounding the event became a key element in the alliance of throne and altar that the monarch was keen to strengthen. The abduction also had a profound personal effect on Stanisław August. He even preserved the clothes he had been wearing that evening as quasi-relics, as if he were the Man of Sorrows. Writing to his intimates, he interpreted his survival as a sign that he was, despite all obstacles, destined to achieve great things for his country. He placed yet greater trust in Divine Providence.

It was probably about a year before Stanisław August's abduction that Catherine II decided to agree to a partition of the Commonwealth. Since the start of her reign the Chernyshev clique, whose power base was in the military, had been pressing for annexations along the Dnieper and Dvina. In the summer of 1767, Russian military engineers made a detailed survey of the north-eastern corner of the Commonwealth. By 1770, the unresolved military struggle and the unfavourable political situation in the Commonwealth had weakened the case for continuing the Petrine policy of controlling the whole of its territory. The Grand Duchy of Lithuania, which was closest to the imperial heartlands, was largely resistant to Russian blandishments. Stanisław August and the Czartoryskis had failed to co-operate fully in restoring Russian hegemony. The empress still held a grudge for their opposition to her wishes regarding the dissidents. This factor continued to operate into the spring of 1771 or even later, as the king and his uncles failed to appreciate the danger in time. The empress also took account of the pressures exerted by the courts of Vienna and Berlin. The partition nevertheless remained her decision. While she was not her own foreign minister, her personal role in the conduct of foreign policy was considerable. She was industrious, skilful and, on the whole, lucky. The manner of her accession to the throne made her particularly sensitive to her prestige and reputation.[13]

Compared to the relatively opaque decision-making in St Petersburg, the roles played by the Austrian and Prussian courts have been better documented since the later nineteenth century. However, those accounts by official historians in Vienna and Berlin require some sceptical revisiting. In 1769 Austria took the opportunity to occupy Spisz, whose mortgage had never been redeemed by the kings of Hungary. The current *rex Hungariæ*, Maria Theresa, did not offer to pay it off now. The following year, on still flimsier pretexts, Habsburg forces crossed the mountain passes to take control of three *starostwa* adjoining the border. An outbreak of pestilence in distant Podolia gave Frederick II the feeble excuse he needed to throw a cordon between his Pomeranian and East Prussian lands. The inhabitants of the cordoned-off areas had to provide quartering and contributions to the Austrian and Prussian military authorities. Two meetings between Frederick and the young Emperor Joseph II (in August 1769 and September 1770) hinted at a putative Austro-Prussian rapprochement. Spectacular Russian successes against Ottoman forces promised extensive Russian gains on the shores of the Black Sea, prompting sabre-rattling from Vienna. The combination of these factors – within and beyond the Commonwealth – probably persuaded the tsaritsa to look favourably on Prussian overtures for a partition made during 1770. The signals about a possible carve-up, given to Frederick and his brother Prince Henry in the autumn of that year, came *after* victories over the Turks had caused Russian prestige to soar. Any partition would be on Catherine's terms. The Russo-Prussian bargain left Austria no real choice but to join in.

Rumours of the partition coincided with the last throes of the Confederacy of Bar. Before dawn on 2 February 1772 a group of confederates managed to take Wawel in a daring assault. The attackers entered via a poorly closed drain, taking the Russian garrison by surprise. Led by a French colonel, Claude-Gabriel de Choisy, they then held out heroically for several weeks against Suvorov's besieging Russian forces (assisted by a Polish detachment under Branicki).

Inflicting heavy casualties, the defenders beat off an attempt to storm the walls on 29 February. Much of the local population was pressed into labour by the Russians, who also exacted provisions and summarily punished those suspected of sabotage. Many houses went up in flames. As the confederates' supplies dwindled, the absence of any prospect of relief forced them to capitulate on 26 April. The Russians failed to honour the agreed terms and about 700 Polish and French defenders of Wawel were walked off to Siberia in chains.[14]

All in all, 5,445 prisoners were officially deported to Russia during and after the Bar insurgency; the actual number may have been much higher. During the long march east, some governors and officers treated the prisoners with kindness and honour, but others were brutal thugs. Most prisoners were released in 1774, but not the unfortunates who reached Tobolsk in Siberia, governed by the sadistic Denis Chicherin. There the prisoners discovered that confederates who had fought for Leszczyński nearly forty years earlier had preceded them, and that the town had been built by Swedes taken captive at Poltava in 1709. Many of those who refused either to join the Russian army or convert to Orthodoxy were flogged to death. A similar fate awaited those who had yielded to this terror but had asked to join their fellow prisoners, finally amnestied by the empress in 1781.[15]

In the late spring and early summer of 1772, Russian and Austrian troops marched up to the new frontiers. And sometimes considerably beyond them. The Prussian cordon had been in place since the previous November. The formal agreement between the three powers was signed in St Petersburg on 5 August 1772 and the partition was officially implemented between 12 and 18 September of that year. Further Prussian and Austrian incursions and annexations continued for several years. The Commonwealth lost almost a third of its territory, and more than a third of its population (Map 3). Frederick II joked about the partition with his characteristic contempt for Christianity: 'This will join the three religions: the Greek, the Catholic and the Calvinist, for we shall take communion of one eucharistic body, which is Poland, and if this is not for the good of our souls, it will surely be a great object for the good of our states.'[16]

The Hohenzollern share was the smallest of the three, but strategically vital. Frederick took nearly all of Royal Prussia, parts of Cujavia and the northern edges of Greater Poland. He now had his stranglehold on the Vistula. Unable to swallow Thorn and Danzig, he decided to throttle them. Thorn was cut off from the Vistula (and thus from the Commonwealth) by the annexation of its own lands. The Prussian monarch took advantage of his army's occupation of Danzig's New

Port to order the collection of the same tolls and fees as those imposed in the city. This doubled the costs of trade through the city and diverted much of it to the newly acquired port of Elbing – which now began to revive. Under pressure from the streets, the Danzig patricians declined a 'compromise' solution involving the cession and lease-back of the New Port. In any case, Frederick aimed to so ruin the city's economy and so vex its inhabitants that they would lose their will to resist him. In March 1775 he was able to impose a one-sided trading regime on Poland. The Danzigers bitterly resented the 12 per cent tolls imposed on transit between their city and the Commonwealth, as well as 2 per cent duties on shipping to and from the port of Danzig. Redefining tariffs, manipulating exchange rates and over-estimating the values of goods allowed Frederick's customs officials to extract still more money from shippers. These extortions may well have amounted to more than the revenues of the entire Crown treasury. This was because, despite the pressure, trade and shipbuilding continued. Volumes, prices and destinations all fluctuated; in the early 1780s even grain exports recovered for a while.

On the banks of the Mottlau, civic demoralization was resisted and cultural life went on. Patrons continued to invest in the arts and architecture – one of the finest examples is the late rococo tenement belonging to the Uphagen family, built between 1775 and 1787. Through a quirky testament, good fortune (until 1945) and a careful restoration this museum gives visitors a glimpse of the otherwise vanished world of late eighteenth-century Danzig patricians.

The Danzigers retained their self-governing institutions. In the seized territories renamed as 'Westpreussen', urban autonomy ended abruptly as officials and military garrisons moved in. Frederick, now officially King *of* Prussia rather than merely King *in* Prussia, made much of his 'civilizing' work – draining marshes, settling colonists and founding schools – in his newly acquired lands. Generations of historians (not all of them German) have echoed his claims. But Hans-Jürgen Bömelburg has demonstrated how the Prussian state's exploitative fiscal, customs and regulatory policies damaged the region's prosperity for decades, while Karin Friedrich has underscored the profound reluctance of Germanophone, Lutheran burghers to embrace Hohenzollern rule. More was at stake than commercial interests. A civic republican spirit had put down deep roots during three centuries of union between Royal Prussia and the Kingdom of Poland.

This spirit was felt in small privately owned small towns as well as in great royal cities, but it was not always 'enlightened'. For example, Wejherowo was governed according to a detailed regulation issued in 1769 by the owner, Ignacy Przebendowski, as well as by Kulm law. At this time over two-thirds of the town's population were Catholics. The town was famed for its Calvary, laid out by the town's founder, Jakub Wejher, in the mid-seventeenth century. On the whole Kashubian- and Polish-speakers tended to be Catholics, while most German-speakers were Lutherans, but there were many exceptions to the rule. In 1772 the mayor and the town council made an act of homage to their new sovereign (in Polish) and were subjected to the *Steuerrat* and the War and Domains Chamber in Marienwerder. In 1774 Ignacy Przebendowski sold the town and estates to his cousin Józef, a Prussian general, and moved to the Commonwealth – a typical family strategy for coping with the partition. The owners had the right to confirm the town councillors and the mayor, but, using the pretext of their joint refusal to permit the settlement of Jews, in 1774 Frederick II had the councillors gaoled. He then tried to impose his own mayor. Faced by the hostility of the 750 or so inhabitants, the royal nominee resigned after a year and the office remained unfilled until 1787. To add insult to injury, the town's name (whose local versions were Wejrowo in Kashubian and Weierfrei in German) was changed to Neustadt-in-Westpreussen. Such was the price of the 'order' and 'progress' symbolized by attempts to enforce fire-safety measures and buildings insurance.

Maria Theresa's tears at the partition moved Frederick to sarcasm, but they probably flowed from her religious and political scruples. They were not shared by either Kaunitz or Joseph II. If Silesia could not be recovered, then compensation for Prussian and Russian gains must be obtained in Poland. Lwów would replace Breslau. The Habsburg Monarchy annexed the lands south of the Vistula as far as Sandomierz, as well as nearly all of the palatinate of Ruthenia, the south-western edge of Volhynia and the western fringes of Podolia. The Austrian share was by far the most populous. The newly acquired territory contained valuable salt deposits at Wieliczka and elsewhere, but it was strategically exposed beyond the Carpathians. Moreover, most of its population of about 2.65 million was mired in poverty – as the critical reports sent back to Vienna by officials and the peripatetic emperor emphasized. Despite the name of the 'Kingdom of Galicia and Lodomeria', derived from the brief reign of Prince Coloman of Hungary over Halych Rus′ in the early thirteenth century, and King Louis's short-lived incorporation of the territory into the Kingdom of Hungary in the 1370s, the 'Galician' szlachta was not allowed to share the privileges of Hungarian nobles. They were soon paying vastly higher taxes. Although peasants would benefit from the limitations Joseph II placed on serfdom and labour services in the 1780s, they were also subjected to the heavy hand of the state. Above all, they were far more likely to be conscripted for arduous military service.

It took time for the unfolding reality to sink in. As late as May 1772 even Stanisław August clung to the hope that Prussian designs on Poland would be restrained by Russia and Austria. In a telling incident the following month, when Austrian forces took over the salt mines at Wieliczka, neither the governor nor Branicki, commanding a nearby Polish-Russian detachment, made more than a token attempt to query the new arrangements. It seems that years of violations of the Commonwealth's sovereignty, political instability, military conflict and enforced contributions had dulled the sensitivities of many nobles. So most made the necessary submissions to their new rulers and got on with their lives. Some quietly hoped for a change of circumstances that would allow them once more 'to be Poles'. Relatively few sold their estates 'beyond the cordon' and moved to the remaining territory of the Commonwealth. Particularly in Galicia, many magnates became *sujets mixtes*. Prince Adam Czartoryski made much of his new rank as an Austrian field marshal. Andrzej Zamoyski lobbied for more than a decade before – in 1786 – he secured a patent from Joseph II which formally permitted his entail, bisected by the new frontier, to continue to function as a single economic unit. The price he had to pay was, on the one hand, to enforce Austrian regulations within his family domains, and on the other, quietly to support the interests of Vienna within the Commonwealth.[17]

Although only half as populous as Galicia, the Russian share was even larger. It is customary – at least among Polish historians – to downplay the significance of this loss to the Commonwealth compared to the Prussian and Austrian slices. However, the prosperous Livonian and Lithuanian lands north of the Dvina and along the Dnieper constituted a strategically and economically important zone for the Russian Empire, long marked out for annexation when the time was right. Boundaries that followed wide rivers were useful obstacles to peasant flight. This huge acquisition facilitated Russia's communications and trade with the Baltic. About half of the Commonwealth's Orthodox population lived here, but they were outnumbered by Uniates. These territories brought Russia, for the first time, substantial populations of Catholics – of both the Latin and Ruthenian rites – and of Jews.

The occupation of these lands began in October 1771, enforced by requisitioning – only the obedient could expect payment. In August 1772 Catherine II ordered landowners to swear fidelity to her within a month or else sell up and leave within three. These unrealistic deadlines were repeatedly extended. Supplementary treaties, finally signed by the Commonwealth with Russia on 15 March 1775 and with Austria and Prussia a day later, allowed a six-year period for *sujets mixtes* to discharge their debts and other obligations in their new jurisdictions, sell up without paying a tax on the sale contract, and move permanently to the other side. During this time they would be freed from double taxation.

So much for the theory. Most of the Grand Duchy's magnates had already suffered sequestrations for failing to assist the Russians during the insurgency. Most estates 'beyond the cordon' were now confiscated. The biggest loser was Karol Radziwiłł, who would remain in exile until 1778. His losses included the latifundium around the small towns of Newel and Siebież, containing 1,230 villages (with 14,406 male souls).[18] Michał Czartoryski lost the Szkłów latifundium. They were not willing to swear allegiance to the empress in order to recover their estates, even if only to sell them afterwards. Besides, these vast landholdings were already being distributed to Russian aristocrats and generals as rewards. On the other hand, magnates who co-operated fully with the Russian authorities were accommodated. A few had performed such valuable services that they were allowed to keep their properties without (publicly) swearing fidelity to the empress. In practice, *sujets mixtes* were constrained politically and their tenure was parlous.

The amputated Commonwealth now resembled a lopsided 'T' placed on its side. These indefensible frontiers were more unlike those of the current, compact borders of the Republic of Poland than any before or since. Less than half of Poland's present territory was part of the Commonwealth between the first and second partitions. Three-quarters of the Commonwealth of that period now lie in Latvia, Lithuania, Belarus and Ukraine. And that was where about two-thirds of the population lived.[19]

Stanisław August comprehended the full horror of the situation when he was officially notified of the annexations in October 1772. He appealed both to the courts of Europe, according to a resolution of the senate council, and to European public opinion against the flagrant illegality of the partition. He succeeded in shaping the coverage of Polish affairs in the semi-official press organ of the French court, the *Gazette de France*, leaving its readers in no doubt as to the coercive character of the ratification. John Lind, the director of the royal Knights' School, sardonically dissected the three powers' legal pretensions in *The Partition of Poland in Seven Dialogues*, published in French and English editions. Caricatures satirizing the greed of Catherine, Frederick and Joseph rolled off the presses. Edmund Burke feared the precedent: 'Poland was but a breakfast, and there are not many Polands to be found – Where will they dine?'[20] French ministers recognized the scale of their disaster, but their British colleagues' reaction was muted. Nine years after the Seven Years' War, the two western powers were too suspicious of each other to undertake any joint action. Indeed, Britain had deterred the French and Spanish navies from attacking the Russian fleet as it sailed from the Baltic to the eastern Mediterranean. After an unhindered voyage, on 5–7 July 1770 the Russians shattered the Ottoman fleet off Chesme (Çeşme).

The king's resistance led the new Russian envoy, Otto Magnus von Stackelberg, to threaten sequestrations, the billeting of troops and further annexations if a confederated sejm were not called in order to ratify the partitions. Stackelberg, only thirty-six years old when he arrived in Warsaw in September 1772, had been schooled by his patron, Panin. The essence of his instructions was to get the partition ratified with all the appearances of legality, and then to exercise stable control over the truncated Commonwealth. The latter entailed a revised constitutional settlement with a weaker monarchy. Behind the Livonian baron's relatively emollient manners was the threat of force: a corps was at his disposal. This and the efforts to act in concert with the ministers of Austria and Prussia, were intended to convince the Poles that resistance was pointless. Stanisław August would protest and procrastinate until the coercion became obvious. Then he would make carefully calibrated concessions to prevent a still worse outcome. The cycle would then begin again. These tactics delayed the inevitable. The Commonwealth would have to inscribe its consent to the amputation of three of its limbs into its own law books. In mid-February 1773, with the agreement of the senate council, the king summoned the sejm. Only at this stage did many nobles begin to grasp the enormity of what had already happened and what was now being demanded.

The three partitioning powers permitted no sejmiks to be held in the newly annexed territories. Divided palatinates and districts moved sejmiks to new locations when necessary, just as the exiled sejmiks for lands ceded to Russia in 1686 continued to meet. However, the sejmik instructions of 1773 and subsequent years offer no evidence of lessons learned from the catastrophe. It has been claimed on this basis that the szlachta was more concerned about the threat to traditional liberties from the new form of government than about the partition.[21] This may overestimate the significance attached to instructions at this time. Elections were considered more important, and Stackelberg failed to procure a majority of pliant envoys. While he and his Austrian and Prussian colleagues lacked the necessary orientation in local politics, the king exercised a discreet but effective influence, especially in Lithuania. Moreover, several sejmiks which broke up without electing envoys protested against the presence of foreign troops and the imprisonment of Barists, and denied the legality of any cession of the Commonwealth's territory. These declarations were entered into castle court records.

While all the known instructions condemned the 'regicides' and many denounced the declaration of an interregnum, much of the language used blurred responsibility. Memories soon became selective. The recess from the Confederacy of Bar demanded by the new sejm confederacy (on pain of confiscation of estates) involved swearing obedience not only to the king, but also to the empress. Given the decomposition of the political scene that had taken place over the previous few years, both Stackelberg and Stanisław August sought to win over former Barists. The ambassador's biggest coup was the venal Crown Treasurer. In return for his submission Teodor Wessel demanded – and in the end received – his enormous arrears of salary. The deadline for the recess was extended and during the next few years many came home without complying fully. One who did not was Kazimierz Pułaski, wanted for his part in the abduction. Forced to move on repeatedly, he finally crossed the Atlantic. He died in the cause of American independence at Savannah in 1779.

Stackelberg selected the unscrupulous Adam Poniński, Crown Master of the Kitchens, to be marshal of the sejm. He would be well rewarded for his obeisance with a licence to pillage and promotion to Treasurer of the Crown. However, any expectations that the partition would be ratified quietly were soon disabused. The first difficulties concerned the holding of the sejm under the aegis of the confederacy formed on 16 April. On 19 April three envoys from the Grand Duchy of Lithuania protested that the king had not summoned a confederated sejm, but a 'free' one. The spectators in attendance cheered them on, until the ministers of the three powers demanded their removal. On the third day of the protest, one of them, Tadeusz Reytan, interposed his body in the entrance to the chamber in an effort to prevent envoys from leaving. They walked over him.

The protesters occupied the chamber for a further day and a half. Exhausted, and having won assurances that they would not suffer repressions, they went home. Their protest satisfied the need felt by the Commonwealth's noble citizens and foreign sympathizers for a heroic, but ineffective gesture. Reytan stressed that he was trying to maintain a 'free' sejm, not break it up. However, if ever a critical situation called out for a virtuous individual to save the Fatherland by invoking the *liberum veto*, this was it. Reytan's failure to prevent the confederated sejm from ratifying the partition proved Stanisław Konarski to have been absolutely correct. If only a handful of virtuous citizens remained, they could not stop a majority, bought or intimidated by a foreign power, from having its way.

In the aftermath of this protest, Stackelberg faced a hostile majority in the sejm, despite his recourse to bribery and intimidation. He reprised the tactic used by Repnin: a plenipotentiary delegation to transact the sejm's business. It was headed by Poniński and filled with his cronies, as well as other ambassadorial clients. As in 1767–68, the 99 (later 105) members of the delegation met in the great hall of the Radziwiłł Palace. Its meetings alternated with theatrical productions. Although there were arguments on particular points, including religion, all but three delegates signed the treaties of partition on 18 September 1773. Thus was the Commonwealth compelled to enter the amputation of its territory into its own laws. Naturally the three treaties also solemnly guaranteed the integrity of the lands remaining to the Commonwealth. Until next time.

Once the amputations had been ratified by the victim, it remained to cauterize the torso by establishing the form of government. This process lasted until the spring of 1775, when the sejm finally concluded. Stackelberg found he had to co-operate with Stanisław August. The king had too many supporters among the envoys to be ignored, while the ambassador's lickspittles could not command sufficient support. The hard bargaining led to compromises. The royal Cabinet made a scrupulous record of the king's increasingly long meetings with the ambassador, creating a source of great value. The thorniest problem was the scaling back of the political rights granted to the dissidents in 1768 – the empress's prestige was at stake. Stackelberg stressed to Stanisław August in January 1774 that 'the affair of the dissidents is regarded by the empress as the principal one, on the success of which depend the others'.[22] The reluctant Russian abandonment of the idea of using the dissidents as a docile political party did facilitate a judicial solution which benefited Protestant nobles – the mixed courts envisaged by the 1768 legislation were to be replaced for appeals involving Evangelicals by the royal assessory courts. This enabled the king to appoint some Protestant judges. Non-Catholic noble citizens were thereby freed from chicanery in the tribunals, dominated by Catholics. Unfortunately, given that priests could not serve as assessory court judges, the only plausible lay Orthodox candidate was the secretary of the Russian Embassy. Progress was somewhat easier regarding trade, royal prerogatives and finances. The king, who had lost revenues from the Wieliczka salt mines and many royal domains, was allowed an adequate civil list of 7 million złotys per annum. However, he lost the right to distribute all but four *starostwa*; the others were to be auctioned off on fifty-year leases as they fell vacant.

Many prerogatives passed to the Permanent Council, which replaced the senate council between the sessions of the sejm. This solution had long been in gestation. On the one hand, antecedents for this collegial executive body could be found in eighteenth-century Polish reformist thought, culminating in Konarski's *On the Means of Effective Councils*. On the other hand, it also owed much to the system which had been designed to weaken the monarchy in Sweden during the 'Age of Liberty' that lasted from the death of Charles XII in 1718 to Gustav III's coup in 1772. Its elective character was weakened by the complex rules for its composition. Every two years the sejm had to choose a council composed of eighteen senators (fifteen temporal and three spiritual) and eighteen members of the Knightly Estate, all carefully balanced among Greater Poland, Lesser Poland and the Grand Duchy of Lithuania. Moreover, one-third of the members would be replaced every two years. The king had the casting vote in the event of a tie. The Council was divided into five departments, for police, justice, the treasury, the military and foreign affairs, which also made collective decisions. They were each serviced by a qualified secretary. However, in cases when commissions, such as those for the treasuries and armies of the Crown and Lithuania, already existed, the departments exercised only supervisory powers. Moreover, all departmental and plenary resolutions of the Permanent Council were subject to amendment or rejection during biennial inspections by the sejm. While the Permanent Council did garner some central executive authority over time, it was emasculated from the start. In the eyes of much of the szlachta, the fact that Russia had imposed the Council was enough to damn it.

Perhaps as great a shock as the bulldozing of the partition treaties through the sejm was the suppression, by Pope Clement XIV on 21 July 1773, of the Society of Jesus. Jesuits were disproportionately numerous among the regular clergy of the Commonwealth, and Poles were disproportionately numerous among the worldwide members of the order. Elsewhere Jesuits were the targets of fierce criticism, not least from other regular clergymen, but they enjoyed much trust from the Polish-Lithuanian nobility and monarch. Amidst plaintive laments, the sejm accepted the suppression during a plenary session on 28 September. The bishops implemented the decision in November. Within the truncated Commonwealth, 1,869 Jesuits in 104 houses were Jesuits no more.[23]

In the Austrian Monarchy, whose rulers had neither desired the suppression nor fought to preserve the Society, the decision was carried out at the same time as in the remaining territories of the Commonwealth. However, Frederick II initially refused to allow the suppression in his Silesian and newly acquired 'West Prussian' territories. There Jesuits survived as Jesuits until 1780. Catherine's freshly annexed lands provided a haven for the order until 1820. These two non-Catholic monarchs acted thus partly to spite the pope and the Bourbon courts. More importantly, they pragmatically wanted to use Jesuits (wholly dependent on their new sovereigns' goodwill) to educate the Catholic populations on terms dictated by themselves. Therefore the partitions of the very country in which Jesuits had enjoyed their greatest popularity created the conditions for the continuous existence of the Society of Jesus between suppression in 1773 and restoration in 1814.

By the terms of the papal *breve*, the Jesuits became secular clergymen. The fate of the Jesuit colleges most concerned the Polish-Lithuanian szlachta. Nobles were faced with an educational cliff-edge if no action were taken – perhaps 20,000 pupils were taught in Jesuit schools.[24] If the suppression was treated as a purely ecclesiastical matter, great wealth and influence would accrue to the bishops, so the sejm decided that the order's property would serve an educational fund. Similar solutions were adopted in other Catholic states, in which the Holy See acquiesced. On 14 October 1773 the sejm established the Commission of National Education. The eight (later twelve) commissioners comprised politicians from across the spectrum, most of them sincerely committed to their task. Wilno University and forty-five colleges and schools remaining in the truncated Commonwealth continued their work under the auspices of the Commission, which enjoined the former Jesuits to stay at their posts. Stackelberg and his superiors were prepared to allow Stanisław August this consolation prize, partly because they underestimated the medium- and long-term effects of the reform.

Unfortunately, the appointed surveyors of the former Jesuit properties could not or would not prevent the looting of land, crops, animals, movables and serfs by the owners of neighbouring estates. Some joined in. In March 1774 the sejm established two distributive commissions, for the Crown and Lithuania respectively, to complete the survey and sell the properties. The ex-Jesuits received far less than the modest annual sum of 300,000 złotys nominally allocated by the sejm for their maintenance, but a substantial annual salary of 8,000 złotys was pocketed by each of the thirty-two commissioners. The latter undervalued many properties, before buying them for themselves, or selling them to their friends and clients. The Educational Fund received much less than the annual 4.5 per cent of the income due from the purchasers of former Jesuit estates. All in all, the Fund was asset-stripped of more than a third of its value within three years.[25]

Within two decades the Commission of National Education would be hailed as probably the greatest achievement of Stanisław August's reign. However, in the short term, most Jesuit colleges were left without funds. With a skeleton staff teaching many fewer pupils, school buildings decayed. Excellent collections of books and instruments were left exposed to the elements. The outlook for the Commonwealth as a whole seemed just as dismal.

— SIX —

THRONE AND ALTAR

Stanisław August's best responses to adversity were artistic. In 1770 he commissioned a commemorative medal (Plate 10). The conventional obverse shows the monarch in antique profile with an inscription that proclaimed him – by grace of God – King of Poland and Grand Duke of Lithuania. The reverse depicts a ship powered by sail and oars, whose crew wear antique-style helmets. The ship lists perilously as it proceeds through a narrow channel of foaming sea, while lightning flashes from the clouds. The twin crags may represent the Russian Empire and the Confederacy of Bar. If so, this expressive protest was reinforced by the Virgilian sentence *NE CEDE MALIS*.[1] This is usually translated as 'Yield not to misfortunes', although it could also be read as 'Yield not to evils'. The words are those uttered by the Cumæan Sibyl in book 6, line 95 of the *Aeneid*, after she has foreseen 'the Tiber foaming with much blood'. Her following injunction is '*sed contra audentior ito*' – 'Go forth against them yet bolder'.

Alas. The Polish-Lithuanian ship of state, having been holed, rendered mast-less, oar-less and driven aground, was plundered by wreckers and stripped of much of its timber. The chief villainess then supervised the repair and refloating of a ship that was now not only less capacious, but even harder to manoeuvre than before. During the dozen years that followed the end of the Partition Sejm, this vessel was all but becalmed. The king was usually allowed to keep one hand on the tiller, but never to steer the ship under sail. Leading crew members grumbled and plotted, but their hopes of replacing him at the helm were disappointed time and again. For the robber-empress who liked to be compared to Minerva,[2] this was – for the time being – the optimal solution. But under the occasionally rippled political surface, strong currents were at work. Polish-Lithuanian society was changing.

During the renewed Russian hegemony that lasted from the defeat of the Confederacy of Bar in 1772 to the inauguration of the Four Years' Sejm in 1788, the results of Stanisław August's legislative efforts were modest. He learned that reforms were best pursued outside the strictly political sphere. After the controversial confederated sejm of 1776, the next five sejms achieved little. These were 'free' sejms in that they were subject – at Russian insistence – to the requirement of unanimity. Scorned and scapegoated by his aristocratic cousins, Stanisław August tried to build a royalist party among wealthy and middling nobles. He enjoyed significant success, not least because he had the support of most Catholic hierarchs. Foremost among them was his surviving younger brother. Michał Jerzy Poniatowski became Primate of Poland in 1785. He epitomized the period's episcopal reformers, when secular and ecclesiastical politics frequently overlapped. The effects of the alliance between 'throne and altar' were tangible in both spheres, but so were the limits.

As the dust settled in the political firmament after the first partition, new stars were born, while old ones dimmed or died. The lodestar of Polish-Lithuanian politics remained St Petersburg, but it became evident that Russian attempts to control the Commonwealth through a 'party' of dissidents and hirelings had failed. Catherine II, mistrusting Stanisław August, partly reverted to the strategy of Elizabeth's reign: maintaining a stalemate between the royal court and its aristocratic opponents. However, Catherine did not intend to restore Poland to the position of relative equilibrium in which it had reposed for much of the Saxon era. The truncated Commonwealth would be a Russian sphere of influence, in which Prussia and Austria were not to meddle. Moreover, she did not rule out a second partition. As Robert Howard Lord put it:

> Her policy after the First Partition was to protect the Poles in their remaining possessions, as long as they made no effort to escape from her control, and as long as no conjuncture in general European affairs rendered it desirable or necessary to purchase the support of the German powers with drafts on the usual treasury – Poland. Within these limits, the Empress was committed to maintaining the existing arrangements.[3]

A novel factor in Polish-Lithuanian politics was the paucity of magnates among royal supporters. The early 1770s saw a generational changing of the guard among the elite. Within a few years several senior figures either died or withdrew from active engagement in politics: they included Michał and August Czartoryski, Franciszek Salezy Potocki, Bishops Kajetan Sołtyk and Adam Krasiński, and Hetmans Jan Klemens Branicki and Wacław Rzewuski. It fell to the formidable Katarzyna Kossakowska, née Potocka, imbued with contempt for Stanisław August, to end the old feud between Potockis and Czartoryskis. In 1772 she arranged the marriage of her favourite nephew, Ignacy Potocki, to Elżbieta, the beautiful daughter of Izabella and Stanisław Lubomirski. Later her sisters Aleksandra, Julia and Konstancja respectively married Ignacy's brother Stanisław Kostka, his distant cousin Jan Potocki, and Seweryn Rzewuski (who had returned from Kaluga with his father Wacław). The king was not invited to the weddings.

Izabella Lubomirska, née Czartoryska, was a noted patron of the arts (Plate 11). Her exquisite taste and insistence on comfort can be admired in her surviving residences (including the spectacular bathroom at Wilanów). She was a migraine-prone and capricious mother-in-law, who paid only the annual interest on her daughters' dowries, but Ignacy and Stanisław Kostka Potocki found a congenial intellectual partner in their uncle by marriage, Adam Kazimierz Czartoryski. The serious Ignacy hesitated over whether to take orders with the Piarists who had schooled him; in the end he sublimated his pedagogical streak into tireless work for the Commission of National Education. The charming Stanisław Kostka was also interested in education and freemasonry, but eventually found his vocation as a collector of antiquities, amateur architect and literary and art critic.

During the turmoil of the past few years, Prince Adam Czartoryski and his wife Izabela, née Flemming, had considered selling up in Poland and settling in England, before they decided otherwise and returned home (Plates 12 and 13). Izabela, it seems, felt a patriotic pang of conscience. They had an 'open marriage', for Adam Kazimierz was unusually tolerant of his wife's affairs even by the standards of the age. He acknowledged all but one of his wife's children as his own, although most were fathered by other men. Less remarkably, he was an accomplished philanderer himself. Perhaps some of Izabella Lubomirska's spleen was prompted by the fact that her sister-in-law had blossomed since she had married Prince Adam as an ugly duckling, recovering from smallpox, in 1761. Izabela Czartoryska's most notable conquests in the mid-1760s had been King Stanisław August and Ambassador Repnin. Among the *beaux* who competed for her favours in the 1770s was Franciszek Ksawery Branicki, who unexpectedly became the key player in the coalition of magnates in opposition to the king (Plate 28).

Branicki had long been a friend of Stanisław August. He had covered himself in gore while fighting against rebellious peasants and insurgent confederates between 1768 and 1772. He had also put the king's case to the empress in St Petersburg. For his trouble he had in 1773–74 been raised to the field hetmanship and then to the grand hetmanship of the Crown. Branicki's promotion piqued the king's elder brother, who had long coveted the hetman's mace. Prince Kazimierz Poniatowski resigned as chamberlain of the Crown, and spent his remaining twenty-seven years in dudgeon, dissipation, debauchery and debt. The 6,000 ducats a year he received from Vienna in recompense for his lost *starostwo* of Spisz was never enough. Branicki, having also received one of the four lucrative *starostwa* left in the king's gift – Biała Cerkiew in the Ukraine – then intrigued against his royal benefactor. Adam Czartoryski accompanied Branicki to St Petersburg in 1775; Ignacy Potocki tagged along a year later.

On the face of it, Branicki's purpose was to restore the hetman's prerogatives to the palmy days of Saxon yore, when his unrelated namesake, Jan Klemens, had swaggered around the Commonwealth. Now Franciszek Ksawery built up a power base in the Crown army. He had many supporters in the notoriously undisciplined National Cavalry. He also had friends, allies and clients in the Crown Military Commission, which he incited to resist the Military Department of the Permanent Council. Above all, Branicki led the opposition's efforts to outbid Stanisław August for the empress's favour. His company was initially enjoyed by Catherine's latest paramour, Grigorii Potemkin, with whom she would probably contract a morganatic marriage and effectively co-rule the Russian Empire. Potemkin, who fired on many intellectual as well as physical cylinders, would later find Branicki a tiresome bore,[4] and from 1774 he was on studiedly polite terms with Stanisław August.[5] However, he saw in the hetman a useful instrument for promoting his own and Russian interests.

From the start Branicki played a double game, posing as the patriot – with respect to Prussia and Austria – in order to deepen Polish dependence on Russia. 'I tell you this as a good Russian and a good Pole,' he wrote to Potemkin in 1775.[6] In 1781 Ksawery would cement his position in St Petersburg by marrying Potemkin's favourite niece and bedmate, Aleksandra Engelhardt. The empress herself signed the marriage contract, an unprecedented distinction.[7] Indeed, 'Sasha' Branicka was so beloved of Catherine that inaccurate gossip even began to circulate in Poland that she was the empress's own natural daughter by her first lover, Sergei Saltykov, whom the Empress Elizabeth had supposedly removed and replaced with an unknown boy who was proclaimed the Grand Duke Paul.[8]

Branicki's exceptional position, effectively a member of the extended imperial family, meant that other magnates discontented with Stanisław August looked to him, his wife and Potemkin to persuade the empress to place her confidence in the 'first families'.[9] Since they could rule the Commonwealth to her satisfaction, they urged the abandonment of Poniatowski who had proved himself unworthy of her support. They also pressed for a change of ambassador because, they alleged, Otto Magnus von Stackelberg had fallen under the influence of the king. This was a truly oligarchic programme – collective rule by a narrow elite. Too rarely has Branicki's leadership been emphasized. Partly this is because no scholar has yet exploited his archive (which may no longer exist). On the other hand, the well-documented cultural role played by Izabela and Adam Kazimierz Czartoryski in the years between the first and second partitions has led generations of scholars to place them on a pedestal, at the head of a morally salubrious, patriotic opposition to a flaccid royal court.[10] The evidence of the king's correspondence, Stackelberg's despatches, their recorded conversations, and snippets of Potemkin's dispersed papers tells a different story. Czartoryski, his wife and his nephews-in-law largely followed the lead of the Crown grand hetman. Prince Adam's studied preference for literary and pedagogical pursuits meant he only intermittently dirtied his hands with politics.

Between the sejms of 1775 and 1776 the opposition fought the king on at least three levels. The first was lobbying at the imperial courts. Leading Austrian *sujets mixtes* asked Maria Theresa to replace Stanisław August with one of her sons, the Archduke Maximilian. Vienna rejected the offer and informed St Petersburg that it had been made (leaving the identity of its proponents to be guessed). Second, the opposition magnates mobilized their clients across the Commonwealth. Linked to this was the third level: appeals to public opinion (which still meant noble opinion). The aristocrats' strategy of outbidding the king in St Petersburg meant that they could not campaign against either the partition or Russian hegemony in the Commonwealth. Instead, in broadsheets, pamphlets and protests registered in local chanceries they and their supporters accused the Permanent Council of usurping the sejm's prerogatives, and of trampling on 'ancient laws'.

Less numerous royalist writers called for modest increases in taxation and the army. They debunked the bucolic legend of peace and prosperity under Augustus III, and identified Stanisław August's wise leadership with the workings of Divine Providence. The most challenging contribution was *Political Thoughts on Civil Liberty*, written by the same Józef Wybicki who had protested against Repnin's sejm of 1767–68 and then joined the Confederacy of Bar. His subsequent legal studies in Leiden had led him to very different conclusions. Rejecting the cult of 'ancient laws', he argued that when circumstances changed, new laws should respond to them. He advocated a stronger, hereditary monarchy coupled with majority voting in the sejm. Drawing on Montesquieu, Wybicki argued that Poland's 'liberty' was meaningless when anarchy and corruption deprived the country's inhabitants of their security and tranquillity.

The king was pleased, but few others were listening. Wybicki's arguments had virtually no impact on the sejmik campaign of 1776. The crucial factor was that Stanisław August persuaded Stackelberg to support a modest strengthening of the Permanent Council and the royal prerogative. This would be accomplished by confederating the sejm of 1776 in advance, within the Permanent Council. On this occasion the ambassador convinced the empress that the alternative was a return to chaos. At some sejmiks Russian troops skirmished with units loyal to Branicki. In the worst incident thirty-six noblemen were killed at Ciechanów. The king also urged the ambassador not to pursue the election of dissidents as envoys. None were chosen. The new papal nuncio, Giovanni Andrea Archetti, kept his joy discreet.[11]

Next in importance to Russian support was the organization of the royalist party. This was lubricated by royal patronage. Although the monarch's distributive power had been much reduced by the legislation of 1773–75, Stanisław August played his remaining cards deftly. At the apex of the hierarchy were senatorial chairs, for which the Permanent Council presented the king with three candidates. Stackelberg tried to reserve decisions on front-row lay senators for himself. He demanded rewards for those who had helped him force through the partition treaties, but given their lack of political credibility, he left most political management to the king. Stanisław August could usually advance his own candidates to bishoprics and lesser castellanies, as well as to the hierarchies of central and local office. He could also present favoured clergymen to the benefices in his gift.

The former steward of Lithuania also knew the value of honorific distinctions. Below the more exclusive order of the White Eagle, created by Augustus II, was the order of St Stanisław, founded in 1765. Most of those honoured had these orders' blue and red ribbons painted in their portraits – testimony to the demand among laymen and clergymen alike. Stanisław August also excelled in writing personal letters. Much of his domestic correspondence (preserved in several dozen fat volumes) was devoted to persuading men of standing to rouse support for royal candidates at the sejmiks which elected envoys to the sejm and deputies to the tribunals.

The king usually had one or more trusted supporters to manage each sejmik. Probably the most important sejmik was for the conjoined palatinates of Greater Poland. The citizens met in front of the venerable parish church of Środa (inside, during inclement weather). Here the monarch came to rely on the business-like Kazimierz Raczyński. At the other end of the Commonwealth, the sejmik for the palatinate of Kiev met at Żytomierz. In these parts the royal strongman was the fearsome Józef Stempkowski, who was rewarded by promotion to castellan, then palatine of Kiev. Sejmiks in northern Mazovia were entrusted to the king's youngest brother, Michał, who finally bowed to family pressure and accepted the episcopal crook and mitre of Płock in 1773.

The political situation in the Grand Duchy of Lithuania was very different. Here the court treasurer, Antoni Tyzenhauz, had won the monarch's gratitude by multiplying revenues from the royal domain lands. Royal forests retreated before the axe, yielding the land to agriculture and proto-industrial enterprises. Settlements even sprung up in the primeval glades of Białowieża. By the mid-1770s Tyzenhauz had created a well-publicized manufacturing complex around Grodno, but it was a fragile achievement, too dependent on the unwilling labour of under-skilled serfs. His grip on political life in the Grodno district was just as tight – he exerted pressure on the petty noble lessees of royal land – and just as vulnerable. After the partition, Tyzenhauz extended his management of the royalist party throughout the Grand Duchy of Lithuania. On the one hand, he delivered many disciplined Lithuanian envoys to the king; on the other, he opposed any diminution of the separate status of the Grand Duchy. Stanisław August's ambitions for a single 'Polish Commonwealth' were put on hold.

The magnate opposition was weaker in Lithuania than in the Crown. There was, admittedly, Michał Kazimierz Ogiński. The Lithuanian Grand Hetman was a cultural dilettante, who also had dabbled in the Confederacy of Bar. Connected by marriage and politics to the Czartoryskis, like them he had suffered Russian sequestrations and confiscations. His remaining wealth and influence paled before the Radziwiłł interest, but the latter was largely a latent force. The head of the clan, Prince Karol, remained in exile for several years after the Barists' defeat.

Tyzenhauz picked up many of his clients, for it was acceptable for clients to abandon patrons who could no longer protect them. The court treasurer's mediation then helped Radziwiłł, encumbered by colossal debts, to return home in 1778. He would co-operate with the court for years to come. In the meantime, the number of Tyzenhauz's enemies grew.

Let us return to the election campaign of 1776. Despite the precautions taken by Stackelberg and Stanisław August, about thirty opposition envoys were elected. Most of these were chosen at sejmiks that split into two factions which then deliberated separately. Normally the sejm decided who had been legally elected. This time the sejm confederacy was formed three days in advance, within the Permanent Council. Royalist envoys and senators then joined it. Among the envoys elected by 'doubled' sejmiks, only those who belonged to the confederacy were deemed legally elected. Royal guards kept the others out of the chamber. A few opposition senators – led by Crown Grand Marshal Stanisław Lubomirski – protested in vain.

These extraordinary means – bordering on a coup d'état – delivered a useful packet of reforms to Stanisław August. He emphasized their limited scope. Addressing the sejm, he enumerated the greater prerogatives of the king of England, while claiming that England was universally considered to be the 'most truly free, and the happiest' nation in Europe. English freedom was sufficiently safeguarded, he argued, by the ability of 'the nation' (in Parliament) to refuse the renewal of taxes.[12] The laws passed in 1776 empowered the Permanent Council to command ministers and commissions, and to interpret the law in doubtful cases, subject to the confirmation of its resolutions by the following sejm. Most importantly, the monarch gained effective control of the Crown and Lithuanian armies, which were henceforth subordinated directly to the Military Department of the Permanent Council. The king also regained the right to promote officers, and direct command of his four guard regiments. A further success was the end to the spoliation of the Commission of National Education, and the sidelining of its chairman, Bishop Ignacy Massalski. The most charitable interpretation would be that Massalski was incapable of managing money – his own or anybody else's. Bishop Michał Poniatowski took firm charge of the Commission, and its finances were soon put in order.[13]

The opposition leaders were incensed. For years they denounced the 'dreadful sejm' of 1776 as a violation of liberty at least as bad as the Partition Sejm of 1773–75. For Branicki, loss of control over the Crown army rankled, but the most persuasive argument at the opposition's disposal was that the new entitlements of the Permanent Council to interpret the law and to order the military execution of court verdicts usurped the legislative and judicial powers of the 'nation'. This was fuel to the fire of orators and writers who warned of creeping royal despotism.

Stanisław August tried to follow up his advantage. He sent his nephew, Prince Stanisław Poniatowski, to St Petersburg. This handsome young prince delivered the king's sincere thanks to the empress, but he achieved little beyond a gracious welcome. Indeed, the pendulum of Russian favour now swung towards the opposition. Catherine's refusal of Stanisław August's request to confederate the sejm of 1778 was compounded when Stackelberg insisted on the election of several opposition candidates to the Permanent Council. Nor did the king's feelers towards the opposition yield any benefits. Subjected to the requirement of unanimity for new laws, this forgettable sejm was barren of reforms.

Catherine's policy did not only reflect her suspicion of Stanisław August. She needed a quiescent Commonwealth as war loomed between Austria and Prussia over the question of the Bavarian Succession (military operations lasted between July 1778 and March 1779). Russia remained formally allied to Prussia. When the crunch came, Catherine supported Frederick in the peace negotiations. She was concerned that Vienna might exploit its Galician *sujets mixtes* to destabilize the Commonwealth. The crisis provoked by the illegal recruiting activities of the Austrian agent Baron Karl Julius, followed by his arrest and trial in Warsaw, was the last thing she needed. St Petersburg forced the Polish side to pay 20,000 ducats in compensation, but also told Vienna to stay out of Polish affairs in future. Joseph II seems to have been playing the Polish card as a minor part of his long-term endeavour to persuade Catherine to switch alliances. Following the War of the Bavarian Succession, the pendulum in St Petersburg swung back towards the king. By 1780 the situation seemed stable enough for Russia to withdraw most of its troops from the Commonwealth.

The departure of most Russian soldiers did not mean that life at the frontiers became tranquil. Stanisław August had made rather too much of Russia's role in the handing back by Prussia and Austria of some of the territories which they had seized beyond the lands specified in the treaties of partition. It was in this context that he told the sejm of 1776: 'I am a friend of the Empress of Russia; I say this as loudly as I do truly, because the interest of my Fatherland requires me to be [her] friend.'[14] In reality, the Habsburgs kept most of their additional gains and Frederick held on to the lion's share of his. Vexations from customs officials and military detachments still afflicted landowners, merchants and peasants in the vicinity of the borders. The Polish side was defenceless, and the Prussian and Austrian commanders knew it. Only in recent years has the analogous situation in the lands adjoining the Russian Empire been revealed.[15]

The partition treaties of 1772 delineated the new Russian frontier thus: the empress and her successors took possession of the lands beyond the Dvina, until the river reached the boundary of the palatinates of Połock and Witebsk, which the new border followed southwards to the point where the three palatinates of Połock, Witebsk and Minsk met. From here it proceeded in a straight line to Orawa, near the source of the Druć, and thence along that river until it flowed into the Dnieper, which from that point southwards marked 'the boundary between the two states, always conserving the boundary possessed by the city of Kiev and its district on the other side of this river'.[16] This sounds clear enough. But the boundaries of the eastern palatinates of the Grand Duchy of Lithuania had never been properly demarcated, so nobody was sure exactly where they were, unless they ran along significant rivers (even then, the status of islands, water meadows and multiple channels was uncertain; the Austrians for several years exploited such a loophole within a stone's throw of Wawel, claiming that the old corridor of the Vistula placed the town of Kazimierz on their side). The point at which three palatinates were thought to meet turned out to be an inaccessible bog.[17] The boundary between places agreed to be in the palatinates of Połock and Witebsk in fact meandered further east than it did on the maps used for the treaties – an inconvenient discovery for the Russians. Russian and Polish commissioners straightened out the frontier between the Dvina and the Druć, placing most of the bisected villages on the Russian side. By 15 July 1775 they had delineated the border all the way to Łojów on the Dnieper.[18]

Below Łojów, however, the border was 'defined' by the 1686 peace treaty between the Commonwealth and Muscovy, although demarcation had never occurred. Initially this had hardly mattered. The Commonwealth's control of the right-bank Ukraine, laid waste by warfare, remained nominal for decades to come. As peace and prosperity returned, Polish lords resettled the borderlands. Their people sometimes came into contact with Russian military colonists and landowners from 'New Serbia' (named after the Serbian settlers offered to

Elizabeth by Maria Theresa). Both sides complained of violations, abductions and thefts, but the Russians had *force majeure* on their side. They demanded, straining the terms of the 1686 treaty, that the Poles abandon all settlements within a strip several kilometres wide, right along the (undemarcated) border. During the *koliivshchyna* and the Confederacy of Bar some Polish magnates had leased their lands to Russian officers. It was difficult to reassert their ownership.

Especially vulnerable were Michał Lubomirski's woods of Nerubaj, located south of a wide bend of the River Taśmin. These extensive woods were coveted by Potemkin, who after the Russo-Turkish war was energetically settling 'New Serbia' (renamed 'Novorossiia'). Lubomirski's foresters were powerless to prevent the cutting down of swathes of woodland and the despatch of the timber down the Dnieper to build the port of Kherson after 1778. The practice of abducting peasants on the pretext that they were runaway serfs from the Russian Empire also intensified. Nothing was wasted: even the women's tresses were hacked off to make wigs.[19] Polish military units were too small and scattered to police the border effectively; they occasionally disrupted minor Russian detachments, but gave way to larger forces.[20]

Complaints made by the Permanent Council to Stackelberg were rebuffed by the misleading assertion that the entire border belt should have been left deserted according to the 1686 treaty. Meanwhile, Russian complaints grew more outlandish: the governor of 'Novorossiia' accused inhabitants of Żabotyn, a settlement belonging to Lubomirski, of penetrating deep into Russian territory and returning (undisturbed) with 178 stolen horses – a tall order indeed. Nevertheless, Stackelberg, like Stanisław August, feared that Potemkin was planning to exploit the Austro-Prussian war over the Bavarian Succession to annex part of the Polish Ukraine. The difficulties the Russian Empire had experienced in supplying the armies fighting the Ottoman Empire underlined the strategic value of these lands. The Warsaw court prepared a thick dossier, mapping the extent of Russian usurpations in the far south-east with precision and beauty (Plate 14),[21] and pressed for demarcation to begin. Potemkin had it delayed until the summer of 1780.

Catherine II's impending switch of alliances seems to have persuaded her finally to agree to the demarcation of the border. She may have feared that Polish protests against Russian annexations could prompt Joseph II to make more trouble in the Commonwealth. Above all, she was determined not to give him a precedent to demand Podolian lands bordering Galicia and Moldavia. The king knew that the commissioners would confirm the loss of most of what had already been seized by Russia. So it proved when they finished their work in January 1781. The Nerubaj woods and much else besides were the price of preventing further annexations.[22] Potemkin, who kept several irons in the fire, then changed tack. His Polish *ius indigenatus*, acquired prudently in 1776, allowed him in 1785 to buy the vast estates centred on Smila, a small town on the northernmost bend of the Taśmin, not far from the Dnieper. He continued his exploitation of the Polish Ukraine by other means.

Russian misbehaviour at the frontier warned Stanisław August not to push his luck. The impossibility of major reform was epitomized by the fate of the work of legal codification. This was entrusted by the sejm of 1776 to Andrzej Zamoyski whose resignation in 1767 of the Crown chancellorship in protest at Repnin's violence had enhanced his reputation for probity. His team, including Józef Wybicki, was authorized to draw on 'natural justice' when existing laws were unclear or obsolete. They got to work in haste – perhaps in excessive haste. The draft code was ready to be presented to the sejm of 1778. Despite – or even partly because of – Wybicki's passionate advocacy of the Code's reforms in his *Patriotic Letters* (1777–78), it stood no chance of success.

The ecclesiastical proposals, limiting papal jurisdiction and restricting monastic professions, angered Nuncio Archetti and many regular clergymen. However, given the anti-clericalism rife among the szlachta, of greater political significance was Stackelberg's displeasure at a minor extension to the royal prerogative of clemency. Moreover, Lithuanian sejmiks voiced opposition to a new code shared with the Polish Crown (although they would have been happy for the Crown provinces to adopt a clarified version of the Third Lithuanian Statute). Most important of all was the fear that the Code's provisions for the peasantry would entail a social and economic upheaval, degrading and ruining the szlachta.

Non-landholding peasants and their families, the clear majority of the population in the countryside, would have been defined as *non adscripti glebæ* (not tied to the soil), their traditional manual tasks now defined by contracts. On completion of their contractual duties, they would be free to leave and seek their fortune on another estate or in a town. So too would the second, fourth and subsequent sons of the smaller category of peasants defined as *glebæ adscripti*, that is, 'settled on a rural estate, without a contract, equipped by the manor with stock and inventory and performing labour service'.[23] Emancipation (a one-way street) would have become much easier to achieve, while the legal position of contracted peasants would have been transformed by enabling them to summon lords before the castle courts. The underlying principle of the Code was that freedom was the normal human condition. The economic impact on medium-sized noble estates, most of which needed unpaid labour to remain viable, could well have been terminal. Just as worrying to spokesmen of the provincial szlachta were the social implications of granting such novel rights to a poverty-stricken peasantry that over the generations had become suspicious, contrary, addicted to alcohol, and sunk in ignorance and superstition. On this point they shared Rousseau's pessimism about the fitness of Poland's serfs for liberty.

Given the torrent of criticism from the sejmiks of 1778, consideration of the Zamoyski Code was postponed until the following sejm. The sejm of 1780 rejected the Code once and for all. In scenes that shocked the 'enlightened' minority, many otherwise co-operative royalist envoys joined in the shredding and trampling of copies. This sejm also saw the public disgrace of Antoni Tyzenhauz. The chastened king once again trimmed back his reformist ambitions in the political arena.

The new decade brought a shift in European geopolitics. Catherine II and Joseph II discreetly concluded an alliance in 1781. The ground had already been prepared by Joseph's journey to meet Catherine at Mohylew the previous year, but they waited until after the death of Maria Theresa, which occurred on 29 November 1780. Their Imperial Majesties sealed their agreement with an initially secret exchange of letters, which avoided tricky questions of precedence. The ageing and toothless Frederick II, once he discovered that he had been jilted by Catherine, again felt isolated and insecure. After having assiduously wooed the tsaritsa in the early 1760s, he had sought to restrain rather than encourage her designs on the Ottoman Empire. However, following her triumphs of 1768–74, Catherine's imagination had been fired by Potemkin's 'Greek plan'. This aimed ultimately at placing her second grandson on the throne of a renewed Byzantine empire. His baptismal name of Constantine was not coincidental. Potemkin angled for a 'Kingdom of Dacia' for himself in Wallachia and Moldavia. Joseph was up for a joint venture, even if it meant undermining the Habsburg–Bourbon alliance. In this respect as well, St Petersburg was reverting to the system of Elizabeth's reign.

For the moment, however, the implications for the Commonwealth were opaque. In the autumn of 1781, Stanisław August took out a long-term insurance policy by travelling to Volhynia, in order to meet the heir to the Russian throne and his wife. Thinly disguised as the Comte and Comtesse du Nord, they were undertaking a voyage to several European countries – significantly not including Prussia. However, while the Grand Duke Paul appreciated his welcome in Poland, he wielded no influence on his mother's foreign policy. Her thanks to the king were coolly conventional. Moreover, he was the pupil of Nikita Panin, whose long career ended that year.[24] Panin's departure exposed Stackelberg. With Branicki married to Potemkin's niece, Stackelberg's anxiety, shared by the king, that Catherine would replace him with an ambassador better disposed towards the opposition magnates seemed well-founded. Still more disturbing were rumours that Potemkin, who liked to keep his options open, had approached Frederick II regarding another partition of the Commonwealth. Yet neither scenario came to pass.

The domestic political stalemate continued, but with the king allowed to remain in possession of more of the chessboard than the opposition. Writing to the Polish envoy in St Petersburg in French and *en clair*, so the message would get through, Stanisław August avowed: 'I only want the good, and after God, I count on Catherine II'.[25] He sometimes persuaded Stackelberg to support the idea of confederating the sejm. However, the incentive – a stable, moderate party oriented towards Russia – failed to sway the empress. Catherine II, through her ambassador, would generally allow the king majorities and tolerate apparently minor improvements, but she was always ready to check him with the opposition. So the five 'free' sejms held between 1778 and 1786 were subject to the requirement of unanimity for 'matters of state'. The consequences were that 'we would need a miracle, therefore, for there to be unanimous consent to make the laws necessary to expand our forces and improve our government'.[26]

As for Russia's new ally, the Julius affair had shown both the potential and the limits of Austrian pressure. With his alliance in the bag, Joseph II had no incentive to encourage the 'Galician party' to cause (too much) trouble in the Commonwealth. He was able, however, to advance his own agenda regarding the Catholic Church. This included rearranging dioceses so that they corresponded to the new frontiers of the Austrian Monarchy. He seized his opportunity when a storm blew up over the Bishop of Cracow.

Kajetan Sołtyk had returned from his captivity in Russia as a hero in 1773, but he soon fell into depression. For almost eight years he rarely emerged from his palace in Cracow, leaving the government of the diocese in the capable hands of the archdeacon. Józef Olechowski had risen from a burgher background after being talent-spotted by the bishop in his saner years. He pursued the goals of enlightened Catholicism: a better-educated, better-disciplined parish clergy, and sober worship. For example, he prohibited the faithful from throwing oats at the parish priest every 26 December, in commemoration of the stoning of St Stephen (this custom must have been fun for the parishioners, but it was not unknown for real stones to be cast at less popular priests). The Cracow curia also had to contend with vexatious decrees issued by the Austrian state authorities concerning the part of the diocese located south of the River Vistula. Partly to secure support against this pressure, during a more lucid interlude in 1775 Sołtyk made Michał Poniatowski his coadjutor with the right of succession.

So matters continued until the tail-end of 1781. Sołtyk started once again to host entertainments and make prodigious bequests. His appalled relatives – apart from one favoured nephew – saw their inheritance draining away. Meanwhile, the re-energized bishop took umbrage against an ambitious clergyman of whom we shall hear much, much more: Hugo Kołłątaj. The latter had quarrelled with the cathedral chapter, which appealed to the bishop. When Sołtyk ruled against Kołłątaj, the latter, as rector of Cracow University, appealed against the bishop – the university's chancellor – to the Commission of National Education. Sołtyk promptly excommunicated Kołłątaj, but he also publicly abused the canons and prelates in vulgar and violent language. The chapter repeatedly appealed to Poniatowski for help, but the bishop-coadjutor was reluctant to step in. Perhaps he wished to avoid aggravating relations with Vienna, strained by the Julius affair. He changed his mind when he learned that Sołtyk was planning to cross the Vistula and conduct a visitation of the Galician part of the diocese. This was partly a question of money: the still enormous revenues would have been payable to the bishop abroad. Moreover, such a step might give the emperor a pretext to divide the diocese immediately, rather than waiting for Sołtyk's death. The Permanent Council agreed to Poniatowski's request to provide a detachment of troops, with whose assistance the chapter of Cracow confined their bishop in the diocesan seminary. At the chapter's request, the bishop-coadjutor assumed the government of the diocese – confirmed in May by the pope. Sołtyk's wits were evidently addled, but to many he remained a national hero. He had recently augmented his popularity by personally administering the last rites and distributing alms. Some Cracovians even attempted to rescue their bishop. The situation troubled the king and his younger brother.

A question of jurisdiction arose – ecclesiastical or secular? Nuncio Archetti appointed two bishops to his own commission. One was the newly minted Bishop of Chełm, Maciej Garnysz. The other was Antoni Okęcki, Bishop of Poznań and Crown grand chancellor. Fear of a clerical stitch-up contributed to the reaction of the opposition magnates to events. Some of them saw an opportunity to embarrass the brothers Poniatowski, and criticized the Permanent Council for supposedly exceeding its competencies. At the monarch's request, it appointed a commission to examine the bishop's health and to make arrangements for his estates. Among the six commissioners was Okęcki. After a wobbly start, the officers of God and Caesar complemented each other. Garnysz presided over the ecclesiastical court which prudently found the canons and prelates guilty of conduct unbecoming towards their bishop (he should have been held in his palace, not the seminary). They were sent on monastic retreat for a month and fined. The commissioners confirmed Sołtyk's illness, nominated curators, mostly from among his relatives, and had him looked after in the episcopal palace at Kielce. Sołtyk soon slipped back into 'melancholy'. His last six years were filled with the notes from the orchestra employed to play for him day and night.

At the fractious, fruitless sejm held in the autumn of 1782, opposition envoys and senators denounced the 'despotism' of the Permanent Council and imputed base motives to the king and his brother. They ignored the fact that Michał Poniatowski received but a fraction of the revenues to cover his costs, which he then devoted to charitable and educational purposes. Sołtyk's curators received the rest. The monies accumulated, to the benefit of his heirs. The magnates and their clients huffed and puffed. They prevented the king from tending his garden ('behold a lost sejm!' he exclaimed),[27] but they could not blow down his house. When the sejm closed, the would-be oligarchs were still out in the cold. They shivered the following year, when Stanisław Lubomirski died. His successor as grand marshal of the Crown, Michał Jerzy Mniszech, was married to the king's favourite niece Urszula. They liked to celebrate their entwined ancestries in the dynastic displays of their residences, but this cultured aristocrat was well travelled and enlightened, usually of like mind to the monarch. Alas, he had a weak speaking voice.

Joseph II, with an eye on Russia, had failed to back the opposition during 'Sołtyk's sejm'. Instead, he had taken advantage of the bishop's incarceration to establish a new ecclesiastical authority for the Galician part of the diocese of Cracow. To gain recognition, he piled pressure on Pius VI, who had journeyed to Vienna in 1782, hoping to persuade the emperor to row back on his ecclesiastical reforms. Enthusiastic crowds had greeted the pontiff, before Joseph made a return visit to Rome two years later. The emperor pressed ahead with his programme – dubbed 'Josephism' by posterity – but generally maintained the proprieties towards the Holy See.[28] Clergy whose benefices remained in the Commonwealth but whose properties lay in Galicia were starved of funds. In 1785 Poniatowski saved what he could. The Convention of Vienna stemmed the flow of revenue to Galician churches and provided one-off compensation for lost funds. Poniatowski assigned some of the money to Cracow University. The pope erected the new diocese of Tarnów the following year.

In retrospect, the sejm of 1784 marked a high point of sorts for Stanisław August. It was the first sejm during his reign to respect the law passed in 1673 which reserved every third sejm to the Grand Duchy of Lithuania. The monarch enjoyed an extended progress to Grodno, visiting fifty noble residences. Very few opposition candidates were elected to this relatively untroubled sejm, which, among other things, authorized the Permanent Council to negotiate the best possible terms for the burgeoning Black Sea trade. A loan was approved to pay off the king's debts, to be redeemed over ten years through the annual *subsidium charitativum* of 700,000 złotys paid by the Catholic clergy of both rites. Afterwards, these revenues would go to the army. Nobody could then have foreseen the consequences of this arrangement.

The ambassadorial-royal duopoly became a three-way relationship when Michał Poniatowski ascended to the primacy, which fell vacant on 26 August 1784 (Plate 16). Stanisław August nominated his brother in the Permanent Council on 9 October, a nomination confirmed by Pius VI on 14 February 1785. On becoming Archbishop of Gniezno, Poniatowski resigned his co-adjutorship of Cracow, but kept the administration. His hopes of repeating the feat – almost three centuries earlier – of another royal brother, Cardinal Frederick Jagiellon, in holding the two dioceses simultaneously, were put on hold. When the time came, Poniatowski expected to gain the necessary dispensations from the *incompatibilitas* enshrined in the laws of Church and Commonwealth. The Holy See was not minded to refuse him. Poniatowski was not principally concerned with the revenues, but with the political influence he could exercise across three palatinates. He also wished to continue as acting chancellor of Cracow University.

The Russian ambassador had insisted that the new primate resign the co-adjutorship of Cracow. Stackelberg was rumoured to be jealous of being outshone by Poniatowski. In a somewhat provocative poem written for Poniatowski's entry into Warsaw for the sejm of 1786, Canon Jan Paweł Woronicz recalled the triumphant entry of Hetman Stanisław Żółkiewski into Warsaw in 1611 after he had crushed a Muscovite army and captured Tsar Vasilii Shuiskii and his brothers. Woronicz likened the light now being shone by the brothers – descendants of the Jagiellons who personified the alliance of Church and nation – to the celestial rays of the inseparable 'two suns': the twins Castor and Pollux. Glory, prosperity and harmony would surely return to Poland through their conjoined wisdom and virtue.[29] The first few years of Poniatowski's primacy marked the apogee of the Stanislavian alliance between throne and altar.

Even after the partition settlement, the King of Poland still controlled a reservoir of ecclesiastical patronage. Stanisław August persuaded the Holy See to grant him the right to nominate two new abbots *in commendam* (of the Cistercian foundations of Ląd and Bledzew) in compensation for the loss to Austria of the Benedictine abbey of Tyniec. The partition had deprived the Commonwealth of four sees – the archbishopric of Lwów and the bishopric of Przemyśl to the Habsburg Monarchy; the prince-bishopric of Warmia and the bishopric of Chełmno to Prussia. The Bishop of Smolensk, whose diocese of three enormous parishes was absorbed by Russia, became a titular hierarch residing in Warsaw. Jurisdiction was ceded to the administrator, Stanisław Siestrzeńcewicz. Catherine II later made this talented and ambitious priest Archbishop of Mohylew, responsible for all the Catholics in the Russian Empire. He allowed neither the finer points of canon law nor sentiment for Poland to impede his rapid ascent. In the early 1780s Rome reluctantly sanctioned the new state of affairs. By this time many Uniate parishes had been 'reclaimed' for Orthodoxy; Siestrzeńcewicz did what he could to facilitate individual transfers from the Ruthenian to the Latin rite.[30] The new frontiers split most of the Commonwealth's other dioceses, forcing their bishops into uneasy relationships with new political masters regarding the parishes 'beyond the cordon'.

From 1775 the Permanent Council presented the king with three candidates for senators, including bishops. In practice Stackelberg allowed the king to nominate most of them, occasionally protecting those most loyal to Russia. The lazy, servile Stefan Giedroyć was thus translated from Livonia to Samogitia in

1781. This paved the way for the ambassador's particular friend, Józef Kossakowski, to become Bishop of Livonia. Following the loss of Polish Livonia to Russia by the partition, this diocese now consisted of ten parishes in Courland and the Pilten district. The latter consisted of three enclaves in the west of Courland, former episcopal domain lands, whose noble families steered a prudent course between the rival claims of the bishops of Livonia and the dukes of Courland. Kossakowski unsuccessfully lobbied for a suffragan to carry out these undemanding duties, while he competed for further benefices. Recognizing his limited prospects of succeeding in the near future to either of the two endowed Lithuanian sees of Wilno and Samogitia, he set his sights on bishoprics in the Polish Crown.

On the whole, however, the quality of the Latin episcopate improved in these years. The king promoted several noblemen from modest or even poor noble families who had proved their worth as auditors, officials and suffragans. When Gabriel Podoski died in 1777, Stackelberg insisted that the primacy go to Antoni Ostrowski – a reliable servant of Russia since 1763.[31] Dogged by ill-health, Ostrowski made little impact on the archdiocese of Gniezno, but his elevation opened one of the better-endowed bishoprics – Włocławek – to the young and energetic Józef Rybiński. In 1780 Antoni Okęcki succeeded the corrupt Andrzej Młodziejowski as Bishop of Poznań. This diocese – the oldest in Poland – included the territorially separated archdeaconry of Warsaw, which meant that the bishop played a leading role in the life of the city and the court. Okęcki, who soon afterwards also became grand chancellor of the Crown, was respected for his integrity and fairmindedness. He was an honest broker in the conflict dividing Warsaw's Lutherans. However, the Russian ambassador supported his nobly born co-religionists against their burgher adversaries. By 1786 Okęcki had had enough of Stackelberg and resigned the great seal. The clergyman who then became vice-chancellor had also succeeded Okęcki – again after a short interlude – as Bishop of Chełm in 1781: Maciej Garnysz. A diminutive snuff-addict, Garnysz loyally served the king and conscientiously carried out his duties, despite his sparse episcopal revenues.

The distant diocese of Kiev benefited from the pastoral care – first as co-adjutor, and then from 1785 as bishop-ordinary – of the wise and mild Kasper Cieciszowski. Two supporters of the Bar confederacy, Adam Krasiński and Feliks Turski, resided in their dioceses of Kamieniec and Łuck respectively, without over-exerting themselves. The greatest impact was made by Michał Poniatowski. Destined by his family for the Church, he was 'not very animated by the spirit of the estate which he professes', as Visconti put it.[32] Poniatowski finally agreed to become Bishop of Płock in 1773. He was elevated to the primacy in 1785 while retaining the administration of Cracow he had taken on in 1782. His co-adjutor and successor in Płock was the learned Krzysztof Szembek. This scion of the Commonwealth's premier episcopal dynasty had contributed to the Zamoyski Code, without endorsing its ecclesiastical provisions.

Poniatowski, Rybiński and – with some reservations – Ignacy Massalski, Bishop of Wilno since 1762, provided a distinct kind of ecclesiastical leadership. This model of 'enlightened Catholicism' has sometimes been applied, perhaps too generally, to the Stanislavian episcopate as a whole. Political and ecclesiastical zeal did not necessarily go hand in hand. The dedicated Cieciszowski was largely apolitical, while neither Giedroyć nor Krasiński, at opposite ends of the political spectrum, were martyrs to their pastoral duties. Poniatowski visited each of his three dioceses – Płock, Cracow and Gniezno – just once. Yet although preoccupied by affairs of state and resident in Warsaw, he and several other bishops were energetic administrators and reformers. They were assisted by industrious, modestly born prelates who were often marked out as future bishops-ordinary. One such was Wojciech Skarszewski, who became Bishop of Chełm in 1790 having been auditor to Rybiński in Włocławek. These were the staff officers who conducted the intensified general visitations and read the obligatory reports sent in by the rural deans. The latter were charged with annual parish visitations.

One of the principal problems encountered by episcopal reformers was pluralism – the simultaneous tenure of several benefices. The best-connected clergymen accumulated not only the choicest morsels – abbeys, canonries and prelatures – but also the more valuable parishes. Such men could pay for the dispensations required by the Tridentine decrees on residence and make themselves useful to monarchical, episcopal or aristocratic patrons. Although the proportion of nobly born resident parish priests seems to have risen in the later eighteenth century, much parish work was still done by men of plebeian birth: execrably paid vicars, poorer incumbents and mendicant friars.

The eastern reaches of the Commonwealth were missionary territory for the Latin rite. Vast parishes spreading over hundreds or even thousands of square kilometres were often consigned to religious orders. This raised the tricky question of the orders' subordination to diocesan bishops in respect of parish work. While this relationship was evidently necessary, some bishops were irritated by questing friars. Poniatowski complained to their provincials about:

> . . . the sending out of friars far from their residences, and in particular for collections, in distraction of the spirit, and other improprieties, such as vain babble, base flattery, gossip and vilification, sowing discord between houses, sometimes importunate and offensive demands for alms, spreading various oddities, fears, falsely strange things (and most distressingly, sometimes supposedly for devotion) and such like; often even worse deeds have habitually been committed many times. Because even the best people, when removed from discipline and closer supervision, often change and are ruined.[33]

Persistent problems were presented by itinerant or vagrant clergymen, some of whom were sexual predators, thieves, drunks or brawlers. More numerous, however, were those clergymen who had not had the good fortune to have been presented to an adequate living by a patron and had taken to the road. Ecclesiastical courts were kept busy by disciplinary cases, and episcopal prisons were rarely empty.

In their efforts to raise standards among the diocesan clergy, reforming bishops altered the curricula in enlarged diocesan seminaries. They often entrusted these to the Priests of the Mission – whose Warsaw seminary had formed Poniatowski and other prominent clergymen. Such bishops prescribed edificatory readings and model homilies, and issued reams of salutary pastoral instructions. Poniatowski published four volumes of ordinances, both as a digest for his successor in Płock and as a model for other dioceses, but his well-meaning advice sometimes provoked mirth: for example, his injunction to parishioners to prevent their children from eating unripe fruit. Poniatowski's endeavours to end the ringing of church bells to ward off thunderbolts, and encourage the installation of lightning conductors, were not always appreciated.[34]

The new model parish priests expected to be moulded by the reformed seminaries were also described in two didactic novels written by bishops – Ignacy Krasicki and Józef Kossakowski. The latter claimed that he had drawn on his own experience as a parish priest. The episcopal novelists praised the straightforward teaching of the Gospel and the Commandments. They satirized the baroque pulpit repertoire of emotional histrionics, wild gesticulations, Latin incrustations, theological disquisitions, metaphysical speculations and confessional polemics. Priests should also refrain from setting sinners ascetic, flesh-mortifying penances in the confessional. Mutual forbearance, social harmony, stability and honest labour were the watchwords.

The latter priority sometimes involved campaigning against the worst abuses of serfdom and for the elementary education of peasant children. Two outstanding preachers, Michał Karpowicz and Wilhelm Kaliński, were beneficed in the vast diocese of Wilno. They belonged to Bishop Massalski's rather worldly circle. In this elegant company, not only the plainer worship, or *divozione regolata* propagated by the learned Neapolitan, Reverend Lodovico Muratori, but also the ideas of the French *économistes*, known as Physiocrats, were discussed. Given the physiocratic convictions that land was the basis of all wealth, and that humans could be educated to be virtuous, the rural parishes of Lithuania must have seemed an ideal *tabula rasa* for enlightened experiments. For a few years Massalski sought to spread elementary schooling, for girls as well as boys, with initially impressive results. Before his enthusiasm had waned, the papal jubilee of 1775, celebrated the following year in the diocese of Wilno, gave Karpowicz the opportunity to preach a series of sermons in which (among some less controversial messages) he expounded on the evils of serfdom. These sermons were printed and reprinted, but made him enemies as well as friends.

Kaliński tried to explain the distinction between 'liberty' and 'licence' to the denizens of an exemplary rural community created by Canon Paweł Brzostowski in his parishes and hereditary estates. The reforms began with the granting of a statute in 1769. Brzostowski's peasants were entitled to leave their farms if they could find a replacement and to appeal against the lord's judgments to the starosta's court. Their labour services were commuted to cash rents. They were even organized into a uniformed militia and an assembly charged with some tasks of self-government. The best farmers were rewarded, the worst named and shamed. The schoolteacher received the relatively generous annual salary of 500 złotys. Brzostowski publicized his reforms, but his neighbours were sceptical, even suspicious of his initiatives. The best testimonies are the peasant militiamen's involvement in the 1794 rising, and the subsequent suppression of his self-governing innovations by the Russian Empire.

Brzostowski's little 'Commonwealth' was exceptional. We should ask what actually changed in most parishes. One reform with unavoidable impact was the reduction in 1775 by Pius VI, at the request of the Polish-Lithuanian bishops, of the number of holy days. For most parishioners that meant more time spent working in the fields, mill or smithy, or at the loom.[35] The reduction did not apply to the Ruthenian rite. The sejmik of Nowogródek complained that the 'Lithuanian province, settled with a greater number of serfs of the Ruthenian rite, from this experiences injury and loss, and days intended for holy observance in the Ruthenian rite are often violated'. It wanted the Commonwealth to ask the Holy See to equalize not only the number of Uniate feasts and fasts, but also the calendar, with the Latin rite.[36]

Another tangible change was the abolition – in some dioceses – of many devotional confraternities and their replacement by less popular confraternities of charity. Reformers believed that the spectacular practice of collective flagellation by hooded confraternities brought religion into disrepute. The practice ceased at the Church of the Holy Cross in Warsaw in 1762, and over the following decades it became rarer in country districts, until at the end of the century it was recalled as a curiosity.[37]

It became much harder for village communities to lynch persons – almost always women – suspected of sorcery. The sejm formally abolished the death penalty for witchcraft in 1776, following a choreographed intervention by Stanisław August. Some although not all bishops frowned on abusive behaviour towards 'infidels', 'schismatics' and 'heretics'. They disciplined priests who baptized Jewish children without their parents' consent. Such hierarchs were generally inclined to permit non-Catholic communities to repair or even build churches, synagogues and mosques. An important turning point was the acquittal by a court presided over by Chancellor Młodziejowski, in 1775, of thirteen Jews accused of the ritual murder of a three-year-old girl from a Mazovian village, because their mutually contradictory confessions had been obtained by torture. The case for the defence, which was put together by an international network of Jews and enlightened sympathizers, also drew attention to the medical evidence, the date of the Passover in 1774, and the disbelief expressed by many popes and Polish monarchs that Jews made ritual use of Christian blood.[38] The following year, in 1776, the same law which ended the capital punishment of sorcerers also abolished judicial torture. The king had a medal struck to commemorate this triumph of enlightenment.

Among the better educated, we may detect a shift over several decades in the perception of ghosts and apparitions – from a real threat to mildly scary entertainment. So testifies the poet Franciszek Karpiński:

> Our father told of how St Joseph from his picture, which was in the room, pronounced the word 'Virtue!'. On Christmas Eve, and also after midnight, he saw the Most Holy Virgin in the sky dressed in a yellow *robe ronde*, he saw

> a spectre; he showed us many vagrants who had been possessed by the Devil; he told many stories about bewitched people and harvests; about those who yielded themselves up to devils; about witches on broomsticks flying out through chimneys for the Bald Mountain. He told of sleepwalkers, who, when touched accidentally at night through a crack by moonlight, went out through that crack on a ray of moonlight. He blindly believed in prognostications, according to the planet under which someone had been born; and he was happy to receive at home vagrant Gipsy women, who told fortunes from palms, eyes and from beans cast on a table or from melted wax poured onto water. Our fathers, like the ancient Greeks and Romans, saw almost everything in imaginary miracles; the greater the belief in and fear of superstition in those times, the more we laugh at them today.[39]

However, persons of all ranks continued to be susceptible to astrologers, fortune tellers and charlatans. Warsaw's high society was as gullible as any in Europe – as the case of 'Count Cagliostro' demonstrates. This fraudster's real name was Giuseppe Balsamo. He arrived in Warsaw in 1780 after he had been expelled from the imperial court in St Petersburg. Stanisław August kept his distance from this aspirant *magus*, but many aristocrats and burghers were fooled by Cagliostro's feats of healing and alchemy. Their secrets supposedly lay in the hermetic mysteries of ancient Egyptian masonic lore. After a few weeks one of his tricks was exposed and the 'count' departed in haste. So much for an eighteenth-century 'age of reason'?

Most historians tend to be more interested in change than continuity. In this case, debate has been conducted between those who have largely welcomed the less sensual, less confrontational style of religion that was advancing in the later eighteenth century, and those who have deplored the cooling of religious ardour among elites. Some have lamented the curtailing of traditional practices, such as Poniatowski's unsuccessful attempts to ban Christmas cribs and Easter graves. These remain much-loved parts of Polish religious practice to this day, even among occasional churchgoers. To some extent these reactions have reflected their authors' differing attitudes towards the transformation of modern Catholicism in the wake of the Second Vatican Council. It is possible to read Poniatowski's ordinances or Massalski's pastoral letters through that prism and find what one is looking for. A bold attempt to investigate what really changed at parish level has led Stanisław Witecki to detect a greater readiness in some dioceses to preach simple Christian morality in stripped-down language. It did not entail an embrace of Enlightenment concepts of the natural world. This pattern, he argues, slowed down the alienation of the rural masses from the ecclesiastical elites for which 'Catholic Enlightenment' has often been reproached.[40]

Vocations to the religious clergy of both sexes may well have fallen in the years after the first partition. They certainly became rarer among the wealthier szlachta. The king thought that most orders purveyed ignorance and fanaticism – but he exempted the teaching orders from his strictures. Several bishops agreed. Krasicki's gentle satires on 'reverend stupidity' in his mock-epic poem *Monachomachia* provoked protests after its publication in 1778. Adam Krasiński was scathing about slothful and greedy monks when Franciscan and Dominican buildings in Kamieniec Podolski obstructed his plans to strengthen the defences of the citadel: 'no gob (*gęba*) is more useless than a monkish one,' he replied to Katarzyna Kossakowska whom the friars had asked to intervene on their behalf.[41] The king and the primate egged him on. Successive papal nuncios suspected Poniatowski and other bishops of wishing to subordinate the religious orders to their jurisdiction, at the expense of the provincials, generals and the Apostolic See.

Following the sumptuous wave of ecclesiastical building that crested in the 1760s, the following decades offer fewer treats to lovers of sacral architecture. Even if one does not share one connoisseur's distaste for the 'ice age' of neoclassicism,[42] there are few major works in that style to enjoy. Foremost is the rebuilding of Wilno Cathedral so that it broadly resembled a Greek temple (Plate 21). More typical was the makeover of Poznań Cathedral with an incongruous portico. Most work was on a smaller scale, while some was effectively private. There were exceptions to the trend – the interior of the Bernardine church at Koło in Greater Poland, rebuilt in 1777–83, is as exuberant as any mid-century work. Moreover, in the north-east of the Commonwealth, the mid-century wave crested later. The tapering towers and rippling curves of the late Vilnan baroque gradually settled into squarer and sparer forms. The quantity and quality of building work might suggest that the impact on the mendicant orders of the disrespectful climate of the late eighteenth century was weaker in the Grand Duchy of Lithuania and Crown Ruthenia than in the western and central parts of the Crown. The jovial Bernardine friar continued to be a familiar figure in taverns and manor houses, while the relative accessibility and emotiveness of preaching and worship in Bernardine churches continued to attract (or distract) the parish faithful. It was surely no accident that when Adam Mickiewicz evoked his childhood homeland in *Pan Tadeusz*, he chose a coarse, brown Bernardine habit for the long atonement of the erstwhile rogue Jacek Soplica.

The unbroken vitality of provincial piety is conveyed by the last eighteenth-century coronations of wonder-working images. Such coronations had increasingly become concentrated in Crown Ruthenia (three more were held after 1772 under Habsburg rule on the basis of permissions granted before the partition). Most were instigated by magnate patrons in monastic churches and served to glorify the donor as well as Christ and his Mother. The swansong of this type of coronation took place on 8 September 1773 at Poczajów. One thousand regular clergy of both rites assisted in the ceremonies at the town's Basilian monastery, along with detachments of the Crown army. The number of communicants was recorded as a symbolically significant 33,300. Whatever the actual number who received the sacrament, it was a great many, and most were Uniates.[43] The costs were largely met by the new church's founder, the already legendary Mikołaj Potocki, former starosta of Kaniów, who was spending his last earthly years doing penance for his spectacular sins of violence and the flesh. Living in a wooden manor house within the monastic compound, 'he joined the monks' morning and evening prayers, admonished the more negligent of them, and despite this kept several girls in his manor house for debauchery, waking them up in the morning for the rosary, which he recited with them, and if one of them should laugh during this prayer, he punished her by beating her back with a pipe stem, so that (he would say) she did not offend God'.[44]

Ceremonies of coronation later took place at the Dominican church at Latyczów in Podolia in 1778, the Franciscan church at Międzyrzec Ostrogski in Volhynia in 1779, and the parish church at Szydłów in Samogitia in 1786. These initiatives came from local bishops and prelates. On 8 September 1786 tens of thousands of people converged on the small town of Szydłów for the festivities attending the crowning of the picture of the Madonna of the Snows and the consecration of the new parish church which housed it. Bishop Giedroyć presided, but it was his suffragan who had made the arrangements in Rome, and the cause had been driven forward by his predecessor Bishop Jan Łopaciński, formerly the local parish priest. Rather than simply rely on the leading noble families, contributions were levied on the inhabitants of the diocese.

The coronation of another miraculous image in the Commonwealth was also planned at this time, although it did not take place until 1796. This was the picture of the Holy Family in the collegiate church at Kalisz, whose coronation was approved by Pius VI in 1783. The image's screen represented the pope, along with the king, the primate and representatives of all estates, supplicating St Joseph to intercede on behalf of Poland (Plate 17). The initiator of the coronation was the custodian, Stanisław Kłossowski, who for decades had devoted himself tirelessly to the *cura animarum* of the parishioners, the cult of St Joseph and the adornment of the church. A Silesian doctor schooled by the Jesuits visited Kalisz in 1791. Johann Kausch admired the elderly priest's kindness and humility, but thought the screen was a '*barrocke Karrikatur*' and a '*monumentum religiosiæ stupiditatis*'. Reverend Kłossowski inhabited a different mental and spiritual world to his visitor, but he too encountered great changes in belief and taste. In the book he wrote detailing the 'miracles and graces' worked by the image, published in 1780, he repeated a classic argument of anti-Enlightenment refutational literature: 'people have long since appeared, who call themselves philosophers, deists, libertines, but should really be called godless. Because although they say they believe in GOD, they do not however accept the Religion revealed by GOD at all.'[45] Such godlessness was most audible in Warsaw. So were its presumed consequences.

— SEVEN —
GROWING PAINS

The sad story told by one Marianna Wróblewska, as recorded by an investigator of the marshal's court in Warsaw on 2 June 1788, may not be representative of life in the city, or even wholly accurate, but it is nonetheless instructive. Three years earlier, at the age of eighteen, Wróblewska had left her mother – a (probably illicit) distiller and brewer – and late stepfather on the promise of marriage made by one Dąbrowski, a cook employed by the Potocki family. Having thus come from Poznań to Warsaw, she discovered that Dąbrowski already had a wife. He proceeded to pimp Marianna's services from a rented lodging in the New Town.* When his wife discovered what was going on and threatened to denounce the girl, the latter went into service with an Italian cook, a Mrs Budzyniowa, for three months, before becoming a kept woman. Marianna first took up with an ex-drummer in the guards regiment called Tomaszewski. After a year and a half she moved on to Rutkowski, a former soldier, now a gardener, who lodged her in a house owned by an unnamed captain. Marianna admitted three thefts while in Warsaw: first, a tablecloth, apron and skirt, from an open dwelling, which were subsequently sold in the New Town, but then returned to the owner, a butcher's wife; second, a furred cape espied through an open window, which was abandoned during the escape; third and finally, textiles, gloves, a fan and a coif, which she sold, leading to her present arrest at the instigation of the owner. For the first theft Marianna had been whipped in the city hall of New Warsaw and lost consciousness. She had also been flogged twice in the barracks of the guard regiment for the 'seduction' of Tomaszewski and Rutkowski; again, so severely that she had fainted.[1]

---

* Warsaw was still divided between the Old Town, dating from the fourteenth century, the New Town, founded in the early fifteenth century, and the extensive *jurydyki* and suburbs. The unification of the agglomeration into a single city was work in progress.

This tale of woe is one of hundreds that have survived, told by men and women who had ended up in Warsaw on the wrong side of the law. Among them were Christians and Jews, runaway serfs and petty nobles, vagrants, thieves, forgers, drunken brawlers, harlots and pimps. Some were let off with a warning, others faced punishments of imprisonment, forced labour, flogging, branding and even death. Expelled through one of the city's so-called gates (in reality, movable barriers placed in gaps in the earthen ramparts erected hastily in 1770 against pestilence), they could reappear the following day at another entrance, often to be caught and punished again. Warsaw's elegant and fragrant courtesans were not likely to face the whippings routinely administered to cheaper prostitutes for the amusement of the crowds. Those accused of crimes before the marshal's court came from all parts of the Commonwealth and from abroad, but about half came from the lands around Warsaw. Only a small minority of those accused were born in the city or its suburbs. Most were economic migrants.[2]

The pulling power of Warsaw was extraordinary, given its lowly status in the Commonwealth's secular and ecclesiastical hierarchies. Its Mazovian hinterland was poor, but the city's economic reach extended into international networks of finance and commerce. By the late 1780s Warsaw's population had topped 90,000, having tripled in three decades to become one of the twenty most populous cities in Europe.[3] Travellers noted the building works, the hazardous traffic, the variety and vigour of economic activity, the diversity of the people, and the rank odour of humans and animals. The symbol of the latter problem was the growing dunghill located just below the Royal Castle. Recognized by the authorities as a scandalous health hazard, no practical alternative was found. Despite efforts dating back to the 1730s, few streets and squares were adequately cobbled and drained, so that the city was by turns muddy and dusty, as well as noisome to the senses.

The dark and crowded Old Town and the lower-storeyed New Town still housed many patrician families. Beyond these areas, wider and more imposing streets included the finest thoroughfare of all, Krakowskie Przedmieście (Cracow Suburb). Carriages entered and exited the gated forecourts of the palaces, not only of magnates and princes of the Church, but also of a new plutocratic elite. The latter filtered the mostly Dutch loans that were now financing consumption. Warsaw became a place to make deals. The financiers were led by Piotr Tepper, who expended much time and money in 'proving' his descent from the noble Scots family of Fergusson. Poland's other principal banker and venture capitalist was the aristocratic Antoni Protazy 'Prot' Potocki; the two exemplified elite convergence. Further out from the centre, wealthy noblemen built houses with gardens. Within the 1770 ramparts, fields, meadows and orchards were still plentiful. The extensive gardens that backed onto both the Saxon Palace and the Krasiński Palace (renamed the Palace of the Commonwealth following its purchase to house offices of state) provided Varsovians of diverse rank with opportunities for licit and illicit amusement amidst the verdure and shadows.

The Saxon Palace was now merely the residence of the elector's ageing diplomatic representative, Franz August Essen. As a result the east–west axis laid out under the Wettin kings reverted to the north–south axis running parallel to the Vistula. The near-continuous presence of Stanisław August's court stimulated the city's growth. Early in his reign the king purchased the suburban estate of Ujazdów. These swampy hunting grounds already contained a small bathhouse (*łazienka*), but in the course of a quarter-century the monarch transformed the estate into the glorious Łazienki park and palace. Beyond the city limits, sometimes at several miles' distance, aristocrats also escaped the stink of summer in their exquisite villas and palaces, surrounded by enchanting gardens. Architects such as Simon Gottlieb Zug, Ephraim Schroeger and Christian Piotr Aigner turned the dreams of their aristocratic patrons into stuccoed pilasters and burbling fountains, while the king employed Domenico Merlini and Johann Christian Kamsetzer to realize his visions. The pulling power of Warsaw is suggested by most architects' foreign names.

A similar phenomenon can be observed among the painters. No fewer than 223 painters have been recorded as active in Stanislavian Warsaw, of whom about seventy were closely connected with the royal court. Foreign-born and trained artists often settled down in the city and showed a marked tendency towards cultural and political Polonization. Polish surnames become commoner towards the end of the century. While – as elsewhere in Europe – painters occupied a less elevated place in the social and artistic hierarchy than either architects or composers, their status was rising. They benefited from the high demand from monarch, magnates and lesser patrons for imagery representing Poland – its peoples, landscapes and heroes. By the 1790s both the supply and demand for art were sufficiently well developed to enable painters to survive the loss of royal patronage and live from the market. We can glimpse this nascent art market in one of Bernardo Bellotto's urban prospects (Plate 18): engravings are being displayed on a wall, examined and sold.[4]

The king's ambition to establish an Academy of Fine Arts in Warsaw was never fully realized, but the royal *Atelier* directed by Marcello Bacciarelli (1731–1818) educated dozens of artists and many of their children. In raising painting from a craft to a liberal art, the *Atelier*, sometimes even called an *Akademia*, prepared the ground for the establishment of a chair in painting at the University of Wilno after the third partition. Having been ennobled by the sejm of 1767–68, Bacciarelli held a prestigious and well-remunerated position as the king's first painter. From 1786 he was also the monarch's director of buildings. As Stanisław August's friend, confidant and principal artistic partner, he made enemies. In a scathing caricature, money pours away as the ass-eared Bacciarelli persuades the king to spend yet more on another architectural scheme (Plate 23).

Below the palaces and churches on the well-aired escarpment, a less appealing odour rose from the slums which stretched down to the riverside. These wooden dwellings, workshops and shacks were vulnerable to landslides or flooding, as were similar buildings in Praga on the right bank of the Vistula. For many of the teeming poor here, life was nasty, brutish and short. Among the consequences of the combined effects of unhealthy surroundings, backbreaking toil, grinding poverty and the incessant demand for carnal pleasures were the hundreds of foundlings accepted annually into the Hospital of the Infant Jesus run by the Priests of the Mission – the largest such institution in the Commonwealth. These numbers rose in line with the city's population, from 206 in 1756 to 748 in 1788, although they spiked in times of crisis – the highest figure recorded was 906 in 1795. Another consequence was the terrifying rate of mortality – fewer than a quarter of the admitted infants survived.[5] Yet, as elsewhere in Europe, the faintest possibility of 'rags to riches' sufficed to keep migrants coming to the city. Some were immortalized by Bernardo Bellotto – also known as Canaletto the Younger.

Having been taught by his uncle Giovanni Antonio Canal (Canaletto the elder), who created the definitive images of Venice, Bellotto made his reputation in Dresden and Vienna. He settled in Warsaw from 1767 until his death in 1780. Bellotto was first employed to represent Stanisław August's election on canvas, and he was the only painter to rival Bacciarelli in royal favour. His *vedute* of Warsaw later served the reconstruction from the rubble left by the German army in 1944. Bellotto depicted the city when it was already populous, bustling and full of scaffolding, but not yet the metropolis it would become by the end of the 1780s. Despite his use of the *camera obscura* and the unvarying, cool, clear light, his works are not 'objective' documentaries. He improved compositions by shifts in placement and scale, while the choice of depicted residences emphasized the monarch's family connections. He did paint views of some recently rebuilt monastic churches with prominent royal or aristocratic founders, but he kept gothic churches and the Old Town at a safe distance. Nevertheless, Bellotto shows us Warsaw's chimney-sweeps at work (Plate 19). They are my stars in a cast of labourers, beggars, hawkers, market traders, craftsmen, carters, cowherds, servants, soldiers, clergy, Jews, burghers, their wives and daughters, military men, ladies and noblemen. Without Bellotto's sensitivity to ordinary folk going about their daily business, Stanislavian Warsaw would be far more remote from us.

Powerful push-factors were also at work. Warsaw's burgeoning population was but one consequence of growth elsewhere. Another was the rising number of vagrants in the countryside, which increasingly disturbed the szlachta. It is not possible precisely to plot the continuing demographic recovery. However, working backwards from a figure of about 8.6 million for the truncated Commonwealth, calculated from the incomplete 1789–90 census, most historical demographers still posit a figure of around 7.7 million immediately after the first partition. They have not accepted a plausible re-computation of the data, yielding figures of about 10 million in 1791 and 9 million in 1773. The increase in population was unevenly spread. One startling estimate for the Grand Duchy of Lithuania has its population rise from 2.66 million in 1775 to 3.61 million in 1790. This would be about as much as the generally accepted increase for the entire Commonwealth. Within the Crown, growth was fastest in the south-east.[6]

Nobles multiplied more rapidly than the population as a whole. There may have been three-quarters of a million of them by 1790, about as many as the still faster-growing Jewish population.[7] Rising agricultural prices and political stability brought a measure of prosperity to nobles of middling means. Landowners in the Ukraine faced Russian depredations, but they could export grain and livestock via the new Black Sea port of Kherson. In these parts of the Commonwealth at least, the wealthiest magnates became even richer.

For the Commonwealth to take full advantage of its trading opportunities, improved communications were required. During the royal progress through the south-west of the Grand Duchy of Lithuania in 1784, Stanisław August saw the expanding network of canals, bridges and roads which were opening up the wetlands of Polesie. At Horodec he inspected a section of a canal which already had four locks and which was soon to link the rivers Muchawiec and Pina. It would ultimately connect the Baltic with the Black Sea via the Bug and the

Vistula, and the Pripet and Dnieper. The potential of this link had been demonstrated earlier that year, when Mateusz Butrymowicz, then judge of the Pińsk castle court, had sent ten canoes all the way to Warsaw. Each was paddled by three archaically attired denizens of the marshes. Local produce, such as honey, mushrooms, wax and tallow, was promptly sold on landing and the flotilla then returned home. Having viewed this exotic spectacle, the king decided to visit the canal. The sejm of 1773–75 had authorized its construction, but the work had proceeded in fits and starts.[8]

'It really seemed to us that we were in Holland,' recorded Bishop Naruszewicz in the official diary of the royal journey of 1784. The ongoing transformation of marsh into pasture, he noted, benefited the local citizenry (most of whom, in the Latin-rite parish of Horodec, bore the surname of either Horehlad or Litwinowicz).[9] At a gala reception in a tented hall, erected in a grove outside Pińsk, illuminations and verses celebrated the route from sea to sea created by the dredging of straight, free-flowing channels through the reeds and sluggish pools. From Pińsk, Stanisław August drove out along Butrymowicz's new 'Volhynian road', carried on causeways across the wetlands, to the family's model estate. He admired dams, ditches, mills, livestock and singing and dancing peasants (who, as Naruszewicz noted in a passage omitted from the published diary, had been encouraged by liberally distributed vodka and beer to show their enthusiasm).[10] The following day, however, the royal party's attempt to sail along a section of Hetman Ogiński's canal faltered in the mud. This canal, begun in 1767 to link the Jasiołda, a tributary of the Pripet, with the Szczara, a tributary of the Niemen, needed widening and deepening.[11] Despite this setback, the king highlighted the progress he had seen in a speech to the sejm in Grodno (Plate 15).[12]

Canals notwithstanding, most of the expansion in the rural economy was quantitative rather than qualitative. Land uncultivated since the mid-seventeenth century was being ploughed. Few landowners experimented with crop rotations or enclosures; fewer still profited from such innovations. Many noble families found themselves under pressure. Partible inheritance weakened the position of those with several children: hence an increased willingness in old houses to marry fortunes made in trade. The rarity of epidemics also helped to fill up the countryside with educated young noblemen with little to inherit. Many sought employment in the law courts, officialdom, the army or the Catholic Church of both rites. Opportunities at magnates' courts were shrinking, as many indebted aristocrats preferred private comforts to public display. Other impecunious nobles sought to live from their wits and pens, or to make a living in trade, even risking their families' noble status. They often sought their fortunes in Warsaw – but sometimes fell by the wayside. Many came from Mazovia, Podlasie and the nearer parts of the Grand Duchy of Lithuania. These lands' characteristic *zaścianki* – villages off the beaten track inhabited by noble families – were becoming overpopulated, while their inhabitants' aspirations were rising. Some of the social origins of the nineteenth-century Polish intelligentsia may be sought on the gently meandering banks of the rivers Narew, Biebrza, Bug and Niemen during the reign of Stanisław August. However, many of those who moved to Warsaw hoped to return to their diminutive family seats and restore them to an imagined former glory. After the city's hammering in the mid-1790s, that is where many of them went, although rarely with the hoped-for fortunes.[13]

For the moment, few of the nobles drawn to Warsaw or other cities became urban citizens, despite the relaxation in 1776 of the derogation laws. Very few of peasant stock made the cut – they were more likely to swell the ranks of the footloose urban poor, scratching a living from casual labour, crime or begging. Jews were ineligible to apply. Although they were barred from residence in Warsaw except during a sejm, Jews were allowed to live, work and trade in the noble and ecclesiastical *jurydyki* on both sides of the river. Many did so; some prospered, others battled destitution. Of the new arrivals accepted as citizens of Old Warsaw, over nine-tenths were already of burgher status. Among these new citizens a growing number were from Royal Prussia and the Reich.[14] Evidently many German-speaking professionals, merchants and craftsmen found Warsaw a more congenial and liberating place in which to live and do business than the heavily taxed and intrusively regulated towns of the Hohenzollern monarchy. The abolition in 1767–68 of legal restrictions on non-Catholic Christians settling in Warsaw (and in other cities) accelerated the trend. Warsaw's Lutheran community constructed an impressive neo-classical church. The foundation stone was laid in 1777 and the completed church was inaugurated in 1781 – on both occasions with pomp and ceremony. It became an attraction for locals and visitors, who liked to climb to the lantern of the dome to admire the best view of the city.[15]

Many other towns and cities in the Commonwealth shared, albeit more modestly, in the phenomenon of urban growth. Within a few years of the partition, Cracow's trading patterns had adjusted to the new situation, and growth resumed in production, consumption and population. As in Cracow, most of Wilno's expansion occurred in its suburbs, but the Lithuanian capital sustained an even livelier cultural scene – especially during sessions of the Tribunal. Wilno's growing pains are suggested by the rising numbers of baptisms of illegitimate children – first in parish churches, and then in the foundling Hospital of the Infant Jesus which opened in 1791. In 1783 a long-awaited court judgment recognized that the Jews were too numerous to be confined to certain quarters of the city, as a 1633 privilege had specified. They could henceforth buy property and reside anywhere except on the 'royal route' from the 'Sharp Gate' (*Ostra Brama*) to the cathedral, and on the street leading to the Troki gate. Their existing properties on those streets were safeguarded. Discriminatory taxation and restrictions on business were abolished, and the *kahal* was entrusted with even more responsibility than hitherto – much to its satisfaction.

A hint of the vitality of town life elsewhere in the Grand Duchy of Lithuania is given by the tax records of 1775 and 1790. Of the royal, ecclesiastical and privately owned settlements noted, seventy were classed as towns and 457 as small towns. Most of the latter were still very rural: the pretext for the sejm of 1776 to remove rights of self-government from all but eleven royal towns. These survivors successfully lobbied to keep their rights to own landed estates. Hearth tax data (a hearth meant an individual dwelling in Lithuania, as opposed to a chimney in the Crown) suggest that the urban population of the Grand Duchy may have climbed to half a million by 1790. The number of hearths counted in Kowno rose from 222 to 540. So many Lutherans and Calvinists arrived from Prussia that the town's elderly Roman Catholic parish priest worried that 'heretical errors' might infect some of his flock – employed by the newcomers as domestic servants. Far to the south-east, Mozyrz posted a steepling increase from 100 to 243 hearths. However, most increases were more modest. Karol Radziwiłł's Słuck, for example, with 809 hearths in 1775, grew at the rate of just one hearth per year, despite the royal permission for a four-weekly fair granted in 1782. Picturesque Troki grew from 102 to 109 hearths; this soporific small town, with its Karaite community, was periodically woken up by a sejmik.[16]

Still faster growth in the urban population, not least of Jews, occurred in the south-east of the Crown, where private towns predominated. The munificence of their magnate proprietors was celebrated in panegyrics declaimed on feast-days. Less sycophantically, rising civic pride in self-governing royal towns was expressed in new or restored municipal buildings, from Żytomierz to Poznań.

The Renaissance-era city hall of Poznań was remodelled in 1781–83. Kazimierz Raczyński, chairman of the city's commission 'of good order' established in 1779, obtained a total of 50,000 złotys from the Crown treasury to this end. The facades and interiors expressed in historical guise a programme of social reform, economic prosperity, cultural and intellectual flowering, strong royal authority and military prowess. The renovated building was topped with a new tower, which became more neo-classical in style as it soared to a monopter and obelisk, topped by an eagle in flight. This startling design is ascribed to the avant-garde Warsaw architect Ephraim Schroeger, but more building work in the city was carried out by Anton Höhne, who hailed from the borders of Bohemia and Saxony. He had earlier worked for Kazimierz Raczyński, and had designed Poznań's impressive Lutheran church, built between 1777 and 1786, as well as the new buildings for the castle court. The royal architect Johann Christian Kamsetzer designed the new guardhouse, built on the market square in 1786–87. Its martial Doric colonnade was surmounted by the coats of arms of the city and the Raczyński family, flanking that of the King and Commonwealth, whose fame was trumpeted to the world. The building proclaimed that the path to prosperity and orderly liberty was through the close co-operation of burghers, nobles and monarch (Plate 20).

The city of Poznań moved towards the integration of its *jurydyki*, suburbs and outlying villages into a single urban organism under its commission *boni ordinis*. Raczyński, the starosta-general, a member of the Permanent Council, court marshal of the Crown and the head of the royalist party in Greater Poland, had the connections, authority and will to get things done. Crucially, he got on well with the patricians. The reduction of religious tensions also helped, given that some of the wealthiest burghers were Germanophone Protestants. Noble and ecclesiastical properties were subjected to municipal taxation. The happy marriage of burgher enterprise and szlachta capital and political protection yielded joint ventures in manufacturing and banking. With barriers crumbling, the pace of trade quickened, especially in products and services for the domestic market. Migrants poured in from the surrounding countryside and further afield, leading to a doubling in the population of the city and its suburbs from 8,000–9,000 in 1777 to as much as 17,000 in 1793.[17] Building land within the city walls became much sought after. Pressured by the commission, the owners of empty or derelict plots erected tenements containing apartments and workshops. Classicizing noble and patrician properties rose on the principal streets, and the number of workshops doubled in fourteen years. Nobles rented space to burghers, and burghers rented space to nobles.

Poznań showcased collaboration between the commission *boni ordinis* and the city council. This was not the case everywhere. As the 1768 law authorizing the establishment of such commissions was rolled out after the partition, overbearing noble and clerical commissioners often clashed with entrenched urban oligarchies. The latter vigorously defended their privileges, while noble and ecclesiastical property owners tried to avoid municipal burdens. Many towns remained stagnant. Olkusz, for example. The local commission *boni ordinis* found this old silver-mining small town in Lesser Poland ruinous, 130 years after the Swedish Deluge. Progress in reordering its governance was slow, and improvements in the use of urban space slower still. Olkusz was also riven by conflicts between Christian burghers and Jews, not least over the sale of alcohol. The commissioners forbade the overburdening of the Jewish community with local taxes. This animosity bore notorious fruit when an accusation of ordering a ritual murder was brought against four senior members of the *kahal* in 1787. This followed the confession – obtained through the illegal use of torture – of a Jewish tailor accused of assaulting and attempting to murder a Christian girl. He was found guilty and executed. However, following the personal intervention of King Stanisław August, who explained that Jews had no use for Christian blood, the elders were found not guilty. This was the last prosecution for ritual murder to be brought in the Commonwealth.

Improvements in the court system resumed. Backlogs were again reduced. Good examples came from the top. Adam Kazimierz Czartoryski was a demonstratively impartial as well as competent marshal of the Lithuanian Tribunal in 1781–82. He could afford the gesture, but he made it more difficult for his successors in the role to hand down blatantly partisan judgments.[18]

The long-standing attraction of the law as a path to social advancement was enhanced by the demographic and economic pressures faced by the szlachta. Most lawyers still learned their trade on the job. The impact of educational reform is debatable. On the one hand, the schools of the Commission of National Education paid more attention to the study of Polish law. On the other hand, several Crown sejmiks complained that these schools no longer taught the kind of Latin used in legal business. In the Grand Duchy of Lithuania and in Crown Ruthenia the official language of legal records changed from Ruthenian to Polish in 1697. Local nobles were well aware, as the Minsk sejmik put it in 1790, that the 'integrity of estates and their tranquil possession by citizens is preserved in the archives of palatinates', but the 'records left after conflagrations are decayed and ever more subject to obliterations, so that the Ruthenian can only be read with great difficulty, and in future will probably become indecipherable'. Sejmiks sporadically resolved to translate crumbling documents into Polish, and to house records in secure archives.[19]

One aspiring young lawyer in the 1780s was Jan Duklan Ochocki. His entertaining although not always reliable memoirs record nobles' perennial interest in lawsuits and the excitement aroused by the tribunals. They also underline the continuing importance of magnate patronage in the Commonwealth's eastern fringes. However, Ochocki's interpretation of the changing times deserves quoting:

> The courts of great lords were then already declining, and had started to change their character; so sons were usually placed under supervision, managing the estate, they were given to the army, or prepared for the clerical calling, or sent to government chancelleries and chambers, tribunals, and land and castle courts.[20]

This testimony is borne out by other careers.

Royal service offered opportunities to a lucky few. Excellent examples are the careers of the brothers Stanisław and Marcin Badeni (born in 1746 and 1751 respectively). Their family was of Italian burgher origin, but any doubts over its nobility were cleared up by a law passed by the sejm in 1768 at the request of the boys' father, Sebastian. Having held the district-level dignity of cupbearer of Winnica since 1750, from 1766 Sebastian supervised the administration of royal domain lands in the palatinate of Cracow. Around this time he placed his eldest son at the royal court. Within a decade Stanisław Badeni was a secretary in the king's Cabinet, where he dealt with domestic correspondence mostly relating to Lesser Poland. The acquired knowledge no doubt helped him to be elected to the sejm for the palatinate of Cracow in 1782 and 1784. As time passed he resided more often on his estates, whence he informed the king of the local political mood. His great-grandson, Kazimierz, would try and fail to resolve the linguistic and national problems of the Austrian half of the Dual Monarchy as its prime minister between 1895 and 1897.

The younger son, Marcin, received only a modest education, but mastered estate management with ease. He gained the trust of the king's nephew. Prince Stanisław Poniatowski, Treasurer of Lithuania from 1784 to 1790, asked Badeni to survey and manage the extensive royal domain lands the prince had leased in the Grand Duchy of Lithuania, following the fall of Antoni Tyzenhauz. Poniatowski collected enlightened plaudits for substituting cash rents for labour services, but it was Badeni who was responsible for ensuring that these changes were implemented profitably. He also took in hand the sole textile manufactory left amidst the debris of Tyzenhauz's ventures, and organized a joint stock company whose shareholders were magnates and wealthy noblemen. The rewards of success later enabled him to buy considerable landed properties in Lesser Poland. He also served the king politically. With the backing of Prince Stanisław, who held two great *starostwa* in the far-south east, Badeni was elected envoy for the palatinate of Bracław in 1784. However, politics was not his forte. Neither Badeni nor the prince could halt the erosion of the royalist position at the Lithuanian sejmiks previously controlled by Tyzenhauz.

The brothers Badeni rose through royal service, illuminating some of the ways in which Stanisław August coped with the diminution of his prerogatives and revenues after the first partition. Especially important was the Cabinet. This organ had developed since its establishment early in the reign. Formally entrusted with matters left to the king by the *pacta conventa* and subsequent legislation, in practice the Cabinet enabled him to conduct a parallel diplomacy. In the years 1775–88 this partly replaced and partly overlapped with the official channel – the Department of Foreign Affairs of the Permanent Council. Stackelberg sometimes demanded to see correspondence, so deciphered despatches and rescripts purposefully left out key fragments. Much of the king's loopy handwriting survives as drafts and corrections on letters carefully written out by Cabinet personnel to his domestic, foreign and diplomatic correspondents. These royal amendments reveal a concern to strike just the right tone with each addressee.

Some of the Cabinet's personnel were foreigners. The most meritorious was the Swiss Maurice Glayre, who was entrusted, among other tasks, with responsibilities relating to France. The longest serving was Reverend Gaetano Ghigiotti, who dealt with Italian and ecclesiastical correspondence. He enjoyed the affection of the brothers Poniatowski, but all too often put his own interests first when acting as a broker for Church patronage – such as paying his gaming debts. Most personnel, however, were Poles. The organizer and first head of the

Cabinet was the experienced Jacek Ogrodzki. He was succeeded by Adam Cieciszowski, who in turn was followed in 1783 by his son-in-law Pius Kiciński.

Few men served king and Commonwealth as well as Kiciński. Born into a modest noble family in the palatinate of Cracow, he entered the Cabinet in 1776. He sought favours for himself and his relations, often gaining them, but never stopped telling the king and primate the unvarnished truth. He even persuaded the spendthrift monarch to economize. It was to Kiciński that the king dictated his most important despatches. Every historian who has worked on these has a debt to Kiciński for his clear and elegant hand. Secretary to the stormy sejm of 1782, he was himself an envoy to the next three. He would play a crucial role at the turning point of the Four Years' Sejm. While Kiciński would memorably employ royalist rhetoric, it was a clerk employed by the Cabinet, Mateusz Czarnek, who provided Polish readers with a translation of the key intellectual component of the king's constitutional vision: Montesquieu's *Spirit of the Laws*.[21]

Much more numerous were the officials employed by the Permanent Council and the Crown and Lithuanian Treasury Commissions, as well as the Commission of National Education. All these institutions were characterized by disciplined record-keeping, formalized procedures, and salaried and hierarchically organized personnel. By the later 1780s the Permanent Council, itself comprising thirty-six salaried councillors, employed about seventy secretaries and clerks ('subalterns'), supposedly chosen on merit. However, it proved impossible to eliminate the practice of buying and selling these positions.

Among the five departments of the Permanent Council, the Department of Foreign Affairs was exceptional. Because Stanisław August had persuaded Stackelberg of the need for a modicum of secrecy and an enhanced role of the monarch in the conduct of foreign policy, the king himself formally headed the department, which had four, rather than eight, elected councillors. The monarch appointed the secretary and subalterns, and some of these persons overlapped with those employed in his Cabinet. The first departmental secretary, for example, was Ogrodzki. The crucial business was still conducted elsewhere: between St Petersburg, the ambassador and the king. From the perspective of plenary sessions it could seem that the department dealt with official notes, border incidents, customs disputes and consular matters. The budget increased in 1776 but was still modest. In these difficult conditions a professional diplomatic service emerged in the years after 1775.

The Commonwealth maintained five permanent diplomatic missions: in St Petersburg, Vienna, Berlin, London and Rome. The first was the most important. It was headed by an alumnus of the Knights' School, Augustyn Deboli. Starting as secretary to his predecessor, he rose through the ranks of chargé d'affaires, resident and finally minister in 1781. As the years passed, he gained a fair knowledge of the Russian court and won the king's trust. For his part Deboli gave his monarch honest advice, free of flattery. Their correspondence is perhaps the single most important source for the political history of the second half of the reign. However, Deboli dealt with the relatively insignificant Vice-Chancellor Ivan Ostermann, while the Russian court channelled more important matters via Stackelberg in Warsaw.[22]

Among the remaining Polish diplomats the trustiest was Franciszek Bukaty. This sturdy Samogitian headed the mission in London. His impecunious condition improved dramatically when he married into the senatorial Prozor family, received the Order of St Stanisław, and after fifteen years' service attained the rank of minister in 1785. The following year he obtained long-term leave, during which his salary would pay off the debts incurred in carrying out his diplomatic duties. His younger cousin kept the mission ticking over in the rank of secretary. Bernard Zabłocki in Berlin was also loyal, but of only limited use given the near-embargo imposed by Frederick II on information. Szymon Corticelli, a Lombard long since established in Poland, was intermittently committed to his work in Vienna. The Commonwealth's envoy to the Holy See, Marquis Tommaso Antici, was a typical eighteenth-century diplomatic *condottiere* whose knowledge of the papal curia could not wholly compensate for his multiple loyalties and personal ambition – which finally brought him a cardinal's hat in 1789. Nine years later, in terror of the French army, he resigned it, and was denied entry to the papal conclave in 1799. Besides these five missions, the king maintained a commissar in Danzig, a consul in Kherson and unofficial agents in France, Venice and Hamburg. The Polish mission sent to Istanbul in 1776, led by Karol Boscamp, proved to be such a success that Russia demanded its closure. However, a part of its activities continued under the cover of the School of Oriental Languages. Compared to the information the school sent to Warsaw, its pedagogical and philological achievements were modest.

The Military Department of the Permanent Council was informally controlled by the king's military chancellery, entrusted to his general-adjutant, Jan Komarzewski. The gradual extension of his influence over the Crown and Lithuanian armies provoked sniping from the hetmans and their allies, some of which concerned his obscure birth. From 1775 the armed forces were organized in divisions. The new regulations introduced for the 'foreign contingent' of infantry and dragoons were far from humanitarian: the brutal punishment of 'running the gauntlet' was retained. Nevertheless they brought proportionality and predictability to military discipline. The guard regiments, whose command Stanisław August recovered in 1776, received preferential treatment, including parade uniforms and a barracks – converted from the royal residence *manqué* of Ujazdów on the outskirts of Warsaw. The department paid attention to the training of surgeons and medical orderlies, and sought to improve equipment, although domestic manufactories could not supply all of the requisite ordnance. The royal Cadet Corps was not subordinated to the department; it continued to educate its students in line with the latest European military thought.

On the other hand, the expansion of the army from the Commonwealth's small annual budget surpluses was excruciatingly slow. The combined factual strength of the Crown and Lithuanian armies reached just 18,342 men in 1786. Furthermore, the number of ordinary soldiers per unit (and thus per officer) was significantly below the European average. All in all, the Commonwealth's armed forces were more comparable to those of minor German and Italian principalities than to those of its three puissant neighbours, whose battle-hardened armies were 200,000, 300,000 and occasionally even 400,000 strong.[23] Attempts to improve recruitment foundered on the immunity of nobles' hereditary land. Few graduates of the Cadet Corps could expect a commission, unless they could buy one. Without a costly system of pensions for retired officers, it was hard to find a viable solution to this problem: the king's attempt in 1776 to prohibit sales from 1784 onwards was struck down by the sejm of that year.

The National Cavalry still consisted of undisciplined 'companions' who were often substituted by their assistants in each 'post'. Senior officers often treated their commands as sinecures – they could rake off some of the monies assigned for provisioning. National Cavalrymen compensated by exploiting the population of the estates on which they were quartered. Any attempts to reform, still less replace this anachronistic bastion of support for the hetmans could expect trouble. Many noblemen, lacking the kind of education required by the artillery, aspired to join the National Cavalry. Even royalists were receptive to calls to reduce the number of foreign officers in the Crown and Lithuanian armies. As heir to the hussar, armoured and light cavalry formations of old, the National Cavalry still enjoyed prestige. Some foreign writers such as Rousseau were taken with the idea of Poles' equestrian prowess and preferred citizen-soldiers to standing armies. Even Catherine II was briefly inclined to find a use for the National Cavalry in 1788.

Departmental records reveal that troops were often used to deal with civil emergencies, criminal gangs and vagrants. The Permanent Council was well aware of the abuses at the frontiers and of illegal foreign military recruitment, but was anxious to avoid confrontations with the forces of the Commonwealth's neighbours. A major expense was housing and feeding the inmates of the Commonwealth's principal gaol for serious delinquents – in the dilapidated fortress at Kamieniec Podolski. The enforcement of verdicts by the army required close co-operation between the Military and Justice Departments of the Permanent Council. Those at the receiving end complained, but creditors, heirs and purchasers were satisfied. Resistance to the soldiers brought a fine of 2,000 złotys and twelve days' imprisonment. The sejms of 1778 and 1784 regulated the intromissory procedure, transferring verdicts of execution from the tribunals to the court judging the case in question. The foray began to move from the realm of custom into that of folklore.

Resolutions interpreting the law were drafted and voted on by the Justice Department before being corrected and endorsed at plenary sessions of the Permanent Council. The number of such resolutions published during each two-year term fluctuated between about fifty and 175. Queries flowed in from lower-level courts, offices and private citizens. Many fewer came, however, from the Grand Duchy of Lithuania – this may reflect the authority of the Third Lithuanian Statute, compared to the diversity of legal practice in the Polish Crown. The matters in doubt included legal documentation, the arbitration of boundary disputes, inheritance law, the rights of separated wives and deaf and dumb persons to make legal transactions, bills of exchange, ministerial salaries, Tatar privileges, fugitive serfs and much else besides. In some cases the resolution simply referred the matter to the appropriate court. Some court officials betrayed ignorance of procedures, competences and statutes; that said, much legislation was poorly drafted. It would take time for the Law Faculties at the reformed universities of Cracow and Wilno to improve the cadre of judges and lawyers. On 16 February 1787 the Council was obliged to reiterate the 1776 sejm's prohibition on the use of torture during judicial investigations. This resolution was issued in a case of church-robbers who had been caught red-handed but then denied their culpability.[24] This was part of a wider tendency to interpret the criminal law in a humanitarian direction – also reflected in recommendations of imprisonment instead of the death penalty. The Council's interpretations also concerned legacies to the Catholic Church, the foundation of parishes, tithes and the rights of clerical presidents at the Crown Tribunal. The temporal jurisdiction was moving cautiously into spheres often considered spiritual.

Three of the thirty-six councillors were bishop-senators, and their co-operation facilitated the activities of the Police Department. The eighteenth-century concept of 'police' involved urban governance, including spatial planning, public health, the care provided to the poor, sick and infirm, the regulation of crafts and trade, military quartering and provisioning, as well as questions of public order, safety, morality and even religion. If the potential for clashes between the servants of God and Caesar was considerable, so too were the opportunities for the 'social disciplining' of the populace by their combined action. This was evident as the department tried to cope with the rising tide of vagrancy. Unable to afford the construction of English-style workhouses, it confined permission to beg for those unable to work to their parish of origin. Its limited efforts to supervise 'hospitals' (most of which only housed a few old, handicapped or dying people) met with a patchy response. Bishops proved more co-operative than religious orders.

The Police Department did not always enjoy a co-operative relationship either with urban authorities or with local starostas. A particular bone of contention was the attempt to enforce the Permanent Council's proclamation of 1777, based on the 1776 law ordaining public auctions of alcohol monopolies and controlled investment of the monies. This measure was intended to curtail abuses. However, the short-term compliance achieved by sending in troops did not win hearts and minds. Doubtless, in some towns interfering bureaucrats dampened whatever local appetite there may have been for reform. The greatest chance of improvements occurred where the starosta and the corporation were in conflict, and one side had appealed to the Permanent Council. In such cases, the department and the commissions *boni ordinis* it supervised could sometimes apply pressure effectively, perhaps improving urban planning and sanitation. Certainly, detailed reports were filed copiously. Perhaps awareness that someone in Warsaw actually cared about the condition of half-forgotten provincial towns was an impulse for change.

The Treasury Department supervised the work of the two Treasury Commissions established in 1764. The department checked the reports sent in by the commissions and presented them to plenary sessions of the Permanent

Council. By the later 1780s it was able to assign the accruing budgetary surpluses as a contingency fund. Most additional expenditure was on military needs, but some went towards paving Warsaw, and rewards were paid to meritorious state functionaries. Monies did not suffice, however, for major investment in communications – such as the dredging of the River Niemen.

The real fiscal business was transacted by the Crown and Lithuanian Treasury Commissions, which had a chequered relationship with the Permanent Council. By the end of the 1780s, the Lithuanian Treasury Commission alone employed 583 customs officers and 476 tax officers of various ranks.[25] Most of these men were recruited from the poorer szlachta, for whom the modest salaries proved sufficiently attractive. After Tyzenhauz's fall, the significance of patron–client relationships changed. Surety bonds, usually put up either by wealthier relatives or well-disposed dignitaries, guaranteed minimum standards of honesty and competence. Merit began to play a greater role in recruitment and promotion. Together the two commissions employed most of the salaried officials of the state.

Fiscally, the Commonwealth functioned smoothly within tight limits. Not the least achievement of the 1776 sejm was an orderly state budget. The unrealistic expectations of the Partition Sejm were soon exposed: instead of a projected combined annual income of about 30 million złotys, enough for an army of 30,000 men, only about 16 million złotys were collected during the seventeen months that followed the sejm. Between 1776 and 1788 the joint annual income of the Crown and Lithuanian treasuries rose slowly from approximately 13,400,000 złotys to about 17,700,000 złotys. The largest contributions came from the hearth tax, paid by the owners of almost all landed and urban property, alcohol excises, the one-and-a-half *kwarta* from leased-out Crown estates, customs duties, the Jewish poll tax, stamp duty, tobacco excise and the clergy's *subsidium charitativum* – charitably reckoned as a tenth of ecclesiastical income.[26]

Expenditure was also trimmed in 1776, starting with the rewards paid to those who had pushed through the partition. Modest surpluses were accumulated and new public debts avoided. Nevertheless, the combined salaries of the Crown and Lithuanian commissioners and treasurers exceeded the total for their centrally located subalterns. Since the 1770s the Crown commission had enjoyed a better reputation for honesty and rigour than its Lithuanian counterpart, but the figures for income and expenditure do not entirely bear out this contrast. While Tyzenhauz indulged his numerous conflicts of interest, by 1786 things had improved considerably.

The work of Michał Kleofas Ogiński for the Lithuanian Treasury shows both the scope for improvements, and the will to make them. He was elected as a commissioner by the 1786 sejm, aged just twenty-one. Not to be confused with his older kinsman, Hetman Michał Kazimierz Ogiński, Michał Kleofas was the son of a palatine of Troki. He learned the ropes at the Lithuanian Treasury Commission's headquarters in Grodno Castle. During his inspections of customs posts located along the River Niemen facing Prussia (for which he claimed no expenses), he realized that the malfunctioning customs system resulted in serious losses. According to the trade 'agreement' of 1768, goods in transit between Prussia and Russia paid only nominal dues per package, without any regard to the size or value of the goods within. But even these loaded provisions were often evaded. Ogiński advocated investment in the number, equipment and remuneration of customs officials, regular inspections by superintendents and commissioners, and obliging lower-ranking officials to report misdemeanours committed by their superiors.

In his description of the customs office at Połąga, a small fishing town belonging to the Bishop of Wilno, Ogiński noted the remains of a nearby harbour at Święta. Permission for its construction, he discovered, had been granted by the sejm to English merchants in 1690, but they were soon accused of bad faith, and the harbour had fallen into disrepair. He prepared a budget for its restoration. Although the River Święta flowed into the Baltic from its source in Courland, Ogiński believed that a canal could be dug to connect it inland with the Niemen (whose mouth was wholly controlled by Prussia), thereby opening a route to the sea for most of the Grand Duchy of Lithuania. In normal times Russian or Prussian objections would have squashed such projects; earlier calls to rebuild this harbour had come to nothing. By the autumn of 1788 such dreams had become feasible, but alas, the Great Sejm did not pursue them. This was despite British interest in reorienting the country's Baltic trade from Russia to the Commonwealth, the enthusiasm of the British consul in Memel, James Durno, and the assurances given by Bukaty in London, that the port in Swięta could be opened. Ogiński repeated these assurances when he undertook a sudden mission to London on his own initiative in the winter of 1790–91. His later path involved some dubious property transactions and composing music. He is best remembered for the lovely polonaise in A-minor, his personal 'Farewell to the Fatherland' after the 1794 Insurrection. Palanga is now independent Lithuania's liveliest seaside resort, with an international airport – on the road to Šventoji.

The development of governance under Stanisław August has been pronounced part of a process of 'bureaucratization' and 'modernization' similar to that often traced for the 'absolutist' or 'well-ordered police state'. These labels can be challenged. Historians in many countries have emphasized the limitations of monarchical 'absolutism', enlightened or otherwise, and have taken greater interest in republican and mixed alternatives.[27] That said, in the Commonwealth of the 1770s and 1780s, we can observe elements of centralization and regulation, as well as more opportunities for careers in officialdom – not only through patronage. This professionalization in government was at odds with the republican ethos of public service. The latter was based on the patriotic duty of free citizens coming together for the common good, rather than on individuals' salaried work in a hierarchical structure. The growing activity of government, which after 1795 would be associated with an impersonal and usually foreign state, was one aspect of the later eighteenth-century cultural confrontation. On the one side were those who wished to move with the times. On the other were those who – for various reasons – were profoundly disturbed by such 'progress'. This culture clash affected nobles and burghers alike; the latter represented themselves as urban citizens, and were just as keen as the former to defend their privileges. So were Jewish communities. On the other hand, a synthesis was expressed by the collegial organization of the organs of central government and the commissions *boni ordinis*. The modest origins and traditional mores of the brothers Badeni pointed to another blend of new and old.

❖

The ideology of limited but efficacious monarchy, resting on a partnership between king and nation, was expounded in words, images and performances. The message of communal harmony and of trust in the prudent shepherd of the flock was preached in major sermons, such as those delivered at the resumptions of the Crown and Lithuanian Tribunals, and especially on the royal nameday of 8 May. This was also when the Order of St Stanisław held its annual celebration at the Church of the Holy Cross in Warsaw. The preachers for these feasts were among the Commonwealth's leading pulpit orators, and many of these homilies were published at royal expense.

The king's aims of order, prosperity and harmony, securing individual citizens' liberty and property, could be declaimed in occasional panegyrics. Occasions included school ceremonies and galas staged by wealthy citizens on royal anniversaries, perhaps in the hope of favour. These aims could also be conveyed through illuminations in provincial towns. Royal progresses afforded opportunities to take the message deep into the provinces. The impact on local communities of a royal visit may have been long lasting. Stanisław August was invariably charming to his hosts. He would remember and compliment their wives and children years later. For example, eight years after meeting them in Polesie in 1784, the king greeted the wife and daughter – 'the polite secretary, who writes a beautiful hand' – of the envoy for Pińsk, Mateusz Butrymowicz.[28]

A favourite royal gift was a snuffbox containing a miniature portrait of the king, like the one immortalized by Adam Mickiewicz, who, drawing on memories of his childhood, wrote:

> A box of gold with diamonds inlaid,
> And King Stanisław in the lid portrayed,
> Who gave it to his father years before,
> Which now in turn the Chamberlain nobly bore.[29]

The original would have been presented to one of the more important of the Mickiewicz family's neighbours during the king's round-about journey to Grodno in 1784. In those parts the magnificent welcome to the king offered by Karol Radziwiłł, including a spectacular staging on the Nieśwież lake of the recent battle for Gibraltar, was long remembered. Last but not least, public thanksgivings were organized when Stanisław August entered Warsaw at the end of his longer journeys.

High culture was often pressed into the service of politics. Among the arts, Stanisław August's expertise was least in music. However, he seems to have enjoyed listening to performances, and he attached importance to the messages conveyed through the theatrical spectacles of opera and ballet. There was gossip about the royal taste in ballerinas, but the king took his responsibilities as patron seriously and continued to support the Tyzenhauz's school for dancers in Grodno, after its founder's fall.

Stanisław August's literary accomplishments are far more impressive. Although he was no poet, much of his memoirs (begun around 1770 but interrupted a few years later) and many of his letters can be described as masterly. The king had few rivals as an orator or as a necessarily anonymous pamphleteer.

The surviving documents of his library amply demonstrate how he read avidly, or was read to, for example while he was being dressed. He was familiar with a wide range of literary genres, both fiction and non-fiction. Besides his native command of Polish and near-native French, he also knew Latin, Italian, English, German and Russian.

The king's greatest passion was for architecture. He has been compared to the conductor of an orchestra, occasionally playing a few bars in practice – several of his sketches have survived.[30] Architecture, with other arts in harness, was best suited for giving form to his ideas. It provided settings for painting and sculpture, drama and music, and through libraries and cabinets, for literature, drawing and numismatics as well. The distinction between the arts and sciences was blurred in cartography and astronomy, such was the beauty of the maps and instruments created at this time. Occasionally the king succumbed to the mindset of a private collector: during the 1794 Insurrection, he was reluctant to lend Kościuszko his maps. On the whole, however, the king's patronage of the arts was firmly subordinated to his political goal of renovating the Commonwealth.

Stanisław August's early building projects, mostly unrealized, showcased monarchical virtues. It is over-interpreting these projects to suggest that having gained the throne, Stanisław August first dreamt of royal 'absolutism', but then saw the error of his ways, and that his later architectural solutions reflected a turn towards 'republican' neo-classicism.[31] The influence of English art, gardens and architecture did increase during his reign, and it is plausible to argue that the Anglo-Palladian idiom symbolized a programme of progress, prosperity and polite liberty. However, the king's architectural and landscaping solutions responded to a range of factors including his personal taste, which always appreciated ornament, while his admiration of the British constitution was a constant.[32]

Royal interiors encouraged constructive dialogue between the Roman ideas of *respublica* and *imperium* and the associated goals of *libertas* and *pax*. An early example was the commissioning of a pair of pictures depicting Julius Caesar's confrontations, first with a monument to Alexander the Great, and then with the severed head of Pompey. One symbolized the dream of universal monarchy; the pendant evoked the terrible price paid for the destruction of republican liberty. The cycle of violence, they implied, ceased under the wise and moderate rule of Augustus, *pater patriæ*. These themes were reprised in the Castle rooms rebuilt in the middle years of the reign. Doubtless it was no accident that as a youthful exercise Stanisław had translated from English into French the first four scenes of Shakespeare's *Julius Caesar*, an ambiguous play that probes the dilemmas of those who strive to defend liberty from the threat of tyranny. He expressed his enthusiasm for this work to his English friends and corrected his own translation after improving his knowledge of the language.[33]

At the Łazienki, three rooms constructed in the first half of the 1790s contained more personal reflections: on fate, time and eternity in the Ballroom; on triumph and weakness in the Solomon Hall or salon; finally and defiantly in the Rotunda which Stanisław August never saw completed, on the attributes of exemplary rulers who made themselves useful to their peoples. In the end, as Jerzy Axer has argued, Stanisław August was left repeating himself, hoping that posterity would listen.[34]

The richest and subtlest of the royal messages were conveyed in the Senatorial Antechamber at the Royal Castle, opened in 1786. They were made explicit by poems penned for the occasion by Naruszewicz and Jan Paweł Woronicz. The room became known as the Knights' Hall, as it served as a space for conversation during sessions of the sejm. It offered a comprehensive lesson in patriotism and history, framed in the language of antiquity. The layout alluded to the triumphal hall of the King of the Latins in the seventh book of Virgil's *Aeneid* with its representations of ancestors. The inscription on the frieze quoted the sixth book (lines 660–64): Aeneas, having arrived in Elysium, saw men who had shed their blood for the Fatherland, priests who had lived pure and pious lives, bards whose songs were worthy of Apollo, those who had discovered ennobling truths, and others whose services had won them remembrance among men. In other words, service to the *patria* could take many forms worthy of commemoration (Plate 22).

This message was illustrated by twenty-two busts and ten painted portraits of Polish heroes, arranged to suggest their conversation, and six large-scale canvases painted by Marcello Bacciarelli. Just one of the latter (albeit one of the two largest) was wholly martial in tone – John III Sobieski triumphant at Vienna. If that suggested that new glories against the Turk might be at hand at Russia's side, then two other pictures celebrated diplomatic achievements: the peace made with the Ottoman Empire in 1621 and the Prussian Homage of 1525. The latter also referred to the composition of the Commonwealth, including its lost territories, as did the depiction of the Union of Lublin. Another canvas showed a royal patron of learning: Władysław Jagiełło refounding Cracow University in 1400. The pendant to Sobieski's victory depicted Casimir the Great listening to the pleas of Polish peasants. To sharpen this point, not all of those portrayed in bronze or oil were nobles: the heroes included the Royal Prussian astronomers Joannes Hevelius and Nicolaus Copernicus. The latter had the place of honour, above the figure of Time and opposite that of Fame. It was politic that most of the Commonwealth's magnate clans were represented – whether by warriors, ministers or bishops. Two Protestants (Hevelius and Lithuanian Grand Hetman Krzysztof II Radziwiłł) made the cut, but no fewer than eleven out of thirty-two were Catholic clergymen. While most of these ecclesiastics were chosen for their services as statesmen, pedagogues, poets, historians or astronomers, the location of Cardinal Stanisław Hosius's portrait vis-à-vis the frieze tells the beholder that he was a priest of unblemished life. Moreover, two of the sculpted clergymen had not yet joined the dead (although their Jesuit order had): the astronomer Marcin Poczobut and the poet and historian Adam Naruszewicz (who worked with the king on the programme).

The Temple of British Worthies in the gardens at Stowe, which the future king had visited in 1754, quoted the same passage of the *Aeneid*. Pointedly, however, at Stowe the reference to pure and pious priests was omitted. Moreover, many of the sixteen British or English heroes sculpted at Stowe (no clergymen among them) had fought for Protestant liberty against monarchs suspected of absolutist and Catholicizing tendencies. In Warsaw, in contrast, two rebellious potentates – Cardinal Zbigniew Oleśnicki and Jerzy Sebastian Lubomirski – were, on reflection, left out. Most of the chosen hetmans were exemplary royalists. The Knights' Hall symbolized a dialogue between Augustan and republican ideas of public service, but it also affirmed the alliance between throne and altar.[35]

The king expended much effort on propagating these sophisticated ideas to metropolitan and provicincial audiences. Yet several historians have pronounced the court party of these years devoid of a political programme. It is clear that in the conditions of Stackelberg's proconsulate Stanisław August could not admit to a programme of constitutional reform derived from his 'Anecdote Historique' of 1763, let alone put such a programme to the 'nation' in the proclamations which summoned the sejmiks that elected envoys to the sejm.[36] The limits of the possible were probably reached in the king's speech to the 1776 sejm. More radical views, such as those of Józef Wybicki, remained at or beyond the margins of acceptable political discourse. Yet the king's unceasing, anodyne message, urging harmony, mutual trust and patriotic co-operation, was part of a wider discourse of renewal that would resonate during the Four Years' Sejm. By that time significant shifts in political language and concepts had occurred. During the 1770s and 1780s a quartet of Piarists – Wincenty Skrzetuski, Antoni Popławski, Hieronim Stroynowski and Konstanty Bogusławski – wrote treatises which moved beyond republican axioms. They cast their arguments in terms of universal and natural law, and individual liberty and property.[37] To solve this puzzle, more research will be required, especially on the flows of information between the royal court on the one hand, and manors and parishes on the other.

The monarch's efforts to win over provincial nobles faced the age-old cultural clash between court and country. Here the classical and Christian heritages of the szlachta merged perfectly. Discoursing against Warsaw – as a godless, sordid den of vice and foreigners – came as naturally to Polish country gentlemen as rants against London came to Squire Western in Henry Fielding's novel *Tom Jones*. Many of those who contrasted the shabby present with the burnished ancestral past denied the need radically to reform the Commonwealth's institutions. Even royalist authors were moved to a nostalgic tone by the Fatherland's situation. Writers usually identified with the Enlightenment tended to assess changing vogues critically. Poets and playwrights balanced their mockery of ignorance, superstition, xenophobia and fanaticism (lumped together as 'Sarmatism') with caustic satires of followers of foolish foreign fashions. Ignacy Krasicki's lapidary warning of the ruinous consequences of indulging a 'fashionable wife' bore a whiff of misogyny. More straightforwardly nostalgic were two lyric poets patronized by the Czartoryskis: Franciszek Karpiński, who returned disillusioned from Warsaw to the countryside, and Franciszek Kniaźnin, who sang of martial heroes who twirled their whiskers and got the girls. All these writers testify to a major cultural shift. Fashions in dress, coiffure, equipage, residential architecture and gardens were all filtering down from Warsaw to the provinces, and from magnates' palaces to moderately wealthy nobles' manors.

Discourse seems to have been out of step with practice. This phenomenon was brilliantly captured – with the benefit of hindsight – by Mickiewicz. In *Pan Tadeusz* he recalls local worthies reminiscing about their youth. At a banquet the studiedly old-fashioned Judge Soplica, having noticed that his distracted nephew has just neglected to fill the goblet of the well-born young lady sitting next to him, contrasts the education and manners of contemporary youth with the courtesy due to all people, but differentiated according to their station in life. He had himself absorbed this code while growing up at a local magnate's court. The judge receives an interesting reply from the chamberlain (whose father had received the snuffbox from Stanisław August). 'Dear Judge, it was still worse of old,' he begins – and later expresses his satisfaction that Polish youths now fight bravely under Napoleon's aegis and have no time for frivolity. It was different a generation or two earlier, 'when it became the mode to ape French ways'. The severest criticism had no effect, because many of those who disliked the new fashions nevertheless adopted them:

> They cried against the dandies, none the less,
> They changed their faith and laws, their speech and dress.

The following two lines help to explain why the 'culture wars' of the Stanislavian period – usually encapsulated in the formula 'whiskers versus periwig', but sometimes as 'Sarmatia versus Europe' – have aroused so much emotion in successive generations of Poles:

> It was a Carnival of knavery,
> Soon followed by a Lent of slavery.[38]

This is not only a perspective from after the third partition of the Commonwealth. It was written following the failure of the 1830–31 Rising, when the Romantic Bards were elaborating their messianic vision of Christ-like national suffering and redemption. However, the theme of impending Divine retribution for the nation's turn away from ancestral piety and virtue towards godless novelties can be found earlier, notably in sermons and pastoral letters penned by Canon Woronicz at the turn of the 1780s and 1790s.[39]

The monarch was fighting an uphill struggle for the hearts and minds of those who 'cried against the dandies', even as they followed their example and sadly shaved off their whiskers or shelled out for new furniture to indulge their wives and children. The prevalent discourse was nostalgic rather than progressive. Stanisław August had declined to cut his tresses and don a *kontusz* for his coronation; he would not make himself look ridiculous two decades later. But some of his contemporaries would take this plunge, and soon. Moreover, most middling and poorer nobles had not changed their attire before traditional dress once more became fashionable. An important factor here was the decision of the

1776 sejm to introduce (non-obligatory) uniforms for the envoys for each palatinate, cut from Polish cloth in the Polish style, to aid identification. The idea was taken up with enthusiasm at many sejmiks, where they were worn by many participating citizens. These uniforms soon evolved subtle distinctions in their colours and patterns, and became symbols of national and local pride (Plate 24).

This cultural shift was articulated and brought into the political arena by Izabela Czartoryska. The opera she commissioned, *The Spartan Mother*, was dedicated to Feliks Potocki, the Commonwealth's richest magnate, but its content and style reflected an effort to 'apply new methods of influencing and consciously adapting to the tastes of the szlachta, which was gradually emancipating itself from the older forms of dependence on magnates'.[40] Following the premiere on 15 June 1786, another aristocrat, Ignacy Potocki, testified to its impact:

> Yesterday Puławy gave us a Graeco-Polish opera, the Spartan Mother. The spectacle was extraordinarily beautiful and civic. Many from Lublin and some from Warsaw thronged the theatre – up to five hundred persons. There were sixty actors and members of the chorus. The opera's verse is the work of Kniaźnin, the prince's secretary. This verse is extraordinarily polished and beautiful. The princess and her sons played the leading roles. Everything was infused with the spirit of knighthood, love of the Fatherland, and in the music and costumes, exquisite taste. Tender tears and civic zeal were the general result of this truly national entertainment.[41]

Czartoryska performed the title role. The opera comprised a series of tableaux, featuring choruses, dialogues and recitatives written by the court poet Kniaźnin and set to music by the court composer Wincenty Lesse. The plot may be briefly summarized: Teona sends her son Likanor (played by the sixteen-year-old Adam Jerzy Czartoryski) to defend Sparta against the Thebans in battle; Likanor returns for reinforcements but goes straight back to the battlefield with his mother's scornful words about courage ringing in his ears; Likanor returns to the city having won a famous victory. The colonnaded staging and the choreography accentuated a stable society in which persons of all social ranks and both sexes knew their place, while burning with love of their shared fatherland. The political implication was that the opposition was ready to unite Poland to fight for freedom, whereas the king passively accepted Russian hegemony.

This was a dishonest, but suggestive narrative. Stackelberg rightly feared the symbolism:

> Among other things there has been a Polish opera at Puławy. In it the princess of the house played the Spartan Mother alongside her two sons. These children have in their quarters a picture of Hannibal swearing an oath of eternal hatred towards the Romans. All this has spread such a perfect confusion of ideas in heads, that the explosion could embarrass the future national assembly, had we not concluded at the preceding ones all the objects of ratification and a few other essential affairs.[42]

An anti-Russian bomb was indeed ticking among the middling szlachta, and neither the king nor his aristocratic opponents would be able to defuse it.

— EIGHT —
FERMENT AND FERMENTATION

In the spring of 1788, Stanisław August was worried that 'the *fermentacya* of minds continues apace, especially among youth'.[1] Should this be translated as 'ferment' or 'fermentation'? The king was worried that his delicately balanced system would be ruined by a rush of enthusiasm – as if too much yeast had been added to the casks of his carefully brewed mild ale. After the high point of the Grodno sejm of 1784, it became more difficult for the monarch to retain control of domestic politics. He travelled across his kingdom to see the empress in 1787, but she did him no favours by keeping him impotently waiting for her answer. The opposition aristocrats recovered their confidence, but the more significant change was in the assertiveness of nobles of middling fortune. We have already explored some of the socio-economic and cultural aspects; it remains to add the educational ingredient to the brew, and to see how it poured into the politics of the Polish 'pre-revolution'.

The cause for which the 'Spartan Mother' sought to rally the provincial szlachta was far from heroic – at least in the short term. The coalition of aspiring oligarchs still sought to outbid the king for the empress's favour. Moreover, the rapid polarization of the Commonwealth's politics had its origins in an unsavoury scandal. An adventuress reputedly of Italian origin, Maria Teresa Neri, the wife of a Russian major called Ogrumov, had twice tried and twice failed to convince the king that opposition magnates were plotting to have him assassinated. So she changed tack. In Warsaw in January 1785 'Dogrumowa' and William Taylor, an English merchant, set up the king's valet, Franciszek Ryx, in an ambiguous conversation overheard by Stanisław Kostka Potocki. This was presented as proof that Ryx and General Komarzewski were planning Czartoryski's murder. Ryx was seized and then held at the suburban residence of Potocki's mother-in-law

Izabella Lubomirska, where he was formally arrested on the orders of Stanisław's brother Ignacy – the court marshal of Lithuania. Komarzewski, who heard the news at the theatre, turned himself in.[2]

When the case came before the court of the Grand Marshal of the Crown, it collapsed because Stanisław Potocki had been counter-sued for defamation, and there were no independent witnesses. Although Potocki was acquitted, Taylor was imprisoned and fined, while 'Dogrumowa', who might have been sentenced to death, was publicly branded on her buttocks and imprisoned for life. The false testimony and several pamphlets carrying the allegations were publicly burnt. On the other hand, every effort was made to appease the magnates who had accused the monarch's servants, and by implication, the king himself, of plotting their deaths. Czartoryski refused to appear and so the court had to fine him for contempt. He left for Vienna. Prince Adam and his sister Izabella Lubomirska made a show of having been injured by a vengeful monarch. They were sustained in their dudgeon by Ignacy and Stanisław Potocki. Franciszek Ksawery Branicki exploited the case.

Ignacy Potocki had been one of the ten judges. He could not alter the obvious verdict, but he managed to insert Branicki's name into the written judgment as a person defamed by 'Dogrumowa'. Branicki loudly proclaimed his outrage at being mentioned, and was not dissuaded when he learned who had been responsible. By the end of 1785 he had obtained the support of Potemkin and Catherine II for the removal of his name from the verdict. By the following summer, when Stackelberg was instructed to seek a compromise solution, the opposition campaign was in full swing. Lavish house parties served to win over wavering magnates – notably the fabulously rich Feliks Potocki – and co-ordinate plans, but were also shows of strength. Well-lubricated entertainments were laid on for local nobles.

In the Grand Duchy of Lithuania the alliance between the royal court and the Radziwiłł interest still held. The opposition performed weakly at most of the sejmiks held to elect envoys in August 1786. One of the few exceptions was Brześć Litewski, where Branicki's nephew Kazimierz Nestor Sapieha won a complete victory. Sapieha's mother, Elżbieta, née Branicka, had persuaded her former lover Stanisław August to grant her then teenage son the lucrative position of general of the Lithuanian artillery. Sapieha's talents were for oratory and high-living – which led to the breakdown of his marriage.

In the Crown, many royalist candidates had a rough ride. The opposition was strongest in the south-east. Branicki's supporters took five of the six mandates for the palatinate of Kiev. In neighbouring Volhynia, royalists accused the hetman's party of re-attiring soldiers in order to swell the numbers of poorer nobles who turned up to the sejmik in Łuck. Rather weakly in the eyes of the law, the royalists held their own sejmik in a nearby village. The bitterest contest took place in Podolia. Here Adam Kazimierz and Izabela Czartoryski were determined to prevail. They dressed their son Adam Jerzy in national costume and taught him electioneering. This sejmik was also doubled: the malcontents controlled the cathedral in Kamieniec, so the royalists went to the Dominican church. The court allegedly passed off the garrison as local nobles, while Prince Czartoryski supposedly carted in his tenants from across the Galician border.

The sejm opened on 2 October 1786. After some stormy sessions and interventions from Stackelberg behind the scenes, it deemed the opposition candidates from Volhynia and the royalist candidates from Podolia legally elected. The deliberations remained fractious; tempers were not calmed by alcohol-fuelled spectators of both sexes mixing among the envoys. The most useful reform agreed was the third proposition from the throne: a devaluation of the złoty against the ducat, which undid most of the damage done by the excessive revaluation of 1766. The first proposition from the throne was the ratification of the Convention of Vienna concluded by Michał Poniatowski regarding the diocese of Cracow and its funds. The primate, having made a splendid entry into Warsaw, endured hours of harangues, before the sejm approved the agreement. Branicki attacked the Military Department of the Permanent Council, while even the generally co-operative Karol Radziwiłł drunkenly threatened the monarch after being denied a favour for a client. After pressure from Stackelberg, a limp compromise finally resolved the Dogrumowa affair: the names of Branicki and Czartoryski were to be excised from the verdict and the whole case consigned to silence. Branicki was rude to the monarch during their 'reconciliation', while Czartoryski's clients fêted his ceremonial entry into Warsaw.

The aristocratic *fronde* was less significant than the signs that ordinary envoys could act in ways that neither the king, nor the magnates, nor the Russian ambassador could control. Branicki was surprised by the fervour aroused by his proposal to exclude foreigners – even naturalized citizens – from army commissions. According to the monarch's non-ciphered account, 'Sarmatian prejudice' forced many who thought proposal absurd to remain silent, for fear of sabre-swinging enthusiasts.[3] The sejm also overturned Komarzewski's reforms of the army regulations. Underlying these outbursts was the desire of many middling nobles to find paid employment for themselves or their kinsmen in an expanded National

Cavalry. Another emotive question was the wording of the protest to the Russian ambassador about a Russian regiment plundering the south-eastern corner of the Commonwealth. The king was unable to rein in some of his own supporters, whose fiery speeches contrasted with his own apparent passivity. Those who had suffered from Prussian depredations in the west stood foursquare alongside the victims of Russian rapacity in the east. This development, which was *not* the result of manipulation by the opposition leaders, would be at the root of the revolt against Russian hegemony in the autumn of 1788.

One of the reasons Stanisław August had taken his eye off the ball was the prospect of meeting the empress. He saw a great opportunity in Catherine's plan to visit the Crimea. He hoped that the anticipated war between Russia and the Ottoman Empire would make the Commonwealth into a desirable ally for Russia. Since the partition he had become more convinced than ever that only such an alliance 'would assure the permanent existence of my Fatherland and make it, as I say, un-attackable'.[4] As Potemkin escorted Catherine down the River Dnieper, Stanisław August might meet her without leaving the Commonwealth's territory (for which he would need the sejm's permission). At the beginning of December 1786 Catherine agreed to a meeting.[5]

With the help of the primate and the Russian ambassador, the king drew up a proposal. Its first point was that the empress would remind the malcontent leaders what they owed the king and deny them hope of her recommendation to office if they persisted in opposition. Requests followed for the conclusion of trading agreements, the withdrawal of the notorious regiment, and the exclusion of Austrian and Prussian interference in the Commonwealth's affairs. The king's wish-list also included a previously confederated sejm and reforms to parliamentary procedure: moving the elections for the Permanent Council and the commissions to the end of the sejm, so that they could not hold up other business, and joining the deliberations of the two chambers (to avoid any repetition of the excesses in the chamber of envoys in 1786). Finally, he requested '*une alliance intime et perpétuelle avec la Russie*'. Stackelberg handed this document to the empress, several weeks before the meeting.[6]

Accompanied by a substantial entourage, Stanisław August left Warsaw on 23 February 1787. He left his younger brother in charge; the king's letters to Pius

Kiciński kept the primate fully briefed. The monarch arrived at Kaniów on 24 March. Upriver, Catherine had entered Kiev on 29 January 1787. While the king waited for the ice floes on the Dnieper to clear, his leading subjects hastened to pay their court to the tsaritsa.

The negotiations began on 20 March at Chwastów, where the king lodged in the residence of the Latin-rite Bishop of Kiev. That evening Potemkin arrived, wearing a Polish uniform and order, accompanied by Stackelberg, Branicki and Prince Charles of Nassau-Siegen (a naturalized Polish noble married to a Polish noblewoman). The king thanked Potemkin for the departure of the regiment, and promises of trading concessions, but Potemkin was soon holding forth on his intentions to found an academy in Iekatineroslav, establish the Piarists in Smila, build palaces, and so forth. On 28–29 March in Kaniów, Stanisław August received another visit, this time from Aleksandr Bezborodko and Stackelberg. Two days later the king sent the ambassador his desiderata.

Catherine's flotilla sailed into view on 6 May. Bezborodko invited the king aboard the empress's galley. Catherine allowed Stanisław August a few minutes' private conversation. The rest of the time was passed in mixed company and in social calls on other galleys. The tsaritsa declined the king's invitation to the evening's ball and supper. The following morning the flotilla sailed on.

Prince Charles de Ligne's wisecrack, that the King of Poland had 'spent three months and three million to see the empress for three hours', begs the question of what might have happened had Stanisław August not traversed his kingdom. In every respect apart from the length of his meeting with Catherine, he had been distinguished by the Russian court. Even Ligne, who had earlier taken it upon himself to advise the king on how to charm the empress, told him as much.[7] The following day Stanisław August felt more optimistic. Catherine sent a message via Stackelberg: she approved of the proposal in principle, but could not yet consider it in detail. Potemkin had, according to Ligne, reproached her for curtailing the interview. In addition to indirect communications via Nassau-Siegen, Potemkin maintained a courteous direct correspondence with Stanisław August for much of 1787 – disquieting Stackelberg. The prince of Taurida even sought the king's permission to found a town in his Polish latifundium, to be named Nowy Stanisławów.[8]

Catherine's treatment of the Poles who had flocked to Kiev also encouraged Stanisław August. She had graciously received Prince Stanisław Poniatowski, the Mniszechs and Naruszewicz, giving the latter a cross, a ring, and an annual pension of 1,500 rubles. Potemkin had taken a shine to the latter. On the other hand, Catherine and Potemkin had disdained Ignacy Potocki and Kazimierz Sapieha. The Branickis remained in the family circle, but Potemkin upbraided the hetman for his disrespect to the king. Had Branicki received Catherine and Potemkin at Biała Cerkiew, he would have scored a political triumph. Had the empress treated Potocki and Sapieha more courteously, their credit would have soared. Had she refused the order of the White Eagle, the king would have been humiliated. Stanisław August prevented the opposition from outbidding him. Although the day after the meeting with the empress he felt despondent that the interview had been so short, by the following day – his nameday – his spirits had risen. Concluding his relation to Kiciński, he thanked God, and gave a hundred ducats to Warsaw hospitals from his personal treasury.[9] The voyage was no fiasco.

Potemkin's agenda remains hard to fathom. Catherine suspected that he wished to make himself independent, while he himself told Stanisław August that he wished Smila to become a fief of the Polish Crown. In practice it was already a state within a state. At the same time as Potemkin was supporting the alliance proposed by Stanisław August, sulking at Catherine and abusing Branicki, he was probably also drawing up plans for a confederacy led by Branicki and Feliks Potocki to seize power in the Commonwealth. Still more audaciously, he had not ruled out using the Cossacks he was recruiting for the Turkish war to raise the populace of the right-bank Ukraine in rebellion. For the moment, however, Potemkin probably saw Stanisław August as his best bet, and contributed to the temporary easing of confessional tensions.[10]

The first partition had removed the Orthodox bishopric of Mohylew and about half of the Orthodox population from the Commonwealth. Concentrations remained in Polesie and Podlasie, but most Orthodox faithful lived in the Polish Ukraine. Here, the nominal allegiance of over a thousand parishes had changed repeatedly since the 1760s, largely depending on the military support available to the rival Orthodox and Uniate hierarchs. Since the mid-1770s the latter had rebuilt and extended their parochial structures. They made strenuous efforts to raise standards among the clergy and to instil a Ruthenian and Catholic credal identity among the laity: a late variant of post-Tridentine confessionalization. By 1788, however, the Polish Ukraine contained almost five hundred Orthodox parishes. Many of these had been founded by Polish magnates; others by Potemkin to serve the growing population of Smila. Equally disturbing to the Uniates was the attraction to almost the entire right-bank populace of the ancient and holy capital of Rus′ – Kiev. Pilgrims to the Monastery of the Caves returned home not only with liturgical books and artefacts, chrisms, blessings and absolutions, but sometimes also with doubts about the Union and hatred of the Poles.

Left largely to their own devices, many Orthodox clergy in the Commonwealth had become slipshod. At least Viktor Sadkovskii thought so. In 1784 the former chaplain of the Russian Embassy in Warsaw became archimandrite (abbot) of Słuck – a centre of Orthodoxy in a Radziwiłł latifundium in the south of the Grand Duchy of Lithuania. Sadkovskii's responsibility for Orthodox faithful in the Commonwealth was confirmed the following year when he was consecrated bishop. His titular see of Pereiaslav was in the left-bank Ukraine, but its actual seat was Słuck. The Uniate hierarchy and the nobility of the palatinate of Kiev protested. Stanisław August, under pressure from both sides, demanded an oath of loyalty. Sadkovskii was in no hurry to comply. He busied himself disciplining lax clergymen and bringing the Orthodox Church in the Commonwealth into line with practices in the Russian Empire. Prayers for the empress were recited according to liturgical books printed in Russia, while her portraits were hung in churches. He also imported priests, mostly from the left-bank Ukraine, for new and vacant parishes. Encountering resistance from local clergymen without knowledge of Russian, he reportedly vowed to eradicate 'your accursed Lithuanian language'.[11] He meant Ruthenian as spoken in the Grand Duchy of Lithuania. This exposes Catherine II's later claims that the populations of what are now Belarus and Ukraine were united in faith and language with the Russian nation. But it also signalled a new determination to subordinate the Orthodox in the Commonwealth to the Holy Synod in St Petersburg. The king began to take the threat seriously.

During the journey east, Stanisław August lavished attention on the Uniate Church. Pupils of the Basilians' school in Włodzimierz welcomed him with panegyrics in Polish, Latin, French, Italian, German and even English. The head of the school, Reverend Julian Antonowicz, would publish the first English grammar in Polish the following year.[12] In 1787 the date of Easter coincided in the two calendars, so during Holy Week, the king ordered court ceremonies to be held in the Ruthenian rite in order to show the populace the essential unity between the two rites. He even washed the feet of twelve old Ruthenes on Maundy Thursday before personally serving them dinner – a local variant on his annual pious ritual, inspired by Christ's act of humility towards his apostles at the Last Supper.[13]

On 18 May 1787, summoned by Stackelberg to Feliks Potocki's gleaming new palace at Tulczyn, Sadkovskii finally swore his oath of loyalty to the king and the Commonwealth. Asked by Stanisław August to arrange this oath, Potemkin and Bezborodko edited the text. It acknowledged the Roman Catholic Church as dominant in the Commonwealth, but it was not clear whether the Russian side thereby acknowledged the Ruthenian rite as co-dominant with the Latin rite. Moreover, the oath contained no promises not to proselytize Catholic souls. The bishop then made a speech in Latin, in which he complained of the oppression of his Church. Stanisław August replied – in Polish – that as the Commonwealth observed the treaties, so he expected Sadkovskii to observe them and his oath, and to help keep the country tranquil. The monarch was less realistic regarding Potocki, who marked the royal visit by freeing the inhabitants of Tulczyn from personal serfdom. Stanisław August even convinced himself that Potocki 'is basically virtuous, and wishes the Fatherland well, and that we can again manage to clasp him to us'. Catherine II had been careful to discriminate in her treatment of the Potockis in Kiev: she snubbed Ignacy, but flattered Feliks. The latter was far from reconciled with the king, but this was the beginning of the end of his flirtation with Puławy (Plate 29).[14]

The king took heart from his brief but lively meeting with Emperor Joseph II at his nephew Prince Stanisław's residence at Korsuń on 11 May. Joseph assured him that he did not want 'a single tree' from Poland. However, the studiedly informal Habsburg found the king's majestic tone 'a bit theatrical for [a] Poniatowski'.[15] For the emperor on his way to tour the Crimea with the empress, meeting the King of Poland was but a diversion.

Stanisław August made his return journey via Cracow. A programme of religious ceremonies and civic welcomes awaited him. Belatedly, he stayed in refurbished apartments in Wawel Castle, and made the traditional pre-coronation royal pilgrimage on foot to Skałka, the site of the martyrdom in 1079 of St Stanisław.[16] Despite the problematic connotations of a bishop who had led resistance to a crowned king, St Stanisław had long served his namesake's court preachers as the model of the good shepherd, when annually on the king's nameday they urged unity and harmony. Since Stanisław August's abduction in 1771, preachers could make more explicit comparisons between king and saint.

The monarch manifested his support for the city's reformed university, admiring its new facilities. An unexpected scandal broke when in the presence of the king, primate and other dignitaries, Reverend Professor Józef Bogucicki read out a 'dissertation' on ecclesiastical history. Bogucicki tore into clerical 'fanaticism', especially the burning at the stake of the Bohemian reformer Jan Hus at Constance in 1415. Such criticism had already been made by enlightened Catholic clergymen in Bohemia. They sought to promote reconciliation with Hus's followers, the still prohibited Utraquists (named for taking communion in both bread and wine).[17] However, Bogucicki's open condemnation of the decision of an ecumenical council of the Catholic Church, believed to be guided by the Holy Spirit, provoked a local backlash against the 'blasphemer' and his supporters. It did not help the professor's cause that he was a neophyte of Jewish origin. The primate sent him off to a country parish until the furore had died down. The king went back to Warsaw and waited for the empress's answer.

The 'Bogucicki affair' exposed tensions regarding the Commission of National Education. At the heart of the new educational system were the universities. After the idea of establishing a completely new university in Warsaw had proved too expensive, the old academies of Cracow and Wilno were renovated. In 1783 the two academies were respectively rechristened as the Principal Schools of the Crown and of the Grand Duchy of Lithuania. These utilitarian names were not accidental. The universities were entrusted with supervising secondary schools in their respective territories. They were also to train schoolmasters. It was hardly surprising that professors found little time for research. Sad to relate, Primate Poniatowski regarded research as a luxury, as did Emperor Joseph II, and many philistine politicians since. His interventionist style – combining the offices of acting chancellor and chairman of the commission – brought mixed blessings to Cracow University. Crucially, he backed Reverend Hugo Kołłątaj, who first as visitor and then as rector (a position he held until 1786), carried out the reform, appointing new talent but making numerous enemies among the older professors and local clergy.

The former Jesuit Marcin Poczobut adopted a less confrontational but no less effective approach after his appointment to the rectorship of Wilno University in 1780. However, his search for foreign expertise did not always yield happy results. The botanist Jean-Emmanuel Gilibert, whom Antoni Tyzenhauz had employed at the medical school in Grodno, reluctantly moved to Wilno in 1781. He left abruptly in 1783. His successor in the Chair of Natural Sciences was

Johann Georg Forster, who had sailed with Captain Cook. Predisposed to find the locals simultaneously barbaric and decadent, Forster hardly knew how to behave in the company of flirtatious Vilnan ladies. He developed such an aversion to Polish that he tried to prevent his daughter from learning the language. Unable to meet his employer's high expectations, including the establishment of a botanical garden, he bought himself out of his remaining contract. By the time a local man, one of Forster's former students, Reverend Professor Stanisław Jundziłł, had established the garden, the Commonwealth had ceased to exist.

The extensive correspondence left by Poczobut indicates that as rector he was able to spend far less time observing the heavens, let alone analysing his observations, than in his happier days as a Jesuit. Ex-Jesuit teachers bombarded him with supplications for benefices and early retirement. Parents lobbied him on behalf of their children. One complained that his sixteen-year-old son had been flogged by the Dominican head of the school at Merecz so severely that the boy's life had been endangered.[18] Another, the Castellan of Brześć Litewski, explained that his son attended the Piarists' school in Dąbrowica and had hitherto been accommodated in the monastery, but Wilno Academy had instructed the school not to let young nobles lodge in the monastery. The castellan pleaded with Poczobut to allow his son to stay another year, as he had no other place to stay. His reasoning deserves quoting, not least because it uses the word 'enlightened' as part of a defensive strategy against the corrupting perils of the modern world:

> I was convinced at home that under the supervision of a virtuous and enlightened monk, and in the shadow of solitude, the boy would allow the inculcation in his heart of those sentiments of religion and innocence, which are without doubt difficult to acquire in the present age.[19]

The father sought the 'shade of isolation' and 'virtuous and enlightened' monastic supervision for his son in a remote place: he correctly reckoned the distance from Warsaw at about sixty miles (420 kilometres as the crow flies, but harder to convey in terms of the travelling conditions of the time). Dąbrowica was located on the slow-flowing river Horyń, a tributary of the equally unhurried Pripet in Polesie. The Piarist college, founded in 1695, had a good reputation.

Poczobut also had to sort out problems caused by undisciplined and drunken pupils. Disorder erupted sporadically in towns right across the Grand Duchy from Kroże in Samogitia to Bobrujsk on the lower Berezyna. In the latter case, during 1790–91 students physically and verbally abused border guards and customs officials – it transpired that a professor's involvement in a tobacco racket lay behind the trouble.[20]

The rector acquired some of his authority at the expense of his neighbour across the narrow street that divided the university from the episcopal palace – the louche and chronically indebted Ignacy Massalski. (Poczobut sometimes also trained his telescopes on the bishop's delightful summer residence of Werki, perched on the bluffs of the River Wilia.) The respect Poczobut enjoyed and his natural tact helped to smooth the systemic transition in the Grand Duchy of Lithuania. Nevertheless, school pro-rectors sometimes complained to him of low enrolment. They blamed this partly on competition from traditional monastic or Protestant schools, either located beyond the frontier or else masquerading as elementary schools. They also lamented the 'unenlightenment' of the noble citizenry. One complained that 'these Samogitians are an unrefined people, they have so fled on vacation, that they are nowhere to be found . . . No good will ever come from these Samogitians. A waste of the Commission's expense. They know absolutely nothing useful. They shame their schools and lessons before the parents.' Despite this, the rector could also read more optimistic assessments, such as that earlier received from the same correspondent: 'the school is ever more populous. The former opinion about schools retreats further, and good opinion increases. They speak better of us. Patience overcomes all.'[21]

The fact that former Jesuits acted as the Commission's visitors to schools staffed predominantly by ex-Jesuit teachers, or else run by other religious orders, helped to manage tensions in the Grand Duchy of Lithuania. But the softer line taken in Lithuania compared to the Crown also ensured that foes of the Society of Jesus, starting with Kołłątaj, have since been prone to accuse the Loyolans of delaying and diluting the reforms. This criticism particularly applies to the implementation of the move to a system in which most teachers were laymen, educated in accordance with enlightened standards at the new universities. Expecting young laymen to follow a quasi-monastic regimen as teachers in former Jesuit schools was asking for trouble. Complaints that they partook in licentious conduct alongside their charges were not always unfounded. These newly minted pedagogues were often regarded with suspicion – even hostility – by ex-Jesuit teachers and parents.

The latter were excoriated by one of the Commission's visitors in the Crown, Reverend Franciszek Salezy Jezierski. In a withering speech delivered in 1785 he accused the older teachers of the school at Łęczyca of sabotaging the programme. He told the pupils – in front of their parents – that they should not 'hold any other class of citizens in contempt', whatever the 'prejudiced public' believed. The spluttering prompted the primate to remove Jezierski from the list of visitors (although he got him the co-adjutorship of a canonry of Cracow).[22]

Despite the long-standing Jesuit and Piarist traditions of public performances by pupils, which from the mid-eighteenth century included scientific experiments, critics derided some of the natural science taught in the Commission's schools as impractical. More damaging was the conviction that the new approach to Latin (the grammatically driven study of classical literature, with fewer hours allocated) left pupils unable to cut a figure at a banquet, funeral or law court. Evidence of contemporary criticism of the Commission and its schools survives, not least in the sejmik instructions of 1788 and 1790. However, some assemblies heaped praise on local schools. The descendants of the exiled nobles of Czernihów commended the local Basilians for inculcating martial values and skills in their pupils:

> When we see with our own eyes the zealous work of the Reverend Basilian Fathers of Włodzimierz, who exercise noble youth not only in their learned subjects according to the statutes of the Most Illustrious Educational Commission, and in numerous foreign languages, always to great advantage, but who also, on days free from lessons exercise them in the knightly art, keeping the proper rules, [they] give [us] sure hope that every year the Fatherland will have people prepared for the army.[23]

The verdict of posterity on the Commission has generally been laudatory – at least as regards secondary and higher education, as far less was achieved at elementary level. Some part of this may derive from taking the Commission's own propaganda at face value, but the reason goes deeper. It fits the commonest grand narrative of the Stanislavian period, that adopted by most admirers of the king: the saving of the Polish nation amidst the destruction of the Polish state. Polish-Lithuanian educational reformers would indeed draw on the Commission's legacy in the early nineteenth century. In popular versions of this grand narrative we are sometimes invited to imagine that the Great Sejm itself was the fruit of the Commission's work. This cannot be literally true – hardly any of the envoys were young enough to have attended its schools. Their formation was most often accomplished by the reformed Piarist and Jesuit colleges of the 1750s and 1760s, and in a few cases (such as Julian Niemcewicz) by the king's own Cadet Corps.

That said, the atmosphere of enlightened but deeply emotional patriotism surrounding the Commission's work bridged political divides. It united Michał Poniatowski with Ignacy Potocki. The enthusiasm must have been infectious. This ethos was not only embedded in the curriculum, but given public expression during events such as the multilingual welcome the monarch received in Włodzimierz on 7 March 1787. In this way the well-publicized cause of 'national education' contributed mightily to the excitement which so worried Stanisław August in the spring of 1788. This ferment(ation) and a change in international circumstances were about to launch the Commonwealth on its meteoric trajectory of light and flame.

As in France, the Polish Revolution only became thinkable once it became possible.[24] In both countries, however, much of the trouble began with an 'aristocratic revolt'. We shall follow some Polish aristocrats to Paris in the aftermath of the Dogrumowa affair.

In the spring of 1787 Princess Izabella Lubomirska was mesmerized. Every morning Monsieur Lamotte, a pupil of Franz Anton Mesmer, would call at her residence in Paris. Lamotte would place vases containing magnetized plants around her bed and then connect them by threads to her thinning hair. The princess told her visitors that her tresses had thickened remarkably since the start of the treatment. Lamotte accompanied Lubomirska and her suite when she decided to tour England. During their crossing of the Channel, he wished to make a magnetic connection between the vessel and the winds, but the alarmed ship's captain almost threw him overboard. By the time the party returned to Paris later in the year, the Mesmerist craze was approaching its zenith. Lubomirska's son-in-law, Stanisław Potocki, visited one of the popular 'magnetic houses', in which patients appeared by turns to fall asleep and awake, to converse and convulse under the influence of magnetism. Decades later, Potocki's companion Julian Niemcewicz claimed to have been the only sceptic in the party.[25]

The French political scene was as mesmerizing as the magnets. Helping the American colonists to gain their independence had cost France dear. The previous autumn the comptroller-general of the royal finances, Viscount Calonne, had convinced Louis XVI that the kingdom was on the verge of bankruptcy. Furthermore, argued Calonne, the only way out of the crisis was through a fundamental reform of the state, society and economy. This would involve a more rational and efficient system of taxes, including a new land tax to be levied without exemptions, the dismantling of trade barriers, and the establishment of provincial assemblies throughout France. The king reluctantly agreed to the plan. However, the handpicked Assembly of Notables, convened to show the support needed to shore up government credit, refused to endorse the reform package without provisions for transparency and external supervision. Louis XVI refused the Notables' demand for a permanent audit commission for the royal finances. Following further protests, the king dissolved the Assembly in May 1787.

The Archbishop of Toulouse, Loménie de Brienne, installed as first minister after Calonne's dismissal, then sought to ram legislation through the kingdom's high courts, the *parlements*. Many of these changes were salutary. They included the abolition of judicial torture and the belated restoration of civil status to Protestants. However, much of merit was lost in the polarized public debate in which accusations of royal despotism and aristocratic and clerical privilege were freely traded. The *parlements* declared that only the Estates-General, which had not met since 1614, had the authority to enact new taxes. Forcible registration of the edicts provoked public demonstrations. The king first ordered the Parlement of Paris into exile, then recalled it to Paris where it was expected to approve a diluted set of measures. However, the flustered monarch forced the registration of the new loans on 19 November 1787, prompting his cousin Philippe, the Duke of Orléans, to protest that this step was illegal. The king blurted out: 'it is legal because I wish it'.[26] The following day, Orléans and others were sent into internal exile by *lettre de cachet* – an arbitrary royal fiat. Public opinion erupted in anger – what better proof could there be of royal despotism? After a winter of discontent, Brienne tried in May 1788 to replace the *parlements* with new jurisdictions. He failed. As popular protests continued across France, government credit collapsed. In August Louis XVI had to recall the Swiss banker Jacques Necker to direct the kingdom's finances, and agree to call the Estates-General the following year. The fallout would sweep away all the intermediary powers and privileges defended so eloquently by the notables and magistrates.

The drama of these events was not lost on Princess Lubomirska's companions. They included, besides Niemcewicz and Stanisław Potocki, another son-in-law

Jan Potocki (who would later write the *Manuscript Found in Saragossa*), her nephew Adam Jerzy Czartoryski, and the latter's democratically inclined Tuscan preceptor, the Abbé Scipione Piattoli, a former Piarist. Besides the Duke of Orléans, among the luminaries who frequented Lubomirska's drawing rooms was the American envoy to France, Thomas Jefferson, who in 1776 had penned the Declaration of Independence.

It was, therefore, a heady mix of republican and anti-monarchical rhetoric that filled the head of the seventeen-year-old Prince Adam Jerzy as he sat down with Piattoli at the end of 1787 to draft an extraordinary project. This plan to seize power in the Commonwealth began with the claim that the szlachta's indignation at the contemptible condition of Poland furnished the opportunity for a secret organization of patriotic lords to lead the nobles against the royal court. At the heart would be a 'Quattuorvirat' – a resonant name inspired by republican Rome. This one would be formed by Seweryn Rzewuski, Feliks Potocki, Adam Kazimierz Czartoryski and an unnamed fourth man. They would be joined by eight further magnates in a 'patriotic congress'. These eight would swear to obey the Quattuorvirat's decisions and provide collateral for a loan of 150,000 ducats. They would join forces to prevail at sejmiks, confederate the palatinates, establish noble militias (under the pretext of defending the frontiers), and win a majority at the sejm. This would allow them to correct abuses and repair the constitution, increase the army to 100,000 men and place it under the command of the Quattuorvirat. An extraordinary committee would assume dictatorial powers. The 'big four' would reside in the south-east. Emanuel Rostworowski pronounced the planned Quattuorvirat a 'mafia organization of magnates', dressed up in the rhetoric of the American Congress at Philadelphia.[27]

Prince Adam Jerzy was idealistic and impressionable. His older relatives doubtless found it easy to convince themselves that what was good for them was good for the Commonwealth. But the time was approaching when 'aristocrat' would be hurled as an insult on the banks of the Seine and the Vistula alike. The discourse of liberty heard in Paris resonated stirringly for the young hope of the 'new *Familia*', for his radical Tuscan preceptor, and for his *Rousseauiste* mother. It is doubtful, however, whether anyone in the Commonwealth fully understood the international ramifications of the turmoil in France – except perhaps for the eccentric genius, Jan Potocki, who witnessed events in the Netherlands at first hand.

In the late summer of 1787 Prussia had taken advantage of France's slide towards bankruptcy to invade and subdue the Dutch Republic. The Netherlands were in the throes of conflict between the Francophile, democratically inclined 'patriots' and the patrician supporters of the Anglophile stadtholder, William V of Orange. When the latter's wife was treated ungallantly by 'patriot' militiamen, her brother King Frederick William II seized the pretext to intervene: within seven weeks, the Prussian army had restored the stadtholder's authority. The following year the Dutch Republic formed the Triple Alliance with Great Britain and Prussia. The humiliating exposure of France's impotence damaged further the credibility of its government, both at home and abroad.

In the country where all the might of Habsburg Spain and Bourbon France had failed in the previous century, Hohenzollern Prussia had triumphed with ease. The corpulent and sensual Frederick William II had felt the barbs of his misanthropic old uncle Frederick II; having at last ascended the throne in 1786, the nephew was keen to prove himself. Crucially, he was free of his predecessor's dread of Russia. Catherine for her part was blithely contemptuous of 'GeGu' – her compound name for the Germanic duo of King George III of Great Britain and Frederick William II (*Ge*orges + *Gu*illaume). The former had infuriated her by his involvement – as elector of Hanover – in the League of German Princes in 1785–86. This successful resistance to Joseph II's plans to exchange the Austrian Netherlands for Bavaria, orchestrated by the wizened Frederick II, had also diminished the significance of Russia's recently acquired role as guarantor of the Holy Roman Empire.

While the Prussians were mopping up in the Netherlands, on 17 August 1787 the Ottoman Empire again imprisoned a Russian ambassador in the fortress of the Seven Towers. His name was Iakov Bulgakov and we shall meet him again. In February 1788 Joseph II came to Russia's aid against the Turks, safe in the knowledge that the ministers of his brother-in-law Louis XVI could not rescue the Porte. The fact that the Ottoman Empire had been the first to declare war saved the French some embarrassment, but the already rancorous Austro-French alliance took another hit. This alliance had served since 1763 to restrain both parties, and thus contributed to the prevention of a general European war, but it did nothing to hold back Russia or Great Britain. Their hegemonic potential was growing.

In the summer of 1788 the Russian and Austrian armies made a painfully slow start against the Turks. At the same time King Gustav III of Sweden (who had thrown off Russian tutelage in 1772) made a pre-emptive strike. He hoped to recover lost territories and mediate in the Ottoman war. After the Swedish artillery rattled windows in St Petersburg, the empress suddenly looked vulnerable. Prussian threats kept Russia's ally Denmark neutral. However, before thus raising the stakes, the Prussian court had recently made a notable attempt to profit from the situation. The recurring scheme concocted by Frederick II's experienced minister Ewald von Hertzberg had several variations that depended on circumstances, but essentially it involved the Prussian acquisition of Danzig, Thorn and parts of Greater Poland. These would be Prussia's 'compensation' for Russian and Austrian gains from the Porte. Poland would regain some or all of Galicia in recompense for its losses to Prussia. Austria's vehement opposition to this unequal bargain was only to be expected, but St Petersburg's rejection of the proposal in May 1788 led Berlin to consider causing trouble for Russia in the Commonwealth. The Hertzberg plan was shelved, but not scrapped.

The opportunities from this diplomatic constellation were slow to register in Poland. During the summer of 1788 the coolest analysis of the situation was penned by Michał Poniatowski. The primate was seeking to keep the Palatine of Sieradz, Michał Walewski, from siding with the opposition (unsuccessfully, as it turned out). Walewski was a kinsman and closet supporter of Branicki, but had ascended the ladder through the favour of the king and his brother. It is worth quoting this letter at length, not least for the unceremonious references to the Commonwealth's neighbours:

> Besides, if it is difficult to expect from human beings (although it would behove Christians) that we should all love each other wholeheartedly, then at least we should suspend particular dislikes, quarrels, private interests, and now think and prudently confer with each other for the sake of our entirety, in such a way so that in not desiring to do too much at once, it would not end with our utter ruin, if we should start acting in a sovereign manner or too briskly. As will probably happen with the king of Sweden, who having received some money, seems seriously to be taking on Muscovy, at this unpredictable moment when the happy Catherine, no longer needing her prepared fleet or her army on the Mediterranean Sea, will turn them entirely on him, with certain help from Denmark, should she require it. The Turks and even the Swedes themselves have forgotten that they are today no longer what they were under Charles XII, and nor are the Muscovites as they were when Peter the Great found them. France is far away from us and has enough to deal with herself. England is only ready to defend her trade everywhere, and in Muscovy to expand it further. The Prussian [wishes] to

> drag Muscovy away from the emperor who weakens his armies and treasuries by his incomprehensible way of fighting a war, and doubtless to gain something at our expense, if we by premature and sovereign actions give him an opportunity to do so. The Turk has too much to deal with, and needed our goodwill in order to wreak destruction on Poland as of old, and abduct her people as slaves, as he did for several centuries, and even during the last war on the estates of Prince Lubomirski, the Palatine of Kiev. This is the true state of Europe and its interests, from which it is easy for an enlightened citizen, who wishes his Fatherland well and is willing to govern himself, to draw out the true consequences.[28]

This was a bucket of cold water. Most of these predictions would come true, but not for some years. And that made all the difference. International events were already taking an unexpected trajectory, bringing new opportunities to the Commonwealth. The Poles' 'sovereign actions' were both a consequence and a cause of that course.

Among the opposition magnates, Ignacy Potocki – snubbed by Catherine in Kiev – was the first major figure to consider seeking a new protector in Berlin. Adam Kazimierz Czartoryski was prepared to listen. He mused about his son-in-law Prince Ludwig of Württemberg, a nephew of Frederick William II, as a potential king of Poland. The 'Quattuorvirat' plan envisaged the negotiation of Poland's alliance with Great Britain, Prussia and the Dutch Republic, while maintaining neutrality in the Russo-Ottoman war. There was uncertainty in Puławy, however, whether other magnates would agree to a pivot away from Russia towards Prussia. Moreover, most of the Puławy set were Austrian *sujets mixtes*, and the two imperial courts were allies engaged in a major war. For the moment, therefore, the talk was of a confederacy, raised in the south-east, and the raising of National Cavalry regiments which would fight the Turks at Russian expense. The consolidation of the magnate coalition proceeded on this basis, but without Feliks Potocki who was dissuaded by Ambassador Stackelberg. Potemkin remained the focus of Branicki's hopes for a confederacy against the throne.

Catherine II's priority in the Commonwealth was stability. She mistrusted Stanisław August, but the last thing she needed was unrest so close to the theatre of war. And such was the likely outcome of the magnates' offer of a confederacy directed against the king. Having learned some lessons from the Bar conflagration, she temporized. Her decision, when at last it came, was a diluted compromise.

She sanctioned a minor increase in the size of the Polish army. Three brigades of Polish cavalry would fight, not as a combined Polish corps, but separately. Their respective commanders would be Branicki, Prince Stanisław Poniatowski and Feliks Potocki. This choice was a sop to both sides as well as to the vacillating Croesus. These troops would be paid for – after the war – by Russia. To facilitate the requisite legislation, the empress consented to the confederation of the sejm. She stipulated that – unlike in 1776 – the sejm should be confederated after it had been inaugurated. This would have fateful consequences.

By the time the Russian counter-proposal finally reached Warsaw in September 1788, much of the provincial szlachta was beyond control. The king could not seize the opportunity he had discerned to mobilize wealthier and middling nobles against the opposition in support of his plan to activate the Commonwealth on the international stage. Youthful minds fermented. Berlin had to deny rumours of an imminent Prussian incursion into Greater Poland, some of which originated from Jan Potocki, who was mindful of what he had seen in the Netherlands. Potocki became the social sensation of the spring of 1788. This largely Francophone aristocrat reattired himself in a short-cut version of the Polish national costume. This he intended as a model for the uniform of the units of sharpshooters which he proposed. He himself funded a formation of sappers (twenty-six men strong). He declaimed his loyalty to the king but urged him to stand up for the dignity of the Commonwealth – regularly insulted by the Russian ambassador. Rostworowski memorably compared Potocki to the count in Mickiewicz's *Pan Tadeusz*: 'He is a crank, I know, and somewhat strange, but a good Pole and not to be refused. In revolutions such men can be used.' A revolution was in the air, but of which sort no one could yet tell.[29]

Turnout was high at the sejmiks of August 1788 (Plate 25). The opposition leaders expected to do better than in 1786. Russia did not rein them in, hoping to defuse tensions in Poland while fighting two wars at once. Similar considerations had prevailed a decade earlier, during the War of the Bavarian Succession. Stanisław August complained that this only encouraged more trouble. Stackelberg agreed, but it made no difference. As usual, the opposition did best in Lesser Poland. Izabela Czartoryska personally supervised the electioneering in Podolia. Faced with cartloads of petty nobles, the court party capitulated. At Lublin, crowds of drunken and brawling noblemen threatened to get out of hand, but after the opposition had taken all six mandates, Elżbieta Sapieżyna, née Branicka, congratulated her 'beloved Spartan woman'.[30] Violence also marred the Volhynian sejmik at Łuck, where Branicki's supporters took five out of six mandates. Elsewhere, keenly contested sejmiks saw a more even division of the spoils, although royalist candidates prevailed in most of Mazovia and Lithuania. Again, a notable exception was Kazimierz Sapieha's stamping ground of Brześć Litewski.

The singular sejmik of Livonia proved a weathercock. Russia had annexed this Lithuano-Polish condominium in 1772, but six years later consented to the reactivation of its sejmik. A water meadow in the River Dvina supplied the venue. Stanisław August compared the Livonian sejmik to the English 'rotten borough' of Old Sarum.[31] However, by the later 1780s the court encountered difficulties even here. In 1788 the opposition candidates turned up in person (this had also worked for the future king himself back in 1756). The sejmik's decision to insist that participants own lands in the Commonwealth further weakened the royalists. To cap it all, Potemkin sent a letter recommending the opposition candidates. They were all elected. As one of them, Niemcewicz, recalled, 'the name of Potemkin, like the head of Medusa, turned everyone to stone'.[32]

Having pored over the results, both sides still expected the monarch to have a majority, but it would be more volatile than at previous sejms. The instructions also provided much food for thought. The king could be satisfied with the support expressed across the Commonwealth for augmenting the army. He was worried, however, by the reluctance to tap noble fortunes and the lack of enthusiasm for war against the Ottoman Empire. His explanation for the pacific mood graded four factors – 'Prussian threats', 'the almost universal hostility to war against the Turks', 'the hostility verging on disgust towards the emperor', and 'the recalling of various injuries sustained from the Russian court and armies'.[33] Perhaps he should have placed that last factor first. An unmistakeable 'noble and provincial voice' broke through the conventional formulae hammered out through influence, negotiation and compromise.[34]

The opposition succeeded in including points hostile to the Permanent Council and/or its Military Department at the sejmiks for the palatinates of Lublin, Brześć Litewski, Sieradz and Volhynia. However, the wording of some instructions hinted at unresolved differences regarding the hetmans' powers. The question expected by the opposition to touch the rawest nerves among the szlachta was the Permanent Council's entitlement to interpret the law. Here the Lublin instruction appealed to republican values: 'Because in a republican state, nothing but the law gives security to citizens; how can this law give security to him who does not have it, because it is subject to arbitrary arbitration?'[35]

Another of Branicki's priorities was the establishment of local militias. The Volhynian instruction cast this as opposition to monarchical forms of government:

> In a free nation each citizen is a participant in government, and so the greatest power and strength should be with the nation; it is difficult for us citizens to maintain numerous armed forces in the monarchical way; we are content with a smaller number of disciplined soldiers.

In case of an invasion, the palatinate would call out a citizens' militia.[36] With this partial exception, no sejmik contested the need to expand the professional army. However, several sejmiks called for the increase to be in the ranks, rather than in officers, while some gave priority to native-born Poles and the National Cavalry.

The king hoped to be given a free hand to steer the Commonwealth to safety. A standard formula to this effect is found in five Lithuanian instructions:

> We are taught by the unhappy experience of our age, that internal disorders and indifference to wars between neighbouring powers provided the occasion to tear away from the Commonwealth its most beautiful provinces. Therefore we want our honourable envoys to lay before His Majesty the King and the Estates of the Commonwealth our care for the entirety and security of our territories in the current circumstances, similar to previous ones, of the war begun between Austria, Muscovy and the Porte. We cannot prescribe anything in detail to our honourable envoys, we oblige them only with love of the Fatherland, that with complete trust in His Majesty regarding the salvation of the Fatherland they should unite their opinions and counsels with the assembled Estates of the Commonwealth, taking the most solemn measures for its security and defence. In which, should a public offering be necessary, our honourable envoys shall gladly agree to this alongside the envoys of other palatinates, with only this reservation, that this offering should be in such a proportion, that it would not entail the ruination of our properties. In which we consign ourselves to the enlightenment and zeal of our honourable envoys.[37]

This wording appears to be a court attempt to impress on the Lithuanian szlachta a sense of peril, requiring trust in the king's leadership, while at the same time offering reassurance that the cost to nobles would be kept to a minimum. However, nearly all Lithuanian sejmiks insisted on exhausting other sources of revenue and cutting government spending before any further burden could be laid on noble fortunes. In this they took the same position as their counterparts in the Polish Crown.

More troubling to the king was the lack of appetite for war. Apart from opposition strongholds in the Crown, the more outspoken sejmiks included Livonia and Mozyrz which demanded 'that they keep intact the friendship and tranquillity maintained until now with the Ottoman Porte according to the treaties'.[38] Expressing an old caveat, the sejmik of Ciechanów in Mazovia added that the expanded army could be used only 'for the particular need of the nation, and not for services to other nations'.[39]

Everywhere nobles looked to throw most or all of the costs of the army onto others. The citizens of the Wołkowysk district noted that the burghers of royal towns provided no labour services, and claimed that peasants on Crown estates performed 'far less' labour than those of nobly owned estates. Therefore those settlements should pay a higher hearth tax.[40] Tensions between laity and clergy also found their outlet. The Orsza instruction was typical in demanding the diminution of 'the excessive revenues of the inactive clergy, and leaving only that which suffices for an honest life according to clerical standards', and assigning the rest to the army.[41]

Several sejmiks also destined educational funds for the army. Religious orders could run the schools. A few instructions affected the king's pride and joy. The szlachta of Wołkowysk, noting that the graduates of the Knights' School could not find commissions as officers, wanted its funds applied to the army. Other ways could be found to train youth for war.[42] Here and there we can glimpse poor nobles' need of gainful employment. The Słonim sejmik not only demanded their exemption from new taxes, but their education as active citizens: 'the impoverished szlachta, having no possibility of education, but authorized by our laws to participate in our deliberations, should become fit for this prerogative'. These indigent brethren were to be promoted to civil offices according to their ability.[43] Such expenditure would require savings elsewhere. The train of professional government ran into the buffers of the republican conviction that public service was a civic duty, not a salaried profession. In general, however, the

Stanislavian era's 'culture clash' is less apparent in the Lithuanian instructions than in those from the Crown. Perhaps the density of powdered periwigs had not yet reached choking levels in most of the Grand Duchy? Closer to Warsaw, foreign attire and travel were denounced: the Sandomierz sejmik demanded a complete ban on all voyages abroad by persons of both sexes.

Taken together, these instructions gave off more heat than light, but amidst the traditionalists' laments were signs of interest in new solutions. The Livonian and Podolian sejmiks favoured a physiocratic land tax. A reflection on the distemper and healing of the body politic emerges from the Kowno instruction. This stated that 'the entire principle of a republican government' depended on the common election of officials, and that therefore 'there is nothing dearer to every nobleman than the free voice'. However, the latter was often a 'playground and vain sign of that freedom'. The envoys were therefore to seek 'among the very first matters of the sejm, a law on the procedure for sejmik deliberations, as a foundation of free government, cleansed from all contradictions, disarray and quibbles, and laid out more clearly'.[44] This call for procedural reform came from an assembly never broken up by the *liberum veto*.

The eagerly anticipated sejm of 1788 shattered all expectations.

— NINE —

REVOLUTION

THE KING WITH THE NATION

At about four o'clock in the morning on 30 May 1792 the sejm prorogued itself. Since it had first met on 6 October 1788, it had sat for 562 sessions.[1] Although it was not able to reconvene, the Four Years' Sejm, also called the Great Sejm, proved the longest parliament in the history of the Commonwealth. Its records are so voluminous that the king could not keep up the custom of fully publishing the official diary of the sejm's deliberations. The diaries of the sejms of 1776 to 1784 each fitted within a single volume. In this case, six folio volumes were printed. If the entire diary had been published thus, forty volumes, about 13,500 pages in all, would have been needed to record about 32,000 interventions and speeches. Most of the original diary of the Four Years' Sejm remains in manuscript.[2] The first four volumes of the official diary (numbered in two tomes, each of two parts) were produced from 1790 onwards at the court press associated with the Educational Commission. They record the sessions from the sejm's inauguration until 6 March 1789. These volumes have a traditional frontispiece, representing the crowned arms of the Commonwealth: the Kingdom of Poland and Grand Duchy of Lithuania quartered around the heraldic symbol of the Poniatowskis – the calf. Very different is the frontispiece of the last two volumes, produced from 1791 onwards by the royal bookseller Michał Gröll, which record the sessions from 16 December 1790 to 7 February 1791. It depicts a victorious personification of liberty, holding a Phrygian-style 'liberty cap' atop a pike. Such a cap evoked revolutionary France. This symbolic transformation of the official record attests a revolution in political culture (Plates 26 and 27).

Revolution is the right word. At the beginning of 1789 the editor of the *Historical, Political and Economic Recorder* promised readers that the periodical would cover 'great events and revolutions of nations, which change their state, government, laws and their relations with other nations', all of which 'entail changes in Europe'.[3] Contemporaries referred to the changes associated with the entirety of the Great Sejm as a 'revolution' in at least five languages. However, most historians have confined the term to the acclamation and implementation of the Constitution of 3 May – if they are prepared to use it at all. Contemporaries used the word 'revolution' for these events too. Some defined or qualified the term. This, for example, is from the official account of the parliamentary session of 3 May 1791:

> A revolution is what I call this important change, constituting an era in the history of the nation, whereby the government of the Commonwealth has begun to be stable and systematic. Similar events in other states carry the characteristics of violence, civil war and the spilling of citizens' blood. This revolution signifies the universal joy of the people which is able to feel its happiness.[4]

The contrast made here is crucial. The change in the Commonwealth, so important that it was deemed revolutionary, concerned the form of government, the way it functioned, and the happiness this change brought to the people. If, on the other hand, the essence of a revolution is a sudden overthrow of one system of government, or even a social order, and its replacement by a different one, in contravention of the existing law and accompanied by violence against established elites and their supporters, then it would be hard to find a revolution in the Commonwealth between 1788 and 1792. Maximilien Robespierre's reaction (in November 1792) to those who said he had blood on his hands is telling: 'Citizens, did you want a revolution without a revolution?'[5] And yet we commonly speak of 'revolutions' in all sorts of contexts, qualified by all kinds of adjectives – even 'gradual'. Much changed in these years, and those changes were both rapid and significant. Emboldened by contemporaries, we may write of a 'Polish Revolution' in 1788–92.[6]

The key to understanding these revolutionary changes is the idea of the 'nation'.[7] This usually meant the 'Polish nation', although citizens of the Grand Duchy of Lithuania spoke freely about both the 'Polish' and 'Lithuanian' nations. Neither usage should be confused with later meanings. The 'Two Nations', characteristic of confederate nomenclature, were distinguished when the status of the Grand Duchy was at stake. Nevertheless, Lithuanian parliamentarians often tried to outdo their brethren from the Crown within the shared political community they all called 'the nation'. The first revolutionary change was the reclaiming by the nation of its sovereignty. By casting off the Russian 'guarantee', the Commonwealth became a player, not a pawn, in international politics. The sejm could make decisions with real consequences for the country's institutions, finances, armed forces and foreign relations. Here at last was an opportunity for the political community to show its mettle. The possibility invited unprecedented public debate. One crucial question concerned the will of the nation. Was it to be articulated by nobles at sejmiks and conveyed to the sejm by mandatory instructions? Or at the sejm, whose members represented 'the entire nation' and used their judgement for its common good?

The latter view of representation facilitated acceptance of the second revolutionary change: in the composition of the nation. Until this point the nation had been synonymous with the szlachta; many, probably most of them, wished to keep it that way. But now another argument was heard: the nation should comprise all inhabitants of the Commonwealth. By the end of the Great Sejm, the point had been carried. Moreover, all persons should enjoy some personal liberty and property under the protection of law and government. A few writers – led by the nobly born Reverend Hugo Kołłątaj – made the radical case that the rights of citizens to participate in public affairs should depend more on their property and education than their birth. This was related to the ongoing economic convergence between burghers and nobles. But for all the notoriety he attracted, Kołłątaj's favoured slogan was a 'mild revolution'.[8]

The third revolutionary change of the Great Sejm was the turn from hard-line noble republicanism towards limited parliamentary monarchy, founded in the sovereignty of a wider Polish nation. Not that republicanism was abandoned – far from it. However, crucial to this turn was an alliance between the king and enough educated and prosperous noble landowners as sufficed to persuade many more nobles to accept significant reforms. Vital to the forging of this alliance was a tide that by 1790 was running strongly against the magnates. By the end of the Polish Revolution, the traditional preference for 'perilous liberty' over 'tranquil servitude' had given way to the celebration of 'orderly freedom', contrasted with 'aristocratic anarchy'. For almost two years, however, Stanisław August had his back to the wall.

On 6 October 1788, in the collegiate church of St John the Baptist in Warsaw, the Bishop of Poznań intoned the Mass to the Holy Spirit which preceded the sejm. The preacher was the same Canon Franciszek Salezy Jezierski who had caused such scandal as a school visitor three years previously. On this solemn occasion, however, he struck a different note. He warned against 'false religion' and reminded the legislators that God would know their innermost thoughts and hold them to account for their deeds.[9]

Having repaired to their chamber in the Royal Castle, the envoys chose Stanisław Małachowski as their marshal. He was the elder brother of the Crown grand chancellor, Jacek Małachowski, who was as unswervingly oriented towards Russia as he was attached to traditional mores. Stanisław Małachowski, however, was on good terms with the opposition leaders. Widely respected for his integrity, patriotism and benevolence, but not suspected of Machiavellian genius, he had the qualities of an honest broker. After the envoys had joined the senators, the king invoked Divine Providence, unity and trust in his opening speech. The sejm then confederated itself. As parliamentary confederacies had a dual structure, Kazimierz Nestor Sapieha – Branicki's mercurial nephew – became marshal of the Lithuanian confederacy alongside Małachowski for the Crown. Małachowski retained the direction of the deliberations of the conjoined assembly of envoys and senators – if direction is the right word. Without either the authority or the temperament to curtail even the most interminable and irrelevant orations, the marshalcy of the sejm would bring him great grief. Not least when Sapieha extemporized at length.

Behind the scenes much hung in the balance. The sejm confederated itself around the Holy Catholic Faith, the entirety of the country, the republican form of government, the royal prerogative, and the existing magistracies. Its declared aims were to augment the army, raise taxes and make unspecified internal improvements.[10] In negotiations just before the sejm was inaugurated, the opposition leaders won an apparently minor amendment to the act. The king had initially proposed to confederate around existing magistracies *and dicasters* – the deletion of the latter cast doubt on the departments of the Permanent Council. Moreover, the opposition leaders only dropped their demand for the explicit safeguarding of the Commonwealth's neutrality after Stackelberg had assured them that his court would not propose an alliance. The king also had to concede that secret voting would follow open voting, should just a single envoy demand it, in all questions except taxes. This would loosen the control of the monarch over his supporters. Nevertheless, Stanisław August still believed he could use his narrow and volatile majority to achieve significant increases in taxation and the army establishment. He might even carry through some modest administrative and judicial reforms, before bringing the sejm safely to a close.

The situation was transformed by the note delivered on Monday 13 October 1788 by the resident Prussian diplomat, Ludwig von Buchholtz. Frederick William II's counsel to the Poles against allying with Russia did more than put the final bullets into the twitching corpse of Stanisław August's plan. His respectful offer of friendship and co-operation for the 'maintenance of the independence, freedom and security of Poland' both flattered and emboldened his audience. Had Buchholtz not heeded local advice to delete phrases about not provoking the Ottoman Empire and proposing the King of Prussia's own guarantee of the Polish form of government, the reception might have been cooler. As it was, the Saxon resident reported 'an unbelievable ferment in all minds and an enthusiasm for the King of Prussia'.[11] Many who had been convinced of the permanence of Russian supremacy now dared to hope for emancipation. During the next few days the opposition's leaders smelled their chance of inflicting a major reverse on the monarch. Their orators spoke stirringly of courage and independence, contrasting these manly qualities with the timid subordination of the king and his courtiers.

Stanisław August advised the sejm first to raise taxes and then to expand the army in line with the additional revenue raised. Read out immediately after the Prussian note, his propositions from the throne fell flat. Instead, the provincial sessions (held separately for Lesser Poland, Greater Poland and Lithuania) and the plenary sessions on 16 and 17 October undammed a torrent of patriotic rhetoric on the need for a strong and numerous army. It would be funded – most assuredly – by spontaneous offerings for the Fatherland. No fewer than 100,000 soldiers would do. At the same time the opposition flagged the danger to liberty in entrusting such a large force to the Military Department of the Permanent Council. In a secret vote the king could only scrape a majority over the text of the oath to be taken by members of the department to the king and Estates. On 20 October the sejm approved a fulsome note of thanks to the King of Prussia. Then Michał Walewski asked Marshal Małachowski to bring forward the first article of the Law on the Army – raising its combined establishment to 100,000. Before it could be read out, members of the sejm and the public in the galleries roared their approval. Stanisław August rose, emotionally gave thanks to Providence and then appealed for the necessary funds. Tears flowed as senators and envoys – in the customary order of precedence – pressed their lips onto the king's outstretched hand.

This show of respect towards the monarch did not last long. While some aristocratic ladies offered to sell their jewels to help fund the army, the opposition leadership had no intention of discussing the necessary taxes before it had resolved the question of control to its satisfaction. The next day Stanisław Kostka Potocki presented a project to replace the Military Department with a Military Commission directly responsible to the sejm. However, the Lithuanian provincial session demanded a separate commission for the Grand Duchy, as had been the case between 1764 and 1776. This step produced an appeal from the provincial session for Lesser Poland for the Lithuanians to expand their project to create one commission for the Commonwealth. Half the members would be from the Grand Duchy and half from the Crown, with alternate presidencies for Lithuanian and Crown hetmans. If this solution bespoke respect for the Commonwealth's dualist heritage, the appeal itself, conveyed to the Lithuanians by a special delegate, was cast in the language of 'one nation' and 'three provinces' that came naturally to nobles from the Crown: 'In constituting the Commonwealth as three provinces, we can stand like three brothers, who if they are joined by unity and love, become safe from every foe.' The Lithuanians agreed to the request.[12]

Once this question had been resolved, the assault on the Military Department began. The battle was fought over four sessions between 24 October and 3 November 1788. For all the off-stage manoeuvring, the vote could only be won by persuading the many waverers. Orators on both sides spared no efforts. Virtually everyone agreed that liberty was imperilled, but within this shared field, rival proto-liberal and republican discourses can be identified. Some royalists warned against an omnipotent sejm unrestrained by checks and balances: it would descend into an 'abyss of absolutism'. Others forecast that the restoration of the hetmans' former powers without adequate civilian control would lead either to 'tyranny', 'repulsive oligarchy' or 'anarchy'. Either way, citizens could not tranquilly enjoy their liberty and property.[13]

However, Montesquieu's dictum that 'power must check power' also served some opposition speakers. They argued that the executive power must be divided to keep it from usurping the legislative and judicial powers. Bishop Sołtyk's incarceration was recalled, as were the sejms of 1773–75 and 1776. Some opposition envoys would admit no impediment whatsoever to national sovereignty – reposing in the sejm. Wojciech Suchodolski, envoy for Chełm and a client of Branicki, accused the royalists of manipulating words. He adroitly turned their contrast between 'anarchy' and 'government' into one between a 'republican government' which brought true security to citizens and a centralized 'monarchy' which threatened their liberty. For their part, royalists complained that the epithet 'true patriot' was being abused to disqualify anyone who thought differently to the opposition. One castellan angrily lectured the 'prejudiced public' for insulting the dignity of the throne and the Estates by its applause and laughter.[14] It was to no avail. The ladies in the galleries, led by Izabela Czartoryska, waved their scarves and cheered on the 'patriot' orators of the opposition. They mocked those who dared to disagree.

The session of 3 November lasted sixteen hours. No fewer than eighty speeches were made during the open voting on whether or not the Military Department should be replaced by a commission. Among the senators, the department commanded a clear majority: seventy to nineteen. A smaller majority of envoys supported a commission. In sum, the department was endorsed by 149 votes to 118, whereupon the opposition demanded a secret vote. When the count was announced, the result was reversed: a majority of 140 to 129 for a commission. The public galleries erupted in rapture.[15]

How would the tsaritsa react to this breach in her guarantee? During the days before the vote, Stanisław August had desperately sought a face-saving 'compromise' which would rename the department as a commission and subordinate it directly to the sejm. The opposition leaders would have none of it. Three Lithuanian aristocrats – Hetman Michał Kazimierz Ogiński, Kazimierz Sapieha and the hitherto dormant Karol Radziwiłł – had even plotted a new confederacy, backed by Prussia, should the king win the vote. Even after the vote, a delay in the legal inscription of the sejm's decision into the records of the Warsaw castle court raised fears that the will of the nation would be frustrated. Stackelberg met the king, the primate and senior royalists in the evening of 5 November 1788. He demanded that they leave Warsaw and 'reconfederate' the provinces against the sejm. They refused. In his official note of protest, read out the following day, Stackelberg threatened the direst consequences of the empress's displeasure if the slightest alteration were made to the form of government she had guaranteed in 1775. The king forestalled a furious reaction to the note by declaring it was his unpopular duty to warn the sejm against breaking treaties and to act in a way 'that I know to be the essential good of the country, or at least its lesser evil'. Russian interests, he argued, were less misaligned with Poland's than those of any other power. He adjourned sessions for four days.[16]

The king's gambit at first seemed to backfire. Among tumultuous scenes many refused to leave the chamber, where Sapieha led cries against the king and

'Muscovy'. The unexpected adjournment exacerbated fears of a coup. Many opposition envoys and a few senators met on the evenings of 6–8 November at Małachowski's house. Branicki's kinsmen and clients demanded the strongest measures in response to the Russian threats. These meetings threatened to become a rival session of the Estates. The leaders of the Puławy set had difficulty in facing down calls for the replacement of the Permanent Council by the sejm in permanent session. Like the king, they preferred a reconvenable sejm. However, the final toned-down requests to the king did include a prolongation of the sejm to 15 December. The monarch was also asked not to adjourn sessions, so often and for so long, without the Estates' agreement. Stanisław August refused to accept that a private gathering could speak for the Commonwealth, but he was shaken. He wrote to Deboli on 7 November that 'the spirit of opposition has so increased hatred towards Muscovy in all estates and kinds of people, that it is almost impossible to believe'.[17]

When the king again addressed the sejm on 10 November 1788 he tried to conciliate the opposition. He launched a slogan: 'the king with the nation, the nation with the king'. Red and white ribbons bearing these words soon went on sale in Warsaw. The first part of the slogan caught on and Stanisław August seemed to regain some popularity. The Estates' reply, read out on 15 November, was drafted in a relatively moderate tone by Ignacy Potocki. It asserted the Poles' right to change their government without breaching any guarantee, but did not explicitly repudiate the Russian guarantee as such.

That same day, however, the sejm demanded the withdrawal of all Russian soldiers from Poland. Their rapacity, combined with the ambassador's arrogance, pushed some habitual supporters of the king's Russian orientation into the arms of the opposition and Prussia. Moreover, the demand presaged problems for military communications between the Russian imperial heartland and the theatre of war against the Ottoman Empire. If the direct route to the besieged port of Ochakov across the right-bank Ukraine was closed, Russian reinforcements and supply columns had to make a long and inconvenient detour via the left bank. The sejm set a number of conditions for further transits in April 1789, but rather than risk another blow to her prestige, the empress informed the sejm at the end of May that Russia would no longer use the transit route across the Polish Ukraine. The strategic importance of this wedge of territory was not lost on her.

The Commonwealth wobbled on a cliff-edge at the start of November 1788. The prospect of intervention in a Polish civil war encouraged Frederick William II to believe that a second partition was feasible. Catherine would learn to respect him! A Prussian corps prepared to cross the border into Greater Poland. Despite his misgivings, Stanisław August preferred to concede defeat and refuse the Russian ambassador's repeated demands than to break with the 'nation'. Some of his opponents would rather have invited in foreign soldiers than suffer their own monarch to win a parliamentary battle.

The King of Prussia was now persuaded to play the long game by his extraordinary envoy to the Commonwealth. Girolamo Lucchesini was destined for St Petersburg, but had stopped in Warsaw. Still only thirty-six, a few years earlier he had memorably answered Frederick II's sardonic question of how long Italian marquises would sell themselves to German princes: for as long as German monarchs were stupid enough to employ them. On another occasion he had disguised himself as a jeweller to gain access to the cathedral chapter of Mainz in order to procure the election of Berlin's candidate as co-adjutor to the archbishop-elector. Now the stolid Buchholtz received instructions to defer to Lucchesini, and the fleet-footed marquis soon had many Polish politicians and their wives eating out of his hand. The marquise, however, fell for the virile Julian Niemcewicz. When she gave birth to a son, Lucchesini tactfully acknowledged the child as his own.

On 20 November a second Prussian note, fine-tuned by Lucchesini, assured the Poles that the King of Prussia wished only to guarantee their independence, respected their right to change their own laws, and had already asked the empress to withdraw her troops from the Commonwealth. This declaration overcame most of the residual fear of reprisals from the two imperial courts, as well as most of the remaining suspicion of Frederick William's intentions. Prussian influence now supplanted Russian. Stackelberg was boycotted socially and left without instructions for almost two months. Unable to rely on Vienna against Berlin, St Petersburg feigned indifference, but was already considering a partition. There was no question of major concessions to the Poles, but the war against the Ottoman Empire took priority. However, this embarrassment of riches drew Berlin further into Polish politics than anticipated; its runaway success could only be exploited by acting like a disinterested friend for longer. So Berlin shelved its plans for military intervention and partition. For the moment, Prussian and Polish interests seemed aligned. Moreover, the interaction between the Prussian, British, Swedish and Saxon diplomats in Warsaw created the impression that alternative alliances were to be had for the asking.

It took the sejm much longer to decide on the command and structure of the army establishment than to decide on the number of men. Following time-honoured procedure, slowed further by the urge of many envoys and senators to parade their patriotic credentials in well-turned rhetoric, the sejm moved one paragraph at a time through the bill establishing the Military Commission. Although on 11 and 12 November the Lithuanians readily conceded that this was to be a joint body of both nations, they carried their point that the commission's seat should alternate between Warsaw and Grodno along with the sejm. Paweł Grabowski, the sole Calvinist envoy, articulated the Lithuanian case:

> The Lithuanian nation joined by the knot of union with the Crown constitutes only one body; we have one king and duke of Lithuania; we form one Commonwealth, but as the Duchy of Lithuania is not a conquered province, but is only for mutual strengthening, for the mutual securing of laws, liberty, integrity and privileges, voluntarily joined with the Crown, it should have one legislative power, even one executive power, but always with the usual alternation, written by law, as is the case for sejms.[18]

For the time being, the Crown and Lithuanian armies remained separately funded and led.

Deeper cracks appeared in the opposition ranks. On the one side were those who would have restored the panoply of powers wielded by the hetmans of yore. On the other were those who sought to limit the four current hetmans to presiding in turn over the commission. On 23 December, when the sejm finally elected the commissioners, Branicki appeared in the sejm, resplendent in a *kontusz*. He expressed joy at the expansion of the army, tinged with regret at his exclusion from military governance. His presence alongside Potemkin at Ochakov was, he claimed, a useful opportunity to study modern warfare. (After a six-month siege, the Russian forces stormed the city on 17 December, before slaughtering men, women and children.)[19]

Branicki had to balance on a thin line. It had not escaped anyone's notice that his partisans had been among the fiercest foes of the king, the Permanent Council and the Russian guarantee. Stackelberg repeatedly criticized the policy of tolerating the opposition led by Branicki and Sapieha. Struggling to convince Polish public opinion of the sincerity of his patriotism, the hetman simultaneously sought to persuade Potemkin that he could 'be useful one day to Russia as a good

Pole'. He blamed the king, the primate and the ambassador for the turn of events and thereby excused the Russophobic rhetoric of his nephew and clients. Judging from the instructions sent to the ambassador, the hetman's explanations seem to have at least partly been accepted. Branicki also sounded out the court of Berlin, which returned the compliment.[20]

During the parliamentary battles the king lost most of his prerogatives of patenting and promoting officers. The loyal head of his military chancellery, General Komarzewski, went abroad after being denied a seat on the commission. Most of the members of this unwieldy body were civilians without significant military experience. Their role was as much to keep watch for dangerous moves from the monarch or the hetmans as it was to organize the recruiting, training, equipping and provisioning of the expanded armed forces.

The court also took a barrage of criticism, some of it justified, directed at its professional diplomats. The traditional model of one-off embassies headed by great lords appealed to the republican ideal of civic service. Several aristocrats volunteered to serve as ambassadors at their own expense, and some of them were duly nominated by the sejm. In practice, most proved more eager to declaim than to depart. Feliks Potocki did not go to St Petersburg, Stanisław Potocki did not go to Paris, and Kazimierz Rzewuski withdrew his candidacy for London. So the Commonwealth's most experienced diplomat, Augustyn Deboli, remained in charge of the mission on the banks of the Neva, while the trusty Franciszek Bukaty returned to England. Stanisław Sołtyk turned down the mission to Vienna, so the job was entrusted to the capable Franciszek Ksawery Woyna. This noble of uncertain parentage had first attracted royal patronage as an author and translator. One of the most famous episodes in the history of the Commonwealth's diplomacy was Jerzy Ossoliński's entry into Rome in 1633, scattering loosely shod golden horseshoes among the populace, so perhaps it was a sign of the times that nobody volunteered for the Holy See.[21] Yet even on the banks of the Tiber, the Commonwealth's representative gained in prestige: Tommaso Antici received his long-desired cardinal's hat in the general promotion shared among the Catholic courts in the spring of 1789.

Polish lords such as the fiery Józef Czartoryski, who did go to Berlin, typically lacked the diplomatic savoir-faire with which their aristocratic counterparts in monarchical states were imbued almost from infancy. Although these high-born envoys acted from patriotic motives and some applied themselves seriously to their tasks, some of them spoke their minds too freely, indulged in wishful thinking, and tired of their jobs after a few months. Without doubt, however, the budget, visibility and number of diplomatic missions increased. The Commonwealth's diplomacy became more socially prestigious, a factor which still counted for much in Europe. Crucially, humbler professionals, rapidly gaining in experience and confidence, assisted and often substituted the high-born amateurs.

On 10 December 1788 the sejm established a deputation to draw up instructions for the Commonwealth's envoys abroad. It soon evolved into the Deputation for Foreign Affairs. Although formally presided over by Chancellor Jacek Małachowski, its *de facto* head was Ignacy Potocki. Republican diplomacy was to be transparent and principled, subordinated to the sovereign nation, embodied in the sejm – as opposed to courtly intrigues. French revolutionary diplomacy would experience a similar cultural shift; however, French inflexibility in the negotiating tent was generally backed up by superiority in numbers and victories in the field. The Poles had no such advantages. In these circumstances, keeping secrets proved impossible, and decision-making hesitant. Ignacy Potocki soon realized this, and began to conduct his own correspondence with key diplomats. Stanisław August kept open his own channels of communication.

The sejm reconvened after the break for Christmas and Epiphany. It was so cold that an envoy suggested moving to a smaller chamber, given the danger to the king's health and the low number of parliamentarians present, but it was decided to stay put.[22] The opposition was determined not only to defeat the monarch, but to prevent him from saving face. When on 8 January 1789 one of the king's supporters introduced a bill to establish a 'National Custodial Council' (*Straż Narodowa*) in place of the Permanent Council, opposition leaders wanted to talk about taxes. Over the next few days attacks on the Permanent Council mounted. On 16 January, when the king proposed to decide the level of taxation, the opposition leaders insisted on first abolishing the Permanent Council.[23]

This decision came on 19 January 1789. The tone of the debate was set by Bishop Szembek of Płock, who had been moving towards the opposition. Invoking Divine Providence, he denounced the Russian guarantee symbolized by the Permanent Council. Stanisław Potocki rebutted the argument for keeping international treaties by exposing those treaties as masks for violence. The royalist argument that the Commonwealth needed government (*rząd*) was answered by Sapieha's call to shatter 'this pillar of *nierząd*'. The word was a double entendre for anarchy and prostitution. Michał Zaleski, envoy for Troki, put the republican case in a nutshell: 'we have the government in ourselves, we have it in sejms'.

When a castellan conceded that the Council could not survive, but asked if it could be abolished courteously, that is, with Stackelberg's agreement, he was shouted down. Opening the voting, the primate declined to express an opinion. Sixty-one senators and envoys followed his example. Only eleven voted to keep the Permanent Council, whereas 120 voted for its abolition.[24] The Russian guarantee was now dead and buried, the sejm was all but omnipotent, and the king little more than a cipher. The clergy were next in line.

In the heady autumn and winter of 1788–89 the champagne of national sovereignty went straight to many unaccustomed heads. After the Russian fetters had been thrown off, almost anything seemed possible. Many royalist envoys began to consider themselves elected representatives of the nation, guided by disinterested patriotism. The weakening bonds between clients and patrons also caused problems for the opposition leaders. The Puławy set might ordinarily have been restrained by Vienna, but Prince Adam Czartoryski explained that he was unable to rein in his own dependants, such as the Livonian envoys, Julian Niemcewicz and the barrel-bellied, bass-voiced Stanisław Kublicki. Perhaps he might have tried harder, but the days when a magnate could calmly vouch for his clients had passed. The Radziwiłł interest melted away during the first few months of the sejm, when Prince Karol was largely absent. Provincial sessions took on more importance in hammering out collective decision-making. This format encouraged solidarity between ordinary envoys.[25] As those envoys became harder to manage, so the sejm's deliberations and decisions became less predictable. Less could be arranged off-stage between the principals, and the importance of both oratorical prowess and public opinion rose accordingly. The Commonwealth's politics moved closer to the republican ideal: 'in a free republican government we should think, act and write not in secret, but openly', as one pamphleteer put it. Yet this author was considered a royalist.[26]

The articulation of the nation's desires fell not only to parliamentarians, but also to the spectating, reading, writing and declaiming 'public' (the Polish word *publiczność* was replacing the Latin *publicum*). A few envoys even invoked the public as the impartial judge of actions and intentions.[27] Before long it would encompass nobles in country manors and burghers in market towns, as well as their wives and daughters. For the moment Warsaw made the running. The city was packed as never before. Landladies and landlords, shopkeepers and restaurateurs, shoemakers and dressmakers, cardsharps and confidence tricksters, errand boys and pickpockets, not to mention pimps and prostitutes – all did a roaring trade. The city's cultural and recreational spaces became politicized. Pleasure gardens such as the Foksal (originally spelled Foxhal, after London's Vauxhall Gardens) thronged with crowds thirsting for political news and gossip, as well as for social and sexual encounters. The charged atmosphere precipitated a pungent bloom of satirical verses and riddles – the latter would ultimately caricature almost every member of the sejm as well as several aristocratic ladies. The novelty of a hot-air balloon prompted one wit to wish that Jean-Pierre Blanchard would take the ambassador, the primate and the Permanent Council on a one-way journey up into the clouds.[28]

Another theme for the rhymesters was the ostentatious discarding of 'French' attire and coiffure in favour of the national style. In the morning of 27 November 1788, to a martial drumbeat, Izabela Czartoryska applied her Spartan scissors to the luxuriant locks of Kazimierz Sapieha. Later that day in the sejm, clad in a splendid *kontusz*, Sapieha demanded that all army officers wear national costume.[29] Several verses lauded the triumph of Polish dress, but a few criticized such gestures as superficial. Moreover, the Sarmatian revival was a two-edged sword. Among the many modestly situated royalist envoys were some who wore the *kontusz* naturally. On 26 January 1789 Pius Kiciński, who would prove one of the sejm's finest orators, mocked the dandified youngsters who wasted their mornings being dressed and coiffed in the latest modes:

> The country has been filled with frock coats, buttons, walking canes, watch-chains, rings, pocket mirrors and other baubles, but we have lacked bold and ridable horses, we have lacked the weapons with which all noble houses were once adorned. It seems that the national spirit is somehow subdued.

The king was not amused. Kiciński assured the monarch of his loyalty, while emphasizing that his priority was to serve the Fatherland and his fellow citizens as an elected envoy. But his words must have also discomfited the powdered Potockis.[30]

Izabela Czartoryska also had a bumpy ride from public opinion. She enjoyed herself as a kind of first lady of Poland in the tableaux and illuminations she choreographed in honour of Stanisław Małachowski in the Krasiński Gardens on

8 May 1789. This event eclipsed the king's nameday celebrations. However, by the summer, the misogynist abuse directed at Czartoryska persuaded her husband to send her and their eldest son abroad. She had become a political liability.

Adam Kazimierz Czartoryski, like some other aristocrats of the opposition, kept open house during the sejm. So did Marshal Małachowski. It was the best of times for respectably dressed Varsovians with an appetite for political conversation over a free dinner. This traditional style of hospitality helped many provincial envoys to prolong their stay in a city of vertiginous prices. However, the similar open table at the Royal Castle gave rise to insults about *pieczeniarze* – those who ate the king's roast meat (*pieczeń*) and then voted as they were told. Even the senatorial rank of castellan became a term of derision. This was partly motivated by aristocratic disdain for the modestly born men promoted by Stanisław August, but it also reflected the court party's dependence on castellans as the bedrock of its voting strength. A target of this discourse was Feliks Potocki, who had resigned as Palatine of Ruthenia and been elected envoy. After he had failed to support the abolition of the Military Department, he was mocked by a rhymester: 'having given up his palatinate, he became a castellan'.[31] Still worse was to be labelled a 'Muscovite'.

The republican conviction that free citizens not only had the right but also the duty to speak and write freely for the public good ran deep. During the four years of the Polish Revolution it bore fruit in about 700 pamphlets and treatises, at least 1,300 printed speeches, and dozens of politicized sermons – printed, so it was usually claimed, by public demand. One author even titled his pamphlet *Me Too*, because, he began, 'everyone writes, everyone answers, even those who were not written to at all'.[32] Most print runs were in the hundreds and some were only in the dozens, but quite a few reached the thousands. Authors and publishers often took the trouble to ensure that works were distributed not only among Warsaw booksellers, but sold also at stalls in provincial market towns, especially when quarterly contracts were being negotiated and exchanged. Some brochures were despatched directly to country manor houses. Pirated editions were quite common, and among those responsible were Basilian monks and Dominican friars, who had easy access to provincial markets. The circulation of political writings in manuscript, so common in the past, continued on a lesser scale, but the debates were shaped by the printed word. Even parliamentary speeches sometimes had more impact in print. Towards the end of the sejm Stanisław August mused: 'Reverend Kołłątaj, the vice-chancellor, made a very long speech, perhaps rather fatiguing to the ear, but which, because of its true erudition, will be very useful to read, when it goes to press.'[33]

The exchanges between the pamphleteers began well before the sejm started, and continued until after it had ceased its deliberations. However, the intensity of the exchanges rose and fell in waves. Discussions on particular topics crested and subsided, merged and diverged. The most substantial treatises tackled multiple problems and so were part of multiple debates. Such was Stanisław Staszic's sprawling *Considerations on the Life of Jan Zamoyski*, which appeared in 1787. It prompted numerous responses, the longest and most thoughtful of which, by the ennobled Danziger Jan Nax, was titled *Considerations on the Considerations*. The most talented writers effortlessly switched between persuasive strategies: logical arguments, emotive appeals, chilling warnings, suggestive juxtapositions and mocking asides. Nearly all authors published anonymously; they often constructed fictional literary personae. Many pamphlets took the forms of letters, dialogues or parables. Alongside scandal-mongering and ephemera, a serious public debate took place about the future of the Commonwealth, summed up by the title of one anonymous brochure, *What is Absolutely Necessary to Establish at this Sejm*.

Most of the proposals adumbrated in the summer and early autumn of 1788 concerned the army and the necessary funds. The polemics on clerical wealth raged on until the middle of 1789, but after the decision had been taken for an establishment of 100,000 men, much of the attention switched to the Commonwealth's executive and legislative institutions. The great majority of these writings can be described as republican. Most authors concurred that since 1775 the Permanent Council had imperilled liberty. In future the bare minimum of central government institutions active between sejms should be strictly subordinated to the 'nation'. This matter was connected to the question of whether the sejm should be in permanent session, as many parliamentarians believed, or merely reconvenable – a solution favoured by the Puławy set and for different reasons by the king. The distinction was rarely as clear as some historians would like. Moreover, while some envoys declaimed about the Commonwealth embodied in the sejm as a 'sovereign mistress',[34] most pamphleteers envisaged that the sejmiks would instruct the sejm and review its decisions. Hugo Kołłątaj, who described the sejm as an omnipotent 'monarch', tried to square this circle in the *Letters of an Anonymous Correspondent* he addressed to Stanisław Małachowski.[35] He also advised the marshal behind the scenes.

Gifted but unorthodox writers such as Nax, who expounded a vision of liberal freedom in response to Staszic's extreme republican subordination of the individual to the nation, and the young Józef Pawlikowski, who urged a stronger monarchy that could defend peasants, burghers, Jews and even the Catholic clergy from oppression by the szlachta, found themselves at the margins of discussion. Pawlikowski came from a family that had lost its noble status through derogation. With another significant exception in Kołłątaj, few authors envisaged far-reaching social transformations. On the other hand, the self-evident need to expand the army naturally led to a search for funds. Few nobles were keen to volunteer their own income, but few dared to refuse it either.

The abolition of the Permanent Council on 19 January 1789 cleared the final obstacle to the discussion of revenue. Parliamentary and public debates had identified two easy targets: starostas and the clergy. Their estates, wrote the appalled nuncio, Ferdinando Maria Saluzzo, 'are erroneously called the free patrimony of the Commonwealth'.[36] They had, it was claimed, received their properties in return for duties; if these duties were not being carried out properly, the Commonwealth had the right to reclaim the lands. Although the timorous nuncio and his superiors in Rome tended to see every attack on ecclesiastical privilege and property as a venomous eighteenth-century hydra spouting fearsome heads of 'enthusiasm', 'patriotism', 'modern philosophy', 'the spirit of novelty and reform' and such like, the argument was not new, but dated back to the sixteenth century. Moreover, the phrase '*patrimonium* of the Commonwealth' featured in the instruction of the sejmik of Zakroczym in 1788.[37] Either way, the clergy faced volleys of criticism. Ecclesiastical authors were forced onto the defensive.

These polemics were voiced in sermons and pamphlets as well as in the sejm. The arguments revolved around several axes: the personal virtues or vices of priests, monks and nuns; their general usefulness or uselessness; their wealth or poverty; and their existing contributions to the public purse. Perhaps the strongest argument made by clerical protagonists was that all citizens should contribute to the common cause in equal proportion to their income. This was countered by the point that lay noblemen, with children to provide for, had far greater outgoings than their clerical brethren, so the latter could afford to pay three times as much in taxes as the former.

The latter conviction was echoed in the swingeing tax imposed on the stamped paper issued for appointment to offices and dignities. Senior clergymen had to pay far more than their nearest lay equivalents. The severity of this blow, followed by the double *kwarta* and new survey imposed on the starostas, concentrated the bishops' minds. They debated among themselves how large an offering might satisfy the sejm. Ignacy Massalski of Wilno argued for taking on responsibility for education. This solution would release funds for the army, while enabling the clergy to shape the next generation. The Crown bishops thought the idea too costly. In the event the episcopal senators had to accept more onerous burdens. The remorseless pressure applied to them during four parliamentary sessions between 12 and 16 March led them to capitulate on terms of a 20 per cent 'offering' from 'stable and sure income'. That was in addition to the existing *subsidium charitativum* of 700,000 złotys per year. Otherwise the sejm would have imposed an even heavier tax without the merest figleaf of assumed papal consent – the phrase '*salve beneplacito apostolico*'. Even this wording was contested as inimical to the sovereignty of the Commonwealth. Warnings that this cult of sovereignty might endanger virtue and religion, and that the Commonwealth should not act like a 'despot', met with the indignant response that a 'despot' aimed to impose on the Estates something they did not desire. As the details were worked out during the days that followed, the poorest secular clergy and religious houses received exemptions or reductions.[38]

The argument that trumped all others was the overwhelming need of the Fatherland. As one envoy asked rhetorically, 'who is poorer than the Fatherland and our Commonwealth?'[39] But once the clergy's offering had been dotted and crossed, that very question challenged the delegates of the szlachta. Would they consent to tax their income at 10 per cent? They would. On 26 March 1789, once procedural objections from two castellans had been swept aside, it took but one speech to stir the sejm into a resonant and repeated roar: '*zgoda!*'. For once Małachowski overruled those who wished to introduce amendments. After a correction matching the wording to the clergy's offering, 'all anticipated the honourable marshal's question with a joyful cry of consent; which, thrice repeated, filled with a sentiment of great sweetness the many assembled spectators sharing the zeal of the sejm, for whom the view of this universal joy became an appreciative reward.' Cathartic tears of joy flowed as senators and envoys lined up to kiss the king's hand.[40]

It is worth reflecting on the argument made that morning by a Lithuanian envoy:

> Where the property of the citizen is the property of the monarchy, there, I say, it is unpleasant to bear the burden of a tax. But with us, where what we are, and what we possess, is ours, then sharing our wealth with the Fatherland becomes pleasant, because it conserves our happiness, because we give it as free men without coercion, not as subjects to a despot, but we ourselves offer the tax to ourselves.[41]

Here was the essence of the republican idea of liberty – free citizens raised taxes for themselves, not for a despotic monarch. While foreign diplomats in Warsaw were sceptical about the decision's implementation, they were impressed by the purposeful unity.

Again, it took time to work out the details. The sejm appointed hundreds of local commissioners – men trusted by their neighbours. During the following months, nobles and clergy handed over what they swore was their tenth or fifth groat at designated collection points. A clergyman who also held an hereditary noble estate paid 20 per cent on his ecclesiastical income and 10 per cent on his secular revenues. During the collection of the new 'offerings' different localities defined 'stable and sure' income variously. The results were similarly mixed. The combined revenues from the offerings on landed and ecclesiastical income reached about 8,500,000 złotys per annum. The annual revenues of the Crown and Lithuanian Treasuries tripled from about 17,700,000 złotys in 1787–88 to about 53,000,000 złotys in 1791–92. However, many contemporaries had hoped for a greater swelling of the Commonwealth's coffers. On 3 March 1790 the sejm restricted the expansion of the army establishment to an initial target of 65,000 men. Although some pamphleteers and parliamentarians assumed perjury by many noble citizens, not in living memory had there been such readiness among the szlachta to contribute to national defence. Among the effects was a marked improvement in the country's creditworthiness. In June 1790 Dutch bankers offered a large loan. The Crown Treasury Commission was able to obtain much better terms than those applying on the domestic credit market: it borrowed just under 7,000,000 złotys repayable at 5 per cent per annum between 1794 and 1806, with an exchange rate margin of 7 per cent. The money arrived in tranches between November 1790 and May 1791.[42]

Debates on revenue intertwined with panic about peasant rebellion in Ruthenia. Although no revolt actually occurred, the fear that it would drew attention to the volatility and vulnerability of the Commonwealth's eastern reaches as nothing else could have done. Stanisław August had touched a raw nerve in his speech of 6 November 1788 against breaking with Russia: he had pointed to the ease with which St Petersburg could incite a new *koliivshchyna*. Some saw this as evidence of his ambition to overthrow noble liberty with the aid of peasant pikes and Russian bayonets. This traditional suspicion was augmented by two further phobias. One was the image of the Ruthenian peasant as a violent and vengeful 'savage'. The other was the fear that Russian pedlars and itinerant 'disuniate' clergymen were inciting a millenarian day of judgement against the hated Poles. On 18 December Kazimierz Sapieha warned of unrest in the Ukraine. Jan Suchorzewski, a maverick envoy for Kalisz, seized the moment to shout: 'fight Muscovy, because we have no worse foe!' The entire chamber, related an incredulous Danish diplomat, repeated the battle-cry – 'fight Muscovy!'[43]

Branicki's kinsmen, allies and clients were also to the fore in denouncing Russia. Perhaps their outbursts were part of a plan agreed with Potemkin; if so, they would have agreed it orally. The hetman did write to his 'dear uncle' that he could not be seen to oppose the Russophobic mood.[44] Potemkin, as ever, had several irons in the fire. One was the formation of confederacies of nobles, as proposed by Branicki. Another was military intervention. Either way, we cannot discount rumours that he was at one stage sending emissaries into the Commonwealth. They could have gauged potential support among the Ruthenian peasantry for an invasion.

On 29 January 1789 the Military Commission placed units of the Crown army in the Ukraine on standby for action. It also issued an irresponsible instruction for Jewish tavern-keepers, millers and such like to spy on the peasants. The official Russian refusal to withdraw troops from the Commonwealth, read out to the sejm on 17 February 1789, only aggravated these festering fears. The cordial relations between Russian commanders and the head of the Crown forces in Ukraine, Feliks Potocki, reinforced the latter's reputation as a 'Muscovite' and discounted his reassuring reports about the peaceable temper of the peasantry. Nevertheless, Branicki and his supporters were unable to persuade the sejm to call out the general levy or to permit confederacies of the szlachta in the Ruthenian palatinates, because of well-founded suspicion of the hetman's intentions. 'Rebellions, rebellions, alleluia, alleluia!' joked a rhymester.[45]

Potemkin backed off. On 17 March 1789 he withdrew soldiers from Smila and announced to his subjects that he would tolerate no rebellion against the Commonwealth. On 23 March, commanded by the empress, the Holy Synod in

St Petersburg forbade prayers for Russian victories in the Commonwealth's Orthodox churches. Too late. Before this news could reach Warsaw, further reports of trouble in the Ukraine interrupted a debate in the sejm on 30 and 31 March. Sapieha carried a motion for the two marshals to issue a proclamation expelling Russian pedlars and vagrant clergymen, and commanding Uniate and Orthodox hierarchs to keep their clergy in order. The sejm decided to reinforce the army in Volhynia, but not to call out the general levy.

During the same night of 30–31 March a nobleman and his wife, together with five serving women, were murdered by two other servants at their home in Volhynia. As the news spread, panic broke out among nobles and Jews across the south-east. Many despatched their wives and children to safe towns, and rumours spread of an imminent invasion. In Warsaw, the doubters could no longer deny the possibility of rebellion. However, Branicki was still unable to win acceptance for his demands to establish local confederacies and to use the National Cavalry to crush the rebels. Such a cure seemed worse than the disease. Bishop Krasiński accepted that a revolt had been planned, but reflected that 'the National Cavalry could sooner force the peasants to rebel, than Muscovite missionaries could encourage them'. He also acknowledged a bitter truth: 'We only need to read the shameless history of our rule in the Ukraine, to admit that we ourselves were the occasion for Cossack rebellions. The beginning of all revolts in the world were poverty, oppression and tyranny.'[46]

After the Easter break, on 17 April the sejm agreed a series of measures. They included the expulsion of all foreign non-Uniate clergymen, tight controls on Russian merchants, an oath of loyalty to the king and Commonwealth on pain of dispossession and banishment, and prayers for the king and Commonwealth instead of foreign rulers. Implementation fell to the commissions that had been established in the south-eastern palatinates after the outbreak of the Russo-Ottoman war to supply the transiting Russian units. As of February 1789 their competencies encompassed public order and the disarmament of peasants.

The Volhynian commission arrested dozens of merchants and priests, and hundreds of peasants. Suspects were routinely tortured for information. It was 'discovered' that Russian pedlars had incited an Easter massacre, but that the planned attacks had been postponed after heavy snows. Dozens of unfortunates were executed after summary trials; many more were brutally flogged. The two servants who had murdered their master and mistress on 30–31 March experienced refinements such as limb-breaking, burning in tar, flaying, drawing and quartering, before their remains went on public display. The Volhynian repressions fell on the Uniate clergy, as Orthodox structures were practically non-existent here. Two priests were among those executed. The local commissioners would only trust the Basilian fathers, not the secular Uniate clergy. The commissions in the other south-eastern palatinates showed restraint. They did not call the citizenry to arms, and they freed most suspects without charge. Although the Kiev commission did find evidence indicating incitement to rebellion by some Orthodox clergymen, it ordered no executions, only whippings for those found guilty. One explanation is that the Volhynian commission contained supporters and clients of Branicki, who had an interest in hysteria, whereas Feliks Potocki, whose influence prevailed on the Bracław and Podolian commissions, had an interest in defusing tensions.

Although the Grand Duchy of Lithuania was largely spared this panic, Bishop Viktor Sadkovskii and some of his clergy were arrested and brought to Warsaw for questioning. The sejm formed a deputation to investigate the purported rebellions. One of the deputies was the Calvinist Paweł Grabowski – testimony to the growing acceptance of Protestants among the Catholic majority. Through the investigation, as well as debates in the sejm and among the pamphleteers, confessional developments in Ruthenia gradually became more comprehensible to outsiders. Perhaps the most dangerous tendency was the ongoing 'Russification' of the Orthodox Church in the Commonwealth. Another source of disquiet was the contemptible condition of most Uniate clergy – in whom was vested the task of 'enlightening' the Ruthenian peasantry about their duties and loyalties. Awareness grew of the need both to raise the prestige of the Union and to cut off the Orthodox from the Holy Synod in St Petersburg. A sign of maturity came in May 1789: the sejm decided to tax Orthodox and Protestant clergy at the same rates as their Catholic counterparts. To do otherwise would have exacerbated grievances.

Both rites of the Catholic Church were affected when the sejm decided to appropriate and redistribute episcopal revenues, starting with those of the bishopric of Cracow. Some of the origins of this drastic step, which for several months threatened a rupture between Rome and Warsaw, lay in the conviction that ecclesiastical lands were the 'patrimony of the Commonwealth'. Others lay deep within a tangled web of 'intrigues and simonies' – as the nuncio put it.[47] This web had first been spun when Michał Poniatowski, on becoming primate in 1785, gave up the co-adjutorship, but retained the administration of the bishopric of Cracow. Immediately after Bishop Sołtyk's death on 30–31 July 1788, several episcopal arachnids asked the king for a better see.

Coming just before the sejmiks, Sołtyk's death could not have happened at a worse time for the primate. His unpopularity worsened during the autumn. The nuncio advised Rome against granting a dispensation to join Gniezno with Cracow, fearing that it might provoke attacks on ecclesiastical privileges and property. For their part, the opposition leaders destined the see of Cracow for Krzysztof Szembek, with Feliks Turski of Łuck moving to the vacated see of Płock. Both revelled in the name of 'patriot'. If Łuck were to fall vacant, Stanisław August could give Adam Naruszewicz an endowed bishopric. The monarch had other ideas. He and the primate came close to striking a bargain with Frederick William II, who wished to make his Catholic cousin Karl von Hohenzollern prince-bishop of Warmia. The incumbent, Ignacy Krasicki, stranded since the partition, would have happily become nominal bishop of Cracow, while Poniatowski continued to supervise the diocese. Almost certainly at the invitation of the king and primate, Krasicki turned up in Warsaw early in July 1789. He began to talk indiscreetly. Lucchesini warned his court that the package, involving compensation for the king's favourite, Naruszewicz, and Stackelberg's favourite, Józef Kossakowski, would diminish Prussian credit in the Commonwealth. The marquis sabotaged the deal by inciting the opposition leaders to unleash their demagogues.

Cometh the hour, speaketh Suchodolski. On 17 July the garrulous envoy for Chełm reprised his project, first introduced into the sejm on 9 January 1789. *Fund for the Army* envisaged the application to the army of the revenue from the estates of the vacant bishopric of Cracow, leaving the future bishop an annual income of 100,000 złotys. This point was agreed that same, sweltering day. Among the absentees were most bishops. Suchodolski, Kublicki and others pressed the argument that the sejm was the sovereign incarnation of the Polish nation. It could therefore act as it saw fit. Suchodolski had invoked the same principle in leading the campaign to attaint and banish the disgraced former treasurer, Adam Poniński.

Stanisław Potocki drafted an amendment providing for the equalization of episcopal revenues and duties. Because he was keen to maintain friendly relations with the nuncio, he persuaded Mateusz Butrymowicz, envoy for Pińsk, to introduce the amendment. This enabled Potocki to remain 'beyond all reproach' (as he explained to his wife).[48] On 24 July the sejm passed the law *Fund for the Army*. As bishoprics became vacant, so the treasury would take over their estates.

In future, it would apply the surplus revenue of the wealthier sees (but not Cracow) to the poorer ones, leaving the bishops-ordinary of the Latin rite with salaries of 100,000 złotys. The law made an exception for future primates, whose duties and expenses justified an income of 200,000 złotys. In the Ruthenian rite, future metropolitans would receive 100,000 złotys a year – a significant reduction. On the other hand most Uniate bishops-ordinary stood to benefit. Not burdened with senatorial duties, they would each have 50,000 złotys a year.[49]

This reference to the senate may have hinted that the metropolitan archbishop of Kiev was being considered for membership. In July 1790 Teodozy Rostocki took his chair – placed after the lowliest bishop-senator of the Latin rite. This tardy and partial fulfilment of one of the terms of the 1595–96 Union of Brest nonetheless boosted the prestige of the Uniate hierarchy. However, the sejm proved resistant to pleas to fund a new bishopric or at least a suffraganship for those territories of the archbishopric of Połock which had remained in the Commonwealth after the partition.

This failure was despite the commitment in the law passed on 24 July 1789 to redraw diocesan boundaries in both rites of the Catholic Church. Such changes required negotiation with the episcopate and the Holy See. The sejm appointed a deputation for the purpose, with a remit to pursue sundry points at issue between laity and clergy. These included tithes, legacies, dowries, monastic profession, seminaries, residence and pluralism, stole fees and the annates paid to Rome. For their part the bishops desired the execution of old laws against 'apostasy' and immoral and 'heretical' writings, as well as measures for the stricter observance of Sundays and holy days. Thanks to the episcopate's explanation of the Church's need of material resources for its spiritual mission, and the reasonableness of the deputation, by May 1790 a compromise had been hammered out. The most contentious points remained as they were, while changes to diocesan boundaries were kept to a minimum. The key to the agreement was that bishops could choose whether to draw their equalized revenues from landed estates in their possession or to collect a salary from the treasury.

This provision sufficed to spare papal blushes, but was unacceptable to Suchodolski. The envoy for Chełm refused to permit any change to *Fund for the Army*. Convention laid down that even a confederated sejm, once it had passed a law, could amend or repeal it only unanimously. In the event, the impasse lasted only a few days: Suchodolski left Warsaw on Branicki's business. Branicki then spoke to Bishop Szembek, suggesting that now would be a good moment to conclude the ecclesiastical matters. The hetman wanted his part in the solution to be kept secret: he feared that Suchodolski would become even more intransigent if he discovered what had happened. Revealed only recently, Branicki's intervention allows us to glimpse how the Polish Revolution altered relations between patrons and clients.[50] The measure passed on 25 May 1790. The following day the sejm decided that bishops would not pay tax on their incomes of 100,000 złotys, given that their overall revenues would already have been reduced by more than the amount of tax.

Thus receded the prospect of schism between Rome and Warsaw. Nevertheless, the episcopal reform remained in principle a radical step – more radical than anything actually implemented by Emperor Joseph II. On the other hand (again in contrast to the Habsburg Monarchy), the religious orders escaped almost unscathed during the Polish Revolution. The reason for this differential treatment of the secular and religious clergy cannot be found in public opinion. Stinging criticism of fat prelates, decrepit monks and useless nuns abounded in pamphlets and sejmik instructions. Several projects envisaged fundamental reform of ecclesiastical temporalities; efforts were made to enact them until the last weeks of the sejm. Such a reform would have closed many monasteries and convents, redeployed many religious clergy to other houses and duties, and applied the remaining orders to education, care of the sick or parish work. Cathedral and collegiate chapters would have been pruned, while the incomes of most of the parish clergy would have been raised. On the other hand, individual religious houses and their superiors continued to be commended and their interests advanced, both in sejmik instructions and in private bills introduced at quieter moments during the sejm's proceedings.

The convenience of the unreformed ecclesiastical system is evident from the fortunes of the commendatory abbots. The royal prerogative, sanctioned by the papacy in the 1737 concordat, of rewarding meritorious bishops and prelates with two-thirds of the revenues of one of thirteen or fourteen abbeys had long drawn criticism. However, the debates on ecclesiastical reforms reveal that some parliamentarians suggested granting abbeys *in commendam*, as well as other benefices, to the new hierarchs rather than find new funds to endow suffragan bishoprics and episcopal seminaries. Nevertheless, when it was rumoured that the reviled Kossakowski stood to receive an abbey, his rival Naruszewicz warned the king that such a grant could provoke '*clamores*, and from such an occasion one of the parliamentarians might propose the abolition or diminution of

1, 2. Twenty-nine years after they had parted as lovers, Catherine II received Stanisław August on her galley on the Dnieper on 6 May 1787. He simulated an eruption of Vesuvius in her honour. This commemorative pair of pictures was part of his diplomatic efforts to gain a Polish-Russian alliance.

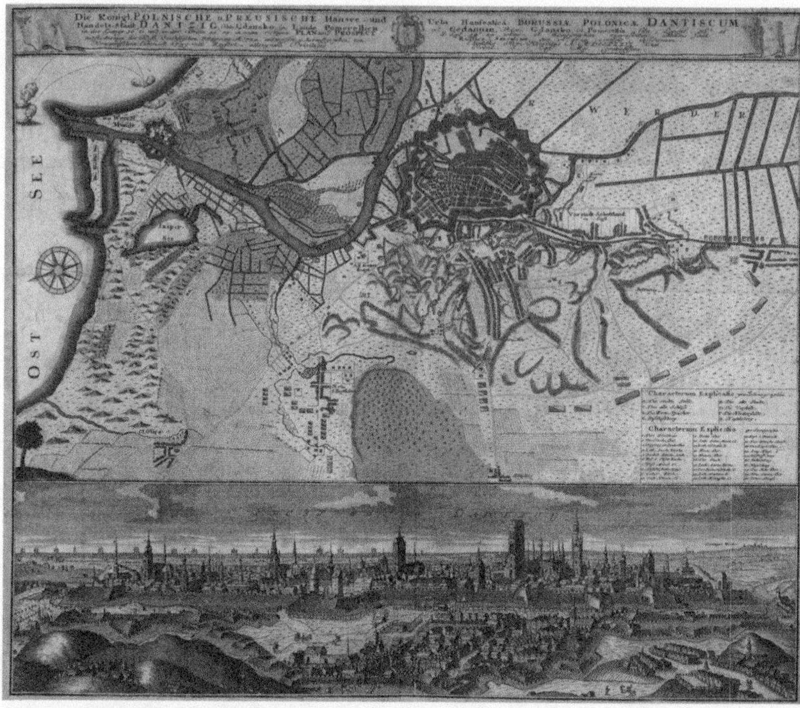

3, 4. Russian intervention decided the royal elections of 1733 and 1764. Much more force was necessary to put Augustus III on the Polish-Lithuanian throne, including a siege of Danzig. As Bernardo Bellotto's commission was intended to show, the election of Stanisław August was far more orderly.

5, 6, 7. The Vilnan baroque rippled across confessional boundaries. Johann Christoph Glaubitz, a Lutheran, also worked for the city's Jewish, Orthodox and Catholic communities. The refurbished Great Synagogue was deceptively large inside, while the University Church of SS. John and John received a new facade. Perhaps the zenith of the style was the Uniate Basilian church at Berezwecz – blown up by the Soviets in 1970.

8, 9, 10. Augustus III sought to win over hearts and minds by wearing national dress following his hastily improvised coronation. In contrast, Stanisław August's carefully planned 'Spanish costume' backfired. By 1770 he was desperately trying to prevent the ship of state sinking as he tried to steer between Russia and the Confederacy of Bar.

NE CEDE MALIS.

11, 12, 13. The intense rivalry between sisters-in-law as patrons, lovers and politicians continues between their partisans to this day. The dazzling Izabella Lubomirska, née Czartoryska, at first patronized her unassuming young cousin who married the Commonwealth's most eligible bachelor, Prince Adam Kazimierz Czartoryski, in 1761. But it was Izabela, née Flemming, who managed to set the magnate opposition's cultural agenda as the 'Spartan Mother'.

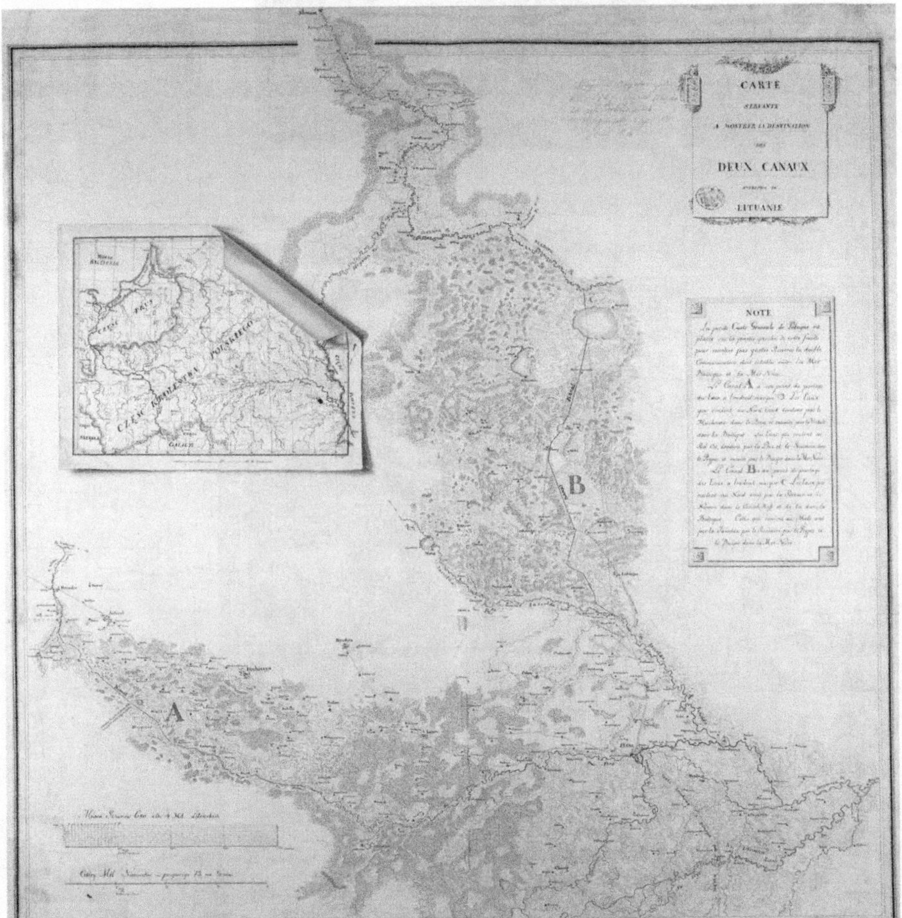

14, 15. Stanisław August's interest in cartography was turned to political and economic as well as scientific ends. In 1780–81 Russian encroachments on the frontier in the far south-east were precisely documented. In 1785 he commissioned a map of the canals he had visited during his progress through the Grand Duchy of Lithuania the previous year.

16, 17. Michał Jerzy Poniatowski, the king's youngest brother, felt no priestly vocation but became an effective reforming bishop and primate, forging a fraternal alliance between throne and altar. He promoted a sober and industrious style of 'enlightened Catholicism', but most believers remained attached to traditional religious practices. On this screen for a wonder-working image of St Joseph in Kalisz, representatives of all ranks, from pope, king and primate to peasant children, pass their supplications heavenwards.

18, 19. Bernardo Bellotto, also known as Canaletto the Younger, depicted Varsovians of all ranks in his prospects of the growing city, commissioned by the king in the 1770s. These pictures served the reconstruction of parts of Warsaw from the rubble after 1945.

20, 21. Stanisław August's reign saw the spread of the neo-classical style which would put down deep roots in Polish-Lithuanian culture. It was employed in municipal architecture, such as the extraordinary tower of Poznań's city hall and the purposeful guardhouse in front, as well as for churches – the most monumental was Wilno's rebuilt cathedral.

22, 23. Stanisław August devoted his energy and resources to the creation of interiors that expressed his vision for the Commonwealth. None were more sophisticated than the Knights' Hall in the Royal Castle, opened in 1786. This national pantheon offered a lesson in patriotism, framed by the poetry of Virgil. However, Stanisław had difficulty in communicating the point of the investment, as this caricature shows. His principal painter and director of buildings, Marcello Bacciarelli, is depicted as an ass, while money drains away.

24, 25. The introduction of voluntary 'uniforms' for the szlachta, subtly differentiated for each palatinate, proved immensely popular and encouraged overlapping local and national patriotism. By the time of the sejmiks which elected envoys to the Great Sejm of 1788–92, aristocratic and royal patrons had to reckon with self-confident tribunes of the middling nobility, with their own ideas on how to repair the Commonwealth.

DYARYUSZ
SEYMU ORDYNARYINEGO
POD ZWIĄZKIEM KONFEDERACYI GENERALNEY
OBOYGA NARODOW
W WARSZAWIE ROZPOCZĘTEGO
ROKU PANSKIEGO 1788.
Tom 1. Część 1.
W WARSZAWIE
w Drukarni Nadworney JKMci i P. Kommissyi Eduk. Narodowey.

DYARYUSZ
SEYMU ORDYNARYINEGO
POD ZWIĄZKIEM KONFEDERACYI GENERALNEY
OBOYGA NARODOW
W PODWOYNYM POSŁOW SKŁADZIE
ZGROMADZONEGO
W WARSZAWIE
Od Dnia 16. Grudnia, Roku 1791.
TOM I. CZĘŚĆ I.
W WARSZAWIE,
w Drukarni Uprzywilejowaney Michała Grölla,
Księgarza Nadwornego Jego Królewskiey Mości.

26, 27. The title pages of the official diary of the Four Years' Sejm suggest the revolution in political culture. The traditional combination of the arms of Poland, Lithuania and the reigning monarch is replaced for the second parliamentary term by a victorious figure of liberty brandishing a French-style Phrygian cap on a pike.

28, 29. The gifted Tyrolean portraitist Giovanni Battista Lampi spent the end of the 1780s in Warsaw. He created similar visions of Franciszek Ksawery Branicki and Feliks Potocki as proud and martial fathers. The two displayed rather less valour when they led the counterrevolutionary Confederacy of Targowica in 1792–93.

30, 31. Jean-Pierre Norblin's sketches have a vibrancy lost in his finished drawings. His first impression of the acclamation of the Constitution of 3 May 1791 dramatizes the role of the king – steadily reduced in later versions. He observed the street fighting in Warsaw on 17–18 April 1794. Here the Russian Embassy is about to be stormed by the insurgents.

32. In exile in St Petersburg after his abdication, the former king became friendly with the French painter Élisabeth Vigée Le Brun. This last portrait of Stanisław August is one of her masterpieces.

abbeys'.[51] This is further evidence for Stanisław August's explanation of the sejm's decision on the bishopric of Cracow in July 1789: everything was governed by a combination of 'enthusiasm and intrigue'.[52] Neither 'enthusiasm' nor 'intrigue' in themselves sufficed to overcome the lack of interest of most parliamentarians in ecclesiastical affairs, but the prospect of both factors working in tandem kept the nuncio '*sempre in timore*'.[53]

It was no coincidence that some of the most radical projects for ecclesiastical reform were hatched in the circle of Reverend Kołłątaj. He envisaged the clergy as one of three service estates, alongside teachers and soldiers, in the vision for the Polish nation and polity, which he revealed in stages to the readers of his *Letters of An Anonymous Correspondent*. He later systematized this vision in his *Political Law of the Polish Nation*, published at the end of 1789. Kołłątaj believed that all inhabitants of the Commonwealth should enjoy personal liberty and security as their inalienable natural right. He therefore urged the abolition of serfdom, without waiting, as Rousseau had advised, for the serfs to be 'enlightened' before they were emancipated. 'There is nothing more terrible in human nature than an enlightened slave,' he hectored the deputation established by the sejm to draft a project for the new form of government.[54] On the other hand, only those with sufficient education and property should enjoy political rights. He proposed two parliamentary chambers: an upper one for landowners, and a lower one for urban proprietors. Kołłątaj's vision of the nation was both less and more than the noble estate defined by birth. Landless nobles, who were often illiterate, faced partial disenfranchisement in this brave new world.

Kołłątaj was the most important of the group of enlightened nobles who took up the cause of the Commonwealth's burghers in the course of 1789. The campaign had begun at the start of the year with a pamphlet printed for the city council of Old Warsaw. The language employed was one of restoration – but those 'ancient' privileges and liberties included participation in the legislature. In March the Varsovians appealed to other royal towns for support. In October they asked the others to send delegates so that a common list of postulates could be agreed. Cracow stood aloof, but the appeal resonated from Połock to Poznań. Many smaller towns in the Grand Duchy of Lithuania that had lost their municipal rights in 1776 joined in the movement – testimony to the survival of civic traditions.

The burghers' draft memorial, penned by Kołłątaj on 23–24 November 1789, contained assurances that they wished to defend the Fatherland together with the szlachta and that they were not aiming at a violent revolution. Nevertheless the king was disturbed by 'prefaces and eloquences obviously borrowed from current French writings'.[55] At his insistence the millenarian language was toned down, but the heavily drawn contrasts between revolutionary violence elsewhere and calm in Poland, as well as the appeal to the Catholic clergy for help, made veiled threats to the szlachta. The towns' demands included self-government, the extension of the noble privilege of *neminem captivabimus* to urban citizens, along with their right to acquire landed estates, and the abolition of barriers to their advance in the army, state administration and the Catholic Church. Most controversially, they demanded representatives in the sejm. Rumours spread that the monarch intended to lead the burghers (and perhaps the peasants and the clergy as well) against the szlachta in a coup – on the twenty-fifth anniversary of his coronation. The recent example of Gustav III's 'revolution' in February 1789 was lost on no one. The Swedish king, with the support of three of the four Estates of the Riksdag, had abolished most of the privileges of the noble Estate, and strengthened his own position in both the executive and the legislature. That he had left parliament the power to agree or refuse taxes impressed few Polish nobles.[56]

Nothing of the kind happened in Warsaw. Instead, on 25 November salutations of 'long live the king with the nation!' welcomed Stanisław August to the illuminated city hall. Two days later it was the venue for the signing of an act whereby the towns pledged to join forces to recover their rights. This, together with the procession of carriages bringing black-clad burghers and their redrafted memorial to the Royal Castle on 2 December made the king nervous. He would only agree to a summary being presented to the sejm by Crown Chancellor Jacek Małachowski, who distorted its sense. The sejm established a deputation for the towns, which then rejected the project submitted by Joachim Chreptowicz, the royalist vice-chancellor of Lithuania, because it provided for forty-four urban envoys to the sejm. The deputation's less generous project was criticized by the seven urban plenipotentiaries appointed by the delegates of the towns in December 1789. Six months later its work ground to a halt.

The burghers' opponents included nobles who wished to move into urban occupations without conceding any convergence from the opposite direction. Foremost was Jacek Jezierski, Castellan of Łuków. While raking in money from commercial ventures, including a Warsaw bath-house that fronted a high-end brothel, he traded insults in print with the tribune of the towns, Jan Baudouin de Courtenay. The two had previously competed in anti-clerical invective. Very different was Franciszek Salezy Jezierski, who parodied his namesake's rhetoric and prejudices, but rebuked Baudouin's cheap shots against the clergy. Canon Jezierski, the former school visitor who had preached the sermon at the sejm's inauguration, proved one of the Polish Revolution's greatest writers. A master of diverse literary forms including the pamphlet, novel, pocket dictionary and catechism, he was in social questions radical, but in religious matters orthodox.

Castellan Jezierski instrumentally compared the burghers' alleged threat of rebellion with the *Humble Request* of the Jewish delegates from a number of royal towns. Offering substantial contributions to the treasury, they particularly wished to extend their right of residence. The Christian burghers of Warsaw and other towns strenuously opposed this postulate. For their part they wanted the abolition of the *jurydyki* in which so many Jews were settled. Numerous Jews were among the thousands of persons crowding into Warsaw, the city's privilege of *de non tolerandis Iudæis* being suspended for the duration of the sejm. Most Christian traders and artisans resented the competition. After much lobbying, Crown Grand Marshal Michał Mniszech did order the Jews to leave the city in April 1790, but within a month many had returned. On 16 May a tumult was sparked by a false rumour that the Jews had killed a Christian tailor called Fuks (who had in fact assaulted Jewish workshops and then temporarily disappeared from view). Although there were no fatalities, many Jews were beaten up and their property looted. The crowd, made up mainly of apprentices, journeymen and masters, stoned the marshal's guard.

In the aftermath of the tumult, Castellan Jezierski voiced noble indignation against the burghers. On 19 June 1790 the sejm appointed a deputation for Jewish affairs, including Jezierski himself. Within two months it had prepared a project that drew on proposals submitted to the sejm by another member of the deputation, Mateusz Butrymowicz. On the one hand, this project assured full religious toleration to all (except those who had abandoned Catholicism). Moreover, Jews would no longer be referred to in public records as 'infidels', but instead as the 'people of the Old Testament'. That label, while much less pejorative, still carried problematic connotations for Jews. On the other hand, Jews would be expected to use the Polish language for all business except strictly religious matters. The Commission of National Education would supervise their schools. Rabbis would be renamed 'teachers', with precautions taken against their extorting money. Banned from producing, distributing or selling alcohol, Jews would be enjoined to take up agriculture and 'useful' crafts and trades.[57] With most civil and economic distinctions between Jews and Christian burghers abolished, the former would be subordinated to the Christian authorities in royal towns. The remnants of Jewish communal authority would therefore depend on noble proprietors. The project pleased few Jews, even among those *maskilim* most supportive of integration. Doubtless it also pleased few Christian burghers.

Subsequent projects both diminished the civic rights envisaged for Jews and the degree of state intervention in Jewish communal affairs, but despite the efforts of Jewish lobbyists and the labours of the Tuscan democrat Scipione Piattoli (who in November 1789 started working for the king), no parliamentary debate was held. Perhaps in the end the sejm would have got round to it, but in May 1792 time ran out. Only some of this reluctance can be ascribed to leading envoys' and senators' support for the Christian burghers. Most parliamentarians simply did not consider the Jewish question a priority. In contrast to Orthodox Christians, Jews were not linked to a hostile neighbouring power. Without a geopolitical imperative to arouse 'enthusiasm', no 'intrigues' could push a reform of the situation of the Commonwealth's Jews up the political agenda.

Essentially the conflict between Christian burghers and urban Jews came down to jurisdiction. For the former, if Jews had to be tolerated within towns at all, they should be subjected to municipal authority and taxes. Above all, they should know their place. Most Jews wished to reside and trade freely in towns, while keeping their communal and cultural autonomy; fearing persecution, they tended to look for state and noble protection. These factors worked against radical, top-down reforms of the kind envisaged by assimilationists such as Kołłątaj. In Lithuania and Ruthenia, the pressure for change was less. There were relatively fewer royal towns than in the western and central parts of the Crown, and fewer of them had the privilege *de non tolerandis Iudæis*. In this landscape, many inhabitants of small towns – Jews and Christians – were not bereft of civic spirit, but they rarely welcomed interference from above.

The attractions of local government by local citizens were felt no less strongly among the szlachta. Bucking the trend of eighteenth-century European administrative thought, the Polish Revolution saw no move towards a 'geometric' system of local administration subordinated to central state institutions. The need to co-ordinate the provisioning, quartering, recruitment and discipline of the expanded army in the localities produced a pragmatic response, one with roots in the noble nation's republican heritage. At the same time many landowners feared the return of the ruinous abuses perpetrated by unpaid soldiers and their over-mighty commanders during the war-torn decades prior to the settlement of 1716–17. Perhaps it was not coincidental that the pressure came first from Lithuanian envoys. Kazimierz Sapieha, the namesake of a notorious late seventeenth-century hetman, took much persuading, before he agreed at a provincial session to introduce the project on behalf of the Grand Duchy of Lithuania.

Civil-Military Commissions of Good Order were established for palatinates, lands and districts by the laws passed unanimously on 17 November 1789 (for the Grand Duchy of Lithuania) and 24 November 1789 (for the Crown).[58] These laws envisaged their 'co-operation' with the Commonwealth's central Military and Treasury Commissions. Their obeisance was reserved for the sejm, at the expense of the sejmiks. Some sejmiks, notably in Greater Poland, had in the past set up analogous bodies for local purposes. The civil-military commissions would convey information to the provinces regarding the work of the sejm and government commissions, while at the same time informing the centre of the situation and economic potential of their respective territories.

Besides handling civil-military relations (including court cases), these commissions were also charged with tasks more often associated with monarchical eighteenth-century 'police states'. These included the collection of statistics, repair of roads and bridges, and supervision of schools, hospitals and their funds. These functions could bring them into conflict with the clergy of various confessions. In the Crown, parish priests were each to maintain an elementary school 'for the enlightenment of the poorer szlachta and the ignorant simple folk', and the commissions were authorized to fine them for non-compliance. In Lithuania, landowners (who might be clergymen) were to maintain a schoolteacher in each village, supervised by the parish priest. Incumbents were also obliged to report the number of persons in their parishes to the commissions. This information would then be passed to the Treasury Commissions which would then estimate the general population from the census data. Although the Crown legislation was more rigorous in this regard than the Lithuanian, clashes could be defused more easily. Besides the sixteen lay noblemen, the Crown commissions contained three nobly born Catholic clergymen. The Lithuanian law made no explicit provision for clerical commissioners, which may explain the relative frequency of disputes in the Grand Duchy.

Most civil-military commissions carried out their tasks admirably. This was partly because of the speed and ease of implementing court verdicts when civil and military authorities acted together. Something must also be allowed for the attraction of participating in the sovereign Commonwealth. The disadvantages of collegial decision-making by gentlemen-amateurs were outweighed by the trust reposed in well over a thousand local men elected at sejmiks by their neighbours to serve their country without pay. The ideal of the accumulation of merit through public service is evident in a possible echo of Rousseau: the provision that participation in a civil-military commission (or at an equivalent level) would be a condition for election as an envoy to the sejm, a deputy to the tribunal, a member of a central commission or to obtain an order. When further institutions of central government were established in 1791, provision was again made for the civil-military commissions to co-operate with and inform the centre. This was because they had proved themselves a success. Two and a quarter centuries later, the Polish Revolution's local government reform remains a marvellous argument for decentralized public administration.

Progress towards wider constitutional reform was slower. On 7 September 1789 the sejm appointed a deputation to compose a project for the form of government. Its nominal chairman was Bishop Krasiński, who had returned to Warsaw after long years in Podolia. Ignacy Potocki took actual charge. He had to contend with obstruction from Suchodolski. Then the Prussian court inadvertently spurred the work forward by making an alliance conditional on an outline of a new constitutional settlement. This was ready on 17 December 1789.

The *Principles for the Correction of the Form of Government*, accepted by the sejm in modified form six days later, left much detail to be decided, especially regarding the executive institutions, but the text distilled the eighteenth-century evolution of noble republicanism. Sovereignty – including the powers to make laws, war and peace, supervise the executive bodies and choose the king and whichever officials would in future be deemed elective – belonged to the 'nation'. However, as a result of the debate, this suspiciously porous term was replaced throughout the document by 'the Commonwealth' or 'the noble estate', as appropriate. The *Principles* assured liberty and equality only to the szlachta, while promising the country's 'inhabitants' the protection of government and the enjoyment of personal property. The draft had contained nothing on royal election or succession, but at the last minute a point was inserted envisaging the 'election of a king of the Roman Catholic religion'. Sovereignty was to repose in ordinary, biennial sejms, but sejmiks would issue envoys with mandatory instructions. The question of the political rights of landless nobles remained unresolved.[59]

It remained to transform these general principles into a full project for the form of government. Ignacy Potocki, who had provided the ideas and momentum during the autumn, became distracted by foreign policy. For much of Europe, including the Commonwealth, the year 1790 proved a hinge of fate.

— TEN —

REVOLUTION

THE NATION WITH THE KING

The Polish Revolution changed course during 1790. The opposition coalition finally broke up, amidst invective about 'true' and 'false patriots'. Stanisław August regained much of his popularity and royalists showed their strength. It became clear to Ignacy Potocki and Hugo Kołłątaj that without the monarch's co-operation they could not lead a wider Polish nation to an enlightened republican future. The sejm had to be prolonged. The sejmiks of November 1790 revealed the extent to which the provincial szlachta had emancipated itself not only from royal or aristocratic patronage, but in Potocki's view, from common sense as well. By the end of the year the conditions for a constitutional compromise were in place, but in the event, the Constitution of 3 May 1791 surpassed all expectations. These shifts can be explained by the moving frames of political discourse. They can also be traced through the high-political choices made by the leading politicians, which bore a close relation to the changing international background.

After holding up well during 1788, the Ottoman Empire was in full retreat during 1789. The fall of Ochakov led to Russian triumphs in Moldavia, while Belgrade fell to the Austrians on 8 October 1789. However, the war had already brought disease, devastation and death well inside the military frontier of the Habsburg Monarchy. The dying Joseph II had poured the last of his energies into his scheme to commute peasant labour services into lesser cash obligations split between lord and state. Revolt was mooted among the nobles of Galicia and Hungary, but in the event the Austrian Netherlands rose up against Joseph's abolition of time-hallowed provinces and privileges. On 11 January 1790 the United Belgian States were proclaimed in Brussels. Joseph revoked some of his reforms before expiring in misery on 20 February. He was succeeded as King of

Hungary and Bohemia, Archduke of Austria and ruler of many other territories, but not yet as Holy Roman Emperor, by his brother Leopold. The new monarch's situation seemed desperate. The court of Berlin and the Sublime Porte had agreed an offensive alliance on 31 January. Frederick William II was sponsoring rebels and preparing to invade the Habsburg Monarchy.

Two perilous, mutually exclusive opportunities came into the Poles' view. The first was to help the Prussians by invading Galicia, part of which they might then keep in exchange for ceding Danzig, Thorn and parts of Greater Poland to the King of Prussia. Although Ignacy Potocki and other prominent 'patriot' leaders were willing to give up the two cities, they baulked at further cessions. They also wanted a favourable trade treaty – which Frederick William II was unwilling to offer. The Deputation for Foreign Affairs rejected the territorial terms, but on 15 March 1790 a less ambitious treaty for a defensive alliance was signed in Berlin, without territorial or trading conditions. The same day Stanisław August shared his misgivings with the sejm, but announced he would accept the nation's decision. He still hoped for an alternative from the two imperial courts. Russia offered nothing, but in the last days of Joseph II's reign, the Austrian chancellor Kaunitz spoke to the Polish minister in Vienna. This was the second opportunity. Kaunitz proposed a defensive alliance, an advantageous contract for salt, and fiscal concessions to Galician *sujets mixtes*. A few days later he hinted that his court rejected the Russian 'guarantee', and sounded out Stanisław August via the Austrian chargé d'affaires in Warsaw. Nevertheless, the deputation, having plumped for Prussia, decided to temporize until Leopold II's position was clarified. Despite the king's pleas, on Lucchesini's advice the deputation did not report Kaunitz's overture to the sejm. Whatever the sincerity of the veteran chancellor's intentions, it must be doubted whether an Austro-Polish alliance was realistic, given the unyielding position of Russia.[1]

On 27 March 1790 the treaty of alliance between the Commonwealth and Prussia was presented to the sejm. This step was taken during a break in the reading out of the long *Relation* of the deputation established to investigate those accused of rebellion in Ruthenia. The report was compiled in such a way as to emphasize the threat from Russia. Michał Zaleski, the deputation's secretary, left nothing to chance. Having quoted a letter from Bishop Sadkovskii to Catherine II, he expressed the hope that an alliance with Prussia would be approved that very day.[2] So it was, and on 29 March the treaty was signed in Warsaw. Both parties guaranteed each other's possessions. Prussia would come to Poland's aid

– if necessary, militarily – in the event of any other power's interference in the Commonwealth's internal affairs. For the Prussian court, what mattered for the moment was Polish help against Austria. Frederick William's gluttonous appetites for Polish territory could be sated later.

The Hohenzollern and the Habsburg girded themselves for battle. In an extraordinary feat, the Austrians mobilized almost half a million men. They matched the Prussian numbers along the northern border, pursued a vigorous campaign against the Turks, and still had enough troops with which to reconquer the Belgian provinces later in the year. The scale of the Austrian preparations impressed Polish witnesses, inducing nervousness at the prospect of war.[3] The Prussian and Austrian negotiators met at Reichenbach in Silesia. Initially, prompted by the British, the Prussians insisted that Austria should make peace with the Ottoman Empire on the basis of the *status quo ante bellum*, thereby renouncing its conquests. However, further variants on Hertzberg's plan for territorial exchange were spun as alternatives, and as the negotiations dragged on, the Austrians reinforced their positions. Frederick William's nerves frayed. He failed to attack while he still held a clear advantage, and was caught out when Leopold II agreed to peace on the basis of the *status quo ante bellum*. Leopold, conscious of the Habsburg Monarchy's need for peace, overruled Kaunitz. The Convention of Reichenbach was signed on 27 July 1790. However, when on 4 August 1791 the representatives of Emperor Leopold II and Sultan Selim III finally signed a peace treaty at Sistovo (Svishtov), a few adjustments were made to the border in favour of the Habsburg Monarchy.

In the meantime, after a two-year, see-sawing struggle, Gustav III fought Catherine II to an honourable draw. On 9 July 1790 the Swedish fleet defeated the Russians in the Gulf of Finland. This blow persuaded Catherine to abandon any territorial ambitions in the north, and also to renounce all restrictions on Swedish sovereignty. The peace treaty of Värälä was signed on 14 August. Ironically, on the same day the Commonwealth's sejm appointed a deputation to negotiate an alliance with the Swedish envoy.

Väräla compounded the impact of Reichenbach on the Commonwealth. As Robert Howard Lord put it, 'the collapse of the proposed attack upon Austria removed the one cogent motive Frederick William had had for desiring the Polish alliance'.[4] The sejm's decision, on 6 September 1790, to forbid by cardinal law any cession or exchange of the Commonwealth's territory confirmed that Prussian and Polish interests were no longer aligned. However, in the short run Reichenbach may have delayed Russian military intervention, as St Petersburg had not ruled out a new partition as a way of resolving the Austro-Prussian standoff. In April 1790 Potemkin had obtained Catherine's consent to 'help' Austria, in the event of a Prusso-Polish attack, by securing the Ukrainian palatinates.[5] As it was, the empress concentrated on another push southwards against the Turks. London and Berlin wished to force Russia as well as Austria to make peace on the basis of the *status quo ante bellum*, but Catherine indignantly rejected the idea. As 1790 drew to an end, the question was whether the British and Prussians were prepared to go to war with Russia. Perhaps the Poles might yet get one last chance, in alliance with Britain, Prussia and the Ottoman Empire, to escape the Russian noose? However, since August, fearing a Russian attack, Stanisław August had done all he could to stall an alliance between the Commonwealth and the Porte.

If 1790 proved a year of near misses for the Commonwealth abroad, at home it brought a turning point. Progress eluded Ignacy Potocki. The stalemate over rights for townsmen resembled the difficulties experienced by the Deputation for the Form of Government. Following a reminder from an impatient sejm in April 1790, the deputation discussed and sometimes mangled Potocki's drafts during June and July. By early August, when the *Project for the Form of Government* was printed (in folio, to accommodate the 658 articles), Potocki knew that arduous struggles lay ahead. Procedure dictated that the project be considered and voted on paragraph by paragraph, subject to innumerable interruptions and amendments. From the very first debates over the cardinal laws, it was evident that no acclamation would clear its path into the statute books. For all the *Project*'s republican safeguards against executive power, its radicalism in social and educational questions would run into obstacles.

The Puławy set had to reckon both with Branicki's faction and the royalists in a three-way contest for the support of independent-minded envoys. The hetman's supporters voiced old-fashioned noble republican stances which 'enlightened' parliamentarians and pamphleteers dismissed as 'prejudices'. Branicki and his allies had long been suspected of 'false patriotism' – of acting in Russian interests, despite their slogans of untrammelled sovereignty and national pride. But not all was well in their camp. Early in August 1790 Kazimierz Sapieha quarelled publicly with Branicki and moved out of his uncle's palace, although not everyone believed that the breach was final.[6]

In contrast, the royalists were beginning to feel the wind in their sails. The king had recovered some of his authority, both among the parliamentarians and the wider public. Two years of listening, yielding and advising had defused much of the inherited mistrust that beset all of the Commonwealth's monarchs. He had displayed the virtues of patience and prudence. In accepting the Prussian alliance against his better judgement, Stanisław August had evidently followed the will of 'the nation'. Would it be unreasonable to expect the nation to restore the prerogatives he had enjoyed when elected to the throne in 1764? The king maintained that he had refrained from exercising some of his prerogatives, such as nominating senators, which naturally reverted to him on the abolition of the Permanent Council. As he had faithfully kept his *pacta conventa*, so 'the nation' should also keep faith with him.

The first indications that the king and the Puławy set might sometimes make common cause against the hetman's faction dated back to the aftermath of the sejm's decision to secularize the properties of the bishopric of Cracow in July 1789. Following this humiliation, the primate departed on a long voyage to Italy, France and England, thereby removing one object of hostility from the opposition's gaze. Stanisław August may or may not have asked his brother to go, but later he represented it as a necessity. Soon after that debacle, by his own account, the king warned the Potockis that 'several gentlemen-orators . . . have ruled the entire sejm for some time . . . They will harry us to ever worse things, if we do not join hands.' The fallout from the affair also damaged the king's relationship with Stackelberg beyond repair.[7]

However, mutual suspicion bedevilled relations between Ignacy Potocki and Stanisław August. Scipione Piattoli, acting as a go-between, briefed the king on work on the *Project for the Form of Government*. The monarch opposed not only the loss of most of his prerogatives and the weakness of the central executive bodies, but also the subordination of the sejm to the sejmiks. By the late summer of 1790 Stanisław August was ready for a trial of strength against Puławy. In the short term, this aligned the royalists with the hetman's faction on some questions, in an appeal to the sentiments of the middling szlachta.[8]

Following the presentation of the *Project* to the sejm on 5 August, it entered deliberation. Criticism was fierce during semi-private conferences at Marshal Małachowski's house. Potocki was already dissatisfied with it. He even mused on 20 August that since Poland was not ready for a pure republic, 'a limited monarchy' would be preferable to 'anarchy'.[9] The most controversial point of the

Project was the proposal that the enervated throne should become 'elective in families' – a euphemism for hereditary succession which deceived nobody. Behind the scenes, Lucchesini did all he could to discourage the supporters of succession and encourage its opponents. The sejm could not even agree on the legality of asking the sejmiks about the succession to the throne.

The sejm did, however, decide on 2 September that the 'holy Roman Catholic Faith of both rites with all the rights of the holy Church *in spiritualibus* in both nations of the Polish Crown and the Grand Duchy of Lithuania, as well as in the provinces appertaining to them, shall be eternally dominant'.[10] The wording of this first cardinal law was the outcome of a fraught debate. The following day the sejm agreed three more laws concerning religion. The second cardinal law specified that the king must be a Catholic, and the queen, if not a Catholic, could not be crowned; the third that abandoning Catholicism for another faith would remain a crime, although without specifying the punishment; and the fourth that persons of confessions hitherto tolerated would be assured 'peace in confession and worship' and freedom from persecution. Stanisław August spoke against restricting toleration only to religions already tolerated, even evoking the horrors of the Inquisition, but after an intemperate intervention from Bishop Krasiński against 'heretics', the point was agreed unanimously.

It is misleading to present the first cardinal law (repeated in briefer form in the Constitution of 3 May) as the culmination of Catholic confessionalization in the Commonwealth.[11] Although the agreement in the 1573 Confederacy of Warsaw to refrain from mutual persecution had been made between equal citizens who were divided in faith, for over a century prior to the 1760s the dominant status of Catholicism had been so obvious that there had been no need to enshrine it in a special law. The various threats to Catholic confessional supremacy during Stanisław August's reign probably made such reassurance necessary.

Battle was also joined over the royal prerogative on 2 September. Małachowski underlined the importance of law, holding up the unwritten British constitution as a model:

> We see how the free English nation keeps its solemn laws which are so strongly inculcated in the citizen, that their spirit might sooner be separated from the body, than a living Englishman from his constitutional law, through which the strength, existence and respect of the English nation are maintained.[12]

This reference probably favoured the royalists, who were well prepared. They sought the definition of the royal prerogative by the 1764 *pacta conventa*. Forced onto the defensive, the opposition leaders denied any threat to the sanctity of the *pacta conventa*, while opposing an explicit confirmation of the king's right to nominate senators and ministers. However, Seweryn Potocki, envoy for Bracław, was less careful. Addressing the monarch, he blamed corruption on 'those sub-lords' who had managed to 'capture your gracious heart' and obtained the 'transfer into their hands of all your graces, in the worst manner'. Royalists strongly defended the king and attacked the magnates. Trying to limit the damage, Ignacy Zakrzewski, envoy for Poznań, acknowledged the trustworthiness of the present king, but in future he wanted the abolition of prerogatives 'which would maintain embedded aristocratic anarchy' in which 'violence is higher than the law'. His alliterative abuse of 'anarchic aristocrats' and 'aristocratic anarchy' was part of the overwhelming discursive tide against the magnates.[13]

The problem of the royal prerogative of nomination returned during the session of 10 September 1790. Seweryn Potocki again insulted the monarch:

> O King! Be content with what the nation, always mindful of the authority of the throne, has been able to offer you. King, do not erode the authority of the nation, because your authority is founded upon it alone; King, do not endeavour to corrupt the nation, because they are the same, whom you are capable of corrupting with money or some will-o'-the-wisps.[14]

Stanisław August picked up the gauntlet at the next session. On 13 September, having again stressed he had kept his side of the *pacta conventa*, he warned that 'from the dead semblance of a king, who would have no power either to reward, or to encourage, you would have no advantage'. He left the chamber, while the sejm resolved the question of his prerogative. Royalist envoys and senators hammered home the argument that in weakening the king, terrible power would be handed to the aristocrats.[15]

Pius Kiciński laid on the sarcasm with a trowel. It was unforgivable for the 'lordlings' not to get the *starostwa* they expected, that poor nobles could become senators and ministers; it caused them infinite suffering that 'any old nobleman has an order', including himself. Kiciński conceded that the king's goodness and pity led him sometimes to give too generously, but he did not corrupt sejms or sejmiks. Instead the king helped the szlachta to resist the lords who wished to dominate them with the help of dazzled burghers, and so the lords sought to destroy the remnants of his prerogatives. With a threatening flourish the envoy for Liw denounced the magnates: 'Those are your lords, your tyrants.'[16]

The sejm unanimously restored the power to nominate senators and ministers to Stanisław August. The brothers Potocki asked the monarch to halt the printing of Kiciński's speech on the grounds that it would prove divisive and hamper work on the new form of government. Stanisław August let it be known he had received their request too late. Of course he approved of the speech's dissemination; it helped seal his recovery of the political initiative. Ignacy Potocki complained about '*cortegiani*' who served the king's private desires while sometimes contradicting him in public.[17] This jaundiced verdict does convey something of Polish revolutionary politics. An independent mind was a prerequisite for respect in public life, while support for the monarch's prerogatives had to be couched in terms of the public good. In other words, royalists also needed to be republicans.

Stanisław August's admirers have celebrated this political comeback.[18] Some of his critics have accused him of cutting a deal with the hetman's faction for the sake of his prerogatives, indulging noble prejudices against the burghers and sabotaging progress towards an enlightened republican form of government.[19] It is possible to take another view. The king had to set at rest fears that he was planning, Swedish-style, to use the burghers to curtail noble liberties. He knew that many envoys jealously guarded the noble monopoly on legislation. Much could be granted to burghers without waving this red flag at nobly born bulls. Royalists diverted the charge of manipulating those deemed unworthy of republican liberty onto the magnates. Moreover, Stanisław August had indeed advanced many talented men from middling noble backgrounds to castellanies. It is a moot point whether election by the sejmiks would have produced a more meritocratic senate. Perhaps the monarch's fears of the effects of drunkenness and ignorance were exaggerated,[20] but there remained sejmiks at which magnates could still cart in many petty and dependent nobles.

Most importantly of all, for the royalists' demagogy to be effective, it had to be plausible. It was. It touched a raw nerve among provincial envoys who had long resented aristocratic hauteur. Stanisław Staszic had set the tone for the year 1790 in his *Warnings for Poland*. In a famous passage he asked repeatedly who for decades had struck each corrupt and cowardly blow against the Fatherland. Each time he answered: 'The Lords'.[21] The royalists sailed with the anti-aristocratic tide with more conviction than the opposition, but they did not create it. Back in 1788–89 a similar discourse had not saved the Permanent Council. By the middle of 1790 circumstances had changed. One factor may have been that over a thousand civil-military commissioners were already making a tangible impact on their localities. The king seized the opportunity to relaunch his efforts to ally himself with middling nobles against the magnates. Generations of historians have berated successive elective kings for not pursuing this very strategy. But the bucking horse of noble opinion had first to be mounted and calmed by the king, before he could ride it towards enlightened reform.

Across the Commonwealth, middling nobles grumbled. They were paying taxes while the politicians prated in Warsaw, with no end in sight. The sejmiks to elect envoys should normally have been held in mid-August 1790, but were delayed to February 1791. Their date was then brought forward to November 1790, but this was linked to the sejm's decision on 12 October that these sejmiks were to elect a new set of envoys, not to replace the existing ones, but to deliberate alongside them. The marshals felt obliged to justify this extraordinary arrangement in a proclamation issued on 25 October: unconventional means and the favour of Divine Providence – they wrote – had brought the casting off of the guarantee, the expansion of the army and a new ally.[22] However, in places the irritation had not abated by the time the sejmiks met. The szlachta of Nowogródek warned against any further extension of envoys' mandates: 'otherwise the usurpation of such power may change them into absolute dictators, damaging and terrible to national liberty'.[23]

The most sensitive question that autumn, both within the sejm and across the country, was succession or election to the throne. The proclamation finally agreed by the sejm on 24 September 1790 asked the 'nation' to agree *vivente rege* to the Elector of Saxony becoming the next monarch. The wording also suggested that hereditary succession was preferable to free election, although this question was not posed explicitly.[24] The precaution made little difference. The Crown field hetman, Seweryn Rzewuski, invested much money, energy and even his name in the cause of defeating hereditary succession. However, he published most of the two dozen or so pamphlets he penned anonymously, creating the impression of a swell of opinion in defence of free royal elections. He even shrugged off the consequences of violent foreign intervention: 'And therefore what could our ancestors see in interregna that is so terrible? That one of them had a village turned into ash? It soon arose again from the ashes.' This nonchalance exposed him to devastating ripostes, especially from Kołłątaj. Kołłątaj also traded insults with Józef Kossakowski after the bishop had spoken out strongly against hereditary succession, and presented the king as a victim of Muscovite violence and aristocratic ambition.[25]

The instructions compiled at the November 1790 sejmiks were even longer and more forthright than those of August 1788. This was partly because of the provision, at Wojciech Suchodolski's insistence, that instructions should be agreed before the election of envoys. The king predicted that 'candidates for envoys, in order only to secure the majority of votes for themselves, will not only not oppose, but help to include all the crankiest points, which the multitude of the least enlightened szlachta will want to cram into the instructions'.[26] So it proved, for example in Greater Poland:

> It is vain even to stay here, when no end is in sight; stubbornness and garrulousness have come from the sejm. In fact every reasonable person retreats from the din, when common sense finds no place . . . They are writing a statute (*konstytucya*), not an instruction, there is a whole day of arguments over one word. It would be enough to settle what has happened until now, but everyone walks around with a sheet full of several or a dozen points.[27]

The assemblies were well attended, with some running to four figures. A few were tumultuous, although violence was rare. 'Sabres were drawn, but it calmed down without anyone being hurt,' reported the Castellan of Sochaczew to the king.[28]

Kołłątaj was verbally abused at some sejmiks, as the story spread that he wished to apply peasant sickles to noble necks. At Lublin, when someone called for the works of the 'anonymous correspondent' to be burnt, others demanded the burning of their author as well. Kołłątaj collected one recommendation for the vice-chancellorship of the Crown (from the Lithuanian sejmik of Wołkowysk), but the palatinates of Sieradz and Volhynia demanded his punishment. Other sejmiks recommended his rivals.

In the Grand Duchy of Lithuania and Livonia, hereditary succession to the throne was supported by six sejmiks but explicitly rejected by ten. In the Crown provinces, only three sejmiks were in favour; eighteen were openly against. The others remained silent on the question. Intense emotions were aroused. For example, the Wyszogród sejmik instructed its envoys: 'as the election of kings is the source of our liberty . . . they shall never permit succession to the throne'.[29] The significant support for the election *vivente rege* of the Elector of Saxony came hedged with conditions. Even sejmiks which permitted hereditary succession demanded restrictions on the prerogatives of Stanisław August's successors.

The sejmik of the palatinate of Kiev, held at Żytomierz, is an especially interesting case. A vote was held, in which 804 voted for succession and 84 for election. Among the latter were the royalist palatine Józef Stempkowski and a republican writer of striking originality, Adam Rzewuski. Among the former were the aristocratic banker 'Prot' Potocki and all of those – about a quarter of the total – who 'signed' by drawing the cross next to their names. The instruction first records that all were convinced of the king's 'caring wish to make his nation happy'. They agreed to the election *vivente rege* of the Elector of Saxony, after whom the 'nation' would choose a male Wettin with the right of succession to the throne. However, because of the danger of '*absolutyzm*', the 'nation' would retain power over army, treasury, diplomacy and 'police'. Clearly the majority was willing to assuage the anxieties of the minority, sharing many of its concerns.[30]

The house of Saxony was as popular as ever. The question requires more research, but perhaps, after a generation had passed, the rotund figure of Augustus III had acquired an aura of regal dignity without responsibility. Memories of the disorder and corruption of the 1750s had dimmed, while few could now remember his election. However, the manifest hostility to hereditary succession shocked Ignacy Potocki. He believed that the instructions '*marquent l'absence du sens commun*'.[31]

The king observed: 'almost everywhere the instructions are filled with old-fashioned oddities, and especially for the spoiling of education'.[32] Many instructions again criticized the Educational Commission. Turning schools over to religious orders would free the educational fund for the army. Most sejmiks desired the return of the Jesuits. This followed an offer published on 10 November 1790 in the *Warsaw Gazette* by its ex-Jesuit editor. Former Jesuits would gladly take on the education of the nation's youth, reliant only on charity and Divine Providence, if the Commonwealth could persuade the pope to restore the Society of Jesus. Although this offer could not have reached the more distant palatinates before the sejmiks began, in the Grand Duchy of Lithuania the ex-Jesuit Marcin

Poczobut co-ordinated the action. Caught between loyalties, the rector of Wilno University strove with mixed results to avoid direct criticism of the commission. The other explanation for the fact that the four south-eastern sejmiks of the Crown failed to support the Jesuit cause could be that the Society of Jesus had historically been weaker in Lesser Poland than in Greater Poland and Lithuania. The Volhynian sejmik, for example, sought to clip the commission's wings. Its instruction favoured the local Piarists and Basilians, but was silent on the Jesuits.[33]

The sejmik instructions of 1790 reveal a noble nation getting accustomed to its recovered sovereignty, jealous of its liberties and privileges, suspicious of professionalization in government, reluctant to pay more taxes, keen to tap ecclesiastical wealth, but as keen as ever to pursue local and provincial interests. The latter included the location of the institutions of the Grand Duchy of Lithuania, such as the Tribunal. Four Mazovian instructions bitterly criticized Jews, but the Volhynian instruction contained a clause in their favour. Lithuanian sejmiks were more likely to forbid the emancipation of the enserfed peasantry, while those in the Crown were more hostile to burghers' participation in the legislature, although often willing to assure their personal liberty. As in 1788, Crown instructions were more likely to demand the wearing of national costume and restrictions on foreign travel.

That said, the differences between the Crown and Lithuanian instructions, in content and rhetoric, are less significant than the similarities. After more than two centuries growing together in parliamentary union, both nations – as well as both components of the conjoined noble nation – shared a common republican culture. A clause of the Samogitian instruction, for example, indicates a mature understanding of liberty:

> . . . it is a condition that civil and political liberty for citizens be guarded and secured. And so not to permit such a form of government which would in any way lead to the infringement of governmental and true freedom, or property, honour or the security of civic life.[34]

These sejmiks also saw the ongoing weakening of magnate influence. Even the Volhynian instruction demanded 'that the country's aristocracy, which is so harmful both in general and in particular, should have no influence by any means either on jurisdiction or deliberations'.[35]

Among the men chosen as envoys, fewer than usual came from magnate families. This was partly because many of the most politically active lords had already been elected in 1788, while most of the others sat in the senate. Despite the new cohort's reputation for youth and inexperience, the differences between them and those elected in 1788 were not that great. For example, the second cohort had an average age of forty years when elected, as opposed to forty-two.[36] A resident Prussian diplomat judged that about two-thirds of the new envoys supported the king. As the year 1790 drew to a close, a hostile observer informed his patron: 'the king says nothing, but he begins to sense that he has the majority of votes in the chamber'.[37] Ignacy Potocki, who conceded that most of the new envoys were chosen '*pas absolument mal*', concluded that the noble nation could not be led from its 'Sarmatian brouhaha' towards 'a happy regeneration' without the full co-operation of the king. That future would involve compromises: between republicanism and monarchism and between enlightenment and tradition.[38]

Ignacy Potocki went to the Royal Castle on 4 December 1790. He invited Stanisław August to take the initiative in drafting the new form of government. The king set to work. He produced the outline of a constitution, titled 'The Daydream of a Good Citizen', which would have placed a stronger executive under the direction of the monarch and given him a substantial role in lawmaking. With Piattoli co-ordinating, Potocki's amendments took the draft in a republican direction, before Stanisław Małachowski helped them to compromise. In mid-March, they brought in Kołłątaj, partly for his turn of phrase. His redaction, finished on 25 March, was quite close both to Stanisław August's concept and structure, and to the final text of the Constitution. The last changes were made towards the end of April, following consultations with trusted envoys and senators. It would henceforth suit all concerned for the king to appear to have taken a back seat. Historians could only guess at the drafting of the Constitution, until in the early 1960s Emanuel Rostworowski assembled and compared the successive versions. He checked these against what could be gleaned from political correspondence and pieced together the whole process – a masterclass in the historian's craft. The king's contribution to the Constitution proved to be much greater than had been supposed. But it was still a compromise.[39]

While the new form of government was being negotiated behind the scenes, Warsaw rocked with mirth. Julian Niemcewicz's hastily written play *The Envoy's Return* brought the reformers' maxims to a recognizable and respectable country manor. For a fortnight after 15 January 1791, this romantic comedy-cum-political satire played to packed houses at the National Theatre. It was then staged in court theatres across the country. The first printed edition sold out, so a second was advertised in mid-February. The titular hero, Walery, was the son of the worthy chamberlain and his virtuous wife. His enlightened patriotism struck a golden mean between the mindless aping of foreign fashion both by the odious Szarmancki, his rival for the hand of the heroine Teresa, and her vacuous mother, and the old-fashioned prejudices aired by her repellent father, the drunkard Starosta Gadulski (a name that implies a windbag). The latter was played by the charismatic and imposing '*primus Poloniae* actor', Karol Boromeusz Świerzawski, whose youthful escapades reputedly included two escapes from incarceration in the tower of Poznań City Hall. Gadulski's verbose utterances parodied 'old republican' pamphleteers and orators. Among the 'prejudices' ridiculed by Niemcewicz was free royal election. This prompted a furious Jan Suchorzewski – three days after the royal première – to demand the exemplary punishment of the author by the sejm court, and the closure of the theatre. The sejm reacted with laughter, as Stanisław August informed his diplomats. However, the king's nephew, Prince Józef Poniatowski, who led Warsaw's fastest set of young blades, also discerned a caricature of himself – Szarmancki. He invited Niemcewicz for a ride in his carriage. The prince drove his horses around the city at such a speed that the playwright took some time to recover from the jolting and shaking.[40]

The sejm was occupied by less amusing matters than Suchorzewski's bluster and Poniatowski's driving. The meandering deliberations of December and January, including much private business, and lengthy speeches of thanks by newly promoted senators, once again demonstrated the need for a reform of procedure. In early January the sejm agreed a temporary regulation. No one could speak on the same matter more than once during debate and once during voting. The marshal would call envoys and senators to speak. He was also to ensure that amendments were relevant to the matter at hand and that a project under discussion could not be interrupted by the introduction of another. On the other hand, it proved impossible to agree either a quorum or a ban on spectators sitting among the envoys.[41]

Further changes followed a debate on 17 and 21 February. According to the law *Protection of Parliamentary Time*, passed with an amendment moved by Pius Kiciński, the sejm would no longer decide projects clause by clause (*categoratim*), which permitted endless amendments, but would either accept them in their entirety or send them back to the relevant sejm deputation for correction. Kiciński's rhetorical tour de force was compared to Mahomet handing down the Koran. He appealed both to the Last Judgement and to the judgement of the public, as he assumed the role of a prophet:

> Almighty God, who today wished to have me as his instrument, that I should put before you these truths with the boldness befitting a Pole, befitting an envoy, will surely inspire all members of the sejm with this same spirit, that you should cast off utterly the remnants of this Russian yoke, which has until now kept you in inactivity.

Kiciński effectively branded anyone who stood by the old form of deliberations as a Muscovite. His demagogy worked – again.[42]

The king was not entirely satisfied. 'I always say this: that in the form of deliberations, it would be best simply to adopt the English method, because that alone is equally far from excessive prolongation, and also from excessive haste,' he wrote to Deboli on 16 March. Three days later he added: 'it seems that something else will still be needed, if our deliberations are to go rapidly and well. Although we are now patching up things as best we can, and despite going in circles, we shall in the end get to the English [form of] government.' It was not only British parliamentary procedure which Stanisław August admired so greatly, but the balanced relationship between Parliament and government, Crown and nation.[43]

The immediate context for these debates on procedure was the reform of the sejmiks. It had suited both Stanisław August and Ignacy Potocki for the sejm to move onto this matter instead of resuming discussion of the cardinal laws – which could prejudice elements of the new Constitution. However, two long debates in early January 1791 had been needed to reach this decision. Marshal Małachowski was obliged to have inscribed into law the cardinal laws agreed back in September 1790. This assuaged fears for those concerning religion. At one stage, faced with obstruction orchestrated by a number of senators, it even looked as though the envoys might walk out and deliberate separately. The king helped to calm the mood. However, he would have wished to avoid the justification for the change of direction, namely that the sejmiks were the source of legislation. One envoy quoted Rousseau's paean to the sejmiks as the 'palladium of liberty'. Most of the *Project for the Form of Government* was shelved, but not forgotten. Although the initiative for the new constitution lay with the monarch, he would have to reckon with self-confident envoys.[44] His opinion of one of the new cohort, Antoni Trębicki (born in 1765), was representative: 'Trembicki, a new envoy for Livonia, a kinsman and protégé of Radziwiłł, the current Palatine of Wilno, very young, but very talented and eloquent, and also too animated, made an incendiary speech.'[45]

Once the sejmiks were under discussion, the most controversial question was whether or not to exclude landless nobles from active participation. Both proponents and opponents of this reform employed an anti-aristocratic discourse. The former evoked malign magnates inebriating and intimidating petty nobles into actions beyond their ken. However, Suchodolski, opposing the measure, sought to turn ordinary landowning nobles into 'aristocrats': 'to destroy equality, preserved by our ancestors with such care, to transfer the government from the generality of the noble estate into the hands of powerful aristocrats alone, will this be to the good of the Fatherland?'[46]

The sejm passed the law *Sejmiks* on 24 March 1791. Building on earlier reforms, this removed active voting rights from landless nobles, except those who leased land worth 100 złotys a year, and from other 'dependants', such as soldiers. It did not settle whether or not nobly born clergymen in possession of landed estates could actively participate in sejmiks. An accompanying law instructed every sejmik to maintain a book of local landowners entitled to participate in its deliberations and votes. Among the other provisions was an attempt to equalize not only the number of envoys, but also the number of sejmiks in each of the Commonwealth's three provinces. However, given attachments to traditional meeting places, perfect parliamentary 'geometry' remained out of reach.[47]

So, for the moment, did the final abandonment of imperative mandates. On 24 March Kiciński cited the English example: 'There, from the moment an envoy learns he has been legally elected, he ceases to be an envoy from a part of the country, and is considered as a representative of the entire nation, and his only precept is the public happiness.'[48] On this occasion even Kiciński was not persuasive enough; for the most important questions put to the sejmiks by the king or future Custodial Council, binding instructions remained.

Next was the reform of royal towns. On 5 April 1791 one of the newly elected envoys, Stanisław Sołtyk of Cracow, introduced a relatively modest project. His bill would have admitted just twelve representatives from the largest cities to the sejm, and restricted their participation to urban matters.[49] Even this went too far for many envoys and senators, who insisted that only nobles were fit to make laws. The following day another newly elected envoy, the elderly Tomasz Dłuski of Lublin, warned of 'absolutism' should such a measure pass. His own project not only excluded burghers from the legislature, but also banned them from buying landed estates. When he was informed that in Lithuania burghers had enjoyed the right since 1775, he amended his project to rescind that right. He was, however, prepared to allow them to rise higher than hitherto in the military and the Catholic Church.[50] There was now no chance of passing the project agreed between Stanisław August, Ignacy Potocki and Kołłątaj, which envisaged forty-eight envoys to represent the burghers in the sejm. According to the king, 'Sarmatian prejudices against the burghers' proved so strong that the best he and others could do was to refer the project to the Constitutional Deputation.[51]

On 14 April the deputation's revised proposal ran into criticism. This project allowed burghers to participate in the Police and Treasury Commissions, but not the sejm. State interference in municipal affairs would be far-reaching.[52] The shadow of the French Revolution hung over the debate, with objections raised to the supposedly threatening tone adopted by the burghers. This stirred another newly elected envoy for Cracow, Aleksander Linowski, to make the case to 'give a Fatherland to those without a Fatherland, to attach to liberty a greater number of souls', strong enough to withstand either the throne or the 'spirit of aristocracy'. Thus might a violent revolution be averted.[53] Stanisław August sought to defuse fears that concessions to the burghers would lead to 'despotism'. On the contrary. He referred to the nobility of Denmark, which suddenly in 1660, 'from unlimited freedom was subjected to the most complete government of absolutism', to show that liberty was best defended by increasing the number of free persons.[54]

The maverick envoy for Kalisz, Suchorzewski, declared that he could not agree to the burghers having a '*vox decisiva*' in the legislature. He introduced a project of his own (although rumour had it that a 'patriot' had given it to him). This provided for twenty-one 'urban plenipotentiaries' who would merely advise the sejm on urban matters. Many opponents of burghers participating in lawmaking supported Suchorzewski, without objecting to the self-government and civil liberties contained in his project. Stanisław August, seeing in this '*omnia essentialia*', except full parliamentary voting rights, invoked Providence and commended the proposal. Supporters of giving the burghers full legislative rights reluctantly yielded and the project was agreed in principle. Two days later the monarch reflected: 'I take it as a visible work of God, that it was through the lips of the crank Suchorzewski that good counsel spoke'.[55]

Suchorzewski's project was reintroduced in a tidier form on 18 April. Małachowski lauded a work which would eliminate 'prejudices held by foreigners about us Poles', 'when they see how the humanity in us is extended towards fellow-citizens, not abasing others in order to raise up ourselves – which we see in the French Revolution'.[56] However, the expected unanimous acclamation did not occur – yet. Several envoys, senators and bishops sought to ensure 'that citizens of the dominant religion settled in towns should have priority over a newcomer of another calling'.[57] Others responded that such a condition would vitiate the aim of encouraging foreigners to settle in Polish towns. Fears of foreign influence being exerted via dissidents, as in the 1760s, were countered by the argument that non-Catholics should not be given cause to seek foreign protection. It was also pointed out that in some towns close to the Silesian border there were hardly any Catholics. In the end, Kazimierz Sapieha's proposal to omit any reference to religion was accepted. With a round of joyous hand-kissing, the project became law.[58] Stanisław August reflected that evening: 'today there were two fanaticisms to combat at once. God gave us the victory. It will not be me who will gather the fruit, but the eyes that see Poland today, and will see her in thirty years' time, will not recognize her.'[59]

Historians have been divided over whether or not to take the king at his word. One interpretation is that a deal between the king and the 'old republicans' set back the cause of a Commonwealth based on property, education and talent, rather than birth. It was not only that commissions in the National Cavalry, and certain ecclesiastical prebends, not to mention bishoprics, remained reserved for the szlachta. The law did not apply to privately owned or clerical towns – the majority of urban settlements. Moreover, the provision for thirty burghers to be ennobled by each sejm could be seen as an attempt to strengthen the noble estate at the expense of its urban competitor.[60] However, the key seems to be Stanisław August's sense of the possible, given his preference for unanimity. He also appreciated that participation as full members of the legislature was not the overriding priority for most burghers.[61]

Despite these limitations, *The Times* of London hailed a 'Revolution in Poland on rational, practicable and liberal principles'.[62] Services of thanksgiving took place right across the Commonwealth, starting with a *Te Deum* in Warsaw on 19 April, attended by the monarch. Many towns prepared to send delegations to the king to express their joyous gratitude on the approaching feast of St Stanisław (8 May). Most expressively, at Warsaw City Hall on 29 April, Stanisław Małachowski led the numerous and often prominent nobles who became urban citizens. The Austrian chargé d'affaires had already concluded that the szlachta had undergone a '*Revolution in der Denkensart*'. The king noted that some diplomats in Warsaw could not conceal their consternation. Indeed, at the courts of Vienna and Berlin, the news caused anxiety about an exodus to Polish towns.[63]

The euphoria manifest on 29 April had not dissipated by the morning of Tuesday 3 May. Something important was afoot. Expectant Varsovians crowded into the public galleries of the senate chamber and thronged the narrow streets adjoining the Royal Castle. Prince Józef Poniatowski's soldiers kept order. The previous evening, the constitutional project, titled the *Law on Government*, had been read out at a meeting in the Radziwiłł Palace. Seven senators and seventy-six envoys had pledged their support. More were canvassed overnight. As most parliamentarians had not yet returned to Warsaw, the reformers hoped for the advantage of surprise. Nevertheless, news had leaked out, and so the introduction of the project was brought forward from 5 to 3 May. The means could only be revolutionary.[64]

Parliamentary procedure envisaged projects being introduced, printed and distributed for three days of 'deliberation', before being debated and thrashed out in the chamber. Moreover, the provision for the succession to the throne in place of free royal elections contravened not only the sejm's own decisions of September 1790 (that the matter would be decided only by three-quarters of sejmik instructions), but also Stanisław August's *pacta conventa*. The only way forward lay in the overwhelming acclamation of the Constitution, without allowing any amendments, as an emergency remedy for a grave crisis. At eleven o'clock in the morning of 3 May Małachowski announced that the Deputation for Foreign Affairs had important matters to report.[65]

Many demanded to be heard, but Stanisław Sołtyk took advantage of the precedence of his own palatinate of Cracow. He referred to alarming news that had reached the deputation. Suchorzewski shouted out: 'I have great and horrible things to reveal!'[66] Although the king urged the reading out of the despatches, Suchorzewski tore off his newly awarded order of St Stanisław and crawled towards the throne until he was permitted to speak. He informed the Estates and the public that he had 'discovered a coup prepared for the destruction of our liberty', and that 'a revolution is plotted similar to the Swedish one, which in introducing a new [form of] government to the country, changed the liberty of the nation into slavery'. He would not be deterred by 'rumours that have been started, that all those who hold a contrary opinion are Muscovites. Because this was done in Sweden, when it was desired to introduce absolutism.' Nor would he be intimidated by the manipulated burghers: 'This is what happened in Sweden as well; one class of citizens was used to put shackles on another.' He was convinced that 'foreign scarecrows are also exaggerated. It is not a foreign, but a domestic enemy that we must fear: not violence, but intrigues, that they should not lead us to despotism, to succession [to the throne], which is the bane of liberty.'[67]

Nevertheless, the sejm silently heard excerpts from diplomatic despatches, creating the impression of an imminent and appalling threat to the Commonwealth's existence. Ignacy Potocki then called on the king to elucidate how the Fatherland could be saved. The monarch dwelt on Poland's critical situation and stated that a suitable project had come to his notice. Having asked to be freed from his *pacta conventa* regarding the succession, he asked for the project to be read out. According to the official record, 'Barely was the reading out finished than the entire chamber shouted out its assent a thousand times.'[68]

In fact, the entire chamber was not in agreement. Faced with vocal protests and demands for discussion, Małachowski thought it prudent to recommend the project to the sejm as the best of all republican forms of government. The king again asked to be freed from his *pacta conventa* regarding the succession. Then,

> when some parliamentarians demanded to speak, others, the larger part, cried *Zgoda!*; confusion arose in the chamber for a while, during which the Honourable Mr Suchorzewski the envoy for Kalisz brought his little son into the middle of the chamber saying: 'I shall kill my own child, so that he should not live to experience the slavery which this project prepares for the country.' But his colleagues led him back to his place.[69]

Suchorzewski's actions nevertheless ensured that the project would be debated at length.[70] Among the 182 envoys and senators present, about 110 are thought to have been in favour of the *Law on Government*, and about thirty to have been opposed. The remainder were as yet undecided – they had only just heard the project read out.[71] Many passionate orations and interventions followed, with frequent appeals both to Providence and to Russophobic and anti-aristocratic slogans. Kiciński was as eloquent as ever. But each time the marshal asked for *zgoda*, protests delayed the final decision.

For the project's opponents, the provisions for the succession to the throne were the greatest sticking point. They managed to have the *pacta conventa* read out. Jan Orłowski, envoy for Podolia, asked rhetorically: 'if a temporary Polish throne interested neighbouring powers, then what would a hereditary one be like, with this absolute government?'[72] Such arguments had already been rejected by Ignacy Zakrzewski who had absorbed Montesquieu's concept of moderate government. He objected to the equation of 'a republican government under a successive throne with despotism'. For 'enlightened nations no longer know despotism today; I find monarchical government moderated even by monarchs themselves, albeit hereditary ones.' Royal elections, claimed Zakrzewski, were not the work of the nation, but only of 'aristocrats in the nation'. A true republican found freedom, he stated, 'when he alone makes his own laws, and is subject to nothing except the law'.[73]

Stanisław Kostka Potocki answered appeals to the verdict of the sejmiks by rejecting his instruction: 'I am ashamed, I say publicly, that my palatinate instructed me to maintain election.' He called on the sejm to rescue freedom – 'not the lawless liberty of aristocrats alone, above equality, but the liberty of everyone, who is counted simply as an inhabitant of the country'. He also dismissed calls to rely on noble militias for defence: 'Probably only the enemy would advise such means of rescue. States stand not on a crowd of armed people, because they are nothing without government, but on good laws and their firm execution.'[74] Similarly, Linowski hailed the day

> on which true government is to be established, destroying the old anarchy, encompassing everything, securing prudent freedom, and for this very certainty restoring a sturdy execution of the laws in Poland, embedding the governmental powers within just limits.[75]

Besides 'government', the key motifs for the project's supporters were urgency and Providence. 'Providence yet gives us a means of saving ourselves in the project that has been put forward. There is no time for deliberation, because even if someone found something bad in it, it would probably be a lesser evil than the destruction of the Fatherland,' stated Kazimierz Rzewuski, envoy for Podolia. He implored the king to ask Małachowski to have the project decided.[76] Stanisław August used the metaphor of the setting and rising sun to emphasize his own disinterest in fixing the succession for the Elector of Saxony. He recalled King John Casimir's prescient warnings of partition in 1661, which had brought about the widespread desire 'to secure for ever, by a lasting law on the government and throne, the tranquillity and happiness of the country'.[77]

Around six o'clock the king heard himself called on to swear to uphold the constitution. When he raised his hand to speak, 'our side took it as a sign of my oath. They stormed towards the throne. And I, seeing that the thing could be done, did it.'[78] He mounted a chair, the better to be seen. Roars of approval greeted his oath, dictated by the Bishop of Cracow, and sworn on the Gospels. Suchorzewski, who had again thrown himself on the floor, was almost trampled underfoot, but 'somehow the giant Kublicki, envoy for Livonia, picked him up and set him on his feet' (Plate 30).[79]

As the scene threatened to become tumultuous, Stanisław August led the throng to the nearby Church of St John the Baptist. At least twenty opponents remained in place, but the triumphant Małachowski and the wavering Sapieha were chaired to the church by their colleagues. After Sapieha had again voiced his doubts on the succession, and again proclaimed he would not divide the nation, the oath was sworn and the *Te Deum* sung, repeated by the thousands filling the streets. The parliamentarians then returned to the Castle. The king asked the marshals to sign the *Law on Government*, and for government magistratures and the army to take the oath without delay. He then adjourned the sitting until Thursday 5 May. The celebrations outside continued long into the night.

The following day Suchorzewski announced he would emigrate to America. The king related that after Suchorzewski was told he would find a stronger executive power there than in Poland, he 'remained in doubt, whether he should abandon Poland forever'.[80] Less risibly, one senator and twenty-seven envoys lodged an official protest in the acts of Warsaw's castle court. They had wanted to do so the previous evening, but the chancery was already closed. Now they were allowed only to declare that they had permitted nothing contrary to 'national liberty, domestic tranquillity and our instruction'. For as the king informed Deboli on 4 May, 'the last article of the act is fearsome to those who would oppose the Revolution'.[81] This was the *Declaration of the Assembled Estates*, read out along with the rest of the *Law on Government* on 3 May.[82]

At the parliamentary session of 5 May the revolutionary means used two days earlier were robed in the legal mantle of unanimity. As the first to be given the floor, Bishop Kossakowski, the chairman of the sejm's Constitutional Deputation, asked how the deputies' oath not to sign a law which had not been passed '*unanimitate vel pluralitate*' could be reconciled with a 'constitution, or law, passed by the voice of the public, when it did not have the usual formalities due to a law'.[83] Linowski then claimed that 'this worthy senator was present in the church when we swore our oath before God, and he raised his consecrated hand, because he felt that God had looked upon an unhappy nation'.[84] Kossakowski did not argue. A unanimous acclamation, suggested by Sapieha, enabled the deputation to sign the law. Signed oaths were presented from the joint Military and Crown Treasury Commissions. An envoy who had demanded the project enter deliberation on 3 May now proposed that all kiss the king's hand, explaining: 'I do not understand why someone should be so obstinate in his opinion, that he would not join himself to unity, when the king is with the nation, and the nation with the king'.[85] After the royal hand had been thoroughly osculated, three other former protesters announced their acceptance of the Constitution. The sejm agreed a measure for the equipping of the army, endorsed Marshal Małachowski's suggestion that he and Sapieha proclaim the joyful news to the nation, and instructed the Constitutional Deputation to draft a more detailed law on the sejm.[86]

The *Law on Government* left much to be resolved later. In this it resembled the comparably brief American Constitution drafted in 1787 and ratified to 1789. Although the *Pacta et Constitutiones Legum Libertatumque Exercitus Zaporoviensis* written by Pylyp Orlyk, Cossack Hetman in exile, in 1710, and the *Regeringsform* accepted by the Swedish Riksdag in 1772 (and as Suchorzewski recalled, amended in Gustav III's favour in 1789) are older acts, the Commonwealth has a strong claim to the first modern written constitution in Europe and the second in the world. The *Law on Government,* which set out the fundamental principles underpinning the Commonwealth's political values, social order and institutions of government, can be considered a constitution in the modern sense of the word.

This usage first joined and then supplanted the traditional meaning of '*konstytucya*' – a statute passed by the sejm. An almanac published early in 1792 reviewed 'four constitutions: the English, which served others as a model, the American, which was formed from it, the Polish, which made use of both, and in the end the French, which has had these three models together before it'.[87] To begin with, however, the keyword was 'government'. Introducing the project, Małachowski invoked the century's two most famous 'republican governments' – the English, and the American, which corrected the faults of the first. The Polish project, he declared, combined the best of both.[88]

The text of the *Law on Government* is structured as a preamble, eleven articles and a declaration.[89] The preamble epitomizes the didactic and persuasive character of the whole. Following a traditional invocation of the Holy Trinity, the 'we' of the text is 'Stanisław August by the grace of God and the will of the nation King of Poland, Grand Duke of Lithuania, Ruthenia, Prussia, Samogitia, Mazovia, Kiev, Volhynia, Podolia, Podlasie, Livonia, Smolensk, Severia and Czernihów together with the confederated Estates representing the Polish nation'. The slogan of 'the king with the nation, the nation with the king' is thus doubly emphasized and sacralized. While the monarch retains a plural and partly archaic set of titles, the nation is singular and Polish.*

Next comes a splendid sentence:

> Persuaded that our common fate depends entirely upon the establishment and rendering perfect a national constitution; convinced by a long train of experience of many longstanding defects in our government, and willing to profit from the present circumstances of Europe, and from the passing moment which has restored us to ourselves; free from the disgraceful shackles of foreign influence; prizing more than life, and every personal happiness, the

* So archaic, in fact, that the old claim to Severia (lost in 1667/86) was only remembered and inserted at the last moment (*Konstytucja 3 Maja*, ed. Grześkowiak-Krwawicz, 61). The word '*naród*' (nation) appears no fewer than thirty-one times in the text (including the *Declaration*), while the adjective '*narodowy*' (national) is employed eleven times. In four of these cases 'nations' figure in the plural, and in just one of these (in the *Declaration*) is there a reference to 'the two nations'. Similarly, only in the *Declaration* do we encounter the phrase 'in the territories of the Polish Crown and the Grand Duchy of Lithuania'. Otherwise Lithuania only appears in the monarchical titles and in a confirmation of privileges granted by Grand Duke Witold (Vytautas). With '*Polska*' (Poland) featuring six times and the adjective '*polski*' fourteen times, the nation in question is Polish, while the '*Ojczyzna*' (Fatherland) mentioned twelve times and the '*kraj*' (country) six times refer to Poland (Butterwick-Pawlikowski, 'Koncepcja narodu', 135–51).

> political existence, external independence and internal liberty of the nation, whose care is entrusted to us; desirous, moreover, to deserve the blessing and gratitude, not only of our contemporaries, but also of future generations, despite the obstacles which can stoke passions in us; for the sake of the public good, for securing our liberty, and saving our Fatherland and her frontiers; we do solemnly establish the present Constitution, which with zeal and firmness we declare sacred and inviolable in every part, till such period as shall be prescribed by law, when the nation, if it should think fit, and deem it necessary, may alter by its express will such articles therein as shall be found inadequate.

Here eight emotive appeals aim at persuasion. The first establishes an imperative: the fate of us all depends on the Constitution. The second is corrective: we have all experienced the faults of the form of government. The third evokes urgency: we need to seize the fleeting opportunity in international affairs. The fourth is about pride: we have recovered our sovereignty. The fifth rests on patriotic virtue, and the sixth on responsibility. The seventh incentive is earning the gratitude of posterity. The eighth flatters the undaunted spirit with which we establish the Constitution. These appeals are made in the name of a double trinity of values: first political existence, independence and freedom, then the general good, freedom and the frontiers (the latter added at a late stage).

The preamble closes with the words 'And this Constitution shall be the standard of all subsequent laws of the present sejm.' This provision, expanded in the *Declaration of the Assembled Estates*, would enable the circumvention or amendment of some inconvenient laws that had already been passed.

The first article confirms the first cardinal law passed in September 1790, proclaiming Roman Catholicism as the 'dominant national religion'. Abandoning Catholicism for another faith remains culpable as 'apostasy', although the penalty is not specified. This unenlightened provision, absent in earlier drafts, was doubtless a nod to the Catholic clergy and much of the provincial nobility. Nevertheless, because 'this same Holy Faith commands us to love our neighbours', not only adherents of hitherto tolerated faiths, but 'all people of whatever confession' are assured freedom of worship and 'the protection of government'. People, not estates.[90] In contrast to the 1573 Confederacy of Warsaw, there was now no question of applying the maxim *cuius dominio, eius religio* to the inhabitants of privately owned towns and villages.[91]

Articles II through IV, concerning nobles, burghers and peasants respectively, deal with the social order. The second article flatters the former, and solemnly confirms their privileges and liberties, but the prudently worded title, 'Nobles [and] landowners', leaves the rights of landless nobles in doubt. The third article simply declares the law on free royal towns part of the Constitution, adding, for the sake of persuasion: 'as a law giving new, true and effectual strength to the free Polish nobility, the security of its liberties and the entirety of the shared Fatherland'.

The fourth article appears at first sight merely to make the peasants an empty promise, albeit with a rhetorically crucial declaration:

> The agricultural populace, from whose hands flows the most plentiful source of the country's riches, which is the most numerous in the nation, consequently forming the most considerable part of its force, from the motives of justice, humanity and Christian duties, as well as our own interest well understood, we receive under the protection of the country's law and government . . .

Serfdom is not abolished – yet. Kołłątaj, whose hand is particularly evident in this article, kept the provisions more general than the king's original proposals, while also changing the title from the demeaning 'Peasants [and] serfs' to 'Peasants [and] villagers'. However, where contracts between lords and villagers exist, they will have to be upheld. All persons immigrating into the 'territories of the Commonwealth' are declared completely free, and moreover, this freedom also belongs to persons returning to the country after an absence. This provision had tremendous potential to undermine serfdom, especially in border regions, because anyone,

> . . . as soon as he sets his foot on Polish land, becomes free and entirely at liberty to exercise his industry, wherever and in whatever manner he pleases, to make contracts to settle, for labour or rent, and until he makes such a contract, is free to settle either in towns or villages, is free to live in Poland, or to return to the country of his choice, after having fulfilled the obligations he may have voluntarily entered into.

This promise of freedom raised the spectre of peasant flight into the Commonwealth, not only from Russia, but also from Prussia and even the

Habsburg Monarchy. Free peasants will be able to pursue their claims in the referendary's courts, according to the eighth article. The road to the end of serfdom was visible to those with eyes to see it.[92]

Articles V through VIII deal with the 'Form of government, or the definition of the public powers', these being the legislative, executive and judicial powers. This triune division, announced in the fifth article, is justified by three aims: 'integrity of territories, civic freedom and order of society in equal balance for ever'. The drafters combined the tripartition of powers with the national sovereignty embodied in the sejm. They also succeeded in blending selected concepts of Enlightenment political thought with Polish constitutional traditions reaching back three centuries or more. In language, as in solutions, the Constitution mixed old and new. Article V expresses in Rousseauvian terms an axiom that had long been taken for granted by noble citizens: 'All power in human society derives from the will of the nation.'

Article VI declares the chamber of envoys the 'representation and composition of the supreme national authority' and the 'temple of legislation'. This chamber duly obtains a far stronger position than the senate, which receives a mere suspensive veto. Envoys are also strengthened with regard to their electors. They are described with emphasis as '*representatives of the entire nation*', thereby ending the imperative character of sejmik instructions, despite the recent law on sejmiks, itself secured by the Constitution. This was a victory for the king, but envoys had become accustomed to legislating for the nation. The phrase was embedded in parliamentary discourse.[93] The change from delegation to representation is anticipated in the preamble, and is here justified thus:

> Because the legislative power cannot be exercised by all, and the nation acts in this regard through its representatives, or freely elected envoys, we enact that envoys elected at sejmiks shall in the legislature and the general needs of the nation be considered as *representatives of the entire nation*, in them reposing our trust.

The sejm will continue to meet biennially, but will be ready to reconvene if needed. Because 'the majority of votes should decide every thing and every where', the *liberum veto*, confederacies and confederated sejms are forever abolished 'as contrary to the spirit of the present Constitution, as overthrowing the government, and as being ruinous to society'. A constituent sejm will revise the Constitution every twenty-five years.

The Constitution applies the Montesquieuvian concept of the division of powers rigorously, but asymmetrically: in favour of the legislature. In contrast to the unequivocal title of the sixth article – 'The sejm or the legislative power', that of the seventh was amended at a very late stage to read: 'The king. The executive power'.[94] This article begins:

> The most perfect government cannot exist or last without an effectual executive power. The happiness of nations depends on just laws, but the good effects of laws flow only from their execution. Experience has taught us that the neglecting of this part of government has overwhelmed Poland with disasters.

The purpose of an executive is then explained – to ensure the observance of laws, not to make or interpret them. Moreover, the executive may not levy taxes 'under any name whatsoever', contract public debts, alter the balance of public expenditure decided by the sejm, declare war or make any final treaty of peace or alliance.

Leaving the 'free Polish nation the right of enacting laws, the power of inspection over all executive power and the choice of officials', the *Law on Government* entrusts executive power to the king in his council, called – as in earlier projects – the Custodial Council of the Laws (the term *Straż Praw* literally means 'guard of the laws'). This body is granted not only supervisory powers, but the real executive responsibilities and decision-making powers demanded by the king. The elected central government commissions (for education, police, the army and the treasury) and the local civil-military commissions are obliged to obey the instructions of the Custodial Council. The king has the right to nominate all ministers, as well as choose five members of the Custodial Council from among them to serve two-year terms as ministers of police, war, the treasury, and two ministers of the seal – one of them for foreign affairs. In addition the Custodial Council comprises the primate as head both of the clergy and of the Commission of National Education, two secretaries, one of them for foreign affairs, and the marshal of the sejm wielding the emergency power to summon the sejm should the king refuse to do so.

Stanisław August had expected the Custodial Council to decide by majority vote, but given the lack of public trust in several ministers, Kołłątaj amended this: 'The King's decision, after all opinions have been heard, should prevail.'

One of the ministers in the Custodial Council will have to countersign each resolution, but a still later amendment prohibits the primate from countersigning. The ministers are to be legally accountable before the sejm court for their actions and counter-signatures. They are also politically responsible to the sejm, which could, by a two-thirds majority of secret votes of the combined houses, force their replacement by the king. Senators and ministers sitting in the Custodial Council or commissions cannot vote upon their own reports, and are present in the senate only to provide explanations demanded by the sejm.

The supremacy of the chamber of envoys thus reduces the significance of the royal prerogative of nominating ministers, bishops and senators; besides, the details are left to later legislation. The king's right to appoint the commanders of the armed forces is also hedged by another late amendment: 'with their free change, however, by the will of the nation'. In general the monarch is envisaged not as an 'absolute monarch, but the father and the head of the nation', in whose name function all courts and magistratures, and who adorns all coins and stamps. Unable to enact anything by himself, his person is sacred and he cannot be held to account by the nation. This symbolically splendid monarchy will be 'elective in regard to families'.[95]

The text justifies this step with an appeal to experience and collective memory:

> Having experienced the fatal effects of interregna, periodically subverting government, and being desirous of assuring the tranquillity of each inhabitant of Polish territory and preventing for ever all influence of foreign powers, remembering the glory and happiness of our Fatherland under families which reigned continuously, and conscious of the need to avert foreigners' ambitions for the throne and to return powerful Poles to the united cultivation of national liberty, we have, from these prudent motives, resolved to grant the Polish throne with the right of succession.

The current Elector of Saxony is to found a dynasty of 'future kings of Poland'. But if he does not beget a son, then his daughter's husband, chosen by the elector with 'the consent of the Estates', will begin the new line of succession.

'Judicial power,' begins the eighth article, 'cannot be administered either by the legislative power, or by the king, but by magistratures established and elected for this end.' This precluded a minister of justice, although one of the chancellors sitting in the Custodial Council as 'minister of the seal' was intended to look after judicial matters. Moreover, administrative courts will be attached to the government commissions. Most judicial matters are reserved to future legislation, but the key point is that sejmiks will elect judges of the courts of the first instance as well as deputies to the *three* tribunals – one for each of the three provinces of the Commonwealth. The highest court of all will be the sejm court, dealing with '*crimina status*' against the king and nation. Its judges will be chosen at the start of each sejm.

Articles IX and X briefly provide for the regency and the education of royal children. Both envisage the leading but accountable role of the Custodial Council. The Educational Commission will devise a curriculum to instil in future kings 'religion, love of virtue, of the Fatherland, of liberty and of the Constitution of the country'. The eleventh article, pointedly titled 'The national armed force', explains: 'The army is but an extract of defensive and regular force from the general mass of national strength.' Sworn to the nation and the king, the army is obliged to obey the executive power and may be used 'in assisting the execution of the law against those that do not obey it'.

The teeth bared here are again manifest in the *Declaration of the Assembled Estates*:

> Whoever should dare to oppose the present Constitution or struggle to damage it, or to disturb the tranquillity of a good nation which begins to be happy through the sowing of mistrust or a perverse interpretation of the Constitution, and much more by forming any insurrection or confederacy in the country, either leading or in any way contributing to it, shall be considered an enemy and traitor to the Fatherland, and a rebel, and shall be punished most severely by the sejm court.

Persuasion, however, was to be more important than threats. The *Declaration* ordains services in all the churches in the country,

> . . . for thanksgiving to God for the gift of a favourable moment to extract Poland from foreign violence and domestic disorder, for the restoration of government, which can most effectively secure our true liberty and the entirety of Poland, for the placing in this way of our Fatherland on a level able to gain true consideration in the eyes of Europe.

Indeed, on both sides of the Atlantic, opinion-formers looked at Poland with new respect, once they had read the rapidly published translations of the Constitution into French, English and German. Stanisław August was delighted by Edmund Burke's favourable contrast of the Polish Revolution with the French.

At home, a critical mass of the szlachta had to be persuaded to embrace the Constitution. The campaign of persuasion began in the text of the *Law on Government*. This was printed in at least fourteen separate editions within a year, a total of between twenty and thirty thousand copies, not counting reprints in the press.[96] The Third of May soon symbolized reclaimed national sovereignty, exercised in order to strengthen the state and preserve its independence at a moment of mortal threat. Celebrations and harmony also became part of the myth, a fact which by no means diminishes their veracity or significance. All this was part of the persuasive strategy adopted by the creators of the Constitution. The language of the *Law on Government* was so didactic that during a celebration in Wilno, Rector Poczobut pronounced it a 'Christian and civic catechism'.[97]

Effective catechisms need both brevity and flexibility. Several subsequent laws moved some way back towards the traditional terms of the Two Nations and the Commonwealth. For critics complained that they could not find '*Rzeczpospolita*' in the text of the Constitution. In fact it appears twice, but incidentally. The creators of the *Law on Government* probably preferred – in this context – to avoid a term which might restrict further changes. Instead the text speaks of the 'nation' and 'Poland'. For it was in its discourse of the Polish nation that the Constitution blazed a trail for posterity.[98]

— ELEVEN —
REVOLUTION
ÇA IRA!

The revolutionary means used on 3 May 1791 were justified to the Polish nation by the need 'to profit from the present circumstances of Europe, and from the passing moment which has restored us to ourselves' – as the preamble put it. Alas, by this time the favourable conjuncture in European affairs had all but vanished. After the signing of the Convention of Reichenbach on 27 July 1790, Prussia no longer had any real interest in supporting the Commonwealth. However, during the first few months of 1791 a new mirage glimmered: a military and commercial alliance with Great Britain, Prussia, the Dutch Republic and the Ottoman Empire against Russia.

The British prime minister, William Pitt the Younger, was determined to pursue the Triple Alliance's objective of forcing the Russian Empire to make peace with the Ottoman Empire on the basis of the *status quo ante bellum*. Among other things, this would involve the return to the Turks of Ochakov, laboriously captured by Potemkin in 1788. Flush from browbeating Spain into retreat over commercial rights in the Nootka Sound (off the Pacific coast of North America), Pitt reiterated the demands in December 1790. Egged on by Berlin, on 27 March 1791 he sent Catherine II a ten-day ultimatum to make peace with the Porte. He ordered a fleet to be made ready to sail to the Baltic. Faced by her sternest test, Catherine was defiant. War loomed.

However, not all British politicians believed that their country's vital interests were at stake. Pitt encountered opposition even within his cabinet. The Russian ambassador in London lobbied opposition politicians, mercantile circles and newspaper editors. His embassy produced dossiers and commissioned pamphlets. In provincial cities public meetings and petitions were organized. Graffiti appeared on public buildings: 'No war with Russia!'. These tactics, heralding the confrontational and public diplomacy of the revolutionary age, proved effective. Pitt's parliamentary majority melted away. Although the Royal Navy was kept in readiness until July, by mid-April it was clear that Britain would not fight Russia. The government withdrew its ultimatum. In July 1791 Britain and Prussia agreed that Russia could annex the lands between the Rivers Boh and Dniester, and within a month the Russian and Ottoman Empires agreed preliminary peace terms at Galatz. After the signing of the final treaty at Jassy on 9 January 1792, the empress could concentrate on Poland.

The argument that weighed heaviest for many Britons was that the country should not sacrifice trade over another Russian fortress on the shores of the Black Sea. Pitt's ministry had for some years been exploring alternative sources of naval stores. Stanisław August had earlier explained why. The British 'could have from Poland all those goods which they need for their fleets, and with this advantage, although apparently for the same price, that in the time that a ship from England can return from St Petersburg once, it could almost return twice from Danzig. And so that almost halves the price.'[1] However, commercial reorientation proved unalluring to British merchants. Moreover, even at the start of 1791 Pitt's government expected the Commonwealth to cede Danzig to Prussia in exchange for better trading conditions. This ignored the reality that the sejm had already ruled out territorial cessions. When in January 1791 the British envoy Daniel Hailes proposed negotiations for a trade treaty and alliance to the Deputation for Foreign Affairs, he also published an anonymous pamphlet urging the yielding of Danzig. This provoked denials of the need to relinquish any territory. All the sejm would agree – after heated debates on 31 March and 1 April – was to authorize the deputation to keep talking to the British. The moment for an alliance passed.

In any case, although Frederick William II was indignant about the British volte-face, it is doubtful whether, in the event of a British–Russian naval clash, the 88,000 troops he had mobilized in East Prussia would have marched into Russian Livonia. His generals and ministers were aghast at the prospect. It is more likely that had push come to shove, Berlin would have cut a deal with St Petersburg at Poland's expense, rather than wait for the grateful Poles to cede Danzig, Thorn and more besides. Potemkin persuaded Catherine to accept just such a bargain, should the need arise. Even if the British and Prussians had attacked Russia, the empress envisaged a flanking counter-attack – in the Commonwealth.[2] In all likelihood Pitt could not have saved Poland.[3] Not unlike Churchill – a hundred and fifty years later.

Nevertheless, while the failure of Pitt's policy is easily explained, it is remarkable that he tried at all. It was not merely revenge for Catherine II's 'Armed

Neutrality' against Britain's control of the seas during the War of American Independence, or even a growing realization that Russian expansion against the Ottoman Empire would sooner or later have to be contained, given the recent thaw in Russo-French relations. Pitt imagined a new international order. According to Paul Schroeder, the 'political and strategic aims . . . involved: splitting Austria from Russia, bludgeoning the Russians into a more friendly attitude, stabilizing Eastern Europe, and, by attaching Poland and possibly Turkey to the Triple Alliance, constructing a broad Federative System to protect the smaller powers of Europe'. The Ochakov crisis inaugurated a long contest for hegemony between Russia, the principal power of the 'heartland' and Britain, the greatest power of the 'coastland', to use geopolitical language. It might conceivably have played out to Poland's advantage. However, the consequences of the British failure proved disastrous for the Commonwealth. Besides recognizing the obstacles of domestic opposition and military and naval logistics, the British elite learned first, that Britain could not mobilize the continent against Russia, and second, that it could not mobilize the continent against revolutionary France without Russian help.[4]

The British failure to harness lesser powers encompassed the Commonwealth. The British expectation that Poland would abandon Danzig was unrealistic, but part of the responsibility for the stalling of negotiations falls to the Poles. Polish diplomats in London lacked clear instructions. After 3 May 1791, although Bukaty successfully promoted the merits of the Polish Revolution to various shades of British public opinion, it was too late to interest Pitt's ministry in the Polish cause. The charge of passivity can be levelled more generally at the Polish-Lithuanian leadership's conduct of foreign policy. Ignacy Potocki declined the ministry of foreign affairs, which went to the royalist Joachim Chreptowicz. The Lithuanian vice-chancellor had a reputation as a Russophile and lacked the political authority openly to seek a compromise with St Petersburg. In any case, the king convinced himself that Russia would not invade Poland, as long as no pretext for intervention was given. This proved a serious error of judgement. Since 1788, the empress had collected plenty of pretexts; she would neither forgive nor forget.[5]

Catherine II was privately outraged by the Constitution of 3 May; she complained to Baron Grimm that revolutionary means had been used to confer 'arbitrary power' on Stanisław August.[6] Nothing and no one, not even Leopold II, could convince her otherwise. Not the least reason for her intransigence was the slight to her prestige. She repeatedly informed Potemkin that as soon as her victorious troops were ready to march, they would restore Russian supremacy in Poland. *How* this was to be done remained unresolved for the moment. She still had to reckon with Austria and Prussia. Until the peace was finalized, she would not reveal her cards. For almost a year, as the sand slipped through the Commonwealth's hourglass, the Russian court maintained public silence on the revolution of the Third of May.[7]

This affected indifference was facilitated by the delay in notifying St Petersburg of the Constitution. As Catherine II explained to Potemkin, 'they have freed us from the trouble of answering them, and prematurely awakening their suspicions regarding our aims tending to the overthrow of this [form of] government and the restoration of their old liberties'.[8] The notification was postponed until, as 1791 drew to a close and Deboli's despatches grew more alarming, the sejm authorized the king to write to the empress. On 24 December he appealed to her greatness of soul, hoping that he would not have to face 'the cruel alternative of failing in what I owe my Fatherland, my nation and my station, or to be regarded by Your Majesty as having crossed her'. Most of Europe had already welcomed 'the work of our present sejm', and it wanted only her approbation. Nothing, he believed, could better become her than to welcome 'the success of a neighbouring government which has for its foundation only a liberty regulated by the laws, and for its end only its own conservation, without the least detrimental object'. In the letter that was finally despatched, which received no reply, the king avoided the facts he had originally included in his draft. Even the word 'Constitution' was missing from the final missive. Stanisław August would not state the obvious to Catherine, namely that the Polish nation had chosen the Elector of Saxony to succeed him. He neither requested her approval of this succession, nor opened negotiations for the alternative solution which the entire leadership seems to have thought necessary.[9] Yet here was the nub of the matter (as the primate realized only too clearly).[10]

After all the polemics for and against hereditary monarchy, the Constitution effectively postponed the choice of a new dynasty for a generation. This was the weakest provision of the *Law on Government.*[11] Adam Krasiński, a veteran partisan of the Saxon cause, warned the king that the *Infantka* Maria Augusta might follow her inclination in choosing a husband. Nobody knew who the next king but one would be. Although the nation desired the elector, it was evident that he would not have a son, so the renewed union with Saxony would end with him. The best solution, concluded the bishop, would be for the *infantka* to thank the Poles for their offer, but decline it.[12]

Ignacy Potocki wanted a Hohenzollern to marry Maria Augusta, sealing the Commonwealth's alliance with Prussia. It was rumoured that Adam Kazimierz Czartoryski intended her for his son Adam Jerzy. Stanisław August hoped that she might marry one of his nephews – on balance he thought Prince Stanisław more suitable than his beloved but hot-headed 'Pepi' – Prince Józef. Elector Frederick Augustus had not been informed in advance of the Poles' decision. He spun out negotiations regarding the royal prerogative. More importantly, he made his acceptance of the offer conditional on the agreement of Prussia, Austria and especially Russia.

In principle, both the emperor and the King of Prussia advised the elector to accept. Frederick William II, suspicious of Russia but always sniffing for more territory, ostentatiously congratulated Frederick Augustus. He was careful, though, not to support the new Constitution, about which he had not been consulted. A reinvigorated Commonwealth, as his minister Hertzberg realized, posed a deadly threat to the future of the Hohenzollern monarchy – especially in the wrong hands. The long-term restoration of the Polish-Saxon union, the solution preferred in Dresden and Vienna, would greatly harm the interests of his kingdom.

For the old Prussophobe Kaunitz, this was the very point. For his part, Leopold II sincerely admired the Polish Constitution and tried – fruitlessly – to persuade Catherine to accept it as part of a new, moral European order, set against the violent revolution in France. However, the emperor did not want a Hohenzollern ruling Poland in the following generation, and he refused to join Prussia and Britain in fighting Russia. Moreover, after his sister Marie-Antoinette and brother-in-law Louis XVI had been intercepted at Varennes as they tried to flee to the Austrian Netherlands in June 1791, he had to deal with the radicalization of the revolution in France. Leopold initially hoped that sabre-rattling would quieten the French. At the same time he tried to hug the Prussians tight, in order to allow the Polish question to be resolved equitably. Ultimately that policy backfired, but for a time after Louis XVI's acceptance of the French Constitution on 13 September 1791, it seemed as though things would settle down in France. Vienna could therefore hope to persuade Berlin and St Petersburg to guarantee a settlement in Poland without territorial changes. In Warsaw, however, the Austro-Prussian rapprochement, sealed at Pillnitz in Saxony in the late summer of 1791, was interpreted too optimistically as joint support for the Commonwealth against Russia. The hopeful interpretation of 'the free constitution' as a reference to that of 3 May was given plausibility by the two courts' resignation from Prussian and Austrian candidatures for the hand of Maria Augusta, but crucially they made no commitment to oppose Russia. Their declaration of abstention from interference in Polish affairs was not – yet – a clear message to St Petersburg that the field was clear, but it was a stage in that process.

To make things still worse, Gustav III, so recently Catherine's enemy, became her ally by the Treaty of Drottningholm, signed on 19 October 1791. This too was directed at revolutionary France, but it was clear that the Poles could expect no help from across the Baltic Sea. That ship had sailed.

The failure of the Polish leadership to grasp the unfavourable geopolitical drift was intrinsically linked to the domestic consolidation of the Polish nation. Wishful thinking about the country's international prospects was a significant factor (not the only one) in persuading so many citizens to support the Constitution. National unity would avert foreign invasion, or so it was believed. The succinct French revolutionary refrain of '*Ça ira*' was translated with more syllables as '*Wszystko pójdzie wyśmienicie*' – 'Everything will go splendidly'. It might have been better put as '*Jakoś to będzie*' – 'It'll be alright on the night'. It is plausible that had the leadership conveyed a more realistic assessment of the situation to the 'nation', it would have worsened internal divisions and thereby facilitated the external intervention which was being prepared. The favourable impression made by the Constitution on public opinion abroad could not compensate for the brutal operation of the eighteenth-century international system. The chorus of praise did, however, help to convince domestic opinion that, as the proclamation issued on 7 May 1791 put it:

> Our Fatherland is already saved, our liberties secured, we are henceforth a free and independent nation; the shackles of slavery and anarchy have been broken by the omnipotent hand of the God of Hosts, which has saved the Fatherland by averting the thunderstorm prepared for her final destruction.[13]

Because it was now widely accepted that the Commonwealth's external vulnerability derived from its internal 'anarchy', it followed that stable government would secure the country's existence. This was an extension of the faith, characteristic of the Enlightenment, in the salutary effects of good laws.[14]

The language of the proclamation of 7 May 1791 was typical of the pro-Constitutional discourse that reached market towns and country manors in the year that followed. This discourse was open to salutary change. In contrast, the discourse of the Constitution's foes lamented the destruction of former liberties, laws and virtues. Proclamations and pastoral letters were read out and nailed to church doors, sermons were preached, and newspapers and pamphlets from Warsaw or Wilno were circulated. During this *annus mirabilis*, the 'miracle of Divine Providence' was trumpeted right across the Commonwealth. Clouds of incense and the smoke of cannonfire wafted the strains of the *Te Deum* heavenwards. Votive masses were typically followed by some combination of processions, banquets, toasts, balls, theatrical tableaux, illuminations and fireworks, as the *sacrum* blended with the *profanum*. In some towns, including Warsaw, separate services of thanksgiving were held in Protestant churches and synagogues. If confessional barriers remained, some social boundaries eroded. During celebrations at Minsk, for example, the noblewomen crossed the floor to the burgesses; henceforth they held their assemblies together. When courts reconvened their sessions and when quarterly transactions were sealed, nobles and burghers could drink fraternal toasts to their shared Fatherland, miraculously saved from the abyss of anarchy and invasion.

Many places saw more than one celebration during this extraordinary year. In Wilno the rejoicing began with the arrival of the news of the Constitution on 8 May – the feast of St Stanisław. The university held a dedicated celebration on 1 July. This included the reading out of Reverend Hieronim Stroynowski's erudite defence of the Constitution. He wove flattery of the Revolution's leaders into philosophical arguments, citing Locke, Rousseau, Montesquieu and Cicero.[15] Further occasions for public joy and fraternization were the elections of urban plenipotentiaries in September 1791, the sejmik to elect deputies to the Lithuanian Tribunal in February 1792, the renewal of the Tribunal on 15 March, and finally the first anniversary of the Constitution. On 3 May 1792 Wilno's clerical professors once again hailed the 'happy revolution'.[16]

In Warsaw, this feast day saw the reception of delegations from the sejmiks bearing votes of thanks for the Constitution. The king laid the foundation stone of the Church of the Highest Providence, promised as a votive offering in the *Declaration of the Assembled Estates.* These decorous ceremonies impressed the papal nuncio, but the French envoy Marie-Louis Descorches, the former Marquis de St-Croix, criticized 'a bizarre mixture of credulity, devotion and immorality . . . a surfeit of religious practices very unsuitable for the growth of true liberal sentiments'. In an earlier report he had conceded that few Poles shared his hostility to traditional religion.[17]

Shortly before this stirring display of unity between Church, monarch and nation, Pius VI agreed to the king's request to translate the feast of St Stanisław. The royal nameday could now be celebrated on the anniversary of the Constitution. The monarch also sought a papal blessing for the Constitution. The Holy See did despatch something of the kind to Warsaw, although the nuncio – still concerned about the extent of the toleration promised by the first article – advised that the wording be as personal to Stanisław August, as benevolent to the nation, and as vague regarding the actual text of the Constitution as possible. The nightmares of Saluzzo and his superiors recurred in the black-clad figure of Kołłątaj. Against the express wishes of most of the bishops, but with the support of Stanisław Małachowski and other envoys, Kołłątaj became Crown vice-chancellor on 17 May 1791. A few months later the Bishop of Cracow, Feliks Turski, finally agreed to make him his co-adjutor with the right of succession. The monarch, who appreciated the new vice-chancellor's aptitude for business more than he feared his ambition, urged him to mend his fences with Rome.

The Holy See was interested, first, in preventing any request for the restoration of the Society of Jesus; second, in excluding ecclesiastical privileges and rights from the scope of the legal codification that was now underway; third, in halting the parliamentary projects for a general reform of the secular and religious clergy, which continued to be refined in Kołłątaj's circle; and, fourth, in stopping the establishment of an Orthodox hierarchy. Regarding the first of these questions, Stanisław August was happy to help, regarding the second and third he was disposed to be conciliatory, but regarding the fourth he would only drop ambiguous hints. It was only after the pope had given his blessing and translated the feast of St Stanisław that on 21 May 1792 the sejm sanctioned an Orthodox hierarchy of an archbishop and three bishops, and a governing consistory composed of clerical and lay members – independent of St Petersburg. These arrangements had been agreed the previous summer between a sejm commission and representatives of the Commonwealth's Orthodox communities gathered at

Pińsk. Although three Catholic bishop-senators tried to stem the tide, their episcopal colleagues were absent from the chamber that day. The result of the vote was 123 to 13.[18]

This debate took place immediately after the reading out to the sejm of the Russian declaration of 18 May, announcing armed intervention. The threat to the Commonwealth could no longer be ignored, but the prevalent response was a call to unity, crossing confessional and linguistic boundaries. According to Stanisław Sołtyk:

> Liberty is our greatest secret against any foreign usurpation, it is the strongest defensive wall against neighbours' invasions; let people speak in different languages, let there be differences between them as regards religion; freedom, when well understood, justice, given strictly to everyone, will unite them most swiftly, and will teach one sentiment, the same expression of their own liberties . . .[19]

The new Orthodox consistory duly ordained thanksgiving and prayers for the Commonwealth. Although by this time two Russian armies had crossed the frontier, the sejm's decision testifies to the fundamental inclusiveness of the Polish Revolution. The primacy of the Catholic Church vis-à-vis other confessions helped to mobilize support for the Constitution among the Catholic clergy and szlachta. However, the honours paid to the 'dominant and national religion' had strict limits. They could not involve the denial of rights and liberties to other Christians, threatening their attachment to the shared Polish Fatherland.

Permitting ourselves hindsight, we know that decisions made in St Petersburg, Berlin, Vienna and Paris would determine the Commonwealth's fate. However, its legacy would to a significant degree depend on how the Polish Revolution's discourse of national salvation through national unity bedded down into reality. At the time, it still seemed in Warsaw that the very survival of the new order was at stake. The greatest domestic political test would be the stance of the sejmiks towards the Constitution. The tone of the November 1790 instructions gave cause for trepidation. The sejmiks to elect deputies to the Crown Tribunal were due to meet on 15 July 1791, but those for the Lithuanian Tribunal only on 14

February 1792. On 26 May 1791 the sejm decided to hold them all in February. This would allow more time to win over the provincial szlachta. The sum of the sejmiks' resolutions would amount to a referendum on the Constitution.

The leadership in Warsaw needed most sejmiks to declare their support in the strongest possible terms, while avoiding open opposition that could serve as a pretext for foreign intervention. Asking Bishop Naruszewicz to use his influence, the king wrote: 'From far and wide they assure me that no foreign power shall invade us, as long as no step against the act of 3 May is taken by our own compatriots.'[20] For several months he and the 'patriot' leaders spared no effort to persuade their supporters to rally support for the Constitution, or at least refrain from opposing it, at the forthcoming sejmiks. However, the abrasive emancipation of the middling szlachta from royal and magnate tutelage had roughened the formerly well-greased channels of patronage. Hearts and minds mattered most, and so the full persuasive armoury was deployed.

The king and his allies distilled the pro-Constitutional discourse developed over the past months into their letters. This is how the monarch wrote to the Castellan of Liw:

> Nothing is more desirable to me than to see the forthcoming sejmiks across the entire country calm, orderly and enlivened by the spirit of our Law on Government of 3 May. This work, in which a miracle of Divine Providence, for the raising up of our Fatherland from her fall, and the threat of her ultimate destruction, is clearly visible, in which every Pole may easily recognize his own and the Fatherland's integrity, liberty, prosperity, is worth its confirmation and praise by the the unanimous consent of the citizenry. I hope that through the virtuous ardour of the enlightened and honest szlachta which will not allow itself to be deceived by semblances and seductions, oaths will even be taken to maintain this Constitution, which in my view is the best suited to save the Commonwealth. God forbid that I should discourage such a praiseworthy intention, eternally securing the fate of our beloved Fatherland. Indeed I expect that if anywhere then it will probably be in the land of Liw, whose favour I have continuously received, that this rite shall most gladly be completed. I spoke of this with the Honourable Chamberlain and Honourable Judge of Liw, who having declared to me their personal inclinations, did not pass over in silence how your leading role, Sir, in the land of Liw, your religion and your civic virtue, as well as your proximity to the location of the sejmik,

> give you the means of preparing and uniting minds in your house, both for the salutary cause of the entire country, and for the preparatory work on the sejmik, for which it is best to reach an early understanding, and in which most benefit will accrue from a complete obedience to the law and procedures relating to the sejmiks. Use, my Castellan, all means to bring about the meeting of minds, and for the confirmation, and if possible the swearing of an oath to our parliamentary deeds on 3 and 5 May. And be sure, that in this you can do nothing more essential, or more graceful, to serve the Commonwealth and myself who places her good above all. In the expectation of the success of your unanimous and joint endeavours, I commend you, Lord Castellan of Liw, to God's care.[21]

First of all, this letter bears witness to the sacral dimension in the campaign. Second, this 'miracle of Divine Providence' is contrasted with the 'semblances and seductions' with which opponents were trying to deceive the 'enlightened and honest szlachta'. Third, it shows how the king had divided responsibilities between the local castellan, chamberlain and judge, to ensure that the sejmik took place in good order and in compliance with the law. Fourth, we see the king's ideal result: an oath to the Constitution.

The swearing of an oath represented the highest level of support for the Constitution. Second-best was a less binding pledge or assurance. This still indicated strong support, but suggests a situation in which pressure for an oath might risk splitting the sejmik in two. After that, where a significant minority expressed its disapproval, the king would settle for a vote of thanks for the Constitution, to be conveyed either by the envoys or by a special delegation. Should the opposition prove very strong, supporters of the Constitution should try to prevent any disapproval being expressed by the sejmik.[22]

Contemporaries interpreted the outcome of the February sejmiks as a triumph for the king and the 'patriots'. To some this was cause for jubilation, to others – an unwelcome surprise. Overall, thirty-seven (47.4 per cent) of the seventy-eight sejmiks swore an oath to the Constitution, and a further twenty (25.6 per cent) made a pledge. Sixteen sejmiks (16.7 per cent) voted thanks and just eight (10.3 per cent) remained silent. Crucially, not a single sejmik criticized the Constitution. Therefore almost three-quarters of the sejmiks expressed strong or very strong support, but at just over a quarter, significant reservations or opposition could not be overcome.[23]

Outcomes depended greatly on local factors. In Cracow an anti-aristocratic tide inundated all opposition. On the first day of the sejmik, the dean of the cathedral dictated the oath from the high altar of St Mary's Church. This act was saluted by cannonfire as nobles and burghers rejoiced. On the other hand, the Lublin sejmik remained silent. Long under the sway of Puławy, it had proved riotous in 1788 and truculent in 1790. If an oath or pledge could not be achieved unanimously, activists sought to word the vote of thanks to demonstrate their understanding of the reforms. For example, the sejmik of Łęczyca recognized that the executive power, 'previously split into parts, and thereby unable to act strongly, is now able to supervise the execution of the laws and make the nation more orderly and happy'.[24]

In Greater and Lesser Poland, a clear but not overwhelming majority of sejmiks expressed strong or very strong support for the Constitution. There were concentrations of silent sejmiks in Mazovia and Podlasie, lands inhabited by numerous poor nobles: by reputation Catholic, conservative and royalist. However, the same could be said of several sejmiks that swore or pledged to support the Constitution. A swathe of sejmiks in the western and northern parts of the Crown confined themselves to voting thanks. The south-east was polarized. In the Grand Duchy of Lithuania, in contrast, no sejmik remained silent, and twenty-seven out of thirty-three swore an oath (Map 4).

Why were Lithuanian sejmiks so much more willing than those of the Crown to swear an oath to the Constitution? A few suggestions have so far been made. First, by the time these sejmiks were held, Lithuanian concerns about the distinctive status of the Grand Duchy had been assuaged, as we shall see. But this does not explain why the Lithuanians were *more* enthusiastic than the nobles of the Crown, only why they were not less so. Second, the reassurances that serfdom had not been abolished may have resonated particularly in the Grand Duchy. In some localities peasants were painfully disabused by the army of their belief that they could now refuse labour services. The Lithuanian instructions of 1790 had been particularly protective of seigneurial powers over peasants. But the same caveat applies. Third, most Lithuanian resolutions pledged to shed blood in defence of national independence. Anti-Muscovite sentiments may have been stronger among the nobles of the Grand Duchy, given their greater exposure to the depredations of Russian soldiers. This same factor might also explain the oaths and pledges in the far south-east of the Crown. It should, however, be borne in mind that most of the Lithuanian and Livonian sejmiks that refrained from swearing an oath either directly bordered the Russian Empire or were sejmiks-in-exile, with significant numbers of *sujets mixtes*. A fourth suggestion is that the political culture of the Grand Duchy of Lithuania was still relatively 'disciplined'. Put bluntly, Lithuanian nobles were more accustomed to carrying out the monarch's wishes. The argument should not be pushed too far: the records of the Wilno sejmik in particular reveal heated debates.[25] Deference had eroded since the days when Tyzenhauz ruled the roost.

In both Lithuania and the Crown, political culture had shifted again since November 1790. At some sejmiks patriotically attired ladies helped to set the tone. Contemporaries marvelled at the orderliness of proceedings, and the care taken to follow the new regulations, established by the March 1791 law on sejmiks and the reform of administrative boundaries passed on 2 November 1791.[26] The new system was showcased at Preny, the principal town of a new district in the palatinate of Troki. The *National and Foreign Gazette* printed the observations of Tomasz Wawrzecki, envoy for Brasław. If this sejmik could have been seen by 'apostles and lovers of the former disorder and disarray in the country and at sejmiks,' he wrote, and 'if they had not yet entirely corrupted their hearts, if they had not completely given their opinions to a foreign will', then they would have venerated the very laws they had calumniated.[27]

Old republicans might not, however, have appreciated the oath sworn by the burghers of Preny, which followed that taken by the szlachta. The burghers were not formal participants in the sejmik, but their presence expressed ongoing fraternization. The official record was signed by about a hundred nobles, but a further fifty nobles marked a cross next to their names. This is one indication that the 'enlightened' elite among the landowning szlachta had not wholly excluded their poorer, illiterate brethren from the political process.[28]

The venue of the new sejmik was the wooden parish church. Here the parish priest Michał Karpowicz preached one of his finest sermons, rapidly published and republished. He distilled the conviction that 'everything will go splendidly' and turned all possible objections to the Constitution against the magnates. The right to elect kings had been enjoyed by the lords alone. Binding instructions had served magnates, who could override the interest of the entire nation. It was true, he said, that 'the gates of the sejmik are closed to the tenants of lords; that servants, vagrants, uncertain persons are forbidden to speak and vote', but leaseholders paying ten złotys in tax could participate. From the carved pulpit flowed encouragement to embrace careers open to talent:

> High birth took all; the merits and talents of the szlachta had to remain abased and neglected. The intrigues and cabals of the aristocrats ruled everywhere; and honesty in poverty was despised. Proud violence achieved everything: and the poor nobles had to grovel before the rich lords. For whence could it have help and support? Unable to divide a tiny piece of ancestral land among several sons and daughters, so that each received one field; in this state, what kind of liberty? What kind of freedom? What kind of noble thinking? Towns were closed to the szlachta on pain of infamy. Workshops, trade, crafts were forbidden to the szlachta as indecent. The army was spare and disorderly, and all the ranks were venal. Hence the abasement of the nobles, and the poverty of their situation compelled them to stick to the party of the rich men, provided with the bread of the Fatherland in *starostwa*, who deluded them that *liberty consists of things always being as they are.*

Karpowicz promised Divine protection for the nation, as long it remained united. So the assembled nobles should respect, love and swear to defend their Constitution, 'so that enlightened nations, in seeing this, should be confirmed in what is already widely said about us abroad: this is a powerful nation! This is a prudent and wise nation! This is a free, humane and rational kingdom! This is noble and enlightened legislation!' *Ça ira*, indeed.[29]

During the last phase of the Polish Revolution the traditional discourse assuming conflict *inter maiestatem ac libertatem* lost its primacy. It was challenged by a discourse of providentially inspired reconciliation – not only between king and nation, but also between 'liberty' and 'government' (*rząd*). In a pamphlet published in the spring of 1792 Aleksander Linowski expressed all this and more:

> It is sad to admit that this holy and estimable name of freedom is so often besmirched on the lips of treacherous tricksters. As many times as national independence has been lost, or as often as it has been desired to preserve anarchy, which is so convenient to personal ambitions, so the expressions of freedom, freedom, and freedom have been heard most loudly in the air. This experience teaches us to know, what to understand by freedom, and what kind of freedom to love – orderly freedom (*wolność rządną*).[30]

After 3 May 1791 other supporters of the Constitution had responded to the complaints by several old republicans (echoing that made by Wojciech Suchodolski on 3 November 1788) that a monarchy had been established in the name of 'government'. A client of Feliks Potocki lamented: 'My God, how the nation allows itself to be deceived by a change of words, the monarchy that has been established is called the firm execution of the law'.[31] But had it? It is time to move from the plane of polemical discourse to those of constitutional law and practice.

To judge the potential of the sovereign Commonwealth, we should ask: what kind of state was emerging from the Polish Revolution? Several historians have concurred that the system of government which took shape throughout the year 1791–92 turned out to be rather more republican than was implied by the lapidary text of the Constitution of 3 May. The protection of liberty concerned the sejm as much as the shaping of government.[32]

The first and most important of the supplementary laws was *Sejms*, passed on 12 and 16 May 1791.[33] Much was retained from the past, including the holding of every third sejm in Grodno. On the other hand, the law empowered the marshal to direct debates and call votes, without being obliged to accept interruptions. Daily sessions would begin at ten in the morning and finish at three in the afternoon. All senators and envoys should be present throughout the sejm, but more realistically the quorum was set at a quarter. The law also reduced the duration of each sejm from ninety-four to seventy days (not counting Sundays and feast days) and envisaged only two fifteen-day prolongations. Without limiting the joint ability of the king and marshal of the sejm to reconvene the sejm, the law defined five cases in which the sejm *must* be reconvened (by the marshal if the king proved dilatory): war, revolution, famine, the death or critical illness of the king, and in case of clashes between the king and his ministers or between the Custodial Council and the commissions. The sejm could directly instruct the commissions and the Council, and overturn their decisions.

The law *Sejms* confirmed the Constitution's abolition of the *liberum veto*, future confederacies and imperative mandates. However, it qualified majority voting. At future sejms, civil laws would require a simple majority of votes, but criminal and constitutional laws would need a majority of two-thirds, and taxation – of three-quarters. The senate's power to suspend legislation would not apply to fiscal measures. Its membership was fixed, in equal proportion for each of the three provinces, at half the number of envoys (later fixed at 102 and

204).[34] Stanisław August kept his right to nominate senators, but future monarchs would choose between two candidates, presented by the relevant sejmik. Many royalists backed this solution. The Elector of Saxony might have expected this question to be settled by negotiation, but most royalists, it transpired, were republicans at heart.

Next was the law filling out the provisions for the extraordinary sejm which would revise the Constitution every twenty-five years. While the Constitutional Deputation should try to ensure that no project for revision contained anything contrary either to an immutable law or the *pacta conventa* of the monarch then reigning, it did not have the power to prevent such projects being brought forward for debate and decision. Moreover, the chamber of envoys would be able to override the objections of the senate.[35]

The law on the sejm court followed. Twelve senators and twenty-four envoys, a third of them from each province, were to be chosen by lot for a two-year term. They were to judge accusations of crimes 'against the nation' and 'against the supreme national government'. The former were crimes 'which violate the public security of the nation, or bring common harm to the entire nation'. They included a 'conspiracy for the overthrow of the free and independent government of the Commonwealth'. Another was corruption among senators, envoys, ministers and senior judges – punishable by the loss of office. In turn, crimes against 'government' encompassed crimes against the king, the sejm and the sejmiks. On the one hand, 'whosoever should incite a rebellion among the common people, or in the army, whoever should incite the szlachta to rebellion or an armed league, with the intention of deposing the reigning king, such a ringleader shall be punished with death'. On the other hand, nothing said or written by a citizen, not forbidden by law, could be treated as a conspiracy or treason. The death penalty was reserved for the most heinous crimes, and nobody could be found guilty except on the basis of reliable testimony or documentary evidence.[36]

On 1 June the sejm passed the law on the Custodial Council, which was defined as the 'royal council for the supervision of the whole, and the execution of the rights given to the king'. This law generally confirmed the *Law on Government*, but it specified that government commissions could remonstrate against the Council's decisions. They could also ask the king or the marshal of the sejm to recall the sejm in order to adjudicate disputes. Should the Council fail to carry out an instruction from the sejm, the marshal (or his deputy) had to send the instruction to the subordinate body concerned. The Council could not directly instruct bodies subordinated to the commissions. Moreover, ministers who were members of the Council could not sit on the commissions. This restriction did not apply, however, to the foreign minister, to whom and the king were entrusted 'all foreign business', save for reports to the Custodial Council on negotiations with foreign powers. Nor did it apply to the primate who chaired the Commission of National Education, but could not countersign resolutions. No provision was made for the king to dismiss ministers before the expiry of their two-year term.[37]

The nomenclature of the Police Commission of the Two Nations, established by law on 17 June 1791, was an early sign that the king's desire that the two nations 'will be just one and the same nation' was not to be fulfilled for the foreseeable future.[38] However, significantly more Lithuanian envoys and senators voted for a single Police Commission than for separate ones. This new body (whose only predecessor had been the Police Department of the Permanent Council, abolished in January 1789) would comprise three senators, including a marshal as chairman, six representatives of the Knightly Estate, and six urban plenipotentiaries, in each case a third being 'from each province', and all being elected for a two-year term by the sejm. The key point was that the Police Commission could not 'establish, enact command or forbid anything which would infringe the natural laws and property of citizens and newcomers, secured by the laws of the Commonwealth'. Nor could it 'interfere under any pretext in another division or in the powers vested in separate authorities and magistratures'. Its authority was confined to free towns of the Commonwealth; it could only advise and warn landowners. Like the Custodial Council, the Police Commission was obliged to protect freedom of speech and publication, with the additional task of looking after authors' rights.[39]

The sejm debated the question of the Treasury Commission in October 1791. Agreement to a single system of taxation for the Commonwealth – the culmination of a long convergence – came easily. On 10 October 1791 Kazimierz Sapieha announced: 'Desirous of bonding both nations closer together in unity and of eliminating the trace of any difference, our province gladly accepts equal taxes with the Crown.' Note the use of 'both nations' and 'our province' in the same sentence. The act was inscribed the following day.[40] Some *koroniarze* were surprised when three days later, after the project for a single commission had been read out, Sapieha announced that the Lithuanian provincial session demanded a separate commission for the Grand Duchy. The Lithuanians stood firm during debates on 14 and 17 October. At stake was the imposition of a solution on the Grand Duchy against its will. The Castellan of Troki best expressed their case: 'in the circumstances of the union, Lithuania cannot be considered as a province with regard to a single body, but as one nation with regard to another'.[41]

On 20 October 1791 Sapieha presented the Lithuanian conditions for joint government commissions: parity in ministers, an equal number of treasury and military commissioners, alternating chairmanship, separate coffers and a separate treasury court located in the Grand Duchy. After a brief discussion, the sejm unanimously acclaimed the law, solemnly titled the *Mutual Assurance of the Two Nations*, which was declared an integral part of the Constitution. For Stanisław August, the point was a timely and unanimous endorsement by the sejm of the Constitution of 3 May.[42] We shall return to this law's afterlife.

The law establishing the Treasury Commission of the Two Nations was passed a week later. Slightly modifying the sense of the *Mutual Assurance*, only the ten noble members of the commission were to be chosen in equal numbers from the two nations. The six urban plenipotentiaries represented three equal provinces. The commission was forbidden much: to collect taxes or fees not sanctioned by law, to establish internal customs posts, to alter external tariffs confirmed by the sejm, to establish monopolies, to apply revenues to any end not specified by law or the express will of the sejm, or to lend or exchange monies in public repositories. Nor could it withhold payments legally due. Above all, it could issue no order 'which would have the character of legislation'.[43]

The division of powers was again applied asymmetrically. The sejm could annul the commission's resolutions and summon accused commissioners before the sejm court. The new Treasury Commission inherited some judicial functions from its two predecessors. Its courts, which remained separate for the Crown and the Grand Duchy of Lithuania, would judge cases of damage to the public treasury and revenues, offences committed by and against its own officials insofar as this regarded their duties, and contractual trade disputes between Poles and foreigners. The commission was expected to look after the balance of trade externally, while removing all barriers to it internally. It thus resumed the work of the general customs established at the start of the reign.

Pending the establishment of a new Military Commission of the Two Nations, the existing commission was plagued by absences. The new project languished amidst fears of royal and ministerial control. It was only passed after a secret ballot of fifty-five to forty votes on 18 May 1792, in the charged atmosphere that followed the delivery of the Russian declaration. The commission would comprise one of the hetmans as chairman, two other senators, six serving officers, and six civilian landowners who were not currently envoys. Only the sejm could authorize the commission to send soldiers abroad. The commission was forbidden to alter the size and pay of the army establishment. As well as functioning as a court martial, the commission's court would judge mutual complaints between civilians and soldiers, handing out civil punishments to the former and military ones to the latter. Otherwise, the commission's powers over civilians were limited to cases of rebellion, violence and theft.[44] There was no time to elect new commissioners before the sejm prorogued itself.

In the judicial sphere, besides the law on the sejm court, the sejm enacted three major sets of legislation. First, a law passed on 3 October 1791 reformed the system of courts for burghers in free (formerly royal) towns. Urban citizens would elect judges, but 'advocates', nominated by the king, would monitor appellate judges' work. Presiding over the courts of the final instance, the assessory courts, would be the vice-chancellors – Kołłątaj and Chreptowicz. The sejm would choose their judges. These were also the highest courts for peasants on Crown estates.[45]

Second, on 5 January 1792 the sejm passed laws which established a consolidated system of local courts to serve nobles and all landowners, in place of the castle and land courts. The new courts dealt with both civil and criminal cases. The monarch lost his remaining powers to nominate judges – all were henceforth to be elected at sejmiks for four-year terms, ready, like envoys to the sejm, to reconvene when necessary. This ended the election or appointment of judges for life, and strengthened citizens' control over the judicial process. Perhaps the Lithuanians were more concerned to retain men of experience, because their law confirmed the existing land court judges for a further four years in the new courts.[46]

Third, on 19 January 1792 the sejm unanimously passed laws for the Crown and Lithuanian Tribunals. Henceforth the Crown Tribunal would be divided into separate Tribunals for Lesser and Greater Poland. These laws followed a disconcerting defeat for the Crown project in a secret ballot on 17 January. The difficulty arose over the provision that in all cases 'clerical and secular deputies shall sit with a decisive vote'. This roused spectres of learned clergymen turning the Tribunal into a consistory court. The other sticking point was the election of clerical judges at the sejmiks. Fears were expressed that chapters and bishops would present only one candidate, rather than two. Chapters' indignation at losing their rights to choose deputies was ignored. No such problems were encountered regarding the Lithuanian Tribunal, in which clerical judges had always been less important than in the Crown. This new law maintained a separate, mixed 'ecclesiastical circle'.[47]

In general, the Polish Revolution did not radically reform the Commonwealth's courts. Access to justice remained differentiated by social estate. The legislation sought to satisfy the needs of the landowning szlachta and propertied burghers. This tendency was exemplified by two laws (inscribed on 3 and 5 December 1791) regarding boundary disputes. Henceforth sejmiks would elect boundary commissioners. The preambles are characteristically didactic. That for the Grand Duchy of Lithuania expresses the wish to 'remedy public tranquillity, sparing the spilling of the innocent blood with which boundaries have often been stained'. That for the Crown emphasizes that 'boundary disputes have most intemperately disturbed neighbourly tranquillity among landowners, damaged the country's economy, and through prolonged and costly lawsuits exhausted citizens' estates'.[48] But perhaps we should not read too much into these words. It seems that the Lithuanian law was implemented smoothly. The partial evidence of sejmik resolutions and delegates' speeches indicates satisfaction with the sejm's judicial reforms.

Taken together, these laws bear out the argument that the political compromise reached before 3 May 1791 created the conditions for the incarnation of the sovereign nation in the chamber of envoys. The legislative power was elevated above the judicial and executive powers. At the same time the sejmiks obtained significant competencies, notably the election of judges. This emergent constitutional settlement drew on the traditions of noble democracy and the experience of the sejm confederacy, as well as on newer currents of constitutional thought or foreign examples. It gained a reassuring legitimacy, for all the length and inflexibility of some of these laws.[49] They are not, however, wholly representative of the condition of the Polish-Lithuanian state in the year that followed 3 May 1791.

In the first place, constitutional laws were but a small proportion of the sejm's legislation. Besides questions of public significance, many largely private matters were also settled by statutes. (This observation applies, to an even greater degree, to the British Parliament.) Moreover, the acceleration was palpable. The 134 parliamentary sessions from 3 May 1791 until 29–30 May 1792 produced more than a twentieth of the entire pre-partition corpus of legislation passed in the Kingdom of Poland and the Commonwealth.[50] This feat of lawmaking would have been impossible without the confederated sejm's reform of procedure. Much went through on the nod, often with relatively few present. Most 'malcontents' had withdrawn by the end of 1791.

However, some questions aroused fierce passions. Although the preference remained for unanimous acclamation, following the thrashing out of a compromise, votes were called regularly, and their results were often close. Such occasional storms were a sign of rude health. Whatever Feliks Potocki's correspondents alleged, the confederated sejm had not become a rubber stamp. On the whole, the institutions and culture of Polish-Lithuanian parliamentarianism functioned constructively and harmoniously. What linked this luminous exercise of 'orderly liberty' to the bonfire of 1788–89 was the untrammelled sovereignty wielded by the representatives of the nation.

The sejm's deliberations were facilitated by a disciplined political caucus. The Association of the Friends of the Government Constitution *Fiat Lux* (often referred to as the Club of the Friends of the Constitution) consolidated less formal groupings after the Constitution had been enacted. It met regularly in rented rooms in the Radziwiłł Palace. Just over a third of the 213 known members were *not* envoys or senators. Among them were the clergymen Michał Ossowski, Hieronim Stroynowski and Scipione Piattoli, the ennobled burgher Franciszek Barss, the nobly born urban plenipotentiary Józef Wybicki, Prince Józef Poniatowski and several other serving officers. Among the parliamentarians in the Club were two bishops – Józef Rybiński and Adam Naruszewicz – and twelve other senators. There were a few aristocrats led by Adam Kazimierz Czartoryski and six Potockis, enlightened royalists such as Pius Kiciński and Aleksander Linowski, and enlightened republicans such as Stanisław Sołtyk and Ignacy Zakrzewski. Seventy-five members of the Association were envoys elected to the sejm in 1790, fifty of them debutants.[51]

The statute obliged all members, including envoys and senators, to support the aims and resolutions of the Club, which were passed by a majority of votes. Projects were read out and amended, and tactics were discussed before key debates. For example, in October 1791 the Association mobilized its members to defeat a motion for the sejmiks to elect government commissioners. According to a pamphlet later inspired by the king in very different circumstances, 'this club was a sejm above the sejm'.[52] In contrast, Kołłątaj later played down its significance. In truth the Association was more than a club, but less than a sejm. Meetings were chaired in turn by every member in alphabetical order. Kołłątaj, Ignacy Potocki and Adam Czartoryski discreetly made the most important political decisions, in consultation with Stanisław Małachowski and the king, neither of whom was a member. The Club is known to have held twenty-one sessions between May and December 1791, but it probably met sporadically until the following spring.

Feliks Potocki's correspondents believed that this diabolical '*klopp*' in Warsaw was modelled on the Jacobin club in Paris.[53] The masonic connections of both the venue (which housed the lodge of the Grand Orient of Poland) and much of the Association membership have exacerbated later suspicions that the Constitution of 3 May was a masonic plot against Catholic Poland. As if the diverse and divided freemasons of the late eighteenth century followed the same political and ideological line . . . Far more significantly, among the Club's members were Julian Niemcewicz and Józef Weyssenhoff, who edited the *National and Foreign Gazette* founded in January 1791. Many government commissioners and three ministers in the Custodial Council (Ignacy Potocki, Tomasz Ostrowski and Joachim Chreptowicz) were also members. So the Association linked the legislative and executive powers at the highest levels, as well as a leading media outlet. In these regards it was akin to a modern political party in government. It eased the co-operation between the king, Potocki, Kołłątaj and their supporters. This defused the potential for constitutional conflict, had the institutions pulled in different directions.[54]

Early in June, Stanisław August nominated the members of the Custodial Council. Ignacy Potocki became minister of police, Chreptowicz minister of foreign affairs and Ostrowski minister of the treasury. These three proved to be the most active ministers. Jacek Małachowski and Franciszek Ksawery Branicki became minister of the seal and minister of war respectively. Better that they spit out than spit in? The king hoped that a broad-bottomed Council would be less likely to provoke the open division that could invite Russian intervention. Małachowski applied himself to his work conscientiously, despite his distaste for the Constitution (he had resigned his office, but the king dissuaded him). Branicki feigned loyalty, but was soon hatching intrigues. After the death of Potemkin on 16 October 1791, he obtained permission to join his wife and sort out her affairs in the Russian Empire. He returned to Warsaw, but in March

1792 he left again for St Petersburg. The ministers were joined in the Council by Stanisław Małachowski and Kazimierz Sapieha. Their job was to communicate with the sejm, although Sapieha did sometimes speak up for his absent uncle Branicki. Finally, when Michał Poniatowski reluctantly returned to Poland in late August 1791, he replaced Bishop Feliks Turski of Cracow, who had deputized for him in the Council.

Stanisław August was well served by the two secretaries he appointed to the Custodial Council. Moreover, seventeen out of the twenty-three regents and clerks had previously worked for the Permanent Council. Ordinary sessions of the Custodial Council were held weekly, first on Tuesdays, later on Thursdays. The king chaired each and every meeting, calling additional ones when necessary – even on Sundays. In total it met eighty-three times between 19 June 1791 and 18 July 1792. The Council received and discussed quarterly reports from the central commissions. It also considered eighty-nine reports from civil-military commissions and diverse complaints made by clergymen, burghers, Jews, peasants, nobles and academies. These petitions indicated confidence from below, given the wider culture of petitioning in early modern Europe. In sum, the king in the Custodial Council made 228 recorded decisions, although some of these simply referred complaints to the relevant government body. The protocols reveal that the monarch participated actively in all sessions and assigned tasks to ministers.[55] Effectively, Stanisław August became his own prime minister. His leadership was apparent to diplomats in Warsaw, but it depended more on trust and confidence than on solidly grounded prerogatives.

After returning from England, Michał Poniatowski might have belonged to the Commonwealth's innermost circle. Initially, things were set fair. The primate caught up with the king, praised the Constitution, and expressed his willingness to work with Ignacy Potocki (to whose care he had consigned the Educational Commission two years previously). On 15 September 1791, when the sejm resumed after the summer break, he made a much anticipated speech. Offering his services, he testified to the great impression produced by the Constitution abroad: 'I was proud to show myself a Pole, hearing the praise and universal respect for the Polish name'.[56] However, the reconciliation soon soured. It hardly mattered that the primate's attempts to introduce Italian-style *conversazioni* failed. With lemonade on offer instead of Hungarian wine and plentiful food, his Friday assemblies were not a success. What counted was Poniatowski's collision with his former protégé, Kołłątaj, and many others over the sale of Crown estates.

The idea of such an auction was not new. Reverend Ossowski had published a proposal early in 1789. Kołłątaj's ascent made such a measure feasible. The project presented to the sejm on 10 October 1791 envisaged the selling off of the Crown estates over five years. On this basis a national bank would annually issue assignats to the value of three million złotys. The primate led the critics. Besides the need to keep faith with existing possessors, which was a question of public trust, their arguments included the costs of a survey, the inflationary danger of paper money, concerns about the land market, and doubts about how much capital might be raised. It was of little avail. On 19 December the sejm voted by 152 to 49 for an immediate sale with compensation for current starostas. However, the sejm rejected the idea of a national bank. Working out the details took so much time that the law was only passed on 24 April 1792, too late to take effect.[57]

This clash revealed tensions among those who supported the Constitution. Among the advocates of an immediate sale of Crown estates were Ignacy and Stanisław Potocki, Ostrowski, Sołtyk and Kiciński. But most bishops and lay senators, as well as a number of envoys, favoured a gradual sale after the death of existing possessors. Following the sejm's decision, starostas' wives boycotted the king's New Year reception. Stanisław August was widely assumed to favour the measure. He had advocated the sale of Crown estates before he was elected king, but he was concerned about malcontents. His absence on the day of the vote was probably no coincidence.

The primate made three passionate speeches against the project. On the second occasion he expressed his

> . . . infinite terror that we should not through incautiousness slip under the appalling light of the street lanterns, with which the French try to extinguish the rays of religion, honour and common sense in the chimerical interpretation of the rights of man and complete equality, placing a Jew, an executioner, a peasant, a Muslim, a noble, a burgher, and a priest together . . .[58]

He had this speech translated into French and printed. This step made his point to Descorches, the revolutionary diplomat with whom he had frozen relations on a point of etiquette. He also sent copies to Rome. While in Paris, Poniatowski had observed the radicalization of the French Revolution. The courteous reception accorded to Catholic French bishops in exile in Protestant England subsequently impressed him. He had met Edmund Burke and generally admired the *Reflections on the Revolution in France*. Writing to his beloved niece Maria Teresa, he contrasted the 'tyrannical liberty' of the French with 'English liberty founded on good laws, balanced by different powers'.[59] Like his elder brother, Michał Jerzy believed the English nation was more secure in its liberty and property than any other nation. However, Stanisław August took longer to reach a similarly critical stance towards the French Revolution.[60]

'Democrats' in the king's entourage worried the primate. Besides Piattoli, there was his fellow Tuscan, Filippo Mazzei. This veteran of the War of American Independence had recently arrived in Poland from Paris. Poniatowski complained privately of the 'impertinences' he suffered not only from envoys linked to Kołłątaj, but also from Kiciński. Nevertheless, he remained loyal to the king and the Constitution. That did not prevent him from asking the Custodial Council to enforce the eleventh cardinal law against publications noxious to religion and morals. Ignacy Potocki, the minister of police, batted away the episcopal request, citing the Council's obligation to maintain freedom of the press. Freedom of expression had long been venerated in Poland as the right – even the duty – of a citizen to give counsel for the common good. While almost nobody conceded a *right* to insult religion, there was little appetite for a crackdown. Disappointed, the primate appealed to the February 1792 sejmiks. He secured resolutions at eight of them. Some of these went well beyond his suggestions, excoriating godless writers and clubs.

This skirmish over freedom of the press shows the potential for the hosts of God and Caesar to contest the meaning of 'orderly liberty'. In this case the secular authorities were reluctant to support the Church hierarchy. More frequently, the Commonwealth's demands on the clergy caused tensions. From 1789, registers of marriages, baptisms and deaths, and information on the population, were required from each Catholic parish. Most clergymen did their best to comply, but such data were not easy to collect and maintain. Some civil-military commissions began to fine recalcitrant priests, and the effects were felt disproportionately in the eastern palatinates. A group of Uniate clergymen petitioned the Custodial Council for relief.[61]

Most religious orders refused to co-operate with the Police Commission's investigation into hospitals, despite episcopal support for the measure. The commission completed its investigation, but there was no time to start merging smaller hospitals into larger facilities. Bishops also assisted the commission's efforts to stem the tide of vagrancy and begging. To facilitate the round-ups that began in Warsaw on 2 November 1791, Bishop Okęcki suspended the right of sanctuary in churches. Persons deemed unfit to work were either taken in by monasteries or convents or sent back to their parishes with a licence to beg. The able-bodied were set to hard labour – at least until they could escape. The commission's instruction to move cemeteries beyond the city limits encountered much passive resistance. However, results were achieved in Grodno, whose parish priest led by example, and in Warsaw, where Okęcki consecrated the extra-mural cemetery at Powązki on 20 May 1792.

Perhaps surprisingly, education was only rarely a point of contention. The strident calls of the November 1790 sejmiks to restore the Jesuits and apply the educational fund to the army produced only weak echoes in the sejm. Doubtless the euphoric atmosphere helped. Instead of being lectured by school visitors or bemused by scientific experiments, parents could watch their sons participating in patriotic galas. Such performances could teach the values of orderly liberty. For example, a march composed by the Basilian pedagogue, Reverend Julian Antonowicz, included the verse:

> Let private interest never seduce you,
> Let the general good rule hearts:
> Unworthy is he, though freeborn,
> Who governs not his passions.[62]

The sejm did not manage to pass a new law on the Commission of National Education. We do not know how far Kołłątaj's ambitions for a 'teaching estate' would have been trimmed back. Nor do we know how far he could have pushed the plans for the commission to supervise seminaries, and the schools of other confessions. But the primate was back in control. He complained to Franciscan provincials about schools that were supposedly parochial, 'but which widely exceed those limits', occupying youth 'with unnecessary learning, most of all Latin – the bad sort'. The orders were welcome to run parish schools in small towns, but 'with the knowledge of the Educational Commission, and according to its regulations'.[63] Some civil-military commissions intensified pressure on the clergy to maintain parish schools. The cause of elementary education was advancing, albeit from a low base and unevenly.

The law on free royal towns was filled out by legislation passed in June 1791.[64] Private and ecclesiastical towns were excluded from its scope, but in September

1791 the episcopate reluctantly put forward a project which would have conferred similar prerogatives on ecclesiastical towns within two years. In principle, municipal elites could henceforth govern the 'free towns of the Commonwealth', but they would have to reckon with an opening up of urban politics to scrutiny and change, both from above and from below. Christian property owners (even of a small workshop) would enjoy the political rights of urban citizens. In practice, this meant that a greater proportion of the population held the franchise in small towns, built predominantly of one-family houses, than in cities, whose tenements were occupied by many families. All inhabitants received civil rights, notably *neminem captivabimus nisi iure victum*, underlining personal dignity. Municipal jurisdiction and taxes encompassed all property-owners and traders, regardless of their estate or religion, thereby ending the autonomy of noble and clerical *jurydyki*. At the same time nobles could trade freely without derogation, and accept urban citizenship and municipal office.

Many nobles were chosen as urban plenipotentiaries to the sejm. These elections, held in September 1791, developed the practice of citizenship. 'Free towns' were grouped into twenty-four divisions, eight in each province of the Commonwealth. The divisional assemblies, composed of deputies elected by the towns, would each elect judges to courts of appeal, civil-military commissioners and a plenipotentiary. Plenipotentiaries could present urban postulates to the sejm, which would assign them to the assessory courts and the Police and Treasury Commissions.

Not every effort to push the boundaries further was successful. Especially in the smaller towns of the Grand Duchy of Lithuania, seventy-four of which now recovered or obtained self-governing status, urban magistrates' ambitions often met resistance from starostas, civil-military commissions, army officers, and noble and ecclesiastical owners of urban properties, who denounced the burghers' enthusiasm as 'insolence'.[65] Townspeople faced overlapping jurisdictions. Clashes were inevitable over the provisioning, billeting, discipline and desertion of soldiers, passports, sanitation, the roads, population records, provision for the poor and sick, the guilds, monopolies, weights and measures, and rural land belonging to towns. Relations between Christians and Jews deteriorated in many places. The Police Commission often ruled in favour of Jewish communities who complained of unfair burdens and restrictions. It also prohibited *kahal* elders from levying unjustified payments or from excommunicating those Jews who refused to pay. Last but not least, it decided that the privilege *neminem captivabimus* included Jewish inhabitants of free towns.

Given this complexity, it was as well that the Police commissioners included such experienced servants of the state as Michał Mniszech, Kazimierz Raczyński and Marcin Badeni. However, all the urban plenipotentiaries chosen for this commission were nobly born – the best known was Wybicki. Confronted with competing interests and stories, it was natural for them to assume that centralization was best. In total the Police Commission employed 158 officials. Half of these were based in Warsaw, half deployed in the provinces. Its budget was more than thrice that of the old Police Department, and the costs drew hostile questions in the sejm. Faced with war in June 1792, the commission also spent modest sums on intelligence agents, who included girls selling oranges.[66]

Such were the problems of success. This survey of the 'state of the union' has shown that in both law and practice it proved impossible fully to implement the constitutional provision that 'three powers shall compose the government of the Polish nation' – if they were indeed intended to be separate and balanced. It is an oversimplification to state that the *Law on Government* introduced the three-way separation of powers. Parts of the judiciary and executive were intertwined, while the legislature was superior to both. The idea of the Polish nation was widening to include all inhabitants of the country, but the older nomenclature of 'the Two Nations' adorned several government bodies. Teething troubles were experienced in the free towns. Expectations had been raised and disappointed in ecclesiastical and private towns, as well as among peasants. The situation was evolving as the initial euphoria ebbed. Even after writing off convinced 'malcontents', it would become more difficult to maintain a balance between those who wished to push the Polish Revolution onwards and those who wished to apply the brakes. Both these tendencies, moreover, could broadly be described as republican. Stanisław August realized that for the foreseeable future the Constitution of 3 May represented a monarchist high tide.[67]

That said, the division between 'republicanism' and 'monarchism' was less clear in practice than it was in theory. In the sixteenth century, as the Commonwealth was taking shape, its noble citizens often made pragmatic political choices, couched in a discourse of security and stability. They moulded their institutions in response to fast-moving events which threatened their property as well as their liberty. With time, these institutions became immemorial customs of the freedom-loving nation.[68] For most of the eighteenth century the plane of discourse was remote from the key political decisions affecting the political community. Not coincidentally, discourse became more uncompromisingly republican. After the

Commonwealth's citizens had regained their power of decision-making in the autumn of 1788, the way was again open to less doctrinaire politics, including elements of limited monarchy. To some extent the new politics was a response to new opportunities and challenges in the international arena, although it was not always realistic or pragmatic. By the final year and a half of the sejm, these shifts were not only apparent in political language, but were bringing about major changes to the hallowed institutions of Polish liberty – such as royal elections.

The content of the *Law on Government* took shape as a clandestine compromise between Stanisław August and Ignacy Potocki. It also took into account both the expectations of landowning nobles and the vision of Hugo Kołłątaj. Once acclaimed, the Constitution broke the mould of Polish politics. The year that followed 3 May 1791 displayed the enormous potential, both of the sovereign Commonwealth to reform its institutions, and of its inhabitants to suffuse those institutions with civic spirit. Within this reformed constitutional framework, a new kind of politics could respond to the economic, social and cultural challenges of the future. Unfortunately, a politics oiled by the conviction '*Ça ira*' proved less able to deal with the challenges presented by the Commonwealth's neighbours.

Looking back over the Polish Revolution, we can see it followed a classic revolutionary trajectory: 'destruction – discussion – creation'.[69] Allowing for overlap, this scheme fits events and processes. The destructive phase involved casualties in administration and diplomacy, the discursive phase used up priceless time, and the creative phase placed too much faith in the salutary effects of good laws and too many restraints on the new executive institutions. Yet the destruction of functioning institutions of government in 1788–89 was intrinsically linked to the recovery of the Commonwealth's sovereignty. The resulting freedom of expression and action enabled parliamentarians and the public to learn that words and decisions had consequences, for which responsibility had to be taken. Finally, the constitutional legislation of 1791–92 was drafted, agreed and often implemented within a transformed political culture, one based on active civic participation. The unthinkable now became thinkable, possible and sometimes even real. In just under four years the wonder is that so much was achieved, rather than so little.

Before taking our leave of the Great Sejm, it remains to indicate a path which the sovereign Commonwealth could have taken. It led far into the future – the future destroyed by the country's neighbours. This path was Kołłątaj's vision. No doubt it would not have been realized in its entirety, but it is unlikely that it would have been rejected outright. For Kołłątaj knew how to choose the order in which he fought his battles. Even before his elevation to the vice-chancellorship, he believed the principle of the protection of law and government for villagers must precede its implementation through more specific laws. In the meantime the 'political constitution' had to be finished, 'in order not to encumber with too many imaginings at once a nation which is so good and sweet, despite many novelties, diametrically opposed to former prejudices'.[70]

On 28 June 1791 Kołłątaj revealed more in a programmatic speech to the sejm:

> Besides, it is not enough for you to rest on political laws alone. Do you want your nation to be indivisible and to last forever under a free [form of] government? You need to give it economic laws, for they will tightly link it to the Polish land. Do you want this nation, free and happy on Polish land, to resist the false lure of novelties and foreign examples? You need to give it moral laws.[71]

So there were to be three constitutions – political, economic and moral. We have seen how the political constitution took shape. The economic constitution, Kołłątaj told the sejm, would involve laws to protect property and labour, and to encourage agriculture, trade and crafts. It probably never got beyond the most general of plans. Some of its principles did appear in the introduction to Ossowski's project for the *starostwa*, published in June 1791. All land would have a hereditary owner. Peasants would obtain their farms in perpetuity; they could sell them with the lord's agreement, but not divide them. Binding contracts would regulate duties, permitting the exchange of labour for rent or vice versa. Thus the sale of Crown estates was to open up far-reaching social changes. However, the law on *starostwa*, finally passed in April 1792, watered these ideas down, like much else. The economic constitution remained work for the future.[72]

Its moral counterpart was just as nebulous. The vice-chancellor told the sejm that the principles of the moral constitution were to be found 'in the purest source of our religion, Christ's Divine rules'. It would depend, moreover, on 'uniform education adapted not only to the enlightenment of minds, but to the strengthening of our character'. To this end he envisaged public games and spectacles. The plans for the Educational Commission provided for the inculcation of a uniform moral and civic spirit. The question of the moral constitution was also linked to legal codification. As Kołłątaj put it in his speech, 'moral laws should provide the principles for good civil and criminal laws'. So codification would provide another way to implement the protection promised to the peasants by the *Law on Government*.[73]

The sejm appointed two deputations for legal codification on 29 June 1791. The vice-chancellor co-chaired the Crown deputation, while his allies were among the Lithuanian deputies. The deputations' joint task was to produce a single *Code of Stanisław August*. This remained unfinished, but surviving materials show the direction taken by their work. The code's prospectus included Kołłątaj's qualification of clergy, teachers and soldiers as 'serving estates'. Fragmentary projects shifted the boundaries of temporal and spiritual authority towards the former, for example regarding matrimony. However, the king reassured the nuncio that the code would include nothing pernicious to the Catholic Church. The deputies took a humane approach to punishment, with the Lithuanians even proposing the abolition of the death penalty. A more traditional element (present in the law on the sejm court) was the right of the accused to the presumption of innocence and to prepare a defence. Inquisitorial torture had been abolished in 1776. The medieval noble privilege of *neminem captivabimus* thus became a principle of procedure. At some point in the future it would have encompassed peasants. For the most part the codified criminal law (as opposed to the court system) would not be differentiated by social rank. Punishments would fit the crime, not the criminal's birth.

This perspective calls to mind the saying that whereas other nations abolished their nobility, the Poles ennobled everyone. The best proof is surely their habit of addressing each other in the third person as *Pani* (Lady) and *Pan* (Lord).[74] My favourite version is that voiced by Gerwazy Rębajło in Adam Mickiewicz's *Pan Tadeusz*. The battle-scarred old warden is surprised and worried by the decision by the new lords of the manor, Tadeusz and Zosia, to free their serfs and endow them with land. 'Freedom's for noblemen, not every man,' he says. Nor is freedom a matter of empty words:

> So following the custom, my advice is
> To make them noble, give them our devices:
> To some Soplica's star and crescent coat

> Of arms, to some the Horeszko demi-goat.
> Rębajło e'en would recognize them then
> As equals and escutcheoned noblemen.
> The sejm will confirm it.[75]

This is one of the less realistic parts of Mickiewicz's masterpiece. However, an earlier example of this idea can be found in a pamphlet from 1790, quoted by Emanuel Rostworowski: 'if nobility is the happiness of the nation, let us ennoble the whole nation'. If this was still a fantasy, it was a fantasy unimaginable elsewhere. The illustrious historian concluded:

> The Great Sejm, in equipping the Commonwealth with reformable institutions and during four years of debate magnificently renewing the temporarily perverted Polish parliamentary tradition, brought Poland into the group of states, whose main constitutional problem in the nineteenth and twentieth centuries was to be the social struggle for universal suffrage.[76]

Things turned out differently, and that is a pity.

— TWELVE —
UNDECLARED WAR

An extraordinary royal council met at the Royal Castle in Warsaw on 23 July 1792. The decision it sanctioned has been passionately debated ever since. Since the Russian invasion on 18 May, the Commonwealth's armies had responded belligerently, making a fighting retreat. The point to be decided on 23 July was whether to cease military operations on the tsaritsa's terms, or whether to fight on in defence of the Constitution of 3 May.

The king convened the meeting. It was composed of all but one member of the Custodial Council and other ministers present in Warsaw. Absent was Crown Grand Hetman Franciszek Ksawery Branicki. He was one of the leaders of the counter-revolutionary confederacy formed under the empress's auspices in St Petersburg on 27 April. Its founding act was post-dated to 14 May at the border town of Targowica. Present in the Castle, however, were Primate Michał Poniatowski, Lithuanian Grand Marshal Ignacy Potocki, Crown Grand Chancellor Jacek Małachowski, Lithuanian Vice-Chancellor Joachim Chreptowicz, Crown Court Treasurer Tomasz Ostrowski, and the two marshals of the sejm confederacy, Stanisław Małachowski and Kazimierz Nestor Sapieha. The other participants were Crown Grand Marshal Michał Mniszech, Crown Vice-Chancellor Hugo Kołłątaj, Lithuanian Court Marshal Stanisław Sołtan, Lithuanian Treasurer Ludwik Tyszkiewicz and Lithuanian Court Treasurer Antoni Dziekoński. Stanisław August's eldest brother, Kazimierz Poniatowski, who held no ministerial office, was present as an observer.

No protocol seems to have been made, and every known version of what was said was created by an interested party. Things may have gone as follows.[1] Opening the meeting, Stanisław August announced that the previous day he had received a reply from Catherine II to his letter of 22 June 1792. In this letter, drafted in consultation with Ignacy Potocki, Chreptowicz, Kołłątaj and the Russian ambassador Iakov Bulgakov, the king had asked the empress for an armistice. He had also explained that Poland needed a better form of government, without the 'continual revolutions' inseparable from interregna, and suggested a solution: that Catherine give the Poles her grandson Constantine as their next king, along with an alliance and commercial treaty.[2] He read out the empress's briefer response: 'This is about the restoration to the Commonwealth of its former liberty and form of government guaranteed by my treaties with it, and overthrown violently by the revolution of 3 May, with scorn for the most sacred laws and specifically the *pacta conventa*.' Moreover, 'the healthiest part' of the Polish nation 'has confederated itself in order to reclaim its rights which have been so unjustly ravished from it', and she had promised it her aid. She expected the king to accede without delay 'to the confederacy formed under my auspices'.[3]

The king then informed the gathering of the longer instruction to the Russian ambassador, which the latter had shown to Chreptowicz. In this rescript, Vice-Chancellor Ostermann conveyed the empress's outrage at the king's letter. The offer of the succession to the throne – ignored in her letter to Stanisław August – was in flagrant contradiction of the laws of election she was defending, and was designed to sow mistrust between the courts of St Petersburg, Vienna and Berlin. The confederacy represented the true Commonwealth; neither it nor the empress recognized the right of either the sejm or the king to demand an armistice, as if this were a war between one power and another. So the king must immediately submit to the confederacy, order the army back to its peacetime quarters, and send away those politicians 'whom the voice of the public justly accuses of hatching these plots'. Otherwise the Russian generals would continue offensive operations.[4]

The king continued his account: faced with these demands, he had sought guarantees regarding the integrity of the Commonwealth's territories, the army establishment, the courts, government commissions and state loans. The ambassador had given only a vague assurance on the first of these. Stanisław August declared to the meeting that nobody could regret more the Russian insistence on destroying the Constitution. However, no help could be expected from abroad. Prussia was preparing for a new partition in the event of continued resistance. In any case, the empty treasury and arsenal, and the diminished army made it impossible to fight on for much longer. It might just be possible to beat one of the two Russian armies in a battle, but the other would remain, and the consequences of losing to either would be catastrophic. Although he avowed his willingness to die for the Constitution, his duty obliged him to consider 'if a desperate step would bring any help'. He asked those present whether he should, as demanded, accede to the Confederacy of Targowica.[5]

The primate answered first: since the Constitution could not be saved, it was imperative to save the country by an immediate accession. This was also the advice of Mniszech, Jacek Małachowski, Kołłątaj, Chreptowicz, Tyszkiewicz and Dziekoński. Mniszech, Tyszkiewicz and Dziekoński also stated for the record that they had not supported the Constitution. Kołłątaj would have preferred direct negotiations with the Russians, but is reported to have concluded: 'today, Sire, it is necessary to accede to the Confederacy of Targowica, not tomorrow; every moment costs us dear, because Poles' blood is spilt'.[6] However, Ignacy Potocki opined that a partition was unlikely and that the army could fight on; hope remained in courage and unforeseen events. He would resign if the king joined the confederacy. Sołtan opposed any negotiations whatsoever. The most belligerent was Ostrowski – he advised the king to join the army south-east of Warsaw and fight a decisive battle. Even if the field were lost, the fight could be sustained in the mountainous country to the south. When the monarch responded that supplies and money would not suffice, Ostrowski countered that in the last resort he should follow the example of John Casimir during the Swedish Deluge of 1655 and retreat to Galicia. Stanisław August riposted that the House of Austria was then allied to the King of Poland; it was now allied to Russia.[7] Potocki, Sołtan and Ostrowski maintained their opposition, urging a general rising. In the end, Stanisław Małachowski declared his support for the continuation of the war. Any negotiations should be conducted directly with the Russian court, not with traitors. The king called a vote. The result is usually given as eight in favour, four against, less often as seven to five; the uncertainty concerns Sapieha.[8]

The following day, 24 July, Stanisław August signed the previously prepared document and sent it to Bulgakov. He promised to accede to the confederacy together with the army. The monarch and the ambassador then communicated the order for an armistice to the respective forces in the field. The next day the king wrote to the empress, hoping that his fulfilment of her wishes would prove his sincerity and that he might reclaim her favour.[9] So ended the Russo-Polish war of 1792 – a war unrecognized by Russia. The trajectory of the Commonwealth now turned away from the bright future promised by the Polish Revolution.

How had matters reached this point? What motivated those Poles who turned to Catherine II for assistance? Was the situation as hopeless as the king and most of the Council maintained? What were the prospects if the war had been continued? What were the consequences of capitulation in these circumstances and on these terms? Finally, what factors lay behind the composition and apparent course of the meeting, and how sincere was the opposition expressed to the decision? Such questions have occupied generations of historians and their readers – not all of them Polish.

Catherine II herself attested the sense of Stanisław August's endeavours to persuade malcontents to accept the Constitution of 3 May. In July 1791 she informed Potemkin of her willingness to give the 'Polish patriots' all necessary help. She added, however, that they should 'set things in motion by assembling a favourable and serious party which would solemnly request from us, as the guarantor of their former liberty, our intervention and assistance'. In the meantime, she needed the acquiescence of Vienna. Berlin had to be prevented from acting against Russia, 'for at least as long as our party in Poland does not augment its strength itself in people and means'. Through the restoration of 'the former Polish liberty' or through a new partition if the King of Prussia proved greedy, Poland would be incapable of troubling Russia again. So Potemkin was to encourage Feliks Potocki to recruit supporters and keep them close. Whether the Commonwealth had a king restrained by hetmans, or no king at all, was of minor importance to the empress. She did want as many official protests as possible, 'in the most expressive and powerful words', against the 'hereditary monarchy established by the Constitution of 3 May'. They should appeal to her as the guarantor of the Commonwealth's cardinal laws. Above all, she needed 'the formation of free confederacies, which in representing the nation, would declare illegal everything that has been or will be done in Warsaw'. It remained to be decided whether their formation should precede or follow the entry of Russian armies into Poland. The former was preferable, but the Polish government and army might take repressive steps against the lovers of liberty.[10]

Running through these points is a theme familiar from the 1764 royal election – the need to have Russian forces invited into Poland to restore and protect Polish liberties. Catherine had no intention of tolerating a well-governed Commonwealth. Indeed, her concern for the malcontents' safety indicates that she realized the Polish state was already growing stronger. Especially after the Constitution had strengthened royal authority, she had lost all faith in the willingness of Stanisław

August to deliver her wishes. She did not want to negotiate with a fellow monarch, but to support one party in Poland against the other. The king underestimated the tsaritsa's determination to destroy the Constitution.[11] He and others in the leadership should have focused on negotiations sooner, while simultaneously preparing for war. Stanisław August was not wrong, however, to believe that assuaging domestic opposition – by overtures to leading malcontents, applying the brakes to radical social reforms, and demonstrating the strong support for the Constitution among the szlachta – would make it much more difficult for Russia to justify military intervention. Such difficulty could perhaps buy time to consolidate the new constitutional order further. Even the elaborate celebrations of the anniversary, risible in hindsight, served a geopolitical purpose.[12] Using such arguments, the king, the primate and their allies succeeded in at least neutralizing many critics of the Constitution.[13] The responsibility for facilitating the Russian invasion of the spring of 1792 rests squarely with the principal counter-revolutionary confederates. They can be called traitors to their country.

Treason is an emotive word. It was used freely at the time, by both sides, and has been used freely ever since, by all sides. Polish political discourse has long used '*targowica!*' as a symbol of treason, a handy insult to hurl at political opponents. It is therefore all the more important to appreciate the legal position in 1791–92. Since 1588 treason had encompassed, relatively precisely by early modern legal standards, 'rebellions in consort with the enemy, revealing state secrets to the enemy, surrendering a castle in cahoots with the enemy, breaching an international alliance, as well as all kinds of offences "*contra Rempublicam*"'. The year 1601 saw the addition of service in the army of a foreign power at war with the Commonwealth. From 1776 the recruitment, abduction and sale of persons to foreign powers, and accepting pensions from foreign courts with the aim of betraying the Fatherland, were also classed as treasonable crimes. The condition attached to the latter offence made it virtually unprovable. When Adam Poniński was accused of treason in 1789, the sejm changed the law to remove this condition, and retrospectively applied the amended law to his conduct in 1772–75. The 1791 law on the sejm court widened the concept further.[14] However complex the motives of the leading confederates, their actions described below easily fit within the definitions of 1588 and 1601. It is not necessary to invoke laws passed by the contested sejms of 1776 and 1788–92 to conclude that Feliks Potocki, Ksawery Branicki, Seweryn Rzewuski, Szymon Kossakowski, Józef Kossakowski and their closest associates committed treason.

The marshal of the Crown Confederacy of Targowica was Feliks Potocki. A slow learner, probably dyslexic and dyspraxic, with a short attention span, he was loved as a child by his mother, but often berated and beaten by his father. At the threshold of adulthood he was traumatized. In October 1770 Feliks defied his father Franciszek Salezy, the possessor of the greatest landed fortune in the Commonwealth, to marry Gertruda Komorowska, the sixteen-year-old daughter of a neighbouring, moderately wealthy nobleman. Soon afterwards Franciszek Salezy had the probably pregnant Gertruda kidnapped by his Cossacks as she tried to escape being confined in a convent, while the cowed Feliks petitioned an ecclesiastical court for annulment of the marriage. Gertruda disappeared into a river. The following year Franciszek Salezy died, leaving his immense riches to his broken son. During the annulment proceedings, the truth of Gertruda's death emerged. A commission of the sejm delegation sentenced some of Franciszek Salezy's servants in absentia for her abduction and drowning. In recognition of his father's 'inattention', Feliks paid substantial compensation to the Komorowskis.

In 1774 Potocki remarried. He espoused his parents' original choice: the talented Józefina Amalia, the daughter and heiress of Jerzy Mniszech and Maria Amalia, née Brühl. Initially he showed her affection, but within a few years it was clear that their union was neither faithful nor happy. He sold off most of her dowry, along with Galician properties of his own, and moved his main residence to Tulczyn, far to the east. Here he erected a classical palace. The frieze above the seventeen-bay facade read 'So that it would always be a free and virtuous residence – erected in the year 1782'. Tulczyn became the thriving capital of a latifundium populated by about a quarter of a million subjects, which brought in rising annual revenues of between a million and a half and three million złotys. Serfs formed what was reputedly a good orchestra, which served the Tulczyn '*operhauz*'. The conductor, Fedorek Kowalczuk, was passed off as 'Teodoro Ferrari'. Potocki liked to play the good master. He was said to be fond of Ukrainian peasant weddings. In 1786 he won plaudits for keeping his serfs nourished and peaceable when famine and rebellion threatened the Ukraine. Order was assured by his Cossacks and militia, the latter recruited from noble leaseholders of his lands.

After Potocki bought the command of the Ukrainian-Podolian division of the Crown army from Józef Stempkowski in 1784, he offered the Commonwealth a regiment with twenty-four artillery pieces. His troops' uniform was based on the national costume. Before the sejm of 1788 he bought the generalship of the Crown artillery from Aloysius Brühl, and resigned as Palatine of Ruthenia. His 'return to the Knightly Estate' enabled him to be elected envoy for Bracław in 1788. However, the popularity augmented by this democratic gesture vanished when he refused to swim with the Russophobic tide. While commanding the Commonwealth's forces in the Ukraine, he attracted opprobrium by manifesting his friendly relations with Russian generals during the rebellion scare of 1789. Stung by the criticism, in November of that year he departed for Vienna. Kept informed by correspondents, he maintained a hostile stance towards the Polish Revolution.

Potocki reached the conclusion, not bereft of logic, that to survive, the Commonwealth must either be a Russian protectorate or a weak, decentralized federation of three centrifugal provinces. A strong monarchy, especially if it was hereditary, would soon destroy liberty, not least because the Polish szlachta was less able to defend its freedom than the entire English people. On the other hand, a powerless monarch was a costly irrelevance. Without a king, opined Potocki, 'authority and liberty would not always be at war'.[15] He confined this ultra-republican world view to the Commonwealth; he supported neither the conversion of republic into monarchy at home, nor monarchy into republic abroad. His views coincided with his personal interests as the heir of an enormous fortune and a mythologized family tradition. Urged to accept the Constitution of 3 May, he haughtily told Stanisław August: 'deign for your own glory and the good of the Fatherland to restore the freedom which the day of the Third of May tore away'.[16] He had earlier written to Potemkin on 14 May 1791, proposing to confederate the eastern palatinates, to be followed by others in turn. The local confederacies would come together in a federative government headed by a president elected for a two-year term. Catherine II had less interest in the exact form of government (as long as it was weak) than in the welcome news that Poland's richest magnate would lead her counter-revolution.[17] He may even have asked her, in the event that the Commonwealth would not regain its liberty, that this 'unhappy father with ten children could choose for his fatherland the countries which have the happiness to be ruled by the great Catherine'.[18]

Potocki's determination was repeatedly stiffened by Seweryn Rzewuski, who joined him in Vienna in 1790. Seweryn had begun his career under the wing of his father Wacław with whom he shared captivity in Russia. Soon after their triumphant return, Seweryn succeeded his father as Crown field hetman. At the sejms of 1773–75 and 1776 he vituperatively attacked Stanisław August. He was a pillar of the 'Galician party' of opposition magnates, not least because of the location of his estates. These links were strengthened in 1782 when he married

Konstancja, née Lubomirska, acquiring three Potocki brothers-in-law. At that year's sejm he threatened recourse to foreign aid. He sought it in 1788–89, only to be rebuffed by both Vienna and Berlin. More inflexible than Potocki, Rzewuski was fixated on restoring the hetmans' former powers and free royal elections. Unlike Potocki, whose Russophilia never wavered, Rzewuski definitively reoriented himself towards St Petersburg only in 1790.

First Potocki, then Rzewuski arrived in Jassy in mid-October 1791, hoping to plan their counterstroke with Potemkin. However, the feverish and restless prince of Taurida had just left town; he died by a desolate Moldavian roadside on 16 October 1791, in the arms of his beloved niece Aleksandra Branicka. To the last he had juggled his plans regarding the Commonwealth, all of which ultimately aimed at an appanage of his own, whether in Poland or Moldavia. Such a principality would have been a haven when Tsarevich Paul ascended the throne. Potemkin was prepared to support a confederacy led by Branicki and Potocki, but also to wage a religious war at the head of his Cossacks and, if need be, to agree a further partition. His death provided Branicki with the excuse to depart Warsaw, so he could sort out his wife's inheritance. The king reluctantly agreed to the hetman's request for leave. Although Potocki and Rzewuski manifested their opposition to the Polish Revolution publicly, while Branicki procrastinated, it was the latter who enjoyed real influence at the Russian court. Contrary to the opinion that his stock plummeted after Potemkin's death, the bereaved Catherine remained solicitous for 'Sasha' and her husband. When the malcontent leaders were back in Jassy, Aleksandr Bezborodko assured them of the empress's support for their planned confederacy. He even agreed to a Russian army of 100,000, but was careful not to endorse any of their divergent projects for the future system of government in Poland.[19]

Potocki was not focused wholly on politics. On 6 December 1791, at a ball in Jassy, he was smitten by Sophie, the wife of Józef de Witte, commandant of Kamieniec Podolski. Of Greek origin, 'Dudu' had been a teenage courtesan in Istanbul. In 1777 she was effectively purchased by Karol Boscamp, a Polish diplomat of Dutch origin, who brought her to Poland. She won Witte's affections and married him. Having taken Warsaw society by storm, during the 1780s she conquered other European cities. In the spring of 1791 she began an affair with Potemkin. The prince of Taurida soon tired of her, but shortly after his death Feliks and Sophie became lovers. The effect on him was startling: 'the murmurer has become a chatterbox'.[20] This extraordinary story merits pursuing to its end. In 1793, following the collapse of his plans, and having consigned his children and latifundium to his wife's care, Feliks and Sophie settled in Hamburg. After the third partition, he returned to Tulczyn, was joined by Sophie and created a gorgeous park in her honour. Following two expensive annulments, they married in 1798. Happiness proved elusive; she cheated on him with his own eldest son. After Feliks's death in 1805, Sophie ditched her stepson and gained control of most of her late husband's fortune. Fifteen years later, however, her own son ejected her from Tulczyn and in 1822 she died in Berlin after a painful illness.[21] Let us return to 1791.

News of Polish magnates supplicating the empress's generals and ministers in Jassy provoked angry scenes in the sejm. Feliks's cousins and the king were unable to calm the mood. At the end of October 1791 the sejm ordered Potocki and Rzewuski to swear an oath to the Constitution and return to duty within three months. Royalists were to the fore in denouncing the magnates in Jassy. As the deadline approached, both Potocki and Rzewuski declared their implacable opposition to the Constitution. The king pleaded with Feliks to relent. His letter was delivered by Stanisław Kostka Potocki, who tearfully tried to win over his equally lachrymose cousin, but the effort achieved nothing. After a stormy debate, on 27 January 1792 the sejm deprived Feliks Potocki and Rzewuski of their ranks. It also abolished the field hetmanships – the Lithuanian one was vacant anyway.

From Jassy, Branicki returned to Warsaw. There he sought to lay a smokescreen of innocence across the malcontents' intentions, while also trying to mobilize his clients, especially in the National Cavalry. Vouched for by Ignacy Potocki and Kołłątaj and having pledged not to act against the Constitution, on 12 March he obtained further leave of absence from the king. This time he headed for St Petersburg. By the time he arrived, the empress had graciously received the others, and the wheels of military intervention were in motion.

The empress's Council of State discussed the situation in Poland on 9 April 1792. According to reports which reached the Swedish ambassador, it was a stormy meeting. The empress's young favourite Platon Zubov argued for immediate military intervention. He and others hoped to acquire latifundia following the annexation of vast territories. Their rival, Bezborodko, is sometimes optimistically cast as the man who might have saved the Commonwealth from Catherine's wrath and Zubov's greed, if only negotiations had been commenced early and pursued vigorously.[22] In fact, for all the animosity between Zubov and Bezborodko, their differences were of degree. The latter preferred a more thoroughly prepared intervention, supported by key Polish-Lithuanian politicians, and with the acquiescence of Vienna and Berlin. At times Bezborodko took the lead in arguing for a partition; at others – Zubov. Prussian diplomats had already picked up hints, including leaked notes and despatches, about the possibility of a new partition. Frederick William feared, however, that it might be too good to be true. Austria, needing Prussian support in the imminent war against revolutionary France, was in no position to oppose Russia. Leopold II had seen this coming. In February he had agreed to dilute the part of the Pillnitz declaration favourable to Poland – substituting an indefinite for a definite article before the words 'free constitution'. His death on 1 March, and the accession of his son Francis as King of Hungary and Bohemia, accelerated the existing drift in Austrian policy. On 12 April (well before any communication from St Petersburg could reach Vienna) the elderly Chancellor Kaunitz, who until mid-March had been pressing for the Saxon succession in Poland, tersely conceded that the Russians could do more or less what they liked there.

Faced with a divided council on 9 April, the empress endorsed Bezborodko's insistence on consulting Austria and Prussia. However, she did not bother to wait for the replies from the courts of Vienna and Berlin, or for answers from key Polish-Lithuanian senators. She delegated these tasks to Bezborodko, except for the letter to the primate, which she dictated herself. In all, almost ninety politicians were identified by Bulgakov and Szymon Kossakowski as probable or potential supporters. Some of them had long been in the embassy's pay; others would resist the temptation. Military operations in the Commonwealth would go ahead anyway, and the malcontents would form a confederacy. If they could muster significant support among the szlachta, so much the better. If not, Catherine was confident her forces would prevail.

The first malcontent to reach the banks of the Neva was Szymon Kossakowski. The erstwhile Barist raider had been reconciled with the king in 1775. However, in 1790 he enlisted in the Russian army with the rank of major-general. The combination of his military experience and talent, inside knowledge of the Commonwealth and its armies, and his friendship with Zubov, gained him the command of one of the four Russian corps that marched into the Grand Duchy of Lithuania in May 1792. Szymon co-ordinated his actions with his elder brother Józef. The Bishop of Livonia stayed first in Warsaw, then in Wilno, dissimulating until the last moment. Together they planned to rule the Grand Duchy in their own interests, and woe to anyone who stood in their way. No longer would the Kossakowskis' vaulting ambitions outrun their means.

The empress dictated the essence of the twenty-three principles regarding the intervention, supposedly agreed among the malcontents. Russia would guarantee a restored republican form of government, enshrining the *liberum veto*, a fully elective and almost powerless monarchy, and the restoration of the hetmans' powers as they had been under Augustus III. The express exclusion of the king from educational matters paid Stanisław August a backhanded compliment. The laws of 1775 would regulate the situation of non-Catholics, but all projects offensive to religion, liberties or the law were to be prohibited.[23]

The act of confederation for the Crown, signed in St Petersburg on 27 April 1792, opens with a register of the sejm's alleged crimes. These included seeking to draw Poland into war with Russia by spreading false rumours, extending its deliberations illegally and removing the rights of nobility from non-possessors. Those who had taken control of the sejm had incited the towns to follow the example of Paris, especially its clubs ('*klopy*'), and wantonly sown 'democratical projects'. This last accusation sat alongside that of turning the Commonwealth into a monarchy. Claiming to be acting on the instructions of their brethren, abiding in their homes, the signatories confederated around the Holy Roman Catholic faith, the equality, liberty and rights of all nobles, the integrity of the Commonwealth's borders, republican government, the laws of union between the Crown and Lithuania, and the maintenance in office of those deprived by the sejm. 'And as the Commonwealth, conquered and in the hands of her overpowering oppressors, cannot by her own strength raise herself up from slavery, nothing else remains to her, but to have trustful recourse to the great Catherine.' The attached supplication was still more servile in tone.[24]

Most of the others who signed the act of confederation were clients of Feliks Potocki. One was a client of Rzewuski. Another was close to both Potocki and Branicki. The company was completed by the maverick republican Jan Suchorzewski, who on 3 May 1792 hosted a banquet parodying the celebrations of the anniversary of the Constitution. Szymon Kossakowski would confederate the Grand Duchy of Lithuania. Potocki became marshal of the Crown confederacy. He was aided by the two hetmans as regimentaries, Dyzma Bończa Tomaszewski (who had authored one of the fiercest pamphlets against the Constitution) as secretary, and the other nine as councillors.[25]

If Catherine II had any doubts at all over invading the Commonwealth in the spring of 1792, these traitors helped her to overcome them. They gave her the figleaf she wanted. The declaration handed by Bulgakov to Chreptowicz on 18 May added further justifications. They included a strong confessional aspect linked to the panic of 1789 – St Petersburg complained of the persecution of Orthodox faithful, especially the incarceration of clergymen, and even of the violation of the embassy chapel. Russian subjects in Poland had been harassed, falsely accused of fomenting rebellion and locked up. Other aspects were geopolitical: the Commonwealth had sided with the Porte and sought its alliance against Russia. It had prevented the movement of supplies and troops via right-bank Ukraine. Last but not least, the empress's name had been insulted in the sejm. Despite these grounds for war, the empress claimed her troops sought only to support and protect those Poles who stood in defence of their freedom against the illegal revolution.[26]

Having delivered the declaration to Chreptowicz, Bulgakov went to see the primate. The ambassador gave him a letter from the empress, dated 19 April, as well as a copy of the declaration. Catherine hoped that Poniatowski would side with the cause of 'patriotism' when

> . . . all good Poles, in uniting to remedy the assaults made on the day of 3 May 1791 on their liberty, and on their legitimate constitution, have invoked my friendship for the Commonwealth, religion and my treaties with her to defend and protect her against the unjust force which oppresses her.[27]

Having read this, the primate voiced the hope that all would be resolved without violence, and went to see the king. That night Bulgakov communicated the declaration to the Prussian and Austrian envoys, as well as politicians oriented towards Russia. The news spread around Warsaw.

The primate certainly consulted the king over the tone and content of his reply to the empress, dated 22 May. Hoping that the empress's resolution was not irrevocable, Michał Poniatowski sought to refute 'the ill-will of some malcontents':

> I am well persuaded that the current order of things in Poland, which is so close to the heart of the nation and which ultimately shows only reforms strictly subordinated to republican principles, far from being incompatible with the maintenance of this desired harmony, could even offer a more useful ally and friend in Poland.[28]

The primate remained faithful to his brother's concept of a Russian alliance with a usefully strengthened Poland. This case should have been put to the empress with renewed vigour immediately after 3 May. Perhaps, however, negotiations at any stage would have been fruitless, such was her wounded pride and determination to keep Poland weak. We cannot be sure, but by this time only sustained military reverses – such as those inflicted on her by Gustav III in very different circumstances – might have persuaded her temporarily to accept a strengthened Commonwealth. Perhaps not even then.

In the meantime a public response was required. On 21 May the Russian declaration was read out to the sejm. The public galleries were packed, and Marshal Małachowski had to demand silence. The king spoke. He began in a tone of dignity and courage. He then moved on to the need for negotiations – with Berlin, Vienna and Dresden. Any road would be taken, but 'rather by the pen, than by the sword'. He hoped that Catherine II could be freed from her misconceptions about the situation in Poland and that her 'tender heart' would lead her to refrain from the threatened severities. He counselled against over-zealous expressions, and asked the sejm to settle various outstanding matters. This was not the defiance many had been hoping for, but nor was it surrender – yet.[29] The rush to complete the sejm's legislation began immediately, with the approval of an Orthodox hierarchy, and lasted until the early hours of 30 May. Despite this urgency, debate was often vigorous. Among the unsuccessful projects was an ambitious reform of the Catholic clergy of both rites. The final project regarding the Jews did not reach the floor of the chamber at all.

The most important measures concerned defence. They had begun to be passed in the few weeks before the declaration was read out, following warnings from Deboli. Powers to sequester malcontents' property and commandeer their private militias served political as much as practical purposes. On 16 April 1792 the law *Readiness for General Defence* authorized a loan of 30 million złotys; a week later the proceeds of the sale of the Crown estates were declared as collateral. A pre-contract was signed with a Dutch bank, but it fell through. On 26 May the sejm increased taxes. Most nobles and clergymen would pay an additional 10 per cent of their income; exempted nobles and clergymen, as well as burghers, would pay an extra instalment of the hearth tax. Peasants would pay a half-instalment. Jews would contribute a double poll tax. Too late. The reduction of all salaries paid by the treasury (except those of ministers to foreign courts) did ease the pressure a little. The *Voluntary Collection for the Universal Defence of the*

Fatherland also had some potential. It was a similar story with the belated restoration on 22 May of the army establishment to 100,000 men (98,515 to be exact), from its 'temporary establishment' of 65,000. These were notional figures, but recruitment continued apace.[30]

A greater difference to the forthcoming campaign was made by the sejm's decisions regarding military command and political authority. The king gained supreme command of the army, the authority to mobilize men, money and supplies as the situation required, and the power to conduct negotiations. Only the conclusion of a final peace treaty was left to the sejm. The king was also allocated two million złotys for his expected expedition to the principal military camp.[31] The British envoy's despatches attest to the accretion of power to the king. 'I think if he be not, at present, he must, shortly, become master of the Country,' wrote Daniel Hailes on 17 April. A week later the caveat had disappeared: 'The hands of His Polish Majesty are now so much strengthened, that He may be said to be entirely master of the Country.' By 26 May the sejm was concluding its business in haste, 'on account of the Dictatorship given by it to His Polish Majesty'.[32] Other diplomats also noted the monarch's strengthened position.[33] The renewed 'republicanization' of the form of government after 3 May was reversed, as responsibilities were heaped on Stanisław August. In the event of defeat, he could be blamed.

The 'patriot' leadership nonetheless shared some responsibility for the conduct of military and foreign policy. On 5 June a War Council was formed to advise the king on logistics and strategy. Most of its members lacked serious military experience. Moreover, all envoys and senators had the right to join the meetings. Hugo Kołłątaj and Ignacy Potocki spoke frequently. The Council was often unable to keep up with events. Nevertheless, the king deferred to its recommendations.

Last-minute diplomatic efforts were undertaken. First came an appeal to Prussia. Chreptowicz gave a note to Lucchesini, and on 31 May 1792 Ignacy Potocki departed for Berlin. Frederick William II refused to honour his alliance with Poland. The pretext, already communicated by Lucchesini, was that he had not been consulted about the Constitution of 3 May. Adam Kazimierz Czartoryski achieved nothing in Vienna either. On 6 June Kaunitz instructed the Austrian chargé d'affaires to puncture the Poles' illusions that Austria would intervene, even diplomatically, on their side. By mid-June it was clear that the Commonwealth was facing the Russian Empire alone.

The two sides were unevenly matched. The passion shown by the sejm and the public in October 1788 for an army of 100,000 men had not been matched by a similar enthusiasm to recruit, equip and above all pay the necessary soldiers. The infantry was under-represented by contemporary standards in relation to the cavalry, and this disproportion was still greater in reality than in the nominal establishment. On the other hand, the noble nation was overcoming its long-standing fears of the military as a threat to its liberty and property. The summer manoeuvres of 1791 proved a great success with the public. Izabela Czartoryska strove to arouse patriotic feelings among soldiers and spectators alike during the exercises of the Lesser Poland division, which took place close to Puławy. Nevertheless, plenty of less glamorous work remained to be done, if the army was to be capable of repelling an invasion.[34]

At the start of hostilities, the actual number of soldiers maintained by the Commonwealth has been estimated at between 57,000 and 65,000. About 45,000 could be fielded. The Commonwealth's army comprised two unequal corps, for the Crown and Grand Duchy of Lithuania respectively. *Toutes proportions gardées*, the Russians matched their deployment. The Polesian marshes, as in many wars before and since, divided the campaign into two theatres (in 1792, a wet summer followed the spring thaw). The Lithuanian corps, minus its guard, which stayed in Warsaw, amounted to about 13,500 men. Reinforcements of 4500 later arrived from the Crown. The numbers of infantry and cavalry were roughly equal, while just over a thousand served in the artillery. Most of the soldiers were untried recruits whose equipment left much to be desired. Their deployment was chaotic. As the war began, the two Lithuanian divisions, commanded by Lieutenant-Generals Józef Judycki and Michał Zabiełło respectively, were dispersed in weak contingents, with smaller units located closer to the frontiers. Overall command rested with Adam Czartoryski's son-in-law, Prince Ludwig of Württemberg. He had served in the army of his uncle, the King of Prussia, and secretly served him still.

Stronger forces were deployed in the south-eastern corner of the Crown. The Ukrainian division of the Crown corps was about 17,000 strong. It too had roughly equal numbers of cavalry and infantry, and fifty-eight pieces of artillery. The divisional commander was Lieutenant-General Poniatowski. Prince Józef, born in 1763, had followed his father Prince Andrzej (died 1773) into the Austrian army. Poniatowski had risen to the rank of colonel and been wounded during the storming of Šabac on the Sava in 1788. In the summer of 1789 the king, who had long taken a special interest in him, had summoned Poniatowski back to Poland, and arranged for him to take acting command of the Ukrainian division. On arrival in Tulczyn, Poniatowski alerted the Military Commission in Warsaw to chronic problems with equipment, quartering, provisioning and training. His requests for reinforcements and supplies were seconded by the king, who wished to confer on him the command of all the Crown forces. During his stays in Warsaw, Prince Józef became the idol of the city's gilded youth. Hearts fluttered as his debts mounted. On 6 May 1792 the Military Council finally confirmed his command of the Crown forces in the south-east, enabling him to return to the Ukraine. He demurred, feeling his inexperience at this level, but his royal uncle insisted. From his service to the House of Austria Józef Poniatowski acquired a preference for disciplined regular troops, a cautious approach to strategy and a solid grasp of logistics. These factors competed with his personal bravery and a soldier's honour. He could only exercise limited authority over the Volhynian division stationed in the rear, only 4,500 strong. Its commander, Lieutenant-General Michał Lubomirski, a militarily inexperienced magnate, was reluctant to accept orders from Poniatowski. Further back, reinforcements from the Greater Poland division were slowly marching east. Finally, 2,750 men garrisoned the fortress of Kamieniec Podolski.

When Prince Józef got back to Tulczyn on 10 May 1792, he reported shortages of almost everything. Many officers were not yet at their posts. In the circumstances, he noted, morale was encouragingly high.[35] Poniatowski then carved up the Ukrainian division into three unequal parts. Two of them took up advance positions to the north-east and south-east respectively, but they were each too weakly manned to be able to take on a Russian corps unaided. This decision has been much criticized, but the point of the advance guards was to watch the enemy.[36] The first of them was commanded by Major-General Michał Wielhorski, son of the defender of the *liberum veto*. He had served alongside Poniatowski in the Austrian army. The commander of the second and smaller division was Major-General Tadeusz Kościuszko.

Kościuszko, born into the middling nobility of Polesie in 1746, was not yet a legend. The king had noticed a talent for drawing in this humble cadet and then instructor in the Knights' School. He sent him on a scholarship to Paris in 1769. Kościuszko remained there for five years, studying the latest ideas on fortification. On his return home, he could not afford to buy an officer's commission. Disappointed in love, he went back to France, and sailed for America, where he joined the Continental Army. His talent for field engineering contributed to several victories over the British. At the end of the war the Americans promoted him to brigadier-general and endowed him with an estate and a sum of money, to be paid in instalments. He consigned these to the care of his friend, Thomas Jefferson, and returned to the Commonwealth in 1784. Yet again he encountered disappointment, although he now had a romantic aura. Finally, in October 1789, the expansion of the army permitted the king to appoint Kościuszko to the rank of major-general in charge of the Greater Polish division. In 1791 he was transferred to the Ukrainian division, acting as its commander during Poniatowski's absence in Warsaw. Kościuszko and his 4,650 men were now exposed to far more numerous Russian forces.

The strategic position was perilous. Because of the geography of the south-eastern corner of the Crown, the best-trained and equipped part of the Commonwealth's armed forces was almost encircled by four Russian corps, totalling 64,000 men. The commander of Russia's 'Ukrainian Army', General Mikhail Kakhovskii, had the forces he needed to engage the Poles from the front while cutting off their retreat. The trap was set. General Mikhail Kutuzov's crack troops were to advance from the south, crossing the Dniester around Mohyłów, linking up beyond Winnica with General Andrei Levanidov's corps coming from the vicinity of Kiev. During the night of 18–19 May General Wilhelm von Derfelden's corps crossed the River Boh and entered the Commonwealth's territory. The others soon followed.

Poniatowski declined to risk a pre-emptive strike against all or part of Levanidov's corps, which faced the longest and hardest march before it could meet the others. He ordered a retreat and concentration at Połonne in Volhynia. With some notable exceptions, the retreating division received little aid from cautious landowners and a mostly indifferent, sometimes hostile populace. Few private militiamen joined the army's ranks. The long march to the north-west proved difficult and dispiriting. The enemy's Cossacks harried the columns, picking off stragglers. Casualties mounted, arduous patrols exhausted the horses, sickness spread, and vital supplies were lost. The king, hoping to open negotiations with the Russian court, urged his nephew to avoid a pitched battle. Doubts assailed the young commander. The resources and revenues of the south-east fell to the enemy. Nevertheless Poniatowski's decisions meant that the core of the Crown army, as well as many outlying units, escaped annihilation at the start of the campaign.

Poniatowski's fatigued division lingered at Lubar. The Russians closed in. From the south-east, Kakhovskii's vanguard inflicted significant losses on

Wielhorski's columns, before the Russian commander called a halt, unsure of the situation. Further north, a feint by Kościuszko sowed sufficient doubt in Levanidov's mind to buy the time for Poniatowski to move on. At Połonne, reached on 15 June, the fortifications and supplies were inadequate for an extended defence. Taking what they could, Poniatowski's forces set off again for Zasław, where Lubomirski's Volhynian division was stationed. The main Russian pursuit was too slow, but the division commanded by General Iraklii Morkov sought to capture the Polish baggage train. Near the village of Zieleńce, Morkov's division, about 11,500 strong, encountered around 3,000 Polish soldiers coming from the west, led by Major-Generals Józef Zajączek and Ludwik Trokin. Early the following morning battle was joined. The Poles defended a ridge along the road between Połonne and Zasław. Poniatowski soon arrived with most of his division, giving a total strength of around 16,000 men. Following extended artillery exchanges, the Russians successively attacked the Polish right, centre and left. Each time the Poles – cavalry and infantry alike – fell back, often in consternation, before rallying. The undaunted Poniatowski, having personally led the counter-attack in the centre, looked to seize the initiative. Morkov, denied reinforcements, decided to withdraw in good order, leaving the Poles in possession of the battlefield. However, after the Poles themselves marched on, two Russian battalions moved back onto the ridge, in an effort to claim victory. The Polish rearguard approached, but given the unfavourable odds, its commander, Kościuszko, decided not to restart the battle.

Zieleńce was not a decisive Polish victory. The Poles had lost over 800 men dead or wounded, as well as 300 horses. They had also used up much ammunition, especially for the artillery. The strategic picture was unchanged. The real significance was moral. Despite tendencies to panic under fire or when charged, the Polish soldiers had managed to recover their courage and wits, stand up to the more experienced Russians, inflict heavier casualties, and force them back. When the news reached Warsaw, spirits soared. It was, as Stanisław August told his nephew, the first time a Polish army had bettered a foreign foe unaided since the reign of John III Sobieski. On the suggestion of Prince Józef, the king established the order of *Virtuti Militari*. The first fifteen officers honoured included Poniatowski, Kościuszko, Wielhorski and Zajączek.[37]

The retreat went on. Lack of supplies, especially ammunition, prevented a longer stand first at Ostróg, then at Dubno. The latter was Lubomirski's divisional headquarters, but he had failed to assemble anything like the supplies required.

Lubomirski lost his separate command to Prince Józef amidst talk of treason. The Poles continued their march west, with Kościuszko's rearguard still holding off the Russians. With a further concentration of men and supplies in progress at Kozienice, located beyond the Vistula south of Warsaw, Poniatowski decided to try to defend the line of the River Bug, between the Galician border and the Polesian marshes. Kamieniec Podolski and its garrison were now cut off. The idea of using Kamieniec as the base for a rising was rejected; the town attracted more refugees than volunteers.[38]

The Poles could not hold the line of the Bug. On 17 July most of Kakhovskii's army crossed the river. The following day he sent his two best corps against the southernmost section of the Polish army, commanded by Kościuszko. The two other Russian corps prevented Polish reinforcements coming from the north. At Dubienka Kościuszko displayed his talent for field fortification. Polish troops held onto their positions on higher ground, even when a Russian cavalry detachment passed through Austrian territory and attacked them from the rear. Kościuszko's division was in danger of being surrounded. After several hours of intense fighting, he ordered a night-time retreat. The Crown corps regrouped to the north-west. Although the battle of Dubienka must formally be counted a Russian victory, the fact that the Poles had resisted a foe that was almost four times as numerous, inflicting about twice as many casualties as they suffered, boosted their morale (Map 5).

The Commonwealth's forces fared worse in the Grand Duchy of Lithuania. The Lithuanian corps, in two divisions, was outnumbered two to one by the 34,000 soldiers commanded by General Mikhail Krechetnikov, arrayed in four corps. The north-western corps, deployed near Dyneburg, was to take Wilno and then spread out as an army of occupation. The south-eastern corps was intended to march due west from Rohaczew, then south into Volhynia, reaching the Bug at Dubienka to cut off Poniatowski, should that prove necessary. Given the watery conditions in Polesie, this was optimistic. The two corps in the middle would start from Połock and Tołoczyn respectively and converge on Grodno. The first and larger of these two corps was commanded by Szymon Kossakowski – albeit under the eye of Krechetnikov himself. The Russian plan envisaged little opposition, presumably as a result of Kossakowski's assurances. This inflexibility might have handed the Lithuanian corps a chance, had its commander been capable of seizing it. It must be regretted that Kościuszko, inexperienced as he was at this level, was not given the command in his native Lithuania.

Most of the Grand Duchy's units, reinforced from the Crown, slowly concentrated in the vicinity of Minsk. And then they waited, while the Russians advanced. The commander of the Lithuanian corps, Prince Ludwig of Württemberg, remained at Wołczyn, on the western fringes of the Grand Duchy, whence he detailed his illnesses in every report. Amidst bewilderment and anger at his inactivity, his wife Maria (prompted by her mother Izabela Czartoryska) petitioned an ecclesiastical court for an annulment of their marriage. Intercepted letters would soon prove that Prince Ludwig was simulating convulsions and fevers in order to paralyze the Lithuanian army. Before his treason was confirmed, on 1 June the king sacked him. The scandal was initially covered up; only on 7 June did the inexperienced Judycki take over the command. The equally green general of the Crown artillery, Stanisław Kostka Potocki, freshly arrived from Warsaw, was continually in dispute with his superior.

Faced by two Russian corps, Judycki ordered a retreat to the south-west. This was shielded by the ferocious defence of the ford over Niemen at Stołpce by the cavalry vanguard commanded by the veteran Tatar, Brigadier Józef Bielak. However, on 11 June General Boris Mellin deployed his forces against the Lithuanians before Mir. While Judycki dithered, the Russian artillery shredded the nerves – and more than a few limbs – of the inexperienced recruits. Several units panicked and fled, forcing a general retreat south and west. Mellin failed to take full advantage, but most of the Grand Duchy could no longer be defended. Judycki, who had left his men behind, was dismissed. His replacement was Michał Zabiełło, a high-living envoy to the Four Years' Sejm. Although he proved more energetic than his two predecessors, he chose not to defend Grodno. His forces were taken by surprise at Zelwa, on the rainy morning of 5 July, and had to retreat further. During the fighting a nineteen-year-old captain, Józef Sułkowski, showed such bravery in holding back the Russians at the bridge, that he was awarded the *Virtuti Militari* cross and promoted to colonel. He would die in Egypt in 1798, as an adjutant to General Bonaparte. At least most of the Lithuanian units avoided encirclement. By the time they fought their last actions, fiercely defending the line of the Bug on 23–24 July, they had hardened into a serious foe for the Russians (Map 6).

On 2/13 July 1792 Catherine's council discussed Stanisław August's request for an armistice and offer of the succession to the throne for her grandson Constantine.

The arguments may well have been long and intense, but the outcome of the meeting proved decisive. The empress's negative reply reached the king on 22 July.[39] The following day he summoned an extraordinary ministerial council to the Royal Castle. The invitation of all the ministers present in Warsaw as well as the members of the Custodial Council gave the king confidence that a majority would endorse his accession to the Confederacy of Targowica. It did. Those who refused – Ignacy Potocki, Tomasz Ostrowski and Stanisław Małachowski – recorded official protests and went abroad. Kazimierz Sapieha may or may not have changed his mind. Before departing from Warsaw, he made a fiery speech to a crowd in the Saxon Garden. The crowd carried him through the streets, before stoning the windows of Jacek Małachowski's palace.[40] Stanisław Małachowski, Sapieha and Potocki would not yet have known that on 21 July the Crown confederacy had indicted them for crimes against the nation and its liberty. They would have known that they would be proscribed from public life, at least in the short term. Kołłątaj, fearing the angry crowds (as well as being held responsible for them), hurriedly left Warsaw after leaving his accession to the confederacy with a friend. When he realized that he too was persona non grata to the counter-revolutionary regime, he performed a volte-face. Safe in Dresden, he covered his tracks by scapegoating the king.

Great was the grief when the king's orders reached the Polish units in the field. Prince Józef obeyed them, but poured out his feelings to his uncle:

> How, Sire, could you hesitate in your choice and not prefer a glorious death worthy of you, with fame, to the remnants of your reign over the remainder of the nation – abased by intrigue, treason, anarchy and weakness? So it is! Sire, it behoved you to sacrifice yourself, to sacrifice us all. What sort of cruel pity is bought by shame and disgrace![41]

It even seems that Poniatowski considered a desperate plan, probably put to him at Puławy by Izabela Czartoryska, to kidnap the king, in order to continue the war in his name. Having failed to persuade his uncle to come to the camp voluntarily, the prince rejected the idea as unlikely to succeed, dangerous and politically counter-productive.[42]

Before reaching this decision, on 26 July Prince Józef heard that some Cossacks in Kakhovskii's vanguard, not yet informed of the ceasefire, had clashed with his own rearguard. He gathered twelve squadrons of cavalry and charged repeatedly, driving the Cossacks back with sheer bravura, until the Poles encountered the massed Russian infantry. Now it was their turn to escape. Twenty Polish cavalrymen died. If Poniatowski sought a warrior's death, it narrowly eluded him – until he rode into the River Elster during the Battle of the Nations at Leipzig on 19 October 1813. Together with Kościuszko, Wielhorski, Zabiełło and many others, he resigned his commission. The king knew that his weak negotiating position would be weaker still without the cream of the officer corps, and vainly tried to persuade them to stay. Prince Józef oversaw the dislocation of the Crown forces to new quarters in the west of the country, looking after his men to the last. However, his manifest contempt for the confederates and the ovations he won from the Warsaw public led the king to hasten his departure. Stanisław August made 'Pepi' a generous settlement – including taking responsibility for his debts, already totalling 20,000 ducats (720,000 złotys).[43] Many of Prince Józef's fellow officers, no less critical of their monarch's decision, had not the wherewithal to resign and emigrate.

The mood on the streets of Warsaw was volatile. The optimistic propaganda of defiance had maintained a belligerent spirit among the public, making this abject capitulation hard to understand. On the other hand, trepidation spread as the Russians approached the city. As prices soared, some of those with something to sell saw a good business opportunity; it was later recalled that the Russian camps resembled markets.

Stanisław August's decision has been debated fiercely ever since. Certainly, the Commonwealth now had no allies willing to offer aid. In the long run, the Commonwealth could not have won a war against the Russian Empire. At some point a Prussian invasion would have been likely – with a view to partition. However, the immediate military situation was not as bad as it seemed to the king. An 'alternative scenario' does not even require the calling-out of the entire nation-in-arms in the French revolutionary manner. By 23 July the bulk of the Crown and Lithuanian regular forces were regrouping and reinforcing. The unbloodied Lithuanian guard regiments were at the king's disposal in Warsaw. Fresh recruits were swelling the forces available. The chronic problems with provisioning and equipment were eased by the shortening lines of supply. Most importantly of all, the Commonwealth's soldiers had proved that they could stand and fight against the battle-hardened Russians. Conversely, the Russians had to deal with over-extended lines of supply after their long and tiring advance westward. Having suffered significant casualties, and having left garrisons in places to bolster the confederates, who had not delivered the promised military and logistical support, their numbers were falling. In sum, the odds were shortening fast. Although Małachowski and Ostrowski had already resigned from the War Council in despair, citing their lack of military expertise, those who remained did not yet favour giving up.

These stock arguments against the premature capitulation have recently been vindicated by Adam Danilczyk's research on Russian political and military correspondence. It transpires that the initial confidence of an easy victory ebbed during the two-month campaign, especially among officers actually involved in the fighting. Despite the exaggerated and boastful reports received in St Peterburg from the generals, Russian courtiers were worried that things were not going as well as expected. Platon Zubov, in a letter to Karl Bühler, the Russian political representative with the confederate leaders, assumed that some concessions would have to be offered to the king. Danilczyk has also discovered that some politicians in St Petersburg expressed pleasant surprise on hearing of the Polish capitulation. A longer armed struggle had been expected, as surely the Poles would wish to gain the best possible negotiating position. The one card left to the political leadership in Warsaw was the possibility – provided by a combination of battle-tested soldiers and public support – of continuing the war. By doing as Catherine wished at this juncture, Stanisław August gave up that one card and abandoned any remaining chance of setting the agenda himself. It is just about possible to imagine two conclusive Polish victories at the gates of Warsaw, which would have sent the scattered remnants of the Russian armies scuttling back home, enabling the Poles to set their own terms. It is also possible to imagine a bloody and calamitous defeat at either the first or the second attempt, as well as a Prussian invasion in the west. Stanisław August and his ministers did not have the benefit of hindsight. However, had the war continued for a while longer, it is at least conceivable that the king would have been able to open direct negotiations with the Russians. Instead, the empress did not have to negotiate with him at all. He followed her instructions.[44]

Stanisław August did *try* to set his terms of access to the Confederacy of Targowica. He hoped to take control of it from within and then negotiate a settlement that would preserve much of the Constitution and allow the 'patriot' leaders to return to public life. Potocki, Kołłątaj, Małachowski and Sapieha initially shared his delusion. Such moves were familiar in eighteenth-century politics; it was not surprising that Stanisław August acted in 1792 more or less as he had in 1772–73. The leaders of the confederacy feared as much. On 24 July the king agreed to follow the empress's demands, joining the confederacy together with the army. But he made no mention of the confederate authorities. Instead, he sent Feliks Potocki an invitation to co-operate in the 'calming of our shared Fatherland'. He then began writing to supporters, explaining the reasons for his decision, and still hoping to save some of the laws of the last sejm. Potocki publicly slapped him down: 'if there was still money, you would not cease shedding the blood of deceived republicans, in order to maintain your new monarchical power'. The king must submit to the confederacy 'as the head of the Estates of the Commonwealth, not as a hetman', for 'Poland is a crowned republic, not a monarchy, not a hereditary kingdom'.[45]

The king's manoeuvre failed utterly. Despite having done all that the Russian ambassador had demanded, and despite the empress's expression of satisfaction at his accession, Stanisław August had to do it again, in the manner desired by Potocki. Otherwise, threatened Bulgakov, he would be left to face 'the fiercest hostility of the confederates'.[46] With no leverage left, on 25 August the king signed a humiliating renunciation of the 'revolutionary Warsaw sejm' and the 'monarcho-democratic government' which had begun to 'transform . . . Poland'.[47] The two confederate Generalcies then showed him their contempt. They removed the guard regiments from royal command, issued a new vow for the Cadet Corps which omitted fidelity to the king, and banned the decorations for those who had recently defended their country and Constitution – a decision that greatly angered soldiers. The monarch's remaining authority crumbled. Towards the end of 1792, with a partition looking increasingly likely, the exiled 'patriots' in Dresden gave up waiting for him to find an acceptable compromise. To prepare the ground for an insurrection, Kołłątaj and Ignacy Potocki penned the pamphlet *On the Establishment and Fall of the Polish Constitution of 3 May*. They scapegoated Stanisław August for the disaster and whitewashed their own role, including the offer of the throne to the Grand Duke Constantine.

— THIRTEEN —
THE AUGEAN STABLES

The undeclared war of 1792 was not a civil war between Poles, but a Russian invasion supplicated and supported by a handful of traitors.[1] As the eight Russian corps had advanced, the Polish-Lithuanian counter-revolutionaries had followed in their baggage-trains. Branicki soon lost hope that the Crown army – even his supposed bastions in the National Cavalry – would submit to his authority. The attempt to form a confederate army proved a fiasco. Something like a regiment was formed in Podolia, mainly from prisoners of war, but many left its ranks at the first opportunity. The confederate councillors initially found it impossible to establish viable local confederacies in Podolia and the Ukraine. Most respectable citizens and substantial landowners had left. Several decades' experience had taught them that the Russian army was hardly the 'friendly' or 'allied' force depicted by confederate propaganda. So it proved this time as well, despite generalized orders to maintain discipline. At Targowica on 24 May, Adam Moszczeński managed to assemble eighty-seven petty noblemen, but could not take the oath as marshal of the Bracław confederacy, 'because there was nobody who could dictate the oath'.[2]

The confederates had begun badly, but things did not improve. Once Feliks Potocki had ceremoniously entered Tulczyn on 11 June, protected by 200 Don Cossacks as well as 300 of his own, he stayed there for over a month. He issued proclamation after proclamation, full of the same empty republican rhetoric as in the act of confederation. In some Podolian parishes, Catholic priests refused to read this verbiage from their pulpits. As persuasion and propaganda failed, forced contributions and quartering were used to bring a few landowning nobles into line. The Podolian confederacy was finally formed on 16 July. The fact that the palatinate of Kiev was confederated only on 21 July 1792 underlines the confederates' weakness. Even at this late stage very few noblemen of independent stature were interested; with one exception the Kievan councillors were clients of either Branicki or Potocki. The former had fewer scruples than the latter. In between his drunken carousing with Russian officers, the hetman had already resorted to intimidation in order to confederate the palatinate of Volhynia at Łuck on 9 July and the palatinate-in-exile of Czernihów at Włodzimierz four days later. Some later accounts may have exaggerated the scale of violence and pillage. Be that as it may, in the end Potocki had to follow suit – on 18 July he issued a proclamation, threatening citizens who refused to join the confederacy with sequestration. Anyone who gave information to the 'enemy' would face death.[3]

After the king's access, the palatinates not yet occupied by the Russians were confederated. Rzewuski and Branicki personally supervised the formation of confederacies at Chełm and Lublin respectively. However, the acts of confederation of most of the remaining palatinates of the Crown reflected a desire to stand by the king. Particularly worrying to the Generalcy was the confederation 'around the king' of the land of Warsaw in the Royal Castle on 2 August. Potocki wrote increasingly impatient letters to the primate in the hope of securing his and the king's co-operation.[4] Meanwhile, the Generalcy ordered the correction of the offending acts. For example, the Mazovian sejmiks of Liw, Ciechanów and Czersk included standard denunciations of the sejm in their amended resolutions. The latter included: 'with despotic declarations it not only forbade resistance to violence, but even to speak against it'. At Liw, a grand total of 147 nobles had 'signed' the revised act of confederation by 12 September, ninety-three of them by tracing the sign of the cross.[5] Although the acts of confederation of the palatinates of Greater Poland and Cracow did not depart from the Targowica formula, very few nobles turned up.

The Bishop of Poznań, Antoni Okęcki, received a summons to a confederate court for not keeping his priests in line. Chastened, he ordered prayers for the confederacy. East of the ceasefire line, many (but by no means most) nobles who had left earlier now returned to their estates and took the requisite oaths of loyalty to the confederacy. In all, the number of councillors of the local confederacies in the Crown approached six hundred.[6] But many were nominated in their absence, and such men often absented themselves from their duties. For the lands west of the Vistula, later accounts of a terrorized szlachta should be treated with a grain of salt. Despite widespread resentment of the onerous confederate regime, most citizens tried to adapt and restore something like a peacetime routine – the harvest needed to be brought in.

The situation was different in the Grand Duchy of Lithuania. Indeed, we cannot properly refer to 'Targowica' there, except as a generalized symbol of treason which entered collective memory. Szymon Kossakowski followed a more traditional procedure: individual districts would be confederated, and only later would they unite into the General Confederacy of the Grand Duchy of Lithuania. Three supporters proclaimed themselves marshals of the confederacies of Połock, Orsza and Brasław respectively, even before the Russians crossed the border. Manning these confederacies proved a problem. In the event just five local confederacies preceded the formation of the General Confederacy in Wilno on 25 June; besides the aforementioned three, the districts of Minsk and Wilno were also confederated, with some difficulty. The last district of the Grand Duchy was not confederated until 15 September. That said, after the invasion had begun, Kossakowski took care to buy support in each district, asking the advancing Russians to respect co-operative nobles while brutally punishing recalcitrant ones. This parody of the 'bottom-up' procedure, like the manifestation of the separateness and equality of the Grand Duchy of Lithuania vis-à-vis the Polish Crown, was doubtless intended to appeal to traditionalist sentiments. So too was the republican and Catholic discourse employed by both confederate leaderships (although it also used metaphors of light, Providence and order, mirroring much of the language of the Polish Revolution). The attraction was limited. No more than four thousand nobles had been pressured into joining the Lithuanian General Confederacy by the time the war ended.[7]

The man designated as marshal of the Lithuanian General Confederacy, Grand Chancellor Aleksander Sapieha, remained passive. His deputy, Szymon Kossakowski, carried out his functions. Although the Lithuanian structures appeared to facilitate the representation of local interests, the brothers Kossakowski made the key decisions. They brandished the stick far more often than the carrot. In most districts, punitive sequestrations, confiscations, levies and quartering encouraged noble landowners to participate in the ceremonies of confederation. As in the Crown, only the king's example significantly increased the number of nobles acceding to the Lithuanian confederacy; it had risen to about 14,000 by January 1793.[8] Wilno finally filled with nobles on 15 August 1792. Citizens who had sat out the war in East Prussia or elsewhere arrived to swear loyalty. Among the councillors at the district and Generalcy levels were many district-level officials – suggesting a degree of pragmatism among local elites. As in the Crown, those districts which confederated 'around the king' had to amend their acts.

They included Nowogródek, whose citizens had sworn to defend the Constitution of 3 May on 8 June.

For the brothers Kossakowski, revenge was sweet. Now it was Bishop Massalski who humbly supplicated his younger co-adjutor. To his credit, Massalski did plead for persecuted clergymen. Repression, censorship, intimidation and extortion were the order of the day. The Generalcy even fixed the exchange rate of the ruble to the złoty higher than in the Crown. This benefited the Kossakowskis, who had access to Russian cash, while reducing the value of those payments that were made to citizens. Many were not. Thus encouraged, Russian soldiers in the Grand Duchy seem to have had fewer scruples about indulging in random plunder and violence than their counterparts in Crown Ruthenia. At the local level some better connected and less scrupulous nobles also took the opportunity to settle old scores at the expense of their neighbours in partisan and abbreviated confederate court proceedings. The Kossakowskis' parading of the separate status of the Grand Duchy of Lithuania served their personal ambitions. Bishop Józef's show of Lithuanian patriotism did not prevent him from procuring a verdict assigning him the secularized estates of the bishopric of Cracow, which he had coveted long before the sejm took them in 1789. Comparisons with Janusz Radziwiłł, who in 1655 had tried to defend Lithuania from Muscovy before reaching a separate deal with Sweden, are misplaced. The Kossakowskis undoubtedly betrayed the Commonwealth, but they betrayed the Grand Duchy of Lithuania in particular.

The Crown and Lithuanian confederacies joined themselves into the General Confederacy of the Two Nations in a bloated ceremony at Brześć Litewski on 11 September. By this time it was clear that Stanisław August's attempt to subvert the counter-revolution had failed, although he encouraged his supporters to accept offices at district level. He often made known his critical stance towards the confederates' decisions and sought to delay their implementation. The Military Commission suspended itself on 20 August, having instructed the Crown and Lithuanian armies – now treated separately – to swear obedience to their respective hetmans. Many units dragged their feet. Branicki, however, had had enough. Once it was clear that the full plumage of the hetmans' powers would not be restored, he handed over command of the Crown army on 23 September to Rzewuski, who just a week later passed it on to Potocki. Potocki let things drift. Meanwhile Szymon Kossakowski, acclaimed as field hetman of the Grand Duchy of Lithuania by the Lithuanian General Confederacy on 25

June, began to restructure the Lithuanian army. The question of whether he sought a cadre for future expansion or simply a source of sinecures remains unresolved. After 11 September the highest domestic political authority rested with the combined Generalcy, whose sessions moved from Brześć to Grodno. However, many matters were still dealt with separately by the Lithuanian Generalcy in Grodno, and by that of the Crown in Brześć.

The best that can be said of the new order in the Crown was that the confederate courts functioned fairly normally. Little else mitigates the record. With the treasury empty, taxes were kept at wartime levels. The Russian army was ever less inclined to pay for supplies or damaged property. The regime restricted the movements of those who refused to accede to the confederacy and routinely opened private correspondence. It tried – ineffectually – to muzzle its critics, introducing preventive censorship and closing down periodicals. Critics became more radical, as connections were maintained with émigrés. Withering satire circulated semi-clandestinely. Warsaw remained a hotbed of revolutionary sentiments and was treated with deep suspicion by General Kakhovskii's occupying force.[9] The counter-revolutionary authorities had good reason to deliberate elsewhere. Burghers lost most of their autonomy, while nobles who had accepted urban citizenship were deprived of their political rights as a punishment for debasing their estate. The regime expelled the French diplomat Marie-Louis Descorches from the Commonwealth. Although both confederacies tried to present themselves as guardians of the Catholic religion and austere republican morality, most Crown bishops kept their distance. One who did not was Wojciech Skarszewski, the principal ecclesiastical pamphleteer of the Polish Revolution, promoted to Bishop of Chełm and Lublin in 1790. He succeeded Kołłątaj as Crown vice-chancellor.

Feliks Potocki sought to use his centralized power to realize his fantasy of a decentralized, ultra-republican Commonwealth.[10] By October 1792 he had concocted the outline of a plan. Three equal provinces would each have ten palatinates and thirty districts (each with an equal number of hearths), ten palatines and thirty castellans, eight ministers, and separate government commissions, watched over by a single weak supervisory council. The sejm would be instructed by prior provincial sessions, the latter having been instructed by the sejmiks. Perhaps Potocki knew snippets of Rousseau, as district-level dignities would be held according to a ladder of seniority, while suitable public service would also be required of ministers and senators. The army of 45,000 would also be symmetrically divided into three parts, each with a general of artillery, while the hetmans for each province would preside in turn over the respective military commission. This was not at all what Branicki, Rzewuski and Kossakowski had in mind. The mode of electing the powerless monarch could be left to the nation to decide.[11] This obsessively 'geometrical' plan reveals that Potocki, despite his protestations to be restoring 'former noble liberty', was in his way a child of the Enlightenment, with scant regard for local traditions and identities. Even the boundary between Lesser and Greater Poland would be redrawn to fit the Commonwealth's political and demographic geography after the first partition. This would leave Potocki without a rival in Crown Ruthenia.[12]

Still more startlingly, Potocki's tripartite division of the Commonwealth would correspond with three ecclesiastical provinces, each with an archbishop and five dioceses. Similar in spirit to the reforms discussed during the Four Years' Sejm were the expectations of the proportionate duties, numbers and endowments of the parish and religious clergy. The combined Generalcy announced all this to the clergy on 3 January 1793. Skarszewski let the nuncio know a little earlier. Saluzzo was especially concerned for the jurisdiction of the Holy See and the independence of the religious orders, but other interests were also at stake. The proclamation made no acknowledgement of the Uniates. To work out the details, the primate in the Crown and the Bishop of Wilno in Lithuania were to convoke assemblies, composed of senior clergymen who had sworn allegiance to the confederacies. This was a nod both to Józef Kossakowski's dualist plans and his expectations of becoming archbishop of Wilno in due course. Although the pope would be expected to approve the reforms, they were first to be submitted to the Generalcy.[13]

Michał Poniatowski dissected these plans. The primate had belatedly – on 8 October 1792 – joined the Confederacy of Targowica on his own terms. He refused to swear an oath of loyalty. Despite some initial hopes, shared with Rome, that the new regime might favour the Church, he had become scathingly critical of the confederates' misrule as the old year drew to a close. At the beginning of December he and the king defended themselves against insinuations of encouraging radicals and made their case for mitigation to the Generalcy. More from a sense of duty than in hope, the primate politely wrote to Potocki, particularly about the ruinous effects of Russian requisitioning.

Poniatowski vented his feelings privately. Before Potocki's 'irrelevancies and absurdities' could become law,

> Poland will for a long time yet be forced to tolerate the arbitrary and inconsistent government established by the Generalcy or its head, which in setting up the police in Warsaw has given the most shocking example of inconsistency and despotism ever seen in Poland, reserving to itself the approval of decrees which hitherto have not been subjected even to revision by sejms, and when it appointed as intendants of this police people who flee the police in almost all Europe.[14]

During a frank exchange of letters with Massalski, who had urged him to co-operate, Poniatowski pointed out the problems that would arise from Potocki's ecclesiastical plans. Moreover, a separate convocation for Lithuania within the province of Gniezno would contravene canon law. The primate also defended the king's policies and prerogatives, and denounced the lawless violence and economic ruin wrought by the confederate regime. Evoking 'disrespected thrones and altars in Europe', he warned against the 'unhappy spirit of novelty, with which France has not only brought itself to the most unforeseen straits, but has infected the minds of the whole world, which it seeks to violate'. After Potocki unceremoniously brushed aside Poniatowski's objections as mere details, the primate and the nuncio tried to mobilize the episcopate to stop the plans.[15] The king even wrote to the empress: 'the proclamations of the confederacy which concern the clergy are even of such a nature which could in part bring on analogous inconveniences to those of which France is the victim'.[16] To try and limit the damage, the primate drafted a point-by-point response to an outline of the Generalcy's constitutional projects. Above all he urged retrenchment, but he was even prepared to concede a form of episcopal election.[17] As it transpired, the plans had been overtaken by events.

On 16 January 1793 in Warsaw, Buchholtz announced that Prussian troops would be crossing into Greater Poland. The note cited the danger of Jacobinism:

> The spirit of French democratism and the maxims of that dreadful sect, seeking to spread everywhere, begin to take root in Poland so far, that the efforts of the Jacobin emissaries find strong support, and many revolutionary clubs openly profess their opinions. Greater Poland is particularly infected by

> this dangerous venom and hides the greatest number of zealous defenders of false patriotism . . .[18]

Perhaps Varsovian radicals were unhappy at being regarded as a lesser threat than their Greater Polish colleagues; we do not know. The Prussian units entered the Commonwealth on 24 January, the day after the signing of a secret treaty of partition in St Petersburg.

Before we examine this catastrophic new blow, it is worth reflecting on the domestic failure of the counter-revolutionary regime. In both the Crown and the Grand Duchy of Lithuania most nobles, especially of middling fortune, were immune to the blandishments of the confederate leaders. Only after the king's accession did more nobles unenthusiastically follow his example. For the vaunted restoration of 'former noble liberty' proved to be empty talk, whether in the Grand Duchy of Lithuania or the Crown. Everyday reality involved – in varying degrees – private interests, corruption, sequestration, confiscation, Russian occupation, economic disruption and onerous burdens of quartering and taxation.

Given the tendency in some quarters to see 'Targowica' as an understandable, if flawed reaction in defence of home-grown, tried and tested republican values, recklessly threatened by enlightened, cosmopolitan, monarchist modernization, it is all the more important to draw the contrast with the authors of the Constitution of 3 May.[19] Anna Grześkowiak-Krwawicz puts it nicely: 'While a "mild revolution" was accomplished in Poland, the counter-revolution was anything but mild.'[20] The leaders of the Polish Revolution abbreviated parliamentary procedure, won the support of the extra-parliamentary public, used threatening language against their opponents, and distributed conventional rewards to influential supporters. That was the extent of their 'plot'. They did not overthrow either the collective or individual liberty of the nobility. *Pace* Branicki, who included a bathetic register of his own and his wife's sufferings in the Volhynian act of confederation, they persecuted no one. Instead, they succeeded in persuading a critical mass of the szlachta to trust them, even among illiterate citizens at the furthest frontiers of the Commonwealth. They rode the waves of ongoing socio-economic, cultural and intellectual changes in the name of 'orderly freedom', and thereby began the deep-rooted, long-term, evolutionary transformation of the Commonwealth's political community – for the better. A client of Potocki's paid them this backhanded compliment: 'Enlightened citizens betray the Fatherland, and they have so confused the lesser citizens, that the shackles which they have put on the latter are understood to be their happiness, and it will not be easy to disabuse them of all this'.[21] The counter-revolutionary plotters discovered that their nostalgic slogans lacked plausibility. Ultimately, these traitors relied on the presence or threat of the Russian army to enforce partial compliance with their endless edicts – well before they were hopelessly compromised by the deal struck between Russia and Prussia in January 1793.

Catherine II had chosen the perfect moment to invade the Commonwealth. The two German courts remained enmeshed in their systemic rivalry, given a further dimension by the war with France. On 20 April 1792 the French legislative assembly had joyously declared war on 'the King of Bohemia and Hungary'. Francis was not yet Holy Roman Emperor, a factor that enabled most German princes to stay neutral until the French invaded the Reich later that year. However, the bellicose King of Prussia had eagerly honoured his alliance, and both sides anticipated an easy victory. Shortly after the news from Paris reached St Petersburg, the final orders were given for the two Russian armies to cross into the Commonwealth. Prussian diplomats started to fish for a partition. Had the war in Poland lasted longer, the King of Prussia might have tried to mediate, or else simply seized what he wanted. Only Frederick William's continuing suspicion of Russia persuaded him to accede in June 1792 to Kaunitz's proposal for the three powers to resolve the situation in Poland jointly. The old chancellor had by this time abandoned the Constitution of 3 May, but still hoped to prevent a partition. As it was, the early subjection of the Commonwealth allowed the empress to reply on 25 August that the Austro-Prussian offer of help was no longer necessary. In the meantime she had reached separate agreements for an alliance with both Vienna and Berlin, and extracted both courts' desiderata without revealing her own. This was, wrote Robert Howard Lord, a 'truly commanding position'.[22] Against the changing backdrop of the war with France, Austrian and Prussian politicians manoeuvred and schemed, not least for the favour of their own monarchs.

The Prussians were initially coy, anxious that openly demanding a new partition might prompt the Poles to throw themselves entirely into the arms of Russia. Such an outcome would have nullified their policy since 1788. So they put forward, in general terms, the idea of indemnifying the German courts for their efforts against revolutionary France. *Sotto voce*, it was suggested that Prussia would receive its indemnity in Poland, whereas Austria would take territories on the Rhine. Behind Kaunitz's back some politicians in Vienna were prepared to take the bait. On 21 March 1792 – even before the outbreak of war – Baron Anton Spielmann foolishly revived Joseph II's old scheme of exchanging the Austrian Netherlands for Bavaria and the Upper Palatinate, in a conversation with the Prussian minister in Vienna. Third time lucky? Berlin might even have committed itself in writing, had Vienna pursued the bargain decisively, although opposition in the Reich would have allowed the Prussians to renege. In Paul Schroeder's metaphor, 'Austria gave hard cash to a notorious swindler in exchange for his conditional promissory note.'[23] It got worse. Some of Spielmann's colleagues pointed out that the exchange would involve a loss of revenue, and also demanded two Franconian principalities, Ansbach and Bayreuth, which the King of Prussia had just purchased. This demand precluded agreement, while encouraging Berlin to pursue expansion in Poland. Kaunitz's long career was over at last. On 19 August he resigned and was replaced as state chancellor by Philipp von Coblenzl. However, pending either the acquisition of Alsace or Bavaria, Vienna wanted Polish territory as security.

Prussian and Russian interests coincided in preventing Austria from taking a share of the Commonwealth, even temporarily. In particular, the recent war against the Ottoman Empire had demonstrated the importance of Russian control over Podolia. Had Vienna demanded an equal share of any second partition of Poland, the idea would have been far less attractive to St Petersburg. As it was, the Austrian pursuit of the Bavarian exchange suited Russia perfectly. Although it was Prussia that lost the battle of Valmy on 20 September 1792, the consequences for Austria were worse. The victorious French followed the Prussians into the Rhineland before invading Belgium. They decisively defeated a smaller Austrian force at Jemappes on 6 November, and within a month they controlled most of the Austrian Netherlands. The prospect of Austrian acquisitions vanished. Vienna, unlike Berlin, did not have the option of withdrawing from the war in the west. The Prussian price for continuing to fight was all of Greater Poland and more besides.

In the end, Catherine was willing to pay that price, not least because she did not have to pay Austria as well. She had long been open to another partition – on her own terms. Such things were part of the eighteenth-century system of indemnification and compensation. St Petersburg had encouraged Berlin and Vienna to state their expectations; the Prussians did so promptly while the

Austrians dithered. By mid-September 1792 St Petersburg was pressing Berlin and Vienna to reach a deal over the Bavarian exchange. After Valmy, the empress's position hardened. She scornfully denied the German courts' right to any indemnification, beyond what they could conquer from France. However, any doubts she may have had about a new partition had passed no later than the beginning of December. On 19 December she issued General Krechetnikov with orders for securing her new territories. He should pay particular attention to Kamieniec Podolski.[24]

Robert Howard Lord argued that 'the Second Partition was not a measure forced upon Catherine II against her will by the importunities of Prussia, but the consummation of the Empress' secret plans and ambitions'.[25] Besides the Prussian threat to withdraw from the war against France, at least three other factors affected the tsaritsa's decision. First, a truncated Poland would be easier to manage. In November she had received a quarrelsome delegation of confederates, led by Branicki, Rzewuski and Kossakowski. They were clearly incapable of stabilizing the Commonwealth which, she genuinely believed, was a hatchery of Jacobinism. As for Stanisław August, he had shown himself utterly untrustworthy and continued to sustain 'hatred towards us and our armies in the Polish nation'. Second, the territories Russia would annex – without Austrian involvement – were of immense strategic and economic value. Platon Zubov and other key advisors had long been eyeing up populous latifundia west of the Dnieper. Third, Catherine had persuaded herself that these lands (and others, as far as the Bug) were historically part of her imperial inheritance, inhabited by a 'nation which is kin to the Russian in terms of descent and religious identity'. These people would gladly cast off the Polish and Catholic yoke.[26] Such wishful thinking about Ukraine affects Russia to this day.

The Austrian condition – an occupation of Polish territory pending the Bavarian exchange – gave Russia and Prussia an incentive to strike a deal speedily and secretly. After six weeks of negotiations they signed the Treaty of St Petersburg on 23 January 1793.[27] Russia dictated the terms. In return for its generous slice of Polish territory, Prussia had to agree to a far larger share for Russia, and to continue the war against France alongside Austria. The two courts undertook in general terms to facilitate the Bavarian exchange. Otherwise, Vienna was left empty-handed. The terms were communicated to the emperor two months later, when he was invited to adhere to the treaty. Francis II angrily dismissed Spielmann and Coblenzl, and consigned foreign policy to Baron Franz von Thugut. As the

Austrians regained Belgium in the spring of 1793, their confidence recovered. Throughout the summer the single-minded Thugut demanded guarantees from Russia and Prussia of Austrian indemnification, whether in Bavaria or Poland. Too late.

The Prussian share – renamed 'Südpreussen' – was substantial, about 58,000 square kilometres. The demarcation line filled most of the salient between Silesia and East Prussia. These lands were inhabited by at least 1,100,000 people. The Russian Empire gained more than four times as much territory – a quarter of a million square kilometres, inhabited by over three million people. Despite Austrian protests, the Russians took all the land right up to the Galician frontier on the River Zbrucz. The new border continued more or less due north until it reached the Dvina at Druja. The empress was not interested, for the moment, in incorporating Courland, where she was settling matters between the duke and his nobility.[28] Remaining to the Commonwealth were 215,000 square kilometres and perhaps four million people. The loss of the best agricultural lands, the principal centres of manufacturing and trade, and the natural channels to the Baltic and Black Seas made the Commonwealth completely dependent on its neighbours (Map 7).

It was hard for the confederates to grasp what was happening. At a session of the combined Generalcy in Grodno on 20 January 1793 a tremulous Feliks Potocki read out the note announcing the Prussian entry into Greater Poland. Jan Suchorzewski roared that everyone must saddle their horses and ride against the invaders. The following day Potocki sent a letter to the empress asking her to confirm the territorial integrity of the Commonwealth. He also protested that the confederacy was perfectly capable of dealing with Jacobins. As rumours spread of a new partition, on 31 January Rzewuski demanded that the general levy of the szlachta fight the Prussians alongside the regular army. However, that very day the new Russian ambassador, Jakob Johann Sievers, arrived in Grodno, and pretended not to know what the Prussians were up to. Four days later he consented to an official protest against the Prussian incursion, which had involved the slaughter of the entire Polish garrison of the border town of Kargowa. On 11 February the Generalcy issued a proclamation placing the szlachta and the king in readiness for general defence. However, together with General Otto Igelström (Kakhovskii's replacement), Sievers prevented both the regular forces from marching against the Prussians and the calling out of the general levy. Prussian and Russian generals took care to avoid mutual misunderstandings, facilitating a smooth and secure takeover in the lands allocated to Prussia. Prussian usurpations beyond the demarcation line agreed by the Treaty of St Petersburg then enabled Sievers to present Russia as the only possible defender of Polish interests. Having abandoned the idea of military resistance to the Prussian advance, on 15 March Potocki set off for St Petersburg on a pointless mission. There, when he began to speak of his fatherland, Catherine interrupted him. '*Votre patrie est ici*,' she said sharply, and stamped her imperial foot.[29]

The partition was proclaimed on 7 April 1793 in the annexed territories. Two days later Sievers and Buchholtz communicated it to the combined Generalcy in Grodno. Sievers also demanded the calling of the sejm; it was obvious that its principal task, as in 1773, would be to ratify the partition. Michał Walewski, deputizing as marshal for Potocki, entered a protest into the acts of the confederacy. His estates were duly sequestered. A few days later Rzewuski also protested. He departed self-righteously for his Galician properties, consoling himself that while the Commonwealth's territory was no longer intact, its liberty had been restored. Walewski capitulated and left Grodno on 28 April. With the leaders of the Crown confederacy absent (Branicki had not returned from St Petersburg), the Kossakowskis and their allies dominated the combined Generalcy. Besides enriching themselves while they could, the Kossakowskis suggested that the empress might take either the whole of the Commonwealth in union, or at least the Grand Duchy of Lithuania. They could govern Lithuania for her.

A new round of homages began. Krechetnikov promised the empress's new subjects religious freedom and the continued enjoyment of their property and privileges, provided they swore an oath of loyalty within a month. Otherwise they would have three months to sell up and leave. *Sujets mixtes* once again had to assess their priorities. For the moment, Kamieniec Podolski, a key Russian strategic objective, remained in Polish hands. Rzewuski ordered its defence. However, the new confederate commandant bowed to local pleas not to provoke Russian punishment. On 2 May 1793 he led the senior Russian officers to the city's cathedral, where he and the notables swore an oath of loyalty to the empress, before handing over the keys to the citadel. The garrison, nobles and clergy, city council, burghers and Jews swore fidelity in a variety of locations. A hundred and one gun salutes were fired from cannons, and the new garrison marched in.[30]

Sievers reported that Rzewuski fell into convulsions of rage on hearing the news. Much good it did him.

The city councils of Danzig and Thorn maintained their contacts with the Commonwealth to the end. On 23 January 1793 Thorn had closed its gates to a unit of the Prussian army, which requested permission to march through the city. The following day the gates were forced open, and Thorn was occupied pending its formal annexation. The Danzigers took note. With popular pressure stiffening patricians' resolve, the city defied an encircling Prussian force for four weeks. The Prussian army took control on 4 April, and promptly incarcerated 180 persons active in organizing resistance. The new authorities lost no time in carrying out a survey to maximize the tax yields. Although the city kept some remnants of self-government, the Hohenzollern monarchy refused to negotiate the terms of incorporation into the Kingdom of Prussia. Berlin insisted that Danzig was part of the territory ceded by the partition treaty – as yet unratified by the Commonwealth. Flags bearing black eagles were hoisted over the city on 15 April.[31]

The second partition disrupted the organization and governance of the Catholic Church. The Latin-rite dioceses of Włocławek, Kiev and Kamieniec now lay entirely beyond the cordons. Bishop Adam Krasiński refused to become a Russian subject, so the episcopal palace in Kamieniec was sequestered, and the diocese abolished. The dioceses of Gniezno, Cracow, Wilno, Poznań, Płock and Łuck were split again. Only the diocese of Samogitia was still untouched. Michał Poniatowski invited King Frederick William II to his archepiscopal estates, in order to negotiate the continuance of the primacy of Poland, and his administration of the Mazovian part of the vacant diocese of Poznań. Worse was in store for Catholics of the Ruthenian rite.

As the confederate regime's position crumbled, on 13 February 1793 the Generalcy invited the king to join it in common counsel, and asked the primate to ordain prayers for the Fatherland at this critical juncture. The next day Stanisław August officially received Sievers at the Royal Castle in Warsaw, and they conversed repeatedly in the following days. They had first met in London back in 1754. On 21 March they listened as Michał Poniatowski preached a strongly worded sermon at the requiem mass for the guillotined Louis XVI. Stanisław August had long compared his situation to that of the French king, and he was horrified by his fate.[32] Earlier Sievers ordered a search for Jacobins in Warsaw, and the royal dentist, Le Fevre, was among the arrested suspects. He was later deported to France.

The king sought to be more active in the diplomatic sphere as well. Two days after the Russo-Prussian treaty was signed, 23 January 1793, he wrote to the empress asking for an alliance and a guarantee of the territorial integrity of the Commonwealth. He offered to abdicate if his debts could be covered. They were already in excess of 30 million złotys. She replied enigmatically four weeks later, blaming the revolutionary sejm for what had happened, and hinting that his obedience would be rewarded.[33] Evident British displeasure at the imminent partition gave him the faintest glimmer of hope, and – in a reversal of the situation during the Ochakov crisis – the Whig press and parliamentarians waxed indignant against the empress. However, after France's declaration of war on Great Britain on 1 February, no aid could be expected from London. Despite Stanisław August's appeal to George III, William Pitt's ministry made no official protest to the Russian and Prussian courts. A Russo-British commercial treaty was signed on 25 March 1793, before the official announcement of the Russian and Prussian annexations. A year later Edmund Burke pronounced: 'Poland might be, in fact, regarded as a country *in the moon*.'[34] With almost no revenue coming in and, given the Warsaw banking crash of February 1793, no possibility of borrowing more, Stanisław August was utterly dependent on Sievers. One argument which the ambassador did not hesitate to use was the possibility of further Prussian annexations. Although the king delayed his departure until 4 April, he had to go to Grodno. It was Lithuania's turn to host the sejm, but the main reason was the Russian fear of Warsaw.

During the spring of 1793, despite receiving the official notification of the partition on 10 April, Stanisław August began to hope that something worthwhile might yet be saved from the wreckage. An oddly shaped Polish state still existed, including Warsaw, Cracow and Wilno. It would be subjected to Russia strategically and constitutionally, but within these strict limits much regarding administration, police, finance, trade and education remained to be decided. Even a vassal state might be governed in an enlightened manner. The king made common ground with two Crown general councillors, Fryderyk Moszyński and Kazimierz Raczyński. Both were advocates of an *état bien policé*. They drafted projects of legislation, communicating them to the king, who commented on them cautiously. Although the Commonwealth's situation was far worse than in the early 1770s, perhaps something could still be gained by a prudently moderate opposition to the new partition, while more could be lost by a refusal to accept that reality. Such were the arguments for the 'Grodno option'.[35]

At the suggestion of Bishop Kossakowski, the Permanent Council reconvened in Grodno to prepare the sejm. The confederates had sworn to preserve the integrity of the country, as Sievers explained to the empress. Nevertheless, only two Crown councillors joined the Lithuanians on 20 April 1793 in summoning their former colleagues. Not everyone who had belonged to the council of 1786–88 was alive, eligible, desirable and available. At Sievers's insistence, the monarch co-opted a further dozen councillors. Even so, the statutory quorum of fifteen persons was rarely met, technically making most sessions invalid. This included the one which on 3 May summoned the sejmiks to elect envoys to the sejm.[36]

Even without the proscribed supporters of the 'revolutionary sejm', turnout was low at the sejmiks held on 27 May 1793. Prussian and Russian soldiers prevented trouble. Sievers calculated that he spent an average of two hundred ducats per envoy in the Grand Duchy of Lithuania, and five hundred in the Crown, but his expectations of their obedience would be disappointed.[37] Although sejmiks were not permitted in the annexed lands, which reduced the overall total of envoys, the number of Lithuanian envoys actually increased. In line with the altered proportions of the Two Nations, seventy-seven envoys were elected in the Crown and fifty-eight in the Grand Duchy. Many of these men had gained public experience during the 1780s. Among the Lithuanian envoys, general councillors, and marshals and councillors of local confederacies were predominant, although some older patterns of patronage were also visible. At most sejmiks the Kossakowskis were unable to nominate their creatures. In the Crown, because of the ongoing decomposition of the Crown Generalcy, there were fewer general councillors, but rather more local marshals and councillors, many of whom had confederated 'around the king'. The king denied any role in the elections, but this seems unlikely, especially in Mazovia.

Signs of discontent were also evident in many instructions, despite the preparation of approved formulae by the confederate authorities.[38] Those of the Grand Duchy of Lithuania were, if anything, more critical than those of the Crown – the Lithuanians had more to complain about. Besides the emphasis on the unchanging terms of the Union, the Lithuanian Statute and separate magistracies located in the Grand Duchy, we find demands for the withdrawal of Russian troops, compensation for the damage they had caused, and even appeals to other powers for help. The Wilno instruction, for example, contained nothing critical of the last sejm or even the French Revolution, but did include this request:

> . . . that the armies of Her Majesty the Empress of All Russia would withdraw from the Polish frontiers as soon as possible, and also according to the very first declaration of Her Imperial Majesty herself and the later notes of His Excellency Mr Sievers Her Ambassador, according to the ongoing verification of all the damages done to citizens from the entry of the Russian armies into the frontiers of the Polish Commonwealth, along with burdensome and repeated forage, provisions and further contributions to this army.[39]

The district of Nowogródek yet again showed its support of the reforms of the Four Years' Sejm, calling for the restoration of the civil-military commissions and the election of land-court judges for four-year terms.[40]

When the sejm opened in Grodno Castle on 17 June, very few senators were present. The only Crown bishop there was Skarszewski, while three Crown ministers – Jacek Małachowski, Mniszech and Raczyński – resigned rather than participate in the ratification of the partition. Moszyński, who replaced Raczyński as court marshal of the Crown, took a full part in the sejm's sessions only after the treaties of partition had been approved. The enduring image of the Grodno Sejm is of a hedonistic blur of balls, parties and excursions. Fortunes were lost and won at the card tables while more than half the country was signed away. Entertainments there were aplenty, and suspicions of a staged farce have never been dispelled. Sievers's memoirs cast the Polish-Lithuanian elite in a most unflattering light – prepared to sell their very souls. However, they also record just how much trouble he encountered in forcing the partition treaties through the sejm.[41]

Sievers had expected some parliamentary resistance, but he was surprised by its intensity and duration. Sessions were prolonged by extended speeches, quibbles over technicalities and procedural manoeuvres. Only a minority of envoys and senators were entirely at the disposition of the ambassador, while most inclined towards silent and passive resistance – up to a point. Decided opposition came from various quarters. Initially, Stanisław August appeared to be behind a group of Mazovian envoys, dubbed 'zealots'. They were not the only ones. Some of the resistance from Lithuanian envoys seems to have been orchestrated by the Kossakowskis, fighting a rearguard action against their critics, and trying to force the ambassador to take them into account. After making an anti-Prussian speech on 6 July, Szymon Kossakowski received a reprimand from St Petersburg, expressly forbidding him to copy Branicki's former behaviour towards Stackelberg. Sievers punished Józef Kossakowski by encouraging the Prussians to quarter soldiers on the secularized estates of the bishopric of Cracow – which the Bishop of Livonia administered. When Sievers and Buchholtz demanded the formation of a delegation to handle both partition treaties, the sejm agreed to a delegation only for the treaty with Russia. Sievers initially went along with this, as it established the pecking order. His tool kit included sequestrations and stopping the king's revenues, as well as temporary arrests of obstructive envoys. So the sejm conferred plenipotentiary powers on the delegation regarding the Russo-Polish treaty. Ratified on 22 July 1793, this treaty confirmed the cession of all the lands taken by Russia according to the Treaty of St Petersburg. It also guaranteed the remaining lands of the Commonwealth, save those to be ceded to Prussia. The form of government was also to be guaranteed and hints were given of an alliance and a favourable trade treaty in future.

Partly because of the revulsion for the treacherous Frederick William II, partly because of Sievers's initial connivance, and partly because of delusions of support from Vienna, the Prusso-Polish treaty proved a far more difficult matter. The delegation demanded several concessions. Buchholtz provisionally agreed to some of these, including commitments to a trade treaty, as well as the evacuation of the image of the Black Madonna of Częstochowa to Cracow. However, Berlin insisted that the treaty be passed in its original form, not for the first time threatening further annexations. Indeed, Prussian usurpations beyond the line agreed by the Treaty of St Petersburg added to the pressure on the sejm – for a while they were even encouraged by Sievers. By this time Prussia's relations with Austria were at breaking point, as Thugut tried to keep up the pressure. Although committed to support the Bavarian exchange, Prussia in reality sought to prevent it. Fortuitously for Berlin, the exchange was opposed by Great Britain. A rapid resolution of the Polish question now suited Russia: it increased Austria's dependence on Russia, prevented further Prussian gains and kept Prussia at war with France. As the parliamentary scenes grew more disorderly, Sievers deported four 'zealots' from Grodno. On 23 September 1793 Russian troops ensured nobody could leave the sejm chamber, and Russian officers were present inside it. The sejm sat for several hours without a word. Finally, in order to forestall the entry of the troops into the chamber, at three or four o'clock in the morning of 24 September the sejm's handsomely paid marshal interpreted the silent response to his threefold request for authorization as consent. The treaty with Prussia was analogous to that with Russia, except for a promise of a trade treaty.

Two days later, the politically bankrupt General Confederacy of the Two Nations was wound up and replaced by the Confederacy of Grodno, formed around the king. One of its first acts was to restore the land courts in place of the confederate courts. Only now was it possible to deal with the new form of government. The framework was defined by what was justly called a pact of subjection, drafted in St Petersburg and passed with only minor amendments on 14 October 1793. Any change to the form of government would require the empress's agreement. The alliance, in which Stanisław August had long sought security for the Commonwealth, was accompanied by a formal prohibition on Poland making any agreements with other states without Russian consent. The Russian Empire would be able to move its soldiers into the Commonwealth (with a few formalities of consultation), and establish its own supply depots. Russian generals would command the joint forces in wartime.

The final stage of the sejm proved more constructive. The Kossakowskis were in full retreat, Bishop Massalski began to co-operate with the king, and Moszyński was in his element. Skarszewski, as the head of the deputation established to verify the confederate regime's disreputable decisions in private matters, saw to it that Józef Kossakowski lost his administration of the estates of the bishopric of Cracow.

The copious legislation of the Grodno sejm fills the final tome of the *Volumina Legum*. Most concerns domestic matters. The Permanent Council returned as a slimmed down, central point of co-ordination, denied the right to interpret the law. Subordinate government commissions were established separately for the Crown and Lithuania. The exception was the reunited Commission of National Education, which the confederate regime had split in two in March 1793 (mainly to access the post-Jesuit educational fund in the Grand Duchy). Rector Poczobut lobbied intensively to try and protect education. In the sejm, the ratio of senators and envoys between the Grand Duchy of Lithuania and the Crown was set at 8:10 – part of the 'political arithmetic' of a rational administrative division. Parliament would be unicameral. Laws were again divided into immutable fundamental laws, matters of state subject to three-quarters majority voting, and lesser matters for which a simple majority would suffice. The sejm would meet only once every four years. The *liberum veto* was thereby abolished, and parliamentary competences were circumscribed to fit the state's lack of sovereignty. So was the royal prerogative. Royal towns had no legislative representation, but burghers kept the privilege of *neminem captivabimus*, possibilities of ennoblement, and some of their reformed self-governing institutions. Civil-military commissions were restored with reduced powers. The civil and military budgets and establishments were contested between the king and Moszyński on one side and Hetmans Kossakowski and Piotr Ożarowski on the other; these matters were settled ambiguously and in haste at the end of the sejm. This mixture of solutions from the sejms of 1767–68, 1773–75, 1776 and 1788–92 was intended to ensure the predictable administration of the diminutive vassal state.

The system established at Grodno never had the chance to prove itself. Across the country, in manor houses, town halls and workshops, expectations had been raised so high during the Polish Revolution and dashed so low during the counter-revolution, that the subtleties of lawmaking and diplomacy seemed an irrelevance. The king, so it appeared, had abased himself and the Commonwealth by consorting with traitors, and for what advantage but his own comfort? Few could appreciate his patient endeavours to appoint more competent and honest men to public office. He might as well have been applying a watering can to the Augean Stables, for he was quite unable to divert the River Styx (something like this analogy might even have occurred to him, for a copy of the Farnese statue of Hercules had recently been installed in the ballroom at the Łazienki). The tsaritsa herself warned Sievers against allowing Stanisław August to promote his own supporters, as opposed to those who had served Russia well. To many, the whole state edifice seemed rotten to the core.[42]

— FOURTEEN —
IMMOLATION

On 1 March 1794 Wojciech Bogusławski's opera *The Presumed Miracle, or Cracovians and Highlanders* premiered at the National Theatre in Warsaw. The packed audience cheered the thinly veiled allusions in a rustic tale of virtuous sub-Cracovian villagers raided by brutish highlanders. An actor pointed at the hated Hetman Ożarowski in his box as he sang lines that threatened a non-miraculous thrashing. After two further performances the censors banned the spectacle. The Russian military authorities had earlier been assured that it contained nothing dangerous.[1]

Cultural life consoled Varsovians in the first months of 1794. Besides the re-amputation and re-subjection of the Commonwealth, the economy was in deep trouble. Many nobles and burghers suffered direct losses from the financial crash of February 1793. Prot Potocki and Piotr Tepper, symbols of elite convergence, saw their banks fail. Both men were also politically bankrupt – Potocki as a general councillor of Targowica, Tepper for mediating the payment of Russian bribes. The knock-on effects were felt by merchants, traders, artisans and hired workers. Warsaw's population shrank along with its prosperity.[2]

By early spring, it was evident that the radicalized French Republic was once again *en marche*. 'Jacobin' sympathies, maliciously exaggerated in previous years, now spread in Cracow and Wilno as well as in Warsaw. Sworn conspirators made headway among the guilds. So the domestic prospects for an insurrection grew, and communication with émigrés intensified. The pamphlet *On the Establishment and Fall of the Polish Constitution of 3 May* provided a compelling, if tendentious narrative of recent events. Safe in Dresden, its principal author, Hugo Kołłątaj, reinvented himself – less Richelieu, more Robespierre.

The pamphlet had been written at the turn of 1792 and 1793, when it had become clear that Stanisław August's gambit had failed and that a second partition was imminent. The patriot leaders in exile chose the path of insurrection.

Throughout 1793 the numbers secretly linked by a sworn association grew. The conspirators were, however, divided between moderates and radicals. The former gravitated towards Ignacy Potocki, and included many former envoys and urban plenipotentiaries to the Four Years' Sejm. They wished to restore the Constitution of 3 May, emphasized the need for careful preparation and to win over conservatively inclined nobles, and planned to rely on the regular army. Some of them envisaged co-operation with Stanisław August. The radicals included military men such as Jóżef Zajączek and Jakub Jasiński. They looked to Kołłątaj for ideas. The gifted writer Józef Pawlikowski, formerly an advocate of 'popular monarchism', was now a decidedly republican democrat. They wished to arm the entire nation and implement far-reaching social reforms at the expense of noble privileges. Many burned to punish 'traitors'. It became clear in the spring of 1793 that a temporary dictatorial power would be required. Tadeusz Kościuszko, whose reputation had soared since Dubienka, was the only credible candidate for the role. Kościuszko's own sympathies were fairly radical, but he would be capable of making pragmatic decisions.

The obvious source of aid was France, which had proclaimed a war of liberation. The obvious person to obtain it was Kościuszko, who alongside George Washington and sixteen others, 'who, through their writings and through their courage, have served the cause of liberty and prepared the emancipation of peoples,' had been made an honorary citizen of France on 26 August 1792.[3] So Kościuszko set off for Paris in January 1793. He received a polite reception, but no promises, and in August returned empty-handed to Saxony. No French revolutionary regime offered the insurgents serious help in men, weapons and money, until, in November 1794, it was too late. Meanwhile, terror became 'the order of the day'. This was partly a pragmatic response to war and counter-revolution, but it also derived from a culture of fear and suspicion present from the start of the Revolution. Under the impact of resistance and invasion, this culture evolved into a Manichaean mindset, dedicated to sanguinary epuration in the name of patriotic virtue.[4] The entire French nation was mobilized for total war by the oft-quoted decree of 23 August 1793 – even old men were commanded to go to the public squares to rouse the courage of the warriors. The advantages and disadvantages of revolutionary, patriotic *élan* versus soldierly discipline may be debated endlessly, but by the winter of 1793–94 the French indisputably fielded more soldiers than the monarchical coalition. They also managed to equip and train them adequately. Not all of the French numerical superiority derived from the *levée en masse* – equally important was the diversion of substantial Prussian and Austrian forces to Poland.[5] Insurrectionary Poland would suffer the odium of being ideologically on the French side without receiving any tangible benefits from the connection.

French help was beseeched by stretching the radicalism of the planned insurrection. Among Kościuszko's rash promises were the suppression of the higher clergy, the immediate abolition of serfdom, and the arming of the entire nation. Vienna, on the other hand, was reassured that no French-style reforms would be undertaken. However, hopes of help from that quarter were illusory. While Austrian policy in 1794 would twist and turn, it never departed from a determination not to be bettered by Prussia. If there had to be a partition, Austria would not be left out again. As usual, St Petersburg would play Vienna and Berlin off against each other. The Poles were on their own.

On Christmas Day 1793 a courier arrived in Warsaw. He conveyed the empress's dismissal of Jakob Sievers and appointment of Otto Igelström as envoy extraordinary and minister plenipotentiary, although without the rank of ambassador. Sievers might well feel aggrieved. Had he not effected the ratification of the partition treaties and subjected the rump of the Commonwealth to Russia? He had done it, moreover, without provoking a new Confederacy of Bar. His policy of stabilization just might have given the Grodno system a chance to bed down. However, he had enemies at the imperial court, especially Platon Zubov. The ageing, irritable tsaritsa felt affronted by the trivial concessions Sievers had made to the Poles in the last phase of the sejm, in particular, the restoration of the right of Polish soldiers to wear the decorations awarded in 1792. Fearing the worst, Stanisław August had to write her an abject letter of apology. He issued a public proclamation that the orders were prohibited; they should be sent to the Permanent Council. After he had left Warsaw, Sievers sent Igelström a coruscating summary of the Commonwealth's principal politicians, with the assurance that he could make them do as he pleased. One of the few persons Sievers genuinely valued was Fryderyk Moszyński, while he reserved his particular ire for the brothers Kossakowski. Igelström was told that 'in the end the confederacy did us more harm than good, through the injustices, violence and pillage which it permitted itself under our protection', and warned that should it be revived, its oppressions might revive the 'crushed party'. Sievers recommended his own course – 'between two rocks'.[6]

Some hope. Igelström showed the king who was boss. He controlled most of the monarch's correspondence and interfered in minor as well as major appointments. When laid low by gout, he summoned the Permanent Council to receive his orders. His network of spies and agents monitored and intimidated the Varsovians. He set an example of arrogant and arbitrary conduct to his own troops vis-à-vis the population, especially in the garrisoned towns. The maintenance of about 30,000 Russian soldiers during the winter of 1793–94 was always going to be resented, even if provisions had been politely and promptly paid for, but the crushing daily reminders of Poles' subservience to Russians could only exacerbate feelings of desperation. The largely unpaid, under-nourished and poorly quartered Polish units could not help but follow the Russians' example in requisitioning. Igelström also interfered in the trade negotiations between the Commonwealth and Prussia, to the latter's advantage.[7]

Did Igelström exceed his instructions or merely carry them out? If the latter – to what end? Perhaps the empress, or others close to her, did not want to stabilize the Commonwealth, but instead to provoke a minor revolt, which could easily be suppressed, and would justify a final partition? The evidence for this surmise amounts to a much later claim made by Igelström to Kołłątaj. Apparently he had received orders for such provocations from unnamed persons in St Petersburg, but had toned them down.[8] Zubov would be the usual suspect here, but Catherine II herself was open to the annihilation of the Polish state, should circumstances require or favour it. For the moment, however, she had no reason to gratify Prussian and Austrian appetites.[9] The fact that in April 1794 Prussia ratified a lopsided trade treaty with the Commonwealth suggests that Berlin was expecting Poland to exist for some time yet.[10]

There is a further argument against the idea of a premeditated provocation of armed revolt. In the spring of 1794 the empress's attention was focused on the Ottoman Empire, which revolutionary France was encouraging to declare war on Austria and Russia. The 'Greek plan' briefly rekindled her imagination. She had some of the Russian occupying forces in Poland relocated to the banks of the Dniester. This meant that if the Commonwealth was to remain securely under Russian control, its armed forces had to be reduced to the level envisaged by the Grodno sejm, sooner than planned by the Military Commissions. To ensure compliance, Igelström threatened to withhold a Russian guarantee on the Dutch loan sought by the Commonwealth. It worked. On 21 and 24 February 1794 the Permanent Council announced the reduction in the army establishments of the Crown and Lithuania respectively, to be effected from 1 and 15 March. The Crown army would be reduced from 23,500 to 8,500 and the Lithuanian army from 12,500 to 6,500. Most of the surplus rank and file were expected to be conscripted into Russian units.

This decision, along with a spate of arrests in Warsaw in early March, precipitated the first act of the rising. Brigadier Antoni Madaliński was not prepared to wait either for his cavalry brigade to be demobilized or for his own arrest as a sworn conspirator. On 12 March he led 1,200 men out of their base at Ostrołęka. The king, fearing this spark would ignite a conflagration that would consume the Commonwealth, paternally urged Madaliński to return to base, as if it was merely a matter of unpaid wages. On 24 March Igelström lost patience and demanded the mass arrest of suspects, without regard for estate, sex or privileges. To its credit, five days later the Permanent Council replied that it had no authority to suspend *neminem captivabimus*. It merely declared that Madaliński would be tried as a rebel by the court of the Crown Military Commission, pending a trial before the sejm court. By this time the insurrection was already under way in Cracow. That was where Madaliński's brigade was headed. It traversed a long arc along the new Prussian frontier, sweeping aside border guards and recruiting volunteers.

Kościuszko had decided to begin the rising in Cracow. Besides the proximity to the Galician frontier, giving him a safe approach, 1,000 Polish soldiers were stationed here. Kościuszko arrived in the late evening of 23 March and met the conspirators. The Polish army was already in control of the city, the Russians having marched out. The following morning, before a vast crowd on the Market Square, Kościuszko swore this oath, dictated by Aleksander Linowski:

> I, Tadeusz Kościuszko, swear in the face of God to the entire Polish Nation, that I shall not use the power entrusted to me for any private oppression, but solely for the defence of the entire frontiers [of the country], the recovery of the sovereignty of the Nation and the consolidation of universal liberty. So help me God and the innocent passion of His Son.

Those powers included the command of the national armed forces and promotions to all military ranks. Within two months, however, he would convoke and choose the members of a National Council which would act as a temporary government.

The acts of the Confederacy of Targowica and the Grodno sejm were declared illegal, thereby restoring the legal status quo of May 1792, but leaving the final constitutional settlement to the victorious Polish nation.[11]

Proclamations were issued to the army, noble citizens, clergy and women. The latter were enjoined to make bandages to stem the flow of blood from the wounds of their brothers, sons and husbands. The szlachta was told: 'Who is not with us, is against us.' Traitors to the Fatherland would face criminal courts.[12] However, the Chief (*Naczelnik*) of the insurrectionary nation trod carefully around noble interests. He dared not proclaim the emancipation of the serfs yet, but he needed tens of thousands of peasant soldiers. Trying to square the circle, he urged the revived Civil-Military Commission of the Palatinate of Cracow to promulgate the halving of labour services for the duration of the campaign. It did not. It merely appealed to nobles to treat their peasant subjects humanely and encourage them to enlist. Alongside the recruits to regular units, formations of scythemen were also organized and hastily given basic training. During an energetic first week in charge, Kościuszko gathered all the forces he could, and initiated the production of more weapons.

The Insurrection caught the Russians and Prussians off guard. Before they could assemble overwhelming forces, Kościuszko had an opportunity for an early success. He tried to reach Warsaw before Igelström's forces there could be reinforced. On 4 April 1794 the Polish army of about 4,000 regulars and 2,000 scythemen found its road north blocked at Racławice by a column of about 3,000 Russians led by Major-General Aleksandr Tornasov. The Russians attacked first. Some of the Polish cavalry scattered. Facing defeat, with Russian reinforcements on their way, Kościuszko led some of his scythemen and regular infantrymen in a counter-attack on the Russian centre; instead of advancing slowly in line, they sprang out of ditches and ran forward. With the advantage of surprise, they captured or disabled several batteries. A further attack by foot soldiers broke the Russian left and won the day. However, the road north was again blocked, this time by Major-General Fedor Denisov's larger force. Kościuszko moved his small, but victorious army back towards Cracow, and schooled the arriving recruits.

The battle of Racławice, although an undoubted tactical success, made little difference at the strategic level. It was, however, a moral triumph which still resonates 225 years later. Representatives of the entire nation, including its most numerous and useful part, had fought for their freedom – and won. It was as if

Article IV of the *Law on Government* was now writ in blood. Aghast at the reports, Igelström evoked all the horrors of the French Revolution in a letter to the Russian commander in Lithuania – Nikolai Repnin. Kościuszko made what he could of the symbolism. As he rode triumphantly back into Cracow on 8 April he wore a peasant coat – a *sukmana*. During the service of thanksgiving held in Wawel Cathedral he promoted the first scytheman to disable a Russian cannon, Wojciech Bartosz, to the rank of ensign in the regiment of Cracovian Grenadiers. A second peasant soldier was similarly promoted. Bartosz took the distinguished-sounding surname of Głowacki. Following Kościuszko's request that Głowacki's workload be lightened and his family looked after in his absence, his lord freed the valiant ensign and his family from all duties and endowed them with their small plot, along with four bushels of wheat, four of rye and four of barley, as well as a cow, a piglet and a sow. There is no record of Głowacki's ennoblement, but in later decades the idea would be absorbed into a self-fulfilling myth – whereas other nations abolished their nobility, the Poles ennobled everyone.

One hundred years later, Racławice was a potent symbol of a nation united. Official centenary commemorations were naturally confined to Galicia and in a more modest way, Poznań. However, the centenary of Kościuszko's death in 1917 occurred after the Germans and Austrians had expelled the Russians from the Kingdom of Poland. The Polish Peasant Party held a great rally at Racławice itself. By this time millions of peasants had become Poles. When independent statehood was regained, they became Polish citizens.

All this was unknowable in the spring of 1794. Kościuszko's next concern was for the families of the enlisted peasants, some of whom were being forced to make up their labour services. The Chief was still encountering obstruction in this regard from the Cracow Civil-Military Commission, although the commission of the palatinate of Sandomierz was more co-operative. When Kościuszko again made camp, further down the Vistula at Połaniec, he was joined by Kołłątaj and Ignacy Potocki. They contributed to the far-reaching proclamation of 7 May. Subject to future approval by the sejm, labour services were reduced by up to half, with more to come in the event of victory, and waived for the families of serving soldiers. Personal serfdom was abolished, so peasants who had discharged their obligations could move elsewhere. If they wished to stay, they had security of tenure. Lords and officials who refused to comply would be tried as criminals, even as traitors. This package might well have given large numbers of peasants an incentive to fight for their homeland. However, the implementation of the measures was patchy at best. The hoped-for mass mobilization did not materialize in the countryside, and the number of noble and peasant volunteers was disappointing.

Things played out very differently in the cities. The victory of Racławice electrified the Varsovians. Igelström's efforts to suppress the news only confirmed its importance. He seemed caught between uncharacteristic mildness and intensified repression. Sensing weakness, the sworn conspirators recovered their nerve and decided to launch the rising, before the Russians had the chance to seize the arsenal, disarm the Polish garrison and make further arrests. At dawn on 17 April – Maundy Thursday – the first shots were fired. Three thousand soldiers of the Polish army and many more ordinary Varsovians fell on the unprepared Russian garrison with pent-up fury. It was a bloodbath (Plate 31). Late on Good Friday, following the failure of negotiations undertaken by the king, Igelström managed to march a column of about 650 soldiers out of the city. Another 2,500 or so got out in other ways. The rest had been killed or taken prisoner. Some of them had tried to surrender and had been killed anyway. The Polish dead and wounded amounted to over 2,000, more than half of them civilians. Much damage was also done to buildings. Many of the wealthier inhabitants of the city felt a sense of shock at the popular fury. The violence provided an opportunity to settle scores at all levels.

The political vacuum was filled in the afternoon of 17 April. The moderate Ignacy Zakrzewski returned to the presidency of Warsaw, and General Stanisław Mokronowski, a royalist, took command of the regular armed forces in the city. On the other hand, crowds led by radicals were still roaming the streets in search of Russian officers and former confederates on Holy Saturday. That day, 2,148 Varsovians, starting with Zakrzewski and Mokronowski and finishing with 340 illiterates, signed (or marked the sign of the cross on) the *Accession of the Citizens and Inhabitants of the City of Warsaw to the Act of National Insurrection Headed by Tadeusz Kościuszko*. A Temporary Replacement Council was formed, chaired by Zakrzewski and dominated by moderates. Of the twenty councillors, fourteen were nobles and six were burghers. The only representative of the ordinary people who had overcome the Russians in the streets was the master-cobbler and sworn conspirator, Jan Kiliński.[13] Two days later a group of mostly young radicals, many of them writers, formed the Club of Polish Jacobins. This tension would define the city's politics for the next six months.

The sworn conspirators in the Grand Duchy of Lithuania included Court Marshal Stanisław Sołtan, Tomasz Wawrzecki, a former envoy to the Four Years' Sejm, the gifted preacher Reverend Michał Karpowicz, and Colonel Jakub Jasiński, a military engineer from Greater Poland, who had won the *Virtuti Militari* cross in July 1792. At the end of March the latter circulated his verse *To the Nation*, calling for the revolutionary overthrow of tyrants. Following the news of Madaliński's march and Kościuszko's oath in Cracow, Szymon Kossakowski ordered arrests of suspects. Jasiński got away. The first act of the Lithuanian Insurrection took place on 16 April 1794 at Szawle, well away from Russian occupying forces. Numerous nobles, who had come for the inaugural session of the Samogitian land courts, joined with units of the Lithuanian army and swore to support the Insurrection. The Szawle Act proclaimed their conviction that it was their duty to

> rescue the salvation of the Fatherland, regain the Commonwealth and the liberties of free citizens . . . to join to the exemplary zeal of brethren and colleagues our own holy ardour, not to spare blood and lives for their restoration of the Fatherland that had been torn from us, for the vanquishing of tyranny and the extermination of traitors . . .[14]

During the next few days the rising spread over Samogitia, and was joined by further army units. The insurgent forces advanced on Wilno. Szymon Kossakowski, realizing events were spiralling out of control, hurried to the Lithuanian capital on 21 April. Finding that his warnings were not taken seriously enough by the Russian commandant, Major-General Nikolai Arsenev, the hetman ordered further arrests and the concentration of the remaining regiments of the Lithuanian army as he prepared to confront the Insurrection.

Too late. During the night of 22–23 April several hundred regular soldiers, supported by much of the population, took control of the city with little bloodshed. Arsenev, who mistakenly believed he was facing superior forces, was among more than a thousand Russians taken prisoner. So was Szymon Kossakowski. He was found hiding behind a chimney in the attic of his quarters, and led in his dressing gown to the Arsenal, where he was locked up. However, the struggle beyond the walls continued until the end of the day, when a Russian force of 2,000 men, having shelled the city and burnt its western suburbs, retreated southwards. On 24 April, in front of the city hall, a crowd witnessed the swearing of the *Act of Insurrection of the Lithuanian Nation*. It reads:

> We the citizens of the province of the Grand Duchy of Lithuania and the inhabitants of the free city of Wilno, giving praise to the Highest Providence, having at last experienced the happy moment of the rising up of the nation from violence and oppressions . . . equally zealous as the citizens of the Crown in the same aim of regaining civic liberty and equality, and also all of those benefits and intentions which are contained in the Cracovian Act, . . . establish this most solemn Act of the Lithuanian Nation, declaring, with the sacrifice of life and property for the defence of ourselves and our common Fatherland, that whosoever is not with us is our enemy, and taking as our slogan either death or victory over our enemies, we do acclaim this present Act.[15]

This wording begins in traditional terms, distinguishing between the (noble) citizens of the province and the burghers of Wilno, before sounding a threatening and national note. The subsequently published *Proclamation of the Insurrection of the Lithuanian Nation* added, among other things, 'the brave French nation together with others give us their friendly hand, and demand our uprising'.[16] On 3 May the leaders in Wilno conferred the command of the Lithuanian insurrectionary forces on Jasiński and shortly afterwards promoted him to lieutenant-general.

The Insurrection enjoyed local superiority, but the leadership in Wilno busied itself with provisioning the Lithuanian army in readiness for the expected counter-attacks. They also propagated their radical message. Couriers skirted lakes and traversed forests to bring proclamations to country parishes. The radical discourse of sacrifice and equality was not to the taste of many nobles, but it did – initially – persuade many Samogitian peasants to enlist.[17] To engage the peasantry at least four proclamations were translated into the Lithuanian language (their vocabulary includes many Lithuanian-inflected Polonisms). It was expected that many parish priests or their vicars would be able to read these out from their pulpits. The truncated borders of the Grand Duchy after the second partition included not only all of Samogitia, but nearly all of the more easterly territories known as *Lithuania propria*. It is a safe bet that the proportion of Lithuanian speakers in the combined population of the Commonwealth had never been as high as it was in 1794.

The Grand Duchy of Lithuania now had its own government, composed mainly of the principal conspirators. Deputations were set up for supply, public safety and the public treasury, along with a criminal court. The first trial, on 25 April, was of Szymon Kossakowski. Found guilty of treason, he was sentenced to death, and his property was confiscated for the Commonwealth. At two o'clock in the afternoon he was led to the gallows in front of the city hall and hanged before a jubilant crowd. The government announced by the *Act of Insurrection* was called the National Provincial Council, but it soon took the name of the Supreme Government Council. This was used interchangeably with the name of the Supreme Lithuanian National Council. Sometimes, especially in communications with Warsaw, the adjective 'Temporary' was inserted. Kościuszko, although a son of the Grand Duchy and acknowledged as the head of the rising, was unhappy with this division of authority. On 21 May he announced that the Lithuanian authorities would be subordinated to the insurrectionary government which was about to be established in Warsaw.

The news of the Vilnan rising and Kossakowski's execution reached Warsaw on 8 May – the king's nameday. That evening a false rumour was spread that Stanisław August, who was taking a carriage ride over to Praga, was trying to escape. Zakrzewski, who had gone to fetch him back, was accused of joining his attempt. As they and others returned, they were met by a turbulent crowd. In all probability this was no misunderstanding, but a deliberate provocation of the populace. By the following morning three gallows had been erected on the Old Town market square, and a fourth on the city's main thoroughfare. A crowd, mostly artisans and soldiers, filled the square and surrounding streets. They burst into the city hall, the seat of the Temporary Replacement Council, and demanded the prisoners. Zakrzewski and his moderate allies had no intention of letting the incarcerated traitors of Targowica escape justice, but wanted due process of law. There was no time for that. A hastily convened criminal court summarily found Piotr Ożarowski, Józef Zabiełło, Józef Ankwicz and Bishop Józef Kossakowski guilty of treason and sentenced them to death. They were taken to the gallows and hanged. Zakrzewski noted that many women of all conditions had cheered on the executioners. It was all over in less than four hours. The Council managed to restore order, and prevent further executions, but having been forced to act against its will, its political course now veered leftwards.

On 24 May 1794 crowds cheered Ignacy Potocki and Hugo Kołłątaj back into Warsaw, twenty-two months after they had left. Empowered by the Chief, they set up an insurrectionary government, the Supreme National Council. Most of the eight councillors, each heading a governmental division, were veterans of the

Four Years' Sejm. Potocki would direct foreign affairs, Kołłątaj the treasury and Zakrewski the Division for Food. The ex-Piarist Franciszek Ksawery Dmochowski (who had helped Kołłątaj and Potocki write *On the Establishment and Fall of the Polish Constitution of 3 May*) was responsible for both education and propaganda. The king asked to be included, but Kościuszko refused. Nevertheless, the noble dominance of the Council (even among the thirty-two deputy councillors, only seven were burghers) and the prominent moderates aroused discontent among radicals, gathering around Jan Kiliński. Kołłątaj discreetly extended his influence, but it seems unlikely that he had the radicals under control.

The successes of the Insurrection in the Crown and Lithuania soon persuaded any residual doubters in St Petersburg that Poland was too troublesome to maintain in any shape or size. By the end of May 1794 Aleksandr Bezborodko had convinced his colleagues that the problem should be resolved once and for all. The Prussian offer of help was accepted, as the best Russian units were still on the Ottoman frontier. Berlin made no secret of its desire for a partition (preferably along the banks of the Vistula, Wieprz and Niemen, plus the coastal parts of Samogitia and Courland, although it also suggested a small buffer-state for Zubov). Meanwhile the dramatic reports sent back to Vienna touched a raw nerve with Francis II and his advisors, who were busy dealing with the Habsburg Monarchy's own 'Jacobins'. If Austria were to lop off some heads of the Jacobin hydra in Poland, it should be able to claim its reward in Polish territory, including compensation for being left out in 1793. Most importantly, Austrian involvement would limit Prussian gains. Vienna would, if it came to a partition, seek the palatinates of Cracow, Sandomierz, Lublin and Chełm, a share of Volhynia and if possible, lands stretching as far as the Narew and even Pińsk. Austrian forces were ordered into position, but they did not cross the border until early July. Kościuszko had left orders for Cracow to be handed over to the Austrians as a 'deposit' should the Prussians approach, but the Austrian military observer hesitated. He waited for written instructions, which arrived on 16 June, the day after the city had opened its gates to the Prussians. On 22 July the Austrian and Prussian ambassadors to St Petersburg were informed that 'the time has come for the three courts to take steps not only for the extinguishing of the last sparks of the fire which has ignited in the neighbouring country, but also for the prevention of any new flame ever arising from the ashes'.[18] For both German powers, the French recovery in the west increased the attraction of easy pickings in the east. And, as usual, Russia could play them off against each other.

The fortunes of war also swung against the Poles. At Szczekociny on 5 June 1794 Kościuszko encountered a joint Russian and Prussian force twice the size of his own. In a hard-fought battle, which initially seemed to be going the Poles' way, they lost about 2,000 men killed or fatally wounded. Among the casualties was Wojciech Głowacki. Kościuszko managed to retreat with most of his army, only to learn that General Derfelden had beaten Lieutenant-General Zajączek's smaller force at Chełm on 8 June, and was engaged in pursuit. With southern Poland lost, the insurrectionary forces pulled back towards Warsaw.

Just as fear of the advancing Prussians and Austrians had sparked the popular violence in Paris on 10 August 1792, so, *toutes proportions gardées*, did fear of Russian and Prussian revenge contribute to the events of 28–29 June 1794 in Warsaw. It was tempting to blame traitors for defeat, and to lynch those at hand. Again a rumour was spread that the king was planning to escape. A ditty sung by the crowds threatened the hanging of the king and the primate. During the night of 27–28 June several gallows went up. One was on Castle Square, another opposite the primate's palace. The king appealed to Kołłątaj to calm the people. Kołłątaj later blamed the slowness and scruples of the insurrectionary courts for what followed, but persons close to him were prominent among the agitators. There is no firm proof he directed the events of 28 June, but he did nothing to prevent or curtail them.

In the morning of 28 June 1794 a large crowd surrounded the seat of the Supreme National Council and demanded the punishment of traitors. Unlike on 8 May, however, the Council did not yield. It defended the impartial judicial process. Its proclamation promising abbreviated procedures – three days – did not work. The crowd dragged Bishop Ignacy Massalski and the Castellan of Przemyśl, Antoni Czetwertyński from their cells, along with several alleged spies, and hauled them to the gallows. The lynching of Massalski, a weak, vain and profligate man, but essentially well intentioned, was unjust. Unlike Kossakowski several weeks earlier, he was not unfrocked before he was hanged. Zakrzewski desperately tried to restore order, but was let down by the militia and the garrison. He did help to save Fryderyk Moszyński from a likely death, but the story that he interposed his own body and cried out that he would rather be hanged himself appears to be a poetic exaggeration.[19]

The king appealed to Kościuszko to use the army in Warsaw. The Chief, suspecting an intrigue sponsored by the enemy, agreed to discipline the populace. Colonel Kiliński was ordered to impress the poorest plebeians into the regular army; he carried out his orders pitilessly. The Jacobin club was closed down as moderates regained the initiative. Kościuszko turned his attention back to the Russian and Prussian forces. During four days of hard fighting over a thirty-kilometre front south of the city, the Poles held up well. Although undefeated, the Russians and Prussians suffered significant casualties. The Chief then deployed his army, 23,000 strong, in a skilfully fortified cordon around Warsaw's left bank. Behind the regular army were the hastily strengthened ramparts dating from 1770, manned by the garrison and a citizens' militia up to 20,000 strong, serving on a rota basis. The production of weapons and ammunition was stepped up.

Frederick William II joined the Prussian army: 30,000 strong. It failed to break through Warsaw's defences on 27 July 1794. The siege then began in earnest. Possession of Warsaw would greatly increase the Prussian bill in the future partition negotiations, and this was reflected in their allies' dispositions. General Fersen's Russian forces offered token assistance, while General Derfelden's corps was redirected to Lithuania. With no immediate threat to Warsaw on the right bank of the Vistula, the forces defending the city against the Prussians could be reinforced and supplies could be brought in by river. Cattle even arrived from Volhynia. The Austrians, deployed well to the south-east, refused to help the Prussians at all. The Prussian heavy artillery began to arrive on 19 August. Thereafter bombardments took their toll. The end of August saw fierce fighting, with heavy casualties on both sides. Disease and desertion decimated the besiegers.

Inside the city, the insurrectionary and municipal authorities tried their best to deal with the orphans and widows, the jobless, the invalids, the sick, mad and dying, the malingerers and the inevitable criminal element. At the same time they had to mobilize all available resources. Metal objects were melted into coin in the former Royal Mint, now nationalized. They also issued paper assignats, received by traders with the utmost reluctance. One of the most unpopular sacrifices required was horses – desperate carters and coachmen protested that their livelihoods were being taken away and their animals mistreated. The stresses of the siege prompted a renewed radicalization. Needing the full commitment of the populace, Kościuszko rowed back on the repressive measures that had followed the events of 28 June. When the courts began to try those accused of being ringleaders, they acquitted many. In the end only eight death sentences were carried out. The king was asked not to visit the ramparts and trenches, for fear of re-stoking rumours of an escape.

It was rumoured – falsely – that the primate had passed plans of the city's defences to the besiegers. Michał Poniatowski died in the night of 11–12 August. His corpse, placed briefly on public display, swelled and blackened in the summer heat, encouraging the wildest conspiracy theories. The falsehood was spread that the primate had taken poison, sent him by the king, in order to avoid execution as a traitor. This calumny has been refuted by research which has explained how these lies first became myth and then 'history'. That said, Poniatowski had probably lost all appetite for life. He had ordered prayers for the Insurrection, and placed ecclesiastical silver and revenues at the disposal of the treasury. But he was convinced that the rising would only accelerate the catastrophic fate of his country, and had fallen into depression. The late primate received honourable exequies, and was laid to rest in the catacombs of the new cemetery at Powązki – outside the ramparts but within the Polish lines. Stationed nearby, his favourite nephew, Prince Józef, who was loyally serving the Insurrection well below his rank, provided a succinct epitaph: 'The Prince Primate has died. I regret him, because he had a rare virtue among us – character.'[20]

The news from the north was not encouraging. The insurrectionary army of the Grand Duchy of Lithuania lost the initiative after the replacement of the charismatic radical Jasiński as commander by the moderate Michał Wielhorski. The last major success of the Lithuanian forces was the capture of Libau on the Baltic coast and the proclamation of an insurrection in Courland on 27 June. It won some support from the local nobility, but more from the duchy's burghers and peasants. To engage the latter, one appeal was printed in Latvian. Many of these peasants, some of the most harshly exploited in Europe, took bloody revenge on their Germanophone lords. As in neighbouring Samogitia, the restoration of order considerably lessened the appeal of the rising to the rural populace. The Russians were soon on the offensive, although mopping up in Courland and Samogitia lasted until September.

On 19 July General Bogdan Knorring tried to storm the defences of Wilno with 8,000 men. The garrison and armed citizens resisted fiercely. After two days' fighting, Knorring called a halt. The bells rang out from the slender towers of the city's churches as votive masses and the *Te Deum* were sung. The deliverance was brief. Reinforced to 12,000 men, Knorring attacked again on 11–12 August. This time the new commander of the Lithuanian forces gave up. He was Antoni

Chlewiński, who had been passed over in favour of Jasiński on 3 May. Wilno capitulated. Chlewiński was accused of treason and later arrested, but nothing was proved before the rising ended. The remaining Lithuanian units retreated towards Grodno, but the effective end of the Insurrection in the Grand Duchy facilitated the Russian drive on Warsaw.

Much better news came from the west. On 20 August 1794 a rising broke out in the Cujavian territories annexed by Prussia in 1793. It spread swiftly across Greater Poland. With his numbers almost halved, and fearing for his communications with Berlin, the King of Prussia abandoned the siege of Warsaw on 5–6 September and headed west. General Fersen retreated south. Warsaw had held out, not least because of the rigorously enforced rota of service by men of all estates, backgrounds and confessions on the ramparts – and their replacement by womenfolk in family businesses. The combination of the Greater Polish insurgents, the small, mobile force sent by Kościuszko into the Prussian rear, commanded by Jan Henryk Dąbrowski (who had learned his military craft in the Saxon army) and Madaliński's detachment, caused Frederick William endless embarrassment. One town after another surrendered to the Poles. The *Te Deum* was sung in Gniezno Cathedral on 27 September. For the first, but not the last time, Józef Wybicki accompanied Dąbrowski. He penned eloquent appeals to all sections of the population. The carnival in Greater Poland could not last beyond six weeks, but it relieved the pressure on Warsaw and humiliated the Hohenzollern. Catherine informed Baron Grimm that she 'broke out into great shrieks of laughter' when she heard the news of his retreat.[21] From this point onwards, the King of Prussia would be asking favours from the empress, rather than inflating his price. As in the aftermath of Valmy and Jemappes in the autumn of 1793, the tsaritsa briefly seemed to reconsider the forthcoming partition; sowing doubt exerted more pressure on the German courts. As Russia dictated its own terms for partition to Austria in the dying months of 1794, Prussia could wait out in the cold.

While these one-sided negotiations were taking place, the Insurrection entered its final phase. Its politics remained finely balanced. On 12 September 1794 a court presided over by Józef Zajączek sentenced Bishop Wojciech Skarszewski to death for treason, principally for his role in the ratification of the partition treaties by the Grodno Sejm. The rejection of the bishop's defence – which boils down to his claim that he had acted for the lesser evil – could also be read as a verdict on the king. The monarch and the new papal nuncio, Lorenzo Litta, begged Kościuszko for clemency. When the Chief relented, moderates approved, but Skarszewski's old rival Kołłątaj was furious. Skarszewski had avoided being lynched on 28 June; now he had escaped again.

In the meantime, on 8 August 1794 the Sublime Porte declared its peaceful intentions. Catherine then ordered Aleksandr Suvorov and his veterans to march against the insurgents. Moving quickly, they crossed the Bug and defeated a Polish force of 5,000 near Terespol on 19 September. Hoping to prevent Suvorov's junction with Fersen's corps, Kościuszko attacked the latter at Maciejowice on 10 October. Outnumbered two to one, he not only lost the hard-fought battle, but was wounded and captured. After the news of the disaster reached Warsaw, the Council conferred the leadership of the rising on Tomasz Wawrzecki – a compromise choice. He had distinguished himself as an envoy to the Four Years' Sejm, but he had no qualifications to be a military dictator.

Had it not been for the end of the rising in Lithuania and the outcome of Maciejowice, the Russians might have waited until the spring for the dénouement of the campaign. As it was, Suvorov grasped the opportunity to end it quickly. Varsovians prepared grimly for another siege, this time with little hope of success. Discipline wavered as troops were relocated from their camps beyond the ramparts to winter quarters inside the city. As the Russians approached, supplies became much more difficult to obtain. The political balance continued to swing between moderates and radicals, and a plot was even hatched to kill the king in order to prevent a capitulation. As morale plummeted, more Varsovians again looked to Stanisław August to save their lives.

Among those who did not give up was a horsetrader born in Samogitia and settled in Warsaw's right-bank suburb of Praga. His name was Berek Joselewicz. Having served on the ramparts and in the trenches with the militia, he had gained permission from Kościuszko to form an all-Jewish light cavalry regiment. This enabled them to wear beards, eat kosher food and whenever possible to keep the Sabbath. By no means every eligible Jew was keen to serve under arms, and nor was every eligible Christian. President Zakrzewski refused almost all requests for exemptions from militia or regular military service. That said, in fighting bravely for a free Poland, thereby confounding every stereotype about their people's alleged lack of martial valour, Joselewicz's 500 and the Jewish militiamen claimed the moral rights of free Polish citizens – just like the scythemen at Racławice. A new chapter began in the interwoven history of Jews and Poles.

Suvorov's forces stormed the inadequate defences of Praga in the early morning of 4 November. In the foggy gloom the impetus was overwhelming.

Zajączek was wounded and traumatized. Jasiński died defending the last bastion. According to tradition, Joselewicz's regiment was almost completely wiped out, although its commander would only die fighting the Austrians in 1809. By nine o'clock in the morning the fighting was over and the slaughter began. The Russian soldiers, some of whose units had taken the brunt of the Warsaw insurrection in April, butchered the defenceless inhabitants, the majority of them Jewish. Russian reports put the total Polish military and civilian casualties at 20,000, although this may have been an exaggeration for effect. This was not the first time Suvorov had played the grim reaper on such a scale. He had unleashed a massacre of the garrison and civilians of Izmail in December 1790. The premeditated slaughter of the people of Praga was calculated to terrorize Warsaw into surrendering.

It worked. That same evening a municipal delegation crossed the river to ask for the terms of capitulation. Before they were received by Suvorov, they were stripped of their valuables. The following day it was agreed that the Polish army would march out of the city by 9 November, while the populace would be disarmed. A crowd of Varsovians surrounded the Royal Castle to prevent the king leaving with the army on 8 November. They feared that otherwise they would share the fate of the people of Praga. As in 1792, Kołłątaj had been among the first to flee. The Russians marched into a silent, shocked Warsaw on 9 November, and Suvorov treated Stanisław August with studiedly eccentric courtesy. Wawrzecki led the insurrectionary army to the camp at Radoszyce, where those who had not already gone home surrendered to General Denisov on 16 November.

The Insurrection was over. With it ends the history of the sovereign Commonwealth. In their different ways the two Polish Revolutions, of 1788–92 and 1794, illuminated the country's vast potential. The greatest success of the former was political: a critical mass of noble citizens was persuaded to follow the evolutionary path of orderly liberty, extended by degrees to ever wider sectors of the population. But the leaders of the Great Sejm neither mobilized the necessary resources, nor wielded those they had with sufficient determination, to give the Commonwealth a reasonable chance of defending its regained sovereignty. The Insurrection, starting from a far worse position, engaged in a desperate fight to recover the nation's sovereignty and dignity. While it never solved the problem of how to win and then keep the support of landlords *and* peasants simultaneously, it did mount a far more intense defence than that offered during the war of 1792. In doing so, the Kościuszko Rising left an inspiring moral legacy to posterity. Its chances of victory were close to zero, and so the decision to launch the Insurrection has often been criticized as suicidal. However, the alternative to immolation was 'slow asphyxiation'. That, writes Jerzy Lukowski, was the likely consequence of 'the king's way'.[22] The Commonwealth's potential for life was never more apparent than in the manner of its death.

Part of this potential was the idea of freedom – not only Polish freedom. 'From America through Paris to Warsaw, the lightning of freedom will proceed all the way to Kamchatka; the tyrants will not realize how speedily they will fall from their eternal and unjust thrones, like so many Lucifers from the heavens,' thundered the suspended priest Florian Jelski in one of his *Civic Sermons by the Warsaw Ramparts*.[23] Tyrants and traitors should tremble before free nations. Free citizens would vanquish despots and their slaves. These messages were conveyed by numerous insurrectionary proclamations, brochures and sermons. It was the cause of freedom that could unite the Commonwealth's peasants, burghers and nobles, its Jews, Muslims, Orthodox, Protestants, and Catholics of both rites, and inspire them to fight for their country. Of course, freedom meant something different to enserfed peasants who longed to be free of labour services, to minority religious communities who wanted to worship publicly in their own sacred languages and in accordance with their own laws and traditions, to entrepreneurs who desired the removal of restrictions on trade, to burghers who wished to be rid of interfering starostas and commissars, to writers who chafed under censorship, and to nobles, for whom it had long encompassed a range of negative and positive freedoms. The dilemmas of how to balance different concepts of liberty did not disappear. Yet in 1794 common to all these understandings of freedom was the conviction that they depended on the collective freedom of the Polish nation to determine the Commonwealth's future. Thus understood, liberty overlapped with ideas of national independence and sovereignty. Poles could neither participate in their own government nor enjoy their lives and property in peace and security under arbitrary foreign rule. This was an old republican axiom well understood two centuries previously, but long since neglected.[24] Sacrifices must be made to defend or recover freedom, but those sacrifices would only minimally and temporarily affect the liberties of citizens. Negative liberty depended on positive liberty. But positive liberty should secure negative liberty, not crush it. Poles could not be forced to be free.

During the Insurrection – unlike under the counter-revolutionary regime – the judicial and executive powers showed great respect for individual rights. The lynchings of 28 June were the exception to the rule. For all their emotive rhetoric against traitors and tyrants, including the slogan 'liberty or death', the Polish and Lithuanian insurrectionary dictatorships bore little resemblance to the Committee of Public Safety in Paris. Some Poles have regretted that, then and since. Perhaps the kind of paranoid terror practised by Robespierre, Saint-Just and their ilk, executing thousands deemed impure and unpatriotic, not just proven traitors like the brothers Kossakowski, would have mobilized more resources and deployed them with fewer scruples against the surrounding monarchies. It might well have prolonged the Insurrection. But a terrorist regime would have besmirched the Commonwealth's republican and Christian values with innocent blood.

'As it was now a question, not merely of how much each Power should take away from the Poles, but of how much each Power should take away from the other two, it proved more difficult than on either of the preceding occasions to reach an agreement about the respective shares.' Thus Robert Howard Lord summed up the negotiation of the third partition.[25] In August 1794 St Petersburg welcomed a new Prussian envoy, a military man with the evocative name of Friedrich Bogislaw Tauentzien von Wittenberg. He felt an autumnal chill after the Hohenzollern retreat from Warsaw. When on 21 October he presented his court's demands for a frontier on the rivers Windau, Niemen, Narew and Vistula, he was curtly told to reduce them by half. Berlin refused. Vienna proved more amenable to Russian pressure, abandoning its hopes of Volhynia. From mid-December, Tauentzien was frozen out as the Austrian ambassador, Ludwig von Coblenzl, negotiated (that is, received) the terms of agreement. On 3 January 1795 Coblenzl signed the Austro-Russian Treaty of St Petersburg, as well as a secret understanding.

The latter envisaged Francis II's accession to the 1793 treaty of St Petersburg, insofar as it concerned the interests of the imperial courts. Austria would support Russia against the Ottoman Empire, while Russia would come to the aid of Austria in the event of a war with Prussia. Russia would also help Austria gain unspecified indemnities for its efforts in the west. According to the treaty, 'the absolute incapacity of the Republic of Poland' to exist under a stable government had led the two courts to recognize 'in their wisdom and in their love of peace and of the happiness of their subjects that it was an indispensable necessity to have recourse . . . to a total partition of this Republic among the neighbouring Powers'.[26] The new Russian frontier would follow the Rivers Bug and Niemen. Austria would take the lands bounded by the Bug, the Vistula and the Pilica. The rest, including Warsaw, was left for Prussia. This relative success for Vienna was still a worse deal than the one Berlin had obtained two years earlier.

It remained to impose this treaty on the King of Prussia. This task was complicated by the situation on the ground. Even before the rising had run its course, Austrian and Prussian commanders raced to occupy Polish lands. Their units occasionally clashed. The temporary demarcation, overseen by the Russian generals, permitted Prussia to retain much of the territory already under its control, including Cracow. Further Prussian forces moved into the disputed areas after Frederick William II's withdrawal from the war against France, effected by the Treaty of Basel on 5 April 1795. Baron Thugut reprised the idea of leaving a small Polish buffer-state, enlarged by previous Prussian acquisitions, only to have it rejected in St Petersburg. Nevertheless, both imperial courts reluctantly prepared for war against Prussia. The British guarantee of a loan of 4,600,000 pounds to Austria on 4 May strengthened Vienna's hand, not least because the Austro-British agreement did not specify where the army promised by Austria for the coming campaign would be used. The two imperial ambassadors officially informed the court of Berlin of the Austro-Russian agreement on 9 August.

Not for the first time, Frederick William's courage wilted. After Austria had yielded a small triangle of Mazovian land between the Bug and the Vistula, the Prussian terms were whittled down to the western fringe of the palatinate of Cracow, not including the city. This was the basis for the final treaties between Prussia and Austria, and Prussia and Russia, signed in St Petersburg on 24 October 1795. The Austrians entered Cracow on 5 January 1796; in return the Russians handed over Warsaw to the Prussians five days later. However, the Austro-Prussian demarcation commission in Lesser Poland continued its fractious work for a further ten months, until the empress herself arbitrated the main disputes. The definitive settlement of the Austro-Prussian border was not finalized until 19 March 1797. Prussia gained 48,000 square kilometres, populated by about a million new subjects. These predominantly sandy and marshy lands were renamed 'Neuostpreussen'. Austria annexed 47,000 square kilometres of more fertile land, inhabited by at least one and half million people, and rechristened its share 'Westgalizien'. Russia took 120,000 square kilometres and at least 1,200,000 subjects for its new 'gubernia' (Map 8).

This time no sejm was required. The king's abdication would suffice to ratify the annihilation of the Commonwealth. The man to obtain it was Nikolai Repnin. As governor of the Lithuanian lands, he was the monarch's guardian in Grodno, following the king's forced departure from Warsaw under armed escort on 7 January 1795. Catherine warned Repnin:

> Many experiences have confirmed to us that this ruler has always been opposed to our interests, that there has been no enterprise directed against us in Poland, at whose head he did not place himself or in which he did not participate. Both this and your old knowledge of his character should command you to maintain the utmost caution towards him.[27]

Yet when Stanisław August arrived in Grodno, he found Repnin a more humane and philosophical man than he remembered. So much had changed since the 1760s, and yet so little. In a despatch of 7 November 1795 the empress explained to Repnin that the practicalities involved in the liquidation of the Polish state, including its financial obligations, required the king's prompt renunciation of the throne and all 'elements of authority concerning the lands which were formerly called Polish'. Moreover, it was essential that the act of abdication should express the 'full conviction of His Majesty of the absolute necessity of the methods which the three powers have employed'.[28]

Stanisław August had first seriously thought of abdication during the sejm of 1766. Twice, in January and June 1793, he had written to the empress, offering to lay down his crown. He believed he had nothing more to offer his country. However, he had to deal with his mountainous debts. Most had been contracted for public purposes, because of the fiscal and financial difficulties so often faced by the Commonwealth. The king felt obliged to protect his servants and creditors, facing destitution. However, he also wished to bargain a comfortable retirement abroad – preferably in Italy – and provision for his closest family. Stanisław August's abdication at another time, such as just before the Grodno Sejm, might have caused Catherine serious trouble. She would have been inconvenienced had he refused to lay down the crown, an act forbidden by Polish law. Had the king told the world – as he had done in 1772–73 – that he was being coerced into acquiescence, he could have embarrassed her. Instead he abdicated on her terms.

Stanisław August's initial draft, dated 23 November 1795, recalled his rejected offer to step down in 1793 (thereby hinting that the current act was involuntary), before declaring his renunciation of the throne and government of the Kingdom of Poland and the Grand Duchy of Lithuania. It contained no acceptance of the partition. This was nowhere near good enough. Repnin made the monarch correct it. The king's next draft half-acknowledged the actions of the three courts, but stopped short of accepting the partition on behalf of the nation. He had to correct it again. After a further attempt to present these unspecified actions as a necessary response to unspecified events, Repnin insisted on a fourth and final version. A crucial paragraph drafted by his assistant was inserted into the text. In close translation it reads:

> Convinced now by experience, that our efforts could no longer be useful to our Fatherland after the unhappy insurrection which having come to her, has again plunged her into her present downfall; considering, moreover, that the measures for the future fate of Poland made necessary by the urgency of the circumstances, to which Her Majesty the Empress of All the Russias and also the other neighbouring powers have had recourse, are the only ones which can assure peace and repose to our fellow-citizens, whose happiness has always been the object of our solicitude; we have in consequence resolved, for love of public tranquillity, to declare as we do declare by this act in the most authentic manner possible, that we freely and voluntarily renounce without exception all our rights regarding the Polish Crown, the Grand Duchy of Lithuania and all their dependencies, as well as all the possessions and belongings of the Crown within the said states.[29]

Stanisław August threw in the towel. On 25 November 1795, the thirty-first anniversary of his coronation, he tearfully signed the act of abdication. Repnin sent it to the empress, along with two letters from the king. One concerned the payment of his own and the state's debts, as well as the sale of his property. The second regarded his plans to go to the Reich or Italy for the sake of his health. He asked whether he could still use the title of king and requested help for his family and for those officers who had bought their commissions. Having meticulously analysed each and every amendment to the successive versions of the act, as well as the relevant correspondence, Zofia Zielińska concludes: 'In November 1795 [the king] saved nothing for the state. The payment of his debts, a comfortable life for himself and those closest to him, finally the hope of regaining his personal liberty, these were not values which could justify Stanisław August in his own eyes.'[30] For three decades the king could reasonably claim that he had consistently striven, 'in every circumstance to do the best for the Fatherland, or at least the least bad, when nothing good could be done at all'.[31] This essentially honourable record had now ended and he knew it. Of course he could not have prevented the third partition, but even Stanisław August's greatest admirers cannot justify either the figleaf of legitimacy he provided for the final destruction of the Commonwealth, or his motives for doing so.

EPILOGUE
SMOKE AND ASH

After his abdication, Stanisław August remained in the Royal Castle in Grodno. Despite Catherine II's encouraging reply to his request to go to Italy (she suggested Rome would suit him),[1] he was not allowed to go there (war broke out in Italy in the spring of 1796). He spent his annual allowance of 200,000 ducats freely, despite the restrictions on his visitors. His correspondence was monitored, which is one reason why so much of it concerns the arts. Marcello Bacciarelli had kept him informed of the ongoing work at the Łazienki in 1795; the following year the ex-king began negotiations to sell much of his property to Frederick William II. They ran into the mire of the general settlement of his debts.

Catherine ordered Stanisław August to move to Moscow in the autumn of 1796, a prospect that filled him with gloom. Her death on 17 November 1796 spared him the journey and raised his hopes that he would be allowed to leave for a cure at Karlsbad. The new emperor, Paul I (who mistakenly believed himself Poniatowski's son), invited the former king to move to St Petersburg instead. There he was greeted with royal honours and installed in the Marble Palace. Shortly afterwards, he did travel to Moscow, along with many other Poles, for Paul's coronation in April 1797. When, during the long service, Stanisław August sat down for a moment, he was instructed to stand up. Having resumed his residence in St Petersburg, his debts began to accumulate again. There were problems with the payment of his allowance and the Marble Palace needed expensive adaptations. Moreover, he rarely refused the many requests he received from Poles for help, and passed on many pleas to the Russian authorities. Conscious that posterity would judge him harshly, Stanisław August spent much of his time writing his memoirs. Before his death he managed to reach 1778. He quoted many documents, in order to explain and justify his actions. Although the later parts contain many striking passages and pen-portraits, overall they are less entertaining than the sparkling account of his youth, which he had penned in the early 1770s.

Stanisław August became a social fixture on the banks of the Neva, not least because of the excellence of his long-serving chef, Paul Tremo (a Huguenot from Berlin). The former king was close to the British ambassador Charles Whitworth, who had been envoy to Poland in 1785–88. He also became friendly with the French émigrée Élisabeth Vigée Le Brun, who painted his last two portraits. One, unfinished, shows Stanisław August stylized as Henri IV of France – an ideal ruler. This frankly embarrassing idea was suggested by his niece, Urszula Mniszech. The other is perhaps the most technically accomplished and psychologically penetrating portrait ever painted of him. It shows the former monarch wearing an ermine robe and the Order of the White Eagle. The viewer's attention follows the melancholy gaze of the large brown eyes well beyond the oval canvas (Plate 32).[2]

By the first weeks of 1798 some of Stanisław August's visitors thought he was showing signs of exhaustion. On 11 February, having drunk his morning cup of broth, he lost consciousness. He recovered briefly, and began his last confession to his chaplain, before losing consciousness again. Emperor Paul came to his bedside, and Archbishop Lorenzo Litta, who had been transferred to St Petersburg on the closure of the Warsaw nunciature, pronounced absolution. At eight o'clock the following morning Stanisław August convulsed and died. His doctor's post-mortem revealed only the signs of apoplexy. The royal body was embalmed before the tsar staged a funeral which cost the colossal sum of 52,000 rubles. The lying in state – twelve days in the Marble Palace and three days in the city's principal Roman Catholic church, dedicated to St Catherine of Alexandria (of course) – featured a *castrum doloris* and catafalque designed by the imperial court architect, Vincenzo Brenna. The funerary liturgy lasted three days. On 8 March, after a requiem mass intoned by Litta, the heavy coffin was interred in the crypt.

This coffin was first opened in 1857. The corpse had almost entirely decomposed, because of the flooding from the Neva. In 1938 the Soviet authorities planned to destroy the church. Before they changed their minds, on 11 July an otherwise ordinary goods train, including a sealed wagon bearing the royal coffin and its contents, crossed the Polish frontier. The embarrassed Polish government tried to keep the matter secret. Four nights later the coffin was walled up in a niche of the church at Wołczyn, where Stanisław had been christened. The priest was even forbidden to say a mass for his soul. However, the Soviet press released the information, forcing the publication of a dry communiqué in Poland. A public debate began on the king's final resting place. Wawel Cathedral was the royal necropolis, but in the meantime it had also become a pantheon for national heroes and bards (Prince Józef Poniatowski, Tadeusz Kościuszko, Adam Mickiewicz, Juliusz Słowacki and most recently, Józef Piłsudski). Many commentators vehemently opposed such honours for Stanisław August. Some proposed St John's Cathedral in Warsaw, while a few proposed to leave him in Wołczyn. The debate was unresolved when the Second World War broke out.

The wrenching westwards of Poland's post-war borders left Wołczyn just inside the Soviet Union. The departing parish priest handed over the keys to the church and the niche to the local village council on 27 April 1945. At some point in the next few days, months or years, the coffin was pillaged. What happened to the skeleton is a matter for speculation. One hopes someone quietly reburied it in a corner of the churchyard, but it may have been profaned. The local collective farm stored chemical fertilizers in the very fine, octagonal baroque church, founded by Stanisław Poniatowski the elder, which soon fell into ruin. Post-war Poland's communist rulers preferred not to raise the matter. As the decrepit dictatorship headed by General Wojciech Jaruzelski desperately sought a way out of the impasse it had created, the Ministry of Culture became more open to pressure from the intelligentsia. Its agreement to send a team of experts to Voŭchin reawakened the public debate interrupted in 1939. Emanuel Rostworowski – a Cracovian – led those who argued that only Wawel would do. Others – mainly Varsovians – preferred St John's Cathedral in Warsaw or the Łazienki, but still others were less kind to the last king's memory. In December 1988 the team crossed the border and drove to Voŭchin. They beheld the ruined church in shock. The coffin was shattered and empty. Soon afterwards they received the remaining fragments of regal fabric, adorned with silver eagles, recovered the previous year by Belarusian scientists. Further fragments were excavated the following spring, and were also taken to Warsaw.

Two hundred years after the Great Sejm, the Polish nation was again in ferment as the communist regime, having run out of money, ideas and time, and shocked at the extent of its own unpopularity, negotiated its own exit with the opposition and the Roman Catholic Church. Poles regained their liberty and sovereignty. The next few years, a time of bitter controversies around the country's transition to political democracy and a market economy, did not facilitate calm discussion of what to do with the largely symbolic remains of the last king of the Commonwealth. A reburial at Wawel was ruled out. Successive governments procrastinated, fearful of antagonizing nationalists and populists. Finally, a replica coffin containing fragments of the royal robes and earth from Voŭchin went on display at the Royal Castle in Warsaw on 12 February 1995 – the 197th anniversary of Stanisław August's death. Thousands filed past, some to pay their respects, others from curiosity. Two days later, following a requiem mass celebrated by the Primate of Poland, Cardinal Józef Glemp, 'King Stanisław August' was interred in St John's Cathedral, where he had been crowned, and where the *Te Deum* had been sung after the acclamation of the Constitution of 3 May. The anachronistic royal titles were carved into the symbolic tomb in the crypt. Except that it was not quite the same church. The cathedral had been rebuilt and re-gothicized after being reduced to rubble by the German army in 1944, while the Red Army waited on the other bank of the Vistula. The Roman Catholic diocese of Pinsk regained the Church of the Holy Trinity at Voŭchin in 2007 and, happy to relate, the restoration is well advanced.

The strange posthumous fate of the Commonwealth's last king is partly paralleled in the fate of its regalia. Most of the objects that have survived to this day were kept in the Cracow Cathedral Treasury or else were found in the royal tombs on Wawel Hill. Others were found in the crypt of Wilno Cathedral in 1931. The digging up of a crown in Sandomierz in 1910 led Lithuanian nationalists to claim it as the royal crown intended for Vytautas the Great in 1430, allegedly stolen by the wicked Poles. In fact the dying King Casimir the Great had probably offered it to the Sandomierz collegiate church.[3] The best-preserved regalia are the crowns, sceptres, orbs and cloaks of the Wettins, kept in Dresden until the National Museum in Warsaw bought some of them in 1925. They returned to the museum from the Soviet Union in 1960. As for the regalia of Stanisław August, an orb and a ceremonial sword from 1764 survived the nineteenth century in Russia, and the Second World War in Canada. They can now be viewed in the Royal Castle in Warsaw. His fragmented burial sword was recovered from Voŭchin.

However beautiful in their own right, these objects are but fragments of what once existed. The principal regalia of the Kingdom of Poland were removed by Prussian officials from the Crown Treasury at Wawel in 1795. In 1836, following inquiries from Tsar Nicholas I, an internal Prussian investigation revealed that the metal objects, including six crowns, had been melted down in 1809, and in 1811 minted into coin on King Frederick William III's orders. However, legends were already circulating as to their purported hiding places, some of them started by the Prussians in order to distract attention from their dastardly deed of destruction, others by Poles in order to comfort their compatriots under foreign rule. They resonated anew under the communist dictatorship, which insisted the regalia no longer existed. Perhaps one day, when one worthy to wear it emerged, like Arthur from the mists of Avalon, would the lost crown of Bolesław the Valiant be rediscovered?

After the abdication other matters remained to be tidied up. The Convention of St Petersburg signed by the three powers on 26 January 1797 established commissions to sort out the debts of the former king, the defunct state and the broken banks. *Sujets mixtes*, including ecclesiastical institutions, would have five years to choose states, sell their properties and move. Just to be on the safe side, a secret addendum bound the three monarchs not to use the title of King of Poland, and to 'abolish everything which can recall the existence of the Kingdom of Poland'.[4]

Some 'former Poles' were already willing to forget. Having long since pledged himself to Catherine II, Feliks Potocki wrote to Seweryn Rzewuski early in 1796: 'I do not speak about the former Poland and Poles. That state has already disappeared, as have so many others in the history of the world. Each former Pole should choose himself a fatherland. I am already a Russian forever.'[5] Few put it as bluntly as this. But then few were in a position to choose their fatherland. Still fewer felt Potocki's intense resentment at being persecuted by his former nation despite all he had done for it (in his own estimation). However, given the long-standing tendency to identify the nation with the state and the state with the nation, many expected that Poland would join those ancient nations 'taken by the flood of history'.[6] For most of those who had survived their Fatherland, life went on, with inevitable adjustments. The rough and ready military administration of the occupied Commonwealth gave way to the more orderly civilian administration of the new provinces of the three monarchies. Former free citizens became subjects of an empress, an emperor or a king, obliged to obey orders – or face the consequences.

'I was ordered to swear that I shall not be free,' wrote the poet Cyprian Godebski.[7] The change of statehood was marked by ceremonies of homage. Across all three partitions, nobles and clergymen, if they wished to keep their privileges and not be forced to emigrate, were expected to travel to the designated town and swear fidelity. In the Grand Duchy of Lithuania these ceremonies had begun even before the Insurrection had been quelled. They were renewed on Catherine's orders in the cold winter of January 1796 – prompting a spate of petitions to be excused from attendance in person. The Austrians and Prussian authorities at least waited until the summer. In Warsaw the oath was received by the minister for South Prussia, Karl Georg von Hoym, at the Royal Castle on 6 July 1796. In a short speech he rejoiced that the disasters wrought by the anarchic habits of the past had been replaced by the tranquil felicity of the rule of law. The oath was first muttered 'through gritted teeth' by the nobles and clergymen assembled in the former senate chamber, then repeated more lustily by a crowd of commoners in the courtyard. The *Te Deum* was sung, cannons fired a hundred salutes, and feasts, balls and illuminations were laid on at the cost of the government.[8]

Such celebratory dinners and balls helped some to drown their sorrows, just as they had in the past, when ratifications of the partitions had been demanded of parliamentarians. Others found them tasteless – even Repnin, it was said. Doubtless few had the pluck of Anna Górecka, who at the ball in Wilno refused a dance to Iakov Bulgakov 'at the funeral of my mother, the Fatherland', although many enjoyed the story. Franciszek Karpiński, who related it in his memoirs, also recalled that a Russian colonel had asked him why he had recited the oath so quietly. The colonel was amused by the poet's reply that 'the Lord God sleeps during our oath' and he had not wanted to wake Him.[9] This was a grimly humorous tale suited to a memoir, but poetry lends itself to grief and despair. These are the prevalent emotions of the poetic legacy of these years. However, the lasting effects of the trauma may have been exaggerated by literary scholars. Most of those who swore oaths to their new rulers in the mid-1790s had no compunction in breaking them, once real hopes of restoring Poland re-emerged a decade later. Many had, after all, successively sworn loyalty to the Constitution of 3 May, the Confederacy of Targowica or Wilno, and the Insurrection.

The relatively warm memory among some Poles of the last half-century of the Austrian Empire (from the 1860s to 1918), at least when compared to collective memories of the Russian and German Empires, bears little relation to the situation in the first years after the third partition. In most respects, conditions were harshest under Austrian rule, largely because Austria bore the brunt of the war against revolutionary and Napoleonic France. All sectors of the population faced greatly increased taxes. From West Galicia alone perhaps 80,000 people were conscripted into the Austrian army between 1796 and 1809.[10] Many never returned home, which needs to be set against the greater judicial protection and limitations on labour services, which were the main gains for the peasantry in the

Austrian and Prussian lands. For many nobles accustomed to having their own way, the experience of dealing with punctilious Austrian and Prussian judges and officials, often commoners, in the largely unfamiliar German language, came as a shock. Taxes also rose for subjects of the King of Prussia, although by less than in Galicia. Although trade between the former lands of the Commonwealth was impeded, other markets became more accessible. Landowners in the Kingdom of Prussia benefited from rising agricultural prices during the eleven years of peace purchased by the 1795 Treaty of Basel with France. After the King of Prussia had left the coalition, the Empress of Russia joined it. Having dealt with 'Jacobinism' in Poland, the screeching harpy of the counter-revolution was at last willing to send her armies into battle against the French Republic. But she died on 17 November 1796, and her son Paul recalled them while they were *en marche*. Russian troops would not fight the French until 1799.

Although the eccentric tsar enjoyed reversing the policies of his unloved and unloving mother, he did not – could not – undo the partitions of the Commonwealth. Paul I did, however, make some gestures to his Polish subjects. Plying Kościuszko with compliments, he released the prisoners of the Insurrection (the principals had been interrogated in the grim Peter and Paul Fortress on an island in the Neva). Perhaps on Repnin's advice, he restored the szlachta's courts and some of its institutions of self-rule in the annexed territories. This was, for the moment, necessary for stability in the 'western gubernia'. The Russian Empire did not have at its disposal a cadre of trained bureaucrats and judges comparable to those of the two German powers, and so much had to be left to local elites. The unquestioning obedience expected by Russian officials was alien to the szlachta's way of life, but the representatives of imperial power could often be bought; they began to be treated rather like the magnate patrons of old. For most landowning nobles in the former Grand Duchy of Lithuania, Volhynia, Podolia and right-bank Ukraine, life proved quite bearable. Overall taxes were lower than in Prussia, let alone Austria, and nobles were personally exempt from the poll tax. Their jurisdiction over the enserfed peasants was bolstered. There is a strong case that under Paul I and Alexander I many wealthier Polish-Lithuanian nobles were co-opted into the privileged elites of the western peripheries of the empire in return for their loyalty. This was a tried and tested strategy of Russian imperial expansion.[11]

Changes were felt more keenly by the poorest nobles, whose status and privileges were questioned and often removed by the new regimes. This process moved most slowly in the Russian Empire. Everywhere indigent nobles lost access to jobs in the modest, but expanding institutions of the Polish state, and on former ecclesiastical and Crown estates. Opportunities dwindled in the diminished aristocratic households. The urban and mercantile occupations opened up to nobles in the last decades of the Commonwealth were now denied under Prussian rule, on pain of derogation. The static conceptions of society embraced by all three partitioning powers halted and even reversed the process of convergence between nobles and burghers. Warsaw, which had offered nobles and would-be nobles alike so many licit and illicit opportunities in the last decades of the Commonwealth, was now a Prussian frontier town whose population in the late 1790s was about half the level of 1791–92. Many other towns, deprived of their self-governing institutions, and suffocated by petty officialdom, stagnated. It must be admitted, however, that the reams of health and safety regulations issued by the Austrian and especially the Prussian authorities were at least well intentioned. In such circumstances service in the armies of the new rulers was widely considered acceptable. Again, the situation was most favourable in the Russian Empire (at least after Catherine had died). Poles could also enter the Russian civil administration.

Catherine claimed that the inhabitants of her annexed lands were of one nation and faith with the Russian people. Even beyond Samogitia and Courland, her claim, repeated by generations of historians in the service of Russian imperial regimes, was far from accurate. Most of the tsaritsa's new subjects were Ruthenian-speaking villagers and burghers. She gave hundreds of thousands of them, living on confiscated estates, to new Russian masters. Her destruction of the Uniate Church would be a problematic task. A major military operation undertaken in 1794 encouraged parishes in the right-bank Ukraine to exchange fidelity to Rome for obedience to St Petersburg. Here the Union had put down shallow roots, but cases of resistance were noted. The Uniate Church proved far more resilient in Volhynia and the former Grand Duchy of Lithuania, but here too, Russian imperial rule would ultimately break the hold of the Catholic Church of both rites over the east Slavic population. The very large numbers of Polish-speaking nobles (many of them landless) and burghers, as well as unassimilated Yiddish-speaking Jews, would give still greater headaches to the Russian imperial bureaucracy for decades to come. The need to have local elites on board provided opportunities to create an expanded network of secondary schools, with the reformed University of Wilno at the apex of the system. As a result, the role of Polish culture in the life of the former Lithuanian, Volhynian, Podolian and Ukrainian lands actually grew in the first three decades or so of Russian rule.

For many diehard patriots, none of this human potential could ever compensate for the loss of independent statehood. Émigrés and conspirators at home took up the insurrectionary legacy. They continued to be divided into radicals and moderates. Most of the legionaries commanded by Jan Henryk Dąbrowski died in Italy, on the Rhine, or on San Domingo, but their cause was immortalized in the jaunty mazurka given words by Józef Wybicki – *Poland has not yet Died* (later changed to *Poland has not yet Perished*). If this proclaimed defiance and confidence, a more hesitant idea of the nation is apparent from the words 'We shall cross the Vistula and the Warta, we shall be Poles'. They also sang 'Bonaparte gave us an example, how we can win'. Others placed their hopes for a restoration of Poland in the rulers of Prussia, Austria or Russia. However, not everyone wanted to rely on a foreign protector. In the title of a pamphlet published in Paris in 1800, Józef Pawlikowski asked a dramatic question: *Can Poles Fight Their Way to Independence?* Yes they could – he answered, provided that the peasantry was emancipated and mobilized to fight.

Within a few years of the third partition, the four principal responses made in the next two centuries by Poles under foreign rule or domination had emerged. All of them had roots in the Stanislavian era, if not earlier. The first three were loyalism, emigration and armed resistance. The last to take shape was what was later called 'organic work'. This strategy often required a degree of dissimulation. Given the impossibility – for the present – of recovering independent statehood, it was vitally important to work just within existing geopolitical limits on the economic, social, cultural, intellectual and above all moral condition of the Polish nation, so that, despite statelessness, it would not be swept away by the 'flood of history'. Should an opportunity arise to reclaim independence, then a well-nourished nation – physically and spiritually – would be better prepared to seize and use it than one emaciated and traumatized by failed risings. This stance, whose permissible limits were so hard to delineate, and which was so vulnerable to the interests and caprices of foreign rulers, was presaged by the policies patiently pursued by Stanisław August before 1788.[12]

Italian has an apt word for the Enlightenment. *L'Illuminismo* evokes the lighting up of what lies within, revealing problems, but also the potential for solutions and growth. In eighteenth-century Polish sources, the word *illuminacje* conjures up the decorations that used lanterns, candles, words and symbols to celebrate feasts, anniversaries and royal progresses. The grandest of these illuminations was the simulated eruption of Vesuvius on the banks of the Dnieper on 6 May 1787. Within a decade the Commonwealth had been blown sky high.

The potential within the Polish-Lithuanian political community was revealed most fully in the Stanislavian generation: men and women born in the middle years of the eighteenth century, educated and matured during the reign of Stanisław August, who continued their activity well into the nineteenth century. Their post-partition achievements were remarkable. Despite the resolution of the partitioning powers to erase the very memory of Poland, the idea of the Polish nation quite soon adapted to the condition of statelessness. Although hopes for the resurrection of the Polish state were repeatedly disappointed, they were never extinguished. In the meantime there was much to do. Cultural, scientific and educational initiatives abounded. Leading aristocratic families assembled and housed collections of books and documents, and opened them to the public.

Prince Adam Jerzy Czartoryski continued the work of the Commission of National Education at the helm of the Vilnan Educational District. However, it was in the central and western lands of the former Commonwealth that the modernizing transformations of the state and society begun in the reign of Stanisław August were most in evidence. The elite of the Stanislavian generation grasped the chance to govern first the Napoleonic Duchy of Warsaw and then the diminutive Kingdom of Poland – in personal union with the Russian Empire. Neither of these was a sovereign state. But nor, except for four years and a few months, was the Stanislavian Commonwealth. By the late 1820s, Warsaw was again thronged and thriving. The art and architecture of mature neo-classicism adorned the capital. The monumental seats of the Bank of Poland, the Society of the Friends of Science and the still unfinished Grand Theatre proclaimed the symbiosis of economic, intellectual and cultural growth. Bertel Thorvaldsen's statues symbolized complementary forms of patriotism: Prince Józef Poniatowski personified the soldiers who had shed their blood for their Fatherland, Nicolaus Copernicus – the discoverers of truths. The lessons of Stanisław August's Knights' Hall at the Royal Castle were now spread across Warsaw's urban space, for the edification of all.[13] But the space permitted by the Russian Empire for liberal politics was shrinking fast, and young minds were again – as in 1787–88 – in ferment.

Light and flame once more turned to smoke and ash after the November Rising of 1830–31. Its defeat finally brought down the curtain on the Stanislavian era. This caesura involved more than a generational change. It meant more, too, than the end of the opportunities for Polish statesmen to govern Polish lands. In exile, the Romantics transfigured the idea of Poland into a community of the spirit, mythologizing its once and future republic. Among such representations, Adam Mickiewicz's epic poem of 1834, *Pan Tadeusz*, was not only one of the most affectionate but also one of the most realistic retrospectives. 'Worship of the swinishness of rural life,' sniffed Juliusz Słowacki, having read the senior Bard's musings on change and continuity in the provincial culture of the Grand Duchy of Lithuania. He later wrote fragments of a more sublime continuation, featuring Napoleon himself as a fallen hero.[14] The defeat of the January Rising of 1863–64 prompted a withering, 'positivist' critique of nostalgia for that vanishing world.

From their academic citadel in Habsburg Cracow, the Polish nation's first generation of scientific, 'positivist' historians delivered a searing verdict on the szlachta and its values. They blamed its incurable 'anarchy' for the downfall of the Commonwealth, complementing the justifications proffered by the official historians of the partitioning monarchies. This apparent conflation of victim and perpetrators sparked an 'optimist' reaction among historians based in Russian-ruled Warsaw as well as in the rival city of Lwów – the Galician capital. The two camps continued their polemics throughout the interwar period, with the 'optimists' gaining ground. But their 'optimism' focused mainly on the transformations of the Stanislavian era. It proved harder to reassess the old Commonwealth in its own terms.[15] After the Second World War, following the imposition of Marxist-Leninist paradigms on Poland's surviving historical establishment, the obligatory framework became one of centuries of feudal oppression followed by the rise of capitalism (after 1764). This did not do much for the reputation of the Commonwealth either. It did, however, provoke another 'optimist' reaction which has gathered momentum since its cautious beginnings in Cracow in the 1960s.

Since the start of the twenty-first century, several Polish historians and political scientists have drawn on the 'republican turn' in Anglophone countries, some to idealize a 'Commonwealth of many nations',[16] others in a more Catholic, neo-Sarmatian idiom.[17] Such is the intensity of the ongoing rehabilitation of the Commonwealth (presented as a model for the United States of America and the European Union alike) that a sense of proportion is often lost. In an echo of some Romantic strictures, the Stanislavian reforms, including the work of the Commission of National Education and the Constitution of 3 May, are sometimes criticized for undermining the authentic 'national spirit'.[18] Another current tendency is to berate the Stanislavian era for introducing a narrower sense of 'Polish nationalism' in place of multi-confessional and multilingual civic patriotism(s).[19] Such arguments have not impressed the new Warsaw school of diplomatic and political history, gathered around Zofia Zielińska. Through painstaking archival research, these historians have conclusively demonstrated that at no point in the eighteenth century was Russia less fundamentally hostile than Prussia to a stronger Commonwealth. They have also, like their academic forebears Jerzy Michalski and Emanuel Rostworowski, strongly approved of Stanisław August's efforts to build a firmly governed and more unitary Polish state.

Particularly interesting – in sovereign Lithuania as well as in sovereign Poland – has been the ongoing re-evaluation of the relationship between the Polish Crown and the Grand Duchy of Lithuania. Even if Kościuszko had cried '*finis Poloniæ*' at Maciejowice (and he almost certainly did not), the defeat of the Insurrection did not herald the end of Poland. Nor did it mean the end of Lithuania. It was, however, the end of the Commonwealth – *finis Reipublicæ*. Once more, we can turn to Mickiewicz:

> True, true, Gerwazy said. How right you are!
> This our Crown and our Lithuania –
> How strange their fortunes are, like man and wife!
> God joins the twain, the devil splits in strife![20]

The hopes of 1812 were dashed. What had been sundered could not be joined together again. Not even by Józef Piłsudski, scion of the Lithuanian szlachta, who adopted Kościuszko's title of the Chief (*Naczelnik*). By the time that Poland and Lithuania were reborn as independent states at the end of the First World War, the ideas of what it meant to be Polish and – still more so – Lithuanian had changed profoundly. Not the least change was in attitudes to political and civil liberty. Both societies by and large accepted the constraints placed on parliamentary democracy following the respective coups by Piłsudski and Antanas Smetona in 1926. Anarchy had been the great sin of the past, which had been severely punished by the partitions. On this, if on little else, Piłsudski concurred with his great political and ideological rival, the 'modern Pole', Roman

Dmowski. Although Piłsudski was enthroned, even in his lifetime, in the pantheon of the Commonwealth's martial heroes, the Commonwealth's libertarian and republican values remained under a cloud. While the authoritarian regimes of Smetona and Piłsudski were mild indeed by the standards of contemporaneous totalitarian dictatorships, they were also distant in spirit from the neo-Roman insurrectionary dictatorships of Kościuszko and his nineteenth-century successors.

Polish and Lithuanian identities could still consubstantiate in the Romantic sphere of the spirit, so beloved of Piłsudski. They could mingle languidly in country manor houses where the traditions of the Grand Duchy of Lithuania were contrasted nostalgically to those of the Polish Crown. They could be bandied about in modish salons where the literary and artistic avant-garde enthused about the folklore, customs and languages of the local peasantry. But in the real world of the late nineteenth and early twentieth centuries, Polishness and Lithuanity were ineluctably riven by sharp social and cultural conflicts – between the assumptions of old elites and the aspirations of rising groups. They collided over questions such as the languages of schooling and worship. Modern Lithuanian nationalists identified the prestige of Polish culture as a mortal threat to their endeavour to build a modern, ethno-linguistic Lithuanian nation. To them it seemed more dangerous than the restrictions imposed by the Russian imperial regime. The trend among both 'modern' Poles and 'young' Lithuanians towards a social-Darwinist understanding of nations locked in an endless struggle for survival and mastery accomplished the rest. Painful as this cleavage was for the minority of 'old' or 'historical' Polonophone Lithuanians, they had to choose. So, for example, in 1918 one brother signed the Lithuanian declaration of independence as Stanislovas Narutovičius, while four years later, his younger sibling became the first elected president of the Second Polish Republic – Gabriel Narutowicz. It did not end well for either of them. The older brother committed suicide in 1932, a decade after the assassination of the younger. Their states did not maintain diplomatic relations, because the Polish incorporation, following a staged mutiny, of the ancient Lithuanian capital city – Vilnius – could not be forgiven. From this perspective, the fact that only a very small minority of Vilnans spoke Lithuanian was neither here nor there.

During the *interbellum*, Polish and Lithuanian schools taught mutually exclusive histories of their nations' former union. The Polish vision emphasized heroic deeds undermined by an anarchic szlachta, treacherous magnates (especially

Lithuanian ones), and at the close, a cowardly king. Lithuanian nationalists wrote off more than half the history of the Grand Duchy of Lithuania as a lamentable period of Polonization, followed by the fall of a failed state that was no longer Lithuanian. Patronizing Poles refused to treat them seriously. There was, however, a kind of consensus about the Constitution of 3 May 1791. This was assumed to have sealed a long-term process whereby the Grand Duchy of Lithuania became the third province of Poland, alongside Lesser and Greater Poland. Poles tended to see this as a natural and desirable outcome, whereas for Lithuanians it summed up the disastrous trajectory of their history after the death of Vytautas the Great in 1430. The ruinous union with Poland had all but destroyed the Lithuanian nation, until, under tsarist rule, it could be reawakened among the Lithuanian-speaking peasantry.

The *Mutual Assurance of the Two Nations* of October 1791 slid into near-oblivion. Then, just before the Second World War, the doyen of modern Lithuanian historians, Adolfas Šapoka, realized its significance: the Constitution of 3 May had not, after all, put an end to the union of the Two Nations; it had not finally incorporated innocent Lithuania into wicked Poland (the very view he had just popularized in the authorized national synthesis of Lithuanian history). On the contrary, because the *Mutual Assurance* became an integral part of the Constitution, the dualist union had been reiterated. However, the Soviet takeover of independent Lithuania prevented the dissemination of his valuable monograph on the Four Years' Sejm. From the end of the nineteenth century onwards, several Polish historians noted the resurgence of dualism after 3 May 1791, but did not celebrate or underline it. A wider impact came during the bicentennial year of 1991, which was also the year in which the restored independence of the Republic of Lithuania was recognized internationally. The legal historian Juliusz Bardach, who had studied at the Stefan Batory University in Wilno in independent Poland, applied the conclusion reached by his predecessors to the cause of reconciliation between modern Poles and modern Lithuanians. His efforts struck a chord as scholars began to read Šapoka's work more frequently in typescript. It was finally published in 2008.

This positive re-evaluation of the *Mutual Assurance* has helped ongoing efforts at improving the often fraught relations between Poland and Lithuania. They have included some joint celebrations of the Constitution of 3 May. Indeed, the *Mutual Assurance* is fast becoming a new myth about that much mythologized act. At the (slight) risk of undermining this geopolitically imperative project of reconciliation, it should be pointed out that while the text of the *Mutual Assurance* repeatedly refers to the Polish Crown and the Grand Duchy of Lithuania, it also uses the singular dative form 'to this double nation' (*oboiemu temu Narodowi*), and emphasizes 'our duty towards our common Fatherland, the Polish Commonwealth'.[21] This point means more than pedantry (useful as pedantry often is to the historian). Such terminological imprecision, however infuriating to constitutional lawyers and modern nationalists alike, reflects a now vanished world when a speech, sermon, sejmik instruction or even the *Act of Insurrection of the Lithuanian Nation* could, occasionally even in the same paragraph, speak of the Grand Duchy of Lithuania, or a Lithuanian province, or a Lithuanian nation, or a Polish nation, or a Polish Commonwealth, or the Kingdom of Poland or some combination thereof. Perhaps this very imprecision helped plural, overlapping identities to co-exist fruitfully within a strong and growing attachment to 'the nation', 'the Fatherland', or, dare one say it, 'Poland'.[22]

This imprecisely defined Poland of old continues to contribute to the cumulative process which has honed the sharper-edged Poland of the early twenty-first century. By its admirers this process is called a living tradition. It can be traced back over more than a thousand years, or about forty generations. This puts into perspective the mere nine generations that have now passed since the immolation of the Commonwealth. The latest attempt at a national synthesis, Andrzej Nowak's magisterial, multi-volume *History of Poland*, is written in a spirit that consciously emulates the *Chronica seu originale regum et principum Poloniæ* of Bishop Wincenty Kadłubek (died 1223, beatified 1764). This spirit seeks meaning in shared stories of the past, replete with moral lessons, hoping to inspire the national community of the future to realize its full potential. Long may it continue.[23]

Historians may be inspired by another nation's story and take up its cause, without their sympathy lowering their critical standards. So it was with the great American diplomatic historian Robert Howard Lord (1885–1954). After publishing his doctoral thesis on the second partition ('the classic example of the moral degeneracy and rottenness of the old monarchical Europe'), he became a full professor at Harvard University. Shortly afterwards he advised President Woodrow Wilson on Polish affairs at the Paris peace conference of 1919. He published a further article on the third partition, the 'crowning iniquity of eighteenth-century diplomacy', resigned his chair, and became a Roman Catholic priest.[24] It is also possible to write responsible, accurate and empathetic history from cosmopolitan, liberal and progressive perspectives. Three illustrious historians of the 'Atlantic Revolution' – Jacques Godechot (1907–1989), Robert Roswell Palmer (1909–2002) and Franco Venturi (1914–1994) – viewed the Polish reforms as a positive example to humanity.[25]

However, politicians, priests, ideologues, social scientists, literati, journalists and, sad to say, amateur and professional historians abound who display no such sophistication or sensitivity. Some of them caricature and manipulate the past for political advantage, career advancement or commercial gain. Others, perhaps more nobly, take shocking liberties with history because they genuinely believe that on such manipulation depend, for example, the future of Catholic Poland, ethnic Lithuania, heroic Ukraine, neo-imperial Russia, or post-national, post-religious Europe. Others just love to shock.[26] Worse still, several states' policies of history and memory involve the criminal law. This can stifle scholarly enquiry as well as public debate.

Still more toxic is the post-modernist orthodoxy that all 'history' is simply a discourse to shore up existing power elites. It must therefore be replaced by other 'metanarratives', arbitrarily constructed without regard for the rules of evidence, to justify the leadership of the 'oppressed' by new elites, self-appointed and self-obsessed. Granted, no work of history can fully represent even a small fragment of the human past, and no historian is ever completely dispassionate. Even historians' cardinal virtue of scepticism can corrode into cynicism. But some endeavours to understand the past – and to apply the understanding of the past to shaping the future – are better founded in the careful and honest interpretation of its surviving traces than are others. Some interpretations are therefore more probable than others. They are closer, in other words, to the truth – the truth which all honest historians should pursue. In contrast, some 'histories' are downright lies, based on the deliberate manipulation, suppression, or even falsification of evidence.

Poland and other nations are now beset by global culture wars, which are sometimes cast for and against a travestied 'Enlightenment'. At a time when neo-Sarmatism takes the form of partly shaven heads, football hooligans' banners and violent computer games, the need is greater than ever for rigorous historical research on the last decades of the old Commonwealth. Such research should not hesitate either to challenge orthodoxies (whether they are time-hallowed or newly fashionable) or to endorse those orthodoxies verified by the balance of evidence.

If the public is not to be left at the mercy of charlatans and fanatics, that research must be communicated, via a range of media, in an accessible manner. This book has sought, however imperfectly, to bring to a wider audience the findings of the best research conducted on the eighteenth-century Commonwealth. Perhaps it has even made some contributions of its own, which may be of interest to specialists. Above all, it has used this research to make an argument. On the whole, it is an optimistic argument for all those who value both individual and collective freedom.

The Stanislavian Commonwealth was not a failed state. It was not put out of its anarchic misery by its better-governed neighbours. In exceptionally unfavourable conditions, this alternately becalmed and battered ship of state managed to catch the wind in its sails. Once it had escaped the doldrums of Russian hegemony in 1788, the Commonwealth sailed into strategically vital waters, threatening its neighbours' geopolitical interests. It also challenged the neighbouring monarchs ideologically. Contrary to the legend of 'lordly Poland' (*panskaia Polsha*), avidly spread by the Bolsheviks, the nobiliary Polish nation, for all its encrusted prejudices, was a political community that belatedly took the path towards encompassing the entire population of the 'territories of the Commonwealth'.

This transformative choice was grounded in the ongoing economic and demographic recovery that had begun in the 1730s. While reaching a *modus vivendi* with the Catholic clergy, once again the Catholic nobility learned to deal with (if not exactly embrace) religious diversity. For the supreme value of the political community was liberty. Many of its members grasped that their individual and collective freedoms depended on stable governance and external independence. Moving beyond the struggle *inter maiestatem ac libertatem*, they came to trust their king, a tireless reformer, to preside over 'orderly freedom'. They refreshed a broadly republican set of civic values with elements of limited and parliamentary monarchy. Contests in the public sphere between reformers and traditionalists precipitated a cultural efflorescence, as well as a naive optimism about Poland's future prospects in what remained a cut-throat international system. All this was achieved through a middle course steered between the Scylla of absolute monarchy and the Charybdis of revolutionary terror. By 1792 the Commonwealth was a going concern, well prepared to sail into the global waters of the nineteenth century. So our ship was repeatedly raked with crossfire and sunk.

GLOSSARY

Castle court (*sąd grodzki*)	A civil and criminal court presided over by a starosta and a castle court judge, nominated by the starosta with jurisdiction over both nobles and burghers.
Commonwealth (*Rzeczpospolita*)	This translation of *Res publica* referred to the state and territories of the union of the Crown of the Kingdom of Poland, the Grand Duchy of Lithuania, Royal Prussia, Livonia and other dominions, as well as to the political community and its values. Once referred to as the Republic of Poland, it is now usually called the Polish-Lithuanian Commonwealth.
Confederacy (*konfederacja*)	A league of nobles, formed in an emergency, either 'around the king' or in opposition to him. The general council (generalcy) of a confederacy could take decisions by majority vote, so a confederated sejm was not subject to the *liberum veto*.
Cossacks	The Zaporozhian Cossacks had been a self-governing army in the service of the king and Commonwealth until the great revolt of 1648; after submitting to Muscovy their autonomy was gradually reduced and finally abolished by Catherine II, who made Potemkin their commander. The term also applied to the Don and Volga Cossacks in the service of the tsars, and to soldiers maintained privately by Polish lords in the Ukraine.
Crown (*Korona, Corona Regni Poloniæ*)	The Crown of the Kingdom of Poland constituted about two-thirds of the Commonwealth's territory after 1569: the term also conveyed the political community of the realm. Also referred to as the Polish Crown.

Crown estates (*królewszczyzny*)	The lands granted to a starosta. Starostas were obliged to pay a quarter of the net revenues to the treasury, but this *kwarta* was notoriously under-assessed.
Grand Duchy of Lithuania (*Wielkie Księstwo Litewskie*)	Fourteenth-century Europe's largest polity first united with the Crown of the Kingdom of Poland in 1385; their evolving union was consolidated at Lublin in 1569, when the Grand Duchy's southern Ruthenian territories were transferred to the Crown. Lithuania maintained its own laws, army, treasury and offices.
Hetman	Commander of the armed forces. The Crown and the Grand Duchy of Lithuania each had a grand and a field hetman. Their prerogatives were curtailed in 1764, 1775 and 1776.
Jurydyka	Noble- or Church-owned land in a royal town, not subject (until 1791) to municipal jurisdiction or guild restrictions.
Koliivshchyna (*koliszczyzna*)	An exceptionally violent, large-scale Cossack and peasant revolt which erupted in the Polish Ukraine in 1768; just as savagely repressed.
Land court (*sąd ziemski*)	A civil and lesser criminal court with jurisdiction over settled nobles, presided over by judges elected by sejmiks.
Landtag	The diet of the Royal Prussian Estates had two chambers: the upper comprised senators and the representatives of the three cities of Danzig, Thorn and Elbing; the lower gathered the nobility of the three Royal Prussian palatinates.
Liberum veto	The right of one or more envoys to refuse consent to a decision or the continued proceedings of the sejm (the latter was known pejoratively as the *liberum rumpo*).
Ministers	The highest offices of the Commonwealth: the grand marshals, grand chancellors, vice-chancellors, court marshals and treasurers of the Crown and Lithuania. From 1768 they were joined as *ex officio* members of the senate by the grand and field hetmans, and from 1775 by the court treasurers. Nominated by the king for life until 1775.

Muscovy (*Moskwa*)	The principality of Rus′ centred on Moscow, whose rulers (styled tsars) controversially claimed imperial dominion over all Rus′ from the late fifteenth century onwards. Transformed into the Russian Empire by Peter I in 1721. 'Muscovite' (*Moskal*) remained a pejorative Polish label for Russians well after the partitions.
Neminem captivabimus nisi iure victum	Privileges issued by King Władysław Jagiełło in 1425, 1430 and 1433 guaranteeing nobles' freedom from imprisonment without a lawful trial and sentence.
Pacta conventa	Effectively the contract of employment agreed with each newly elected monarch. They incorporated the more general Henrician Articles drawn up for Henri Valois in 1573. If the king broke the pacts, his noble subjects were entitled to refuse him obedience.
Permanent Council (*Rada Nieustająca*)	Established by the sejm of 1773–75 as a central supervisory and executive body to replace the Senate Council. Composed of the king and eighteen senators and eighteen envoys elected by the sejm. Took on some royal prerogatives. Strengthened in 1776, abolished in 1789.
Primate (*prymas*)	The archbishop of Gniezno held the title and precedence of primate of Poland. He acted as *interrex* during an interregnum.
Prussia	The lands of the pagan Prussian tribes were conquered by the Teutonic Order. In 1454 the western part of the Order's state united with the Crown of the Kingdom of Poland as Royal Prussia. The terms of union were often contested. In 1525 the remaining eastern part became the vassal Duchy of Prussia under the Hohenzollerns, who gained sovereignty in 1657 and became Kings *in* Prussia from 1701. Following the first partition of the Commonwealth in 1772, Royal (or Polish) Prussia was renamed West Prussia, to distinguish it from East (formerly Ducal) Prussia, and the Hohenzollerns became Kings *of* Prussia.

Rus′	Originally referred to a people, then to their lands. Kievan Rus′ fell apart in the thirteenth century under the impact of the Mongols. Its legacy was contested principally by the Grand Duchy of Lithuania and Muscovy.
Russia	A medieval Latin translation of Rus′, also mediated by the Byzantine Greek *Rhossia* and the Russian *Rossiia*. Refers here to the Russian Empire (*Rossiiskaia Imperia*) proclaimed by Peter I in 1721.
Ruthenia (*Ruś*)	Another medieval Latin translation of Rus′. Refers here to the lands of post-Kievan Rus′ which remained in the Commonwealth after the mid-seventeenth century (they now comprise all of Belarus, about half of Ukraine and the easternmost fringes of Poland). 'Red Ruthenia' (formerly the southern part of the principality of Halych-Rus′ and later the eastern half of Habsburg Galicia) formed the palatinate of Ruthenia.
Ruthenian (*ruskii*)	The east Slavic language and dialects spoken in the Grand Duchy of Lithuania and the Ruthenian lands of the Polish Crown, which later developed into modern Belarusian and Ukrainian. Chancery Ruthenian was the legal language of these lands until 1697.
Sarmatism (*sarmatyzm*)	The theory of the Polish szlachta's descent from ancient Sarmatians led to the identification of the Commonwealth with 'Sarmatia' and begat a distinctive 'Sarmatian' culture and lifestyle. Later eighteenth-century reformers' mockery of traditional mores and superstitions as 'Sarmatism' have spurred ongoing 'neo-Sarmatian' revivals.
Sejm	The Commonwealth's parliament or diet, composed of three Estates: the king, the senate and the knighthood, whose envoys were elected by sejmiks and composed the Chamber of Envoys.
Sejmik	A dietine or assembly of the nobility of a land, district, palatinate or group of palatinates. Some sejmiks elected envoys to the sejm, others judges to the Tribunals, others dealt with local business and elected local officials.

Senate (*senat*) — The upper chamber of the sejm, presided over by the monarch, comprising archbishops and bishops, palatines, castellans, the starosta of Samogitia and ministers. The king nominated senators for life until 1775.

Senate Council — Originally composed of senators nominated by the sejm to reside by the monarch between sejms. It became a forum of all available senators which the king could summon for advice and decisions. Replaced by the Permanent Council in 1775.

Starosta (*capitaneus*) — The holder of a *starostwo*, originally the office of a royal representative. Some *starostwa* had judicial responsibilities; others did not, but the latter tended to be best endowed with Crown estates.

Szlachta — The nobility, comprising 6–8 per cent of the Commonwealth's population in the eighteenth century.

Tribunal (*trybunał*) — The supreme courts of appeal for the nobility of the Crown and the Grand Duchy of Lithuania, whose lay judges were elected by sejmiks.

Ukraine (*Ukraina*) — Referred in the eighteenth century to a smaller area than today's Republic of Ukraine. Divided into the Russian Ukraine on the left bank of the River Dnieper, and the Polish Ukraine on most of the right bank. The latter comprised the palatinates of Kiev and Bracław, more rarely including those of Podolia and Volhynia.

Uniates (*unici*) — The 1595–96 Union of Brest divided the Commonwealth's Orthodox Christians into those who united with the Catholic Church – called Uniates – and those who did not (pejoratively called 'disuniates'). In the eighteenth-century Commonwealth, the Uniate Church was called the Ruthenian or Greek Rite, as opposed to the Latin Rite, of the Catholic Church. Suppressed in the Russian Empire after the partitions, the Uniate Church flourished in the Habsburg Monarchy, where the two rites were called the Greek Catholic and Roman Catholic Churches.

GAZETTEER

There is no fully satisfactory way of rendering place names in early modern East-Central Europe. The ownership of many places has since been bitterly contested, and for many people their names still thrum with emotion. Given the paucity of acceptable English names, I have preferred the versions that reflect the dominant culture of the time and place in question (usually Polish or German), rather than those applicable now. This is however an imperfect approximation; we should not forget early modern multilingualism. The version usually used in the book is given in **bold**; the version in the official language of the state currently in possession is given in *italics*.

English/Other	*Polish*	*Lithuanian*	*Latvian*	*Belarusian*	*Ukrainian*	*Russian*	*German*	*Yiddish*
	Berezwecz			*Beraz´vechcha, Hlybokae*				
(river)	**Berezyna**			*Biarezina*		Berezina		
	Biała Cerkiew				*Bila Tserkva*	Belaia Tserkov		Shvartze Timme
	Bobrujsk			*Babruisk*		Bobruisk		Babruysk
(river)	**Boh**				*Pivdennyi Buh*	Iuzhnii Bug		
	Bracław				*Bratslav*	Bratslav		Broslev
	Brasław	Breslauja		*Braslaŭ*		Braslav		Breslev
	Wrocław						**Breslau**	
	Brody				*Brody*			Brod
Brest	**Brześć Litewski**	Brasta		*Brest/ Berastse*	Berestia	Brest-Litovsk		Brisk
(river)	***Bug***			*Zakhodni Buh*	*Zakhidnyi Buh*	Zapadnii Bug		
	Chełm				Kholm			Khelem
	Chełmno						Kulm	
	Chocim				*Khotyn*			
	Chołopienicze			*Khalopenichy*		Kholopenichy		Khalopenits
	Chwastów				*Fastiv*			Khvastev
Courland	Kurlandia		*Kurzeme*				Kurland	

English/Other	*Polish*	*Lithuanian*	*Latvian*	*Belarusian*	*Ukrainian*	*Russian*	*German*	*Yiddish*
Cracow	*Kraków*							Kroke
Cujavia	*Kujawy*							
	Czehryń				*Chyhyryn*			
	Czernihów				*Chernihiv*	Chernigov		Tshernikhev
	Dąbrowica				*Dubrovytsia*	Dubrovytsia		Dombrevits
	Gdańsk						**Danzig**	Dantsk
River Dnieper	Dniepr			*Dniapro*		*Dnepr*		*Dnipro*
River Dniester	Dniestr				*Dnister*	Dnestr		
(river)	**Druć**			*Druts′*		Drut′		
	Druja			*Druia*		Druia		Drue
	Dynemunt		*Daugavgrīva*				**Dünamünde**	
(river)	Dźwina		*Daugava*	*Dzvina*		***Dvina***		Düna
	Dyneburg	Daugpilis	*Daugavpils*	Dzvinsk		Dvinsk	Dünaburg	Deneborg
					Dnipro	**Ekatineroslav**		
	Elbląg						**Elbing**	
Galați (Romanian)	Gałacz				Halats	Galats	**Galatz**	
Greater Poland	*Wielkopolska*							
	Grodno	Gardinas		*Hrodna*		Grodno		Grodne
	Hadziacz				***Hadiach***			
	Horodec			*Horodets*				Horodets

English/Other	*Polish*	*Lithuanian*	*Latvian*	*Belarusian*	*Ukrainian*	*Russian*	*German*	*Yiddish*
(river)	**Horyń**			*Haryn´*	*Horyn´*			
	Humań				*Uman´*			Human
	Jasiołda			*Iaselda*				
Iaşi (Moldova, Romanian)	**Jassy**				Ias´	Iass´	**Jassy**	Yas
	Kamieniec Podolski				*Kamianets´ Podil´s´kyi*			
	Kaniów				*Kaniv*	Kanev		Konev
	Kargowa						Unruhstadt	
Karlovy Vary (Czech)							**Karlsbad**	
	Kijów				*Kyiv*	**Kiev**		
	Królewiec					*Kaliningrad*	**Königsberg**	
	Korsuń				*Korsun*			Korsn
	Kowno	*Kaunas*		Koŭno		Kovno	Kauen	Kovne
	Krewo	Krėva		***Kreva***				
	Kroże	*Kražiai*						Krozh
	Krystynopol				*Chervonohrad*			Krisnipole
	Latyczów				*Letychiv*			
Lesser Poland	*Małopolska*							
	Lipawa		*Liepāja*				**Libau**	Libave

English/Other	*Polish*	*Lithuanian*	*Latvian*	*Belarusian*	*Ukrainian*	*Russian*	*German*	*Yiddish*
	Lida	Lyda		*Lida*		Lida		
Livonia	Inflanty	Livonija	Livonija/ Inflantija			Lifliandia	Livland	
	Łojów			*Loieŭ*				Loev
	Lubar				*Liubar*			Luber
	Łuck				*Luts′k*			Loytsk
	Lwów				*L′viv*	L′vov	Lemberg	Lemberik
	Kwidzyń						**Marienwerder**	
Mazovia	*Mazowsze*							
	Merecz	*Merkinė*				Merech′		Meretch
	Międzyrzecz Ostrogski				*Mezhyrich*			
	Mińsk	Minskas		***Minsk****/Mensk*		**Minsk**		Mintsik
	Mohylew			*Mahilioŭ*		Mogilev		Molev
	Mohyłów				*Mohyliv*			Mohilev
	Motrenin				*Motronyn*			
(river)	*Motława*						**Mottlau**	
	Mozyrz	Mozyrius		*Mazyr*		Mozyr		Mazhir
	Mścisław	Mstislavlis		*Mstsislaŭ*		Mstislavl′		
(river)	**Muchawiec**			*Mukhavets*				
	Nerubaj				*Nerubai*			

English/Other	*Polish*	*Lithuanian*	*Latvian*	*Belarusian*	*Ukrainian*	*Russian*	*German*	*Yiddish*
	Newel			Nevel′		*Nevel′*		
(river)	**Niemen**	*Nemunas*		*Neman*		*Neman*	Memel	
	Nieśwież			*Niasvizh*		Nesvizh		Nezvizh
	Nowogródek	Naugardukas		*Navahrudak*		Novogrudok		Navaredok
	Oczaków				*Ochakiv*	**Ochakov**		
	Olita	*Alytus*						Alite
	Oliwa						**Oliva**	
	Orawa			*Orava*		Orava		
	Orsza	Orša		*Orsha*		Orsha		Orshe
	Ostróg				*Ostroh*			Ostre
	Oszmiany	Ašmena		*Ashmiany*		Oshmiany		Oshmene
	Perejasław				***Pereiaslav***	Pereiaslavl		
	Piltyń		*Piltene*				**Pilten**	
	Pińsk	Pinskas		Pinsk	Pynsk			Pintsk
	Poczajów				*Pochaiv*	Pochaev		
Podolia	Podole				*Podillia*	Podole		Podole
Podlachia	***Podlasie***	Palenkė		Padliashsha	Pidlissia			Podlashe
	Połąga	*Palanga*						Palonge
Polesia	***Polesie***			*Palesse*	*Polissia*	*Polese*		
	Połock	Polockas		*Polatsk*		Polotsk		Polotsk
	Połonne				*Polonne*			Polone

English/Other	***Polish***	***Lithuanian***	***Latvian***	***Belarusian***	***Ukrainian***	***Russian***	***German***	***Yiddish***
	Poznań						Posen	Poyzn
	Preny	*Prieniai*						Pren
River Pripet	Prypeć			*Pripiats´*	*Pripiat´*	Pripiat´		
Prussia	Prusy						Preussen	
	Przemyśl				Peremyshl´			Peremisle
	Dzierżoniów						**Reichenbach**	
	Rohaczew			*Rahachoŭ*		Rogachev		
Ruthenia / Russia	*Ruś / Rosja*	Rusija	Krievija	***Rus´*** */ Rasiia*	***Rus´*** */ Rosiia*	***Rus´*** */ Rossiia*	Ruthenien/ Russland	Rusland
	Rzeczyca	Rečica		*Rechytsa*		Rechytsa		Retshitse
Samogitia	Żmudź	*Žemaitija*						
Semigallia	Semigalia		*Zemgale*				Semgallen	
Severia	Siewierz				*Siveria*	*Severshchina*		
	Siebież					*Sebezh*		
	Słonim	Slanimas		*Slonim*		Slonim		Slonim
	Słuck	Sluckas		*Slutsk*		Slutsk		Slutsk
	Smiła				***Smila***			Smile
	Smoleńsk	Smolenskas				**Smolensk**		
Spiš (Slovak)	**Spisz**						Zips	
	Starodub	Starodubas				*Starodub*		
	Suwałki	Suvalkai						Suvalk

English/Other	*Polish*	*Lithuanian*	*Latvian*	*Belarusian*	*Ukrainian*	*Russian*	*German*	*Yiddish*
	Święta	*Šventoji*						
	Szawle	*Šiauliai*						Shavl
	Szczara			*Shchara*				
	Szkłów			*Shkloŭ*		Shklov		Shklov
	Szydłów	*Šiluva*						Shidleve
	Targowica				*Torhovytsia*			
(river)	**Taśmin**				*Tiasmyn*			
	Toruń						**Thorn**	
	Tołoczyn			*Talachyn*		Tolochin		Talatshin
	Troki	*Trakai*		Troki				Trok
	Tulczyn				*Tul´chyn*			Toltshin
	Upita	*Upytė*						Upine
	Uszacz			*Ushachy*		Ushachy		Ushach
River Vistula	*Wisła*						Weichsel	
Volhynia	Wołyń				*Volyn´*			Volin
	Warmia						Ermland	
Warsaw	*Warszawa*						Warschau	Varshe
	Welawa	Vėluva				*Znamensk*	**Wehlau**	
Wejrowo (Kashubian)	***Wejherowo***						Weierfrei/ Neustadt-in-Westpreussen	

English/Other	*Polish*	*Lithuanian*	*Latvian*	*Belarusian*	*Ukrainian*	*Russian*	*German*	*Yiddish*
	Werki	*Verkiai*						
(river)	**Wilia**	*Neris*		*Viliia*				
	Wilkomierz	*Ukmergė*						Vilkomir
	Wilno	*Vilnius*		Vil´nia		Vil´na	Wilna	Vilne
(river)	Windawa	*Venta*	*Venta*				**Windau**	
	Winnica				*Vinnytsia*	Vinnitsa		Vinitse
	Wiśniowiec				*Vyshnivets´*			Vishnifits
	Witebsk	*Vitebskas*		*Vitsebsk*		Vitebsk		Vitepsk
	Włodzimierz (Wołyński)				*Volodymyr Volyns´kyi*	Vladimir Volynskii		Ludmer
	Wołczyn			*Voŭchin*				
	Wołkowysk	Valkaviskas		*Vaŭkavysk*				Valkevisk
	Wschowa						Fraustadt	
	Żabotyn				*Zhabotyn*			
Zaporozhian Sich	Sicz Zaporoska				*Zaporiz´ka Sich*	Zaporozhskaia Sech´		
	Zasław				*Iziaslav*			Zaslev
(river)	**Zbrucz**				*Zbruch*			
	Zieleńce				*Zelentsi*			
	Żytomierz				*Zhytomyr*	Zhitomir		Zhitomer

NOTES

Most of the primary and secondary sources on which this book is based are in Polish and few readers will be able to consult them. I have therefore shortened the notes compared to the Polish edition. I have not referenced every statement or argument, but only quotations and very specific intellectual debts. In place of a bibliography, I have provided a guide to the principal literature on which each chapter is based, giving priority to works in English. To save space, many subtitles of books, journals and articles have been omitted, and only the primary place of publication is given for books. This is Warsaw unless stated otherwise. Shortened titles are employed for subsequent citations. My apologies to the translators I have excised. The abbreviations listed below are also employed in the notes.

ABBREVIATIONS

AAV ANV	Archivio Apostolico Vaticano, Archivo della Nunziatura Apostolica a Varsavia
AGAD	Archiwum Główne Akt Dawnych, Warsaw
AMS	Archiwum Księży Misjonarzy na Stradomiu, Cracow
APH	*Acta Poloniae Historica*
APP	Archiwum Publiczne Potockich, AGAD
ASC	Archiwum Sejmu Czteroletniego, AGAD
BC	Biblioteka Czartoryskich, Cracow
BEN	*Biblioteka Epoki Nowożytnej*
BGdPAN	Biblioteka Gdańska Polskiej Akademii Nauk
BHS	*Biuletyn Historii Sztuki*
BPAUiPAN	Biblioteka Polskiej Akademii Umiejętności i Polskiej Akademii Nauk, Cracow
Bo insza jest rzecz zdradzić	*Bo insza jest rzecz zdradzić, insza dać się złudzić. Problem zdrady w Polsce przełomu XVIII i XIX w.*, ed. Anna Grześkowiak-Krwawicz, 1995
BZNiO	Biblioteka Zakładu Narodowego im. Ossolińskich, Wrocław
Constitution and Reform	*Constitution and Reform in Eighteenth-Century Poland: The Constitution of 3 May 1791*, ed. Samuel Fiszman, Bloomington, IN, 1997
Correspondance	*Correspondance de Stanislas-Auguste avec Catherine II et ses plus proches collaborateurs (1764–1796)*, ed. Zofia Zielińska, Cracow, 2015
CPH	*Czasopismo Prawno-Historyczne*

Dwór, plebania	*Dwór, plebania, rodzina chłopska. Studia z dziejów wsi polskiej XVII i XVIII wieku*, ed. Magdalena Ślusarska, 1998
Dyaryusz 1788	*Dyaryusz Seymu Ordynaryinego pod związkiem Konfederacyi Generalney Oboyga Narodów w Warszawie rozpoczętego roku pańskiego 1788*, 2 vols (4 parts) Warsaw: Drukarnia Nadworna JKMci P. Kommissyi Eduk: Narodowey, 1790
Dyaryusz 1790	*Dyaryusz Seymu Ordynaryinego pod związkiem Konfederacyi Generalney Oboyga Narodów w podwoynym składzie zgromadzonego w Warszawie od dnia 16 grudnia roku 1790*, 1 volume (2 parts), Warsaw: Michał Gröll, 1791
HGd	*Historia Gdańska*, vol. 3, parts 1–2, ed. Edmund Cieślak, Gdańsk, 1993
HJ	*Historical Journal*
HUS	*Harvard Ukrainian Studies*
JfGO	*Jahrbücher für Geschichte Osteuropas*
Kalinka, *Ostatnie lata*	Walerian Kalinka, *Ostatnie lata panowania Stanisława Augusta*, part 2, *Dokumenta do historyi drugiego i trzeciego podziału*, 2nd edn, Cracow, 1891
KH	*Kwartalnik Historyczny*
Konfederacja barska	*Konfederacja barska. Jej konteksty i tradycje*, ed. Anna Buchmann and Adam Danilczyk, 2009
Korespondencja Naruszewicza	*Korespondencja Adama Naruszewicza 1762–1796*, ed. Julian Platt and Tadeusz Mikulski, Wrocław, 1959
KPSAAD	*Korespondencja polityczna Stanisława Augusta. Augustyn Deboli*, ed. Ewa Zielińska and Adam Danilczyk, *1780*: 2012, *1781*: 2015, *1782*: 2017
LDKSI	*Lietuvios Didžiosios Kunigaikštytės seimelių instrukcijos (1788–1792)*, ed. Robertas Jurgaitis et al., Vilnius, 2015
LHS	*Lithuanian Historical Studies*
LLVPD	*Lenkijos-Lietuvos valstybės padalijimų dokumentai*, i: *Sankt Peterburgo konvencijos*, ed. Ramunė Šmigelskytė-Stukienė, Vilnius, 2008
LVIA SA	Lietuvos valstybės istorijos archyvas, Senoji aktai, Vilnius
MDSC	*Materiały do dziejów Sejmu Czteroletniego*, 6 vols, ed. Janusz Woliński et al., Wrocław, 1955–69
Michalski, *SH*	Jerzy Michalski, *Studia historyczne z XVIII i XIX wieku*, 2 vols, 2007
Między Konstytucją	*Między Konstytucją a Targowicą. Korespondencja i pisma polityczne prymasa Michała Jerzego Poniatowskiego z lat 1791–1793*, ed. Angela Sołtys, 2018
My i oni	*My i oni. Społeczeństwo nowożytnej Rzeczypospolitej wobec państwa*, ed. Wojciech Kriegseisen, 2016
NP	*Nasza Przeszłość*
Pamiętniki SA	*Pamiętniki Stanisława Augusta i ich bohaterowie*, ed. Anna Grześkowiak-Krwawicz, 2015
Pan Tadeusz	Adam Mickiewicz, *Pan Tadeusz or the Last Foray in Lithuania*, trans. Kenneth R. MacKenzie, 7th bilingual edn, Łomianki, 2009

PH	*Przegląd Historyczny*
PNH	*Przegląd Nauk Historycznych*
Polish-Lithuanian Monarchy	*The Polish-Lithuanian Monarchy in European Context, c. 1500–1795*, ed. Richard Butterwick, Basingstoke, 2001
Powstanie kościuszkowskie	*Powstanie kościuszkowskie Z dziejów polityczno-społecznych*, ed. Janusz Wojtasik, 1997
Prusy 1701–1806	*Prusy w okresie monarchii absolutnej (1701–1806)*, ed. Bohdan Wachowiak, Poznań, 2010
PSB	*Polski Słownik Biograficzny*, 52 vols to date, Cracow, Wrocław and Warsaw, 1935–
RL	*Rocznik Lituanistyczny*
Rok Monarchii	*„Rok Monarchii Konstytucyjnej". Piśmiennictwo polskie lat 1791–1792 wobec Konstytucji 3 Maja*, ed. Teresa Kostkiewiczowa, 1992
SA	Stanisław August
SA, *Mémoires*	Stanislas Auguste, *Mémoires*, ed. Anna Grześkowiak-Krwawicz and Dominique Triaire, Paris, 2012
SAOKP	*Stanisław August. Ostatni król Polski. Polityk – mecenas – reformator 1764–1795*, exhibition catalogue, ed. Angela Sołtys, 2011
SARz	*Stanisław August i jego Rzeczpospolita. Dramat państwa, odrodzenie narodu*, ed. Angela Sołtys and Zofia Zielińska, 2013
SEER	*Slavonic and East European Review*
SH	*Studia Historyczne*
SIRIO	*Sbornik Imperatorskogo Russkogo Istoricheskogo Obshchestva*, 148 vols, St Petersburg, 1867–1916
Social and Cultural Relations	*Social and Cultural Relations in the Grand Duchy of Lithuania: Microhistories*, ed. Richard Butterwick and Wioletta Pawlikowska, New York, 2019
SVEC	*Studies on Voltaire and the Eighteenth Century*
Theiner	*Vetera monumenta Poloniae et Lithuaniae*, ed. Augustinus Theiner, iv, Rome, 1864
TNA FO 62	The National Archives, Kew, Foreign Office 62 (Poland)
Trudne stulecia	*Trudne stulecia. Studia z dziejów XVII i XVIII wieku ofiarowane Profesorowi Jerzemu Michalskiemu*, ed. Łukasz Kądziela et al., 1994
Viešosios ir privačios erdvės	*Viešosios ir privačios erdvės XVIII amžiaus Lietuvos Didžiojoje Kunigaikštytėje*, ed. Ramunė Šmigelskytė-Stukienė, Vilnius, 2008
VL	*Volumina Legum*, vols i–viii: St Petersburg, 1859–60, ix: Cracow, 1889, x: Poznań, 1952
VUB	Vilniaus universiteto biblioteka
Wartości polityczne	*Wartości polityczne Rzeczypospolitej Obojga Narodów. Struktury aksjologiczne i granice cywilizacyjne*, ed. Anna Grześkowiak-Krwawicz and Jerzy Axer, 2017
W cieniu	*W cieniu wojen i rozbiorów. Studia z dziejów Rzeczypospolitej XVIII i początków XIX wieku*, ed. Urszula Kosińska et al., 2014
WO	*Wiek Oświecenia*

W podróży	*W podróży przez wiek osiemnasty . . . Studia i szkice z epoki nowożytnej*, ed. Adam Perłakowski et al., Cracow, 2015
ZH	*Zapiski Historyczne*
ZP	Zbiór Popielów, AGAD
Życie kulturalne	*Życie kulturalne i religijność w czasach Stanisława Augusta Poniatowskiego*, ed. Marian Marek Drozdowski, 1991
200 rocznica	*200 rocznica powstania kościuszkowskiego*, ed. Henryk Kocój, Katowice, 1994

PROLOGUE

1. Adam Naruszewicz, *Dziennik podróży Króla Jegomości Stanisława Augusta na Ukrainę i do innych Ziem Koronnych roku 1787*, 1788, 188, quoted after Magdalena Bober-Jankowska, 'Proza diariuszowa Adama Naruszewicza', doctoral thesis, Stefan Cardinal Wyszyński University, Warsaw, 2016, 126.
2. Simon Dixon, *Catherine the Great*, Harlow, 2001, 156.
3. Stanisław August was initially accompanied by – besides Bezborodko and Bariatynskii – his niece Urszula, her husband Michał Mniszech, his nephew Prince Stanisław Poniatowski, Ludwik Tyszkiewicz (the husband of another royal niece, Konstancja), the British envoy to Poland, Charles Whitworth, and the two princes, Ligne and Nassau-Siegen. The latter acted as the king's unofficial ambassador to Nassau's new patron – Potemkin. Several others, including Naruszewicz and Konstanty Plater, joined the party later. Cf. Naruszewicz, *Dziennik podróży Stanisława Augusta na Ukrainę*, 290–308; *Podróż króla Stanisława Augusta do Kaniowa w roku 1787 podług listów Kazimierza Konstantego de Broel Platera, starosty inflantskiego, opisana przez J. I. Kraszewskiego*, Wilno, 1860, 258–59.
4. I follow Urszula Mniszech's letter to her mother, Ludwika Zamoyska, 7 May 1787, in 'Listy Pani Mniszchowej', trans. and ed. Józef Ignacy Kraszewski, *Rocznik Towarzystwa Historyczno-Literackiego w Paryżu. Rok 1866*, 174–231 (212–15). Cf. the copy made from the French original, part of an 'Extrait des feuilles de Kiew de l'année 1787', ed. Andrzej Edward Koźmian, in *Wyciągi Piotrowickie*, Wrocław, 1842, 31–36.
5. Charles Whitworth to Francis Osborne, Marquess of Camarthen, Kaniów, 7 May 1787, TNA FO 62, 2, fols 113–14. In his previous despatch of 29 April, Whitworth, on learning the schedule, had expected that the king would have next to no opportunity for business; in Kiev, any hint of politics curtailed conversation with the empress (loc. cit., fols 109–12).
6. Diary of Aleksandr Khrapovitskii, quoted after Kalinka, *Ostatnie lata*, ii, 38 n. 1.
7. The judgement of Isabel de Madariaga (1919–2014), shared with me in 2005.
8. Catherine II to Friedrich Melchior Grimm, 26 April/7 May 1787, *SIRIO*, xxiii, 408.
9. Quoted after Przemysław Wątroba, 'Wezuwiusz w Kaniowie – realizacje Jakuba Kubickiego z okazji spotkania Stanisława Augusta i Katarzyny II w maju 1787 r.', in *SARz*, 195–211 (at 208).
10. Philip Mansel, *Prince of Europe: The Life of Charles-Joseph de Ligne*, London, 2003, 122.
11. SA to Augustyn Deboli, 3 May 1788, quoted after Emanuel Rostworowski, *Sprawa aukcji wojska na tle sytuacji politycznej przed sejmem Czteroletnim*, 1957, 224.
12. Charles Yorke to William Warburton, 1 August 1754, quoted more fully at p. 84.
13. *LLVPD*, i, 307.
14. J. H. Elliott, 'A Europe of Composite Monarchies', *Past & Present*, 137, 1992, 48–71.
15. Richard Butterwick, 'Lawmaking in a Post-Composite State? The Polish-Lithuanian Commonwealth in the Eighteenth Century', in *The Eighteenth-Century Composite State: Representative Institutions in Ireland and Europe*, ed. D. W. Hayton, John Bergin and James Kelly, Basingstoke, 2010, 221–43.
16. Robert Howard Lord, *The Second Partition of Poland*, Cambridge, MA, 1915, 485–87.

CHAPTER 1: COMMONWEALTH

1. Adapted from R. J. W. Evans, *The Making of the Habsburg Monarchy*, Oxford, 1979, 447.
2. Robert Frost, *The Oxford History of Poland-Lithuania*, i: *The Making of the Polish-Lithuanian Union, 1385–1569*, Oxford, 2015, 47.
3. Ibid., i, 493–94.
4. See David M. Althoen, *That Noble Quest: From True Nobility to Enlightened Society in the Polish-Lithuanian Commonwealth*, 1550–1830, s.l., 2000.
5. Frost, *Oxford History*, i, 349.
6. Cf. Caroline Robbins, *The Eighteenth-Century Commonwealthman*, Cambridge, MA, 1959.
7. See Teresa Bałuk-Ulewiczowa, *Goslicius's Ideal Senator and His Cultural Impact over the Centuries: Shakespearean Reflections*, Cracow, 2009.
8. *VL*, ii, 124.
9. Władysław Konopczyński, *Dzieje Polski nowożytnej*, 3rd edn, 1986, ii, 114.
10. *Pan Tadeusz*, II, 699–726 (pp. 94–95).
11. Klaus Zernack, 'Negative Polenpolitik als Grundlage deutsch-russischer Diplomätie in der Machtpolitik des 18. Jahrhunderts', in *Russland und Deutschland*, ed. Uwe Liszkowski, Stuttgart, 1974, 144-59; Urszula Kosińska, '*Liberum veto* jako narzędzie niszczenia sejmów przez państwa ościenne w czasach Augusta II', *BEN*, 4/1, 2016, 127–61.

CHAPTER 2: IMPASSE

1. Emanuel Rostworowski, 'Polska w układzie sił politycznych Europy XVIII wieku', in *Polska w epoce Oświecenia*, ed. Bogusław Leśnodorski, 1971, 11–59 (at 15–17).
2. Newsletter, 23 July 1733: *Od Augusta Mocnego do Augusta III. Doniesienia z Warszawy Andrzeja Cichockiego z lat 1732–1734*, ed. Jerzy Dygdała, 2016, 303.
3. Newsletter, 3 September 1733, ibid., 318.
4. Newsletter, 17 September 1733, ibid., 333.
5. On the bombastic words and sublime music, see Norman Davies, *God's Playground: A History of Poland*, 1st edn, Oxford, 1981, i, 505–07.
6. *VL*, vi, 282–320.
7. Jacek Staszewski, introduction to Józef Feldman, *Stanisław Leszczyński*, 3rd edn, 1984, 10–11; Władysław Konopczyński, 'Narodziny nowoczesnej idei niepodległości Polski (1733–1773)', in *Pamiętnik V Zjazdu Historyków Polskich*, Lwów, 1930, i, 462–75; cf. Jerzy Dygdała, 'Urażone magnackie ambicje czy racja stanu?', in *Spory o państwo w dobie nowożytnej*, ed. Zbigniew Anusik, Łódź, 2007, 187–99.
8. John P. LeDonne, *Russia and the World, 1700–1917: The Geopolitics of Expansion and Containment*, New York, 1996, 34. See Evgeny V. Anisimov, *Empress Elizabeth*, Gulf Breeze, FL, 1995.
9. Zofia Zielińska adumbrated this thesis in her *Walka „Familii" o reformę Rzeczypospolitej 1743–1752*, 1983, 18–19, 55–158; she confirmed it, using Russian archival sources, in eadem, 'Rosja wobec polskich planów aukcji wojska w 1740 roku', *Ikonotheka*, 13, 1998, 241–57; eadem, 'Rosja wobec polskich planów aukcji wojska w 1738 r.', *KH*, 107/3, 2000, 3–25; eadem, *Studia z dziejów stosunków polsko-rosyjskich w XVIII wieku*, 2001, 9–59.
10. Z. Zielińska, *Walka „Familii"*, 164, 185–88, 244–45, 275–79, 294–98, 306–07, 317–19, 338–39.
11. *VL*, v, 14.
12. The Sallustian motto was also popular among Royal Prussian burghers, who discerned 'tranquil servitude' in the Hohenzollern territories: Karin Friedrich, *The Other Prussia: Royal Prussia, Poland and Liberty, 1569–1772*, Cambridge, 2000, 115, 221.
13. Jacek Staszewski, *August III Sas*, Wrocław, 1989, 209–19, 226–28, 259–62, offers a more nuanced view of Brühl than Konopczyński, *Dzieje*, ii, 134–36.
14. 'Concordatum . . .', in Theiner, iv, 123–29; for the negotiations, see Jerzy Dygdała, *Adam Stanisław Grabowski (1698–1766)*, Olsztyn, 1994, 36–40.

15. Teofil Długosz, 'Biskupi polscy XVII i XVIII wieku', *Roczniki Teologiczno-Kanoniczne*, 5/2, 1958, 73–98.
16. Stanisław Konarski, *O skutecznym rad sposobie* [1760–63], quoted after Maria Czeppe, 'Budowanie wpływów dworu na prowincji w ostatnich latach panowania Augusta III', in *Dwór a kraj*, ed. Ryszard Skowron, Cracow, 2003, 547–58 (at 547).
17. Rafał Jeleński [?] to Samuel Jeleński, Nowogródek, 30 November 1750, quoted after Dariusz Rolnik, 'Symbioza miasta, dworu i wsi jako podstawa funkcjonowania Jeleńskich w życiu publicznym Litwy czasów stanisławowskich', in *Miestas – dvaras – kaimas*, ed. Ramunė Šmigelskytė-Stukienė, Vilnius, 2018, 157–77 (at 164–65).
18. The sceptical stance of Wojciech Kriegseisen, 'Zmierzch staropolskiej polityki, czyli o niektórych cechach polskiej kultury politycznej przełomu XVII i XVIII wieku', in *Zmierzch kultury staropolskiej*, ed. Urszula Augustyniak and Andrzej Karpiński, 1997, 15–39, also fits the reign of Augustus III. It is the guiding assumption of Jerzy Lukowski, *Liberty's Folly: The Polish-Lithuanian Commonwealth in the Eighteenth Century*, London, 1991, 165–75.
19. Władysław Konopczyński, *Polscy pisarze polityczni XVIII wieku*, 2nd edn, Cracow, 2012, concentrated on exceptional authors. Anna Grześkowiak-Krwawicz, *Dyskurs polityczny w Rzeczypospolitej Obojga Narodów*, Toruń, 2018, 19–23, selects treatises and pamphlets with some level of abstraction in order to elucidate shared concepts.
20. Konarski, *O skutecznym rad sposobie*, quoted after Jerzy Lukowski, 'Stanisław Konarski (1700–1772) [*sic*]: A Polish Machiavelli?', in *Enlightenment and Catholicism in Europe: A Transnational History*, ed. Jeffrey D. Burson and Ulrich L. Lehner, Notre Dame, IN, 2014, 433–53 (at 444).
21. [Józef Andrzej Załuski?], *Opisanie krótkie niektórych interesów wewnętrznych Najjaśniejszej Rzeczypospolitej Polskiej w roku 1762*, ed. Monika Wyszomirska and Adam Perłakowski, Cracow, 2011, 34, cf. Grześkowiak-Krwawicz, *Dyskurs*, 60.
22. Franz A. J. Szabo, *The Seven Years War in Europe 1756–1763*, Harlow, 2008, 421–23, 430; *Die königliche Jagdresidenz Hubertusburg und der Frieden von 1763*, exhibition catalogue, Dresden, 2013.

CHAPTER 3: *SACRUM* AND *PROFANUM*

1. For a fuller exposition, see Richard Butterwick-Pawlikowski, 'Między oświeceniem a katolicyzmem, czyli o katolickim oświeceniu i oświeconym katolicyzmie', *WO*, 30, 2014, 11–55.
2. Adam Zamoyski, *The Last King of Poland*, London, 1992, 13–14; Krystyna Zienkowska, *Stanisław August Poniatowski*, Wrocław, 1998, 6–8.
3. Instruction, Środa, 24 August 1744, *Akta sejmikowe województw poznańskiego i kaliskiego. Lata 1733–1763*, ed. Michał Zwierzykowski, 2015, 356.
4. Instruction, Środa, 22 August 1746, ibid., 411.
5. Henryk Palkij, *Sejmy 1736 i 1738 roku*, Cracow, 2000, 143.
6. Instruction, Środa, 24 August 1744, *Akta sejmikowe województw poznańskiego i kaliskiego*, 354.
7. Mikołaj Szołtysek, *Rethinking East-Central Europe: Family Systems and Co-Residence in the Polish-Lithuanian Commonwealth*, 2 vols, Bern, 2015.
8. Tomasz Wiślicz, 'Kobieta i przemoc w środowisku plebejskim w Rzeczypospolitej czasów saskich', in *Między barokiem a oświeceniem. Radości i troski dnia codziennego*, ed. Stanisław Achremczyk, Olsztyn, 2006, 389–96.
9. Cezary Kuklo, *Demografia Rzeczypospolitej przedrozbiorowej*, 2009, 210–16. Cf. Emanuel Rostworowski, 'Ilu było w Rzeczypospolitej obywateli szlachty?', *KH*, 94/3, 1987, 3–40, for an estimate of 14 million by 1772.
10. Zigmantas Kiaupa, *Trumpasis XVIII amžius (1733–1795 m.)*, vii/1 of *Lietuvos istorija*, Vilnius, 2012, 253–58.
11. Leonid Żytkowicz, 'Grain Yields in Poland, Bohemia, Hungary and Slovakia in the 16th to 18th Centuries', *APH*, 24, 1971, 51–72; Jerzy Lukowski, 'The Peasantry of Poland-Lithuania on the Eve of the French Revolution', *History of European Ideas*, 12/3, 1990, 377–93 (at 383–84).
12. Kuklo, *Demografia*, 234–36.

13. Paweł Maciejko, *The Mixed Multitude: Jacob Frank and the Frankist Movement, 1755–1816*, Philadelphia, PA, 2011, 10.
14. Ibid., 92–126; SA, *Mémoires*, 72.
15. Anna Lepalczyk, 'Sytuacja społeczna kowieńskich ewangelików w świetle tumultu z 1765 roku', *XVIII amžiaus studijos*, 4, 2018, 269–83.
16. Tomasz Kempa, *Konflikty wyznaniowe w Wilnie od początku reformacji do końca XVII wieku*, Toruń, 2016, 583.
17. SA, *Mémoires*, 109.
18. The city's lobbying moved up a gear during interregna: e.g. 'Documenta zum Recess des Interregni seit dem Absterben Ihr: Königl. Majest. Augusti III. bis auf die Ihr: Königl. Majest. Stanislao Augusto von dieser Stadt geleitete Huldigung ab A° 1764 d. 31 July. usque ad A° 1765. d. 31. July. N° 447_1012. Vol: II', BGdPAN, XV fol. 70b. Here were also recorded extracts from acts of the Royal Prussian and General Confederacies (in Polish) as well as correspondence (in French and German) with Russian generals.
19. Kuklo, *Demografia*, 234–36; Jerzy Dygdała, *Polityka Torunia wobec władz Rzeczypospolitej w latach 1764–1772*, 1977, 14.
20. Friedrich, *The Other Prussia*, 108–20.
21. Juljan Nieć, *Młodość ostatniego elekta. St. A. Poniatowski, 1732–1764*, Cracow, 1935, 5–17. Given that Stanisław was just seven years old when he left Danzig, Friedrich, *The Other Prussia*, 200–02, makes too much of Lengnich's influence on the future king. However, the latter probably did read the *Historia Poloniæ*.
22. I have learned much from Filippo Soramel, 'Gottfried Lengnich – History and Sovereignty', BA dissertation, UCL, 2018.
23. Stanisław Poniatowski, *List ziemianina do pewnego przyjaciela z inszego województwa*, in Klemens Kantecki, *Stanisław Poniatowski kasztelan krakowski, ojciec Stanisława Augusta*, 2 vols, Poznań, 1880, ii, lxxxix–civ.

CHAPTER 4: *'A NEW CREATION OF THE POLISH WORLD'*

1. Quoted after Zofia Zielińska, '„Nowe świata polskiego stworzenie". Stanisław August – reformator 1764–1767', in *SARz*, 9–32 (at 15).
2. Paul W. Schroeder, *The Transformation of European Politics 1763–1848*, Oxford, 1994, 47.
3. Z. Zielińska, *Walka „Familii"*, 327, 337–39.
4. Agnieszka Whelan, 'Gesture and Performance: Princess Izabela Czartoryska and Her Gardens, 1770–1831', doctoral thesis, UCL, 2013, act I, scene II, 'A prophetic wedding', 65–75; Thomas Wroughton cited in Richard Butterwick, *Poland's Last King and English Culture: Stanisław August Poniatowski, 1732–1798*, Oxford, 1998, 125.
5. SA, *Mémoires*, 243.
6. Butterwick, *Poland's Last King*, 146–55; Juljan Nieć, 'Stanisława A. Poniatowskiego plan reformy Rzeczypospolitej', *Historia*, 3, 1933, 11–18; Emanuel Rostworowski, *Ostatni król Rzeczypospolitej*, 1966, 33–42, 216–18.
7. [Charles-Louis de] Montesquieu, *The Spirit of the Laws*, trans. and ed. Anne M. Cohler et al., Cambridge, 1989, 157.
8. SA to Charles Yorke, 6 October 1764, quoted after Butterwick, *Poland's Last King*, 165.
9. Yorke to William Warburton, 1 August 1754, quoted ibid., 123.
10. Richard Butterwick, 'The Enlightened Monarchy of Stanisław August Poniatowski (1764–1795)', in *Polish-Lithuanian Monarchy*, 193–218 (at 195); see also Emanuel Mateusz Rostworowski, 'Edukacja ostatniego króla (1765–1772)', in idem, *Popioły i korzenie*, Cracow, 1985, 61–73.
11. Quoted after Z. Zielińska, '„Nowe świata polskiego stworzenie"', 12.
12. Zofia Zielińska, *Polska w okowach „systemu północnego" 1763–1766*, Cracow, 2012, 39–41, 44, 67–79, 100–12, emphasizes that the alliance was concluded on Russian terms; cf. H. M. Scott, *The Emergence of the Eastern Powers, 1756–1775*, Cambridge, 2001, 107–09, 112–17, who argues it was a success for Frederick.

13. SA, *Mémoires*, 289–90.
14. Andrzej Zamoyski, *Mowa na sejmie convocationis dnia 16 maja 1764*..., quoted after Anna Grześkowiak-Krwawicz, *Queen Liberty: The Concept of Freedom in the Polish-Lithuanian Commonwealth*, Leiden, 2012, 8; see Bogusław Leśnodorski, 'Mowa Andrzeja Zamoyskiego na konwokacji 1764 r.', in *Księga pamiątkowa 150-lecia Archiwum Głównego Akt Dawnych w Warszawie*, 1958, 383–99.
15. Proclamation of August Alexander... Czartoryski, Warsaw, 12 May 1764, copy in BGdPAN, Nl. 108, fol. 8.
16. Z. Zielińska, *Polska w okowach*, 63–65, 90–98, 126–33, 175–76.
17. An *ostensible* instruction not to mention any candidate – prompted by the opposition of the Porte to Poniatowski (feared as a potential husband for Catherine) – was already on its way to the Russian envoys. Keyserlingk allowed Poniatowski to believe that he had exceeded his instructions to get him the throne. Z. Zielińska, *Polska w okowach*, 178–81; cf. SA, *Mémoires*, 304–05; *Oratio illustrissimi et excellentissimi S. R. I. Comitis Hermanni Caroli à Keyserling*..., s.l.d., copy in BGdPAN, XV f. 70b, fols 379–82.
18. *VL*, vii, 107–32. I thank Maciej Olex-Szczytowski for lending me his bound volume, *Akt elekcyi*..., of the acts and constitutions of 1764.
19. Z. Zielińska, *Polska w okowach*, 204–09.
20. Jean Fabre, *Stanislas-Auguste Poniatowski et l'Europe des lumières*, Paris, 1952, 85–86, 90–91; Edmund Cieślak, *Stanisław Leszczyński*, Wrocław, 1994, 248.
21. *VL*, vii, 97–103 (quotations at 99, 97).
22. Quoted after Zamoyski, *Last King*, 100, although I have changed his 'state' back to 'Fatherland' for '*Ojczyzna*'.
23. Jerzy Michalski, *Stanisław August Poniatowski*, 2009, 98.
24. SA, *Mémoires*, 304.
25. Antonio Eugenio Visconti to Luigi Torrigani, 24 September 1766, in Theiner, iv, 94.
26. A copy of the instruction is in BGdPAN, XV f. 70b, fols 164–67v. (no. 669).
27. Tadeusz Korzon, *Wewnętrzne dzieje Polski za Stanisława Augusta*, 2nd edn, Cracow, 1897–98, iii, 133–36; Marian Drozdowski, *Podstawy finansowe działalności państwowej w Polsce 1764–1793*, 1975, 22–24.
28. Visconti to Torrigani, 24 September 1766, in Theiner, iv, 97.
29. Emanuel M. Rostworowski, 'Religijność i polityka wyznaniowa Stanisława Augusta', in *Życie kulturalne*, 11–24 (at 16). On Stanisław August and Visconti, see Ewa Manikowska, *Sztuka – ceremoniał – informacja. Studium wokół królewskich kolekcji Stanisława Augusta*, 2007, 21–55.
30. Andrzej Zamoyski quoted after Paweł Zając, 'Wokół planów nowego kształtu relacji Rzeczypospolitej ze Stolicą Apostolską na progu panowania Stanisława Augusta Poniatowskiego, 1764–1766', *Kościół w Polsce. Dzieje i kultura*, 15, 2016, 33–54 (at 43).
31. Larry Wolff, *The Vatican and Poland in the Age of the Partitions*, New York, 1988, 246–47.
32. Z. Zielińska, *Polska w okowach*, 256–357; SA to Catherine II, 3 December 1765, *Correspondance*, 73–75; Catherine II to SA, 28 March/8 April 1766, *SIRIO*, lxvii, 492–96.
33. Visconti to Torrigani, 5 December 1764, Theiner, iv, 35–36.
34. SA to Yorke, 28 November 1764, quoted after Butterwick, *Poland's Last King*, 162.
35. Isabel de Madariaga, *Russia in the Age of Catherine the Great*, New Haven, CT, 1981, 197–201.
36. Gédéon Benoît to Frederick II, 3 September 1766, quoted after Z. Zielińska, *Polska w okowach*, 497.
37. Cf. Dygdała, *Polityka Torunia*, 71–92, 129, 191–97, with Friedrich, *The Other Prussia*, 203–14.
38. SA to Charles Lee, 20 November 1767/March 1768, quoted after Butterwick, *Poland's Last King*, 164–65.
39. SA to Catherine II, 5 October 1766, *Correspondance*, 92–96.
40. Catherine II to SA, 6/17 October 1766, *SIRIO*, lxvii, 149–55.
41. Załuski quoted after M[aria] Cecylia Łubieńska, *Sprawa dysydencka 1764–1766*, 1911, 114–15.
42. The declarations are printed in Theiner, iv, 109–15.

43. Visconti to Torrigani, 19 November 1766, in Theiner, iv, 102; Clement XIII to Władysław Łubieński, 6 September 1766, ibid., iv, 108. Visconti's audience and speech, and Zamoyski's reply: ibid., iv, 122–29.
44. Visconti to Torrigani, 26 November 1766, in Theiner, iv, 102.
45. Nikolai Repnin to Kazimierz Poniatowski, 22 June 1767 (quotation); Kajetan Ignacy Sołtyk to Visconti, Borzęcin, 25 June 1767; also Józef Chyżewski to Visconti, Cracow, 3 July 1767, all in Theiner, iv, 162–63; Visconti to Torrigani, 24 June, 1 July, 8 July, 18 July 1767, ibid., iv, 214–17; SA to Catherine II, 24 June, 24 July 1767, *Correspondance*, 117–20; Catherine II to SA, 27 June/8 July 1767, *SIRIO*, lxvii, 382–84.
46. Cf. Rostworowski, *Ostatni król*, 55.
47. Catherine II to SA, 28 March/8 April 1768, *SIRIO*, lxxxvii, 69. See Z. Zielińska's commentaries to the *Correspondance*, 131–52.

CHAPTER 5: MARTYRDOMS

1. Durini was a cultured *literato*: Magdalena Wrana, *Angelo Maria Durini*, Cracow, 2013. He has been criticized for political partisanship in excess of his instructions, but Wojciech Kęder has sought to rehabilitate him as a loyal and zealous defender of the Holy See and the Roman Catholic Church: *Stolica Apostolska wobec Rzeczypospolitej w okresie konfederacji barskiej 1767–1773*, Opole, 2006. Without doubt, Durini was bereft of diplomatic finesse: see Paweł Zając, 'Warszawska misja nuncjusza Angelo Duriniego od jej inauguracji do końca pierwszego roku konfederacji barskiej', *KH*, 126/3, 2019, 481–529. The nuncio even deemed Stanisław Konarski's 1769 refutation of freethinkers suspiciously Gallican, and accused him of conniving at religious indifference and immorality. Following representations from the king, Rome recalled Durini in 1772. See Władysław Konopczyński, *Stanisław Konarski*, 1926, 281–97.
2. Quoted after Konopczyński, *Dzieje*, ii, 191.
3. Stanisław Kryciński, *Łemkowszczyzna po obu stronach Karpat*, Rzeszów, 2016, 276–89.
4. SA to Catherine II, 26 January, 17 July 1769, 21 February 1770, *Correspondance*, 164–69, 182–85, 205–08; Catherine II to SA, 26 March/6 April 1769, 31 March/11 April 1770, *SIRIO*, lxxxvii, 362–67, xciii, 50–53.
5. Jerzy Michalski, *Rousseau and Polish Republicanism*, 2015, 26–28, 61–62, 101, 140.
6. My thanks to Graham Clure for arguing this case to me, on the basis of his forthcoming book. I make my own argument in 'Challenges for the Commonwealth: The Counsel of Jean-Jacques Rousseau', *XVIII amžiaus studijos*, 3, 2016, 33–42. Cf. Franco Venturi, *The End of the Old Regime in Europe, 1768–1776*, Princeton, NJ, 1989, 193–99.
7. Jean-Jacques Rousseau, *Considérations sur le gouvernement de Pologne et sur sa réforme projetée*, ed. Jean Fabre, in Rousseau, *Oeuvres complètes*, ed. Bernard Gagnebin and Marcel Raymond, iii, Paris, 1964, 958–61, 966–71, 979–80, 1003–04.
8. Ibid., iii, 954–55, 975–1003, 1020–36.
9. Jerzy Lukowski, *Disorderly Liberty: The Political Culture of the Polish-Lithuanian Commonwealth in the Eighteenth Century*, London, 2010, 78, 137–39; cf. Grześkowiak-Krwawicz, *Dyskurs*, 285–93.
10. Quoted after Władysław Konopczyński, *Konfederacja barska*, 2nd edn, 1991, i, 415.
11. *Suum cuique*, s.l.d., [1771]; on the content, see Konopczyński, *Konfederacja barska*, ii, 891–93; idem, *Polscy pisarze polityczni*, 159–61; on the authorship, see Jerzy Michalski, 'O rzekomych i rzeczywistych pismach Andrzeja Zamoyskiego', in Michalski, *SH*, i, 135–59.
12. Konopczyński, *Konfederacja barska*, ii, 576–80.
13. Dixon, *Catherine the Great*, 2001, 155–77 and passim.
14. Konopczyński, *Konfederacja barska*, ii, 627–35, 640, 654–55, 657.
15. Ibid., ii, 733–38.
16. Frederick II to Prince Henry of Prussia, 9 April 1772, quoted after Albert Sorel, *La Question d'Orient au XVIII siècle*, 4th edn, Paris, 1902, 207.
17. Curtis G. Murphy, *From Citizens to Subjects: City, State and the Enlightenment in Poland, Ukraine and Belarus*, Pittsburgh, PA, 2018, 143–47; Lukowski, *Liberty's Folly*, 35.

18. I have learned much from Paul Marsh, the author of 'The History of Nevel from the Earliest Times until 1772', MPhil. thesis, UCL, 2011.
19. Emanuel Rostworowski, 'Miasta i mieszczanie w ustroju Trzeciego Maja', in *Sejm Czteroletni i jego tradycje*, ed. Jerzy Kowecki, 1991, 138–51 (at 138, 144).
20. Edmund Burke to A. H. von Borcke, 17 January 1774, quoted in N. Davies, *God's Playground*, i, 570.
21. 'Rejtan i dylematy Polaków w dobie pierwszego rozbioru', in Michalski, *SH*, i, 160–201 (at 185–87); Jerzy Lukowski, *The Partitions of Poland: 1772, 1793, 1795*, Harlow, 1999, 85–86, 105–09.
22. Conversation of 30 January 1774, *Entretiens du roi Stanislas-Auguste avec Otto Magnus von Stackelberg (1773–1775)*, ed. Dorota Dukwicz and Ewa Zielińska, 2017, 121.
23. Jan Poplatek, *Komisja Edukacji Narodowej. Udział byłych Jezuitów*, Cracow, 1974, 31–41.
24. Stanisław Bednarski, *Upadek i odrodzenie szkolnictwa jezuickiego w Polsce* [1933], reprint Cracow, 2003, 112–18.
25. *VL*, viii, 152–57, 537–38. Władysław Maria Grabski, *U podstaw wielkiej reformy*, Łódź, 1984, 86–96.

CHAPTER 6: THRONE AND ALTAR

1. *SAOKP*, 104. According to the Saxon envoy, the medal was struck in tribute to the *Familia* – the oarsmen represent Michał and August Czartoryski, Andrzej Zamoyski, Stanisław Lubomirski, Jan Borch and Antoni Przeździecki. Konopczyński, *Konfederacja barska*, i, 362.
2. Susan Tipton, 'Die Russische Minerva. Katharina die Große und die Ikonographie der Aufklärung', in *Katharina die Grosse*, exhibition catalogue, ed. Hans Ottomeyer and Susan Tipton, Kassel, 1997, 73–80.
3. Lord, *Second Partition*, 64.
4. Richard Butterwick, *Polska Rewolucja a Kościół katolicki 1788–1792*, Cracow, 2012, 219.
5. Their correspondence began on 2 April 1774 with the king's compliments on Potemkin's victories and the Order of the White Eagle: *Correspondance*, 286. The king began to ask Potemkin to pass his requests to the empress, just as he had hitherto approached Panin.
6. Franciszek Ksawery Branicki to Grigorii Potemkin, 9 April 1775, quoted after *Correspondance*, 310 n. 292.
7. Adam Cieciszowski to Augustyn Deboli, Warsaw, 17 December 1781, in *KPSAAD 1781*, 432–33.
8. This implausible story, so reminiscent of the 'warming pan' story concocted about Prince James Francis Edward Stuart, was presented as undoubted fact by Henryk Mościcki, 'Branicka Aleksandra', *PSB*, ii, 393–96, and Władysław Konopczyński, 'Branicki Franciszek Ksawery', *PSB*, ii, 398–401. It has since been repeated by, *inter alia*, Rostworowski, *Ostatni król*, 96. Cf. Simon Sebag Montefiore, *Prince of Princes: The Life of Potemkin*, London, 2000, 189–90. I am grateful to Isabel de Madariaga and Simon Dixon for clearing up my doubts.
9. In a telling vignette, a year *before* Aleksandra Engelhardt married Branicki, Ignacy Potocki reportedly sent her a letter, enclosing another for the empress, so that he might be appointed Crown vice-chancellor. The king commented that Potocki could have been seduced by the impression given by Branicki and Aleksandra's brother, Vasilii Engelhardt, of the power of this connection, which was already beginning to worry Stackelberg – who soon found out about the approach. Deboli to Cieciszowski, 24 October 1780, SA to Deboli, 6 November, 13 November 1780, Deboli to SA, 24 November 1780, *KPSAAD 1780*, 231–33, 237–39, 246–48, 259–65.
10. E.g. Ludwik Dębicki, *Puławy (1762–1830)*, Lwów, 1887, i, 1–219; Alina Aleksandrowicz, 'Sejm Czteroletni i Konstytucja 3 Maja w kręgu Puław', in *Rok Monarchii*, 195–249 (at 195–212); more moderately: Zamoyski, *Last King*, 282–83.
11. Jerzy Michalski, 'Sprawa wyboru posłów dysydentów na sejm 1776 roku', in *Kultura staropolska – kultura europejska*, 1997, 273–80; Wolff, *Vatican and Poland*, 118–23; August Sułkowski to Giovanni Andrea Archetti, 18 July 1776, Archetti to Sułkowski, [18 July 1776], Archetti to

Opizio Pallavicini, 24 July 1776, in *Acta Nuntiaturae Polonae*, tome 54, *Ioannes Andreas Archetti (1776–1784)*, ed. Paweł Zając, Cracow, 2013, i, 500–01, 531–33.

12. *Mowa Króla JMci na seymie dnia 23. Septembris 1776. miana* [1776]. The king translated and recorded it in SA, *Mémoires*, 619–22.
13. Ambroise Jobert, *La Commission d'Education Nationale en Pologne (1773–1794)*, Paris, 1941, 224–28; Grabski, *U podstaw wielkiej reformy*, 96–120, 271–75; Butterwick, *Polska Rewolucja*, 190–91.
14. *Mowa Króla JMci . . . 29 Augusti 1776 miana.*
15. See Ewa Zielińska, 'Sprawa polsko-rosyjskiej komisji granicznej w latach 1778–1780', in *W cieniu*, 339–68'. The problem was discussed by the king and ambassador throughout 1775: *Entretiens*, 178–217; the vexatious conduct of the forces commanded by Branicki's future brother-in-law Vasilii Engelhardt embarrassed the king in 1780: SA to Deboli, 25 September, 23 October, 1 November, 13 November 1780, *KPSAAD 1780*, 209–11, 228–30, 235–36, 246–48. In 1783 further incursions and abductions took place in the district of Rzeczyca: SA to Catherine II, 28 August 1783, Catherine II to SA, 15/26 September 1783, *Correspondance*, 410–13.
16. *LLVPD*, i, 124, 151, 180–81.
17. Ramunė Šmigelskytė-Stukienė, 'Abiejų Tautų Respublikos sienos su Rusija demarkavino problemos 1774–1775 metais', *Lietuvos istorijos metraštis*, 2005/2, 53–68.
18. Władysław Konopczyński, *Pierwszy rozbior Polski*, Cracow, 2010, 264–65.
19. I owe this information to the kindness of Ewa Zielińska.
20. On one such incident, see SA to Deboli, 26 June 1780, *KPSAAD 1780*, 122–24.
21. My thanks to Ewa Zielińska for drawing my attention to these maps.
22. *Correspondance*, map 6.
23. *Zbiór praw sądowych . . .*, quoted by Lukowski, *Disorderly Liberty*, 113.
24. SA to Catherine II, 12 August, 5 November 1781, Catherine II to SA, 12/23 August, 10/21 November 1781, and commentaries, *Correspondance*, 394–401; see also David L. Ransel, 'An Ambivalent Legacy: The Education of Grand Duke Paul', in *Paul I: A Reassessment of His Life and Reign*, ed. Hugh Ragsdale, Pittsburgh, PA, 1979, 1–16.
25. SA to Deboli, 9 September 1782, *KPSAAD 1782*, 218–20 (at 219).
26. Cieciszowski to Deboli, 20 September 1780, *KPSAAD 1780*, 206–07.
27. SA to Deboli, 4 November 1782, *KPSAAD 1782*, 268–71 (at 268).
28. See Derek Beales, *Joseph II*, ii: *Against the World, 1780–1790*, Cambridge, 2009, 214–38, 271–332, 353–55.
29. Jan Paweł Woronicz, 'Na wjazd . . . Michała Jerzego Ciołka Poniatowskiego [. . .]', in idem, *Pisma wybrane*, ed. Małgorzata Nesteruk and Zofia Rejman, Wrocław, 2002, 11–22.
30. Cf. SA to Deboli, 18 December 1780, *KPSAAD 1780*, 304–06: 'I am all the more desirous of learning the final effect of the pope's letter to the empress, when the news from Belorussia increasingly confirms the daily diminution of Uniatism. Ninety Ruthenian Uniate churches have already been changed to non-Uniate ones. The Russians seem to connive here and there at the Uniates declaring themselves Latin Catholics, but even this, however, is generally not without difficulty.'
31. Z. Zielińska, commentary to SA to Nikita Panin, 21 April 1777, *Correspondance*, 343–45.
32. Visconti to Torrigani, 24 September 1766, in Theiner, iv, 96.
33. Michał Poniatowski to Reformed, Observant and Conventual Franciscan Provincials, 22 August 1786, quoted after Butterwick, *Polska Rewolucja*, 133.
34. Jędrzej Kitowicz, *Pamiętniki czyli historia polska*, ed. Przemysława Matuszewska and Zofia Lewinówna, 1971, 423–24.
35. Jan Kracik, '„Nieposłuszne Kościołowi Dziatki". Reakcja społeczna na papieską redukcję świąt w Polsce w 1775 roku', *Analecta Cracoviensia*, 26, 1995, 501–09.
36. Nowogródek instruction, 20 August 1788: *LDKSI*, 222.
37. Kitowicz, *Pamiętniki*, 352; idem, *Opis obyczajów za panowania Augusta III*, ed. Zbigniew Goliński, 1999 edn, 42–44.
38. François Guesnet, 'Jewish Intercession and the Abolition of Torture in Poland-Lithuania, 1776', lecture delivered at UCL, 14 November 2019.

39. Franciszek Karpiński, *Historia mego wieku i ludzi, z którymi żyłem*, ed. Roman Sobol, 1987, 26–27.
40. Stanisław Witecki, *Przekaz kulturowy w parafiach katolickich na obszarze Rzeczypospolitej Obojga Narodów czasów stanisławowskich*, Cracow, 2018, esp. 328–37.
41. Adam Krasiński to Katarzyna Kossakowska, 9 October 1791, quoted after Butterwick, *Polska Rewolucja*, 638.
42. Cf. Mariusz Karpowicz, *Sztuki polskiej drogi dziwne*, Bydgoszcz, 1994, 150.
43. Andrzej J. Baranowski, *Koronacje wizerunków maryjnych w czasach baroku*, 2003, 59–64, 198–99.
44. Karpiński, *Historia mego wieku*, 96–99 (quotation at 98); see Zofia Zielińska, 'Potocki Mikołaj Bazyli', *PSB*, xxviii, 113–15.
45. Ewa Andrzejewska, *Ks. Stanisław Józef Kłossowski (1726–1798)*, Kalisz, 2010, quotations at 87–88, 130–31; cf. Butterwick, *Polska Rewolucja*, 622.

CHAPTER 7: GROWING PAINS

1. *Z rontem marszałkowskim przez Warszawę (zeznania oskarżonych z lat 1787–1794)*, ed. Zofia Turska, 1961, 255–58.
2. Ibid., statistics at 6.
3. Barbara Grochulska, *Warszawa na mapie Polski stanisławowskiej*, 1980, 26–30.
4. Aleksandra Bernatowicz, *Malarze w Warszawie czasów Stanisława Augusta*, 2016, 282–83.
5. Kuklo, *Demografia*, 392–400; Monika Maludzińska, *„Próżnowanie stało się powszechnym nałogiem". Żebracy i włóczędzy w stanisławowskiej Warszawie*, 2014, 147–53.
6. The higher figures are from Kiaupa, *Trumpasis XVIII amžius*, i, 253–58; Rostworowski, 'Ilu było . . . szlachty?'; idem, 'Miasta i mieszczanie'; cf. lower estimates in Jerzy Ochmański, 'Zaludnienie Litwy w roku 1790', *Zeszyty Naukowe Uniwersytetu Adama Mickiewicza*, Historia, 7, 1967, 269–79; Kuklo, *Demografia*, 210–16. Part of the problem of estimating population is the different definition of 'hearth' in the Crown and Lithuania, as well as the fact that households tended to be somewhat larger in the east.
7. Rostworowski, 'Ilu było . . . szlachty?'. If his estimate for the number of nobles were to be accepted while retaining most demographers' estimate of 8.6 million for the overall population, then the proportion of nobles would rise from 7.5 per cent to 8.7 per cent.
8. Adam Naruszewicz, *Dyjaryjusz podróży Jego Królewskiej Mości na sejm grodzieński*, ed. Magdalena Bober-Jankowska, 2008, 297–99. For an in-depth analysis, see Bober-Jankowska, 'Proza diariuszowa Adama Naruszewicza'.
9. Naruszewicz, *Dyjaryjusz podróży*, 34–37; the names of the parishioners are listed ibid., 281.
10. Ibid., 47–50; cf. 301–14.
11. Ibid., 53–54; cf. 315–17.
12. *Dyaryusz seymu wolnego ordynaryinego grodzieńskiego sześcioniedzielnego roku pańskiego MDCCLXXXIV* . . ., 1785, 293.
13. Maciej Janowski, *Narodziny inteligencji 1750–1831*, 2008, 54–60.
14. Kuklo, *Demografia*, 265–66.
15. See *Ewangelicki Kościół Świętej Trójcy w Warszawie*, ed. Karol Guttmejer, 2017; on the view: Andrzej Zahorski, *Warszawa w powstaniu kościuszkowskim*, 1985, 5–7.
16. Kiaupa, *Trumpasis XVIII amžius*, i, 176–88. The privilege for a fair in Słuck issued by Stanisław August on 18 November 1782 is in BGdPAN, akc. 4233-D-2000; on Kowno, see Lepalczyk, 'Sytuacja społeczna kowieńskich ewangelików', 276; Revd Franciszek Michał Frąckiewicz (b. 1717, who had personally beaten the Lutheran pastor in 1765) quoted after *Vyskupo Ignoto Jokūbo Masalskio Kauno dekanato vizitacija 1782 m.*, ed. Vytautas Jogėla, Vilnius, 2001, 88–90.
17. *Dzieje Poznania*, i: *Do roku 1793*, ed. Jerzy Topolski, 1988, 830–33.
18. Daniel Stone, *Polish Politics and National Reform, 1775–1788*, New York, 1976, 48; Tadeusz Frączyk, *Adam Kazimierz Czartoryski*, Cracow, 2012, 392–94.
19. Minsk instruction, 21 November 1790: *LDKSI*, 334. On the decline of Ruthenian, see Andrzej B. Zakrzewski, *Wielkie Księstwo Litewskie*, 2013, 255–61; on archives: idem, *Sejmiki*

Wielkiego Księstwa Litewskiego XVI–XVIII w. Ustrój i funkcjonowanie: sejmik trocki, 2000, 201–02.

20. *Pamiętniki Jana Duklana Ochockiego*, ed. Józef Ignacy Kraszewski, 2nd edn, 1910, i, 10; Antoni Mączak, *Klientela. Nieformalne systemy władzy w Polsce i Europie XVI–XVIII w.*, 2nd edn, 2000, 274–84; cf. Tadeusz Srogosz, *Między wojną a modernizacją*, Częstochowa, 2016, 148.
21. *Dzieła pana de Montesquieu*, 2 vols, *Duch, czyli treść praw*, Leipzig, 1777; see Władysław Smoleński, *Monteskjusz w Polsce w wieku XVIII*, 1927.
22. On Ostermann's weakening position, see Dixon, *Catherine the Great*, 2001, 154–55.
23. Rostworowski, *Sprawa aukcji wojska*, 62–65, 136–40.
24. *Zbiór rezolucji interpretacyjnych Rady Nieustającej z lat 1786–1788*, ed. Marcin Głuszak, Łódź, 2014, 88–89.
25. Ramunė Šmigelskytė-Stukienė et al., *Modernios administracijos tapsmas Lietuvoje: valstybės institucijų raida 1764–1794 metais*, Vilnius, 2014, 276–79.
26. Differences in accounting practices and calendars make it hard to provide precise figures. I have adapted those in Marian Drozdowski, *Podstawy finansowe*, 59–132; cf. Korzon, *Wewnętrzne dzieje*, iii, 160–79.
27. E.g. Šmigelskytė-Stukienė et al., *Modernios administracijos tapsmas Lietuvoje*, 11–26, 31–94, 611–12; Łukasz Kądziela, *Między zdradą a służbą Rzeczypospolitej. Fryderyk Moszyński w latach 1792–1793*, 1993, 364–65. A harbinger of change in Poland was Józef Andrzej Gierowski, *The Polish-Lithuanian Commonwealth in the XVIIIth Century*, Cracow, 1996; for the wider picture, cf. Marc Raeff, *The Well-Ordered Police State*, New Haven, CT, 1983; with Nicholas Henshall, *The Myth of Absolutism*, 2nd edn, London, 2017.
28. SA to Mateusz Butrymowicz, Biblioteka Jagiellońska 5993, fasc. XVI, n.p.
29. *Pan Tadeusz*, I, 758–61, with a slight change at line 759 (p. 42). Most such snuffboxes were made of silver, but even so much was spent on these and other gifts, peaking in 1792 at 76,000 ducats: Magdalena Górska, 'Symbolika panowania Stanisława Augusta', in *SARz*, 33–50, 49.
30. Marek Kwiatkowski, *Stanisław August. Król-architekt*, Wrocław, 1983, 257.
31. Ibid., 40 and passim; Andrzej Rottermund, *Zamek Warszawski w epoce Oświecenia*, 1989, 74–75, 92–102, 105–11; idem, 'Program polityczny i formy jego realizacji w najważniejszych inicjatywach królewskich', in *SAOKP*, 116–22; Artur Badach, 'Inicjatywy artystyczne z pierwszych lat panowania Stanisława Augusta – ewolucja form i treści', ibid., 62–69; Bogusław Pfeiffer, *Rex et Patria*, 2012, 148–61.
32. Barbara Arciszewska, 'Pałac na wyspie i wyspiarski klasycyzm', lecture at the Royal Łazienki, 1 July 2017; eadem, *Classicism and Modernity: Architectural Thought in Eighteenth-Century Britain*, 2010; Mikołaj Getka-Kenig, 'Bringing Order out of Chaos: Stanisław August's Political Patronage of Architectural Classicism in the Late Eighteenth-Century Polish-Lithuanian Commonwealth', *Central Europe*, 16/2, 2018, 81–104; cf. Butterwick, *Poland's Last King*, 159–65, 191–93, 199–222.
33. Butterwick, *Poland's Last King*, 81, 97–98, 108, 178–82.
34. Jerzy Axer, 'Tropem łacińskich inskrypcji Stanisława Augusta', in *Łazienki Królewskie. Nowe świadectwa – nowe znaczenia*, ed. Maria Poprzęcka and Daria Majewska, 2013, 27–33 (at 33).
35. Andrzej Rottermund, 'Echo podróży do Anglii w Przedpokoju Senatorskim Zamku Królewskiego w Warszawie', in *De Gustibus*, ed. Robert Pasieczny et al., 1996, 33–40, cf. John Dixon Hunt, *Gardens and the Picturesque*, Cambridge, MA, 1992, 83–84; *SAOKP*, 330–32; Richard Butterwick-Pawlikowski, 'Chrześcijanin i obywatel w dyskursie politycznym drugiej połowy XVIII wieku', in *Wartości polityczne*, 175–95 (at 192–95).
36. Michalski, *Stanisław August Poniatowski*, 46–47; similarly: Lukowski, *Liberty's Folly*, 214–15; Witold Filipczak, *Sejm 1778 roku*, 2000, 32; idem, *Życie sejmikowe prowincji wielkopolskiej w latach 1780–1786*, Łódź, 2012, 36; Andrzej Stroynowski, *Opozycja sejmowa w dobie rządów Rady Nieustającej*, Łódź, 2005, 203.
37. Grześkowiak-Krwawicz, *Dyskurs*, 61–63, 69, 80, 88–91, 114, 119–20, 134, 165–70, 213, 285–87, 396–98.
38. *Pan Tadeusz*, I, 412, 416, 431–34 (p. 24). See Jerzy Michalski, 'Osiemnastowieczne realia *Pana Tadeusza*', in Michalski, *SH*, i, 530–52 (at 532–36).

39. Butterwick, *Polska Rewolucja*, 493–95.
40. Rostworowski, *Sprawa aukcji wojska*, 126.
41. Ignacy Potocki to Seweryn Rzewuski, 16 June 1786, quoted ibid., 270.
42. Otto von Stackelberg to Ivan Ostermann, 27 June/8 July 1786, quoted after Adam Danilczyk, *W kręgu afery Dogrumowej. Sejm 1786 roku*, 2010, 76.

CHAPTER 8: FERMENT AND FERMENTATION

1. SA to Deboli, 3 May 1788, quoted after Rostworowski, *Sprawa aukcji wojska*, 224.
2. Danilczyk, *W kręgu afery Dogrumowej*, 37–38; for Neri and her attempt to convince the king that he was in danger from Branicki: SA to Deboli, 7 October 1782, *KPSAAD 1782*, 246–48.
3. Quoted in Rostworowski, *Sprawa aukcji wojska*, 222–23.
4. SA to Deboli, 7 January 1784, quoted after Butterwick, *Polska Rewolucja*, 234.
5. SA to Catherine II, 22 November 1786, Catherine II to SA, 4/15 December 1786, *Correspondance*, 417–18, 422.
6. Z. Zielińska, 'Stanisław August i Otto Stackelberg u progu wojny rosyjsko-tureckiej (marzec-październik 1787)', *KH*, 107/4, 2000, 3–20 (at 4–6).
7. Mansel, *Prince of Europe*, 121–22.
8. Z. Zielińska, 'Listy Stanisława Augusta z podróży do Kaniowa (1787)', *KH*, 110/4, 2003, 71–124 (at 84–98); eadem, 'Stanisław August i Otto Stackelberg u progu wojny', 11–12; SA to Kiciński, Kaniów, 8 May 1787, in Kalinka, *Ostatnie lata*, ii, 33–44; Potemkin to SA, 25 April 1787; the king agreed, adding that he would have named the town Grzegorzyn: SA to Potemkin, 26 April 1787, *Correspondance*, 434–39 (both letters in French and Polish versions).
9. SA to Kiciński, Wiśniowiec, 12 March 1787, Chwastów, 21 March 1787, Kaniów, 5 April, 17 April, 8 May 1787, in Kalinka, *Ostatnie lata*, ii, 8, 11, 24, 30, 35, 39, 43; SA to Charles de Nassau-Siegen, 7 May 1787, in Z. Zielińska, 'Listy Stanisława Augusta z podróży do Kaniowa', 118.
10. Cf. Montefiore, *Prince of Princes*, 360–62, 365–67.
11. Aleksy Deruga, 'Kościół prawosławny a sprawa „buntu" w 1789 roku we wschodnich województwach Rzeczypospolitej', *Ateneum Wileńskie*, 13/2, 1938, 175–269 (at 181–85).
12. *Powitanie Nayiaśnieyszeyszego Stanisława Augusta Krola i Pana Naszego przeieżdżaiącego przez Włodzimierz do Kaniowa od szkoł tamecznych pod dozorem Bazylianow prowincyi litewskiey roku 1787. dnia 7. marca z aktow szkolnych wyięte*, [1787]; Julian Antonowicz, *Grammatyka dla Polaków chcących się uczyć angielskiego języka*, 1788; Butterwick, *Poland's Last King*, 175.
13. Rostworowski, 'Religijność', 19.
14. SA to Pius Kiciński, 19 May 1787, in Kalinka, *Ostatnie lata*, ii, 53; see Emanuel Rostworowski, 'Potocki Stanisław Szczęsny', *PSB*, xxxviii, 183–202 (at 188).
15. SA to Kiciński, Korsuń, 11 May 1787, in Kalinka, *Ostatnie lata*, ii, 44–48; Joseph II to Wenzel Anton von Kaunitz, Kherson, 15 May 1787, in *Joseph II, Leopold II und Kaunitz. Ihr Briefwechsel*, ed. Adolph Beer, Vienna, 1873, 259–60. I owe a photocopy to the kindness of Derek Beales. See Zamoyski, *Last King*, 298–99.
16. Stanisław August's visit to Cracow was recorded by Naruszewicz, *Dyaryusz podrozy Nayiaśnieyszego Stanisława Augusta krola polskiego na Ukrainę*, 210–49.
17. Ulrich L. Lehner, *The Catholic Enlightenment: The Forgotten History of a Global Movement*, New York, 2016, 60–62.
18. Józef Wiszniewski to Marcin Poczobut, Merecz, 19 November 1790, VUB F2 DC 49, fol. 108.
19. Józef Niemirowicz-Szczytt to Poczobut, Warsaw, 17 September 1788, VUB F2 DC 47, fol. 171.
20. Wioletta Pawlikowska-Butterwick and Richard Butterwick-Pawlikowski, 'Najjaśniejsza gwiazda wileńska. Ksiądz rektor Marcin Poczobut w ostatnich latach Rzeczypospolitej', *XVIII amžiaus studijos*, 2, 2015, 88–101 (at 92–93); Aldona Prašmantaitė, 'Dėl Lietuvos katalikų dvasininkijos dalyvavimo Edukacinės Komisjos veikloje', *XVIII amžiaus studijos*, 2, 2015, 55–71 (at 65–67).

21. Letters from Mikołaj Wieliczko to Poczobut, 1783–84, quoted in Poplatek, *Komisja Edukacji Narodowej*, 298–99.
22. Władysław Smoleński, *Kuźnica kołłątajowska*, 2nd edn, 1949, 30–40; Jobert, *La Commission d'Éducation Nationale*, 354–55.
23. Czernihów instruction, 1788: BZNiO 6848, p. 14.
24. Cf. William Doyle, *Origins of the French Revolution*, 3rd edn, Oxford, 1999, 38.
25. Julian Ursyn Niemcewicz, *Pamiętniki czasów moich*, ed. Jan Dihm, 1957, i, 243–44.
26. Doyle, *Origins*, 103.
27. Rostworowski, *Sprawa aukcji wojska*, 204–08.
28. BZNiO, 6847/I, iii, part 1, pp. 137–38. Walerian Kalinka transcribed this letter from an unspecified source, but did not refer to it directly in his *Sejm Czteroletni*. On Walewski, see Hanna Żerek-Kleszcz, 'Michał Walewski (podkomorzy krakowski, wojewoda sieradzki) i jego korespondencja ze Stanisławem Augustem w latach 1776–1787', *Rocznik Łódzki*, 48, 2001, 47–65; Angela Sołtys, *Opat z San Michele. Grand Tour prymasa Poniatowskiego i jego kolekcje*, 2008, 204.
29. See Rostworowski, 'Debiut polityczny Jana Potockiego w r. 1788', *PH*, 47/4, 1956, 685–711;', 708; *Pan Tadeusz*, VI, 278–80 (p. 276).
30. Elżbieta Sapieżyna to Adam Kazimierz Czartoryski, Kodeń, 20 August 1788, quoted after Jerzy Michalski, 'Sejmiki poselskie 1788 roku', in Michalski, *SH*, i, 217–84 (at 239).
31. SA to Filippo Mazzei, 19 January 1791, cited after Butterwick, 'Lawmaking in a Post-Composite State?', 233.
32. Niemcewicz, *Pamiętniki*, i, 261–62.
33. SA to Deboli, 1 October 1788, quoted after Michalski, 'Sejmiki poselskie 1788', 274.
34. Rostworowski, *Sprawa aukcji wojska*, 222.
35. Lublin instruction, 18–20 August 1788: BPAUiPAN 8326, fol. 463.
36. Volhynian instruction, 19 August 1788: ZP 130, p. 390.
37. Wilkomierz instruction, 19 August 1788: *LDKSI*, 74–75. Cf. identical or near-identical phrasing in the instructions of Połock (199), Nowogródek (219), Orsza (274–75) and Minsk (322–23).
38. Mozyrz instruction, 18 August 1788: *LDKSI*, 343.
39. Ciechanów instruction, 18 August 1788: BPAUiPAN 8318, fol. 359.
40. Wołkowysk instruction, 18 August 1788: *LDKSI*, 255.
41. Orsza instruction (the sejmik met at Chołopienicze), 19 August 1788: *LDKSI*, 276.
42. Wołkowysk instruction, 18 August 1788: *LDKSI*, 256. See Andrzej Zakrzewski, 'Szkoła Rycerska – Między Koroną a Litwą' in *Szkoła Rycerska Kadetów Jego Królewskiej Mości i Rzeczypospolitej*, ed. Waldemar Bednaruk and Kamil Jaszczuk, Lublin, 2016, 35–42 (at 38–39).
43. Słonim instruction, 18 August 1788: *LDKSI*, 237–39.
44. Kowno instruction, 18 August 1788: *LDKSI*, 143.

CHAPTER 9: REVOLUTION: THE KING WITH THE NATION

1. ASC 24, fol. 9v; *VL*, ix, 469–70.
2. Bernard Krakowski, *Oratorstwo polityczne na forum Sejmu Czteroletniego*, Gdańsk, 1968, 19–25; *Dyaryusz 1788*; *Dyaryusz 1790*. Sessions 1–71, 98–198 and 327 are available online (www.wbc.poznan.pl/dlibra). AGAD has now made available scans of the entire ASC.
3. Piotr Świtkowski, *Pamiętnik Historyczno-Polityczno-Ekonomiczne*, quoted after Anna Grześkowiak-Krwawicz, 'Konstytucja 3 Maja. Rewolucja – prawo – dokument', in *Konstytucja 3 Maja 1791 na podstawie tekstu Ustawy Rządowej z Archiwum Sejmu Czteroletniego*, ed. Anna Grześkowiak-Krwawicz, 2018, 5–52 (at 5).
4. From the foreword to *Dzień trzeciego maja roku 1791*, 1791.
5. Quoted after Peter McPhee, *Liberty or Death: The French Revolution*, New Haven, CT, 2016, xii.
6. Richard Butterwick, *The Polish Revolution and the Catholic Church 1788–1792: A Political History*, Oxford, 2012, 7–9. Cf. Anna Grześkowiak-Krwawicz, *Czy rewolucja może być legalna?*,

2012. R. H. Lord wrote of 'this revolution' and 'the Polish Revolution' regarding the sejm in his *Second Partition*, 101, 105.

7. See Richard Butterwick-Pawlikowski, 'Koncepcja narodu w polskim dyskursie końca XVIII wieku. Rozważania nad Konstytucją 3 maja', in *O ziemię naszą, nie waszą. Ideowe aspekty procesów narodowotwórczych w Europie Środkowej i Wschodniej*, ed. Łukasz Adamski, 2017, 135–51. Cf. Andrzej Walicki, *The Enlightenment and the Birth of Modern Nationhood: Polish Political Thought from Noble Republicanism to Tadeusz Kościuszko*, Notre Dame, IN, 2000.
8. Hugo Kołłątaj, *Listy anonima i Prawo polityczne narodu polskiego*, ed. Bogusław Leśnodorski and Helena Wereszycka, 2 vols, 1954, i, 167, 254. He borrowed the term from Gaetano Filangieri: see Bogusław Leśnodorski, '„Łagodna rewolucja" w starciu z despotyzmem', *CPH*, 27/1, 1975, 187–95.
9. Franciszek Salezy Jezierski, *Kazanie przed stanami Rzeczypospolitej na sejmie w roku 1788*, in idem, *Wybór pism*, ed. Zdzisław Skwarczyński, intr. Jerzy Ziomek, 1952, 53–64.
10. *VL*, ix, 46–47.
11. The Prussian note is printed in *Dyaryusz 1788*, i/1, 33–35; Franz August Essen to Heinrich Gottlob Stutterheim, 15 October 1788, quoted after Butterwick, *Polish Revolution*, 54.
12. Walerian Stroynowski, 25 October 1788, quoted after Butterwick, *Polska Rewolucja*, 289.
13. These debates are recorded in *Dyaryusz 1788*, i/1, 93–323; quotations after Butterwick, *Polska Rewolucja*, 288–92.
14. Wojciech Suchodolski, 3 November 1788; Chryzanty Opacki, 24 October 1788, both quoted after Butterwick, *Polish Revolution*, 56, 58.
15. Walerian Kalinka, *Sejm Czteroletni*, 1991, i, 176–78.
16. The king's speech is quoted at length by Michalski, *Stanisław August Poniatowski*, 52.
17. Quoted after Kalinka, *Sejm Czteroletni*, i, 191.
18. *Dyaryusz 1788*, i/2, 36, 52–73, quotation at 65.
19. Ibid., i/2, 554–56. See Montefiore, *Prince of Princes*, 404–14.
20. Branicki to Potemkin, 19 January 1789, quoted after Zofia Zielińska, 'Listy Ksawerego Branickiego do Grigorija Potiomkina (1788–1789)', in *Świat pogranicza*, ed. Mirosław Nagielski et al., 2003, 283–306 (at 306); eadem, *Studia z dziejów stosunków polsko-rosyjskich*, 172–94, 208; Bronisław Dembiński, *Polska na przełomie*, 1913, 181–82.
21. Cf. Hanna Osiecka-Samsonowicz, *Polskie uroczystości w barokowym Rzymie 1587–1696*, 2012, 77–99.
22. Franciszek Kwilecki, 7 January 1789, *Dyaryusz 1788*, ii/1, 4.
23. Ibid., ii/1, 19, 183–84.
24. Ibid., ii/ 1, 184–266, quotations at 197, 205.
25. Wojciech Szczygielski, *Sejm Wielki 1788–1792*, Łódź, 2015, 38–39.
26. Ignacy Łobarzewski, quoted after Anna Grześkowiak-Krwawicz, *O formę rządu czy o rząd dusz? Publicystyka polityczna Sejmu Czteroletniego*, 2000, 18.
27. Examples in Butterwick, *Polska Rewolucja*, 292–93, 699, 714.
28. 'Do Blancharda balonisty', in *Wiersze polityczne Sejmu Czteroletniego*, i, *1788–1789*, ed. Edmund Rabowicz and Krystyna Maksimowicz, 1998, 202–03.
29. ''Książę marszałek Sapieha przebierający się po polsku', ibid., i, 65.
30. *Dyaryusz 1788*, ii/1, 290–93; Kiciński to SA, 28 January 1789, both quoted in Richard Butterwick, 'Faworyt – demagog? Pius Kiciński na Sejmie Czteroletnim', in *Faworyci i opozycjoniści*, ed. Mariusz Markiewicz and Ryszard Skowron, Cracow, 2006, 485–93 (at 487–88). This alignment had been prefigured at the sejm of 1780, when royalists had demanded that National Cavalry officers and the hetmans wear Polish dress, while the latters' partisans, led by Suchodolski, had resisted: Witold Filipczak, 'Wojsko i obronność Rzeczypospolitej na sejmie w 1780 r.', in *Między obowiązkami, przywilejami a prawem Rzeczypospolitej XVI–XVIII wieku*, ed. Anna Kalinowska et al., 2018, 263–80 (at 278–79).
31. 'Do Jmci Pana Potockiego generała artylerii koronnej', in *Wiersze polityczne*, i, 184–85.
32. *I ja też*, s.l.d. [1790], 1.
33. SA to Deboli, 12 November 1791, quoted after Richard Butterwick, 'Political Discourses of the Polish Revolution, 1788–1792', *English Historical Review*, 120/487, 2005, 695–731 (at 700).

34. E.g. Wojciech Suchodolski, 21 July 1789, quoted after Butterwick, *Polish Revolution*, 120.
35. Kołłątaj, *Listy anonima*, ii, 97.
36. Ferdinando Maria Saluzzo to Ignazio Boncompagni, 11 January 1789, AAV ANV 66, fols 243–44.
37. Quoted in Butterwick, *Polish Revolution*, 43.
38. Ibid., 87–88.
39. Aleksander Zieliński, envoy for Nur, 12 March 1789, quoted ibid., 83.
40. Kalinka, *Sejm Czteroletni*, i, 388–90; Butterwick, *Polska Rewolucja*, 380–82.
41. Tadeusz Matuszewic, quoted after Butterwick, *Polska Rewolucja*, 381.
42. The severity of Kalinka, *Sejm Czteroletni*, i, 390–93, 432–35, was moderated by Korzon, *Wewnętrzne dzieje*, v, 15–16. See Roman Rybarski, *Skarbowość Polski w dobie rozbiorów*, Cracow, 1937, 272–335, 376–83; Marian Drozdowski, *Podstawy finansowe*, 140–65.
43. *Dyaryusz . . . 1788*, i/2, 501–17; SA to Deboli, 20 December 1788, ZP 417, fol. 674; Michalski, 'Zmierzch prokonsulatu', 486.
44. Branicki to Potemkin, 19 January 1789, in Z. Zielińska, 'Listy Ksawerego Branickiego', 306.
45. 'Ewangelia św. Ksawerego . . .', quoted after Rostworowski, *Ostatni król*, 165.
46. Adam Krasiński to Piotr Małachowski, 6 April and 3 April 1789, quoted after Butterwick, *Polska Rewolucja*, 396.
47. Saluzzo to Carlo Federici, 22 July 1789, quoted after Butterwick, *Polish Revolution*, 118.
48. Stanisław Kostka Potocki to Aleksandra Potocka, 22 July, 24 July 1789, quoted ibid., 123.
49. *VL*, ix, 103–05.
50. Krzysztof Szembek to Feliks Turski, undated, quoted in Butterwick, *Polish Revolution*, 178.
51. Naruszewicz to SA, 8 September 1790, *Korespondencja Naruszewicza*, 370–71.
52. SA to Deboli, 22 July 1789, quoted in Butterwick, *Polish Revolution*, 126.
53. Saluzzo to Francesco Zelada, 2 December 1789, quoted after Butterwick, *Polska Rewolucja*, 535 n. 20; in translation: Wolff, *Vatican and Poland*, 186.
54. Kołłątaj, *Listy anonima*, ii, 174.
55. SA to Deboli, 28 November 1789, in *MDSC*, ii, 321–22.
56. Gabriela Majewska, *Szwecja. Kraj – ludzie – rządy w polskiej opinii II połowy XVIII wieku*, Gdańsk, 2004, 280–81, 291–97, 318–20, 333, 338–40, 352, 355.
57. *Reforma Żydów. Projekt od Deputacyi do tego wyznaczonej*, in *MDSC*, vi, 215–28 (quotations at 216, 217, 222).
58. *VL*, ix, 136–42, 146–56.
59. Emanuel Rostworowski, *Legendy i fakty XVIII wieku*, 1963, 292–99; Zofia Zielińska, *„O sukcesyi tronu w Polszcze" 1787–1790*, 1991, 107–10.

CHAPTER 10: *REVOLUTION: THE NATION WITH THE KING*

1. See SA's correspondence with Franciszek Ksawery Woyna and Ignacy Pokubiatto between 16 February and 24 March 1790, *Korespondencja polityczna Stanisława Augusta. Wiedeń*, i: *1788–1790*, ed. Monika Jusupović and Adam Danilczyk, 2016, 154–64; Dariusz Nawrot, *Działania dyplomacji polskiej w Wiedniu w latach 1788–1792*, Katowice, 1999, 43–50.
2. Kamil Paździor, 'Polityka Sejmu Czteroletniego wobec Kościołów wschodnich', doctoral thesis, Uniwersity of Silesia in Katowice, 2000, 106–11.
3. Jerzy Michalski, '„Wszystko pójdzie wyśmienicie". O politycznym optymizmie po 3 maja', in Michalski, *SH*, i, 323–34 (at 323).
4. Lord, *Second Partition*, 151.
5. Ibid., 137–40.
6. Rostworowski, *Ostatni król*, 166–71; Butterwick, *Polska Rewolucja*, 646.
7. Butterwick, *Polska Rewolucja*, 457–67 (quotation of SA to Deboli, 12 August 1789, at 460–61); for the primate's voyage, see Sołtys, *Opat z San Michele*, 56–197.
8. Krystyna Zienkowska, *Sławetni i urodzeni. Ruch polityczny mieszczaństwa w dobie Sejmu Czteroletniego*, 1976, 117–28, pushed this argument much further.
9. Quoted after Rostworowski, *Legendy i fakty*, 323.
10. *VL*, ix, 203.

11. *Pace* Urszula Augustyniak, *History of the Polish-Lithuanian Commonwealth: Society – State – Culture*, Frankfurt, 2015, 168, 205.
12. Diary, ASC 9, fols 19–20.
13. Diary, ASC 9, fols 3–32, quotations at fols 9 (Zakrzewski), 21–22 (Potocki: *Przymówienie się . . . Seweryna Potockiego . . . 2 września 1790 . . .*).
14. *Przymówienie się . . . Seweryna Potockiego . . . 10 września 1790 . . .*, ASC 9, fols 209–10v.
15. Diary, ASC 9, fols 226–60, quotation at 235.
16. *Głos . . . Piusa Kicińskiego . . . 13 września 1790. po wyiściu Króla . . .*, ASC 9, fols 238–41.
17. SA to Deboli, 15 September 1790, ZP 420, fols 974–76; Ignacy Potocki to Elie Aloe, 15 September 1790, APP 277, fols 321–22.
18. E.g. Kalinka, *Sejm Czteroletni*, ii, 383.
19. E.g. Zienkowska, *Stanisław August Poniatowski*, 322–26.
20. SA to Deboli, 17 November 1790, quoted in Rostworowski, *Legendy i fakty*, 343–44.
21. Stanisław Staszic, *Przestrogi dla Polski*, ed. Stefan Czarnowski, 3rd edn, Wrocław, 2008, 79–81.
22. Stanisław Małachowski and Kazimierz Nestor Sapieha, *Wszem w obec y każdemu z osobna, komu o tym wiedzieć będzie należało . . .*, 25 October 1790, in *Dyaryusz 1790*, i/1, pp. vii–xii. SA, *Uniwersał powtorny na seymiki*, 17 October 1790.
23. Nowogródek instruction: *LDKSI*, 226–27.
24. S. Małachowski and K. N. Sapieha, *Wszem w obec y każdemu z osobna, komu o tym wiedzieć należy . . .*, 24 September 1790.
25. Seweryn Rzewuski, *O sukcesyi tronu w Polszcze. Rzecz krótka*, quoted after Zofia Zielińska, *Republikanizm spod znaku buławy. Publicystyka Seweryna Rzewuskiego z lat 1788–1790*, 1988, 109; see also Grześkowiak-Krwawicz, *O formę rządu*, 217–61.
26. SA to Deboli, 17 November 1790, quoted after Rostworowski, *Legendy i fakty*, 343.
27. Antoni Gorzeński to SA, Środa, 19 November 1790, quoted after Butterwick, *Polska Rewolucja*, 664–65.
28. Adam Lasocki to SA, Sochaczew, 16 November 1790, BC 728, fol. 515.
29. Wyszogród instruction, 24 November 1790: BPAUiPAN 8352, fols 373–80 (at 374).
30. Kiev instruction, 22 November 1790: Archiwum Narodowe, Cracow, Archiwum Podhoreckie X 4/17; record of vote: ZP 130, pp. 503–18.
31. I. Potocki to Aloe, 24 November 1790, quoted after Rostworowski, *Legendy i fakty*, 344.
32. SA to Deboli, 21 November 1790, quoted ibid., 344.
33. [Stefan Łuskina], *Ofiara ex-Jezuitów z własnych swych osób dla Rzeczypospolitej uczyniona roku 1790*, supplement *gratis* to *Gazeta Warszawska*, 10 November 1790; Volhynian instruction in Czesław Nanke, *Szlachta wołyńska wobec Konstytucyi Trzeciego Maja*, Lwów, 1907, 82–89. Piotr Stolarski, *Friars on the Frontier: Catholic Renewal and the Dominican Order in Southeastern Poland, 1594–1648*, Farnham, 2010, shows the deep roots of 'God's dogs' in these parts.
34. Samogitian instruction, 19 November 1790: *LDKSI*, 171.
35. Volhynian instruction, in Nanke, *Szlachta wołyńska*, 89. *Pace* Szczygielski (*Sejm Wielki*, 92–93, 99–101), who can only explain the inconvenient conservatism of the instructions by assuming the continuing strength of magnate patronage at most sejmiks.
36. Jerzy Kowecki, 'Posłowie – debiutanci na Sejmie Czteroletnim', in *Wiek XVIII. Polska i świat*, ed. Andrzej Zahorski, 1974, 195–210.
37. August Friedrich von Goltz to Frederick William II, 20 November 1790, quoted in Kalinka, *Sejm Czteroletni*, ii, 427; Adam Moszczeński to Feliks Potocki, Warsaw, 22 December 1790, quoted after Szczygielski, *Sejm Wielki*, 101.
38. I. Potocki to Aloe, 1 December 1790, quoted in Rostworowski, *Legendy i fakty*, 346.
39. Rostworowski, *Legendy i fakty*, 265–464.
40. Jan Dihm, *Niemcewicz jako polityk i publicysta w czasie Sejmu Czteroletniego*, Cracow, 1928, 82–97; Karol Zbyszewski, *Niemcewicz od przodu i tyłu* [1939], 4th edn, 1991, 172–74. Krzysztof Kurek, 'Świerzawski Karol Boromeusz', *PSB*, li, 354–56. SA to Franciszek Bukaty, 19 January 1791, in Kalinka, *Ostatnie lata*, ii, 177.
41. *VL*, ix, 202–03.

42. Longer quotation in Butterwick, *Polska Rewolucja*, 698–99; Kalinka, *Sejm Czteroletni*, ii, 442–43; Krakowski, *Oratorstwo*, 165; *VL*, ix, 209–10.
43. SA to Deboli, 16 March and 19 March 1791, ZP 413, fols 52–53, 54–55, quoted in Rostworowski, *Ostatni król*, 212, 217–18.
44. Szczygielski, *Sejm Wielki*, 104–11.
45. SA to Deboli, 5 February 1791, ZP 413, fols 25–26.
46. Suchodolski, 10 February 1791, quoted after Jerzy Michalski, *Witaj majowa jutrzenko*, Cracow, 1999, 49.
47. The law was not inscribed until 28 May 1791: *VL*, ix, 233–40. Łukasz Kądziela, 'Local Government Reform during the Four-Year Diet', in *Constitution and Reform*, 379–96 (at 380–81); cf. Lukowski, *Disorderly Liberty*, 237–38.
48. Kiciński quoted after Szczygielski, *Sejm Wielki*, 126.
49. Stanisław Sołtyk, *Projekt . . . przywrócenie praw miastom koronnym i litewskim*, in *MDSC*, iv, 66.
50. Tomasz Dłuski, 6 April 1791, quoted after Butterwick, *Polish Revolution*, 242; idem, 'Projekt obok projektu od deputacyi prawa miejskie rozważającej podanego', in *MDSC*, iv, 67–68.
51. SA to Deboli, 9 April 1791, ZP 413, fols 68–69.
52. 'Miasta', in *MDSC*, iv, 75–88.
53. Aleksander Linowski, 14 April 1791, quoted after Butterwick, *Polska Rewolucja*, 702.
54. SA, 14 April 1791, Diary, ASC 17, fols 260–65.
55. Diary, ASC 17, fols 248–49; SA to Deboli, 16 April 1791, ZP 413, fol. 72; Kalinka, *Sejm Czteroletni*, ii, 450.
56. Diary, ASC 17, fol. 268.
57. Józef Radzicki, envoy for Zakroczym, 18 April 1791, Diary, ASC 17, fol. 271.
58. The law is republished in *Konstytucja 3 Maja*, ed. Jerzy Kowecki, 1981, 111–23.
59. SA to Gaetano Ghigiotti, 18 April 1791, quoted after Butterwick, *Polish Revolution*, 246.
60. Zienkowska, *Sławetni i urodzeni*, 162–74.
61. Zofia Zielińska, 'Suchorzewski Jan', *PSB*, xlv, 320; Szczygielski, *Sejm Wielki*, 142–46.
62. Quoted after Grześkowiak-Krwawicz, 'Konstytucja 3 Maja. Rewolucja – Prawo – Dokument', 14.
63. Benedikt de Caché to Wenzel Anton von Kaunitz, 27 April 1791, quoted after Butterwick, *Polish Revolution*, 247; SA to Deboli, 20 April 1791, ZP 413, fol. 75; Kalinka, *Sejm Czteroletni*, ii, 458.
64. Rostworowski, *Ostatni król*, 231–34.
65. The principal source for the events of 3 and 5 May 1791 is the official diary of the sejm compiled by Antoni Siarczyński. This was edited and published, with the help of his brother, Revd Franciszek Siarczyński, for the sessions of 3 and 5 May as *Dzień trzeci maja roku 1791*, Warsaw: M. Gröll, 1791. The preface of this authorized version contains an appeal for trust: 'I have endeavoured to provide a faithful description of the Revolution of the third of May for the contemporary, and perhaps the future public (*Powszechności*) . . . I was a conscious witness of the entire Work, careful in preserving the memory, exact in gathering the circumstances, honest in presenting them.' Although far from impartial, especially in its general introduction (1–8), frequent comments on the impact of 'patriot' speakers, and extended conclusion, it makes a point of quoting the project's opponents in full, and its record of what was said in the two sessions has not hitherto been challenged. It should be compared with the fair copy of the MS diary (ASC 19, fols 23–40 [3 May], fols 75–89 [5 May]) in which, however, several speeches are not recorded, being supplied separately (not all of which are in ASC 19). Besides minor variations in spelling and punctuation, most differences are in word order, which in the published version was altered slightly to emphasize the historic moment. Some differences are pointed out below. These changes were probably made for additional persuasive effect, but some speakers may have corrected the record to provide a more accurate version. The fair copy is an edited version of the secretary's notes and materials supplied by speakers, but for now it is as close as we can get to what was actually said. A critical edition of the sejm diary for 3 and 5 May 1791 would be of great help to scholars and students.

66. *Dzień trzeci maja*, 13.
67. Ibid., 14–22.
68. Ibid., 61.
69. Ibid., 65.
70. On Suchorzewski's arguments and gestures, see Grześkowiak-Krwawicz, *Czy rewolucja może być legalna?*, 17, 25, 28–29, 63, 83–84, 160–62.
71. The figures of 111 and 32 given by Jan Dihm, *Trzeci Maj*, Cracow, 1932, 12–20, seem implausibly precise.
72. *Głos . . . Jana Onufrego Orłowskiego . . . 3. maia roku 1791 . . .*, s.l.d., in ASC 19, fols 43–44. This speech is noted, but not quoted in *Dzień trzeci maja*, 119.
73. *Dzień trzeci maja*, 74–82.
74. Ibid., 98–105.
75. Ibid., 88.
76. Diary, ASC 19, fol. 34. The reference to Providence was omitted in *Dzień trzeci maja*, 134–35.
77. *Dzień trzeci maja*, 138–39.
78. SA to Deboli, 4 May 1791, ZP 413, fol. 82.
79. Niemcewicz, *Pamiętniki*, i, 338.
80. SA to Deboli, 7 May 1791, ZP 413, fols 85–86.
81. SA to Deboli, 4 May 1791, ZP 413, fol. 82.
82. Anna Grześkowiak-Krwawicz, 'Deklaracja Stanów Zgromadzonych z 5 czy 3 maja 1791 roku?', *KH*, 99/1, 1992, 106–11. Besides the evidence therein, the copy of the *Law on Government* read out on 3 May has the *Declaration* as an integral part of the text, with the two marshals' signatures below. This version, with some revealing late corrections, is in ASC 20, fols 91–101, published as *Konstytucja 3 Maja 1791 na podstawie tekstu Ustawy Rządowej z Archiwum Sejmu Czteroletniego*, ed. Anna Grześkowiak-Krwawicz, 2018, 61–82. The two better-known copies, probably made by royal scribes on 4 May, omit the *Declaration*, with the signatures of the marshals and the Constitutional Deputation following Article XI. The copy in AGAD, Tzw. Metryka Litewska, VII, 4, fols 75–82 (reproduced in *Konstytucja 3 Maja 1791. Faksymile rękopisu*, ed. Józef Płocha, Wrocław, 1991), was probably the basis for the version inscribed into the acts of the Warsaw Castle Court, and thence for most subsequent printed versions. The copy in APP 100, vol. 2, pp. 74–84, was chosen for the first critical edition, *Konstytucja 3 Maja*, ed. Jerzy Kowecki, intr. Bogusław Leśnodorski, 1981. This was ready in 1971, but the Communist dictatorship only permitted publication during another Polish Revolution. It then rolled off the presses of the 'October Revolution Printing House'.
83. Diary, ASC 19, fol. 75. Cf. *Dzień trzeci maja*, 177: 'As the Law of Government was passed by the voice of the Sejm and the Public, it did not take the usual path of formalities.'
84. Diary, ASC 19, fol. 76v. Cf. the longer version in *Dzień trzeci maja*, 181–82.
85. Tadeusz Korsak, quoted after *Dzień trzeci maja*, 195.
86. Diary, ASC 19, fols 88v–89.
87. *Kalendarzyk polityczny na rok przestępny 1792*, s.l.d. [1792], quoted after Grześkowiak-Krwawicz, 'Konstytucja 3 Maja. Rewolucja – Prawo – Dokument', 27.
88. *Dzień trzeci maja*, 63.
89. All quotations have been checked against *Konstytucja 3 Maja*, ed. Grześkowiak-Krwawicz. I have made use of the eloquent translation made – it seems – by Franciszek Bukaty, *New Constitution of the Government of Poland*, London, 1791, reprinted in the *Annual Register*, 1791 (at 177–200), but in places I have translated more precisely. For a good modern alternative, see Lukowski, *Disorderly Liberty*, 260–71.
90. Grześkowiak-Krwawicz, 'Konstytucja 3 Maja. Rewolucja – Prawo – Dokument', 18.
91. Cf. *VL*, ii, 124.
92. Less optimistically: Jerzy Michalski, '„Wolność" i „własność" chłopska w polskiej myśli reformatorskiej XVIII wieku', in Michalski, *SH*, ii, 130–205 (at 195–96).
93. E.g., on 27 July 1790 the Volhynian envoy Wojciech Świętosławski thus opposed leaving a decision on funding a new Uniate bishopric of Połock to a Lithuanian provincial session: 'We

are all representatives of the nation, we should all decide together', quoted after Butterwick, *Polska Rewolucja*, 589.

94. Rostworowski, *Legendy i fakty*, 431–42. In subsequent manuscript and printed copies the full stop became a comma.
95. Krystyna Zienkowska, 'Sukcesja tronu w Ustawie Rządowej 3 Maja 1791 roku – koncepcja władzy czy symbol suwerenności?', in *Konstytucja 3 Maja. Prawo – polityka – symbol*, ed. Anna Grześkowiak-Krwawicz, 1992, 51–64.
96. *Konstytucja 3 Maja*, ed. Kowecki, 56–57.
97. Poczobut quoted after Magdalena Ślusarska, 'Konstytucja 3 Maja w kaznodziejstwie okolicznościowym lat 1791–1792', in *Rok Monarchii*, 153–75 (at 163).
98. Butterwick-Pawlikowski, 'Koncepcja narodu', 143, 146–49; Anna Grześkowiak-Krwawicz, 'Spór o Ustawę Rządową jako zderzenie dwóch dyskursów politycznych?', *WO*, 31, 2015, 195–212 (at 197–200).

CHAPTER 11: *REVOLUTION: ÇA IRA!*

1. SA to Pokubiatto, 25 September 1790, *Korespondencja polityczna Stanisława Augusta. Wiedeń*, i, 209.
2. Lord, *Second Partition*, 183.
3. Zofia Libiszowska, *Życie polskie w Londynie w XVIII wieku*, 1972, 114–37.
4. Schroeder, *Transformation*, 79–82.
5. Jerzy Michalski, 'Dyplomacja polska w latach 1764–1795', in *Historia dyplomacji polskiej*, ii, ed. Zbigniew Wójcik, 1982, 483–705 (at 646–47, 657, 670); cf. Zbigniew Anusik, 'Rzeczpospolita wobec Rosji w ostatniej fazie obrad Sejmu Wielkiego (1791–1792)', *PNH*, 16/2, 2017, 71–118 (at 80–83, 95–97); idem, 'Rzeczpospolita wobec wojny wschodniej (1787–1792) i wojny szwedzko–rosysjskiej (1788–1790)', in *Polska wobec wielkich konfliktów w Europie nowożytnej*, ed. Ryszard Skowron, Cracow, 2009, 145–86 (at 169–73).
6. Catherine II to Grimm, 10/21 May 1791, *SIRIO*, xxiii, 535.
7. Anusik, 'Rzeczpospolita wobec Rosji', 113, is convinced that given the divided positions at the Russian court and the empress's willingness to consider a variety of scenarios, much of the constitutional settlement could have been saved by prompt and decisive negotiations with Russia. He polemicizes with Emanuel Rostworowski (*Maj 1791–maj 1792*, 1985, 28) who saw no such possibilities of an understanding, given Catherine's determination to end the Commonwealth's emancipation. Ultimately this argument comes down to how much more of the domestic settlement might have been rescued, compared – as a minimum – to its survivals in the system of government established by the Grodno sejm of 1793. There was no question of Poland being permitted an autonomous role in European politics, so either the form of government would have reflected a lack of sovereignty, as it had before 1788, or the country would have been much smaller, as it was between 1815 and 1830, or both. Cf. Rostworowski, *Ostatni król*, 258–65, 299–300.
8. Catherine II to Potemkin, 18/29 July 1792, translation in Kalinka, *Ostatnie lata*, ii, 127–32 (at 127–28).
9. SA to Catherine II, 24 December 1791, and the unsent draft, entirely in the king's hand, in *Correspondance*, 506–08.
10. Michał Poniatowski to Jacek Małachowski, 29 December 1792, in *Między Konstytucją*, 115–18.
11. Kalinka, *Sejm Czteroletni*, ii, 526–29; Lord, *Second Partition*, 488–89.
12. Krasiński to SA, 28 January 1792, quoted in Władysław Smoleński, *Ostatni rok Sejmu Wielkiego* [1897], reprint Poznań, 2006, 451–54.
13. Stanisław Małachowski and Kazimierz Sapieha, *Wszem w obec, i każdemu z osobna komu o tym wiedzieć należy* [. . .], Warsaw, 7 May 1791, in *Za czy przeciw Ustawie Rządowej*, ed. Anna Grześkowiak-Krwawicz, 1992, 24–29 (at 24).
14. Michalski, '„Wszystko pójdzie wyśmienicie"', 324–28.
15. Hieronim Stroynowski, *Mowa o konstytucji rządu . . .*, ed. Ewa M. Ziółek, Lublin, 2009; see Lukowski, *Disorderly Liberty*, 243–45.

16. Jan Nepomucen Kossakowski, *Kazanie o Jedności, Zgodzie i Pokoiu . . .*, Wilno, 1792.
17. Marie-Louis Descorches to Charles Dumouriez, 9 May 1792, idem, 'Mémoire sur les événements arrivés en Pologne . . .', 6 January 1792, quoted in Butterwick, *Polish Revolution*, 269, 280; see Franciszka Sawicka, 'Uroczystości dla uczczenia pierwszej rocznicy Konstytucji 3 Maja', in *Rok Monarchii*, 177–94.
18. Paździor, 'Polityka Sejmu Czteroletniego', 370–82.
19. Stanisław Sołtyk, 21 May 1792, quoted after Butterwick, *Polish Revolution*, 308.
20. SA to Naruszewicz, 13 January 1792, *Korespondencja Naruszewicza*, 408–09.
21. SA to Krzysztof Cieszkowski, 6 February 1792, BC 920, pp. 511–12.
22. Wojciech Szczygielski, *Referendum trzeciomajowe. Sejmiki lutowe 1792 roku*, Łódź, 1994, 51–68.
23. Ibid., 362–96.
24. *Laudum* of the Łęczyca sejmik: BPAUiPAN 8330, fol. 831.
25. Acts of the Wilno sejmik: LVIA SA 4236, pp. 533–68; Robertas Jurgaitis kindly sent me photographs.
26. *VL*, ix, 326–38.
27. Quoted after Szczygielski, *Referendum*, 314.
28. This 'exclusion' has been criticized by Korzon, *Wewnętrzne dzieje*, i, 272–73; Jerzy Łojek, *Ku naprawie Rzeczypospolitej. Konstytucja 3 Maja*, 1988, 97; Janusz Tazbir, 'Próby zrozumienia racji targowiczan', in *Trudne stulecia*, 235–44 (at 240); Daniel Beauvois, *Pouvoir russe et noblesse polonaise en Ukraine 1793–1830*, Paris, 2003, 40–49, but applauded by Szczygielski, *Sejm Wielki*, 124–25.
29. Quotations from Michał Franciszek Karpowicz, *Kazanie . . . na pierwszym ufundowaniu powiatu preńskiego . . . 14 lutego . . .*, Wilno, 1792. See Richard Butterwick, 'Between Anti-Enlightenment and Enlightened Catholicism: Provincial Preachers in Late Eighteenth-Century Poland-Lithuania', in *Peripheries of the Enlightenment*, ed. Richard Butterwick et al., *SVEC*, 2008:1, 201–28 (at 222–24).
30. [Aleksander Linowski], *Doniesienie pilne współobywatelom z Warszawy*, in *Za czy przeciw Ustawie Rządowej?*, ed. Anna Grześkowiak-Krwawicz, 1992, 272–80 (at 280).
31. Suchodolski quoted in Butterwick, *Polish Revolution*, 56; Benedykt Hulewicz to Feliks Potocki, 8 March 1792, BC 3474, p. 153.
32. E.g. Smoleński, *Ostatni rok*, 417–20; Rostworowski, *Ostatni król*, 248–49; Łukasz Kądziela, *Od Konstytucji do Insurekcji. Studia nad dziejami Rzeczypospolitej w latach 1791–1794*, 2011, 26–27; Daniel Stone, 'The First (and Only) Year of the May 3 Constitution', *Canadian Slavonic Papers*, 35/1–2, 1993, 69–86 (at 85); Lukowski, *Disorderly Liberty*, 245.
33. *VL*, ix, 250–66.
34. *VL*, ix, 326.
35. *VL*, ix, 241–43.
36. *VL*, ix, 243–50.
37. *VL*, ix, 266–70.
38. *VL*, ix, 277–87; SA quoted after Rostworowski, *Legendy i fakty*, 451.
39. *VL*, ix, 278.
40. *VL*, ix, 315; Sapieha quoted after Jerzy Michalski, 'Zagadnienie unii polsko-litewskiej w czasach Stanisława Augusta', in Michalski, *SH*, i, 44–73 (at 61).
41. Konstanty Plater quoted ibid., 64.
42. *VL*, ix, 316–17; SA to Deboli, 22 October 1791, cited in Butterwick, *Poland's Last King*, 303.
43. *VL*, ix, 319–26.
44. *VL*, ix, 457–64.
45. *VL*, ix, 301–13.
46. *VL*, ix, 370–79, 406–11.
47. *VL*, ix, 381–94; Butterwick, *Polska Rewolucja*, 778–84.
48. *VL*, ix, 346–61 (at 346), ix, 361–66 (at 361).
49. Szczygielski, *Sejm Wielki*, 160–71, is more positive than Smoleński, *Ostatni rok*, 420; Rostworowski, *Ostatni król*, 248–89; Jerzy Michalski, *Konstytucja 3 Maja*, 1985, 58; and Kądziela, *Od Konstytucji do Insurekcji*, 26–28.

50. In the ninth of the ten volumes of the *Volumina Legum*, the Four Years Sejm's laws and resolutions begin on p. 46 and end on p. 470. They vary in length either side of the *Law on Government* at pp. 220–26. Cf. Peter Jupp, *The Governing of Britain 1688–1848*, London, 2006, 219–25.
51. See Jerzy Kowecki, 'Pierwsze stronnictwo polityczne w Polsce w XVIII wieku', in *Dzieje kultury politycznej w Polsce*, ed. Józef Andrzej Gierowski, 1977, 117–35.
52. *Obrona Stanisława Augusta*, quoted after Adam Skałkowski, 'Towarzystwo Przyjaciół Konstytucji 3 Maja', *Pamiętnik Biblioteki Kórnickiej*, 2, 1930, 50–83 (at 51).
53. Rostworowski, *Ostatni król*, 241–43.
54. Stone, 'The First (and Only) Year', 85–86.
55. Józef Wojakowski, *Straż Praw*, 1982, 103–04, 115–21, 131–55; cf. Derek Beales, 'Joseph II, Petitions and the Public Sphere', in *Cultures of Power in Europe during the Long Eighteenth Century*, ed. Hamish Scott and Brendan Simms, Cambridge, 2007, 249–68.
56. Poniatowski, 15 September 1791, quoted after Butterwick, *Polish Revolution*, 281.
57. The problem is discussed, not always fortuitously, by Andrzej Stroynowski, *Reforma królewszyczyzn na Sejmie Czteroletnim*, an issue of *Acta Universitatis Lodziensis*, seria 1, Folia Historica 69, 1979; and Wojciech Szafrański, *Prace prawnicze Hugona Kołłątaja*, Poznań, 2005, 51–76. Cf. Maria Pasztor, *Hugo Kołłątaj na Sejmie Wielkim w latach 1791–1792*, 1991, 173–83. Fiscal historians have endorsed some of the primate's arguments: Rybarski, *Skarbowość*, 345–54, 456–58; Marian Drozdowski, *Podstawy finansowe*, 163–64.
58. Poniatowski, 5 December 1791, quoted after Butterwick, *Polish Revolution*, 282.
59. Poniatowski to Maria Teresa Tyszkiewiczowa, 15 February 1791, quoted ibid., 283.
60. Jerzy Michalski, 'Stanisław August obserwatorem rewolucji francuskiej', in Michalski, *SH*, i, 500–14, concentrates on the king's sympathies for the Revolution expressed to Mazzei in 1789–90. During 1791 the monarch's letters to Deboli (in ZP 413) reveal an increasingly critical stance.
61. Wojakowski, *Straż Praw*, 148, 171; for examples of compliance: Jerzy Gordziejew, *Komisje Porządkowe Cywilno-Wojskowe w Wielkim Księstwie Litewskim w okresie Sejmu Czteroletniego (1789–1792)*, Cracow, 2010, 57–60.
62. 'Marsz studentów szkół włodzimierskich przez ks. Juliana Antonowicza, prefekta szkół tychże napisany', in *Komisja Edukacji Narodowej*, ed. Stanisław Tync, Wrocław, 1954, 540–43.
63. Poniatowski to Conventual, Observant and Reformed Franciscan provincials, 26 March 1792, quoted after Butterwick, *Polska Rewolucja*, 797.
64. *VL*, ix, 291–98.
65. Jankowski to I. Potocki, 8 October 1791, quoted after Zienkowska, *Sławetni i urodzeni*, 216.
66. Zahorski, *Centralne instytucje policyjne*, 121–33; Šmigelskytė-Stukienė et al., *Modernios administracijos tapsmas Lietuvoje*, 383–93.
67. Rostworowski, *Ostatni król*, 255.
68. Felicia Roşu, *Elective Monarchy in Transylvania and Poland-Lithuania, 1569–1587*, Oxford, 2017, 13–15 and passim. Miia Ijäs, *Res Publica Redefined? The Polish-Lithuanian Transition Period of the 1560s and 1570s in the Context of Central European State Formation Processes*, Frankfurt, 2016, also emphasizes external pressures.
69. Grześkowiak-Krwawicz, 'Konstytucja 3 Maja. Rewolucja – Prawo – Dokument', 8–12, 22–23.
70. Hugo Kołłątaj to Jan Śniadecki, quoted after Rostworowski, *Ostatni król*, 247; Pasztor, *Hugo Kołłątaj*, 172–73.
71. Hugo Kołłątaj, 28 June 1792, quoted after Pasztor, *Hugo Kołłątaj*, 171.
72. Rostworowski, *Ostatni król*, 250–53.
73. Kołłątaj quoted after Pasztor, *Hugo Kołłątaj*, 193; Emanuel Mateusz Rostworowski, 'Ksiądz Kołłątaj i trzy konstytucje: polityczna, ekonomiczna, moralna', in idem, *Popioły i korzenie*, Cracow, 1985, 138–50 (at 146–48).
74. Norman Davies, *Heart of Europe: A Short History of Poland*, 1st edn, Oxford, 1984, 331–33.
75. *Pan Tadeusz*, XII, 539, 557–64 (pp. 556–58, with minor modifications).
76. Emanuel Mateusz Rostworowski, 'Naprawa Rzeczypospolitej (w 190 rocznicę Konstytucji 3 Maja)', in idem, *Popioły i korzenie*, 133–37 (at 136–37). The high regard expressed in the 1830s

by Polonophile German liberals for the Constitution, as an example for their own monarchs and nobilities to follow, is noted by Tadeusz Cegielski and Łukasz Kądziela, *Rozbiory Polski*, 1990, 340. For a cautionary note, cf. Michalski, '„Wolność" i „własność" chłopska', 202–05.

CHAPTER 12: UNDECLARED WAR

1. The Russian ambassador Iakov Bulgakov despatched his version to St Petersburg on 27 July 1792, and it was summarized by Sergei Solovev in 1863. It is published in Polish translation by Szymon Askenazy, *Przymierze polsko-pruskie*, 3rd edn, Cracow, 1919, 298–300. The course of the meeting had already been contested: first by Hugo Kołłątaj, Ignacy Potocki and Franciszek Ksawery Dmochowski in *O ustanowieniu i upadku Konstytucyi polskiey 3-go maia 1791*, published in 1793, supposedly in Leipzig, as a kind of manifesto for an uprising. A response, *Uwagi nad książką pod tytułem: O ustanowieniu i upadku Konstytucyi polskiey 3 Maja*, was written in 1794–95 under the king's supervision, but only published in 1868 as 'Mikołaja Wolskiego *Obrona Stanisława Augusta*', ed. Bronisław Zaleski, in *Roczniki Towarzystwa Historyczno-Literackiego w Paryżu, Rok 1867*, Paris, 1868, 1–252 (at 231–35). Kołłątaj's role had already been exposed, although it was not yet widely believed, by Aleksander Linowski, *List do przyiaciela, odkrywaiący wszystkie czynności Kołłątaja w czasie insurrekcyi pisany roku 1795*, s.l. (at 8–12), republished twice in 1846, and Jan Komarzewski, *Coup d'oeil rapide sur les causes réelles de la décadence de la Pologne*, Paris, 1807, 244–46. The first scholarly account was Leon Wegner, 'Hugo Kołłątaj na posiedzeniu rady królewskiej z dnia 23 lipca 1792', *Rocznik Towarzystwa Przyjaciół Nauk Poznańskiego*, 5, 1869, 1–68. These and other sources are discussed in the reconstruction of the meeting by Jerzy Łojek, *Geneza i obalenie Konstytucji 3 Maja*, Lublin, 1986, 404–18 (a recombination in one volume of two books he had earlier had to publish separately) while Łojek's use and abuse of these sources is critically reviewed by Zofia Zielińska, in *PH*, 69/2, 1978, 317–36 (at 331–33). On Wolski's *Obrona*, the publication of which in 1868 also contained the king's own shorter *Zdanie o królu polskim* (at 10–28), first published anonymously in Danzig in 1792, see Emanuel Rostworowski, *Legendy i fakty*, 487–506. The standard accounts of the meeting are Władysław Smoleński, *Konfederacya targowicka* [1903], reprint Poznań, 2006, 210–16; Rostworowski, *Ostatni król*, 297–99.
2. SA to Catherine II, 22 June 1792, in *Correspondance*, 510–13.
3. Catherine II to SA, 2/13 July 1792, in *Correspondance*, 513–14.
4. Rostworowski, *Ostatni król*, 295–97.
5. 'Mikołaja Wolskiego *Obrona Stanisława Augusta*', 231–32.
6. Ibid., 232.
7. These arguments were first revealed in *Zdanie o królu polskim*, albeit without direct reference to the council of 23 July 1792 ('Mikołaja Wolskiego *Obrona Stanisława Augusta*', 26–27).
8. According to Bulgakov (in Askenazy, *Przymierze*, 299), Sapieha declared he would follow the king's example, giving a result of 8:4. He changed his mind the following day. However, Komarzewski, *Coup d'oeil*, 245, gave the result of the vote as 7:5; this, combined with a note by Stanisław August dated 25 July and the memoirs of General Stanisław Wodzicki furnished Łojek (*Geneza i obalenie*, 412, 415–16) with grounds to argue that Sapieha had opposed the king's decision on 23 July. Moreover, according to 'Mikołaja Wolskiego *Obrona Stanisława Augusta*', 234, 'what Marshal Małachowski and Prince Marshal Sapieha said at this council, they express in the contents of the manifestos inscribed by them'.
9. SA to Catherine II, 25 July 1792, in *Correspondance*, 516–17.
10. Catherine II to Potemkin, 18/29 July 1792, translation in Kalinka, *Ostatnie lata*, ii, 127–32 (quotations at 128, 130–31). The meanings of this rescript (and its less decisive predecessor of 16/27 May 1792) have been much debated. Cf. *inter alia*, Lord, *Second Partition*, 245–47; Rostworowski, *Ostatni król*, 261–65; Madariaga, *Russia*, 420–25, 428; Cegielski and Kądziela, *Rozbiory*, 235–36; Montefiore, *Prince of Princes*, 478–79; Adam Danilczyk, *Targowica czyli zdrada*, 2016, 69–71. NB. Schroeder, *Transformation*, 84–86, follows Jerzy Łojek ('The International Crisis of 1791: Poland Between the Triple Alliance and Russia', *East Central*

Europe, 2/1, 1975, 1–63) in downplaying the significance of these rescripts, wrongly assuming Potemkin's fall from favour.

11. Madariaga, *Russia*, 430, cites 'a note to the College of Foreign Affairs of December 1791, in which she bluntly stated that she would never agree to the new order which had been introduced in Poland in breach of a treaty, without consulting her, and to the accompaniment of many insults'.
12. SA to Deboli, 5 May 1792, quoted in Butterwick, *Polska Rewolucja*, 769.
13. Stone, 'The First (and Only) Year', 83–84; Sołtys, 'Między Konstytucją a Targowicą' in *Miedzy Konstytucją*, 32–34; Michał Zaleski, *Pamiętniki Michała Zaleskiego*, ed. Bronisław Zaleski, Poznań, 1879, 204–06.
14. Adam Lityński, 'Zdrada kraju w polskim prawie karnym końca XVIII wieku', in *Bo insza jest rzecz zdradzić*, 9–30 (quotation at 9); *VL*, ii, 251–52, 388–89, viii, 542, ix, 245.
15. Feliks Potocki to Seweryn Rzewuski, 11 August 1788, quoted after Rostworowski, 'Potocki Stanisław Szczęsny', *PSB*, xxxviii, 191
16. Potocki to SA, 30 May 1791, quoted after Rostworowski, *Ostatni król*, 272.
17. Potocki to Potemkin, 14 May 1791, in Lord, *Second Partition*, 527–28.
18. Draft of Potocki to Catherine II, quoted after Rostworowski, 'Potocki Stanisław Szczęsny', *PSB*, xxxviii, 193.
19. Montefiore, *Prince of Princes*, 2–10, 472–96; Smoleński, *Ostatni rok*, 187–88, 191–97. Polish translations of nine reports from Vasilii Popov to Catherine II from Jassy, between 4/15 October–30 November/11 December 1791, are in Kalinka, *Ostatnie lata*, ii, 133–40.
20. Deboli to SA, quoted after Rostworowski, 'Potocki Stanisław Szczęsny', *PSB*, xxviii, 194.
21. See Agata Roćko, 'Mieć w sobie „to coś". Zofia Potocka – fenomen piękna czy intelligencji emocjonalnej?', in *Słynne kobiety w Rzeczypospolitej XVIII wieku*, ed. Agata Roćko and Magdalena Górska, 2017, 131–48; cf. Montefiore, *Prince of Princes*, 460–61, and the sensationalist Jerzy Łojek, *Dzieje pięknej Bitynki*, 6th edn, 1995.
22. This argument is made forcefully by Łojek, *Geneza i obalenie*, 224–25, 264–66; with more nuance by Anusik, 'Rzeczpospolita wobec wojny wschodniej', 174–81.
23. Smoleński, *Konfederacya targowicka*, 24–27.
24. *Akt Konfederacyi Generalney wolney Koronney* in *Zbiur* [*sic*] *wszystkich druków Konfederacyi Targowickiey y Wileńskiey*, 1792, 17–56; the petition is quoted by Danilczyk, *Targowica*, 87–88.
25. Z. Zielińska, 'Suchorzewski Jan', *PSB*, xlv, 321. The other councillors were Jerzy Wielhorski, Adam Moszczeński, Leon Hulewicz, Antoni Złotnicki, Jan Świejkowski, Jan Zagórski, Michał Kobylecki and Prince Antoni Czetwertyński, Castellan of Przemyśl.
26. The note was delivered in handwritten Russian and French versions and printed Russian and Polish versions. SA to Franciszek Bukaty, 19 May 1792, in Kalinka, *Ostatnie lata*, ii, 220–21. It was published in *Gazeta Warszawska* on 23 May 1792.
27. Catherine II to Poniatowski, 19 April 1792, copy in AMS, Poniatowski I 27, pp. 55–56.
28. Poniatowski to Catherine II, Poniatowski to Bulgakov, Jabłonna, 22 May 1792, both in Kalinka, *Ostatnie lata*, ii, 72–74.
29. SA, 21 May 1792, quoted at length in Smoleński, *Ostatni rok*, 398–400.
30. *VL*, ix, 431, 441, 442–45, 449–50, 452, 454–56; Leonard Ratajczyk, *Wojsko i obronność Rzeczypospolitej 1788–1792*, 1975, 63–100, 112–16.
31. *VL*, ix, 421, 423–24, 447, 454.
32. Daniel Hailes to William, Baron Grenville, 14 April 1792 (no. 39), 17 April 1792 (no. 40), 25 April 1792 (no. 42), 26 May 1792 (no. 48), TNA FO 62/5.
33. E.g. Benedikt de Caché to Wenzel von Kaunitz, 18 April 1792, Vienna, Österreichisches Staatsarchiv, Haus-, Hof- und Staatsarchiv, Polen II 54, fol. 23 (no. 877); Marie Descorches to Charles Dumouriez, 23 April 1792, Paris, Archives du Ministère des Affaires Étrangères, Correspondance Politique, Pologne 319, fol. 207 (no. 45); Saluzzo to Zelada, 18 April 1792, AAV ANV 67, fol. 145.
34. Rostworowski, *Ostatni król*, 245; Dariusz Rolnik, 'Społeczeństwo szlacheckie Rzeczypospolitej a wojsko w czasie Sejmu Czteroletniego i w okresie rządów konfederacji targowickiej (1788–1793)', in *Społeczeństwo Staropolskie*, seria nowa, iv, 2015, 309–34 (at 318–27); on the

manoeuvres and their cultural choreography, see Ratajczyk, *Wojsko i obronność*, 304–16; Aleksandrowicz, 'Sejm Czteroletni', 233–42; Andrzej Michalski, 'Obóz wojskowy pod Gołębiem w 1791 roku', in *Studia Wojskowe*, iii, ed. Tomasz Ciesielski, Zabrze, 2009, 265–94.
35. Bronisław Pawłowski, *Od konfederacji barskiej do powstania styczniowego*, 1962, 163–64.
36. Adam Wolański, *Wojna polsko-rosyjska 1792 r.*, 2nd/3rd edn, 1996, 41–69, criticizes Poniatowski's decision; Pawłowski, *Od konfederacji barskiej*, 167–69, explains and defends it.
37. Wolański, *Wojna polsko-rosyjska*, 171–78; Pawłowski, *Od konfederacji barskiej*, 181–83.
38. Renata Król-Mazur, *Miasto trzech nacji. Studia z dziejów Kamieńca Podolskiego XVIII wieku*, Cracow, 2008, 567–74.
39. Łojek, *Geneza i obalenie*, 370–79, and Anusik, 'Rzeczpospolita wobec wojny wschodniej', 181–83 (on the basis of Curt von Stedingk's despatches), argue that the arguments were long and intense, before Zubov, Morkov and Popov finally convinced a wavering Catherine not to make any concessions. Bezborodko and Ostermann are again identified as moderates. The evidence is not conclusive.
40. According to the primate, Sapieha was drunk: Poniatowski to Augustyn Middleton, 25 July 1792, in *Między Konstytucją*, 121–23.
41. Józef Poniatowski to SA, 26 July 1792, quoted after Smoleński, *Konfederacja targowicka*, 225.
42. Szymon Askenazy, *Książę Józef Poniatowski 1763–1813*, 2nd edn, 1910, reprint Poznań, 2006, 34–37, 249–53; Jerzy Skowronek, *Książę Józef Poniatowski*, Wrocław, 1986, 60–62, 268.
43. Skowronek, *Książę Józef*, 62–65.
44. Adam Danilczyk, 'Rosja wobec Rzeczypospolitej w okresie konfederacji targowickiej. Nowe spojrzenie', unpublished paper delivered to the conference *Konstytucja 3 Maja versus Targowica*, at the Instytut Historii PAN, Warsaw, 13 May 2014; idem, *Targowica*, 154–61; cf. Łojek, *Geneza i obalenie*, 376–79, 402–03.
45. SA to Feliks Potocki, 24 July 1792, Potocki to SA, 2 August 1792, both quoted in full in Smoleński, *Konfederacya targowicka*, 217–18, 235–37.
46. Catherine II to SA, 3/14 August 1792; 'Pro memoria pour M. de Bułhakow'; SA to Catherine II, 26 August 1792, in *Correspondance*, 517–22.
47. The second accession is quoted in full in Smoleński, *Konfederacya targowicka*, 296–97.

CHAPTER 13: THE AUGEAN STABLES

1. *Pace* Schroeder, *Transformation*, 104–05.
2. Adam Moszczeński to Feliks Potocki, Targowica, 25 May 1792, quoted after Smoleński, *Konfederacya targowicka*, 69–70.
3. Rostworowski, 'Potocki Stanisław Szczęsny', *PSB*, xxviii, 195.
4. Potocki to Poniatowski, 2, 7, 13 and 22 August 1792, in *Między Konstytucją*, 124–28, 132–34.
5. Copies of the acts of the Liw confederacy of 6 and 30 August 1792 are in BPAUiPAN 8322, fols 624–25, 629–35, of the Ciechanów confederacy of 7 and 28 August 1792 in BPAUiPAN 8318, fols 384–87, 388–92, and of the Czersk confederacy of 9 and 24 August 1792 are in BPAUiPAN 8320, fols 516–18, 519–24.
6. Dariusz Rolnik, *Szlachta koronna wobec konfederacji targowickiej*, Katowice, 2000, 150–61.
7. Ramunė Šmigelskytė-Stukienė, *Lietuvos Didžiosios Kunigaikštystes konfederacijos susidarymas ir veikla 1792–1793*, Vilnius, 2003, 98.
8. Ibid., 262.
9. *Wiersze polityczne czasu konfederacji targowickiej i sejmu grodzieńskiego 1793 roku*, ed. Krystyna Maksimowicz, Gdańsk, 2008; *Tajna korespondencja z Warszawy do Ignacego Potockiego 1792–1794*, ed. Maria Rymszyna and Andrzej Zahorski, 1961.
10. Wojciech Stanek, *Konfederacje generalne koronne w XVIII wieku*, Toruń, 1991, 225–26, argues that the eighteenth-century tendency to concentrate power in the central organs of general confederacies culminated in that of Targowica.
11. Smoleński, *Konfederacya targowicka*, 311–12.

12. Quotations from the summary of Potocki's reply to the primate, sent by Ignacy Massalski from Grodno on 23 January 1793, in Kądziela, *Od Konstytucji do Insurekcji*, 164–65.
13. Proclamation of 3 January 1793, in Richard Butterwick-Pawlikowski, '„Z istotnego przekonania". O postawie prymasa Michała Jerzego Poniatowskiego wobec Targowicy raz jeszcze', in *W cieniu*, 429–48 (at 442–44).
14. Poniatowski to Ghigiotti, 27 December 1792 (probably intended for Prince Stanisław Poniatowski in Rome), in *Między Konstytucją*, 164–73 (at 172–73); also Poniatowski to Kazimierz Raczyński, 2 December 1792, Raczyński to Potocki, 3 December 1792, Poniatowski to Potocki, 19 December 1792, 145–59.
15. The correspondence is in Kądziela, *Od Konstytucji do Insurekcji* (quotations from Poniatowski to Massalski, 16 January 1793, at 158–64) and Butterwick-Pawlikowski, '„Z istotnego przekonania"', 444–48.
16. SA to Catherine II, 'Pro memoria', 25 January 1793, *Correspondance*, 525–27 (at 527).
17. 'Wypis objaśnień i informacji, jakie były dawane przez konsyliarzów Generalności względem przyszłej formy rządu, w Grodnie, dnia 15 lutego tworzyć się mającej'; 'Uwagi nad niektóremi punktami tego wypisu', in *Między Konstytucją*, 173–89.
18. Quoted after Smoleński, *Konfederacya targowicka*, 366–67.
19. According to Andrzej Sulima Kamiński, *Historia Rzeczypospolitej wielu narodów 1505–1795*, Lublin, 2000, 227: 'the widespread support given by noble multitudes [*sic!*] to the infelicitous Confederacy of Targowica was not only an expression of thoughtlessness or national treason, but also a desperate defence of free citizenship against a royal plot'. For a similar perspective, see Tazbir, 'Próby zrozumienia racji targowiczan'.
20. Grześkowiak-Krwawicz, 'Konstytucja 3 Maja. Rewolucja – Prawo – Dokument', 24.
21. Moszczeński to Potocki, 25 May 1792, quoted after Smoleński, *Konfederacya targowicka*, 70.
22. Lord, *Second Partition*, 309.
23. Schroeder, *Transformation*, 106.
24. On Catherine's *ukaz* of 8/19 December 1792, see Smoleński, *Konfederacya targowicka*, 381.
25. Lord, *Second Partition*, xvi; also 497–502.
26. Catherine II to Jakob Johann Sievers of 22 December 1792/2 January 1793 quoted after Smoleński, *Konfederacya targowicka*, 385; see also Wojciech Kriegseisen, 'Katarzyna II jako mediewistka. Przyczynek do genezy drugiego rozbioru', *KH*, 111/3, 2004, 126–40.
27. The Treaty of St Petersburg is published in *Consolidated Treaty Series*, ed. Clive Parry, 231 vols, Dobbs Ferry, NY, 1969–81, li, 451–58.
28. Kądziela, *Od Konstytucji do Insurekcji*, 139–40.
29. Catherine II quoted after Smoleński, *Konfederacya targowicka*, 422.
30. Król-Mazur, *Miasto trzech nacji*, 584–93.
31. Jerzy Wojtowicz, 'Walka Gdańska i Torunia przeciwko pruskiej zaborczości 1772–1793', in *Historia Pomorza*, ii/2, *Pomorze Wschodnie w latach 1657–1815*, ed. Gerard Labuda, Poznań, 1984, 617–22; Czesław Bernat, 'Zabór Gdańska przez Prusy i prawno-ustrojowe tego konsekwencje', in *HGd*, iii/2, 16–37.
32. On Stanisław August's interest in Louis XVI, and some parallels, see Richard Butterwick, '„Król z narodem, naród z królem". Porównanie Stanisława Augusta Poniatowskiego z Ludwikiem XIV w latach 1788–1792', *WO*, 16, 115–32; Piotr Ugniewski, *Ludwik XVI – Stanisław August. Propagandowe wizerunki równoległe*, 2014.
33. SA to Catherine II, 25 January 1793, Catherine II to SA, 9/20 February 1793, *Correspondance*, 522–25, 534–36.
34. Burke, 6 March 1794, quoted after Lord, *Second Partition*, 445; see Zofia Libiszowska, 'Prasa i publicystyka angielska wobec drugiego rozbioru Polski', *Rocznik Historii Czasopiśmiennictwa Polskiego*, 12/3, 1973, 299–325.
35. Kądziela, *Od Konstytucji do Insurekcji*, 167–80.
36. Ibid., 199–208.
37. Lukowski, *Partitions*, 156.
38. A model instruction for the Crown is in APP 96, pp. 228–30.
39. Wilno instruction: LVIA SA 4238, pp. 1675–78 (at 1677).

40. Šmigelskytė-Stukienė, *Lietuvos Didžiosios Kunigaikštystes konfederacijos susidarymas*, 233–34.
41. Jakob Johann Sievers, *Jak doprowadziłem do drugiego rozbioru Polski*, 3rd Polish edn, ed. Barbara Grochulska and Piotr Ugniewski, 1992.
42. Madariaga, *Russia*, 439–40.

CHAPTER 14: IMMOLATION

1. Wacław Tokarz, *Rozprawy i szkice*, 1959, i, 141–50.
2. Grochulska, *Warszawa na mapie*, 190–234; eadem, 'Echa upadłości warszawskich bankierów', in *Wiek XVIII. Polska i świat*, ed. Andrzej Zahorski, 1974, 245–54.
3. Quoted after McPhee, *Liberty or Death*, 159.
4. Ibid., 114–15, 140, 149–273; François Furet, *Revolutionary France 1770–1880*, Oxford, 1992, 134–42; Timothy Tackett, *The Coming of the Terror in the French Revolution*, Cambridge, MA, 2015.
5. T. C. W. Blanning, *The French Revolutionary Wars 1787–1792*, London, 1996, 64–69, 91–144.
6. Sievers, *Jak doprowadziłem do drugiego rozbioru Polski*, 171–81; Sievers to Otto Igelström, Grodno, 28 January 1794, ibid., 183–90 (quotations at 190); SA to Catherine II, 29 January 1794, SA to Platon Zubov, 29 January 1794; Catherine II to SA, 27 February/9 March 1794, Zubov to SA, 28 February/10 March 1794, *Correspondance*, 590–95.
7. Kądziela, *Od Konstytucji do Insurekcji*, 296–97.
8. Zahorski, *Warszawa w powstaniu*, 52–57; Lukowski, *Partitions*, 161.
9. Robert Howard Lord, 'The Third Partition of Poland', *S[EE]R*, 3, 1924/25, 481–98 (at 482); Madariaga, *Russia*, 437–38; Dixon, *Catherine the Great*, 2001, 171.
10. Kądziela, *Od Konstytucji do Insurekcji*, 303–11.
11. Andrzej Zahorski, *Naczelnik w sukmanie*, Cracow, 1990, 22–26 (quotation at 24).
12. Andrzej Woltanowski, 'Tadeusz Kościuszko i pierwszy etap reform włościańskich (28 marca–1 maja 1794 r.)', *PH*, 78/1, 1987, 19–44 (at 21–25); idem, 'Kształtowanie opinii publicznej podczas powstania', in *Powstanie kościuszkowskie*, 80–111 (at 81–83).
13. Zahorski, *Warszawa w powstaniu*, 103, 106.
14. Quoted after Bartłomiej Szyndler, *Powstanie kościuszkowskie 1794*, 1994, 123.
15. Quoted ibid., 130.
16. Quoted after Władysław Zajewski, 'Wilno w rewolucji 1794 roku', in *200 rocznica*, 103–32 (at 104).
17. Repnin regarded the Samogitian peasants as incorrigibly rebellious: Leonid Żytkowicz, 'Rozwarstwienie chłopstwa a gospodarka na Żmudzi w 2 połowie XVII i w XVIII wieku', in *Społeczeństwo staropolskie*, ii, 1979, 229–314 (at 305).
18. Quoted after Cegielski and Kądziela, *Rozbiory*, 308.
19. Łukasz Kądziela, *Fryderyk Moszyński w insurekcji kościuszkowskiej*, 2004, 68–87.
20. Józef Poniatowski to Stanisław Mokronowski, Powązki, 19 August 1794, quoted after Sołtys, *Opat z San Michele*, 49.
21. Catherine II to Grimm, quoted after Lord, 'Third Partition', 491.
22. Lukowski, *Partitions*, 165.
23. Quoted after Grześkowiak-Krwawicz, *Queen Liberty*, 119.
24. Ibid., 101–20.
25. Lord, 'Third Partition', 481.
26. Quoted after Lord, 'Third Partition', 495; published in *LLVPD*, i, 236–39.
27. Catherine II to Nikolai Repnin 1794, 23 November/4 December 1794, quoted after Borys Nosow, 'Polityka Rosji na początku panowania Stanisława Augusta, 1764 – początek 1765 r.', in *SARz*, 81–99 (at 82). I am grateful to Zofia Zielińska for her guidance on this point.
28. Catherine II to Repnin, 27 October/7 November 1795, quoted in Zofia Zielińska, 'Geneza i treść aktu abdykacji Stanisława Augusta', *Studia Źródłoznawcze*, 51, 2013, 43–68 (at 51).
29. Ibid., 63–64.
30. Ibid., 66–67; SA to Catherine II, 25 November and 26 November 1795, *Correspondance*, 634–41.

31. Draft of SA to Ignacy Zakrzewski, 22 April 1794, quoted after Zbigniew Góralski, *Stanisław August w insurekcji kościuszkowskiej*, 1988, 73–74.

EPILOGUE: SMOKE AND ASH

1. Catherine II to SA, 21 December 1795/1 January 1796, *Correspondance*, 642–63.
2. *SAOKP*, 479–80; Zamoyski, *Last King*, 450–51; Piotr Skowroński, 'Presumcja równania się Henrykowi IV. Stanisław August a legenda pierwszego Burbona na tronie francuskim', *Pamiętnik Teatralny*, 67/4, 2018, 113–29.
3. The story of the Polish theft of Vytautas's crown is debunked by Rimvydas Petrauskas, 'Korona Witolda: niedoszła koronacja i jej późniejsza legenda historyczna', in *Tradycja – metody przekazywania i formy upamiętnienia w państwie polsko-litewskim*, ed. Urszula Augustyniak, 2011, 13–23.
4. Lukowski, *Partitions*, 182; *LLVPD*, i, 307.
5. Potocki to Rzewuski, Humań, 4 January 1796, in Emanuel Rostworowski, 'Korespondencja Szczęsnego Potockiego z Sewerynem Rzewuskim z l. 1788–1796', *PH*, 45/4, 1954, 722–40 (at 740).
6. Tadeusz Czacki, quoted after Jarosław Czubaty, '"What is to be Done when the Motherland has Died?", The Moods and Attitudes of Poles after the Third Partition 1795–1806', *Central Europe*, 7/2, 2009, 95–109 (at 98).
7. Quoted ibid., 100.
8. Jarosław Czubaty, *Księstwo Warszawskie (1807–1815)*, 2011, 12–13.
9. Karpiński, *Historia mego wieku*, 174–75.
10. Czubaty, *Księstwo Warszawskie*, 16.
11. Simon Dixon, *The Modernisation of Russia 1676–1825*, Cambridge, 1998, 50–53.
12. Davies, *Heart of Europe*, 175–214; Cegielski and Kądziela, *Rozbiory*, 327–29.
13. Stanisław Lorentz and Andrzej Rottermund, *Klasycyzm w Polsce*, 1984, 48–51, 176–88, 213–15.
14. Quoted after Zofia Stefanowska, *Mapa romantyzmu polskiego*, 2014, 119.
15. See John D. Stanley, 'Introduction', in *Nation and History: Polish Historians from the Enlightenment to the Second World War*, ed. Peter Brock et al., Toronto, 2006, 3–17.
16. E.g. Kamiński, *Historia Rzeczypospolitej wielu narodów*.
17. E.g. Włodzimierz Biernacki, *Myśl polityczna I Rzeczypospolitej*, Cracow, 2011.
18. Cf. Zdzisław Libera, 'Adam Mickiewicz o Konstytucji 3 Maja', in *Konstytucja 3 Maja. Prawo – polityka – symbol*, ed. Anna Grześkowiak-Krwawicz, 1992, 99–108.
19. Friedrich, *The Other Prussia*, 211–18.
20. *Pan Tadeusz*, XI, 338–41 (adapted from p. 502).
21. *VL*, ix, 316.
22. Richard Butterwick, '*Finis Poloniae, finis Lituaniae, finis Reipublicae*?', in *Lietuvos Didžiosios Kunigaikštijos tradicija ir tautiniai naratyvai*, ed. Alfredas Bumblauskas and Grigorijus Potašenko, Vilnius, 2009, 105–114; Ramunė Šmigelskytė-Stukienė, '„Wielkie Księstwo" i „prowincja litewska" w piśmiennictwie politycznym okresu rozbiorów', *Europa Orientalis*, 1, 2009, 349–63.
23. Andrzej Nowak, *Dzieje Polski*, Cracow, 2014– . The first four volumes have reached 1572.
24. Lord, *Second Partition*, 504; idem, 'Third Partition', 482; Jerzy Łojek, 'Robert Howard Lord – uczony niezwykły', foreword to Robert Howard Lord, *Drugi Rozbiór Polski*, 1973.
25. Jacques Godechot, *France and the Atlantic Revolution of the Eighteenth Century, 1770–1799*, New York, 1965, esp. 135–38; R. R. Palmer, *The Age of the Democratic Revolution: A Political History of Europe and America, 1760–1800* [1959–64], updated edn, Princeton, NJ, 2014, 307–25, 437–46, 482–90; Venturi, *The End of the Old Regime in Europe, 1768–1776*, 172–234; idem, *The End of the Old Regime in Europe, 1776–1789*, Princeton, NJ, 1991, ii, 784–87, 907–47.
26. For example, the writer Jarosław Marek Rymkiewicz not only glorifies revolutionary violence, but repeats the falsehood that Michał Poniatowski committed suicide, in his *Wieszanie*, 2007, esp. 152–61. Unfortunately this book purports to be a work of history, not historical fiction.

FURTHER READING

PROLOGUE

Catherine II and her empire are covered magisterially by Isabel de Madariaga, *Russia in the Age of Catherine the Great*, New Haven, CT, 1981 (the progress to the Crimea at 359–73); see also Simon Dixon, *Catherine the Great*, Harlow, 2001; idem, *Catherine the Great*, London, 2009; John T. Alexander, *Catherine the Great*, New York, 1989; Simon Sebag Montefiore, *Prince of Princes: The Life of Potemkin*, London, 2000.

On Stanisław August, see the elegant biography by Adam Zamoyski, *The Last King of Poland*, London, 1992 (on the Kaniów expedition: 292–306); Richard Butterwick, *Poland's Last King and English Culture: Stanisław August Poniatowski, 1732–1798*, Oxford, 1998; idem, 'The Enlightened Monarchy of Stanisław August Poniatowski (1764–1795)', in *Polish-Lithuanian Monarchy*, 193–218; the inspirational Jean Fabre, *Stanislas-Auguste Poniatowski et l'Europe des lumières. Étude de cosmopolitisme*, Paris, 1952; the lucid Emanuel Rostworowski, *Ostatni król Rzeczypospolitej*, 1966; and the authoritative Jerzy Michalski, *Stanisław August Poniatowski*, 2009.

The politics of the Kaniów summit are explained by Robert Howard Lord, *The Second Partition of Poland: A Study in Diplomatic History*, Cambridge, MA, 1915, 82–91; Zofia Zielińska, ' „Król wydał trzy miliony, czekał trzy miesiące, by widzieć Katarzynę przez trzy godziny" – po co ta podróż?', in *SARz*, 183–94; eadem, 'Stanisław August i Otto Stackelberg u progu wojny rosyjsko-tureckiej (marzec-październik 1787)', *KH*, 107/4, 2000, 3–20. For the question of an alliance, see Emanuel Rostworowski, *Sprawa aukcji wojska na tle sytuacji politycznej przed sejmem Czteroletnim*, 1957, 177–202; Jerzy Michalski, *Polska wobec wojny o sukcesję bawarską*, Wrocław, 1964; idem, 'Problematyka aliansu polsko-rosyskiego w czasach Stanisława Augusta. Lata 1764–1766'; in Michalski, *SH*, i, 335–61; idem, 'Dwie misje księcia Stanisława', in Michalski, *SH*, i, 376–92; idem, 'Sprawa przymierza polsko-rosyjskiego w dobie aneksji Krymu', in Michalski, *SH*, i, 420–48; idem, 'Zmierzch prokonsulatu Stackelberga', in Michalski, *SH*, i, 449–99. Stanisław August's moods can be followed in the letters published in Kalinka, *Ostatnie lata*, ii, 5–64; and Zofia Zielińska, 'Listy Stanisława Augusta z podróży do Kaniowa (1787)', *KH*, 110/4, 2003, 71–124.

For the show: Przemysław Wątroba, 'Wezuwiusz w Kaniowie – realizacje Jakuba Kubickiego z okazji spotkania Stanisława Augusta i Katarzyny II w maju 1787 r.', in *SARz*, 195–211 (at 208); *SAOKP*, 439–41; cf. Franco Venturi, *The End of the Old Regime in Europe, 1776–1789*, Princeton, NJ, 1991, ii, 786.

On the geopolitics (rooted in Halford John Mackinder's 'heartland' theory, first published in 'The Geographical Pivot of History', *Geographical Journal*, 23/4, 1904, 421–37), see John P. LeDonne, *Russia and the World, 1700–1917: The Geopolitics of Expansion and Containment*, New York, 1996; idem, *The Grand Strategy of the Russian Empire, 1650–1831*, New York, 2004; also Andrzej Nowak, *History and Geopolitics: A Contest for Eastern Europe*, 2008; Zofia Zielińska, 'Poland between Prussia and Russia in the Eighteenth Century', in *Constitution and Reform*, 87–111; cf. Simon Dixon, *The Modernisation of Russia 1676–1825*, Cambridge, 1998, 27–56, who emphasizes the primacy of Russia's rivalry with the Ottoman Empire and the role of French weakness; see also Christopher Duffy, *Russia's Military Way to the West*, London, 1981; Brian

Davies, *Empire and Military Revolution in Eastern Europe: Russia's Turkish Wars in the Eighteenth Century*, London, 2011.

On the international system, see Paul W. Schroeder, *The Transformation of European Politics 1763–1848*, Oxford, 1994; H. M. Scott, *The Birth of a Great Power System, 1740–1815*, Harlow, 2006; M. S. Anderson, 'Eighteenth-Century Theories of the Balance of Power', in *Studies in Diplomatic History*, ed. Ragnhild Hatton and M. S. Anderson, London, 1970, 183–98; T. C. W. Blanning, *Origins of the French Revolutionary Wars*, Harlow, 1986, 1–68.

The partitions are explained within this system by Jerzy Lukowski, *The Partitions of Poland: 1772, 1793, 1795*, Harlow, 1999; Emanuel Rostworowski, 'Polska w układzie sił politycznych Europy XVIII wieku', in *Polska w epoce Oświecenia*, ed. Bogusław Leśnodorski, 1971, 11–59; Michael G. Müller, *Die Teilungen Polens*, Munich, 1984; Tadeusz Cegielski and Łukasz Kądziela, *Rozbiory Polski*, 1990; Robert Frost, 'The Impact of War: The Holy Roman Empire and Poland-Lithuania', in *The Holy Roman Empire 1495–1806*, ed. R. J. W. Evans and Peter H. Wilson, Leiden, 2012, 239–57; Michael G. Müller, 'Koniec dwu republik: rozbiory Polski i rozpad starej Rzeszy', in idem, *Zrozumieć polską historię*, Poznań, 2012, 349–54.

Jerzy Lukowski, *Liberty's Folly: The Polish-Lithuanian Commonwealth in the Eighteenth Century*, London, 1991, offers a fairly 'pessimist' interpretation of its subject; Józef Andrzej Gierowski, *The Polish-Lithuanian Commonwealth in the XVIIIth Century*, Cracow, 1996, belongs to the 'optimist' school.

1 COMMONWEALTH

On medieval Poland, Lithuania and Prussia, see Paul W. Knoll, *The Rise of the Polish Monarchy: Piast Poland in East-Central Europe, 1320–1370*, Chicago, IL, 1972; S. C. Rowell, *Lithuania Ascending: A Pagan Empire within East-Central Europe, 1295–1345*, Cambridge, 1994; Darius Baronas and S. C. Rowell, The *Conversion of Lithuania: From Pagan Barbarians to Late Medieval Christians*, Vilnius, [2015]; Robert Frost, *The Oxford History of Poland-Lithuania*, i: *The Making of the Polish-Lithuanian Union, 1385–1569*, Oxford, 2015; Michael Burleigh, *Prussian Society and the German Order: An Aristocratic Corporation in Crisis, c. 1410–1466*, Cambridge, 1985; Karin Friedrich, *Brandenburg-Prussia, 1466–1806: The Rise of a Composite State*, Basingstoke, 2012, 7–21.

Two general histories are Daniel Stone, *The Polish-Lithuanian State, 1386–1795*, Seattle, WA, 2001; Urszula Augustyniak, *History of the Polish-Lithuanian Commonwealth: Society – State – Culture*, Frankfurt, 2015; for some of the Commonwealth's constituent parts and peoples, see Karin Friedrich, *The Other Prussia: Royal Prussia, Poland and Liberty, 1569–1772*, Cambridge, 2000; Almut Bues, *Der Herzogtum Kurland und der Norden der polnisch-litauischen Adelsrepublik im 16. und 17. Jahrhundert*, Giessen, 2001; Bogusław Dybaś, 'Wasale, baronowie, panowie bracia. Szlachta inflancka, kurlandzka i piltyńska wobec Rzeczypospolitej w XVI–XVIII wieku', in *My i oni*, 99–129; *Under a Common Sky: Ethnic Groups of the Commonwealth of Poland and Lithuania*, ed. Michał Kopczyński and Wojciech Tygielski, 2017. The military rise and fall of the Commonwealth are explained by Robert I. Frost, *The Northern Wars: War, State and Society in Northeastern Europe, 1558–1721*, Harlow, 2000.

On the parliamentary system, see Anna Sucheni-Grabowska, 'The Origin and Development of the Polish Parliamentary System through the End of the Seventeenth Century', in *Constitution and Reform*, 13–50; *The Polish Parliament at the Summit of its Development*, ed. Władysław Czapliński, Wrocław, 1985; *Historia sejmu polskiego*, i, ed. Jerzy Michalski, 1984; *Sejm Królestwa Polskiego i Rzeczypospolitej Obojga Narodów a europejskie reprezentacje stanowe*, ed. Dariusz Kupisz and Wacław Uruszczak, 2019; Władysław Konopczyński's classic *Liberum veto* [1918], 2nd edn, Cracow, 2002, appeared in an abridged French edn: *Le Liberum veto*, Paris, 1930; for the latest research: *Liberum veto*, issue of *BEN*, 4/1, 2016.

The role of the monarchy can be approached via *The Polish-Lithuanian Monarchy*, esp. the introduction (1–24) and the contrasting chapters by Jerzy Lukowski ('The Szlachta and the Monarchy: Reflections on the Struggle *inter maiestatem ac libertatem*', 132–49) and Robert Frost

('Obsequious Disrespect: The Problem of Royal Power in the Polish-Lithuanian Commonwealth under the Vasas, 1587–1668', 150–71); see also Felicia Roşu, *Elective Monarchy in Transylvania and Poland-Lithuania, 1569–1587*, Oxford, 2017; Urszula Augustyniak, *Wazowie i „królowie rodacy". Studium władzy królewskiej w Rzeczypospolitej XVII wieku*, 1999.

On political ideas, discourse and values, see Anna Grześkowiak-Krwawicz, *Queen Liberty: The Concept of Freedom in the Polish-Lithuanian Commonwealth*, Leiden, 2012; eadem, 'Noble Republicanism in the Polish-Lithuanian Commonwealth: An Attempt at Description', *APH*, 103, 2011, 31–65; eadem, *Dyskurs polityczny w Rzeczypospolitej Obojga Narodów*, Toruń, 2018; Karin Friedrich, 'Polish-Lithuanian Political Thought, 1450–1700' in Howell Lloyd et al. (eds), *History of European Political Thought, 1450–1700*, New Haven, CT, 2007, 409–47; *Citizenship and Identity in a Multinational Commonwealth: Poland-Lithuania in Context, 1550–1772*, ed. Karin Friedrich and Barbara Pendzich, Leiden, 2009; Benedict Wagner-Rundell, *Common Wealth, Common Good: The Politics of Virtue in Early Modern Poland-Lithuania*, Oxford, 2015; Dorota Pietrzyk-Reeves, *Polish Republican Discourse in the Sixteenth Century*, Cambridge, 2020; cf. Quentin Skinner, *Liberty before Liberalism*, Cambridge, 1998.

For confessional developments, see, *inter alia*, Natalia Nowakowska, *King Sigismund of Poland and Martin Luther: The Reformation before Confessionalization*, Oxford, 2018; Wojciech Kriegseisen, *Between State and Church: Confessional Relations from Reformation to Enlightenment: Poland-Lithuania – Germany – Netherlands*, Frankfurt, 2016; Piotr Wilczek, *Polonia Reformata: Essays on the Polish Reformation(s)*, Göttingen, 2016; Janusz Tazbir, *A State without Stakes: Polish Religious Toleration in the Sixteenth and Seventeenth Centuries*, 1973; Piotr Stolarski, 'Dominican-Jesuit Rivalry and the Politics of Catholic Renewal in Poland, 1564–1648', *Journal of Ecclesiastical History*, 62/2, 2011, 255–72; Hanna Mazheika, 'From Text to Network: Confessional Contacts and Migration between Early Modern Britain and the Grand Duchy of Lithuania', University of Aberdeen doctoral thesis, 2019; Marzena Liedke, *Od prawosławia do katolicyzmu. Ruscy możni i szlachta Wielkiego Księstwa Litewskiego wobec wyznań reformacyjnych*, Białystok, 2004; Tomasz Kempa, *Wobec kontrreformacji. Protestanci i prawosławni w obronie swobód wyznaniowych w Rzeczypospolitej w końcu XVI i w pierwszej połowie XVII wieku*, Toruń, 2007.

On Ruthenia and the Ukraine, see especially Borys Gudziak, *Crisis and Reform: The Kyivan Metropolitanate, the Patriarchate of Constantinople, and the Genesis of the Union of Brest*, Cambridge, MA, 1998; Frank Sysyn, 'The Social Causes of the Khmel'nyts'kyi Uprising', in *Religion and Culture in Early Modern Russia and Ukraine*, ed. Samuel Baron and Nancy Shields Kollmann, DeKalb, IL, 1997, 52–70; idem, 'Orthodoxy and Revolt: The Role of Religion in the Seventeenth-Century Ukrainian Uprising against the Polish-Lithuanian Commonwealth', in *Religion and the Early Modern State*, ed. James D. Tracy and Marguerite Ragnow, Cambridge, 2004, 154–84; Serhii Plokhy, *The Cossacks and Religion in Early Modern Ukraine*, Oxford, 2001; idem, *The Origins of the Slavic Nations: Premodern Identities in Russia, Ukraine and Belarus*, Cambridge, 2006; Henryk Litwin, 'Catholicisation among the Ruthenian Nobility and Assimilation Processes in the Ukraine during the years 1569–1648', *APH*, 55, 1987, 57–83; Andrzej Sulima Kamiński, 'The Cossack Experiment in Szlachta Democracy', *HUS*, 1, 1977, 178–97; and the classic Myhailo Hrushevsky, *History of Ukraine-Rus'*, ed. Frank Sysyn et al., vols 4, 6–10, Edmonton, 1999–2017.

For the seventeenth-century political and constitutional crisis, see especially Robert Frost, *After the Deluge: Poland-Lithuania and the Second Northern War 1655–1660*, Cambridge, 1993; idem, '*Initium calamitatis regnum*? John Casimir and Monarchical Power in Poland-Lithuania, 1648–1668', *European History Quarterly*, 16/2, 1986, 181–207; idem, 'The Ethiopian and the Elephant? Queen Louise Marie Gonzaga and Queenship in an Elective Monarchy, 1645–1667', *SEER*, 91/4, 2013, 787–817; Henryk Olszewski, 'The Political System and Political Thought in Poland during the Reign of John Sobieski', *APH*, 52, 1986, 87–104; Gierowski, *Polish-Lithuanian Commonwealth*, 5–59; on the tipping point vis-à-vis Muscovy: Andrzej Sulima Kamiński, *Republic Versus Autocracy: Poland-Lithuania and Russia, 1686–1697*, Cambridge, MA, 1993; Kyril Koczegarow, *Rzeczpospolita a Rosja w latach 1680–1686*, 2017.

On the Great Northern War and Polish-Lithuanian responses, see also L. R. Lewitter, 'Russia, Poland and the Baltic, 1697–1721', *HJ*, 11/1, 1968, 3–34; Robert I. Frost, ' "Everyone Understood what it Meant": The Impact of the Battle of Poltava on the Polish-Lithuanian Commonwealth',

HUS, 31/1, 2009, 159–76; Mindaugas Šapoka, *Warfare, Loyalty and Rebellion: The Grand Duchy of Lithuania and the Great Northern War, 1709–1717*, London, 2017; Jacek Burdowicz-Nowicki, *Piotr I, August II i Rzeczpospolita 1697–1706*, Cracow, 2010; Józef Feldman, *Polska w dobie wielkiej wojnie północnej 1704–1709*, Cracow, 1925; Andrzej S. Kamiński, *Konfederacja sandomierska wobec Rosji w okresie poaltransztadzkim 1706–1709*, Wrocław, 1969; Jarosław Porazinski, *Epiphania Poloniae*, Toruń, 1999; Józef Gierowski, *Między saskim absolutyzmem a złotą wolnością*, Wrocław, 1953; *Rzeczpospolita w dobie wielkiej wojny północnej*, ed. Jadwiga Muszyńska, Kielce, 2001.

For the 1716–17 settlement and its effects, see Michał Nycz, *Geneza reform skarbowych sejmu niemego*, Poznań, 1938; Tomasz Ciesielski, *Armia koronna w czasach Augusta III*, 2009, 20–127, 203–15; idem, 'Armia Wielkiego Księstwa Litewskiego w latach 1717–1775', in *Studia z dziejów Wielkiego Księstwa Litewskiego*, ed. Sławomir Górzyński and Mirosław Nagielski, 2014, 59–94; *Sejm Niemy. Miedzy mitem a reformą państwa*, ed. Michał Zwierzykowski, 2019.

For Augustus II and his efforts to get out of jail, see Mariusz Markiewicz, 'The Functioning of the Monarchy during the Reigns of the Electors of Saxony, 1697–1763', in *Polish-Lithuanian Monarchy*, 172–92; L. R. Lewitter, 'Poland, Russia and the Treaty of Vienna of 5 January 1719', *HJ*, 13/1, 1970, 3–30; Urszula Kosińska, *Sejm 1719–1720*, 2003; eadem, *August II w poszukiwaniu sojusznika*, 2012; Jacek Staszewski, *August II Mocny*, Wrocław, 1998. Tim Blanning's biography is eagerly awaited.

For comparisons, see Nicholas Henshall, *The Zenith of European Monarchy and its Elites: The Politics of Culture, 1650–1750*, Basingstoke, 2010; Tim Blanning, *The Pursuit of Glory: Europe 1648–1815*, London, 2007, 195–285, 393–455; Jerzy Lukowski, *The European Nobility in the Eighteenth Century*, Basingstoke, 2003.

2 IMPASSE

The struggle for the Polish-Lithuanian throne is narrated from various perspectives by Lukowski, *Liberty's Folly*, 155–61; Józef Feldman, *Stanisław Leszczyński*, 3rd edn, 1984, 170–79; Edmund Cieślak, *W obronie Króla Stanisława Leszczyńskiego*, Gdańsk, 1986; Jacek Staszewski, *August III Sas*, Wrocław, 1989, 138–53; Feliksas Sliesoriūnas, 'The General Confederation of the Grand Duchy of Lithuania (1734–1736)', *LHS*, 8, 2003, 61–94. On the pamphleteering, see Jerzy Dygdała, 'Antistanisławowska i prosaska publicystyka doby bezkrólewia 1733 roku', *KH*, 109/2, 2002, 41–59; Rafał Niedziela, *Pisma polityczne w okresie bezkrólewia i wojny o tron Polski po śmierci Augusta II Mocnego (1733–1736)*, Cracow, 2005. For the diplomacy, see Urszula Kosińska, 'Could a Portuguese Prince become King of Poland? The Candidacy of Don Manuel de Brangança for the Polish Throne in the Years 1729–33', *SEER*, 94/3, 2016, 497–508; Emanuel Rostworowski, *O polską koronę. Polityka Francji w latach 1725–1733*, Wrocław, 1958; Jerzy Dygdała, 'Gra pozorów: zabiegi dyplomacji cesarskiej o rosyjską interwencję w Rzeczypospolitej w 1733 r.', in *W cieniu*, 137–60; idem, 'Rywalizacja dyplomatów cesarskiego i francuskiego w Polsce 1733 roku', in *Polska wobec wielkich konfliktów w Europie nowożytnej*, ed. Ryszard Skowron, Cracow, 2009, 495–512; Andrej Macuk, 'Polityka rosyjska w Rzeczypospolitej w 1733 roku a kandydatura „Piasta"', *Klio*, 29/2, 2014, 41–110. On the wider war, see Michael Hochedlinger, *Austria's Wars of Emergence 1683–1797*, Harlow, 2003, 208–12. On Leszczyński's later years, see also *Stanisław Leszczyński. Król polski księciem Lotaryngii*, exhibition catalogue, 2005; Anne Muratori-Philip, *Le roi Stanislas*, Paris, 2000; Edmund Cieślak, *Stanisław Leszczyński*, Wrocław, 1994, 181–254.

The domestic and international politics of Augustus III's reign are covered by Władysław Konopczyński, *Dzieje Polski nowożytnej*, 2nd edn, 1986, ii, 139–66; Mariusz Markiewicz, *Historia Polski 1492–1795*, 2nd edn, Cracow, 2004, 631–46; Michael G. Müller, *Polen zwischen Preußen und Rußland. Souveränitätskrise und Reformpolitik 1736–1752*, Berlin, 1983; Henryk Palkij, *Sejmy 1736 i 1738 roku*, Cracow, 2000; Zofia Zielińska, *Walka „Familii" o reformę Rzeczypospolitej 1743–1752*, 1983; Tomasz Ciesielski, '„Alarmy konfederackie" w pierwszej połowie panowania Augusta III', in *Król a prawo stanów do oporu*, ed. Mariusz Markiewicz et al., Cracow, 2010, 341–52; Tomasz Szwaciński, 'Finał sejmu 1754 r. w relacjach rosyjskich i brytyjskich', *BEN*, 4/1, 2016, 163–93; on Courland, see Klauspeter Strohm, *Die Kurländische Frage (1700–1763)*, Berlin, 1999;

for wider perspectives see Emanuel Rostworowski, 'Podbój Śląska przez Prusy a pierwszy rozbiór Polski', *PH*, 63/3, 1972, 389–412; Michael G. Müller, 'Polska i Niemcy w układzie sił politycznych Europy XVIII wieku', in *Polska i Niemcy w okresie Oświecenia*, Poznań, 1986, 71–81; idem, 'Rußland und der Siebenjährige Krieg', *JfGO*, 28, 1980, 198–219.

The Polish policies of Frederick II have been exposed by Władysław Konopczyński, *Fryderyk Wielki a Polska*, Poznań, 1947, 65–68, 77–81; Stanisław Salmonowicz, *Fryderyk Wielki*, 3rd edn, Wrocław, 1996, 86–95; Józef Gierowski, 'Szlachta mazowiecka wobec sąsiada pruskiego', in idem, *Na szlakach Rzeczypospolitej w nowożytnej Europie*, Cracow, 2007, 175–88; Andrzej Kamieński, 'Polityka polska Fryderyka II i pierwszy rozbiór Polski', in *Prusy 1701–1806*, 284–344; Jörg K. Hoensch, 'Manipulacje walutowe Fryderyka II w okresie wojny siedmioletniej i ich wpływ na polską reformę monetarną z roku 1765–1766', *Roczniki Historyczne*, 39, 1973, 41–104; Klaus Zernack, 'Das preussische Königtum und die polnische Republik im europäischen Mächtesystem des 18. Jahrhunderts', *Jahrbücher für die Geschichte Mittel- und Ostdeutschlands*, 30, 1981, 4–20.

On 'parties', see Władysław Konopczyński, 'Z dziejów naszej partyjności', in idem, *Mrok i świt*, 1911, 1–36; Katarzyna Kuras, 'Partie i fakcje w schyłkowym okresie rządów Augusta III Sasa', *PNH*, 12/1, 2013, 61–90. On the *Familia*, see also eadem, *Współpracownicy i klienci Augusta A. Czartoryskiego w czasach saskich*, Cracow, 2010; Klemens Kantecki, *Stanisław Poniatowski kasztelan krakowski, ojciec Stanisława Augusta*, 2 vols, Poznań, 1880; Andrzej Link-Lenczowski, 'Stanisław Poniatowski', *PSB*, xxvii, 471–81; Urszula Kosińska, 'Stanisław Poniatowski, niezwykły ojciec Stanisława Augusta', in *Pamiętniki SA*, 88–111. On the Potockis, Kazimierz Waliszewski, *Potoccy i Czartoryscy*, Cracow, 1887, i, 3–108, retains much value. See also Andrzej Link-Lenczowski, 'Potocki Józef', *PSB*, xxviii, 59–72; Barbara Grosfeld, 'Potocki Antoni', *PSB*, xxvii, 782–90; Maria Czeppe, 'Potocki Franciszek Salezy', *PSB*, xxvii, 814–23. On Branicki and his clients: Elzbieta Kowecka, *Dwór „najrządniejszego w Polszcze magnata"*, 1991; Anna Oleńska, *Jan Klemens Branicki „Sarmata nowoczesny"*, 2011; Teresa Zielińska, 'Klientela w otoczeniu Jana Klemensa Branickiego kasztelana krakowskiego i hetmana wielkiego koronnego około połowy XVIII wieku', in *Patron i dwór*, ed. Ewa Dubas-Urwanowicz and Jerzy Urwanowicz, 2006, 209–23; Ciesielski, *Armia koronna*, 128–47, 569–82. On Jerzy Mniszech, see Maria Czeppe, *Kamaryla Pana z Dukli*, 1998.

On politics in the Grand Duchy of Lithuania, see Andrei Matsuk, *Barats'ba mahnatskich hrupovan u VKL (1717–1763 hh.)*, Minsk, 2010; Andrej Macuk, 'Stronnictwo sapieżyńskie w powiatach Wielkiego Księstwa Litewskiego za panowania Augusta III', in *Studia z dziejów Wielkiego Księstwa Litewskiego*, ed. Sławomir Górzyński and Mirosław Nagielski, 2014, 287–318; Zofia Zielińska, 'Mechanizm sejmikowy i klientela radziwiłłowska za Sasów', *PH*, 62/3, 1971, 397–410; Hanna Dymnicka-Wołoszyńska, 'Radziwiłł Michał Kazimierz', *PSB*, xxx, 299–306, eadem, 'Radziwiłł, Hieronim Florian', *PSB*, xxx, 185–88; Jerzy Michalski, 'Radziwiłł Karol Stanisław', *PSB*, xxx, 248–62; Tomasz Szwaciński, 'Tumult wileński 1755 roku i jego reperkusje', *RL*, 2, 2016, 107–26; Monika Jusupović, *Prowincjonalna elita litewska w XVIII wieku*, 2014; for the earlier period, see Gintautas Sliesoriūnas, *Lietuvos Didžioji Kunigaikštytė vidaus karo iškvarėse*, Vilnius, 2000; Przemysław P. Romaniuk, 'Instytucjonalne podstawy hegemonii Sapiehów w Wielkim Księstwie Litewskim w drugiej połowie XVII wieku', in *W cieniu*, 29–37.

On the magnates' socio-political role, see Robert I. Frost, 'The Nobility of Poland-Lithuania, 1569–1795', in *The European Nobilities in the Seventeenth and Eighteenth Centuries*, ed. H. M. Scott, 1st edn, Harlow, 1995, ii, 183–222; the classic work for this period is Teresa Zielińska, *Magnateria polska epoki saskiej*, Wrocław, 1977. For the concept of 'unequal friendship', see Antoni Mączak, *Klientela. Nieformalne systemy władzy w Polsce i Europie XVI–XVIII w.*, 2nd edn, 2000; idem, *Nierówna przyjaźń*, Wrocław, 2003, esp. 159–207. On magnates' officials, see Teresa Zielińska, 'Oficjaliści w dobrach magnackich w XVIII wieku jako urzędnicy ziemscy', in *Świat pogranicza*, ed. Mirosław Nagielski et al., 2003, 267–81; on their militias: Tomasz Ciesielski, 'Milicje magnackie i ich potencjał militarny w połowie XVIII wieku', in *Wobec króla i Rzeczypospolitej*, ed. Ewa Dubas-Urwanowicz and Jerzy Urwanowicz, Cracow, 2012, 773–92; Maria Pasztor, 'Milicje magnackie Radziwiłłów', in *Trudne stulecia*, 140–46; Valdas Rakutis, 'Valstybinė ir privati kariuomenė Lietuvos Didžioje Kunigaikštystėje XVIII a. viduryje', in *Viešosios ir privačios erdvės*, 106–20.

FURTHER READING

On the sejmiks, see Jerzy Michalski, 'Les diétines polonaises au XVIII siècle', *APH*, 12, 1965, 87–107; Andrzej B. Zakrzewski, *Sejmiki Wielkiego Księstwa Litewskiego XVI–XVIII w. Ustrój i funkcjonowanie: sejmik trocki*, 2000; Robertas Jurgaitis, *Nuo bajoriškosios savivaldos iki parlamentarizmo: Vilniaus seimelio veikla 1717–1795 m.*, Vilnius, 2016; Michał Zwierzykowski, *Komisja skarbowa poznańska*, Poznań, 2003; idem, 'Geneza i funkcjonowanie chorągwi policyjnej województw poznańskiego i kaliskiego w latach 1734–1767', in *W podróży*, 117–34; idem, '*Liberum veto* w praktyce wielkopolskiej działalności sejmikowej', *BEN*, 4/1, 2016, 97–125; Wiesław Bondyra, *Reprezentacja sejmowa Rusi Czerwonej w czasach saskich*, Lublin, 2005.

The functioning of other institutions is explored by Markiewicz, 'The Functioning of the Monarchy'; idem, 'Rzeczpospolita bez sejmu. Funkcjonowanie państwa', in *Miedzy barokiem a oświeceniem*, ed. Krystyna Stasiewicz and Stanisław Achremczyk, Olsztyn, 1996, 175–80; idem, *Rady senatorskie Augusta II (1697–1733)*, Wrocław, 1988; idem, 'Rady senatu za Augusta III', *Zeszyty Naukowe Uniwersytetu Jagiellońskiego*, 614, 1985, 69–89; Dariusz Makiłła, *Władza wykonawcza w Rzeczypospolitej*, Toruń, 2003; Adam Perłakowski, *Jan Jerzy Przebendowski jako podskarbi wielki koronny (1703–1729)*, Cracow, 2004; Jerzy Michalski, *Studia nad reformą sądownictwa i prawa sądowego w XVIII w.*, part 1, Wrocław, 1958; Wojciech Stanek, *Konfederacje generalne koronne w XVIII wieku*, Toruń, 1991. On careers in Dresden, see Jacek Staszewski, *Polacy w osiemnastowiecznym Dreźnie*, Wrocław, 1986, 51–146; Adam Perłakowski, *Kariera i upadek królewskiego faworyta*, Cracow, 2013.

Political ideas and discourse have been excavated by Jerzy Lukowski, *Disorderly Liberty: The Political Culture of the Polish-Lithuanian Commonwealth in the Eighteenth Century*, London, 2010; idem, 'Political Ideas among the Polish Nobility in the Eighteenth Century (to 1788)', *SEER*, 82/1, 2004, 1–26; idem, 'The Szlachta and their Ancestors in the Eighteenth Century', *KH*, 111/3, 2004, 3, 161–82; and less scathingly by Grześkowiak-Krwawicz, *Queen Liberty*; Wagner-Rundell, *Common Wealth, Common Good.* See also Władysław Konopczyński, *Polscy pisarze polityczni XVIII wieku*, 2nd edn, Cracow, 2012; Henryk Olszewski, *Doktryny prawno-ustrojowe czasów saskich (1697–1740)*, 1961; Jerzy Michalski, 'Z problematyki republikańskiego nurtu w polskiej reformatorskiej myśli politycznej w XVIII wieku', *KH*, 90/2, 1983, 327–38; Andrzej Rosner, 'Uwagi o języku politycznym czasów saskich', in *Polska czasów saskich*, ed. Mieczysław Wzrosek, Białystok, 1986, 263–73; Monika Wyszomirska, *Między obroną wolności a naprawą państwa. Rzeczpospolita jako przedmiot polemik politycznych w dobie panowania Augusta III (1734–1763)*, 2009; Michał Zwierzykowski, ' „*Sine iustitia in libertate* żyć nie chcemy". Prawo i sprawiedliwość w dyskursie politycznym kampanii sejmowych lat 1696–1762', in *Wartości polityczne*, 264–88.

On Konarski's political thought and language, see also Jerzy Lukowski, 'Stanisław Konarski (1700–1772) [*sic*]: A Polish Machiavelli?', in *Enlightenment and Catholicism in Europe: A Transnational History*, ed. Jeffrey D. Burson and Ulrich L. Lehner, Notre Dame, IN, 2014, 433–53; Anna Grześkowiak-Krwawicz, 'Stanisław Konarski o wolności i anarchii', *WO*, 20, 2004, 71–88; eadem, '„Nowe wino w starych butelkach". O języku politycznym Stanisława Konarskiego', *WO*, 32, 2016, 11–28; Władysław Konopczyński, *Stanisław Konarski*, 1926, 185–221.

On the Catholic hierarchy, see Richard Butterwick-Pawlikowski, 'Kościół katolicki a państwo w Rzeczypospolitej za Augusta III i Stanisława Augusta', in *My i oni*, 317–54. On the Protestants, see Wojciech Kriegseisen, *Ewangelicy polscy i litewscy w epoce saskiej*, 1996.

For the confessional situation in Ruthenia, see Barbara Skinner, *The Western Front of the Eastern Church: Uniate and Orthodox Conflict in Eighteenth-Century Poland, Ukraine, Belarus, and Russia*, DeKalb, IL, 2009; eadem, 'Borderlands of Faith: Reconsidering the Origins of a Ukrainian Tragedy', *Slavic Review*, 64/1, 2005, 88–116; Sofia Senyk, 'Religious Conflict in Dnepr Ukraine in the 18th Century', *Orientalia Christiana Periodica*, 73/1, 2007, 5–59; Bogumił Szady, *The Geography of Religious and Confessional Structures in the Crown of the Polish Kingdom in the Second Half of the Eighteenth Century*, Berlin, 2019, 76–170; Antoni Mironowicz, *Diecezja białoruska w XVII i XVIII wieku*, Białystok, 2008; Andrzej Gil and Ihor Skoczylas, *Kościoły wschodnie w państwie polsko-litewskim w procesie przemian i adaptacji: metropolia kijowska w latach 1458–1795*, Lublin, 2014; Ludomir Bieńkowski, 'Organizacja kościoła wschodniego w Polsce', in *Kościół w Polsce*, ed. Jerzy Kłoczowski, Cracow, 1969, ii, 779–1049; Stanisław Nabywaniec, *Unicka archidiecezja kijowska w okresie rządów arcybiskupa metropolity Felicjana Filipa Wołodkowicza 1762–1778*, Rzeszów, 1998, 38–65; Dorota

Wereda, *Biskupi unickiej metropolii kijowskiej w XVIII wieku*, Siedlce, 2013; cf. Dariusz Ciołka, *Latynizacja Kościoła unickiego w Rzeczypospolitej po synodzie zamojskim*, [Białystok, 2014].

For the confessional aspects of Russian policy (and their limits), see L. R. Lewitter, 'Peter the Great and the Polish Dissenters', *SEER*, 33/1, 1954, 75–101; Jacek Burdowicz-Nowicki, 'Polityka Piotra I w związku ze sprawą toruńską 1724 r.', in *W cieniu*, 78–103; Urszula Kosińska, '*L'affaire secrète*, czyli nieznany plan rozbioru Polski z lat 1724–1726', in *W cieniu*, 105–35; Aleksy Deruga, *Piotr Wielki a unici i unja koscielna (1700–1711)*, Wilno, 1936. On the demographic factor, see Robert E. Jones, 'Runaway Peasants and Russian Motives for the Partitions of Poland', in *Imperial Russian Foreign Policy*, ed. Hugh Ragsdale, Cambridge, 1993, 103–16.

3 *SACRUM* AND *PROFANUM*

On Konarski's life and career, see Lukowski, 'Stanisław Konarski'; Konopczyński, *Stanisław Konarski*; *Stanisław Konarski. Pedagog – polityk – filozof*, ed. Jadwiga Zjętarska, 2004. For the Piarist and Jesuit educational reforms, see also Richard Butterwick-Pawlikowski, 'Before and After Suppression: Jesuits and Former Jesuits in the Polish-Lithuanian Commonwealth, c. 1750–1795', in *Jesuit Survival and Restoration: A Global History, 1773–1900*, ed. Robert A. Maryks and Jonathan Wright, Leiden, 2015, 51–66; Kazimierz Puchowski, 'Collegium Nobilium Stanisława Konarskiego a elitarne instytucje wychowawcze zakonów nauczających w Europie', *WO*, 20, 2004, 11–70; idem, *Jezuickie kolegia szlacheckie Rzeczypospolitej Obojga Narodów*, Gdańsk, 2007; Stanisław Bednarski, *Upadek i odrodzenie szkolnictwa jezuickiego w Polsce* [1933], reprint Cracow, 2003; Ludwik Piechnik, *Dzieje Akademii Wileńskiej*, 4 vols, Rome, 1983–90; idem, 'Przemiany w szkolnictwie jezuickim w Polsce XVIII wieku', in *Z dziejów szkolnictwa jezuickiego w Polsce*, Cracow, 1994, 183–209; *Wkład pijarów do nauki i kultury Polsce XVII–XIX w.*, ed. Irena Stasiewicz-Jasiukowa, 1993; Asta Vaškelienė, 'Etikietas ir butis reformuotoje XVIII a. antrosios pusės Lietuvos Didžiosios Kunigaikštystės pijorų edukacijoje', *XVIII amžiaus studijos*, 4, 2018, 73–96. For wider comparisons, see Stanisław Janeczek, *Edukacja oświeceniowa a szkoła tradycyjna*, Lublin, 2008. On the seminaries of the Priests of the Mission, see Sławomir Zabraniak, *Stan duchowieństwa a religijność w archidiakonatach: kaliskim, uniejowskim i wieluńskim (1660–1763)*, Rzeszów, 2012, 129–86; Tomasz Chachulski, 'Pisarze polskiego oświecenia w Kościele Świętego Krzyża', in *Księga Pamiątkowa. Kościół Świętego Krzyża w Warszawie*, ed. T. Chachulski, 1996, 105–21; Zofia Zielińska, 'Śliwicki Piotr Hiacynt', *PSB*, l, 586–91.

These reforms are considered within the context of 'Catholic Enlightenment' and 'enlightened Catholicism' by Richard Butterwick, 'Catholicism and Enlightenment in Poland-Lithuania', in *A Companion to the Catholic Enlightenment in Europe*, ed. Ulrich L. Lehner and Michael Printy, Leiden, 2010, 297–358; Stanisław Janeczek, 'Ideały wychowawcze i dydaktyczne w szkolnictwie pijarskim a „Oświecenie chrześcijańskie"', *NP*, 82, 1994, 115–61; idem, *Oświecenie chrześcijańskie*, Lublin, 1994; idem, 'Czym była oświeceniowa philosophia recentiorum?', *Kwartalnik Filozoficzny*, 1998/1, 115–28; Irena Stasiewicz-Jasiukowa, 'Rola oświeconego katolicyzmu w rozwoju myśli naukowej i pedagogicznej we wczesnym polskim Oświeceniu', *Analecta*, 7/1, 1998, 79–92. Compare the situation in the Reich: Ulrich L. Lehner, *Enlightened Monks: The German Benedictines 1740–1803*, Oxford, 2011; Richard van Dülmen, 'Antijesuitismus und katholische Aufklärung in Deutschland', *Historisches Jahrbuch*, 89, 1969, 52–80; and more broadly: Ulrich L. Lehner, *The Catholic Enlightenment: The Forgotten History of a Global Movement*, New York, 2016; *A Companion to the Catholic Enlightenment*; and *Catholicism and Enlightenment in Europe: A Transnational History*.

The episcopal and pastoral dimensions of 'enlightened Catholicism' in Poland-Lithuania are also discussed by Magdalena Ślusarska, 'Oświeceniowe modele biskupa, plebana i parafii' in *Dwór, plebania*, 37–53; Jerzy Dygdała, 'U początków katolickiego oświecenia w Polsce. Z działalności kościelnej biskupów Andrzeja Stanisława Załuskiego i Adama Stanisława Grabowskiego', in *Między barokiem a oświeceniem*, ed. Krystyna Stasiewicz and Stanisław Achremczyk, Olsztyn, 1996, 181–88; Jan Kracik, 'Ewangelicznie i rozumnie. Oświecenie katolickie', *Znak*, 451/12, 1992, 57–69; idem, 'Biskupa krakowskiego Andrzeja Stanisława Załuskiego działalność w duchu katolickiego oświecenia', *Prace Naukowe WSP w Częstochowie*, 1997/4, 91–100; Bogusław Dygdała, *Struktury parafialne diecezji chełmińskiej w XVII–XVIII wieku*, Toruń, 2009, 55, 83–91, 232–33, 261–62. For comparisons with Catholic Germany, see also Ulrich L. Lehner, 'Johann Nikolaus von Hontheim's Febronius: A Censored Bishop and his Ecclesiology', *Church History and Religious Culture*, 88, 2008, 93–121; Michael Printy, *Enlightenment and the Creation of German Catholicism*, Cambridge, 2009; and for a still wider picture: Owen Chadwick, *The Popes and European Revolution*, Oxford, 1981.

On rites of passage, especially funerals, see Maria Bogucka, *The Lost World of the "Sarmatians"*, 1996; Tomasz Wiślicz, 'Peasant Funerals in Early Modern Poland', *APH*, 82, 2000, 49–80; Juliusz A. Chrościcki, *Pompa funebris*, 1974; Tomasz Ciesielski, 'Pogrzeby wojskowe w czasach saskich', in *Wesela, chrzciny i pogrzeby w XVI–XVIII wieku*, ed. Henryk Suchojad, 2001, 217–33; Andrea Mariani, 'Rola jezuitów w pogrzebach szlachty polsko-litewskiej w XVIII wieku', *NP*, 119, 2013, 177–96; Zabraniak, *Stan duchowieństwa*, 256–308, 339–46; Agnieszka Jakuboszczak, *Rodzina i rodzinność szlachcianek wielkopolskich w XVIII wieku*, Poznań, 177–92. Jędrzej Kitowicz, *Opis obyczajów za panowania Augusta III*, ed. Zbigniew Goliński, 1999 edn, is an unrivalled source for nobles' customs and religiosity. On almanacs, see Bogdan Rok, *Kalendarze polskie czasów saskich*, Wrocław, 1985; Małgorzata Gorczyńska, *Popularyzacja wiedzy w polskich kalendarzach okresu Oświecenia (1737–1821)*, Lublin, 1999; Maciej Janik, *Polskie kalendarze astrologiczne epoki saskiej*, 2003.

On bequests, see Bożena Popiołek, 'Polisa na życie wieczne. Zagadnienie miłosiedzia w czasach saskich', *NP*, 118, 2012, 143–56; three studies of chaplaincy are Karolina Stojek-Sawicka, *Duchowieństwo katolickie w życiu Radziwiłłów Nieświeskich w XVIII wieku*, Toruń, 2011; Andrea Mariani, 'Duszpasterstwo jezuitów nieświeskich w XVII–XVIII wieku', *RL*, 2, 2016, 47–91; idem, 'Aktywność jezuickich kapelanów nadwornych prowincji litewskiej', *RL*, 1, 2015, 37–82. Parishes are surveyed by Stanisław Litak, *Parafie w Rzeczypospolitej w XVI–XVIII wieku*, Lublin, 2004. For popular religiosity, see idem, 'Ze studiów nad religijnością niższych warstw społecznych w Rzeczpospolitej w XVIII wieku', *Przegląd Humanistyczny*, 40/1, 1996, 163–73; and numerous works by Tomasz Wiślicz, including ' "Miraculous Sites" in the Early Modern Polish-Lithuanian Commonwealth', in *Religion und Magie in Ostmitteleuropa*, ed. Thomas Wünsch, Berlin, 2006, 287–99; idem, 'Ex-votos in the World of Objects of Polish Peasants in the Early Modern Times', *APH*, 102, 2010, 175–81; idem, 'Shepherds of the Catholic Flock: Polish Parochial Clergy, Popular Religion, and the Reception of the Council of Trent', in *Gelehrte Geistlichkeit – geistliche Gelehrte*, ed. Luise Schorn-Schütte, Berlin, 2012, 25–52; idem, *Zarobić na duszne zbawienie. Religijność chłopów małopolskich od połowy XVI do końca XVIII wieku*, Warsaw, 2001; idem, 'Naród chłopski? Społeczna, religijna i narodowa tożsamość chłopów we wczesnonowożytnej Polsce', in *Między barokiem a oświeceniem. Społeczeństwo stanowe*, ed. Stanisław Achremczyk and Jerzy Kielbik, Olsztyn, 2013, 52–65. For wonder-working images, see Jan Kracik, 'Święte obrazy wśród grzesznych Sarmatów', *NP*, 76, 1991, 141–92; for the problems of the lower clergy: idem, *Prawie wielebni*, Cracow, 2011.

On missions, see Jerzy Flaga, *Działalność duszpasterska zakonów w drugiej połowie XVIII wieku 1767–1772*, Lublin, 1986, 141–330; Agnieszka Wieczorek, *Misje ludowe Zgromadzenia Księży Misjonarzy św. Wincentego a Paulo na terenie Rzeczypospolitej od połowy XVIII do początku XIX wieku*, Toruń, 2014; Stanisław Roszak, 'Tradycja i reforma w działalności misjonarzy na kresach w czasach saskich', in *Miedzy barokiem a oświeceniem. Obyczaje czasów saskich*, ed. Krystyna Stasiewicz and Stanisław Achremczyk, Olsztyn, 2000, 202–07.

Tensions between the szlachta and the Catholic clergy are discussed by Janusz Tazbir, 'Staropolski antyklerykalizm', *KH*, 109/3, 2002, 13–22; Urszula Augustyniak, *Państwo świeckie czy księże?*, 2013, 22–128; Wojciech Kriegseisen, ' „Krzywda nad wszystkie krzywdy – hiberna w Polszcze"', *Barok*, 8/1, 2001, 19–37; Mariusz Markiewicz, 'Problem antyklerykalizmu w czasach saskich', in *Rzeczpospolita wielu wyznań*, ed. Adam Kaźmierczyk et al., Cracow, 2004, 341–47; Robert Kozyrski, *Duchowieństwo, kościoły i religia w w dokumentach sejmików województwa ruskiego*, Lublin, 2013. On clerical judges to the Tribunals, see Henryk Karbownik, 'Deputaci duchowni na Trybunałach Koronnym i Litewskim', in *Kościół i prawo*, 10, 1992, 185–202; Waldemar Bednaruk, *Trybunał Koronny*, Lublin, 2008, 101–27, 134–42, 199–271; and the introduction to *Deputaci*

Trybunału Głównego Wielkiego Księstwa Litewskiego 1697–1794, ed. Andrzej Rachuba and Przemysław P. Romaniuk, 2004.

On Garczyński, see Lukowski, *Disorderly Liberty*, 57–61; Władysław Konopczyński, 'Garczyński Stefan', *PSB*, vii, 275–77; Emanuel Rostworowski, 'Spór Stefana Garczyńskiego z braćmi Załuskimi o rolę duchowieństwa w Anatomii Rzeczypospolitej', in *O naprawę Rzeczypospolitej XVII–XVIII w.*, 1965, 213–30.

The condition of the peasantry and the rural economy can be approached via Lukowski, *Liberty's Folly*, 29–61; idem, 'The Peasantry of Poland-Lithuania on the Eve of the French Revolution', *History of European Ideas*, 12/3, 1990, 377–93; Jan Rutkowski, *Poddaństwo włościan w XVIII wieku w Polsce i niektórych innych krajach Europy*, Poznań, 1921; Witold Kula, *An Economic Theory of the Feudal System*, 2nd edn, London, 1986; Jacek Kochanowicz, 'The Polish Economy and the Evolution of Dependency', in *The Origins of Backwardness in Eastern Europe*, ed. Daniel Chirot, Berkeley, CA, 1989, 92–130; idem, 'Between Submission and Violence: Peasant Resistance in the Polish Manorial Economy of the Eighteenth Century', in idem, *Backwardness and Modernization: Poland and Eastern Europe in the 16th–20th Centuries*, Aldershot, 2006, 34–63; for further cases of resistance and conflict, see Tomasz Wiślicz, 'Bunt chłopski w starostwie libuskim w latach 1755–1758', *Klio*, 25/2, 2013, 143–67; idem, 'Afera Tomasza Kobcza, czyli o samorządności chłopów na wsi przedrozbiorowej', in *W podróży*, 197–211; M. J. Lech, 'Wojsko W. Ks. Litewskiego w dobie saskiej w walce z ruchami chłopskimi na Białorusi', *Rocznik Białostocki*, 2, 1961, 101–40; Dominikas Burba, 'Valstiečių dalyvavimas smurtinose bajorų nusikaltimose, XVIII amžiaus Vilniaus pavieto pilies ir žemės teismųknygų duomenimis', *XVIII amžiaus studijos*, 3, 2016, 282–301; Jerzy Topolski, *Położenie i walka klasowa chłopów w XVIII w. w dobrach arcybiskupstwa gnieźnieńskiego*, 1956; Alicja Falniowska-Gradowska, 'Dwór a gromada wiejska w województwie krakowskim w XVIII wieku', in *Studia nad gospodarką, społeczeństwem i rodziną w Europie późnofeudalnej*, ed. Jerzy Topolski and Cezary Kuklo, Lublin, 1987, 269–81; Władysław A. Serczyk, *Hajdamacy*, Cracow, 1972. For the clergy as mediators, see Magdalena Ślusarska, 'Powinność i należytość. Wzajemne relacje między właścicielami dóbr a społecznością wiejską w świetle kazań z epoki stanisławowskiej', in *Dwór, plebania*, 69–102.

Regional diversities are explored in Władysław Rusiński, *Osady tzw. „Olędrów" w dawnym województwie poznańskim*, Cracow, 1947; Maria Paradowska, *Bambrzy*, Poznań, 1998; Marian Szczepaniak, 'Spożycie piwa i gorzałki oraz dochody feudalne z propinacji na wsi wielkopolskiej u schyłku XVIII wieku', *Roczniki Dziejów Społecznych i Gospodarczych*, 29, 1968, 87–103; Jerzy Topolski, 'Uwagi o strukturze gospodarczo-społecznej Wielkopolski w XVIII wieku, czyli dlaczego na jej terenie nie było żydowskich karczmarzy', in *Żydzi w Wielkopolsce na przestrzeni dziejów*, ed. Jerzy Topolski and Krzysztof Modelski, 2nd edn, Poznań, 1999, 71–82; Leonid Żytkowicz, 'Rozwarstwienie chłopstwa a gospodarka na Żmudzi w 2 połowie XVII i w XVIII wieku', in *Społeczeństwo staropolskie*, ii, 1979, 229–314; Alicja Makowska, 'Pracownicy najemni wielkiej własności ma przykładzie dóbr sandomierskich Czartoryskich w XVIII wieku', ibid., 315–37; Edmund Kizik, 'Mennonites', in *Under a Common Sky: Ethnic Groups of the Commonwealth of Poland and Lithuania*, ed. Michał Kopczyński and Wojciech Tygielski, 2017, 226–43.

A strong case for significant economic growth, continuing into the next reign, is made by Jerzy Topolski, 'Gospodarka', in *Polska w epoce Oświecenia*, ed. Bogusław Leśnodorski, 1971, 171–211. On demography, see Cezary Kuklo, *Demografia Rzeczypospolitej przedrozbiorowej*, 2009; for the consequences of epidemics: Andrzej Karpiński, *W walce z niewidzianym wrogiem. Epidemie chorób zakaźnych w Rzeczypospolitej w XVI–XVIII wieku*, 2000, 193–222.

On towns, see Andrzej Wyrobisz, 'Functional Types of Polish Towns in the 16th–18th Century', *Journal of European Economic History*, 12/1, 1983, 69–103; Curtis G. Murphy, *From Citizens to Subjects: City, State and the Enlightenment in Poland, Ukraine and Belarus*, Pittsburgh, PA, 2018; cf. the gloomier depiction in Lukowski, *Liberty's Folly*, 62–85.

The literature on Jewish communities starts with Antony Polonsky, *The Jews in Poland and Russia*, i: *1350 to 1881*, Oxford, 2010, 40–90; and Gershon D. Hundert, *Jews in Poland-Lithuania in the Eighteenth Century*, Berkeley, CA, 2004. Studies include idem, *The Jews in a Polish Private Town: The Case of Opatów in the Eighteenth Century*, Baltimore, MD, 1992; Moshe J. Rosman, *The Lord's Jews: Magnate-Jewish Relations in the Polish-Lithuanian Commonwealth during the 18th Century*, Cambridge, MA, 1990; Adam Teller, *Money, Power and Influence in Eighteenth-Century*

Lithuania: The Jews on the Radziwiłł Estates, Stanford, CA, 2016; Anna Michałowska-Mycielska, *The Jewish Community: Authority and Social Control in Poznań and Swarzędz 1650–1793*, 2019; Adam Kaźmierczyk, *Żydzi w dobrach prywatnych w świetle sądowniczej i administracyjnej praktyki dóbr magnackich w wiekach XVI–XVIII*, Cracow, 2002; Stefan Gąsiorowski, *Chrześcijanie i Żydzi w Żółkwi w XVII i XVIII wieku*, Cracow, 2001; Jacob Goldberg, *Żydzi w społeczeństwie, gospodarce i kulturze Rzeczypospolitej szlacheckiej*, Cracow, 2012, 1–18; Yvonne Kleinmann, 'Städtische Gemeinschaft. Christen und Juden im frühneuzeitlichen Rzeszów', *Osteuropa*, 62/10, 2012, 3–24.

On Jewish religious movements, see also Marcin Wodziński, *Haskallah and Hasidism in the Kingdom of Poland*, Oxford, 2005, 9–33; Paweł Maciejko, *The Mixed Multitude: Jacob Frank and the Frankist Movement, 1755–1816*, Philadelphia, PA, 2011. Regarding the blood libel, see Zenon Guldon and Jacek Wijaczka, 'The Accusation of Ritual Murder in Poland', *Polin*, 10, 1997, 97–140. On conversions, see Magda Teter, 'Jewish Conversions to Catholicism in the Polish-Lithuanian Commonwealth of the Seventeenth and Eighteenth Centuries', *Jewish History*, 17/3, 2003, 257–83; Goldberg, *Żydzi w społeczeństwie*, 207–65; Adam Kaźmierczyk, *Rodziłem się Żydem. Konwersje Żydów w Rzeczypospolitej XVII–XVIII wieku*, Cracow, 2015; cf. Małgorzata Borkowska, 'Dzieje zgromadzenia Mariae Vitae czyli mariawitek', *NP*, 93, 2000, 107–52.

On confessional geography, see Szady, *The Geography of Religious and Confessional Structures*; Józef Gierowski, 'Przestrzeń etnograficzno-geograficzna Rzeczypospolitej Polsko-Litewskiej', in idem, *Na szlakach Rzeczypospolitej w nowożytnej Europie*, Cracow, 2008, 557–72; Stanisław Litak, *Atlas Kościoła łacińskiego w Rzeczypospolitej Obojga Narodów w XVIII wieku*, Lublin, 2006, 116–47, 155–69; Witold Kołbuk, *Kościoły wschodnie w Rzeczypospolitej około 1772 roku*, Lublin, 1998; Dzianis Liseichykau, 'Zasięg osadnictwa ruskiej społeczności etniczno-wyznaniowej w Wielkim Księstwie Litewskim od końca XVII do połowy XVIII wieku', *RL*, 3, 2017, 121–33.

On Wilno, see David Frick, *Kith, Kin and Neighbors: Communities and Confessions in Seventeenth-Century Wilno*, Ithaca, NY, 2013; Polonsky, *The Jews in Poland and Russia*, i, 76–82; Martynas Jakulis, 'The Poor and the Community: The Lutheran Charitable System in Eighteenth-Century Wilna', in *Social and Cultural Relations*, 47–60; Tomasz Kempa, *Konflikty wyznaniowe w Wilnie od początku reformacji do końca XVII wieku*, Toruń, 2016, 473–635; Urszula Anna Pawluczuk, *Osiemnastowieczne Wilno – miasta wielu religii i wyznań*, Białystok, 2015; Bernadetta Manyś, *Uroczystości rodzinne w Wilnie za Augusta III (1733–1763)*, Poznań, 2015. On Vilnan architecture: Tojana Račiunaitė and Arūnas Sverdiolas, *Baroque in Lithuania*, Vilnius, 2007; Stanisław Lorentz, *Jan Krzysztof Glaubitz. Architekt wileński XVIII wieku*, 1937; Władysław Tatarkiewicz, *Dwa baroki, krakowski i wileński*, Cracow, 1946; Jerzy Kowalczyk, 'Późnobarokowa architektura Wilna i jej europejskie związki', *BHS*, 55/2–3, 1993, 169–97; a double issue of *BHS*, 73/3–4, 2011; Mariusz Karpowicz, *Wileńska odmiana architektury XVIII wieku*, 2012; for Crown Ruthenia, see idem, *Sztuki polskiej drogi dziwne*, Bydgoszcz, 1994, 127–74; Andrzej Betlej, *Paweł Giżycki SJ*, Cracow, 2003; Jerzy Kowalczyk, *Świątynie późnobarokowe na kresach*, 2006.

For the confessional situation in Royal Prussia, see Sławomir Kościelak, 'Dzieje wyznaniowe Prus Królewskich w XVI–XVIII w.', in *Prusy Królewskie. Społeczeństwo – kultura – gospodarka 1454–1772*, ed. Edmund Kizik, Gdańsk, 2012, 204–63; idem, *Katolicy w protestanckim Gdansku od drugiej połowy XVI do końca XVIII wieku*, Gdańsk, 2012, esp. 387–441; Edmund Cieślak, 'Mieszkańcy Gdańska w życiu codziennym', in *HGd*, iii/1, 640–67; Jan Baszanowski, 'Statystyka wyznań a zagadnienia etniczne Gdańska w XVII–XVIII wieku', *ZH*, 54/1, 1989, 57–82; Elżbieta Paprocka, *Tolerowani i nielubiani. Katolicy w Elblągu w drugiej połowie XVII i w XVIII wieku*, 2009; Janusz Tandecki, 'Zmiany terytorialne i demograficzne', in *Historia Elbląga*, ii/2: *(1626–1772)*, ed. Andrzej Groth, Gdańsk, 1997, 66–79; Krzysztof Mikulski, 'Obcy w oblężonej twierdzy protestantyzmu – zbiorowy portret katolików toruńskich', in *Rzeczpospolita wielu wyznań*, ed. Adam Kaźmierczyk et al., Cracow, 293–310; Filip Wolański, 'Kaznodzieje Braci Mniejszych Regularnej Obserwancji w Prusach Królewskich i Warmii w epoce saskiej', in *W podróży*, 213–20; B. Dygdała, *Struktury parafialne diecezji chełmińskiej*, 193–95, 214–21, 236–47. For the Tumult of Thorn and its ramifications, see also Stanisław Salmonowicz, 'The Toruń Uproar of 1724', *APH*, 47, 1983, 55–79; Jerzy Dygdała, *Polityka Torunia wobec władz Rzeczypospolitej w latach 1764–1772*, 1977, 15–30, 38; Grzegorz Król, 'Anglia wobec wydarzeń toruńskich 1724 roku', *ZH*, 56/1, 1991, 25–46.

FURTHER READING

For Royal Prussian politics, see Friedrich, *The Other Prussia*, 189–216; Jerzy Dygdała, *Życie polityczne Prus Królewskich u schyłku ich związku w Rzecząpospolitą w XVIII wieku*, 1984, 13–94; idem, 'Dzieje polityczne Prus Królewskich do rozbiorów Rzeczypospolitej', in *Prusy Królewskie. Społeczeństwo – kultura – gospodarka 1454–1772*, ed. Edmund Kizik, Gdańsk, 2012, 72–94; idem, 'Szlachta Prus Królewskich wobec kryzysu Rzeczypospolitej w XVIII w.', in *My i oni*, 287–315; Edmund Cieślak, 'Konflikty polityczne i społeczne w Gdańsku w latach 1748–1752', in *HGd*, iii/1, 542–78; idem, 'Udział Gdańska w życiu politycznym Prus Królewskich i Rzeczypospolitej', in *HGd*, iii/1, 596–617; Krzysztof Mikulski, 'Szlachta i patrycjat w Prusach Królewskich w XV–XVIII wieku', in *Prusy Książęce i Prusy Królewskie w XVI–XVIII wieku*, ed. Jacek Wijaczka, Kielce, 1997, 97–109. For the fate of Elbing, see *Historia Elbląga*, ii/2, 5–65, 80–119.

On Royal Prussian intellectual and cultural life, see Karin Friedrich, 'The Urban Enlightenment in Eighteenth-Century Royal Prussia', in *Raison universelle et cultures nationales au siècle des lumières*, ed. David Bell et al., Paris, 1998, 11–29; *HGd*, iii/1, 321–484, 618–723; Stanisław Salmonowicz, *Prusy Królewskie w XVII–XVIII wieku*, Toruń, 2002; Anna Grześkowiak-Krwawicz, *Gdańsk oświecony/Die Aufklärung in Danzig*, 1998; Piotr Paluchowski, *Danziger Erfahrungen w latach 1737–1793*, 2013.

Mid-eighteenth-century learned circles are reconsidered by Stanisław Roszak, *Koniec świata sarmackich erudytów*, Toruń, 2012; see also Jarosław Kurkowski, *Warszawskie czasopisma uczone doby Augusta III*, 1994; Irena Stasiewicz-Jasiukowa, 'Recepcja poglądów Christiana Wolffa w środowiskach katolickich polskiego Oświecenia', *Analecta*, 1998/2, 53–69.

On the cultural tensions of the era, see Jerzy Michalski, 'Sarmatyzm a europeizacja Polski w XVIII wieku', in Michalski, *SH*, ii, 7–36; *Sarmatyzm. Sen o potędze*, exhibition catalogue, ed. Beata Biedrońska-Słota, Cracow, 2010; Agata Roćko, *Kontusz i frak*, 2015; *Polski Grand Tour w XVIII i początkach XIX wieku*, ed. Agata Roćko, 2014; *Staropolskie podróżowanie*, ed. Bogdan Rok and Filip Wolański, iv, Cracow, 2016; *Dwory magnackie w XVIII wieku*, ed. Teresa Kostkiewiczowa and Agata Roćko, 2006; Tadeusz Bernatowicz, *Mitra i buława. Królewskie ambicje książąt w sztuce Rzeczypospolitej szlacheckiej (1697–1763)*, 2011; Oleńska, *Jan Klemens Branicki*.

For the Czartoryskis' plans and their fate, see Jerzy Michalski, 'Plan Czartoryskich naprawy Rzeczypospolitej', in Michalski, *SH*, i, 11–26; Zofia Zielińska, *Studia z dziejów polsko-rosyjskich w XVIII wieku*, 2001, 60–89; Butterwick, *Poland's Last King*, 146–55.

4 'A NEW CREATION OF THE POLISH WORLD'

The main foundation of most of this chapter is Zofia Zielińska, *Polska w okowach „systemu północnego" 1763–1766*, Cracow, 2012. For the international dimensions, see also H. M. Scott, *The Emergence of the Eastern Powers, 1756–1775*, Cambridge, 2001, 11–182; Schroeder, *Transformation*, 3–52; Franz A. J. Szabo, *The Seven Years War in Europe 1756–1763*, Harlow, 2008; Müller, 'Rußland und der Siebenjährige Krieg'; LeDonne, *Russia and the World*, 38–41, 237–40; Madariaga, *Russia*, 187–204; D. M. Griffiths, 'The Rise and Fall of the Northern System: Court Politics and Foreign Policy in the First Half of Catherine II's Reign', *Canadian-American Slavic Studies*, 4, 1970, 547–69; Tim Blanning, *Frederick the Great: King of Prussia*, London, 2015, 254–85; Boris V. Nosov, *Ustanovlenie rossiiskogo gospodstva w Rechi Pospolitoi 1756–1768 gg.*, Moscow, 2004; Borys Nosow [Boris Nosov], 'Polityka Rosji na początku panowania Stanisława Augusta, 1764 – początek 1765 r.', in *SARz*, 81–99; Michalski, 'Problematyka aliansu polsko-rosyjskiego'.

For overviews of the reforms of 1764–66, see Lukowski, *Liberty's Folly*, 179–80, 186–90; Jörg K. Hoensch, *Sozialverfassung und politische Reform. Polen im vorrevolutionären Zeitalter*, Cologne, 1973. For the fiscal reforms, see idem, 'Die Streit um dem polnischen Generalzoll 1764–1766', *JfGO*, 18, 1970, 356–88; Marek Woźnicki, 'Reforma ceł i podatków w Rzeczypospolitej w latach 1764–1766', *Annales Universitatis Mariae Curie-Skłodowska*, 49/1–2, 2014, 151–66; Marian Drozdowski, *Podstawy finansowe działalności państwowej w Polsce 1764–1793*, 1975. On the botched monetary reform, see also Jerzy Dygdała, 'Wielkie miasta Prus Królewskich wobec reformy menniczej z lat 1765–1766', *ZH*, 41/3, 1976, 105–23. The judicial reforms are explained by Ramunė Šmigelskytė-Stukienė, 'The Modernisation of the Court System in the Grand Duchy of Lithuania: Changes to the Organisation of the Local District Courts and Regulation of Judges' Duties in 1764–1793', *LHS*, 21, 2017, 1–30; and Jerzy Michalski, 'Reforma sądownictwa na sejmie konwokacyjnym 1764 roku', in Michalski, *SH*, i, 27–43. On parliamentary changes, see Jerzy Michalski, 'Sejm w czasach panowania Stanisława Augusta', in *Historia sejmu polskiego*, i, 350–419 (at 350–61). On the relationship between the Crown and Lithuania, see Jerzy Malec, 'Próby ściślejszego zespolenia Litwy z Koroną w latach 1764–1788', *Lituano-Slavica Posnaniensia. Studia Historica*, 2, 1987, 167–85; Vydas Dolinskas, 'Lietuvos Didžiosos Kunigaikštytės politinio gyvenimo aktualijos ir Lietuvos atstovųveikla 1764 m. konvokaciniame seime', in *Lietuvos Didžiosos Kunigaikštytės istorijos atodangos*, ed. Vydas Dolinskas et al., Vilnius, 2016, 468–517.

On the transition to the new reign, see Jerzy Dygdała, 'Lojalni urzędnicy Wettynów i Stanisława Augusta Poniatowskiego', in *W służbie obcych monarchów i państw*, ed. Tomasz Ciesielski, 2015, 219–36; Jerzy Michalski, 'Ogrodzki Jacek', *PSB*, xxiii, 648–51. On the king's relationship with his family, see Zamoyski, *Last King*, 123–26; Zofia Zielińska, 'Królewska familia – książęta Czartoryscy', in *Pamiętniki SA*, 112–39; eadem, 'Poniatowski Kazimierz', *PSB*, xxvii, 444–53; Emanuel Rostworowski, 'Poniatowski Andrzej', *PSB*, xxvii, 412–20; and the jaundiced Stanisław Lubomirski, *Pod władzą księcia Repnina*, ed. Jerzy Łojek, 1971, esp. 68–97. For the king's private finances, see Maciej Wojtyński, *Szkatuła prywatna króla Stanisława Augusta*, 2003.

For Stanisław August's early cultural and educational initiatives, see Zamoyski, *Last King*, 101–20, 131–37; Butterwick, *Poland's Last King*, 159–73, 178–89, 201–02, 239–41; idem, 'What is Enlightenment (*oświecenie*)? Some Polish Answers, 1765–1820', *Central Europe*, 3/1, 2005, 19–37 (at 23–24); Andrzej Rottermund, *Zamek Warszawski w epoce Oświecenia*, 1989, 92–98; Jakub Pokora, *Obraz Najjaśniejszego Pana Stanisława Augusta (1764–1770)*, 1993; Bogusław Pfeiffer, *Rex et Patria*, 2012, 134–48; Magdalena Górska, 'Symbolika panowania Stanisława Augusta', in *SARz*, 33–50; Jerzy Dygdała, 'Wizerunek barokowego Sarmaty i oświeconego Europejczyka, czyli August III Wettyn i Stanisław August Poniatowski', *Wieki Stare i Nowe*, 6/11, 2014, 38–57; Kamilla Mrozowska, *Szkoła Rycerska Stanisława Augusta Poniatowskiego (1764–1794)*, Wrocław, 1961; Zofia Sinko, *„Monitor" wobec angielskiego „Spectatora"*, Wrocław, 1956; Elżbieta Aleksandrowska, '„Monitor" 1765–1785. Rekonesans dziejów redakcji i ideologii', in *„Monitor" 1765–1785. Wybór*, ed. Elżbieta Aleksandrowska, Wrocław 1976; Tadeusz Frączyk, *Adam Kazimierz Czartoryski*, Cracow, 2012; Mieczysław Klimowicz, *Oświecenie*, 4th edn, 1980, 91–101.

Domestic politics and noble mentalities are analysed by George Tadeusz Lukowski, *The 'Szlachta' and the Confederacy of Radom, 1764–1767/68: A Study of the Polish Nobility*, Rome, 1977; see also Tomasz Szwaciński, 'Sejmiki poselskie przed konwokacją 1764 r.', *KH*, 113/1, 2006, 19–56; Dygdała, *Życie polityczne Prus Królewskich*, 57–187; idem, 'U początków polityki wewnętrznej Stanisława Augusta w latach 1764–1768', *WO*, 15, 1999, 111–34; Rozalia Kosińska, 'Sejmiki poselskie 1766 roku', *KH*, 125/4, 2018, 861–99.

On Church–state relations and the dissident question, see Jerzy T. Lukowski, 'The Papacy, Poland, Russia and Religious Reform, 1764–8', *Journal of Ecclesiastical History*, 39/1, 1988, 66–92; Barbara Skinner, 'Khmelnytsky's Shadow: The Confessional Legacy', in *Citizenship and Identity in a Multinational Commonwealth*, ed. Karin Friedrich and Barbara M. Pendzich, Leiden, 2009, 149–169; Jerzy Tadeusz Łukowski, 'Watykan wobec ostatniego polskiego bezkrólewia', *KH*, 98/1, 1991, 21–30; Maciej Loret, 'Rzym a Polska w początkach panowania Stanisława Augusta', *Przegląd Współczesny*, 23/6, 1927, 214–35, 501–17; Paweł Zając, 'Wokół planów nowego kształtu relacji Rzeczypospolitej ze Stolicą Apostolską na progu panowania Stanisława Augusta Poniatowskiego, 1764–1766', *Kościół w Polsce. Dzieje i kultura*, 15, 2016, 33–54; M[aria] Cecylia Łubieńska, *Sprawa dysydencka 1764–1766*, 1911; Jerzy Dygdała, 'Wokół kwestii dysydenckiej w początkowym okresie panowania Stanisława Augusta', *Czasy Nowożytne*, 31, 2018, 257–78; Kazimierz Rudnicki, *Biskup Kajetan Sołtyk 1715–1788*, Cracow, 1906; Maria Czeppe, 'Sołtyk Kajetan Ignacy', *PSB*, xl, 386–404; Emanuel Rostworowski 'Podoski Gabriel', *PSB*, xxvii, 149–61; Jerzy Michalski, 'Sprawa dysydencka a zagadnienia gospodarcze w pierwszych latach panowania Stanisława Augusta', *PH*, 40/3, 1949, 156–63; Wojciech Kriegseisen, 'Dysydenci i dyzunici w Rzeczypospolitej epoki stanisławowskiej', in *SARz*, 51–62; Mariusz Markiewicz, 'Polscy dysydenci w polityce europejskiej w XVIII wieku', in *Polska wobec wielkich konfliktów w Europie nowożytnej*, ed. Ryszard Skowron, Cracow, 2009, 456–63.

FURTHER READING

5 MARTYRDOMS

The standard work on the Confederacy of Bar remains the eruditely detailed and emotionally charged *opus vitæ*: Władysław Konopczyński, *Konfederacja barska*, 2 vols [1936–38], 2nd edn, 1991. In English, see Lukowski, *Liberty's Folly*, 197–203. On the prior of Bar, see Wacław Szczygielski, 'Jandołowicz Marek', *PSB*, x, 499–502; Emanuel Rostworowski, 'Ksiądz Marek i proroctwa polityczne', in *Przemiany tradycji barskiej. Studia*, ed. Zofia Stefanowska, Cracow, 1970, 29–57. On religious fervour, see Magdalena Ślusarska, ' „My mocą Boga wsparci, ocalając wiarę" – motywy religijne i obrzędowe konfederacji barskiej', in *Konfederacja barska*, 157–81.

For the confederacy's outbreak, see also Emanuel Rostworowski, 'Z dziejów genezy konfederacji barskiej', *Zeszyty Naukowe WAP*, Seria Historyczne, 1964, 11/37, 147–57. On the *koliivshchyna*, see B. Skinner, 'Borderlands of Faith'; eadem, *Western Front*, 132–33; Zenon E. Kohut, 'Myths Old and New: The Haidamak Movement and the Koliivschyna in Recent Historiography', *HUS*, 1/3, 1977, 359–78; Władysław A. Serczyk, *Koliszczyzna*, Cracow, 1968; idem, 'Melchizedek Znaczko-Jaworski i klasztor motreninski przed wybuchem koliszczyzny', *SH*, 11/3, 1968, 297–322; Tadeusz Srogosz, *Między wojną a modernizacją*, Częstochowa, 2016, 83–100; Władylena W. Sokyrska and Tadeusz Srogosz, 'Hajdamacy i koliszczyzna w polskiej i ukraińskiej historiografii', *PNH*, 16/2, 2017, 7–41.

Wacław Szczygielski, *Konfederacja barska w Wielkopolsce*, 1970, is a fine regional study. For the later stages of the confederacy, see Jerzy Michalski, *Schyłek konfederacji barskiej*, Wrocław, 1970. On two swashbuckling confederates who chose different paths later, see Vydas Dolinskas, *Simonas Kosakovskis*, Vilnius, 2003, 163–317; Władysław Konopczyński, *Kazimierz Pułaski*, Cracow, 1931. The king's stance is reassessed by Zofia Zielińska, 'Stanisław August wobec konfederacji i konfederatów barskich', in *Konfederacja barska*, 117–30. For his abduction, see Zamoyski, *Last King*, 187–92; Piotr Ugniewski, ' „Szkaradny występek królobójstwa" w międzynarodowej propagandzie Stanisława Augusta', *PH*, 95/2, 2004, 327–47; Zdzisław Żygulski junior, 'Garnitur nieszczęśliwości Króla Stanisława Augusta', *Roczniki Humanistyczne*, 47/4, 1999, 237–48; *SAOKP*, 106–08.

On Rousseau and Mably's interactions with the confederacy, see Jerzy Michalski, *Rousseau and Polish Republicanism*, 2015 (available online); idem, *Sarmacki republikanizm w oczach Francuza. Mably i konfederaci barscy*, Wrocław, 1995. For Stanisław August's reaction, see Jean Fabre, *Stanislas-Auguste Poniatowski et les hommes de lettres français*, Cracow, 1936, 25–28 (cf. idem, *Stanislas-Auguste Poniatowski et l'Europe des lumières*, 343–47); Jochen Schlobach, 'Lumières en France, princes éclairés et le roi Stanislas-Auguste Poniatowski', *Kwartalnik Neofilologiczny*, 42, 1995, 93–107 (at 100); Richard Butterwick, 'Polite Liberty or *l'esprit monarchique*? Stanisław August Poniatowski, Jean-Jacques Rousseau and *politesse* in England', *SVEC*, 2003:7, 249–70.

For an overview of the first partition, which distills the older historiography while allowing for greater Russian agency, see Lukowski, *Partitions*, 48–81. Władysław Konopczyński, *Pierwszy rozbior Polski*, Cracow, 2010, published six decades after it was written, is essential, despite its understandable Germanophobia. Most scholars have rejected the Austrocentric interpretation of Herbert H. Kaplan, *The First Partition of Poland*, New York, 1962; cf. Derek Beales, *Joseph II*, 2 vols, Cambridge, 1987–2009, i, 278–300. Schroeder, *Transformation*, 11–19; and Scott, *Emergence*, 187–224, interpret the partition as the workings of the international system. Dorota Dukwicz, 'The Internal Situation in the Polish-Lithuanian Commonwealth (1769–1771) and the Origins of the First Partition (in the Light of Russian Sources)', *APH*, 103, 2011, 67–84, has particular explanatory force. See also Madariaga, *Russia*, 203–36; LeDonne, *Russia and the World*, 42–47, 103–04, 241–43, 295–97; Brian L. Davies, *The Russo-Turkish War, 1768–1774*, London, 2016; Jones, 'Runaway Peasants'; M. S. Anderson, 'Great Britain and the Russian Fleet, 1769–1770', *SEER*, 31, 1952–53, 148–63; Albert Sorel, *La Question d'Orient au XVIII siècle*, 4th edn, Paris, 1902; Boris Nosov, 'Politika Rossii v Litve vo vremia barskoi konfederatsii 1768–1772 gg.', in *Viešosios ir privačios erdvės*, 317–31; Jerzy T. Lukowski, 'Guarantee or Annexation: A Note on Russian Plans to Acquire Polish Territory prior to the First Partition of Poland', *Bulletin of the Institute of Historical Research*, 56/133, 1983, 60–65; Emanuel Rostworowski, 'Podbój Śląska przez Prusy a pierwszy rozbiór Polski', *PH*, 63/2, 1972, 389–412.

FURTHER READING

For nobles' reactions to the partition, see Ramunė Šmigelskytė-Stukienė, '*Les Sujets mixtes*: The Problem of Double Subordination in the Period of the Partition of the Polish-Lithuanian Commonwealth, and the Case of Mykolas Kleopas Oginskis', *LHS*, 19, 2014, 111–34 (at 115–23); Jerzy Michalski, 'Rejtan i dylematy Polaków w dobie pierwszego rozbioru', in Michalski, *SH*, i, 160–201; Dorota Dukwicz, 'Czy rozbiór był wstrząsem?', in *My i oni*, 355–77; Piotr Skowroński, 'Ani z twarzą, ani z tarczą. Kilka słów o wyrzekaniu się konfederacji barskiej', *Kronos*, 46/3, 2018, 204–16. For the king's efforts to influence foreign opinion, see D. B. Horn, *British Public Opinion and the First Partition of Poland*, Edinburgh, 1945; Piotr Ugniewski, *Media i dyplomacja. „Gazette de France" o sejmie rozbiorowym 1773–1775*, 2006; On further annexations, see Jerzy Topolski, 'Pruskie uzurpacje graniczne w dobie pierwszego rozbioru Polski (1772–1777)', *Zeszyty Naukowe Uniwersytetu Adama Mickiewicza. Historia*, 8, 1968, 51–75; Jerzy Michalski, 'Sprawa zwrotu ponadtraktatowych nabytków austriackich i pruskich po pierwszym rozbiorze', *KH*, 112/1, 2005, 77–127.

For the impact on Royal Prussia, see Hans-Jürgen Bömelburg, *Zwischen polnischer Ständegesellschaft und preussischem Obrigkeitsstaat. Vom Königlichen Preussen zu Westpreussen (1756–1806)*, Munich, 1995; Friedrich, *Brandenburg-Prussia*, 91–93; eadem, 'The Development of the Prussian Town, 1720–1815', in *The Rise of Prussia 1700–1830*, ed. Philip G. Dwyer, Harlow, 2000, 129–50 (at 145–49); eadem, *The Other Prussia*, 214–21; Dariusz Łukasiewicz, 'Przejęcie Prus Królewskich przez administrację pruską', in *Prusy 1701–1806*, 344–48. For a traditional view: Walther Hubatsch, *Frederick the Great*, London, 1973, 181–89. The case against the Hohenzollern monarchy is conceded by Blanning, *Frederick the Great*, 294–95; see also Edmund Cieślak, 'Pruska agresja ekonomiczna i polityczna wobec Gdańska w okresie rozbiorowym', Edmund Cieślak and Jerzy Trzoska, 'Handel i żegluga gdańska w XVIII w.'; Jerzy Stankiewicz, 'Przemiany przestrzenne i demograficzne Gdańska w XVIII wieku', all in *HGd*, iii/1, at 578–95, 402–03, 414, 335–38; Jerzy Wojtowicz, 'Walka Gdańska i Torunia przeciwko pruskiej zaborczości 1772–1793', in *Historia Pomorza*, ii/2, *Pomorze Wschodnie w latach 1657–1815*, ed. Gerard Labuda, Poznań, 1984, 617–22; J. Dygdała, *Polityka Torunia*, 188–90; *Historia Wejherowa*, ed. Józef Borzyszkowski, Wejherowo, 1998; Andrzej Groth, 'Wejherowo w roku 1778', *Rocznik Gdański*, 65/1–2, 2005, 143–49; idem, 'Wykaz właścicieli i gruntów w Wejherowie z 1788 r.', *Rocznik Gdański*, 65/1–2, 2005, 191–96.

On Galicia, see Beales, *Joseph II*, i, 363–66; Horst Glassl, *Das Österreichische Einrichtungswerk in Galizien (1772–1790)*, Wiesbaden, 1975; Miloš Řezník, *Neuorientierung einer Elite. Aristokratie, Ständewesen und Loyalität in Galizien (1772–1795)*, Frankfurt, 2016; Tomasz Wiślicz, 'Józefinizm na galicyjskiej wsi: Trześniów 1784–1790', in *Galicja – mozaika nie tylko narodowa*, ed. Urszula Jakubowska, 2014, ii, 13–21. On the salt problem, see Grażyna Bałtruszajtys, 'Kłopoty z solą u schyłku Rzeczypospolitej', in *Wiek XVIII. Polska i świat*, ed. Andrzej Zahorski, 1974, 225–43.

For the partition sejm and the constitutional settlement, the fundamental Władysław Konopczyński, *Geneza i ustanowienie Rady Nieustającej* [1917], 2nd edn, Cracow, 2014, is joined by the work of Dorota Dukwicz. See her 'Restricted Sovereignty of the Sejm. The Plenipotentiary Delegation and Ratification of the First Partition Treaty', in *Separation of Powers and Parliamentarism, the Past and the Present*, ed. Wacław Uruszczak et al., 2007, 454–67; eadem, 'Ambasador Otto Magnus von Stackelberg wobec króla Stanisława Augusta w przededniu sejmu rozbiorowego w latach 1773–1775', *WO*, 15, 1999, 95–109; eadem, *Rosja wobec sejmu rozbiorowego warszawskiego (1772–1775)*, 2015; eadem, 'Sekretne wydatki rosyjskiej ambasady w Warszawie w latach 1772–1790', in *Gospodarka, społeczeństwo, kultura w dziejach nowożytnych*, ed. Andrzej Karpiński et al., 2010, 449–65; Zofia Zielińska, 'Poniński Adam', *PSB*, xxvii, 504–12; Michalski, 'Rejtan'; cf. Jonas Nordin, 'The Monarchy in the Swedish Age of Liberty (1719–1772)', in *Scandinavia in the Age of Revolution*, ed. Pasi Ihalainen et al., Farnham, 2011, 29–40. See also Piotr Skowroński, 'Zmagania o kształt sejmu 1773–1775 r.', *KH* 127/2, 2020, 233–72; idem, 'Radziwiłł Palace in Warsaw during Two Delegation Sejms (1767–1768, 1773–1775)', *Journal of Heritage Conservation*, 55, 2018, 67–74.

On the suppression of the Jesuits, see Chadwick, *The Popes and European Revolution*, 260–66, 345–85; Derek Beales, *Prosperity and Plunder: European Catholic Monasteries in the Age of Revolution, 1650–1815*, Cambridge, 2003, 143–68; idem, 'Maria Theresa, Joseph II and the Suppression of the Jesuits', in idem, *Enlightenment and Reform in Eighteenth-Century Europe*, London, 2005, 207–26; for the suppression in Poland-Lithuania and the establishment of the

Educational Commission, see Butterwick-Pawlikowski, 'Before and After Suppression'; Jan Poplatek, *Komisja Edukacji Narodowej. Udział byłych Jezuitów*, Cracow, 1974; Władysław Smoleński, 'Żywioły zachowawcze i Komisya Edukacyjna', in idem, *Pisma Historyczne*, Cracow, 1901, ii, 95–206 (at 99–105, 120–22); Dorota Dukwicz, ' „L'Humanité . . . m'oblige à contribuer aux progrès de l'instruction en Pologne" – czyli o kulisach ustanowienia Komisji Edukacji Narodowej', *PH*, 109/1, 2018, 73–93; Ambroise Jobert, *La Commission d'Education Nationale en Pologne (1773–1794)*, Paris, 1941. On Jesuit survival, see Marek Inglot, 'The Society of Jesus in the Russian Empire (1772–1820) and the Restoration of the Order', in *Jesuit Survival and Restoration: A Global History, 1773–1900*, ed. Robert A. Maryks and Jonathan Wright, Leiden, 2015, 67–82; Maciej Loret, *Kościół katolicki a Katarzyna II, 1772–1784*, Cracow, 1910, 29–30, 65–85, 119–95.

6 THRONE AND ALTAR

The political history of the period is succinctly presented by Daniel Stone, *Polish Politics and National Reform, 1775–1788*, New York, 1976; see also Lukowski, *Partitions*, 101–22. The key decisions regarding the Commonwealth were made in St Petersburg, against the background of shifting alliances, on which see Madariaga, *Russia*, 383–91; LeDonne, *Russia and the World*, 48, 105–09, 243; Dixon, *Catherine the Great*, 2001, 164–68; Beales, *Joseph II*, i, 431–38, ii, 104–23; Blanning, *Frederick the Great*, 307–10; Jerzy Michalski, 'Fryderyk Wielki i Grzegorz Potemkin w latach kryzysu przymierza prusko-rosyjskiego', in Michalski, *SH*, i, 401–19.

For the interaction of international and domestic politics, see Michalski, *Polska wobec wojny o sukcesję bawarską*; idem, 'Do dziejów stronnictwa austriackiego i polskiej polityki Austrii po pierwszym rozbiorze', in Michalski, *SH*, i, 393–400; idem, 'Dwie misje księcia Stanisława'; idem, 'Zmierzch prokonsulatu Stackelberga', 449–52; idem, 'Sprawa przymierza polsko-rosyjskiego w dobie aneksji Krymu', in Michalski, *SH*, i, 420–48; Z. Zielińska, *Studia z dziejów stosunków polsko-rosyjskich*, 136–59; Ewa Zielińska, 'Rzeczpospolita wobec zbliżenia rosyjsko-austriackiego na początku lat osiemdziesiątych XVIII w. Sprawy Barona Karla Juliusa i Biskupa Kajetana Sołtyka', doctoral thesis, IH PAN, 2004; eadem, 'Otto Magnus Stackelberg wobec projektu skonfederowania sejmu 1782 roku', *KH*, 106/4, 1999, 73–87.

The situation at the frontiers is revealed by Konopczyński, *Pierwszy rozbior*, 240–86; Topolski, 'Pruskie uzurpacje'; Michalski, 'Sprawa zwrotu'; and especially by Ewa Zielińska, 'Sprawa polsko-rosyjskiej komisji granicznej w latach 1778–1780', in *W cieniu*, 339–68.

On the magnate opposition, see Jerzy Michalski, 'Opozycja magnacka i jej cele w początkach Sejmu Czteroletniego', in Michalski, *SH*, i, 285–304 (at 286–89); idem, 'Początki opozycyjnej działalności Franciszka Ksawerego Branickiego', *KH*, 113/2, 2006, 75–132; idem, 'O zmianę rosyjskiego ambasadora w Warszawie (zabiegi magnackiej opozycji w latach 1775–1776)', *KH*, 109/3, 2002, 147–60; 'Konflikt między kuzynami (Stanisław August i Adam Kazimierz Czartoryski w latach 1775–1776)', in *Literatura – historia – dziedzictwo*, ed. Tomasz Chachulski and Anna Grześkowiak-Krwawicz, 2006, 430–38; Dorota Dukwicz, 'Stanisław August w świetle korespondencji z Franciszkiem Ksawerym Branickim 1769–1770', in *W cieniu*, 278–309; eadem, 'Od przyjaźni do wrogości. Franciszek Ksawery Branicki i Stanisław August', in *Pamiętniki SA*, 292–313. Andrzej Stroynowski, *Opozycja sejmowa w dobie rządów Rady Nieustającej*, Łódź, 2005, tends to take the opposition leaders at their word. For a local study: Maria Wisińska, 'Opozycja magnacka w Sieradzkiem w latach 1785–1790', *Rocznik Łódzki*, 32, 1982, 67–109.

On other members of the opposition, see also Bernard Krakowski, 'Kossakowska z Potockich Katarzyna', *PSB*, xiv, 255–60; Jerzy Michalski, 'Lubomirska z Czartoryskich Izabela (Elżbieta)', *PSB*, xvii, 625–29; Zofia Zielińska, 'Potocki Ignacy', *PSB*, xxviii, 1–17; Barbara Grochulska, 'Potocki Stanisław Kostka', *PSB*, xxviii, 158–70; Jerzy Michalski and Alina Nowak-Romanowicz, 'Ogiński, Michał Kazimierz', *PSB*, xxiii, 624–30.

On aristocratic patronage of the arts, see Agnieszka Whelan, 'Gesture and Performance: Princess Izabela Czartoryska and Her Gardens, 1770–1831', doctoral thesis, UCL, 2013; Frączyk, *Adam Kazimierz Czartoryski*; Bożenna Majewska-Maszkowska, *Mecenat artystyczny Izabelli z Czartoryskich*

Lubomirskiej (1736–1836), Wrocław, 1976; Jolanta Polanowska, *Stanisław Kostka Potocki: twórczość architekta amatora, przedstawiciela neoklasycyzmu i nurtu picturesque*, 2 vols, 2009; and several essays in *Słynne kobiety w Rzeczypospolitej XVIII wieku*, ed. Agata Roćko and Magdalena Górska, 2017.

The royalist party has usually been studied within the context of local parliamentary politics: Jerzy Michalski, 'Sejmiki poselskie 1788 roku', in Michalski, *SH*, i, 217–84, set the standard. For the Crown, much detail is provided by Witold Filipczak, *Sejm 1778 roku*, 2000, 32–37, 46–112; *Życie sejmikowe prowincji wielkopolskiej w latach 1780–1786*, Łódź, 2012; idem, 'Stronnictwo regalistyczne w województwie kijowskim 1780–1782', *PNH*, 8/1, 2009, 79–104; idem, 'Sejmiki województwa płockiego 1780–1786', *PNH*, 8/2, 2009, 23–62; idem, 'Aktywność sejmikowa regalistów w województwie rawskim w latach 1780–1786', *Rocznik Łódzki*, 47, 2010, 11–39; idem, 'Sejmiki ziemi nurskiej 1780–1786', *PNH*, 13/1, 2014, 23–62; idem, 'Sejmiki ziemi zakroczymskiej 1778–1786', *PNH*, 14/2, 2015, 85–121; idem, 'Relacje między liderami stronnictwa regalistycznego na terenie Ukrainy w latach 1783–1784', in *Historia na źródłach oparta*, ed. Andrzej Stroynowski, Częstochowa, 2017, 667–80; idem, 'Sejmiki ziemi wiskiej 1780–1786', in *Sic erat in votis*, ed. Małgorzata Karkocha and Piotr Robak, Łódź, 2017, i, 321–50; see also Srogosz, *Między wojną a modernizacją*, 139–66.

On two leading royalists, see Jerzy Dygdała, 'Raczyński Kazimierz', *PSB*, xxix, 644–53; Andrzej Rosner, 'Mniszech Michał Jerzy Wandalin', *PSB*, xxi, 480–84; Marek Bratuń, *„Ten wykwintny, wykształcony Europejczyk": zagraniczne studia i podróże edukacyjne Michała Jerzego Wandalina Mniszcha*, Opole, 2002. Management in the Grand Duchy of Lithuania was delegated: see Stanisław Kościałkowski, *Antoni Tyzenhauz. Podskarbi nadworny litewski*, 2 vols, London, 1970–71; Jerzy Michalski, 'Wokół powrotu Karola Radziwiłła z emigracji pobarskiej', *KH*, 106/4, 1999, 21–72.

On the battle of ideas and shifts in discourse, see Lukowski, *Disorderly Liberty*, 138–63; Grześkowiak-Krwawicz, *Dyskurs*, passim; Jerzy Michalski, 'Publicystyka i parapublicystyka doby sejmu 1776 roku', *KH*, 105/1, 1998, 21–64. For two bold tracts: Józef Wybicki, *Myśli polityczne o wolności cywilnej*, ed. Zbigniew Nowak, intr. Emanuel Rostworowski, Wrocław, 1984; idem, *Listy patriotyczne*, ed. Kazimierz Opałek, Wrocław, 1955.

The Zamoyski Code is incisively analysed by Lukowski, *Disorderly Liberty*, 109–20; see also Ewa Borkowska-Bagieńska, *„Zbiór Praw Sądowych" Andrzeja Zamoyskiego*, Poznań, 1986; Jerzy Michalski, '„Wolność" i „własność" chłopska w polskiej myśli reformatorskiej XVIII wieku', in Michalski, *SH*, ii, 130–205 (at 144–60); Mieczysław Tarnawski, *Kodeks Zamoyskiego na tle stosunków kościelno-państwowych*, Lwów, 1916; Adam Skałkowski, *Biskup Szembek a kodeks Zamoyskiego*, in idem, *Fragmenty*, Poznań, 1928, 197–211; Richard Butterwick, *Polska Rewolucja a Kościół katolicki 1788–1792*, Cracow, 2012, 210–16; Krystyna Adolphowa, 'Szlachta litewska wobec Zbioru Praw Andrzeja Zamoyskiego', in *Księga Koła Historyków Uniwersytetu Stefana Batorego*, Wilno, 1933, 156–88; Jerzy Malec, 'Walka szlachty litewskiej o zachowanie III Statutu w drugiej połowie XVIII wieku', *CPH*, 44/1–2, 1992, 65–72.

On the Sołtyk affair, see E. Zielińska, 'Rzeczpospolita wobec zbliżenia rosyjsko-austriackiego', 299–354; Rudnicki, *Biskup Kajetan Sołtyk*, 192–200; Czeppe, 'Sołtyk Kajetan Ignacy', *PSB*, xl, 397–402; Michał Pęckowski, *Józef Olechowski, archidiakon i sufragan krakowski 1735–1806*, Cracow, 1926; Paweł Zając, 'Giovanni Andrea Archetti i Stanisław August Poniatowski', *KH*, 123/2, 2016, 279–311 (at 301–03).

On Michał Poniatowski's rise, see Zofia Zielińska, 'Poniatowski Michał Jerzy', *PSB*, xxvii, 455–71; Angela Sołtys, *Opat z San Michele. Grand Tour prymasa Poniatowskiego i jego kolekcje*, 2008, 29–42; Butterwick, *Polska Rewolucja*, 109–11, 219–26.

For the impact of the partition on the Catholic Church, see B. Skinner, *Western Front*, 144–68; Loret, *Kościół katolicki a Katarzyna II*; Zygmunt Szultka, 'Stosunki wyznaniowe i kościelne w Prusach w XVIII w.' in *Prusy 1701–1806*, 745–88 (at 772–80); Władysław Chotkowski, *Historya polityczna Kościoła w Galicyi za rządów Marii Teresy*, 2 vols, Cracow, 1909; Jan Krętosz, *Archidiecezja lwowska obrządku łacińskiego w okresie józefinizmu*, Katowice, 1996; Stanisław Grodziski, 'Gubernium lwowskie a kuria krakowska po pierwszym rozbiorze Polski', in idem, *Studia galicyjskie*, Cracow, 2007, 41–52; Glassl, *Das österreichische Enrichtungswerk*, 135–47.

FURTHER READING

For the Latin-rite episcopate and the reforms some bishops promoted, see Butterwick, *Polska Rewolucja*, 109–33, 140–46, 171–77, 184–86, 201, 626–30; Ślusarska, 'Oświeceniowe modele biskupa, plebana i parafii'; Rafał Szczurowski, *Zaradzić potrzebom doczesnym i wiecznym. Idee oświecenia w Kościele katolickim w Polsce*, Cracow, 2014; Stanisław Witecki, *Przekaz kulturowy w parafiach katolickich na obszarze Rzeczypospolitej Obojga Narodów czasów stanisławowskich*, Cracow, 2018, 51–121; Michał Grzybowski, 'Kościelna działalność Michała Jerzego Poniatowskiego biskupa płockiego', *Studia z Historii Kościoła w Polsce*, 7, 1983, 5–225; Tadeusz Kasabuła, *Ignacy Massalski, biskup wileński*, Lublin, 1998; Eligijus Raila, 'Vilniaus vyskupas Ignotas Masalskis ir katališka apšvieta', in *Kultūros istorijos tyrenėjimai*, Vilnius, 1997, iii, 92–146; Jan Wysocki, *Józef Ignacy Rybiński biskup włocławski i pomorski 1777–1806*, Rome, 1967; Wojciech Jerzy Górczyk, 'Diecezja kamieniecka w drugiej połowie XVIII wieku. Czasy pontyfikatu Adama Stanisława Krasińskiego', *NP*, 130, 2018, 75–114; Aldona Prašmantaitė, *Žemaičių vyskupas Juozopas Arnulfas Giedraitis*, Vilnius, 2000, 48–80; Martyna Deszczyńska and Ewa Zielińska, 'Skarszewski Wojciech', *PSB*, xxxviii, 50–61. On the parish clergy, see Stanisław Litak, 'Duchowieństwo polskie w okresie Oświecenia', *WO*, 5, 1988, 91–110; idem, *Parafie*, 125–216; Kracik, *Prawie wielebni*.

Enlightened initiatives in the diocese of Wilno are also covered in Ambroise Jobert, *Magnats polonais et physiocrates français (1767–1774)*, Paris, 1941; idem, *La Commission d'Éducation Nationale*, 203–10; Eligijus Raila, *Ignotas ignotus. Vilniaus vyskupas Ignotas Jokūbas Masalskis*, 142–93; Magdalena Ślusarska, 'Michał Franciszek Karpowicz', in *Pisarze polskiego oświecenia*, ed. Teresa Kostkiewiczowa and Zbigniew Goliński, 3 vols, 1992–96, ii, 74–98; eadem, 'Powinność i należytość'; Lesław Gruszczyński, 'Z problematyki politycznej w kazaniach katolickich okresu stanisławowskiego', *Acta Universitatis Lodziensis. Folia Historica*, 49, 1993, 13–34; Massalski's circle was recorded by Wilhelm Kaliński, *Dziennik*, ed. Łukasz Kurdybacha, Wrocław, 1968; and Józef Kossakowski, *Pamiętniki Józefa Kossakowskiego, biskupa inflanckiego*, ed. Adam Darowski, 1891.

On Brzostowski's model community, see the sceptical Emanuel Rostworowski, 'Reforma pawłowska Pawła Ksawerego Brzostowskiego (1767–1795)', *PH*, 44/1, 1953, 102–52; cf. Julian Bartyś, *Rzeczpospolita Pawłowska na tle reform włościańskich*, 1982, Magdalena Górska, 'Paweł Ksawery Brzostowski – autoportret ustawodawcy i mecenasa', in *Dwór, plebania*, 103–21; *Povilas Ksaveras Bžostovskis – Paulavos respublika*, ed. Aurelija Arlauskienė, Vilnius, 2014. The 'constitution' is republished in Valdas Rakutis, '1769 m. kovo 10 d. Pavlovo Respublikos nuostatai', in *Praeities pėdsakas*, ed. Egidijus Aleksandravičius et al., Vilnius, 2007, 389–416 (at 391–404).

The abolition of torture and trials for witchcraft is discussed by Stanisław Waltoś, 'L'Abolition de torture et des procès contre les sorcières en Pologne', *Archiwum Iuridicum Cracoviense*, 11, 1978, 109–11; Zenon Guldon and Jacek Wijaczka, *Procesy o mordy rytualne w Polsce w XVI–XVIII wieku*, Kielce, 1995, 87–88, 151–59; Jerzy Michalski, 'Jeszcze o konstytucji sejmu 1776 roku „Konwikcje w sprawach kryminalnych"', in Michalski, *SH*, i, 202–16; Władysław Smoleński, *Przewrót umysłowy w Polsce wieku XVIII*, 4th edn, 1979, 114–15.

On attitudes to magic and paranormal phenomena, see Danuta Kowalewska, *Magia i astrologia w literaturze polskiego oświecenia*, Toruń, 2009; Michał Otorowski, *Cagliostro w Warszawie*, 2012; Tadeusz Cegielski, 'Domek Biały i hermetyczno-alchemiczne zainteresowania Stanisława Augusta', in *Łazienki Królewskie. Nowe świadectwa – nowe znaczenia*, ed. Maria Poprzęcka, 2013, 59–73. Regarding religiosity, cf. Janusz Pasierb, 'Religijność polska w okresie Oświecenia', in *Życie kulturalne*, 49–58; Kracik, 'Ewangelicznie i rozumnie'; with Karol Górski, *Zarys dziejów duchowości w Polsce*, Cracow, 1986, 213–65. On the Bernardines, see Filip Wolański, *Kaznodziejstwo bernardyńskie w staropolskim systemie komunikacji społecznej schyłku epoki saskiej*, Toruń, 2012. For coronations of images, see Andrzej J. Baranowski, *Koronacje wizerunków maryjnych w czasach baroku*, 2003.

Trends in ecclesiastical architecture can be observed via Przemysław Wątroba, 'Nurt klasycystyczny w architekturze ostatniej ćwierci XVIII w. w Wilnie i na Wileńszczyźnie', in *W kręgu wileńskiego klasycyzmu*, exhibition catalogue, ed. Elżbieta Charazińska and Ryszard Bobrow, 2000, 177–80; Karpowicz, *Wileńska odmiana*, 127–28; Stanisław Lorentz and Andrzej Rottermund, *Klasycyzm w Polsce*, 1984; Račiunaitė and Sverdiolas, *Baroque*; Piotr Maluśkiewicz, *Baroque churches in Wielkopolska*, Poznań, 2006.

FURTHER READING

7 GROWING PAINS

On Warsaw and Varsovians, see Zamoyski, *Last King*, 253–56, 261–63; *Warszawa w wieku Oświecenia*, ed. Andrzej Zahorski, Wrocław, 1986; Anna Berdecka and Irena Turnau, *Życie codzienne w Warszawie okresu Oświecenia*, 1969; Barbara Grochulska, *Warszawa na mapie Polski stanisławowskiej*, 1980; eadem, 'Statystyka ludnościowa Warszawy w drugiej połowie XVIII wieku', *PH*, 45/4, 1954, 586–608; Monika Maludzińska, *„Próżnowanie stało się powszechnym nałogiem". Żebracy i włóczędzy w stanisławowskiej Warszawie*, 2014; on vagrancy more generally, see Jerzy Michalski, 'Problematyka ludności luźnej w pierwszej połowie panowania Stanisława Augusta', in *Cała historia to dzieje ludzi . . .*, ed. Cezary Kukło and Piotr Guzowski, Białystok, 2004, 311–22; on single women, see Cezary Kuklo, *Kobieta samotna w społeczeństwie miejskim u schyłku Rzeczypospolitej szlacheckiej*, Białystok, 1998; on immigration, see Marta Kuc-Czerep, 'Gospodarczy wymiar niemieckojęzycznej migracji do osiemnastowiecznej Warszawy', in *Skąd się biorą warszawiacy?* ed. Katarzyna Wagner et al., 2016, 59–72; eadem, 'Niemieckojęzyczni mieszkańcy osiemnastowiecznej Warszawy', doctoral thesis, IH PAN, 2018, 27–150; on architects, see *Słownik architektów i budowniczych środowiska warszawskiego XV–XVIII wieku*, ed. Paweł Migasiewicz et al., 2016; on painters: Aleksandra Bernatowicz, *Malarze w Warszawie czasów Stanisława Augusta*, 2016.

For Bacciarelli and Bellotto, see also Alina Chyczewska, *Marcello Bacciarelli 1731–1818*, Wrocław, 1973; Anita Chiron-Mrozowska, 'Marcello Bacciarelli i jego Malarnia', in *SAOKP*, 340–55; *Marcello Bacciarelli. Najpiekniejsze portrety*, exhibition catalogue, ed. Dorota Juszczak, 2018; *Bacciarelli. Studia o malarzu królewskim, dyrektorze, nauczycielu, opiekunie sztuk*, ed. Andrzej Pieńkos, 2018; Mieczysław Wallis, *Canaletto. Malarz Warszawy*, 7th edn, 1983; Alberto Rizzi, *Canaletto w Warszawie*, 2006; Rottermund, *Zamek Warszawski*, 112–21.

On economic developments, see, *inter alia*, Lukowski, *Liberty's Folly*, 26–37, 215–16; Topolski, 'Gospodarka'; Janina Leskiewiczowa, *Dobra osieckie w okresie gospodarki folwarczno-pańszczyźnianej XVI–XVIII w.*, Wrocław, 1957, 63–75; Emanuel Rostworowski, 'Miasta i mieszczanie w ustroju Trzeciego Maja', in *Sejm Czteroletni i jego tradycje*, ed. Jerzy Kowecki, 1991, 138–51; Mariusz Kulczykowski, 'Kraków jako ośrodek towarowy Małopolskiej Zachodniej w drugiej połowie XVIII wieku', in *Studia z Historii Społeczno-Gospodarczej Małopolski*, 6, 1963, 5–156; Mirosław Frančić, 'Kraków produkujący i konsumujący', ibid., 157–77.

On Wilno, see Polonsky, *The Jews in Poland and Russia*, i, 79–80; Zigmantas Kiaupa, *Trumpasis XVIII amžius (1733–1795 m.)*, vol. vii/1 of *Lietuvos istorija*, Vilnius, 2012, 180–81; Martynas Jakulis, 'Pamestinukų globa XVIII amžiaus Vilniuje', *XVIII amžiaus studijos*, 3, 2016, 193–209; Magdalena Ślusarska, 'Życie kulturalne Wilna w czasach stanisławowskich', *XVIII amžiaus studijos*, 1, 2014, 298–311. On the reduction of recognized towns in Lithuania, see Zigmantas Kiaupa, 'Kaip tvarkėsi Lietuvos mažieji miestai po 1776 m. įstatymo', in *Lietuvos Didžiosos Kunigaikštytės istorijos atodangos*, ed. Vydas Dolinskas et al., Vilnius, 2016, 519–28; Liudas Glemža, 'Delegaci miasta Kowna na sejmach Rzeczypospolitej w drugiej połowie XVIII wieku', *RL*, 3, 2017, 155–72 (at 157–60). On Poznań, see *Dzieje Poznania*, i: *Do roku 1793*, ed. Jerzy Topolski, 1988, 799–811, 830–89; Zofia Ostrowska-Kębłowska, *Architektura i budownictwo w Poznaniu w latach 1780–1880*, 2nd edn, Poznań, 2009, 27–107; Lorentz and Rottermund, *Klasycyzm*, 137–42; Bogna Tyszkiewicz, *Komisja Dobrego Porządku w Poznaniu 1780–1784*, 2nd edn, Poznań, 2005.

Murphy, *From Citizens to Subjects*, 50–87, 223–26, critically interprets changes in urban governance. On Olkusz, see Przemysław Jędrzejewski, 'Działalność Komisji *Boni Ordinis* dla miast wielkorządów krakowskich w latach osiemdziesiątych XVIII stulecia', *KH*, 124/2, 2017, 237–65; Guldon and Wijaczka, *Procesy o mordy rytualne*, 41.

On professionalization in government, see Ramunė Šmigelskytė-Stukienė, 'From Clientage Structure to a New Social Group: The Formation of the Group of Public Servants in the Grand Duchy of Lithuania in the Late Eighteenth Century', in *Social and Cultural Relations*, 148–65; Maciej Mycielski, *Marcin Badeni*, 1994, 11–33. The Cabinet is studied by Maria Rymszyna, *Gabinet Stanisława Augusta*, 1962; see also Witold Łukaszewicz, 'Glayre Piotr Maurycy', *PSB*, viii, 40–42; Jan Reychman, 'Ghigiotti Kajetan', *PSB*, vii, 417–18; Jerzy Michalski, 'Kiciński Pius', *PSB*, xii, 383–85. For the functioning of the Permanent Council and its departments, see Aleksander

Czaja, *Między tronem, buławą a dworem petersburskim. Z dziejów Rady Nieustającej 1786–1789*, 1988; Ramunė Šmigelskytė-Stukienė, Eduardas Brusokas, Liudas Glemža, Robertas Jurgaitis and Valdas Rakutis, *Modernios administracijos tapsmas Lietuvoje: valstybės institucijų raida 1764–1794 metais*, Vilnius, 2014, 176–310.

On the Department of Foreign Affairs and the diplomatic service, see Jerzy Michalski, 'Dyplomacja polska w latach 1764–1795', in *Historia dyplomacji polskiej*, ii: *1572–1795*, ed. Zbigniew Wójcik, 1982, 483–705 (at 585–604); Zofia Libiszowska, *Misja polska w Londynie w latach 1769–1795*, Łódź, 1966, 43–78; eadem, *Życie polskie w Londynie w XVIII wieku*, 1972, 70–109; Jan Reychman, *Życie polskie w Stambule w XVIII wieku*, 1959, 31–32, 40–50, 66–97; on Antici: Maciej Loret, *Życie polskie w Rzymie w XVIII wieku*, Rome, 1930, 38, 107–12; Gaetano Platania, *"Varsavia e Roma". Tommaso Antici un diplomatico nel '700*, Salerno, 1980; Ewa Manikowska, *Sztuka – ceremoniał – informacja. Studium wokół królewskich kolekcji Stanisława Augusta*, 2007; Paweł Zając, 'Tomasz Antici, rewolucja i cierpienia Kościoła w korespondencji kardynała Franciszka Herzana z lat 1798–1799', in *Od Kijowa do Rzymu*, ed. Mariusz R. Drozdowski and Katarzyna Wiszowata-Walczak, Białystok, 2012, 807–34.

On the Military Department and the army, see also Rostworowski, *Sprawa aukcji wojska*, passim; Andrzej Zahorski, 'Komarzewski Jan Baptysta', *PSB*, xiii, 380–83; Wojciech Organiściak, 'Polskie *Artykuły Wojskowe* z 1775 roku', *KH*, 109/1, 2002, 41–59; Witold Filipczak, 'Wojsko i obronność Rzeczypospolitej na sejmie w 1780 r.', in *Między obowiązkami, przywilejami a prawem Rzeczypospolitej XVI–XVIII wieku*, ed. Anna Kalinowska et al., 2018, 263–80.

The activity of the Justice Department is also explored in Marcin Głuszak, 'Rezolucje interpretacyjne Rady Nieustającej', *CPH*, 65/2, 2013, 73–101; *Zbiór rezolucji interpretacyjnych Rady Nieustającej z lat 1786–1788*, ed. Marcin Głuszak, Łódź, 2014. On the Police Department, compare Murphy's criticism with Andrzej Zahorski, *Centralne instytucje policyjne w Polsce w dobie rozbiorów*, 1959, 30–58. On 'hospitals', see Tadeusz Srogosz, *Problemy sanitarno-zdrowotne w działalności administracji Rzeczypospolitej w okresie stanisławowskim*, Łódź, 1993, 122–52; Marian Surdacki, *Opieka społeczna w Wielkopolsce zachodniej w XVII i XVIII wieku*, Lublin, 1992; Paweł Staniszewski, *Szpitalnictwo kościelne w archidiakonacie łęczyckim i łowickim do 1795 roku*, 2004.

The work of the Treasury Department and the Treasury Commissions is also assessed in Tadeusz Korzon, *Wewnętrzne dzieje Polski za Stanisława Augusta*, 2nd edn, Cracow, 1897–98, iii; Marian Drozdowski, *Podstawy finansowe*; Kościałkowski, *Tyzenhauz*, ii, 220–71. For the case study, see Ramunė Šmigelskytė-Stukienė, *Michał Kleofas Ogiński. Politician, Diplomat and Minister (1786–1794)*, Vilnius, 2015, esp. 61–78; see also Libiszowska, *Życie polskie w Londynie*, 122–31; Andrzej Załuski, *The Times and Music of Michał Kleofas Ogiński (1765–1833)*, London, 1997.

For Stanisław August's patronage of the arts, see also *Treasures of a Polish King: Stanislaus Augustus as Patron and Collector*, exhibition catalogue, Dulwich, 1992; *SAOKP*, passim; Zamoyski, *Last King*, 234–41, 256–58; Butterwick, *Poland's Last King*, 172–222, 231–35; Fabre, *Stanislas-Auguste Poniatowski et l'Europe des lumières*, 365–95. On music and dance, see Alina Żórawska-Witkowska, *Muzyka na dworze i w teatrze Stanisława Augusta*, 1995; Bożena Mamontowicz-Łojek, *Tancerze Króla Stanisława Augusta 1774–1798*, 2005. On literary matters, see also Zdzisław Libera, 'Stanisław August Poniatowski – opiekuń i miłośnik literatury', in *Życie kulturalne*, 85–99; Tomasz Chachulski, 'Stanisław August i współcześni mu pisarze', in *SARz*, 347–62; *Biblioteka Stanisława Augusta na zamku warszawskim*, ed. Jadwiga Rudnicka, Wrocław, 1988; Józef Wojakowski, 'Biblioteka Kozienicka Stanisława Augusta', *Z badań nad polskimi księgozbiorami i materiałami*, 5, 1981, 99–139. For the rise of a literary system, see Jan IJ. Van der Meer, *Literary Activities and Attitudes in the Stanislavian Age in Poland (1764–1795): A Social System?*, Amsterdam, 2002. For the monarch as author, see Jerzy Michalski, 'Stanisław August Poniatowski (1732–1798)', in *Pisarze polskiego oświecenia*, ed. Teresa Kostkiewiczowa and Zbigniew Goliński, 1992–96, i, 371–98; Teresa Kostkiewiczowa, *Pamiętniki Stanisława Augusta na nowo odkryte*, 2015.

On royal architectural initiatives, see also Marek Kwiatkowski, *Stanisław August. Król-architekt*, Wrocław, 1983; Andrzej Rottermund, *Zamek warszawski*. On the messages conveyed, see also Tadeusz Dobrowolski, 'Program Sali Balowej Pałacu Łazienkowskiego', in *Curia maior*, 1990, 131–44; idem, 'Antyk w Przedpokoju Senatorskim Zamku Królewskiego w Warszawie', *Kronika Zamkowa*, 35/1, 1995, 5–24; Zuzanna Prószyńska, *Zegary Stanisława Augusta*, 1994, 87–119;

Jerzy Axer, 'Stanisław August jako Oktawian August', in *Łacina jako język elit*, ed. Jerzy Axer, 2004, 251–58; Pfeiffer, *Rex et patria*, 163–75.

The king's ideology is discussed by Richard Butterwick, 'Positive and Negative Liberty in Eighteenth-Century Poland', in *Liberté: Héritage du passé ou idée des lumières?*, ed. Anna Grześkowiak-Krwawicz and Izabella Zatorska, Cracow, 2003, 62–69. On the sermons preached on royal anniversaries, see Magdalena Ślusarska, 'Królewskie kaznodziejstwo okolicznościowe czasów Stanisława Augusta Poniatowskiego', *Napis*, 1, 1994, 135–52.

On cultural clashes, see Zamoyski, *Last King*, 277–83; Jerzy Michalski, '„Warszawa" czyli o antystołecznych nastrojach w czasach Stanisława Augusta', in Michalski, *SH*, ii, 37–96; idem, 'Sarmatyzm a europeizacja Polski'; Teresa Kostkiewiczowa, *Polski wiek świateł*, Wrocław, 2002, 25–90; Roćko, *Kontusz i frak*. For the *Spartan Mother*, see Whelan, 'Gesture and Performance', Act IV, 218–35; Aleksandrowicz, 'Sejm Czteroletni', 196–211.

8 FERMENT AND FERMENTATION

Political events are distilled by Stone, *Polish Politics*, 64–74. On the 'Dogrumowa affair' and the 1786 sejm, see Adam Danilczyk, *W kręgu afery Dogrumowej. Sejm 1786 roku*, 2010. Rostworowski, *Sprawa aukcji wojska*, illuminates more than the politics of the army. Local and national parliamentary politics receive detailed coverage in Filipczak, *Życie sejmikowe*; see also idem, 'Rozdwojone wołyńskie sejmiki poselskie 1786 r.', *Res Historica*, 36, 2013, 163–90; Butterwick, *Polska Rewolucja*, 226–80; Kazimierz Marian Morawski, *Ignacy Potocki*, i: *1750–1788*, 1911. On the Kaniów summit, see the works cited for the Prologue; for its aftermath and the sejmiks of 1788, see also Rostworowski, *Ostatni król*, 104–07, 114–48; Zofia Zielińska, 'Geneza upadku orientacji rosyjskiej u progu Sejmu Czteroletniego w opinii ambasadora Stackelberga', *WO*, 15, 1999, 57–93; Michalski, 'Sejmiki poselskie 1788 roku'; idem, 'Zmierzch prokonsulatu', 458–62; Adolfas Šapoka, *Lietuva reforma seimo metu. Iki 1791 m. gegužės 3 d. konstitucijos*, Vilnius, 2008, 157–71; Andrzej Stroynowski, 'Sprawa aukcji wojska w litewskich instrukcjach poselskich z 1788 r.', in *Staropolski ogląd świata*, ed. Elżbieta Kociak et al., Toruń, 2017, 389–99.

On Kazimierz Sapieha and his mother, see Łukasz Kądziela, 'Sapieha Kazimierz Nestor', *PSB*, xxxv, 52–67; Maria Czeppe, 'Sapieżyna Elżbieta', *PSB*, xxxv, 163–67; Witold Filipczak, 'Stanisław August i Elżbieta Sapieżyna. Spór wokół losów sejmu 1782 roku', in *Władza i polityka w czasach nowożytnych*, ed. Zbigniew Anusik, Łódź, 2011, 53–75; Szymon Piotr Dąbrowski, 'Między królem a hetmanem. Działalność Elżbiety Sapieżyny w świetle jej korespondencji ze Stanisławem Augustem i Franciszkiem Ksawerym Branickim', in *Słynne kobiety w Rzeczypospolitej XVIII wieku*, ed. Agata Roćko and Magdalena Górska, 2017, 241–58.

For Orthodox–Uniate rivalry, see Skinner, *Western Front*, 45–47, 133–43, 168–83; Szady, *The Geography of Religious and Confessional Structures*, 148–56; Gil and Skoczylas, *Kościoły wschodnie*, 386–89, 394–96, 401–04; Witecki, *Przekaz kulturowy*, 108–11; Eugeniusz Sakowicz, *Kościół prawosławny w Polsce w epoce Sejmu Wielkiego 1788–1792*, 1935, 3–5; Tadeusz Śliwa, 'Sadkowski Wasyl, imię zakonne Wiktor', *PSB*, xxxiv, 278–80; Aleksy Deruga, 'Kościół prawosławny a sprawa „buntu" w 1789 roku we wschodnich województwach Rzeczypospolitej', *Ateneum Wileńskie*, 13/2, 1938, 175–269.

For the universities, see Jobert, *La Commission d'Éducation Nationale*, 234–52; Janina Kamińska, 'Komisja Edukacji Narodowej a reforma uniwersytetów', *XVIII amžiaus studijos*, 2, 2015, 72–87; Mirosława Chamcówna, *Uniwersytet Jagielloński w dobie Komisji Edukacji Narodowej*, 2 vols, Wrocław, 1957–59; Katarzyna Karaskiewicz, 'Prymasa Poniatowskiego potyczki w Akademii Krakowskiej', *PH*, 88/1, 1997, 53–71; Marian Skrzypek, 'Sprawa Józefa Bogucickiego', *Przegląd Humanistyczny*, 42/1, 1998, 1–11; Janina Kamińska, *Universitas Vilnensis. Akademia Wileńska i Szkoła Główna Wielkiego Księstwa Litewskiego 1773–1792*, Pułtusk, 2004, 64–65, 72–73, 131–41; eadem, *Universitas Vilnensis 1793–1803*, 2012, 199–206. On Gilibert and Forster, see also Kościałkowski, *Tyzenhauz*, i, 380–409; Laimonas Briedis, *Vilnius: City of Strangers*, Vilnius, 2008, 63–78. On Poczobut, see also Wioletta Pawlikowska-Butterwick and Richard Butterwick-Pawlikowski, 'Najjaśniejsza gwiazda wileńska. Ksiądz rektor Marcin Poczobut w ostatnich latach Rzeczypospolitej', *XVIII amžiaus studijos*, 2, 2015, 88–101.

On secondary schools and their teachers, see Jobert, *La Commission d'Éducation Nationale*, 263–74; Kamilla Mrozowska, *Funkcjonowanie systemu szkolnego Komisji Edukacji Narodowej na terenie Korony w latach 1783–1793*, Wrocław, 1985; Irena Szybiak, *Szkolnictwo Komisji Edukacji Narodowej w Wielkim Księstwie Litewskim*, Wrocław, 1973; eadem, 'Portret zbiorowy nauczycieli szkół średnich Komisji Edukacji Narodowej', *WO*, 5, 1988, 55–68; Ryszard W. Wołoszyński, *Między tradycją a reformą. Nauczyciele w Polsce w XVIII wieku*, Piotrków Trybunalski, 2000; Poplatek, *Komisja Edukacji Narodowej*. On the szlachta's reaction to the reforms, see Władysław Smoleński, 'Żywioły zachowawcze i Komisya Edukacyjna', in idem, *Pisma Historyczne*, Cracow, 1901, ii, 95–201; Jan Hulewicz, 'Opinia publiczna wobec Komisji Edukacji Narodowej', in Henryk Barycz and Jan Hulewicz (eds), *Studia z dziejów kultury polskiej*, 1949, 401–43; Butterwick, *Polska Rewolucja*, 272–73, 667–75, 682–87. For press coverage, see Magdalena Ślusarska, 'Działalność Komisji Edukacji Narodowej na Litwie w świetle „Gazet Wileńskich"', *XVIII amžiaus studijos*, 2, 2015, 102–21.

On Piattoli, see Venturi, *The End of the Old Regime in Europe, 1776–1789*, ii, 941–47; Emanuel Rostworowski, 'Piattoli Scipione', *PSB*, xxv, 818–28. On Jan Potocki, see idem, 'Debiut polityczny Jana Potockiego w r. 1788', *PH*, 47/4, 1956, 685–711; Nina Taylor-Terlecka, 'Jan Potocki and his Milieu: The Cultural Context', *Comparative Criticism*, 24, 2002, 55–77.

For events in France and the international situation in the later 1780s, see William Doyle, *Origins of the French Revolution*, 3rd edn, Oxford, 1999, 45–107; Peter McPhee, *Liberty or Death: The French Revolution*, New Haven, CT, 2016, 39–57; Blanning, *Origins of the French Revolutionary Wars*, 42–59; idem, 'That Horrid Electorate or "*Ma Patrie germanique*"? George III, Hanover and the Fürstenbund of 1785', *HJ*, 20/2, 1977, 311–44; Schroeder, *Transformation*, 35–61; Lord, *Second Partition*, 64–91; LeDonne, *Russia and the World*, 52–57, 245–46; Madariaga, *Russia*, 391–405; Dixon, *Catherine the Great*, 2001, 168–70.

9 REVOLUTION: THE KING WITH THE NATION

Walerian Kalinka, *Sejm Czteroletni* [1880–87], 4th edn, 2 vols, 1991, remains historians' go-to work on the Four Years' Sejm as far as 3 May 1791. Vol. 1 reaches the end of 1789. The most extensive treatment in English, albeit profiled, is Richard Butterwick, *The Polish Revolution and the Catholic Church 1788–1792: A Political History*, Oxford, 2012. The longer Polish version, *Polska Rewolucja a Kościół katolicki 1788–1792*, Cracow, 2012, is wider in scope. For an interpretation of the sejm's trajectory, see idem, 'Political Discourses of the Polish Revolution, 1788–1792', *English Historical Review*, 120/487, 2005, 695–731. See also the accounts in Zamoyski, *Last King*, 306–24; Lukowski, *Liberty's Folly*, 239–47. Lukowski, *Disorderly Liberty*, 163–222, straddles political ideas and practice. Jerzy Michalski, *Witaj majowa jutrzenko*, Cracow, 1999, is a reliable summary. His studies 'Zmierzch prokonsulatu' and 'Opozycja magnacka' (Michalski, *SH*, i, 285–304, 449–99) are seminal for the politics of 1788–89. Rostworowski, *Ostatni król*, 148–71, still dazzles. Wojciech Szczygielski distils his own research and views into *Sejm Wielki 1788–1792*, Łódź, 2015. Socio-political transformations are the focus of Yvonne Kleinmann, 'Der Vierjährige Sejm – Von der Adelsrepublik zur Staatsbürgergesellschaft?', in *Polen in der Europäischen Geschichte*, ed. Michael G. Müller, Stuttgart, 2014, ii, 529–66.

On the Commonwealth's international situation and diplomacy (to the end of 1789), see Lord, *Second Partition*, 92–120; Michalski, 'Dyplomacja', 633, 657–67; Bronisław Dembiński, *Polska na przełomie*, 1913; Józef Dutkiewicz, 'Prusy i Polska w dobie sejmu czteroletniego w świetle korespondencji dyplomatycznej pruskiej', *PH*, 33/1, 1935, 59–88; Z. Zielińska, *Studia z dziejów stosunków polsko-rosyjskich*, 170–247. For Polish missions, see also Libiszowska, *Misja polska w Londynie*, 79–85; Dariusz Nawrot, *Działania dyplomacji polskiej w Wiedniu w latach 1788–1792*, Katowice, 1999; Zbigniew Anusik, *Misja polska w Sztokholmie w latach 1789–1795*, Łódź, 1993; Maciej Kucharski, *Działalność dyplomacji polskiej w Berlinie w latach 1788–1792*, Katowice, 2000. For the old and new styles of diplomacy, cf. Hamish Scott, 'Diplomatic Culture in Old Regime Europe', in *Cultures of Power in Europe during the Long Eighteenth Century*, ed. Hamish Scott and Brendan Simms, Cambridge, 2007, 58–85, with Linda Frey and Marsha Frey, *The Culture of French Revolutionary Diplomacy*, Cham, 2018.

Military matters are covered by Leonard Ratajczyk, *Wojsko i obronność Rzeczypospolitej 1788–1792*, 1975; Emanuel Rostworowski, 'Z dziejów genezy Targowicy. Sprawa kawalerii narodowej w dobie Sejmu Czteroletniego', *PH*, 45/1, 1954, 14–35; fiscal questions by Korzon, *Wewnętrzne dzieje*, iii, 203–353; Roman Rybarski, *Skarbowość Polski w dobie rozbiorów*, Cracow, 1937, 272–335, 376–83; Drozdowski, *Podstawy finansowe*, 140–65. Ecclesiastical policies, dealt with by Kalinka and Butterwick, can be compared with those in the Habsburg Monarchy, on which see Beales, *Joseph II*, i, 439–79; ii, 68–103, 214–38, 271–332, 597–99; P. G. M. Dickson, 'Joseph II's Reshaping of the Austrian Church', *HJ*, 36/1, 1993, 89–114.

On the rebellion scare and its impact, covering the Union and Orthodoxy alike, the best work is Kamil Paździor, 'Polityka Sejmu Czteroletniego wobec Kościołów wschodnich', doctoral thesis, University of Silesia in Katowice, 2000; More accessibly, see Richard Butterwick, 'Deconfessionalization? The Policy of the Polish Revolution towards Ruthenia, 1788–1792', *Central Europe*, 6/2, 2008, 91–121; B. Skinner, *Western Front*, 185–90; see also Tomasz Hen, ' "Rabid Ruthenian": *L'Homme Sauvage* of the Late Eighteenth-Century Polish-Lithuanian Semiosphere', *APH*, 105, 2012, 121–55; Deruga, 'Kościół Prawosławny'; Sakowicz, *Kościół prawosławny*, 92–142; Srogosz, *Między wojną a modernizacją*, 121–28.

For a nuanced discussion of the contested powers, duration and functioning of the sejm, see Anna Grześkowiak-Krwawicz, 'Rządzący, nieustanny, do zwołania gotowy… Dyskusje o władzy i funkcjonowaniu sejmu w początkach Sejmu Czteroletniego', in *W cieniu*, 405–27; see also Jerzy Michalski, 'Kilka uwag o koncepcji sejmu rządzącego w XVIII wieku', in Michalski, *SH*, i, 74–80. Wojciech Szczygielski distinguishes too precisely between a sejm in permanent session and a reconvenable sejm: idem, 'Sejm nieustający. Batalia parlamentarna o jego urzeczywistnienie i rola w życiu politycznym Rzeczypospolitej u schyłku XVIII wieku', *PNH*, 1/1, 2002, 33–70; idem, 'Sejm gotowy i władza typu Straży', *PNH*, 2/1, 2003, 65–87.

On the marshal of the sejm, see Edmund Machalski, *Stanisław Małachowski marszałek Sejmu Czteroletniego*, Poznań, 1936; Bartłomiej Szyndler, *Stanisław Nałęcz Małachowski 1736–1809*, 1979; Andrzej Zahorski, 'Małachowski Stanisław', *PSB*, xix, 415–20; cf. his brother the chancellor: idem, 'Małachowski Jacek', *PSB*, xix, 393–96. For the marshal of the Lithuanian confederacy, see Krystyna Maksimowicz, 'O talentach Kazimierza Nestora Sapiehy w świetle obserwatorów życia publicznego drugiej połowy XVIII wieku', in *Kultura parlamentarna epoki staropolskiej*, ed. Andrzej Stroynowski, 2013, 483–93. On the disintegrating Radziwiłł interest, see also Maciej Kucharski, 'Karol Radziwiłł Panie Kochanku jako przywódca opozycji antykrólewskiej w dobie Sejmu Czteroletniego', in *Radziwiłłowie*, ed. Krzysztof Stępnik, Lublin, 2003, 403–14. On two garrulous envoys, see Monika Podgórzak, 'Suchodolski Wojciech', *PSB*, xlv, 303–11; Zofia Zielińska, 'Suchorzewski Jan', *PSB*, xlv, 315–24. On the lapidary Julian Niemcewicz, see Jan Dihm, *Niemcewicz jako polityk i publicysta w czasie Sejmu Czteroletniego*, Cracow, 1928; his patron is discussed by Monika Jusupović, 'Działalność Adama Kazimierza Czartoryskiego na początku Sejmu Czteroletniego', *KH*, 116/3, 2009, 43–72; Frączyk, *Adam Kazimierz Czartoryski*, 398–404; on his patroness's fortunes, see Izabela Czartoryska, née Flemming, *Tour through England: Diary from Travels around England and Scotland in 1790*, ed. Agnieszka Whelan, trans. Agnieszka Whelan and Zdzisław Żygulski junior, 2015, 13–16.

On parliamentary oratory, see Bernard Krakowski, *Oratorstwo polityczne na forum Sejmu Czteroletniego*, Gdańsk, 1968; for political sermons, see Magdalena Ślusarska, 'Sejm Czteroletni w okolicznościowym kaznodziejstwie lat 1788–1790', in *Ku reformie państwa i odrodzeniu moralnemu człowieka*, ed. Piotr Żbikowski, Rzeszów, 1992, 65–80; on political verses, see Krystyna Maksimowicz, *Poezja polityczna a Sejm Czteroletni*, Gdańsk, 2000.

On pamphlets and treatises, see Anna Grześkowiak-Krwawicz, 'Political and Social Literature during the Four-Year Diet', in *Constitution and Reform*, 175–201; eadem, *O formę rządu czy o rząd dusz? Publicystyka polityczna Sejmu Czteroletniego*, 2000; Konopczyński, *Polscy pisarze polityczni*, 253–567; regarding the clergy, see Butterwick, *Polish Revolution*, 65–78, 133–45, 164–66, 272–77. On Józef Pawlikowski, see Emanuel Rostworowski, *Legendy i fakty XVIII wieku*, 1963, 195–264; on Franciszek Salezy Jezierski, see also Teresa Kostkiewiczowa, *Oświecenie. Próg naszej współczesności*, 1994, 220–35.

The best book on the urban movement is Krystyna Zienkowska, *Sławetni i urodzeni. Ruch polityczny mieszczaństwa w dobie Sejmu Czteroletniego*, 1976; see also Władysław Smoleński,

Mieszczaństwo warszawskie w końcu wieku XVIII [1917], 2nd edn, 1976; for Lithuania, see Liudas Glemža, *Lietuvos Didžiosios Kunigaikštytės miestų sąjūdis 1789–1792 metais*, Kaunas, 2010; on a noble entrepreneur and polemicist, see Krystyna Zienkowska, *Jacek Jezierski kasztelan łukowski (1722–1805)*, 1963.

On the intertwined position of Jews, see Polonsky, *The Jews in Poland and Russia*, i, 210–19; Artur Eisenbach, *The Emancipation of the Jews in Poland 1780–1870*, Oxford, 1991, 1–112; Richard Butterwick-Pawlikowski, 'Jews in the Discourses of the Polish Enlightenment', *Polin*, 27, 2015, 45–62; Murphy, *From Citizens to Subjects*, 86–117; Krystyna Zienkowska, ' "The Jews have Killed a Tailor": The Socio-Political Background of a Pogrom in Warsaw in 1790', *Polin*, 3, 1988, 78–101; eadem, 'Citizens or Inhabitants? The Attempt to Reform the Status of Jews during the Four Years' Sejm', *APH*, 76, 1997, 31–52; Goldberg, *Żydzi w społeczeństwie*, 19–34; Jerzy Michalski, 'Sejmowe projekty reform położenia ludności żydowskiej w Polsce w latach 1788–1792', in Michalski, *SH*, i, 305–22.

On the civil-military commissions, see Łukasz Kądziela, 'Local Government Reform during the Four-Year Diet', in *Constitution and Reform*, 379–96; Korzon, *Wewnętrzne dzieje*, v, 196–32; Jerzy Gordziejew, *Komisje Porządkowe Cywilno-Wojskowe w Wielkim Księstwie Litewskim w okresie Sejmu Czteroletniego (1789–1792)*, Cracow, 2010; idem, 'Wokół genezy administracji lokalnej w Wielkim Księstwie Litewskim', *RL*, 3, 2017, 183–222.

10 REVOLUTION: THE NATION WITH THE KING

Kalinka, *Sejm Czteroletni*, vol. 2, remains the most important account of the middle third of the Great Sejm. For the international situation in 1789–90, see Lord, *Second Partition*, 121–52; Schroeder, *Transformation*, 61–67; Hochedlinger, *Austria's Wars of Emergence*, 383–96; Beales, *Joseph II*, ii, 587–93; Madariaga, *Russia*, 408–16; LeDonne, *Russia and the World*, 49–50; Dembiński, *Polska na przełomie*, 280–321; Z. Zielińska, *Studia z dziejów polsko-rosyjskich*, 231–46; Zbigniew Anusik, 'Rzeczpospolita wobec wojny wschodniej (1787–1792) i wojny szwedzko-rosysjskiej (1788–1790)', in *Polska wobec wielkich konfliktów w Europie nowożytnej*, ed. Ryszard Skowron, Cracow, 2009, 145–86 (at 159–68); idem, 'O szwedzki alians', *Acta Universitatis Lodziensis. Folia Historica*, 57, 1996, 77–106; Władysław Konopczyński, *Polska a Szwecja* [1926], 2nd edn, Cracow, 2016, 327–49.

On the *Projekt do formy rządu* (s.l.d. [1790]), and the three-way contest between enlightened republicans, traditionalists and royalists, see Butterwick, 'Political Discourses', 717–24; Rostworowski, *Legendy i fakty*, 285–343; idem, *Ostatni król*, 172–92; Bogusław Leśnodorski, *Dzieło Sejmu Czteroletniego*, Wrocław, 1951, 149–63; Szczygielski, *Sejm Wielki*, 73–115; for the question of the succession, see Zofia Zielińska, *„O sukcesyi tronu w Polszcze" 1787–1790*, 1991, 107–223. For the November 1790 sejmiks, see Butterwick, *Polish Revolution*, 216–35; Lukowski, *Disorderly Liberty*, 195–203, 218–19, 236–38; A. Šapoka, *Lietuva reformų seimo metu*, 319–77.

On the negotiation and drafting of the Constitution of 3 May, see Rostworowski, *Legendy i fakty*, 265–464; idem, *Ostatni król*, 204–32. For the law on free royal towns, see Krystyna Zienkowska, 'Reforms Relating to the Third Estate', in *Constitution and Reform*, 329–55; eadem, *Sławetni i urodzeni*, 112–78. On the reform of the sejmiks and its implementation, see Adam Lityński, *Sejmiki ziemskie 1764–1793*, Katowice, 1988; Andrzej B. Zakrzewski, 'Sejmiki litewskie epoki Sejmu Wielkiego. Między tradycją a innowacją?', *XVIII amžiaus studijos*, 1, 2014, 54–75; Jacek Sobczak, 'Reforma sejmików na sejmie czteroletnim i jej realizacja w Wielkopolsce', *Roczniki Historyczne*, 46, 1980, 67–98; idem, 'Organizacja i działalność sejmiku województwa płockiego po reformie w 1791 r.', *Notatki płockie*, 4/113, 1982, 14–20; Ramunė Šmigelskytė-Stukienė, 'Lietuvos Didžiosios Kunigaikštystės naujųjų pavietų seimelių vietos parinkimo ir įrengimo problema 1792–1794 metais', in *Lietuvos Didžiosios Kunigaikštystės istorijos atodangos*, ed. Vydas Dolinskas et al., Vilnius, 2016, 529–44.

The events of 2–5 May 1791 are retold by Zamoyski, *Last King*, 337–44. On the Constitution, see, *inter alia*, Jerzy Lukowski, 'Recasting Utopia: Montesquieu, Rousseau and the Polish

Constitution of 3 May 1791', *HJ*, 37/1, 1994, 65–87; idem, *Disorderly Liberty*, 223–49, which compares the *Law on Government* with subsequent legislation and the 1790 *Project for the Form of Government*; Jerzy Michalski, 'The Meaning of the Constitution of 3 May', in *Constitution and Reform*, 251–86; Zbigniew Szcząska, 'The Fundamental Principles Concerning the Political System in the 3 May, 1791 Government Statute', ibid., 287–308; Butterwick, *Poland's Last King*, 139–43, 285–309, which compares it with the British constitution; Rostworowski, *Ostatni król*, 219–31, which compares the final text with the drafts; and Leśnodorski, *Dzieło Sejmu Czteroletniego*, 205–445, which integrates subsequent legislation. On 'representatives', see also Adam Lityński, 'Status posła po Konstytucji 3 maja', in *Pierwsza w Europie. 200 rocznica Konstytucji 3 maja 1791–1991*, ed. Henryk Kocój, Katowice, 1988, 53–68.

For 'Western' reactions, see Norman Davies, ' "The Languor of so Remote an Interest": British Attitudes to Poland, 1772–1832', *Oxford Slavonic Papers*, new series, 16, 1983, 79–90; Samuel Fiszman, 'European and American Opinions of the Constitution of 3 May', in *Constitution and Reform*, 453–95; Zofia Libiszowska, 'Edmund Burke a Polska', *KH*, 77/1, 1970, 63–76; eadem, 'Odgłosy Konstytucji 3 maja na Zachodzie', in *Konstytucja 3 maja w tradycji i kulturze polskiej*, ed. Alina Barszczewska-Krupa, Łódź, 1991, i, 70–81; Grześkowiak-Krwawicz, *Czy rewolucja może być legalna?*, 107–54.

11 REVOLUTION: *ÇA IRA!*

The best account of the international situation in 1791 remains Lord, *Second Partition*, 153–247. See also Schroeder, *Transformation*, 86–93; Madariaga, *Russia*, 416–26; LeDonne, *Russia and the World*, 297–300; John Ehrman, *The Younger Pitt*, ii, London, 1983, ch. 1; Jeremy Black, *British Foreign Policy in an Age of Revolutions, 1783–1793*, Cambridge, 1994, 270–328; Blanning, *Origins of the French Revolutionary Wars*, 80–89; Hochedlinger, *Austria's Wars of Emergence*, 403–05; Lukowski, *Partitions*, 142–43; Cegielski and Kądziela, *Rozbiory*, 217–29; Zofia Libiszowska, 'Międzynarodowe powikłania sukcesji saskiej', in *Konstytucja 3 Maja. Prawo – polityka – symbol*, ed. Anna Grześkowiak-Krwawicz, 1992, 65–74; Zbigniew Anusik, 'Rzeczpospolita wobec Rosji w ostatniej fazie obrad Sejmu Wielkiego (1791–1792)', *PNH*, 16/2, 2017, 71–118.

The standard account of the final year of the Four Years' Sejm, Władysław Smoleński, *Ostatni rok Sejmu Wielkiego* [1897], reprint Poznań, 2006, does not rival Kalinka's achievement. See Daniel Stone, 'The First (and Only) Year of the May 3 Constitution', *Canadian Slavonic Papers*, 35/1–2, 1993, 69–86; Łukasz Kądziela: *Od Konstytucji do Insurekcji. Studia nad dziejami Rzeczypospolitej w latach 1791–1794*, 2011, 25–41. Butterwick, *Polish Revolution*, 252–314, offers an ecclesiastical lens on various questions. On the visionary vice-chancellor, see Maria Pasztor, *Hugo Kołłątaj na Sejmie Wielkim w latach 1791–1792*, 1991; Emanuel Rostworowski, 'Ksiądz Kołłątaj i trzy konstytucje: polityczna, ekonomiczna, moralna', in idem, *Popioły i korzenie*, Cracow, 1985, 138–50. For the sense of optimism, see Michalski, ' „Wszystko pójdzie wyśmienicie" ', in Michalski, *SH*, i, 323–34. On the sejmiks of February 1792, see Wojciech Szczygielski, *Referendum trzeciomajowe. Sejmiki lutowe 1792 roku*, Łódź, 1994; Jacek Sobczak, 'Zreformowane sejmiki litewskie wobec Konstytucji 3 Maja', in *Profesor Henryk Łowmiański*, ed. Krzysztof Pietkiewicz and Artur Kijas, Poznań, 1995, 165–182; Ramunė Šmigelskytė-Stukienė. 'O referendum Konstytucji 3 Maja raz jeszcze. Sejmiki egzulanckie i inflanckie 1792 roku', *SH*, 49/2, 2016, 233–47. For the polemics, see Grześkowiak-Krwawicz, *O formę rządu*, 318–37; eadem, 'Spór o Ustawę Rządową jako zderzenie dwóch dyskursów politycznych?', *WO*, 31, 2015, 195–212; Butterwick, 'Political Discourses', 726–30.

On the impacts of the urban reform, compare the caustic Murphy, *From Citizens to Subjects*, 86–117, with Lukowski, *Disorderly Liberty*, 223–25, 235, 247; Zienkowska, *Sławetni i urodzeni*, 179–290; Rostworowski, 'Miasta i mieszczanie', 149–51; Grażyna Bałtruszajtys, '„Zgromadzenia ludu miejskiego" według projektów i ustaw Sejmu Czteroletniego', in *Parlament, prawo, ludzie*, ed. Stanisław Russocki and Wanda Sudnik, 1996, 47–54; Glemža, *Lietuvos Didžiosios Kunigaikštytės miestų sąjūdis*, 75–194; Zigmantas Kiaupa, 'Współdziałanie mieszczan i szlachty na rzecz poprawy sytuacji prawnej mieszczan w dobie Sejmu Czteroletniego', *RL*, 3, 2017, 173–81.

The Custodial Council and the government commissions are presented in Šmigelskytė-Stukienė et al., *Modernios administracijos tapsmas Lietuvoje*, 312–412; for the view from the civil-military commissions, see Gordziejew, *Komisje Porządkowe*. For particular bodies, see Józef Wojakowski, *Straż Praw*, 1982; Zahorski, *Centralne instytucje policyjne*, 59–205; Grażyna Bałtruszajtys, *Sądownictwo Komisji Skarbowych w sprawach handlowych i przemysłowych (1764–1795)*, 1977. On 'hospitals' and paupers, see Maludzińska, *„Próżnowanie stało się powszechnym nałogiem"*, 282–370; Tadeusz Srogosz, 'Próby reform szpitalnictwa w Wilnie u schyłku I Rzeczypospolitej', in *Studia z dziejów Wielkiego Księstwa Litewskiego*, ed. Sławomir Górzyński and Mirosław Nagielski, 2014, 403–13. For the Military Commission: A. Šapoka, *Lietuva reformų seimo metu*, 234–91. On schools, see Jobert, *La Commission d'Education Nationale*, 332, 404–39; Korzon, *Wewnętrzne dzieje*, v, 212–17; Janina Ender, 'Sprawy oświatowe w okresie Sejmu Czteroletniego', *Rozprawy z Dziejów Oświaty*, 4, 1961, 35–86; Tadeusz Mizia, 'Komisje cywilno-wojskowe a szkolnictwo parafialne w okresie Sejmu Czteroletniego', *Rozprawy z Dziejów Oświaty*, 6, 1963, 40–92; Kamil Paździor, 'Edukacja jako narzędzie polityki wyznaniowej Sejmu Wielkiego wobec innowierców', *NP*, 100, 2003, 329–66; Katarzyna Buczek, *Hugo Kołłątaj i edukacja*, 2007. On the Polish-Lithuanian union, see Jerzy Michalski, 'Zagadnienie unii polsko-litewskiej w czasach Stanisława Augusta', in Michalski, *SH*, i, 44–73.

On the judicial and legal reforms, see Šmigelskytė-Stukienė, 'The Modernisation of the Court System', 17–22; Adam Lityński, 'The Reform of the Criminal Law during the Four-Year Diet', in *Constitution and Reform*, 397–421 (at 407–18); Jacek Sobczak, *Wielkopolskie sądy ziemiańskie*, 1977; Andrzej Abramski, 'Z dziejów sądu ziemiańskiego województwa sieradzkiego w 1792 roku', in *Pierwsza w Europie. 200 rocznica Konstytucji 3 Maja 1791–1991*, ed. Henryk Kocój, Katowice, 1989, 96–111; Ramunė Šmigelskytė-Stukienė, 'Išmatouoti erdves: ribų komisijų įkūrijmas ir jųveikla 1791–1792 metais', in *Viešosios ir privačios erdvės*, 222–51.

On the Club of the Friends of the Constitution, see Jerzy Kowecki, 'Pierwsze stronnictwo polityczne w Polsce w XVIII wieku', in *Dzieje kultury politycznej w Polsce*, ed. Józef Andrzej Gierowski, 1977, 117–35; idem, 'Klub Radziwiłłowski w Warszawie w 1791 roku', *WO*, 6, 1989, 85–123; Adam Skałkowski, 'Towarzystwo Przyjaciół Konstytucji 3 Maja', *Pamiętnik Biblioteki Kórnickiej*, 2, 1930, 50–83. For Mazzei, see Venturi, *The End of the Old Regime in Europe 1776–1789*, i, 82–143. On Primate Poniatowski, see also Angela Sołtys, 'Między Konstytucją a Targowicą', in *Miedzy Konstytucją*, 22–34; for his nightmares, see *inter alia*, Nigel Aston, *Religion and Revolution in France 1780–1804*, Basingstoke, 2000, 140–62.

12 UNDECLARED WAR

The policies of Russia, Prussia and Austria are best explained by Lord, *Second Partition*, 243–309. See also Madariaga, *Russia*, 426–33; Lukowski, *Partitions*, 144–47; Cegielski and Kądziela, *Rozbiory*, 235–41. On the desperate Polish diplomatic efforts, see also Bronisław Dembiński, 'Misja Ignacego Potockiego w Berlinie w roku 1792', *KH*, 51/1–2, 1937, 171–88; Nawrot, *Działania dyplomacji polskiej w Wiedniu*, 113–23.

The standard work on the Confederacy of Targowica remains Władysław Smoleński, *Konfederacya targowicka* [1903], reprint Poznań, 2006. For its early stages, see idem, *Ostatni rok*, 47–79, 147–231, 301–19. See also Rostworowski, 'Z dziejów genezy Targowicy. Sprawa kawalerii narodowej'; idem, *Ostatni król*, 288–307. Although Adam Danilczyk, *Targowica czyli zdrada*, 2016, has no notes or bibliography, it incorporates otherwise unpublished research in Russian archives. On the leading traitors, see Rostworowski, 'Potocki Stanisław Szczęsny', *PSB*, xxviii, 183–202; Zofia Zielińska, 'Rzewuski Seweryn', *PSB*, xxxiv, 138–51; eadem, 'Seweryn Rzewuski – pułapki republikanizmu', in *Bo insza jest rzecz zdradzić*, 31–47; Konopczyński, 'Branicki Franciszek Ksawery', *PSB*, ii, 398–401; idem, 'Kossakowski Szymon Marcin', *PSB*, xiv, 288–93; Dolinskas, *Simonas Kosakovskis*; Andrzej Zahorski, 'Kossakowski Józef Kazimierz', *PSB*, xiv, 269–72. For the General Confederacy of the Grand Duchy of Lithuania, see Ramunė Šmigelskytė-Stukienė, *Lietuvos Didžiosios Kunigaikštystes konfederacijos susidarymas ir veikla 1792–1793*, Vilnius, 2003; for the Crown Confederacy: Dariusz Rolnik, *Szlachta koronna wobec konfederacji targowickiej*, Katowice, 2000.

The most detailed treatment of the Russo-Polish war (originally published in two volumes in 1909–22/24 under the pen name Tadeusz Soplica) is Adam Wolański, *Wojna polsko-rosyjska 1792 r.*, 2nd/3rd edn, 1996. See also Bronisław Pawłowski, *Od konfederacji barskiej do powstania styczniowego*, 1962, 78–190; and Jerzy Skowronek, *Książę Józef Poniatowski*, Wrocław, 1986, 7–50. For the stance of the nobility, see Dariusz Rolnik, 'Szlachta koronna Rzeczypospolitej wobec wojny polsko–rosyjskiej 1792 roku', *SH*, 43/2, 2000, 215–33.

Biographies of Kościuszko abound, not all of them hagiographic. See, *inter alia*, Monica M. Gardner, *Kościuszko: A Biography*, 2nd edn, London, 1942; Miecislaus Haiman, *Kościuszko in the American Revolution*, 2nd edn, New York, 1975; idem, *Kościuszko: Leader and Exile*, 2nd edn, New York, 1977; James S. Pula, *Thaddeus Kościuszko: The Purest Son of Liberty*, New York, 1999; Alex Storozynski, *The Peasant Prince: Thaddeus Kosciuszko and the Age of Revolution*, New York, 2009; Tadeusz Korzon, *Kościuszko – biografia z dokumentów wysnuta*, 1st edn, Cracow, 1894; Adam Skałkowski, *Kościuszko w świetle nowych badań*, Poznań, 1925; Stanisław Herbst, 'Kościuszko Andrzej Tadeusz Bonawentura', *PSB*, xiv, 430–40; Jan Dihm, *Kościuszko nieznany*, Wrocław, 1969; Bartłomiej Szyndler, *Tadeusz Kościuszko 1746–1817*, 1991; Katarzyna Jedynakiewicz, *Osobowość i życie codzienne Tadeusza Kościuszki*, Łódź, 1996.

13 THE AUGEAN STABLES

Confederate misrule is exposed by Smoleński, *Konfederacya targowicka*; Danilczyk, *Targowica*, 130–40; less categorically by Rolnik, *Szlachta koronna wobec konfederacji targowickiej*. For the Grand Duchy of Lithuania, including the Grodno Sejm, see Šmigelskytė-Stukienė, *Lietuvos Didžiosios Kunigaikštystes konfederacijos susidarymas*; eadem, 'Livonijos vyskupo Juozapo Kazimiero Kosakovskio LDK vizija antropo valstybės padalijimo akivaizdoje', *Lietuvos Istorijos Metraštis*, 2001:1, 73–86; Dolinskas, *Simonas Kosakovskis*, 501–722. For the attempts of the confederates to form an army loyal to themselves, see Wolański, *Wojna polsko-rosyjska*, passim; Wacław Tokarz, *Rozprawy i szkice*, 1959, ii, 42–56; Rostworowski, 'Z dziejów genezy Targowicy', 32–34. On the mixed implications for the Catholic Church, see Butterwick, *Polska Rewolucja*, 862–77. On the primate, see Sołtys, 'Między Konstytucją a Targowicą', 35–81; Łukasz Kądziela, *Od Konstytucji do Insurekcji*, 155–66; Richard Butterwick-Pawlikowski, ' „Z istotnego przekonania". O postawie prymasa Michała Jerzego Poniatowskiego wobec Targowicy raz jeszcze', in *W cieniu*, 429–48.

For the second partition and its wider contexts, see Lord, *Second Partition*, 255–73, 299–445, 471–79, 552–56; Lukowski, *Partitions*, 148–61; Schroeder, *Transformation*, 104–24, 142–43; Madariaga, *Russia*, 433–40; T. C. W. Blanning, *The French Revolutionary Wars 1787–1792*, London, 1996, 72–82, 88–91; Hochedlinger, *Austria's Wars of Emergence*, 406–20; Cegielski and Kądziela, *Rozbiory*, 247–75, 285–86; Adam Danilczyk, 'Rosja, Austria i II rozbiór Rzeczypospolitej', in *W cieniu*, 449–65.

The Grodno Sejm was reassessed by Łukasz Kądziela, whose collected articles form *Od Konstytucji do Insurekcji*. His *magnum opus* is a meticulous analysis of politics and reforms: *Między zdradą a służbą Rzeczypospolitej. Fryderyk Moszyński w latach 1792–1793*, 1993. See also Tokarz, *Rozprawy i szkice*, i, 115–40. On the relationship between the Crown and Lithuania, see also Jerzy Malec, 'Sejm grodzieński 1793 roku a unia polsko-litewska', in *Parlament, prawo, ludzie*, ed. Stanisław Russocki and Wanda Sudnik, 1996, 148–53. For the lacerating account of the Russian ambassador, see Jakob Johann Sievers, *Jak doprowadziłem do drugiego rozbioru Polski*, 3rd Polish edn, ed. Barbara Grochulska and Piotr Ugniewski, 1992.

14 IMMOLATION

For an accessible summary of the Insurrection, see Lukowski, *Liberty's Folly*, 256–63; for an evaluation: Jerzy Kowecki, 'The Kościuszko Insurrection: Continuation and Radicalization of Change', in *Constitution and Reform*, 497–518. Bartłomiej Szyndler, *Powstanie kościuszkowskie 1794*, 1994, provides a general history; Andrzej Zahorski, *Naczelnik w sukmanie*, Cracow, 1990, is briefer. See also the biographies of Kościuszko listed above.

FURTHER READING

On the Insurrection's preparation and precipitation, see Andrzej Zahorski, 'Geneza insurekcji', in *Powstanie kościuszkowskie*, 16–29; Tokarz, *Rozprawy i szkice*, i, 167–90, 201–61, ii, 57–190. On Warsaw, see idem, *Warszawa przed wybuchem powstania 17 kwietnia 1794*, Cracow, 1911; idem, *Insurekcja Warszawska (17 i 18 kwietnia 1794* r.), Lwów, 1934; Andrzej Zahorski, *Warszawa w powstaniu kościuszkowskim*, 2nd edn, 1985; idem, *Ignacy Wyssogota Zakrzewski*, 1963; Dariusz Nawrot, 'Echa zwycięstwa pod Racławicami w Warszawie w 1794 roku', in *200 rocznica*, 170–80. For the Insurrection in Lithuania, see Henryk Mościcki, *Generał Jasiński i powstanie kościuszkowskie*, 1917; Zdzisław Sułek, *Sprysiężenie Jakuba Jasińskiego*, 1982; Zdzisław Maciej Zachmacz, *Jakub Jasiński. Generał i poeta*, 1995; Kiaupa, *Trumpasis XVIII amžius*, i, 262–91; Władysław Zajewski, 'Wilno w rewolucji 1794 roku', in *200 rocznica*, 103–32; Dolinskas, *Simonas Kosakovskis*, 722–746; Jerzy Urwanowicz, 'Organizacja i uwarunkowania władz insurekcyjnych na Litwie', in *Z dziejów kultury prawnej*, ed. Anna Rosner et al., 2004, 433–43; Eduardas Brusokas, 'Lietuvos Didžiosios Kunigaikštystės Visuomenės saugumo deputacijos organizacijos ir veiklos bruožai 1794 m.', *XVIII amžiaus studijos*, 1, 2014, 148–64. On the insurrectionary government, see Zbigniew Góralski, 'Ustrój powstania kościuszkowskiego', in *Powstanie kościuszkowskie*, 30–49.

'Jacobins' are presented – and applauded – by Bogusław Leśnodorski, *Polscy jakobini*, 1960 (abridged French edn: *Les Jacobins polonais*, Paris, 1965). Compare Zbigniew Góralski, *Stanisław August w insurekcji kościuszkowskiej*, 1988, and Łukasz Kądziela, *Fryderyk Moszyński w insurekcji kościuszkowskiej*, 2004 – this unfinished, posthumously published monograph gives a detailed analysis of the arrest, interrogations and investigations of Moszyński, illuminating the Insurrection's judicial system. Falsehoods about the primate's death are exposed by Andrzej Woltanowski, 'Czarna legenda o śmierci prymasa Poniatowskiego', *KH*, 94/4, 1987, 25–62; see also Sołtys, *Opat z San Michele*, 47–49. On insurrectionary propaganda, see Andrzej Woltanowski, 'Kształtowanie opinii publicznej podczas powstania', in *Powstanie kościuszkowskie*, 80–111; for its distribution to country parishes: Richard Butterwick, 'Propaganda in the Parishes: Local Communication during the Insurrection of 1794', and Michał Gochna, 'The Route Map of Dean Szymon Waraxa's Courier', both in *Social and Cultural Relations*, 215–34, 235–37. On Wybicki, see Edyta Pętkowska, *Biografia intelektualna Józefa Wybickiego w latach 1794–1806*, 2016.

On the peasant question and its military ramifications, see Jerzy Kowecki, *Uniwersał Połaniecki i sprawa jego realizacji*, 1957; idem, *Pospolite ruszenie w insurekcji 1794 roku*, 1963; Andrzej Woltanowski, 'Tadeusz Kościuszko i pierwszy etap reform włościańskich (28 marca–1 maja 1794 r.)', *PH*, 78/1, 1987, 19–44; Mirosław Francič, 'Sprawa chłopska w insurekcji kościuszkowskiej', in *Powstanie kościuszkowskie*, 72–79; Marcin Konarski, 'Reflections on the Legal Situation of Peasants during the Kościuszko Uprising of 1794', *Review of Comparative Law*, 35, 2018, 41–72. For the long-term significance, see Dariusz Rolnik, 'Obchody setnej rocznicy insurekcji kościuszkowskiej w Galicji', in *200 rocznica*, 218–34; Magdalena Micińska, 'Obchody rocznic powstania kościuszkowskiego w latach 1894–1917', in *Powstanie kościuszkowskie*, 112–29. On Jews, see Józef Andrzej Gierowski, 'The Jews in the Kościuszko Insurrection', in *„Der letzte Ritter und erste Bürger in Osten Europas": Kościuszko, das aufständische Reformpolen und die Verbundheit zwischen Polen und der Schweiz*, ed. Heiko Haumann and Jerzy Skowronek, Basel, 1996, 192–99; *Księga pamiątkowa ku czci Berka Joselewicza*, ed. Majer Bałaban, 1934.

Military fortunes are also narrated by Stanisław Herbst, *Z dziejów wojskowych powstania kościuszkowskiego 1794 roku*, 1983; Jan Lubicz-Pachoński, *Bitwa pod Racławicami*, 1984; Jan Pachoński, *Generał Jan Henryk Dąbrowski 1755–1818*, 2nd edn, 1987, 69–97. On arms production and supply, see Andrzej Zahorski, *Uzbrojenie i przemyśl zbrojeniowy w powstaniu kościuszkowskim*, 1957.

On the international situation and the third partition, see Robert Howard Lord, 'The Third Partition of Poland', *S[EE]R*, 3, 1924/25, 481–98; Schroeder, *Transformation*, 124–56; Lukowski, *Partitions*, 161–80; Madariaga, *Russia*, 441–51; Hochedlinger, *Austria's Wars of Emergence*, 412–14, 421–23; Cegielski and Kądziela, *Rozbiory*, 288–326; Zbigniew Góralski, *Austria a trzeci rozbiór Polski*, 1979. Stanisław August's abdication is dissected by Zofia Zielińska, 'Geneza i treść aktu abdykacji Stanisława Augusta', *Studia Źródłoznawcze*, 51, 2013, 43–68. For his guardian, see Leonid Żytkowicz, *Rządy Repnina na Litwie w latach 1794–1797*, Wilno, 1938.

FURTHER READING

EPILOGUE: SMOKE AND ASH

On Stanisław August's last years, see Zamoyski, *Last King*, 432–52; Maria Żywirska, *Ostatnie lata życia króla Stanisława Augusta*, 1975; Michalski, *Stanisław August Poniatowski*, 80–83, 102. On his memoirs, see Anna Grześkowiak-Krwawicz's introduction to *Pamiętniki króla Stanisława Augusta. Antologia*, 2013, 7–42; and Kostkiewiczowa, *Pamiętniki Stanisława Augusta*. For his reputation, see Andrzej Zahorski, *Spór o Stanisława Augusta*, 1988. On his three funerals, see Butterwick, *Poland's Last King*, 1–2; Aleksandra Zgorzelska, *Powrót króla*, 1991; *SAOKP*, 481–84. On the regalia, see Michał Rożek, *Polskie koronacje i korony*, Cracow, 1987, 97–144; for survivals: *Pod jedną koroną. 300-lecie unii polsko-saskiej*, exhibition catalogue, 1997, 89–90, 105, 108–11; *SAOKP*, 485–87.

Poles' adjustments to their new rulers and the accompanying moral dilemmas are superbly analysed by Jarosław Czubaty, *Zasada „dwóch sumień". Normy postępowania i granice kompromisu politycznego Polaków w sytuacjach wyboru (1795–1815)*, 2005; idem, ' "What is to be Done when the Motherland has Died?" The Moods and Attitudes of Poles after the Third Partition 1795–1806', *Central Europe*, 7/2, 2009, 95–109. See also the sparkling prologue to his *Księstwo Warszawskie (1807–1815)*, 2011, 12–56 (mostly omitted from the abridged edn: *The Duchy of Warsaw (1807–1815): A Napoleonic Outpost in Central Europe*, London, 2016). On conspiracies, see Maryan Kukiel, *Próby powstańcze po trzecim rozbiorze 1795–1797* [1912], reprint Poznań, 2006. More generally, see Stefan Kieniewicz, *Historia Polski 1795–1918*, 9th edn, 1997, 21–38; Stanisław Grodziski, *Polska w czasach przełomu (1764–1815)*, Cracow, 1999, 210–38; Zgymunt Szultka, 'Społeczno-ekonomiczne aspekty drugiego i trzeciego rozbioru Polski i innych nabytków terytorialnych Prus', in *Prusy 1701–1806*, 730–38; Dariusz Łukasiewicz, 'Kultura polska w Prusach do roku 1806', ibid., 895–901; Żytkowicz, *Rządy Repnina*.

On poetic trauma, see Marek Nalepa, *Takie życie dziś nasze, gdy Polska ustaje . . . Pisarze stanisławowscy a upadek Rzeczypospolitej*, Wrocław, 2002; Piotr Żbikowski, *W pierwszych latach narodowej niewoli. Schyłek polskiego oświecenia i zwiastuny romantyzmu*, Wrocław, 2007, 9–261; cf. Tomasz Chachulski, 'Oświeceniowe dylematy sumień, czyli Franciszka Karpińskiego przysięgi na wierność', in *Bo insza jest rzecz zdradzić*, 177–85.

On the new tsar, see *Paul I: A Reassessment of His Life and Reign*, ed. Hugh Ragsdale, Pittsburgh, PA, 1979; Roderick McGrew, *Paul I of Russia, 1754–1801*, Oxford, 1992. For consequences of the partitions in the Russian Empire see, *inter alia*, Hubert Zawadzki, *A Man of Honour: Adam Czartoryski as a Statesman of Russia and Poland, 1795–1831*, Oxford, 1993; Murphy, *From Citizens to Subjects*, 153–236; B. Skinner, *Western Front*, 199–225; Gil and Skoczylas, *Kościoły wschodnie*, 411–26; John D. Klier, *Russia Gathers her Jews: The Origins of the "Jewish Question" in Russia, 1772–1825*, DeKalb, IL, 1986; Daniel Beauvois, *Pouvoir russe et noblesse polonaise en Ukraine 1793–1830*, Paris, 2003; idem, *Le Noble, le serf et le revizor: La noblesse polonaise entre le tsarisme et les masses ukrainiennes (1831–1863)*, Paris, 1985; idem, *La Bataille de la terre en Ukraine (1863–1914). Les Polonais et les conflits socioethniques*, Lille, 1993; idem, *Lumières et société en Europe de l'Est: l'Université de Vilna et les écoles polonaises de l'Empire russe*, 2 vols, Paris, 1977.

The Polish-Lithuanian parting of the ways is discussed by Timothy Snyder, *The Reconstruction of Nations: Poland, Ukraine, Lithuania, Belarus, 1569–1999*, New Haven, CT, 2003; Robert Frost, 'Ordering the Kaleidoscope: The Construction of Identities in the Lands of the Polish-Lithuanian Commonwealth since 1569', in *Power and the Nation in European History*, ed. Len Scales and Oliver Zimmer, Cambridge, 2005, 212–31; Dangiras Mačiulis and Darius Staliūnas, *Lithuanian Nationalism and the Vilnius Question, 1883–1940*, Marburg, 2015; Darius Staliūnas, 'Nowoczesna Litwa – czy istniała alternatywa dla modelu państwa narodowego?', *KH*, 125/2, 2018, 403–25. The Belarusian claim to the inheritance of the Grand Duchy of Lithuania is presented in Uladzimir Arloŭ and Zmicier Hierasimovič, *Belarus. The Epoch of the Grand Duchy of Lithuania: An Illustrated History*, Minsk, 2018.

On Lithuanian and Polish attitudes to the Constitution of 3 May, see Rasa Čepaitienė, 'Gegužės 3-iosios konstitucija Lietuvių istorinėje atmintyje', *XVIII amžiaus studijos*, 1, 2014, 76–96; Alfredas Bumblauskas, 'Konstytucja 3 Maja a amnezja historyczna Litwy i Polski', in *Pamięć chwili, która nas samym sobie wróciła . . . Wykłady trzeciomajowe w Trybunale Konstytucyjnym*, ed. Andrzej

Rzepliński et al., 2016, 91–102. For the Mutual Assurance of the Two Nations, see A. Šapoka, *Lietuva reforma seimo metu*, 444–46; Smoleński, *Ostatni rok*, 126–28; Rostworowski, *Legendy i fakty*, 451–53; Jerzy Malec, 'Problem stosunku Polski do Litwy w dobie Sejmu Czteroletniego', *CPH*, 34/1, 1982, 31–50; Michalski, 'Zagadnienie unii polsko-litewskiej'; Juliusz Bardach, 'The Constitution of 3 May and the Mutual Guarantee of the Two Nations', in *Constitution and Reform*, 357–78 (original: 'Konstytucja 3 Maja a unia polsko-litewska', *PH*, 82/3–4, 1991, 383–410); Zigmantas Kiaupa, 'The Rise of the Mutual Guarantee of the Two Nations', in *Europa unii i federacji*, ed. Krzysztof Ślusarek, Cracow, 2004, 91–98.

INDEX

Terms explained in the glossary and persons in the genealogical table are given in **bold**. Unless mentioned in the text, alternative versions of place names are provided only in the gazetteer.

Printed and bound by CPI Group (UK) Ltd, Croydon, CR0 4YY

09/07/2025

14700990-0001